Strategies and Applications of Islamic Entrepreneurship

Ahmad Rafiki
Universitas Medan Area, Indonesia

Alfatih Gessan Pananjung
Bahrain Institute of Banking and Finance, Bahrain

Muhammad Dharma Tuah Putra Nasution
Universitas Pembangunan Panca Budi, Indonesia

IGI Global
PUBLISHER of TIMELY KNOWLEDGE

A volume in the Advances in Logistics, Operations, and Management Science (ALOMS) Book Series

Published in the United States of America by
IGI Global
Business Science Reference (an imprint of IGI Global)
701 E. Chocolate Avenue
Hershey PA, USA 17033
Tel: 717-533-8845
Fax: 717-533-8661
E-mail: cust@igi-global.com
Web site: http://www.igi-global.com

Library of Congress Cataloging-in-Publication Data

Names: Rafiki, Ahmad, 1981- editor. | Nasution, Muhammad Dharma Tuah Putra, 1974- editor.
Title: Strategies and applications of Islamic entrepreneurship / edited by Ahmad Rafiki, Alfatih Gessan Pananjung, and Muhammad Dharma Tuah Putra Nasution.
Description: Hershe, PAy : Business Science Reference, [2023] | Includes bibliographical references and index. | Summary: "As many countries are now looking for alternative ways of doing business with a focus on preserving ethics, morals, and values, it is important to understand and consider Islamic business. Islamic business, management, and entrepreneurship are topics that are discussed by many scholars; however, researchers in some countries have yet to comprehensively understand and implement current models, strategies, and applications. Strategies and Applications of Islamic Entrepreneurship considers all aspects of Islamic business, management, and entrepreneurship. The book also provides the best practices and challenges of implementing Islamic business models. Covering key topics such as Islamic marketing, Islamic business environments, and Muslim countries, this premier reference source is ideal for managers, business owners, policymakers, industry professionals, researchers, academicians, scholars, instructors, and students"-- Provided by publisher.
Identifiers: LCCN 2023027752 (print) | LCCN 2023027753 (ebook) | ISBN 9781668475195 (hardcover) | ISBN 9781668475201 (paperback) | ISBN 9781668475218 (ebook)
Subjects: LCSH: Management--Islamic countries. | Business enterprises--Islamic countries. | Entrepreneurship--Islamic countries. | Business--Religious aspects--Islam. | Entrepreneurship--Religious aspects--Islam.
Classification: LCC HD70.I74 S77 2023 (print) | LCC HD70.I74 (ebook) | DDC 338/.04--dc23/eng/20230615
LC record available at https://lccn.loc.gov/2023027752
LC ebook record available at https://lccn.loc.gov/2023027753

This book is published in the IGI Global book series Advances in Logistics, Operations, and Management Science (ALOMS) (ISSN: 2327-350X; eISSN: 2327-3518)

British Cataloguing in Publication Data
A Cataloguing in Publication record for this book is available from the British Library.

For electronic access to this publication, please contact: eresources@igi-global.com.

Advances in Logistics, Operations, and Management Science (ALOMS) Book Series

John Wang
Montclair State University, USA

ISSN:2327-350X
EISSN:2327-3518

Mission

Operations research and management science continue to influence business processes, administration, and management information systems, particularly in covering the application methods for decision-making processes. New case studies and applications on management science, operations management, social sciences, and other behavioral sciences have been incorporated into business and organizations real-world objectives.

The **Advances in Logistics, Operations, and Management Science** (ALOMS) Book Series provides a collection of reference publications on the current trends, applications, theories, and practices in the management science field. Providing relevant and current research, this series and its individual publications would be useful for academics, researchers, scholars, and practitioners interested in improving decision making models and business functions.

Coverage

- Political Science
- Risk Management
- Decision analysis and decision support
- Production Management
- Operations Management
- Services management
- Computing and information technologies
- Information Management
- Finance
- Organizational Behavior

IGI Global is currently accepting manuscripts for publication within this series. To submit a proposal for a volume in this series, please contact our Acquisition Editors at Acquisitions@igi-global.com or visit: http://www.igi-global.com/publish/.

The Advances in Logistics, Operations, and Management Science (ALOMS) Book Series (ISSN 2327-350X) is published by IGI Global, 701 E. Chocolate Avenue, Hershey, PA 17033-1240, USA, www.igi-global.com. This series is composed of titles available for purchase individually; each title is edited to be contextually exclusive from any other title within the series. For pricing and ordering information please visit http://www.igi-global.com/book-series/advances-logistics-operations-management-science/37170. Postmaster: Send all address changes to above address.

Titles in this Series

For a list of additional titles in this series, please visit: www.igi-global.com/book-series

Climate Change Management and Social Innovations for Sustainable Global Organization
Sumita Dave (Amity University, Raipur, India) Monica Sainy (Amity University, Raipur, India) Disha Sharma (Amity University, Raipur, India) and Anupam Singh (University of Stirling, UK)
Engineering Science Reference • copyright 2023 • 313pp • H/C (ISBN: 9781668495032) • US $250.00 (our price)

Technological Innovation Driving Sustainable Entrepreneurial Growth in Developing Nations
Nana Yaw Asabere (Accra Technical University, Ghana) Glenn Kwabena Gyimah (Accra Technical University, Ghana) Amevi Acakpovi (Accra Technical University, Ghana) and Florence Plockey (Accra Technical University, Ghana)
Business Science Reference • copyright 2023 • 452pp • H/C (ISBN: 9781668498439) • US $250.00 (our price)

Emerging Technologies and Digital Transformation in the Manufacturing Industry
Fernando Ortiz-Rodriguez (Tamaulipas Autonomous University, Mexico) Sanju Tiwari (Tamaulipas Autonomous University, Mexico) Luis Manuel Hernández-González (INDEX, Mexico) and Agustin Tiburcio (INDEX, Mexico)
Business Science Reference • copyright 2023 • 291pp • H/C (ISBN: 9781668480885) • US $250.00 (our price)

Transformational Leadership Styles, Management Strategies, and Communication for Global Leaders
Darcia Ann Marie Roache (University of Saskatchewan, Canada & Capilano University, Canada & University Canada West, Canada & University of the People, USA)
Business Science Reference • copyright 2023 • 532pp • H/C (ISBN: 9781668488225) • US $250.00 (our price)

Black Women's Formal and Informal Ways of Leadership Actualizing the Vision of a More Equitable Workplace
Audrey D. Bowser (Arkansas State University, USA) Kimberley M. Davis (University of Arkansas at Pine Bluff, USA) and Natalie A. Johnson-Leslie (Arkansas State University, USA)
Information Science Reference • copyright 2023 • 340pp • H/C (ISBN: 9781668438275) • US $215.00 (our price)

Multidisciplinary Approaches to Organizational Governance During Health Crises
Carla Sofia Vicente Negrão (CeBER, University of Coimbra, Portugal) Isabel Guerreiro Pimentel Maia (Centre for Business and Economics Research, University of Coimbra, Portugal) and João António Furtado Brito (University of Cape Verde, Cape Verde)
Business Science Reference • copyright 2023 • 300pp • H/C (ISBN: 9781799892137) • US $250.00 (our price)

New Perspectives and Possibilities in Strategic Management in the 21st Century Between Tradition and Modernity

IGI Global
PUBLISHER of TIMELY KNOWLEDGE

701 East Chocolate Avenue, Hershey, PA 17033, USA
Tel: 717-533-8845 x100 • Fax: 717-533-8661
E-Mail: cust@igi-global.com • www.igi-global.com

Table of Contents

Detailed Table of Contents

The aim of this chapter is to explore the capabilities of chatbots in the domain of marketing communication, with a particular focus on their potential application within the halal industry. It also analyzes the escalation in chatbot adoption across various business sectors. Furthermore, the chapter delves into the significance of adopting chatbots in Halal marketing communication. This includes an analysis of the challenges that may arise and capitalize on opportunities to successfully engage and captivate the intended audience. Likewise, this chapter sheds light on the areas of research that require further investigation and outlines potential avenues for future exploration regarding the adoption of chatbots in the context of Halal marketing. Hence, the contribution of this chapter lies in providing a comprehensive analysis of the challenges, opportunities, and positive outcomes associated with the chatbots. By doing so, it enriches existing knowledge and may serve as a basis for future research agendas.

The chapter aims to explore factors, values, and education driving Islamic entrepreneurial initiatives, and their impact on economic development. It emphasizes integrating Islamic principles into new business creation. The study also examines roles of absorption capacity, financial development, Islamic debt financing, and family background in Islamic entrepreneurship. By linking Islamic teachings and entrepreneurial pursuits, the Initiative enhances understanding and promotes ethical, sustainable business. It values Islamic work ethics and management team insights to foster Islamic-based enterprises. The chapter guides entrepreneurs, policymakers, and researchers in nurturing Islamic entrepreneurship, contributing to knowledge and future research. Insights can fuel positive transformations in the evolving entrepreneurial landscape.

Rooted in sharia values, Islamic finance should have the eligibility to lead microfinance in contributing to financial inclusion in Islamic countries in the Maghreb region. However, Islamic microfinance in this region has not been going well. At least when compared to the Southeast Asian region, Islamic

This study investigated the implementation of value intermediation by strengthening the Islamic social capital (ISC) information in Indonesia's Baitul Maal Wat Tamwil institution (BMTI) activities. ISC dimensions are considered an intangible resource that reinforces BMTI and plays a crucial role in its development in Indonesia. ISC consisted of four categories: networking, norms, trust, and spirituality. Thus, this chapter aimed to examine the stakeholder's perception of the importance of ISC as value intermediation in Indonesia's BMT. The study found that the respondents perceived ISC as valuable information for decision-making in BMT activities. Additionally, the mean for the importance of spiritual information is higher than that of networking, norms, and trust. The findings of the ANOVA revealed that the perceptions of spiritual, networking, norms, and trust confirmed the significance in the importance perception of the four categories.

The purpose of this study is to explore the factors that influence Muslim Consumers in purchasing halal products through the digital marketplace, using the unified theory of acceptance and use of technology (UTAUT). The approach of this study was based on the UTAUT's constructs such as performance expectancy, effort expectancy, social influence, and facilitating conditions toward behavioral intention and use behavior. There were 296 data collected through an online questionnaire from Muslim consumers in Indonesia by using the purposive sampling method. The structural equation modeling (SEM) Amos application was used to analyze the data of this study. The results of this study indicated that performance expectancy and social influence significantly affected the behavioral intention of Muslim consumers in purchasing halal products through the digital marketplace. On the other hand, effort expectancy had no significant effect on behavioral intention.

This study aims to explore various facets of entrepreneurship, particularly Islamic entrepreneurship, from a religious perspective, with a focus on its practice within the context of Bangladesh. In Bangladesh, diverse social enterprises, some profit-driven and rooted in Islamic principles like Zakat and Waqf, exemplify Islamic entrepreneurship. Examples include the Baitul Mukarram complex and the Islamic Bank Hospital, which generate income, promote Islamic culture, and address social needs. Social Islamic Bank Ltd. employs Cash Waqf, while organizations like Muslim Aid Bangladesh focus on economic empowerment. These approaches showcase the blend of profit motives, social impact, and religious values in Bangladeshi Islamic entrepreneurship.

Preface

Islamic entrepreneurship, a subject that has captured the attention of scholars, practitioners, and policymakers alike, continues to evolve and grow in significance. In many parts of the world, research on this topic is still in its nascent stages, with a pressing need for comprehensive exploration of models, strategies, and applications related to Islamic entrepreneurship. This reference book is an endeavor to meet this need by compiling a comprehensive array of chapters and topics encompassing all aspects of Islamic entrepreneurship.

The contemporary business landscape is witnessing a paradigm shift, with an increasing number of individuals and entities seeking alternative approaches that align with ethical principles, morals, and values. Islamic entrepreneurship, deeply rooted in Islamic thought, offers a compelling alternative. This book aims to shed light on Islamic entrepreneurship in comparison to conventional concepts, empowering practitioners, businessmen, academicians, and policymakers to make informed decisions and adapt to the changing dynamics of the business world.

Within these pages, readers will find invaluable insights and best practices shared by numerous authors who have dedicated their expertise to the field of Islamic entrepreneurship. It is our hope that policymakers can draw upon the knowledge contained herein to formulate and execute strategies that resonate with Islamic principles and values. This book also paves the way for the emergence of various models and frameworks that can serve as reference points for individuals across diverse sectors.

This comprehensive reference work caters to a wide readership, including students, academicians, practitioners, businessmen, entrepreneurs, and policymakers. It delves into the world of Islamic business concepts, principles, and the application of *Maqasid Shariah* in business practices. It explores the realm of halal products and industries, Islamic financing schemes, and best practices in Islamic entrepreneurship. Furthermore, it provides insights into businesses in Muslim-majority countries, the intersection of Islamic business with digitalization, the business environment within an Islamic context, and the role of Islamic business institutions.

Entrepreneurship is not limited by geographical boundaries, and this book embraces a global perspective. It delves into Islamic new venture creation, marketing strategies for small firms, global Islamic marketing, and the intricacies of Islamic retailing. Throughout the book, readers will find a rich tapestry of ideas and practices that can be applied in various business contexts.

We believe that this reference book will serve as a valuable resource for researchers, enabling them to delve deeper into the field of Islamic entrepreneurship. As a culmination of diverse perspectives, it also provides a platform for the comparison of existing business concepts with Islamic principles, offering readers a holistic view of the subject.

As editors, our goal was to create a comprehensive compendium that not only elucidates the nuances of Islamic entrepreneurship but also empowers individuals and organizations to make informed choices in the pursuit of ethical and value-driven business practices. We extend our gratitude to all the contributors who have shared their expertise and insights, making this book a reality.

Strategies and Applications of Islamic Entrepreneurship is a testament to the continued growth and relevance of Islamic entrepreneurship in the global business landscape. We hope it serves as a source of knowledge and inspiration for all those who seek to navigate the dynamic world of business while upholding the values and principles advocated by Islamic though.

CHAPTER OVERVIEW

Chapter 1: "Social Media Influencers - A Dynamic Impact for Halal Brands? A Review and Future Research Agenda"

In this chapter, the authors delve into the evolving landscape of marketing, exploring the influential role of social media influencers in promoting Halal brands. They meticulously examine the intricate connections between social media influencers, consumer attitudes, and perceptions. This comprehensive review offers valuable insights for marketers, advertisers, and scholars, shedding light on the changing dynamics of marketing in the digital age and the nuances of brand perception.

Chapter 2: "Understanding the Behavior of *Qardhul Hassan* Borrowers in Nano-Entrepreneurship: A Field Experiment of Islamic Nanofinance"

This chapter embarks on a field experiment to delve into the financial behavior of nano-entrepreneurs who utilize *qardhul hassan* in Indonesia. By providing insights into the financial management of nano-entrepreneurs, this research aims to inform policymakers and the Islamic microfinance industry. The study offers crucial data on serving underserved communities and filling the gap in Islamic microfinance.

Chapter 3: "Is it Practicable to Utilize AI-Powered Chatbots in Halal Marketing Communications?"

This chapter investigates the potential applications of chatbots in the realm of marketing communications, with a specific focus on the Halal industry. It examines the rising adoption of chatbots across various sectors and their significance in Halal marketing. The authors analyze both challenges and opportunities, offering valuable insights for businesses looking to engage their audience through innovative technologies in the Halal market.

Chapter 4: "Islamic Entrepreneurship Nurturing New Ventures through Islamic Principles"

This chapter explores the factors, values, and education that drive Islamic entrepreneurial initiatives and their impact on economic development. By integrating Islamic principles into new business creation, the study sheds light on the role of Islamic teachings and work ethics in fostering ethical, sustainable businesses. The chapter provides guidance for entrepreneurs, policymakers, and researchers, offering the potential for positive transformations in the entrepreneurial landscape.

Chapter 5: "Islamic Quadruple Helix, Social Finance Partnership for Developing Digital Financial Inclusion in Maghreb Region"

Focusing on the Maghreb region, this chapter investigates the potential of Islamic finance and social finance partnerships to accelerate financial inclusion. It examines the current state of Islamic finance in the region and proposes the Islamic Quadruple Helix approach as a means to bridge the financial inclusion gap. The chapter also maps out the digital financial inclusion ecosystem, emphasizing the importance of multi-stakeholder involvement.

Chapter 6: "Exploring Factors Influencing International Muslim Tourists' Intentions Towards Homestays in Sabah, Malaysia"

This chapter delves into the factors influencing the intentions of international Muslim tourists to stay in homestays in Sabah, Malaysia. It explores the significance of halal image, halal awareness, and religiosity in shaping tourists' preferences. The findings have implications for marketers and operators in Sabah's tourism industry, aiming to attract Muslim tourists while contributing to rural socio-economic development.

Chapter 7: "How Islamic Relational Capital Being Explored"

This chapter develops a relational capital model from an Islamic perspective, focusing on conflict management, customer satisfaction, networking, mutual respect, Islamic good governance, and the production of halal *toyyiban* products. By examining the importance of these elements in Islamic relational capital, the study provides guidelines for policymakers and organizations to enhance competitiveness, offering insights for both academics and practitioners.

Chapter 8: "Harnessing Islamic Entrepreneurship for the Belt and Road Initiative: Opportunities, Challenges, and Future Directions"

This chapter explores the potential synergy between Islamic business practices and the Belt and Road Initiative (BRI). It evaluates how Islamic business principles can contribute to the sustainability goals of the BRI and discusses the challenges of adapting digital processes to Sharia law. The chapter offers suggestions for future research to tap into the transformative force of Islamic entrepreneurship in global economic policies.

Chapter 9: "Involvement of Women in Islamic Finance in Pakistan: Challenges and Prospects"

This chapter investigates the challenges faced by women and the prospects available for them in Islamic finance in Pakistan. Through interviews with women in academia and industry, it sheds light on gender-related issues, opportunities, and efforts to overcome barriers. The findings may motivate women to pursue careers in Islamic finance and encourage policy changes to support gender diversity in the sector.

Chapter 10: "Islamic Marketing for Small Firms Value"

In this chapter, the authors examine the influence of Islamic marketing on the value of small enterprises. They analyze marketing strategies aligned with Islamic principles that cater to Muslim consumers and differentiate small businesses in competitive markets. The study dissects the intricate relationship between Islamic marketing, small business value, and relevant factors, providing guidance for small enterprises operating in Islamic markets.

Chapter 11: "Entrepreneurial intentions from an Islamic Perspective: A Case Study of Muslim Entrepreneurs in Pakistan"

This chapter delves into the concept of entrepreneurial intentions from an Islamic perspective, focusing on honesty and worship of Allah as key traits. Through a survey of Muslim business owners in Pakistan, the study explores the motivations and characteristics that drive entrepreneurial activities. The research provides insights into the intersection of Islamic values and entrepreneurship, emphasizing the importance of ethics and spirituality in business endeavors.

Chapter 12: "Exploring the Multifaceted Landscape of Halal Branding: Challenges, Opportunities, and Cross-Cultural Dynamics"

This chapter offers a comprehensive exploration of challenges and opportunities in Halal branding, encompassing marketing, consumer behavior, culture, and religion. It examines the global appeal of the Halal market, the complex link between Halal branding and consumer behavior, and strategic implications for businesses. The chapter calls for further research to develop branding frameworks tailored to the nuances of the Halal market, offering valuable insights for academics, marketers, and businesses.

Chapter 13: "Strategizing Islamic Medicine Marketing Through Social Media: The Case of Northern Nigeria"

This chapter investigates the role of social media in marketing Islamic medicine in Northern Nigeria. It explores how social media platforms are used for awareness creation and product visibility. The study highlights the prospects and challenges of leveraging social media in the promotion of Islamic medicine, emphasizing the need for regulatory measures in the industry.

Chapter 14: "Value-Based Intermediation - The Islamic Social Capital Perspective in Baitul Maal Wat Tamwil Institutions (BMTIs) in Indonesia"

This chapter explores the implementation of value intermediation through Islamic Social Capital (ISC) in Indonesia's Baitul Maal Wat Tamwil institutions (BMTIs). It delves into the dimensions of ISC, including networking, norms, trust, and spirituality, and examines their significance in decision-making within BMT activities. The study offers insights into the importance of ISC in reinforcing BMTIs and contributes to understanding the role of social capital in Islamic finance.

Chapter 15: "Using the Unified Theory of Acceptance and Use of Technology to Explore the Factors Influencing Muslim Consumer in Purchasing Halal Product Through Digitalization"

This chapter investigates the factors influencing Muslim consumers' purchasing behavior of Halal products through digital marketplaces, employing the Unified Theory of Acceptance and Use of Technology (UTAUT). The study analyzes constructs such as Performance Expectancy, Effort Expectancy, Social Influence, and Facilitating Conditions in relation to Behavioral Intention and Use Behavior. The findings provide insights into the role of technology in Halal product consumption and inform future research directions.

Chapter 16: "Islamic Entrepreneurship Application and Its Strategies: A Case Study of Bangladesh"

This chapter delves into the multifaceted landscape of entrepreneurship, particularly Islamic entrepreneurship, within Bangladesh. It explores the practices of diverse social enterprises rooted in Islamic principles, offering examples such as the Baitul Mukarram complex and Islamic Bank Hospital. The chapter highlights the blend of profit motives, social impact, and religious values in Bangladeshi Islamic entrepreneurship, serving as a valuable case study for understanding entrepreneurship in a religious context.

IN SUMMARY

As we reach the conclusion of this meticulously curated reference book, *Strategies and Applications of Islamic Entrepreneurship*, we reflect on the journey through the diverse and dynamic landscape of Islamic entrepreneurship. This comprehensive compilation of chapters, contributed by esteemed scholars from various corners of the world, has illuminated the multifaceted dimensions of Islamic entrepreneurship in the contemporary global context.

Throughout the chapters, we have explored a rich tapestry of topics, each contributing to our understanding of how Islamic entrepreneurship is shaping the business world and influencing economic and social development. From the innovative role of social media influencers in promoting Halal brands to the profound impact of Islamic principles on new business creation, each chapter offers unique insights and valuable knowledge.

Our journey took us from Indonesia, where nanofinance is transforming the lives of underserved communities, to the Maghreb region, where the Islamic Quadruple Helix approach is paving the way for financial inclusion. We ventured into the intricacies of Islamic medicine marketing in Northern Nigeria and the challenges and opportunities of Halal branding across cultures.

We also explored the vital role of women in Islamic finance in Pakistan, the ethical dimensions of Islamic marketing for small firms, and the significance of relational capital from an Islamic perspective. The intersection of technology and Islamic finance was examined, and the entrepreneurial intentions of Muslim business owners in Pakistan were studied, emphasizing the fusion of ethics and spirituality in business pursuits.

We concluded our journey by delving into the transformative potential of Islamic entrepreneurship within the context of the Belt and Road Initiative and Bangladesh's diverse social enterprises, which exemplify the harmonious coexistence of profit motives and social values.

In each of these chapters, we have witnessed the dynamic nature of Islamic entrepreneurship, a force that not only fosters economic growth but also upholds ethical and moral principles. It is a force that bridges the gap between traditional values and the modern business world, offering innovative solutions to contemporary challenges.

As editors, we are immensely grateful to all the contributors who shared their expertise and research findings, making this reference book a valuable resource for scholars, practitioners, policymakers, and students. The collective knowledge contained within these pages serves as a testament to the ongoing evolution and relevance of Islamic entrepreneurship in today's global business landscape.

We hope that this book inspires further exploration and research in the field of Islamic entrepreneurship. May it empower individuals, organizations, and nations to embrace ethical and value-driven business practices while fostering economic growth and social development. As we conclude this journey, we invite all readers to continue their exploration of Islamic entrepreneurship, for it is a field filled with endless opportunities and enduring principles that shape a better future for all.

Ahmad Rafiki
Universitas Medan Area, Indonesia

Alfatih Gessan Pananjung
Bahrain Institute of Banking and Finance, Bahrain

Muhammad Dharma Tuah Putra Nasution
Universitas Pembangunan Panca Budi, Indonesia

Chapter 1
Social Media Influencers:
A Dynamic Impact for Halal Brands? A Review and Future Research Agenda

Yossie Rossanty
https://orcid.org/0000-0001-9556-8958
Universitas Pembangunan Panca Budi, Indonesia

Yolanda Masnita
Universitas Trisakti, Jakarta, Indonesia

Sri Vandayuli Riorini
Universitas Trisakti, Jakarta, Indonesia

Muhammad Dharma Tuah Putra Nasution
https://orcid.org/0000-0002-4671-0230
Universitas Pembangunan Panca Budi, Indonesia

ABSTRACT

In the realm of marketing, the rise of influencer marketing and its integration with social media platforms have brought about a significant change in communication strategies. This convergence has led to a transformative shift in the marketing field. This study aims to investigate the diverse roles of social media influencers in promoting Halal brands. Specifically, it focuses on how influencers shape consumer attitudes and perceptions. The research also examines the complex interactions among influencers, opinion leaders, and endorsers in modern marketing. These insights are valuable for marketers, advertisers, and scholars. By offering a comprehensive understanding, this study enriches our knowledge of the evolving marketing landscape, the impact of social media on consumer behavior, and the intricate aspects of brand perceptions. This contributes to existing knowledge and provides a basis for future research.

INTRODUCTION

Research on social media influencers is a pertinent and captivating area of study for both academicians and practitioners alike. The ascendancy of influencer marketing coupled with the utilization of social

DOI: 10.4018/978-1-6684-7519-5.ch001

media platforms for advertising and brand endorsement has undeniably revolutionized the marketing landscape (Veirman et al., 2017). Discerning the efficacy of influencer marketing strategies and the variables that mold consumer perceptions and attitudes towards both influencers and brands stands as an imperative for marketers and businesses.

One sphere of investigation gravitates toward the impact of follower count on influencer effectiveness. Indeed, studies have unveiled that influencers boasting a substantial following are perceived as more popular and likable, a dynamic that can exert a positive influence on brand perceptions (Abidin, 2016). Nonetheless, the relationship between follower count and influencer effectiveness isn't always linear, necessitating further exploration to unravel the scenarios in which follower count emerges as a significant factor in influencer marketing (Abidin, 2016).

Another captivating arena of inquiry pertains to the role of product divergence in influencer marketing. Collaborating with influencers commanding vast followings might not universally be the optimal choice for promoting divergent products, as it could potentially dilute the perceived uniqueness of the brand and impact brand attitudes (Veirman et al., 2017). Discerning the judicious selection of influencers tailored to specific product categories, along with gauging the resonance of influencer-product alignment, becomes indispensable for effective influencer marketing strategies (Veirman et al., 2017).

The realm of research on social media influencers also delves into the realm of engagement between influencers and their followers. These studies unveil insights into the nature of influencer-follower dynamics and the variables propelling engagement (Zhang, 2022). Gaining a nuanced understanding of engagement mechanisms and the factors that catalyze robust influencer-follower relationships can elucidate influencer marketing strategies and aid brands in fostering meaningful connections with their target audience (Zhang, 2022).

This avenue of research in influencer marketing casts its interdisciplinary net widely, intersecting realms ranging from computer science, psychology, and business to medicine (Yildiz, 2022; Rizqi & Riorini, 2022; Abidin, 2016; Zhang, 2022; Zhang & Earp, 2020; Khan et al., 2022). Investigations have encompassed diverse aspects, from the profiles of social media users to the impact of influencers on consumer behavior and the efficacy of influencer marketing strategies (Yildiz, 2022; Rizqi & Riorini, 2022). Furthermore, studies have delved into impression management tactics adopted by influencers, the correlation between social media posts and academic citations, and the influence of influencers on the realm of digital marketing (Abidin, 2016; Zhang, 2022; Zhang & Earp, 2020; Khan et al., 2022). This interdisciplinary approach converges to furnish a holistic grasp of the influence and repercussions of social media influencers across diverse contexts (Yildiz, 2022; Rizqi & Riorini, 2022).

Similarly, delving into research on the impact of social media influencers on Halal brands emerges as a compelling necessity for myriad reasons. First and foremost, social media influencers have ascended as formidable agents of influence, meticulously shaping consumer attitudes, perceptions, and purchase tendencies (Handriana et al., 2020). Navigating the intricacies of how social media influencers can adeptly champion Halal brands and mold consumer behaviors emerges as an essential contemplation for marketers and enterprises deeply entrenched in the Halal market.

Secondly, the Halal market is undergoing a rapid expansion, encompassing not only Muslim-majority countries but also non-Muslim nations with substantial Muslim populations (Ali et al., 2018). Research centered on social media influencers holds the potential to empower businesses to tap into this burgeoning market. By discerning the preferences, needs, and aspirations of Muslim consumers, and comprehending how social media influencers can serve as conduits for promoting Halal brands, enterprises can strategically position themselves for success.

Thirdly, the influence wielded by social media influencers on Halal brands transcends conventional marketing and consumer behavior realms. It extends its reach into the domain of representing and shaping perceptions of Islam and Muslim identity in the digital realm (Gümüş & Onurlubas, 2023). Investigation in this arena possesses the capacity to enrich our understanding of the intricate interplay between religion, branding, and the landscape of social media within the context of Halal brands.

The primary objective of this study is to comprehensively investigate the multifaceted role that social media influencers assume within the domain of Halal brands. Specifically, the study aims to enhance our understanding of how the influence exerted by social media influencers intricately molds consumer attitudes and perceptions pertaining to Halal brands. Moreover, the study delves into the complex interplay and symbiotic relationships among social media influencers, opinion leaders, and endorsers within the contemporary marketing landscape. The insights gleaned from this study hold considerable significance for marketers and advertisers, affording them the opportunity to refine their influencer selection processes, craft strategies tailored to the distinctive attributes of Halal brands, and cultivate authentic connections with their intended audience. Additionally, scholars and researchers stand to gain profound insights into the ever-evolving panorama of marketing, the transformative impact of social media on consumer behaviors, and the intricate dynamics that underpin brand perceptions.

Halal Brand

Halal brands encompass products or services that adhere to Islamic law (Ali et al., 2018), ensuring their compatibility with the dietary guidelines of Muslims. These products are formally certified as Halal, signifying their permissibility for consumption. The essence of the Halal brand transcends mere products, intertwining religious convictions, ethical sourcing, and conscientious production practices that align with Islamic principles (Awan et al., 2015). Importantly, the domain of Halal extends beyond the realm of food, permeating diverse sectors such as cosmetics, finance, and tourism (Ali et al., 2018).

In the domain of Halal branding, celebrity endorsers emerge as influential architects of consumer perceptions and purchasing decisions. Notably, celebrity endorsements exert a tangible impact on customers' decision-making processes, amplifying their propensity to opt for Halal products (Awan et al., 2015). The orchestration of Halal marketing and branding practices, including strategic sales promotions and celebrity endorsements, undeniably molds customer behavior, steering them towards the sphere of Halal offerings (Awan et al., 2015). The strategic incorporation of influencers within this framework augments the brand's credibility and authenticity, effectively tapping into consumers' perception of these individuals as trustworthy sources of information (Awan et al., 2015).

The emergence of social media platforms has further catalyzed the fusion of influencers and Halal brands. Influencers are equipped to vividly exhibit Halal products to their followers, an audience often deeply engaged with the immersive realms of web 2.0 technology (Alalwan et al., 2017). By aligning with influencers, Halal brands are not only bolstered but also curated to resonate within their target demographic (Ali et al., 2018). This resonance generates a positive spillover effect, subtly influencing consumers' intentions to opt for Halal brands.

Crucially, marketing facets, including advertising and branding, punctuate the landscape of Halal product purchase intent (Awan et al., 2015). It becomes evident that meticulously crafted marketing campaigns, attuned to the tenets of Halal, possess the potential to amplify the visibility and desirability of Halal products and services (Awan et al., 2015). The interconnected factors of Halal marketing practices, personal and societal perceptions, and the presence of Halal certifications collectively navigate consumers towards reliance on Halal branding and, in turn, fuel their intention to opt for these offerings (Awan et al., 2015).

To sum up, the construct of Halal brands encapsulates products adhering to Islamic law. Celebrity endorsers and influencers intricately shape consumer perceptions and buying decisions, with marketing-related facets serving as pivotal touchpoints in propelling Halal purchase intent. This intricate interplay underscores the multifaceted dynamics within the domain of Halal branding and its resonance among consumers.

Social Media Influencer

A social media influencer embodies an individual who has amassed a substantial following across platforms like Instagram, YouTube, or TikTok. They wield the prowess to sway opinions, behaviors, and purchasing determinations of their followers (Abidin, 2016). Often specializing in particular niches such as fashion, beauty, fitness, travel, or gastronomy, these influencers intricately collaborate with brands to endorse products or services before their audience (Abidin, 2016).

In the realm of digital marketing, social media influencers have ascended as potent entities, capable of engaging sizable follower bases who entrust and esteem their insights and recommendations (Abidin, 2016). Employing their unique personal brand and authenticity, they foster connections with their audience, frequently sharing personal narratives, experiences, and insights (Abidin, 2016). Through their content, these influencers hold the power to mold consumer sentiments, inclinations, and purchasing intents—rendering them prized allies for brands aiming to reach and captivate distinct target markets (Abidin, 2016).

The significance of delving into research on social media influencers is multi-fold. Primarily, it furnishes marketers and advertisers with a lens to decipher the efficacy of influencer marketing strategies and the components that underpin fruitful influencer-brand synergies (Abidin, 2016). By scrutinizing the attributes, actions, and repercussions of social media influencers, researchers can offer insights into how brands can adroitly harness influencer collaborations to heighten brand visibility, credibility, and sales (Abidin, 2016).

Secondarily, research concerning social media influencers contributes profoundly to the comprehension of consumer behavior in the digital epoch. This line of inquiry delves into how individuals perceive and engage with influencers, the motivations underpinning their following and interaction, and the impact of influencer content on consumer sentiments and actions (Taillon et al., 2020). Such knowledge empowers marketers and advertisers to construct precise and impactful influencer marketing endeavors, resonating harmoniously with their target audience.

Moreover, delving into research on social media influencers can illuminate the ethical considerations and challenges intertwined with influencer marketing. This exploration probes matters like transparency, authenticity, and the potential for deceptive practices in influencer-brand collaborations (Taillon et al., 2020). Understanding these ethical dimensions holds paramount importance for both influencers and brands, ensuring the perpetuation of trust and credibility within their audience ecosystem.

Impactful Dynamics: Social Media Influencers, Opinion Leaders, and Endorsers in Marketing

In the dynamic realm of contemporary marketing, the symbiotic interplay between influential figures and brand communication strategies has become a focal point of exploration. As businesses strive to navigate the ever-evolving landscape of consumer engagement, the roles of social media influencers, opinion leaders, and endorsers have emerged as pivotal agents of influence. Each with its distinct attributes and nuances, this trio forms a spectrum of impact that extends beyond traditional advertising methodologies.

Social Media Influencers

In the realm of social media influencers, we encounter individuals who have masterfully cultivated substantial followings across various digital platforms. Their content creation is honed to specific niches, seamlessly bridging the gap between diverse interests and audience engagement. Crucially, they wield an unparalleled capacity to sway opinions, shape behaviors, and steer purchasing decisions within their cohort of followers (Shiner, 2020). By forging connections rooted in authenticity and personal branding, influencers become conduits of influence. This symbiotic relationship often extends to brand collaborations, wherein the promotion of products and services takes center stage (Shiner, 2020).

Opinion Leaders

The echelon of opinion leaders is populated by individuals lauded for their extensive knowledge and profound influence within distinct domains. Their eminence stems from being recognized as authorities or experts in their chosen fields. An essential facet of their influence rests in their aptitude for molding opinions and behaviors, largely a consequence of their persuasive acumen (Pepitone et al., 1957). It's pertinent to note that their impact transcends mere follower counts, as they wield the trust and esteem of their peers and adherents within their specific sphere (Pepitone et al., 1957).

Endorsers

Endorsers, on the other hand, fulfill the role of advocates by championing products, services, or brands through public support. Often encompassing celebrities, athletes, and prominent figures, their endorsement functions as a conduit for elevating brand credibility and visibility. This dynamic is aptly harnessed within advertising and marketing campaigns, where their credibility is leveraged to foster brand trust and consumer confidence (Segovia-Villarreal & Rosa-Díaz, 2022). Here, endorsers embody a nexus of recognition and reputation, channeling their influence to magnify brand resonance (Segovia-Villarreal & Rosa-Díaz, 2022).

In a nutshell, the synthesis of social media influencers, opinion leaders, and endorsers within the marketing realm unveils a dynamic triad, each with distinct attributes that collectively shape the intricate facets of consumer engagement. The ensuing table encapsulates the distilled essence of these definitions (see. Table.1).

Embedded within these concepts are interconnected threads, yet each possesses nuanced distinctions that delineate their distinct roles within the marketing tapestry. Within these contrasts lies the key to understanding their individuality, a facet that illuminates their unique contributions:

Table 1. Conceptual definitions

Concept	Definitions	Key authors
Social Media Influencers	Social media influencers are individuals who have amassed a substantial following on various social media platforms.	(Shiner, 2020)
Opinion Leaders	Opinion leaders are individuals who are acknowledged as knowledgeable and influential within specific domains or fields of interest.	(Chen et al., 2022) (Pepitone et al., 1957)
Endorsers	Endorsers are individuals or entities that publicly support or recommend a particular product, service, or brand.	(Segovia-Villarreal & Rosa-Díaz, 2022)

Social Media Influencers

Social media influencers are individuals who have cultivated substantial followings across various platforms. Concentrating on specific niches such as fashion, beauty, fitness, or travel, they yield the power to influence opinions, behaviors, and purchasing decisions within their follower base (Shiner, 2020). At the heart of their allure lies the ability to harness personal authenticity, fostering genuine connections with their audience. The hallmark of their impact is often seen in collaborations with brands to endorse products or services, exemplifying their capacity for engagement within the social media realm.

Opinion Leaders

Opinion leaders emerge as authoritative figures and founts of knowledge within designated domains or areas of expertise (Chen et al., 2022). Revered for their deep understanding, they possess the capacity to mold viewpoints and guide behaviors. Their influence stems from cultivated expertise, lived experiences, and their esteemed standing within their respective fields. Their persuasion proficiency further solidifies their role in shaping perspectives. Unlike social media influencers, their impact might not hinge on follower numbers; instead, it centers on the trust and respect of peers and adherents within their specific sphere.

Endorsers

In contrast, endorsers encompass individuals and entities that publicly champion products, services, or brands (Wang et al., 2022). This category notably includes celebrities, athletes, and widely recognized figures. Their endorsement functions as a conduit, infusing credibility and reputation to amplify brand visibility and consumer confidence (Wang et al., 2022). While they share commonalities with influencers and opinion leaders, endorsers may not actively cultivate ongoing audience relationships or exhibit vigorous engagement on social platforms.

In synthesis, social media influencers thrive through extensive reach and interactive prowess (Shiner, 2020). Opinion leaders wield influence through domain expertise and esteemed recognition (Chen et al., 2022). Endorsers bolster brands with their established credibility and stature (Wang et al., 2022). The synergy of these roles weaves a multifaceted fabric that molds the marketing and communication landscape. The ensuing table encapsulates the distilled essence of these discerning differences (see Table.2).

Building upon the insights distilled from the referenced works, a comprehensive panorama of the typologies inherent to social media influencers, opinion leaders, and endorsers comes into view.

Table 2. Conceptual differences

Concept	Description	Key authors
Social Media Influencers	Individuals with a substantial social media following who create and share content in specific niches. They have the power to influence opinions, behaviors, and purchasing decisions of followers through personal brand and authenticity. Collaborate with brands to promote products/services and engage with their audience on social platforms.	(Shiner, 2020)
Opinion Leaders	Individuals recognized as experts in specific domains. They influence others' opinions and behaviors through knowledge and persuasive abilities. Trusted and respected within their field, may not have a large social media following.	(Chen et al., 2022)
Endorsers	Individuals/entities publicly supporting or recommending products/brands. Enhance brand awareness, credibility, and consumer trust. Often include celebrities, athletes, or well-known personalities in advertising campaigns.	(Wang et al., 2022)

Social Media Influencers

Within the realm of social media influencers, a meticulous typology takes form, illuminating their multidimensional personas. Central to this classification lies the intricate analysis of two pivotal factors: the scale of followers amassed and the depth of engagement fostered within their audience, a discourse underscored by Frangi et al. (2019). A closer scrutiny unveils a more nuanced vista, one that encapsulates the distinct niches or specialized domains to which each influencer dedicates their content creation—a dimension artfully articulated by the insights of Zak and Hasprova (2020).

Moreover, this labyrinthine landscape gains complexity as we delve into the diverse array of content these influencers conjure, spanning realms such as lifestyle, fashion, fitness, and myriad other realms, as posited by Zak and Hasprova (2020). It becomes patently clear that the intangible attributes of authenticity and relatability exhibited by these influencers assume significant roles in differentiation and categorization within this vibrant milieu (Zak & Hasprova, 2020).

Opinion Leaders

The sphere of opinion leaders, likewise, unveils a typology rooted in their profound influence and capacity to sculpt multifaceted discourses. Foundational to this classification lies the dimensions of domain-specific impact and influence, a bedrock concept aptly expounded by Frangi et al. (2019). Expanding upon this foundation, the classification gains finesse by delving into the depths of erudition and expertise each opinion leader wields within their chosen purview, a facet eloquently explicated by Frangi et al. (2019).

Remarkably, a distinctive facet emerges, encapsulating their adeptness in shaping viewpoints and guiding the actions of their contemporaries—an aspect elucidated by Frangi et al. (2019). A nuanced stratum of classification unfurls as we contemplate the extent of their sway over pivotal societal figures, including regulators and political stalwarts, culminating in a comprehensive framework of categorization (Frangi et al., 2019).

Endorsers

The typology of endorsers unfurls its own intricacies, tethered to their ability to extend support and bestow their reputation upon products, services, or brands. This terrain is textured with distinct categories, each hinged upon the archetypal persona they embody—encompassing luminaries, athletes, and domain authorities—a revelation astutely unveiled by Zak and Hasprova (2020). A deeper plunge into this classification unravels the quotient of credibility and trustworthiness projected by an endorser, a pivotal differentiator dissected by Zak and Hasprova (2020).

Furthermore, the harmonization of personal values and ethical convictions with the products or brands they champion introduces another facet of classification within the sphere of endorsers, an insight eloquently articulated by Zak and Hasprova (2020). Ultimately, this taxonomy culminates by unraveling the pivotal role endorsers assume in steering consumer attitudes, influencing decision-making processes, and personifying brand role models—a discourse expounded by Zak and Hasprova (2020).

In a holistic summation, the dimensions that underpin social media influencers, opinion leaders, and endorsers weave a tapestry of intricate categorization, underscoring their diverse roles and profound ramifications for marketing strategies and brand positioning in the ever-evolving contemporary landscape. The ensuing table encapsulates the distilled essence of these typologies (see. Table.3).

Influence Unveiled: Taxonomies of Social Media Influencers, Opinion Leaders, and Endorsers in Contemporary Marketing

Amidst the intricate fabric of modern marketing, where consumer behavior evolves through the interplay of digital platforms, interpersonal connections, and shifting trends, the roles of social media influencers, opinion leaders, and endorsers have risen as pivotal focal points of inquiry. As businesses navigate this complex landscape, comprehending the nuanced dimensions and classifications within these personas becomes paramount. These classifications, derived from scholarly research and empirical insights, furnish a comprehensive framework to fathom the intricacies propelling their influence and impact in today's dynamic marketing milieu. Your text maintains a sophisticated and informative tone while effectively conveying the

Table 3. Typologies

Concept	Categories	Differentiating Factors	References
Social Media Influencers	Based on followers and engagement levels	Number of followers, level of engagement.	Frangi et al. (2019) Zak & Hasprova (2020)
	Based on niche/expertise	Specific areas of focus.	
	Based on content type.	Content themes such as lifestyle, fashion, fitness.	
	Based on authenticity and relatability.	Authenticity and relatability levels.	
Opinion Leaders	Based on domain or expertise.	Specific fields or domains of influence.	Frangi et al. (2019)
	Based on knowledge and recognized expertise.	Levels of expertise and knowledge.	
	Based on ability to shape opinions and actions.	Influential power to shape opinions and actions.	
	Based on influence on key social actors.	Impact on regulators, political leaders, etc.	
Endorsers	Based on type.	Categories like celebrities, athletes, experts.	Zak & Hasprova (2020)
	Based on credibility and trustworthiness.	Levels of credibility and trust.	
	Based on alignment with personal values.	Match between personal values and endorsed products/brands.	
	Based on impact on consumer attitudes and decisions	Influence on consumer attitudes and decision-making processes.	

Social Media Influencers

Delving into the realm of social media influencers, we uncover a well-structured framework built upon fundamental dimensions. Chief among these dimensions are metrics such as follower count and the level of engagement, as elucidated by the meticulous studies of Frangi et al. (2019). Venturing deeper, these influencers are classified based on the specific niches to which they passionately dedicate their content, a categorization eloquently expounded upon by Frangi et al. (2019). A more intricate landscape of classification emerges when we contemplate the essence of their crafted content, spanning from lifestyle narratives to nuances like fashion and fitness—a panoramic view vividly depicted by Zak and Hasprova (2020). Delving even further, the intangible qualities of authenticity and relatability they exude add another layer of distinction within this taxonomy, expertly emphasized by Zak and Hasprova (2020).

Opinion Leaders

Exploring the realm of social media influencers, we uncover a well-structured framework built upon fundamental dimensions. Chief among these dimensions are metrics such as follower count and the level of engagement, as elucidated by the meticulous studies of Frangi et al. (2019). Venturing deeper, these influencers are classified based on the specific niches to which they passionately dedicate their content—a categorization eloquently expounded upon by Frangi et al. (2019). A more intricate landscape of classification emerges when we contemplate the essence of their crafted content, spanning from lifestyle narratives to nuances like fashion and fitness—a panoramic view vividly depicted by Zak and Hasprova (2020). Delving even further, the intangible qualities of authenticity and relatability they exude add another layer of distinction within this taxonomy, expertly emphasized by Zak and Hasprova (2020).

Endorsers

The taxonomy underlying endorsers weaves a tapestry of roles, each anchored in their capacity to champion products, services, or brands. These diverse personas acquire distinct classifications, encompassing archetypes ranging from luminaries and athletes to domain experts—a design philosophy gleaned from the insightful work of Zak and Hasprova (2020). Delving deeper, the equilibrium struck between credibility and trustworthiness becomes a cornerstone, exerting palpable influence on their classification schema—a facet meticulously explored by Zak and Hasprova (2020). Furthermore, the synergy they cultivate between personal ethos and the brands they endorse becomes a defining factor within this taxonomy, aligning harmoniously with Zak and Hasprova's (2020) discerning perspective. The culmination of this taxonomy underscores their pivotal role in shaping consumer attitudes, guiding decisions, and embodying brand ethos—a realization illuminated by the erudition of Zak and Hasprova (2020). The ensuing table encapsulates the distilled essence of these intricate taxonomies (see. Table. 4).

In the domain of endorsers, the classification follows a distinct trajectory, revolving around the amalgamation of credibility and brand advocacy. These figures, often distinguished personalities, lend their reputation to endorse products, thus bolstering brand credibility and consumer trust. Their attributes encompass the roles they undertake as brand advocates and the alignment between their personal ethos and the brands they champion. The taxonomy of endorsers extends to their pivotal function in shaping advertising campaigns, cultivating brand loyalty, and guiding consumer choices. Their influence re-

Table 4. Taxonomies

Categories	Social Media Influencers	Opinion Leaders	Endorsers
Differentiation	Number of followers and engagement	Specific niche or area of expertise	Type of endorsers (e.g., celebrities, athletes, experts)
	Type of content created	Level of knowledge and recognized expertise	Level of credibility and trustworthiness
Additional Factors	Authenticity and relatability	Ability to shape opinions and influence actions	Alignment between personal values and endorsed products/brands
Influence Level	Moderate to high	Moderate to high	Variable depending on credibility, trustworthiness, and impact on consumer attitudes
Key authors: (Frangi et al., 2019) (Zak & Hasprova, 2020)			

verberates through their classification, encapsulating their capacity to epitomize brand ideals and steer consumer preferences.

In essence, the confluence of inherent attributes that define social media influencers, opinion leaders, and endorsers creates a vibrant mosaic of their roles in contemporary marketing. This comprehensive exploration unveils the intricacies underpinning their impact, offering insights into their distinct taxonomies that contribute to orchestrating consumer perceptions, behaviors, and engagement. As we navigate this taxonomy, we uncover the threads interweaving the dynamic tapestry of influence within the modern marketing landscape.

Social Media Influencers

Within the sphere of social media influencers, a unique constellation of markers distinguishes their role. These individuals command a substantial following across diverse social platforms, a phenomenon substantiated by the empirical insights of Cha et al. (2010). Beyond mere numerical presence, influencers craft and disseminate content intricately tied to specific niches, channeling narratives that resonate with their audience's aspirations and preferences—an essence underscored by Cha et al. (2010).

More profoundly, their influence transcends opinions to shape behaviors and guide purchasing decisions of their dedicated followers, a dynamic rooted in the astute observations of Cha et al. (2010). However, their impact isn't solely tied to numbers; they adeptly weave their personal brand and authenticity, forging connections with their audience that transcend the digital realm, a facet spotlighted by Cha et al. (2010). Notably, these influencers actively engage in meaningful dialogues with their followers, nurturing an ecosystem of interaction and engagement that amplifies their influence, as articulated by Cha et al. (2010).

Opinion Leaders

Within the galaxy of opinion leaders, a unique constellation of attributes emerges, depicting individuals of significant renown and influence. Emerging from diverse domains or specialized fields, these leaders radiate inherent depth of knowledge and impact resonating within their scholarly realms—an embodiment elucidated through the analyses of Cha et al. (2010) and Taillon et al. (2020). It's within these distinctive domains that they ascend to the pinnacle of authority, their words echoing as beacons of wisdom—a perception solidified by the discernment of Cha et al. (2010) and Taillon et al. (2020). Their potency lies not only in shaping viewpoints but also in directing actions, harnessing sagacity and persuasive prowess to catalyze transformative shifts, as substantiated by Cha et al. (2010) and Taillon et al. (2020). Remarkably, their following might not necessarily scale the peaks of social media metrics; however, their stature as luminaries of knowledge remains undisputed among peers and followers within their distinct domain—an insight upheld by the narratives of Cha et al. (2010) and Taillon et al. (2020).

Endorsers

Navigating the realm of endorsers unveils a distinctive tapestry of traits converging to amplify their role as brand advocates. Emerging from the fabric of individuals or entities, endorsers traverse the path of public support or endorsement for products, services, or brands—an emblematic facet firmly rooted in the findings of Magnini et al. (2010) and Kapitan & Silvera (2015). This journey often includes luminaries, athletes, and renowned figures who seamlessly lend their reputation and credibility to underscore the endorsement of a specific product or brand—an influential role that intricately shapes marketing strategies, as unveiled by Magnini et al. (2010). Their presence within advertising and marketing campaigns takes on a transformative mantle, elevating brand awareness, infusing it with credibility, and nurturing consumer trust—a trajectory harmonizing impeccably with the explorations of Magnini et al. (2010) and Kapitan & Silvera (2015). The following table encapsulates the distilled essence of these attributes (see. Table.5).

The intricate tapestry of social media influencers, opinion leaders, and endorsers unfolds through dimensions that intricately define their distinctive roles. With a comprehensive understanding drawn from scholarly references, the contours of each archetype emerge with compelling clarity, capturing the essence of their influence and impact.

Social Media Influencers

Venturing into the realm of social media influencers, their dimensions crystallize into defining elements of their influence. At the forefront, the level of activity and engagement on social media platforms unfurls

Table 5. Key characteristics

Characteristics		
Social Media Influencers	**Opinion Leaders**	**Endorsers**
Have a significant following on social media platforms (Cha et al., 2010).	Seen as experts or authorities in their respective fields (Cha et al., 2010; Taillon et al., 2020).	Often include celebrities, athletes, or well-known personalities (Magnini et al., 2010).
Create and share content related to specific niches (Cha et al., 2010).	Level of knowledge and recognized expertise	Level of credibility and trustworthiness
Have the ability to influence the opinions, behaviors, and purchasing decisions of their followers (Cha et al., 2010).	Shape the opinions and behaviors of others through their knowledge and persuasive abilities (Cha et al., 2010; Taillon et al., 2020).	Lend their credibility and reputation to endorse a particular product or brand (Magnini et al., 2010).
Leverage their personal brand and authenticity to establish connections with their audience (Cha et al., 2010).	May not necessarily have a large following on social media but are respected and trusted by their peers or followers within their specific domain (Cha et al., 2010; Taillon et al., 2020).	Used in advertising and marketing campaigns to enhance brand awareness, credibility, and consumer trust (Magnini et al., 2010; Kapitan & Silvera, 2015).
Engage with their followers on social media platforms (Cha et al., 2010).		

as a critical gauge of their reach and resonance, a revelation rooted in the empirical insights of Frangi et al. (2019). This facet seamlessly aligns with their unique ability to disseminate knowledge, shape opinions, and catalyze actionable responses within the digital landscape, as discerningly analyzed by Frangi et al. (2019). Anchored in the pillars of dedication, honed expertise, and acknowledged knowledge within specific domains, their reputation forms a foundational bedrock, as meticulously outlined in Frangi et al.'s (2019) research. The latent potential to transcend their influencer role and ascend into the echelons of opinion leaders emerges as a latent opportunity, fueled by robust network support and profound engagement with peers' content—an evolution elegantly unveiled by Frangi et al. (2019). Furthermore, this taxonomy extends its influence to advocacy campaigns, where influencers become pivotal in shaping framing paradigms and mobilizing actions, weaving a complex influencer ecosystem, as illuminated by Frangi et al. (2019).

Opinion Leaders

Transitioning to opinion leaders, a symphony of attributes converges to shape their influential stature. Comparable to virtuosos of knowledge, they navigate specific realms with intricate expertise, wielding profound influence, as underscored by Xu et al. (2018). This authority extends into the sphere of molding opinions and behaviors, their intellectual prowess akin to a rudder guiding public sentiment—an observation meticulously explored by Xu et al. (2018). Source attributes come to the forefront in this taxonomy, serving as markers of credibility and gravitas, elements encompassing account type, verification, and media type, all orchestrating their nuanced influence within public discourse, as detailed by Xu et al. (2018). Their influence reverberates through user engagement in intricate discussion networks, their insights sparking interaction and dialogue—an aspect eloquently probed by Xu et al. (2018). This taxonomy culminates by recognizing their potent potential to steer discourse and ignite engagement across the spectrum of social media platforms, a phenomenon validated within Xu et al.'s (2018) seminal research.

Endorsers

In the domain of endorsers, dimensions form the bedrock of their role as brand advocates. Foremost among these dimensions is their unequivocal public support and endorsement of products, services, or brands—an integral role magnified within Kühn & Riesmeyer's (2021) study. This dimension seamlessly intertwines with credibility and reputation, amplifying brand awareness and fostering consumer trust—an attribute deftly examined by Kühn & Riesmeyer (2021). Embodying their intrinsic role, endorsers galvanize advertising and marketing campaigns, magnifying brand credibility and nurturing the art of persuasion—a dimension intricately explored within Kühn & Riesmeyer's (2021) research.

Additionally, the dimension of serving as brand role models assumes prominence, their influence emanating as a guiding light, shaping consumer behavior and preferences—an attribute thoughtfully dissected by Kühn & Riesmeyer (2021). This taxonomy reaches its zenith as endorsers transform into embodiments of influence, brand ambassadors whose sway resonates through the corridors of consumer choice—an undeniable truth echoing within Kühn & Riesmeyer's (2021) insightful scholarship. The ensuing table encapsulates the distilled essence of these dimensions (see. Table.6).

Table 6. Key dimensions

Dimensions		
Social Media Influencers	**Opinion Leaders**	**Endorsers**
Level of activity and engagement on social media platforms (Frangi et al., 2019).	Knowledgeable and influential in specific domains or areas of interest (Xu et al., 2018).	Publicly support or recommend a product, service, or brand (Kühn & Riesmeyer, 2021).
Ability to disseminate knowledge, shape opinions, and influence actions of other users (Frangi et al., 2019).	Ability to shape opinions and behaviors of others through knowledge and persuasive abilities (Xu et al., 2018).	Credibility and reputation that enhance brand awareness and consumer trust (Kühn & Riesmeyer, 2021).
Reputation based on dedication, expertise, and recognized knowledge in a specific field (Frangi et al., 2019).	Source attributes such as account type, account verification, and media type (Xu et al., 2018).	Role in advertising and marketing campaigns to enhance brand credibility and persuasion (Kühn & Riesmeyer, 2021).
Potential to become opinion leaders based on a supportive network and engagement with others' content (Frangi et al., 2019).	Influence on user engagement in public discourse and discussion networks (Xu et al., 2018).	Potential to serve as brand role models and influence consumer behavior (Kühn & Riesmeyer, 2021).
Opportunity to impact campaign framing and mobilizing in advocacy campaigns (Frangi et al., 2019).	Potential to lead the discourse and drive engagement on social media platforms (Xu et al., 2018).	

Navigating Complexities: Unraveling Challenges and Opportunities Faced by Social Media Influencers, Opinion Leaders, and Endorsers

Amid the landscape of challenges, social media influencers, opinion leaders, and endorsers navigate a myriad of complexities, each with its unique set of hurdles and intricacies. These challenges, as discerned through the insightful lenses of various scholars, converge to shape a nuanced tapestry of impediments faced by these key figures.

Social Media Influencers

Within the realm of social media influencers, the contours of their challenges come to light, illuminated by the research of Veirman et al. (2017). A primary challenge that looms large is the perpetual quest to maintain authenticity and credibility within an influencer landscape that teems with saturation, a quest underscored by Veirman et al. (2017). This authenticity must coexist harmoniously with the balancing act of navigating popularity and likeability, while also navigating the intricate terrain of opinion leadership, as aptly delineated by Veirman et al. (2017).

Moreover, the intricate dynamics of follower count and followee ratios add a layer of complexity, where the impact of these numbers on likeability and popularity necessitates astute management, an endeavor meticulously investigated within Veirman et al.'s (2017) scholarship. The challenge of ensuring effective promotion of divergent products without diluting brand uniqueness occupies a pivotal juncture, wherein strategic alignment and promotion become a delicate art, a pursuit that finds resonance within Veirman et al.'s (2017) insightful study.

Opinion Leaders

Transitioning to the realm of opinion leaders, a rich tapestry of challenges unfolds, as discerned through scholarly inquiry. As expounded by Chen et al. (2022), the rapidly evolving dynamics of social media platforms and the fluid currents of online discourse pose a formidable challenge, one that compels opinion leaders to recalibrate their strategies with alacrity. In this labyrinthine realm, the challenge of managing the impact and influence of their opinions on followers and public sentiment emerges as a constant undercurrent, a challenge that assumes multifaceted dimensions, as evidenced by Chen et al. (2022). Within this milieu, the bane of political and religious polarization in online environments emerges as an onerous challenge, where opinion leaders must traverse treacherous terrains with sagacity and poise, as highlighted by Kazkaz (2020).

Simultaneously, the shift from traditional to digital paradigms ushers in a transformative challenge, where the nuanced art of adaptation becomes imperative, a transformation parsed meticulously by Balci et al. (2022). These challenges are compounded by the responsibility of ensuring the accuracy and reliability of information disseminated to followers, a formidable responsibility that resonates within the scholarship of Indriani et al. (2022). Moreover, the complexity of persuasive messaging and the looming potential for biases to creep in manifest as further challenges, as elegantly dissected by Balci et al. (2022).

Endorsers

Stepping into the arena of endorsers, the spectrum of challenges converges to illuminate a unique set of tribulations that they confront. Foremost among these is the intricate task of perpetuating credibility and trustworthiness as brand representatives, a mantle of authenticity that is inherently challenged by the dynamics of endorsement, a challenge that requires sagacious navigation. In tandem, the endeavor to balance their personal reputation with the weight of brand endorsements emerges as a tightrope walk, where equilibrium becomes pivotal, a challenge that underscores the duality of their role. The challenge extends into ensuring an unwavering alignment between their personal values and the ethos of the products or brands they endorse, a tango that necessitates meticulous scrutiny and congruence.

Crucially, the challenge of managing the potential impact of endorsements on their personal brand image emerges as a looming frontier, where the symbiotic dance between their personal identity and endorsed entities assumes paramount significance. This intricate choreography of challenges collectively encapsulates the dynamic landscape navigated by endorsers, a landscape where every move must be calculated with precision to maintain equilibrium and integrity. The ensuing table encapsulates the distilled essence of these challenges (see. Table.7)

In the dynamic landscape of contemporary marketing, where digital interactions and consumer engagement hold paramount importance, the roles of social media influencers, opinion leaders, and endorsers have emerged as pivotal nodes in the fabric of brand communication. These influential figures have become the subjects of intensive scholarly investigation, shedding light on both the challenges they face and the opportunities they present. As businesses strive to adapt to the evolving dynamics of consumer behavior and harness the power of these personas, a comprehensive understanding of the potential opportunities they offer becomes imperative.

The realm of opportunities beckons within the realm of social media influencers, opinion leaders, and endorsers, each brimming with distinctive potentialities as illuminated by the discerning perspectives of renowned scholars.

Table 7. Key challenges

Key Challenges		
Social Media Influencers	**Opinion Leaders**	**Endorsers**
Maintaining authenticity and credibility in a saturated influencer market.	Navigating the changing dynamics of social media platforms and online discourse.	Maintaining credibility and trustworthiness as brand representatives.
Balancing popularity and likeability with perceptions of opinion leadership.	Managing the influence and impact of their opinions on followers and public opinion.	Balancing personal reputation with brand endorsements.
Managing the impact of the number of followers and followees on likeability and popularity.	Addressing the challenges of political and religious polarization in online environments.	Ensuring alignment between personal values and endorsed products or brands.
Ensuring effective promotion of divergent products without compromising brand uniqueness.	Adapting to the transition from traditional to digital mindsets and platforms.	Managing the potential impact of endorsement on personal brand image.
Key authors: (Veirman et al., 2017; Chen et al., 2022; Kazkaz, 2020; Balci et al., 2022).		

Social Media Influencers

Navigating the sphere of social media influencers, a panorama of remarkable prospects unfolds, rooted in the insightful observations of Veirman et al. (2017). The foremost of these prospects stems from the seamless capacity to forge connections and captivate a vast audience across the sprawling expanse of social media platforms—a dynamic underscored by Veirman et al. (2017). Within this realm of engagement, a potent opportunity arises to augment brand awareness and cultivate a favorable brand attitude, a goal that comes to fruition through strategic partnerships with influencers, a narrative deeply resonant within Veirman et al.'s (2017) scholarship. The fusion of popularity and likability translates into a unique ability to influence consumer behavior, imbuing a tangible sphere of influence within the social media ecosystem, a phenomenon meticulously scrutinized by Veirman et al. (2017).

In parallel, a compelling avenue manifests in the ability to tailor product or service promotions with surgical precision, targeting a discerning audience entrenched within specific niches—a phenomenon meticulously outlined by Veirman et al. (2017). Noteworthy is the art of crafting narratives that brim with authenticity and relatability, narratives that harmoniously reverberate with followers and underscore the ingenuity articulated by Veirman et al. (2017).

Opinion Leaders

Transitioning to the realm of opinion leaders, an array of distinctive opportunities comes into sharp focus, illuminated through the perceptive lens of Balci et al. (2022). At the forefront of these vistas is the remarkable potential to exert influence over a substantial cohort of internet denizens—a potential capable of igniting transformative societal change—a testament to the potency of opinion leaders, as lauded by Balci et al. (2022). Within this realm, the opportunity to mold opinions and attitudes spanning the spectrum of social existence, politics, and products, emerges as a potent conduit—an opportunity crafted by Balci et al. (2022). The mantle of catalyzing discourse and amplifying engagement within the expansive realm of social media platforms becomes a hallmark, echoing the potential to lead and stimulate discussions—an aspect vividly illuminated by Balci et al. (2022).

Remarkably, this influential stature provides the opportunity to disseminate information that resonates with trust and reliability, lending a layer of credibility to the stature of opinion leadership, an accolade chronicled by Balci et al. (2022). The realm of influencing public perceptions and decision-making processes emerges as a pinnacle, where the potential to shape societal perspectives resonates powerfully, as extolled by Balci et al. (2022).

Endorsers

Venturing into the domain of endorsers, a tapestry of dynamic opportunities unfolds, as elucidated by the discerning insights of Balci et al. (2022). At the core of these prospects lies the profound ability to amplify brand credibility and imbue trustworthiness through the conduit of endorsements—an ability that takes tangible form, meticulously chronicled by Balci et al. (2022). In parallel, the prospect of elevating brand awareness and exposure through strategic alignment with endorsers unfurls as a compelling narrative, where the synergy between brand and endorser reverberates with impactful resonance, as illuminated by Balci et al. (2022). Central to this landscape is the unique ability to harness the formidable reputation and pervasive influence of endorsers, channeling their sway to nudge consumer behavior towards a desired trajectory—an artistry adroitly explored within Balci et al.'s (2022) scholarship. It is within these folds of influence that endorsers step into the role of brand role models, wielding an intrinsic power to shape consumer preferences and orchestrate choices—a narrative that resonates with profound significance within Balci et al.'s (2022) discourse.

The ensuing table encapsulates the distilled essence of these myriad opportunities, painting a comprehensive picture of the dynamic potentialities that beckon within the realms of influencers, opinion leaders, and endorsers (see. Table.8).

Table 8. Key opportunities

Key Opportunities		
Social Media Influencers	**Opinion Leaders**	**Endorsers**
Ability to reach and engage with a large audience on social media platforms.	Influence over a sizable mass of internet users and potential to drive social change.	Ability to enhance brand credibility and trustworthiness through endorsements.
Potential to enhance brand awareness and brand attitude through collaborations with influencers.	Ability to shape opinions and attitudes on various topics, including social life, politics, and products.	Potential to increase brand awareness and exposure through association with endorsers.
Opportunity to leverage popularity and likeability to influence consumer behavior.	Potential to lead the discourse and drive engagement on social media platforms.	Opportunity to leverage the reputation and influence of endorsers to influence consumer behavior.
Potential to promote products or services to a targeted audience within specific niches.	Opportunity to provide trusted and reliable information to followers.	Ability to serve as brand role models and influence consumer preferences and choices.
Ability to create authentic and relatable content that resonates with followers.	Ability to influence public perceptions and decision-making processes.	
Key authors: (Veirman et al., 2017; Balci et al., 2022)		

CONCLUSION

In the dynamic landscape of evolving marketing paradigms, an exciting avenue for research emerges at the crossroads of social media influencers and the realm of Halal brands. As the global demand for Halal products and services continues its ascent, a profound inquiry beckons into how influencers can skillfully convey the unique essence of Halal brands. This exploration assumes paramount significance, aiming to unravel the intricate dynamics and untapped potential that arise when influential figures engage with the intricate tapestry of Halal offerings. This research agenda aspires to chart an illuminating course, one that navigates the interplay between influential voices and the distinctive dimensions of Halal brands, thereby steering the trajectory of consumer preferences and behaviors.

Within this fertile research terrain, a compelling narrative unfolds, probing into strategic dimensions that warrant meticulous investigation. The first dimension ventures into the intersection of cultural alignment and authenticity. This inquiry seeks to comprehend how social media influencers can organically intertwine their content with the cultural and religious bedrock that defines Halal brands. The resonance of such alignment with consumer perceptions and its effect on diverse audiences come to the fore.

Another avenue delves into the pivotal role played by religious influencers in advocating for Halal brands. This exploration aims to illuminate the potency of influencers deeply immersed in the nuances of Halal requirements. By deciphering how they artfully convey brand attributes to devout consumers, this dimension uncovers an aspect of influence deeply entwined with authenticity.

Moving forward, the spotlight turns to the realm of digital storytelling for Halal Brands. This narrative-driven investigation seeks to unveil the potential of influencers employing digital storytelling techniques. Such techniques, it is posited, possess the power to convey the ethos and values of Halal brands, creating a narrative bridge that resonates with consumers seeking alignment with their beliefs.

Venturing further, the spotlight shifts to the realm of Halal lifestyle influencers. Here, a captivating study unravels the impact of lifestyle influencers seamlessly integrating Halal products and services into the broader tapestry of lifestyle narratives. The potency of influencers endorsing a holistic approach to Halal living surfaces, potentially elevating engagement.

Within tight-knit communities, the sway of micro-influencers on Halal brand perception comes into focus. This exploration seeks to fathom how micro-influencers wield influence, offering personalized recommendations that forge trust and impact the perception and adoption of Halal brands.

Awareness campaigns find their place in this narrative, too. Investigating the influence of social media influencers in spearheading campaigns to educate consumers about the significance of Halal certifications, this dimension delves into their role as educators and advocates, bridging awareness gaps.

Trust-building mechanisms underpin the subsequent inquiry. It unearths the intricate ways in which influencer endorsements construct trust and credibility for Halal brands. Through their voice, influencers become instrumental in bridging the chasm of trust that often exists between brands and consumers.

Innovation shines through engagement strategies, where influencers foster a sense of community among Halal brand enthusiasts. The impact of influencer-led discussions, challenges, and interactive content on forging this sense of belonging surfaces.

The selection of influencers tailored to Halal brands finds its niche, too. Developing a framework to identify influencers whose values align with the authenticity and values of Halal brands, this investigation aims to set the criteria for selecting harmonious influencers.

Finally, a pivotal dimension tackles impact measurement on consumer behavior. This is a metric-focused endeavor, aimed at forging methodologies that gauge the influence of social media influencers on consumer behavior towards Halal brands. The nexus between influencer engagement and purchase decisions stands under scrutiny here.

In sum, these interdisciplinary inquiries map out a journey of enlightenment, a journey that offers insights into the strategic prowess of social media influencers in propelling Halal brands to the forefront of consumer consciousness, while honoring the rich tapestry of cultural and religious sensitivities that weave the narrative of Halal offerings.

REFERENCES

Abidin, C. (2016). Visibility labour: Engaging with Influencers' fashion brands and# OOTD advertorial campaigns on Instagram. *Media International Australia, Incorporating Culture & Policy*, *161*(1), 86–100. doi:10.1177/1329878X16665177

Alalwan, A. A., Rana, N. P., Dwivedi, Y. K., & Algharabat, R. (2017). Social media in marketing: A review and analysis of the existing literature. *Telematics and Informatics*, *34*(7), 1177–1190. doi:10.1016/j.tele.2017.05.008

Ali, A., Xiaoling, G., Sherwani, M., & Ali, A. (2018). Antecedents of consumers' Halal brand purchase intention: An integrated approach. *Management Decision*, *56*(4), 715–735. doi:10.1108/MD-11-2016-0785

Awan, H. M., Siddiquei, A. N., & Haider, Z. (2015). Factors affecting Halal purchase intention–evidence from Pakistan's Halal food sector. *Management Research Review*, *38*(6), 640–660. doi:10.1108/MRR-01-2014-0022

Balci, E. V., Tiryaki, S., & Karakuş, M. (2022). Exploring the transformation of opinion leaders from a traditional to a digital mindset. *International Journal of Organizational Leadership, 11*(Special Issue 2022), 36-50.

Cha, M., Haddadi, H., Benevenuto, F., & Gummadi, K. (2010, May). Measuring user influence in twitter: The million follower fallacy. In *Proceedings of the international AAAI conference on web and social media* (Vol. 4, No. 1, pp. 10-17). 10.1609/icwsm.v4i1.14033

Chen, J., Wang, H., & Chao, X. (2022). Cross-platform opinion dynamics in competitive travel advertising: A coupled networks' insight. *Frontiers in Psychology*, *13*, 1003242. doi:10.3389/fpsyg.2022.1003242 PMID:36389514

Frangi, L., Zhang, T., & Hebdon, R. (2020). Tweeting and retweeting for fight for $15: Unions as dinosaur opinion leaders? *British Journal of Industrial Relations*, *58*(2), 301–335. doi:10.1111/bjir.12482

Gümüş, N., & Onurlubas, E. (2023). Investigation of Factors Affecting Generation Z's Halal Cosmetics Adoption. *Marketing and Management of Innovations*, *14*(1), 1–11. doi:10.21272/mmi.2023.1-01

Handriana, T., Yulianti, P., Kurniawati, M., Arina, N. A., Aisyah, R. A., Ayu Aryani, M. G., & Wandira, R. K. (2021). Purchase behavior of millennial female generation on Halal cosmetic products. *Journal of Islamic Marketing*, *12*(7), 1295–1315. doi:10.1108/JIMA-11-2019-0235

Indriani, S. S., Limilia, P., & Alam, P. W. (2022). Opinion Leaders and Health Information: A Systematic Literature Review in Indonesia. In *Proceedings of International Conference on Communication Science*, (pp. 737-744). IEEE. 10.29303/iccsproceeding.v2i1.110

Kapitan, S., & Silvera, D. H. (2016). From digital media influencers to celebrity endorsers: Attributions drive endorser effectiveness. *Marketing Letters, 27*(2), 553–567. doi:10.100711002-015-9363-0

Katz, E., Lazarsfeld, P. F., & Roper, E. (2017). Personal influence: The part played by people in the flow of mass communications. *The American Journal of Psychology, 70*(1), 157.

Kazkaz, L. (2020). Role of New Opinion Leaders on Social Media in Political and Religious Polarization (Jordanian case study). *Lebanese Science Journal, 21*(2), 211–229. doi:10.22453/LSJ-021.2.211-229

Khan, S., Zaman, I., Khan, M. I., & Musleha, Z. (2022). Role of Influencers in Digital Marketing: The moderating impact of follower's interaction. *Gmjacs, 12*(1), 15–43. doi:10.59263/gmjacs.12.01.2022.218

Kühn, J., & Riesmeyer, C. (2021). Brand Endorsers with Role Model Function. MedienPädagogik. *Zeitschrift Für Theorie Und Praxis der Medienbildung, 43*(43), 67–96. doi:10.21240/mpaed/43/2021.07.25.X

Magnini, V. P., Garcia, C., & Honeycutt, E. D. Jr. (2010). Identifying the attributes of an effective restaurant chain endorser. *Cornell Hospitality Quarterly, 51*(2), 238–250. doi:10.1177/1938965510363669

Rizqi, S. S., & Riorini, S. V. (2022). The Stimulus of Loyalty to Beauty Product Influencer on Social Media. *The Management Journal of Binaniaga, 7*(2), 197–212. doi:10.33062/mjb.v7i2.10

Segovia-Villarreal, M., & Rosa-Díaz, I. M. (2022). Promoting Sustainable Lifestyle Habits:"Real Food" and Social Media in Spain. *Foods, 11*(2), 224. doi:10.3390/foods11020224 PMID:35053956

Shiner, L. (2020). *Something ordinary to something navy- exploring influencer arielle charnas' use of parasocial interaction techniques on instagram.*

Taillon, B. J., Mueller, S. M., Kowalczyk, C. M., & Jones, D. N. (2020). Understanding the relationships between social media influencers and their followers: The moderating role of closeness. *Journal of Product and Brand Management, 29*(6), 767–782. doi:10.1108/JPBM-03-2019-2292

Veirman, M., Cauberghe, V., & Hudders, L. (2017). Marketing through Instagram influencers: The impact of number of followers and product divergence on brand attitude. *International Journal of Advertising, 36*(5), 798–828. doi:10.1080/02650487.2017.1348035

Wang, S. W., Huang, C. Y., & Sun, C. T. (2022). Multiagent Diffusion and Opinion Dynamics Model Interaction Effects on Controversial Products. *IEEE Access : Practical Innovations, Open Solutions, 10*, 115252–115270. doi:10.1109/ACCESS.2022.3218719

Xu, Q., Yu, N., & Song, Y. (2018). User engagement in public discourse on genetically modified organisms: The role of opinion leaders on social media. *Science Communication, 40*(6), 691–717. doi:10.1177/1075547018806526

Yildiz, S. Y. (2022). Instagram Influencerlarının Cinsiyetine Göre Tüketici Profillerinin Belirlenmesi. *Cumhuriyet Üniversitesi İktisadi ve İdari Bilimler Dergisi, 23*(4), 943–953. doi:10.37880/cumuiibf.1130303

Zak, S., & Hasprova, M. (2020). The role of influencers in the consumer decision-making process. In *SHS web of conferences* (Vol. 74, p. 03014). EDP Sciences. doi:10.1051hsconf/20207403014

Zhang, D., & Earp, B. E. (2020). Correlation between social media posts and academic citations of orthopaedic research. *JAAOS Global Research & Reviews, 4*(9).

Zhang, W. (2022). The Engagement Between Social Media Influencers and Their Followers on Instagram: A Case Study of# StopAsianHate. *Rangahau Aranga Aut Graduate Review, 1*(3).

Chapter 2
Understanding the Behavior of Qardhul Hassan Borrowers in Nano-Entrepreneurship:
A Field Experiment of Islamic Nanofinance

Khairunnisa Musari
https://orcid.org/0000-0003-0525-9903
Kiai Haji Achmad Siddiq State Islamic University, Indonesia

Nur Alifah Fajariyah
https://orcid.org/0000-0002-7752-2873
Kiai Haji Achmad Siddiq State Islamic University, Indonesia

Khusnul Khotimah
Kiai Haji Achmad Siddiq State Islamic University, Indonesia

ABSTRACT

Most emerging countries have communities categorized as excluded and underserved, unbanked and underbanked, the bottom of the pyramid (BoP), and ultra poor which have no ability to access bank financing. They are often victims of loan sharks. They should be a target of microfinance, but most banks and also microfinance institutions (MFIs) do not yet do well in serving them. Likewise, Islamic microfinance in fact has also not succeeded in reaching these people. Islamic nanofinance through qardhul hassan is promoted as a new paradigm to fill the Islamic microfinance gap. Through a field experiment for eight months by providing a fund IDR5 million with a maximum loan IDR1 million to provide nanofinancing, this study investigated the financial behavior of the nano-entrepreneurs in managing the qardhul hassan in Indonesia. The outcome of this study is expected to be input for policymakers, especially for the Islamic micro-industry, to come up with financing schemes according to the characteristics of these communities.

INTRODUCTION

Most emerging countries have very poor people in large numbers. They have no ability to access bank financing, particularly in rural areas. Asian Development Bank [ADB] (2000), Robinson (2001), Morduch

DOI: 10.4018/978-1-6684-7519-5.ch002

& Haley (2002), Segrado (2005), and Leikem (2012) mentioned that microfinance is a powerful and effective tool for poverty alleviation. However, Duvall (2004), Bateman (2011), Parpart (2014), Mahanti (2018), Musari & Simanjuntak (2016), Musari (2016b, 2019, 2020b, 2020c) found the microfinance institutions (MFIs) in some countries charge high rates to poor people, although they are bit lower than local loan sharks interest rates. Nevertheless, the rates of small loans to poor people are generally more expensive than the rate of normal commercial banks.

In order to provide more opportunities for financial services for the impoverished, meager income, and very low enterprises, then come to the term 'nanofinance'. Not many literature reviews about nanofinance. The presence of nanofinance has not been accepted as much awareness as microfinance in theoretical work. However, Pathak & Sriram (2004), Mahanti (2008), Ray (2008), Parpart (2014), Chonlaworn & Pongpirodom (2015), Musari & Simanjuntak (2016), Musari (2016b, 2020b, 2020c) highlighted that nanofinance practices can be found in some Asian countries like Thailand, India, Cambodia, and also Indonesia.

Referring to Mahanti (2008) and Musari (2016b, 2017c, 2020b, 2020c), it can be drawn a common thread related to nanofinance. Its missions are to permit the people in the bottom of the pyramid (BoP) to have easier access to obtain financing, to encourage people in BoP to have (small) business; and to avoid them to go to the loanshark. Generally, the user of nanofinance is women with ultra micro businesses ---or can also be called as nano enterprises, and afterward in this paper will be called so--- which have no access to capital from banks and also MFIs because have no guarantee or collateral.

In Indonesia, nano economy is a representation of the face of the people's economy (Musari, 2020a) and nanofinance also can address the gap of Islamic microfinance (Musari, 2017b). To encourage the existence of Islamic nanofinance as a new paradigm to fill the Islamic microfinance gap, qardhul hassan as a better contract (Musari, 2017c, 2019, 2020c, 2020d).

METHOD

By using a qualitative approach, this applied research using a field experiment in Situbondo, East Java Province, with the nanofinance project name "Rumah Qardhul Hassan (RQH)" or House of Qardhul Hassan. RQH allocated IDR5 million as capital with a maximum loan of IDR1 million to understand the behavior of *qardhul hassan* borrowers in managing the funds for eight months.

The target of this field experiment was people who are categorized as excluded and underserved, unbanked and underbanked, BoP, and very poor/ultra poor as well as ultra micro/super micro enterprises. Then, Situbondo was chosen as the experimental location because the widest micro small medium enterprises (MSMEs) network that the research team could access was in this regency. By considering the need to make sure the borrowers to open-heart in providing information, this experiment must find the close relationship between borrowers and the RQH operator which is an extension of the research team.

Furthermore, a field experiment was taken in this study to find the characteristic of borrowers as representatives of nano enterprises and ultra-micro communities, their reason to access nanofinance, what is the mindset of them regarding 'debt', their ability to pay this soft loan, etc. In order to establish the validity of a number of findings in the field, this study also confirmed them by interviewing a practitioner of an Islamic bank.

By understanding the behavior of nanofinance borrowers, the outcome of this study is expected to be input for stakeholders, particularly to policymakers and Islamic micro-industries, to come up with financing schemes according to the financial behavior of communities categorized as excluded and underserved, unbanked and underbanked, BoP, and ultra poor in managing the borrowing fund.

RESULT AND DISCUSSIONS

Nano-Entrepreneurs

Worldwide, microfinance plays a key role in providing financial services to the poor. Microfinance helps mitigate vulnerability to shocks, such as sickness as well as natural disasters, and develops enterprises. Microfinance plays an important role in the development of the country and in alleviating poverty. According to The Micro Credit Summit, microfinance actually is 'programs extend small loans to very poor for self-employment projects that generate income, allowing them to care for themselves and their families'. So, there are 'very poor' not just 'poor' which should be a target of microfinance too. The community group 'very poor' or also often called ultra poor or ultra micro or super micro is often neglected in microfinance.

In Indonesia, businesses are classified into categories of MSMEs, as well as large enterprises. For MSMEs, the criteria of the classification is regulated under Article 35 of Government Regulation No. 7 of 2021 on the Ease, Protection, and Empowerment of Cooperatives and MSMEs ("IGR No. 7/2021"). Table 1 shows the current criteria which distinguish MSMEs based on their business capital (excluding land and business buildings) and sales annual. These criteria are the latest criteria currently in effect.

Referring to IGR No.7/2021, the lowest business group in Indonesia's economic pyramid structure is micro-enterprises. In the field, many economic activities for which the value of business capital and annual sales under the criteria of the micro-enterprises as within the IGR No.7/2021. According to Musari & Simanjuntak (2016), most banks in Indonesia have not accommodated people or businesses with conditions under the micro-enterprises criteria. The classification of credit or financing in Indonesian banks just is categorized into MSMEs, but their microfinance in fact does not cover the 'very poor/ultra poor/ultra micro/super micro' which consist the very low income and very micro enterprises. In other words, microfinance in the term of the bank actually does not service the real micro society.

Table 1. The criteria for MSMEs

Type of Enterprises	MSMEs Classification	
	Based on Business Capital (excluding Land and Business Buildings)	**Based on Sales Annual**
Micro Enterprises	Enterprises with the maximum business capital criteria of IDR1 billion.	Enterprises with the maximum annual sales criteria of IDR2 billion.
Small Enterprises	Enterprises with the business capital criteria between IDR1 billion up to IDR5 billion.	Enterprises with the annual sales criteria between IDR2 billion up to IDR15 billion.
Medium Enterprises	Enterprises with the business capital between IDR5 billion up to IDR10 billion.	Enterprises with the annual sales criteria between IDR15 billion up to IDR50 billion.

Source: IGR No. 7/2021

Previously, Ascarya & Sanrego (2007) also mentioned that MSMEs classification in Indonesia should be redefined to reach the 'very poor/ultra poor/super micro/ultra micro' as well as to assist and lead them to expand their businesses up until survive, larger, and self-reliant. At that time, micro-enterprises still was defined as businesses with assets of IDR10-100 million and credit limits of IDR5–50 million. So, the super micro or ultra micro-enterprises could be defined as businesses with assets less than IDR10 million and a credit limit of less than IDR5 million. Likewise, the survey by The Asia Foundation (2003) found that MFI in Indonesia was defined as an institution (bank or nonbank) that provides loans with a ceiling of Rp 50 million per customer.

The situation of very poor/ultra poor people or ultra micro/super micro enterprises which are neglected from access to formal financial institutions, especially banks, also occurs in a number of countries, particularly in emerging countries. This is also what sparked the emergence of a new term which became known as 'nanofinance'. So, the term of microfinance needs to be redefined and nanofinance, even picofinance, should be promoted as the financial services for the very micro society, namely very poor/ultra poor people and/or ultra micro/super micro enterprise.

Furthermore, The Asia Foundation (2003)'s survey recommended nonbank MFIs can be an alternative for the micro-enterprises and/or the poor to access financial services. Banks are considered too bureaucratic by most of the micro-enterprises and/or the poor. Banks are also incapable to serve the poorest strata because the cost of small loan services was exorbitant. This consideration of profitability is believed to affect banks' reluctance to allocate microfinance.

However, around the world, the size of microfinance is very likely to vary between countries. Referring to World Bank (1978), microenterprises can be defined differently. It depends on the country's stage of development, policy objectives, and administration. Thus, microfinance also should be defined differently. Likewise with nanofinance. Table 2 shows a comparison of the value of financing or credit on nanofinance in Indonesia, Cambodia, Thailand, and India.

Characteristics of Borrowers

Through field experiments, this study would like to know the characteristics of nanofinance borrowers. When the practice of nanofinance in a number of countries targets women as borrowers, this experiment did not limit the gender of the borrowers. Whoever comes and the nanofinance capital was still available, the operator of RQH will distribute the fund. While microfinance generally provides funding to communities to build or develop productive businesses, this field experiment does not require the use of loan funds for businesses. However, the operator of this nanofinance project encourages the funds to be used for productive activities.

Table 3 shows the characteristics of nanofinance borrowers obtained during the eight months of the field experiment. The IDR 5,000,000 capital used was only able to help provide soft loans to seven people. When the idle funds are empty or no money was returned or the available funds do not meet the borrower's funding needs, the operator does not serve loans even though borrowers come.

Based on Table 3, the general characteristics of nanofinance borrowers are: having no monthly steady income; no payroll; no financial history or have, but limited financial history; and no collateral. Their income is not regular and they don't always get income every day. Some of them come to RQH with the reason: emergency needs (for healthcare), working capital, debt payment, social needs, and daily needs (for food). Indeed, the nanofinance concept actually is helping the very poor with emergency needs, such

Table 2. Comparison of nanofinance in four countries

	India	Thailand	Cambodia	Indonesia
The Concept of Financial Institution	Nanofinance Institution (NonGovernment Organization)	NonBank, Limited Company or Public Company (under Bank of Thailand as regulator)	Cooperative/ Microfinance Institution (Non Government Organization)	Cooperative/ Microfinance Institution (under Department of Cooperative and MSMEs or Financial Services Authority (OJK)
Mission	Avoid the very poor women to go to the moneylenders, encourage the very poor to be independent and have the minimum necessities to live a decent life, build sufficient internal financial.	Allow the grassroots to have easier access to obtain credits, to tackle the problem of informal loans, ease the loan shark problem and promote better access to capital that would expand occupational opportunities of the borrowers.	Avoid the high interest of rural/local bank.	Avoid the people to go to the moneylenders and encourage the people to have (small) business.
Credit Needs	Emergency needs	Emergency needs	Livelihood activities.	Business, but also for emergency
Loan Size	Up to Rs 2,000 Equal to IDR 360,713 ~ USD 24.22 (Rs 1 ≈ IDR 180.36; Rs 1 ≈ USD 0.012) on June 8, 2023.	Up to Bt 100,000 Equal to IDR 42,675,450 ~ USD 2,865 (Bt 1 ≈ IDR 426.71; Bt 1 ≈ USD 2,864) on June 8, 2023.	Up to USD100 Equal to IDR 1,489,825 (USD 1 ≈ IDR 14,898) on June 8, 2023.	IDR50,000- 1,000,000
Interest Rate	-	Not exceeding 36% per year	<1.8% per month	0.5% per week
Repayment Periods	< 1 years	2-3 years		10 weeks
Collateral/ Guarantees	No collateral required	No collateral required	No collateral required	No collateral required

Source: Developed from Musari (2016b)

as food, healthcare, education, death, wedding, daily livelihood, small trading or very micro-enterprises (Musari, 2016a, 2016b, 2017a, 2017b, 2019, 2020b, 2020c).

Generally, the field experiment found the borrowing behavior of borrowers can be influenced by internal and external factors. Internal factors are elements that are influenced by individual conditions while external factors are elements that are influenced beyond the individual control. This study found at least five internal and external factors that influence the nanofinance borrowing behaviors of borrowers.

INTERNAL FACTORS

The Emergency and Daily Needs

Based on the investigation result of the borrowers, the main reason for them to find the nanofinance is to meet their urgent basic needs, particularly daily fulfillment. In Maslow's Hierarchy of Needs (1943), human behavior is driven by their needs. The need hierarchy model shows that the most basic level is the fulfillment of physiological needs, so this indicates that the very poor/ultra poor people or ultra micro/ super micro enterprises still focus on physiological fulfillment.

Ensuring physiological fulfillment, in Islamic economics perspective, is the need of human beings to preserve their true nature or innate goodness *(fitrah)*. The fulfillment of this need can be temporarily

Table 3. The characteristics of Qardhul Hassan borrowers

NAME	Zainul	Oos	Siti	Fajar	Siti	Yoyok	Saiful	Kiki
SEX	Male	Female	Female	Female	Female	Male	Male	Female
NUMBER OF DEPENDENTS	3	1	4	1	4	5	1	1
HUSBAND/WIFE	1	0	0	1	0	1	1	1
CHILDREN	2	1	4	0	4	2	0	0
OTHERS	0	0	0	0	0	2	0	0
AGE	32	49	60	39	60	50	23	18
OCCUPATION								
- Main Job	Meatball Sliders	Vegetables Peddlers	Pensionary	Honorary	Pensionary	Street Vendor	Coolie	Freelance
- Side Job	-	Consignment	-	Freelance	-	Freelance	Freelance	-
INCOME PER MONTH								
- Average (IDR)	250,000	75,000	3,000,000	400,000	3,000,000	300,000	1,200,000	600,000
- Extra Income (IDR)	-	25,000	-	200,000	-	100,000	100,000	200,000
EXPENSES								
- Average (IDR)	50,000	30,000	1,500,000	1,500,000	1,500,000	50,000	35,000	50,000
- Working Capital (IDR)	200,000	200,000	2,000,000	-	2,000,000	200,000	-	200,000
THE INTENDED USE	Emergency Needs	Working Capital	Emergency Needs	Debt payment	Debt payment	Social Needs	Working Capital	Daily Needs
LOAN								
Amount (IDR)	500,000	500,000	1,000,000	500,000	1,000,000	700,000	250,000	600,000
Borrowing Period	3 months	3 months	2 months	3 months	22 days	3 months	4 months	3 months
Payment System								
- Instalment system	Once Payment	Weeekly	Once Payment	Monthly	Once Payment	Once Payment	Weekly	Daily
- Total Payment (IDR)	Paid off	200,000	Paid off	-	-	-	-	20,000

Source: Documentation of Authors

postponed. Even so, this need must still be met because it can result in insecurity in human life. Chapra (2008) explained that the Islamic worldview and its values also address the dire need for the security of life.

Helping the Family Economy

For female borrowers, most of their motivation to borrow is to help their husbands in the family economy. The money which is given by their husbands not enough to meet their living needs, including to meet the educational needs of their children, so the wives feel an obligation to complete it spontaneously even without the husband's permission as expressed by Mrs. Kiki,

"...I'm trapped and I don't know where to borrow anymore. The children have not paid the school tuition for two months, Ma'am. If I didn't pay for it, we can not get the certificate. I've been desperately looking for a job washing and ironing, but I could not find it, Ma'am... I didn't tell my husband, what a pity, his business is going down."

Based on the information above, borrowing behavior is based on the ultra group's spontaneity in seeking the fastest alternative to solve the problems of life's necessities. This indicates that the communities categorized as excluded and underserved, unbanked and underbanked, BoP, and ultra poor do not have some alternative choices in solving the problems.

Capital Needs

A factor that also influences borrowing behavior is the need for capital to open a business. In the Theory of Capital Structure, Modigliani & Miller (1958) and Myers (2001) mentioned that many different media can supply capital, one of them being pure debt instruments that dominate the capital structure. In Islamic Economics, the concept of debt and receivables were regulated in Surah Al-Baqarah: 280, *"And if (the debtor) is in trouble, then give him toughness until he has plenty. And giving charity (some or all of the debt) is better for you, if you knew."*

Islam has provided guidelines for paying debts. The concept of accounts payable in Islam is applied to financing. This financing is of a business nature and social in nature. One type of financing is *qardhul hassan.* For the ultra group, this financing provides a breath of fresh air because there is no interest charged to the borrower, flexible terms, and no collateral to be submitted. The experience of transacting at RQH using the *qardhul hassan* contract makes them become loyal customers of RQH as mentioned by Mrs. Siti when she borrowed for the second time,

"Ma'am, if I may borrow again, Ma'am, InsyaAllah, I will pay for the harvest later... I've tried to have a qardhu house from the start, I don't bother going anywhere anymore. If you don't need a survey here, it's fast, there's no interest, I'm just glad I borrowed it here".

Zainul also conveyed the same thing when he was going to borrow for the second time,

"... Ma'am, I'm here to borrow again five hundred thousand for trade purposes... Oh God, how could they have the heart, they've been given a free loan and we decide when to pay it, Ma'am, check it out, don't worry about it. Let it be, Ma'am... Let me pray all the borrowers will pay and this RQH keep running well. Gosh, Sist... You have a lot of rewards, like you help poor people so as not borrow from a moneylender (mindring)".

Lifestyle

One of the reasons for borrowers to access the *qardhul hassan* was caused by the snowball effect of debt as a result of mistakes in interpreting and managing finances as well as lifestyle. As stated by Fajar,

"I'm stuck in debt. At first, I needed money for buying a motorcycle after seeing a debt offer on my mobile phone. I received a sizable installment and finally, I could not pay it."

The same thing was conveyed by Mrs. Susi, a prospective borrower of nanofinance, but did not meet by RQH because the fund need was too large for RQH's capital,

"...I have been so confused and caused a lot of needs, I have been borrowing three times for my daughter's wedding parties, and if I don't pay back soon they will make fun of me."

Debt Unawareness

The emergence of ignorance of debt is caused by an inadequate religious understanding of the concept of debt. This creates an 'easygoing' character for some borrowers towards the obligation to repay the loan. Coupled with the lack of knowledge and lack of experience in obtaining and managing large amounts of money, this causes excessive consumption patterns when getting large amounts of money. Islam has warned about the dangers of debt, as conveyed in the hadith, the Prophet said, *"Whoever dies with a debt, then later (on the Day of Resurrection) there will be no dinar and dirham to pay it off. But there is only good or bad (to pay it off)."* (Narrated by Ibn Majah).

THE EXTERNAL FACTORS

Culture Cost

Culture also influences someone in debt. The culture of gatherings and *gotong royong* has experienced a shift in values so that this creates very high social costs. A study by Handayani (2016) indicated that Javanese and Madurese cultural values have a correlation with debt, one of which is the *guyub* culture. This friendly culture is a form of social donation in the form of financial and reciprocal and has social sanctions in the form of a negative image. The shift in cultural meanings and values raises demands for the necessities of life that are higher than their financial capabilities. This field experiment also found similar as conveyed by Mrs. Zein, as follows,

"I need to increase my capital, the capital for trading is not enough for wholesalers, because there are many extra needs. Because I ve already been married off my kids, so I must give more changes as the return. Otherwise, people will talk about me later and I will be billed to the house by the one who has the celebration (hajat)."

Financial Management

This field experiment found that all borrowers have problems in financial management. This is mainly due to the low literacy caused by the low level of education. Islam has highlighted the importance of financial management, as the word of Allah SWT, "*...And no one know (with certainty) what he will strive for tomorrow. And no one know on which earth he will die."* (QS. Luqman: 34).

And the words of the Prophet in a history, *"Allah will give mercy to someone who strives from good, spends moderately and can set aside excess to guard on a day when he is poor and in need."* (Narrated by Ahmad and Muslim).

No doubt, the weaknesses of financial management will lead to financial problems. One of them is the debt trap. For the people who are categorized as excluded and underserved, unbanked and underbanked, BoP, and ultra poor or nano enterprises, the income below the minimum wage will cause an inability to fulfill their physiological needs, coupled with consumptive behavior, and also the need to be accepted in social life causing a multiplier effect in the long term, namely the inability to settle their debts.

Social Cost for Having a Prestigious

Character is a person's personality that is formed from various experiences he has gone through. The behavior of nano society who cannot manage finances and respond to money is mostly the cause of this character as well as an "easy going" attitude towards debt. Lack of knowledge as well as less experience in getting large amounts of money causes excessive consumption patterns when earning large amounts of money. This is expressed by Kiki's husband who prefers to buy jewelry compared to paying debts if he gets an *arisan*,

"...I actually had an arisan money last month, and Kiki and I bought jewelry to wear to the Party. After that, the price dropped a lot and I used it for shopping for washing machines and household needs... How many times have I paid off this debt, the last time I bought (online) clothes through my mobile phone...".

Business Clarity

The characteristics of nano society in running a business are still dominated by a trial and error system due to limited skills and minimal business knowledge. Most of them will imitate businesses that are considered viral and will switch to other businesses in the short term. This was conveyed by Mr. Haru, a Risk Manager at an Islamic bank,

"Most of them, if they try, they just try, they are desperate... Yes, that's because of limited capital, limited skills, limited job opportunities, so they try any business whatever business can be produced... At the end they can't pay for the reason that the merchandise doesn't sell." and many also run to become migrant workers in the end."

Business Failure

Business failures caused by natural factors and business risks. The seasonal factor is the main factor in business failure for entrepreneurs who rely on their business on the seasons. As stated by Mrs. Siti when borrowing from the RQH,

"My harvest failed, this month it rained non-stop. Many crops are failing now. Where's the little capital? This is just for the harvest, it seems that it is not enough to cover the cost of the harvest."

The same thing was conveyed by Broher Saiful,

"I apologize.. I can't pay because my merchandise is empty. Most of the people who buy are in debt and have not paid up until now. I'm waiting for them to pay before they can pay in installments..."

Overall, the results of this field experiment showed that from eight times financing, only two financings were repaid in full. While the other six financings were not paid off. Even, four of them were not refunded at all. This indicates that the probability of these people experiencing default is very large. Studying the behavior of these community groups for eight months, this field experiment result recommends for nanofinance program with assistance, both to improve financial literacy and skills. Then, the source of funding for implementing nanofinance must comes from low-cost funds, such as: Islamic social finance, namely *zakat, infaq, shadaqa*, and productive *waqf;* social funds; and corporate social responsibility (CSR).

CONCLUSION

Nanofinance is another concept of microfinance in order to address the financial inclusion problems which do not reach the people who are categorized as excluded and underserved, unbanked and underbanked, BoP, and ultra poor in managing the borrowing fund. The nanofinance borrowers have characteristics: no steady income, no payroll, no financial history, and no collateral. The borrowing behavior from these community groups is influenced by internal and external factors. The internal factors include: the urgent needs, helping the family economy, capital needs, lifestyle, and debt unawareness. The external factors include: culture cost, financial management, social cost for having a prestigious, business clarity, and business failure. This study recommends for nanofinance program to be facilitated by the assistance, both to improve financial literacy and skills. Then, the source of funding for implementing nanofinance must comes from low-cost funds.

REFERENCES

Aaminou, M. W. (2022). *Towards a better financial inclusion in Maghreb countries: Insights on the role of Islamic microfinance and fintech (Research Report No. 22).* İstanbul: Research Center for Islamic Economics (IKAM).

ADB. (2000). *Finance for the poor: microfinance development strategy.* Asian Development Bank (ADB).

Ascarya & Sanrego. Y. D. (2007). *Redefine micro, small, and medium enterprises classification and the potency of baitul maal wa tamwiel as intermediary institutions in Indonesia.* Paper was presented at UBD-IRTI International Conference on Inclusive Islamic Financial Sector Development "Enhancing Islamic Financial Services for Micro and Medium Sized Enterprises (MMEs)", Empire Hotel and Country Club, Negara Brunei Darussalam.

Bateman, M. (2011). *Microfinance as a development and poverty reduction policy: is it everything it's cracked up to be?* Overseas Development Institute (ODI). www.odi.org.uk/50years

Chapra, M. U. (2008). *The Islamic vision of development in the light of maqasid al-shari'ah.* (Occasional Paper No. 15). The International Institute of Islamic Thought (IIIT)

Ditlmann, R., & Paluck, E. L. (2015). Field experiments. In J. D. Wright (Ed.), *International encyclopedia of the social & behavioral sciences* (2nd ed., Vol. 9, pp. 128–134). Elsevier. doi:10.1016/B978-0-08-097086-8.10542-2

Handayani, S. A. (2016). Money and the culture of debt in the ex-cresidence of Besuki in cross history. *Paramita: Historical Studies Journal, 26*(2), 203–216.

Leikem, K. (2012). Microfinance: a tool for poverty reduction? *Senior Honors Projects.* Digital Commons. https://digitalcommons.uri.edu/srhonorsprog/300

Mahanti, J. (2008). Women helping women through nano finance institution. *Ashanet.* http://www.ashanet.org/detroit/Projects/BISWA/Nano_Finance_Report_ Jan2008.pdf

Maslow, A. H. (1943). A theory of human motivation. *Psychological Review, 50*(4), 370–396. doi:10.1037/h0054346

Modigliani, F., & Miller, M. H. (1958). The cost of capital, corporation finance and the theory of investment. *The American Economic Review, 48*(3), 261–297.

Morduch, J., & Haley, B. (2002). *Analysis of the effects of microfinance on poverty reduction.* (NYU Wagner Working Paper No. 1014). New York University. https://www.nyu.edu/wagner/workingpapers.html

Musari, K. (2016a). Economic sustainability for Islamic nanofinance through sukuk-waqf linkage program (case study in Indonesia). [IJISEF]. *International Journal of Islamic Economics and Finance Studies, 2*(3), 73–94.

Musari, K. (2016b). Redefining the Islamic nanofinance and its institutional strengthening: lesson learned from Asian countries. A paper was presented at *11th International Conference on Islamic Economics and Finance (ICIEF).* Institution Kulliyyah of Economics and Management Sciences International Islamic University Malaysia (IIUM).

Musari, K. (2017a). Nanofinance. *Jawa Pos Radar Jember Daily Newspaper*, Perspektif.

Musari, K. (2017b). Nanofinance, addressing the Islamic microfinance gap through global Islamic humanitarian institution. In Proceeding of Conference on *Philanthropy for Humanitarian Aid 2017 "Philantrophy for Humanitarian Aid as Mechanism to Alleviate Poverty and Maintain Human Dignity."* International Research Centre of Islamic Economics and Finance (IRCIEF).

Musari, K. (2017c). *Promoting qardhul hassan in nanofinance to against the moneylender (case study Indonesia, Cambodia, Brunei, Vietnam, and Thailand).* A paper was presented at the 2nd Studia Islamika International Conference 2017 "Southeast Asian Islam: Religious Radicalism, Democracy, and Global Trends," Post-Graduate School of State Islamic University Syarif Hidayatullah, Jakarta.

Musari, K. (2019). Promoting qard al-hasan in nanofinance to counter the moneylender in Southeast Asia. *Studia Islamica, 26*(1), 1–16. doi:10.15408di.v26i1.5990

Musari, K. (2020a). Nanoeconomics, people's economy in post-pandemic. *Portal Jember, Pikiran Rakyat Media Network*, Opini. https://portaljember.pikiran-rakyat.com/opini/pr-16392575/refleksi-hari-lahir-pancasila-1-juni-ekonomi-nano-ekonomi-kera kyatan-pasca-pandemi?page=5

Musari, K. (2020b). Islamic nanofinance for the very poor by women, hopes for addressing the Islamic microfinance gap. In T. Azid & J. L. Ward-Batts (Eds.), *Economic empowerment of women in the Islamic world: theory and practice* (pp. 265–286). World Scientific Publishing. doi:10.1142/9789811212154_0013

Musari, K. (2020c). The loan shark in ASEAN: can nanofinance with qardhul hassan deal with it? lesson learned from bank wakaf mikro in Indonesia. In P. Ordoñez de Pablos, M. Almunawar, & M. Abduh (Eds.), *Economics, business, and Islamic finance in ASEAN economics community* (pp. 252–277). IGI Global. doi:10.4018/978-1-7998-2257-8.ch012

Musari, K., & Simanjuntak, R. (2016). Nanofinance, redefinition of microfinance for the very micro society through philanthropy linkage program (case study in Indonesia, Cambodia, Thailand, India). [AARJSH]. *Asian Academic Research Journal of Social Sciences and Humanities*, *3*(4), 455–463.

Myers, S. C. (2001). Capital structure. *The Journal of Economic Perspectives*, *15*(2), 81–102. doi:10.1257/jep.15.2.81

Parpart, E. (2014, October 25). BOT considers 'nano-financing' for grass-roots people. *The Nation*. https://www.nationmultimedia.com/business/BOT-considers-nano-financing-for-grass-roots-peopl-30246202.html

Ray, A. K. (2008). Self-help groups, micro finance and political economy. In B. J. Deb, K. Sengupta, & B. D. Ray (Eds.), *Globalization and north east India* (pp. 21–35). Ashok Kumar Mittal.

Robinson, M. (2001). *The microfinance revolution: sustainable finance for the poor*. World Bank. doi:10.1596/0-8213-4524-9

Segrado, C. (2005). *Islamic microfinance and socially responsible investments*. Meda Project, University of Torino, August.

The Asia Foundation. (2003). *Microfinance services in Indonesia: a survey of institutions in 6 provinces*. The Asia Foundation.

World Bank. 1978. Employment and development of small enterprises. Washington DC: World Bank.

ADDITIONAL READINGS

Hidayat, S. E., & Musari, K. (2023). Towards the global halal msmes hub through the digitally-enabled society: an institutional arrangement with Islamic n-tuple helix. In A. Rafiki (Ed.), Digitalization in Halal Management. (forthcoming). Springer.

Musari, K. (2022). P2P lending & philanthropy platform: a new face of asian digital financial inclusion (evidence from Indonesia). In M. N. Almunawar, Z. Islam, and P. Ordóñez de Pablos (Eds.), Digital transformation management: challenges and futures in the Asian digital economy (pp. 185-206). New York, NY: Informa UK Limited, Taylor & Francis/Routledge. doi:10.4324/9781003224532

KEY TERMS & DEFINITIONS

Arisan: A common term for a regular social gathering between friends and relatives who save in money to be won in turns through a lucky draw.

Gotong Royong: Mutual cooperation; An Indonesian national identity; An Indonesian cultural value; Communal work is a gathering for mutually accomplishing a task or for communal fundraising; Communal work provided manual labour to others.

Guyub: An ancient concept or something like a local wisdom in the Javanese and some ethnic in Indonesia that living in a community where joy is shared and pain is consoled which bring individuals together in happier, healthier communities.

Qardhul Hassan: Soft loan, zero-return loan, charitable loan, beautiful loan, benevolent loan, or voluntary loan.

Chapter 3
Is It Practical to Utilize AI-Powered Chatbots in Halal Marketing Communications?

Muhammad Dharma Tuah Putra Nasution
https://orcid.org/0000-0002-4671-0230
Universitas Pembangunan Panca Budi, Indonesia

Endang Sulistya Rini
Universitas Sumatera Utara, North Sumatera, Indonesia

Beby Karina Fawzeea Sembiring Sembiring
Universitas Sumatera Utara, North Sumatera, Indonesia

Amlys Syahputra Silalahi
Universitas Sumatera Utara, North Sumatera, Indonesia

Cut Kesuma Pahlufi
University of Surrey, UK

ABSTRACT

The aim of this chapter is to explore the capabilities of chatbots in the domain of marketing communication, with a particular focus on their potential application within the halal industry. It also analyzes the escalation in chatbot adoption across various business sectors. Furthermore, the chapter delves into the significance of adopting chatbots in Halal marketing communication. This includes an analysis of the challenges that may arise and capitalize on opportunities to successfully engage and captivate the intended audience. Likewise, this chapter sheds light on the areas of research that require further investigation and outlines potential avenues for future exploration regarding the adoption of chatbots in the context of Halal marketing. Hence, the contribution of this chapter lies in providing a comprehensive analysis of the challenges, opportunities, and positive outcomes associated with the chatbots. By doing so, it enriches existing knowledge and may serve as a basis for future research agendas.

DOI: 10.4018/978-1-6684-7519-5.ch003

INTRODUCTION

The intersection of halal marketing and technology adoption has catalyzed a significant surge within the burgeoning halal industry. A plethora of erudite scholars have embarked on comprehensive inquiries into the integration of technology within this realm, illuminating diverse facets of this intricate convergence.

In a seminal study by Hendayani and her esteemed colleagues (2019), the nexus between the adoption of blockchain technology and firms' competitive prowess came under scholarly scrutiny, with the mediation of Halal supply chain performance in focus. The researchers unveiled a compelling narrative: the affirmative and substantial embrace of blockchain technology yields a direct impact on both Halal supply chain performance and the competitive vigor of firms. Furthermore, their inquiry unveiled a nuanced chain reaction, whereby blockchain technology's influence on firm competitiveness is artfully mediated through its impact on the performance of the Halal supply chain.

In a harmonious resonance, Kamarulzaman et al. (2022) orchestrated a comprehensive exploration into the determinants shaping the intentions of small and medium-sized enterprises (SMEs) within the food industry, intent on embracing a halal traceability system. Their astute study showcased a tapestry of pivotal factors steering the intentions of food SMEs. These encompassed the cadence of sales turnover, the perceived utility, and ease of adoption, and the intricate interplay of technological, organizational, and environmental dimensions, all weaving together a comprehensive narrative.

Aligned with this symphony of exploration, Azmi et al. (2018) embarked on a meticulous journey to discern the factors underpinning the adoption of Halal standards in businesses operating within the Halal industry. Their study adroitly categorized these factors into three distinct domains: technological, organizational, and environmental. The technological sphere bore factors such as compatibility and perceived benefits, while the organizational sphere enfolded dimensions such as management support, organizational readiness, awareness, understanding, anticipated business benefits, and the vital facet of Halal integrity. Conversely, the environmental realm resonated with influences stemming from government support, competitive pressures, consumer dynamics, and the clarion call of Halal market demand.

In a congruent cadence, Masudin et al. (2021) orchestrated an exploration to discern the correlation between employees' readiness to embrace technology and the intricate dance of performance within halal logistics, enmeshed in the realms of halal meat retailing and manufacturing. Their revelations resounded with clarity: employees' preparedness to embrace technological strides invariably enhances the efficacy of halal logistics operations. Similarly, Ahmad Tarmizi et al. (2020) delved into the integration of Internet of Things (IoT) technology within halal agro-food SMEs in Malaysia, unearthing a landscape where this transformative technology's adoption remains a gradual endeavor.

In a crescendo of exploration, Berakon and colleagues (2023) embarked on a captivating voyage, peering into the determinants shaping the intention to leverage halal tourism applications among Muslim travelers. This study, etched against Indonesia's rich cultural tapestry, unveiled trust as a pivotal mediator, interweaving perceived ease of use and utility with individual intentions. The symphony continued with the revelation that halal knowledge exerts a positive and statistically substantial impact on individual intentions. In contrast, the tenor of religious devotion, while present, lacked statistical significance in influencing individual intentions.

Furthermore, the significance of halal entrepreneurs in the halal travel industry was emphatically underscored by Battour et al. (2021). Their work highlights the pressing need for the adoption of innovative and technological strategies, paving the way for scalable, digitally enabled business models in anticipation of imminent industry developments. Adding to this discourse, Mukherjee and colleagues

(2023) embarked on a study that delved into the myriad digital technologies employed in the realm of Halal tourism, uncovering the challenges faced by the sector. This investigation unveiled a spectrum of digital tools ranging from cyber-physical systems to the internet of things, cloud computing, big data, artificial intelligence, and advanced robotics, all collectively enhancing the landscape of Halal tourism.

In a similar vein, the study conducted by Battour et al. (2022) delved into the potential of artificial intelligence (AI) in redefining the tourism experience for Muslim travelers throughout their journey. This study echoed the sentiment that AI possesses the capacity to enhance the Muslim tourism experience by seamlessly integrating it into every facet of the journey – from meticulous planning to comfortable stays and comprehensive evaluation.

The burgeoning popularity of AI-powered chatbots in the marketing sphere is underscored by their adeptness in delivering tailored and streamlined customer support. The adoption of chatbots is becoming increasingly ubiquitous, being harnessed in a plethora of marketing contexts. These contexts range from aiding consumers in navigating intricate e-commerce platforms to providing real-time solutions to product-related queries, offering personalized consumer guidance, and even functioning as digital concierges (Adam et al., 2021; Shumanov & Johnson, 2021). Notably, multiple scholarly inquiries have engaged in a rigorous exploration of the pivotal role of chatbots within the marketing landscape. These scholarly endeavors delve into diverse facets, encompassing their effects, utility, and the attendant challenges they present (Ovuakporaye, 2022; Sujata et al., 2019). Such research collectively underscores the promising potential of chatbots in elevating the efficacy and impact of the marketing domain.

Recent studies have meticulously examined the profound impact of chatbots on integrated marketing communication within business settings, revealing a compelling correlation with impulsive purchasing tendencies and the inclination for repeat purchases (Lo Presti et al., 2021; Mostafa & Kasamani, 2022). A significant study by Tsai et al. (2021) shed light on the remarkable potential of chatbots' anthropomorphic profile design, amplifying the positive outcomes of social presence communication through intricate psychological mediators. By harnessing the capabilities of chatbots, enterprises can bolster their competitive edge and embark on the initial stages of embracing advanced digital marketing tools (Illescas-Manzano et al., 2021). It is perceptible that chatbots occupy an eminent stance within marketing communication, exerting a tangible influence on consumer behavior and substantively contributing to the refinement of the holistic customer experience.

Massaro (2022) advances the perspective that chatbots have attained pivotal significance in the realm of strategic marketing, capitalizing on sentiment analysis and capitalizing on cutting-edge customer experience enhancements. Scholars have painstakingly delved into the intricate dynamics between consumers and chatbots, probing their ramifications on customer engagement and behavioral outcomes, notably within the domain of e-commerce (Torres & Delgado, 2022). As such, chatbots have unequivocally transformed into indispensable marketing tools, furnishing tailored and efficient customer assistance that bolsters integrated marketing communication, enriches social presence communication, and fosters enhanced customer engagement. However, Attar et al. (2022) present a cogent argument that propels the necessity for further research, an imperative step to fortify the theoretical underpinnings and methodological frameworks of digital marketing and e-commerce, thereby unleashing the full spectrum of chatbot potential across diverse domains. This underscores, comprehensively, the paramount importance of chatbots in the intricate marketing landscape, concurrently accentuating the unswerving need for perpetual research endeavors in this dynamic arena.

Hence, the objective of this paper encompasses a dual-fold approach: firstly, to embark on an in-depth exploration of chatbots, unraveling their distinct attributes and intricacies; and secondly, to meticulously discern and delineate the inherent challenges and prospects entrenched within the realm of halal marketing communication. The latter aims to meticulously identify the underpinning challenges and burgeoning prospects intrinsic to halal marketing communication. Given the relative dearth of cohesive discourse surrounding this subject matter and the nascent nature of this topic, a judicious decision was taken to embark upon preliminary research for the present study. The crux of this paper lies in furnishing a comprehensive and thorough analysis of the challenges and opportunities that traverse this landscape, underscored by the potential positive ramifications arising from the integration of chatbots. It is noteworthy that this endeavor has the potential to establish a solid foundational base for prospective research agendas.

GROWING IN THE HALAL MARKET

The emergence of the global halal market as a prominent growth sector within the global economy has been a noteworthy phenomenon, transcending geographical and cultural boundaries (Elasrag, 2016). This market has gained prominence by meticulously catering to the unique needs of Muslim consumers, adhering to the principles of Islamic law. Its scope encompasses an impressive spectrum of products and services, ranging from food and pharmaceuticals to cosmetics, fashion, media, and even finance (Marković & Stošić-Mihajlović, 2022). What was once predominantly concentrated in Muslim-majority countries has now successfully extended its reach to encompass non-Muslim-majority regions such as Europe, Canada, Australia, and the United States (Ruiz-Bejarano, 2017). This expansion vividly reflects the global prevalence of the halal market, which effectively addresses the distinctive requirements of Muslim consumers across a diverse range of sectors.

At the core of the halal market's operation lies the fundamental and mandatory requirement for halal certification. This certification framework serves as a steadfast mechanism for ensuring strict compliance with Islamic regulations, offering a genuine assurance that the concerned products or services are entirely devoid of any haram (prohibited) elements (Alia & Ahmada, 2023). The certification process, as elucidated by Elasrag (2016), is not merely a cursory exercise; rather, it is a comprehensive and meticulous scrutiny of the entire supply chain, commencing from the sourcing of raw materials and extending to the final product. This comprehensive process bestows upon Muslim consumers a profound sense of confidence and reassurance, signifying that the products they consume align with their religious beliefs and requirements.

Another captivating aspect of the halal market's dynamics is the increasing demand for its products and services among non-Muslim consumers. This intriguing shift, as illuminated by Aziz and Chok (2013), underscores that the halal market has transcended religious boundaries. It has successfully attracted consumers who may not identify as Muslim but are drawn to the market's offerings due to their inherent qualities of high quality and health-consciousness. This paradigm shift underscores the evolving landscape of consumer preferences, where individuals seek products and services that align with their ethical considerations and desire for superior quality. The halal market offers a range of products that are not only free from harmful ingredients but are also produced using ethical and sustainable practices (Ali & Suleiman, 2016). This indicates that the growing popularity of the halal market reflects the shift towards halal consciousness.

The escalating demand for halal products and services among non-Muslim consumers has paved novel pathways for enterprises to venture into the halal market and broaden their consumer base (Elasrag,

2016). Nonetheless, enterprises treading within the realm of the halal market are met with distinctive challenges that necessitate strategic resolution for the attainment of triumph. One such formidable challenge is the lack of standardized halal certification protocols, with the certification process diverging across countries and a conspicuous absence of a universal benchmark (Elasrag, 2016). This conspicuous absence in standardization confounds both consumers and enterprises alike, erecting barriers for market expansion and hampering the endeavor to allure a more extensive clientele.

A parallel hurdle in the halal market resides in the perceptual terrain, where certain consumers harbor reservations about halal products being perceived as subpar or of inferior quality. As per the insights proffered by Aziz and Chok (2013), a segment of consumers entertains the notion that halal offerings may exhibit diminished taste or compromised healthfulness compared to their non-halal counterparts. This entrenched perception poses a palpable obstruction for enterprises endeavoring to penetrate uncharted markets and expand their market reach.

Nonetheless, it's imperative to underscore that the halal market unfurls a distinct panorama of opportunities for enterprises. The burgeoning demand for halal products and services, kindled by the fervor of both Muslim and non-Muslim consumers, crystallizes a propitious opening for businesses to diversify their consumer base and venture into this burgeoning sector (Ali & Suleiman, 2016). By proffering high-caliber and health-conscious offerings that cater adeptly to the sensibilities of both Muslim and non-Muslim patrons, enterprises have the potential to carve out a distinctive niche for themselves, diverging markedly from the competitive landscape.

In summation, the halal market, while replete with its intricate web of challenges, also holds an alluring tapestry of prospects for astute businesses. Despite the hurdles presented by non-standardized certification procedures and misperceptions around product quality, the surging demand emanating from the intersection of Muslim and non-Muslim consumers unveils a precious avenue for businesses to not just participate, but flourish. By adeptly catering to the discerning preferences of a diverse array of consumers with premium-quality and wellness-centric offerings, businesses can effectively etch their presence onto this dynamic terrain and craft a unique and commanding market identity.

CHARTING THE TRANSFORMATIVE LANDSCAPE OF CHATBOTS IN MARKETING COMMUNICATION: INSIGHTS AND APPLICATIONS

The burgeoning importance of chatbots within marketing communication has witnessed a notable ascent in recent years. A plethora of scholarly investigations have cast a spotlight on the escalating significance of chatbots in shaping the landscape of marketing communication. A case in point is the study by Van den Broeck et al. (2019), which delved into the efficacy of chatbot advertising, elucidating that the perceived intrusiveness stands as a pivotal determinant of chatbot advertising effectiveness. Notably, they underscored the pivotal role played by the perceived usefulness and helpfulness of chatbot interactions in shaping users' overall experiences.

In a similar vein, Tsai et al. (2021) illuminated the swift assimilation of chatbots across a diverse array of industries, spotlighting their pivotal function in facilitating social and intimate dialogues with consumers. The researchers also brought to the fore the potential of chatbots to elevate consumer satisfaction and potentially emerge as the forthcoming frontier in business communication channels. Notably, Tsai et al. (2021) also advanced the proposition that the incorporation of anthropomorphic profiles in chatbot design could accentuate the positive outcomes of social presence communication by leveraging

Table 1. Key aspects of chatbots in marketing communication

Aspect	Description and Applications	Key Authors
Importance of Chatbots in Marketing Communication	- Chatbots have gained substantial importance in recent years. - Academic studies emphasize their significance in marketing communication. - Chatbots' roles include enhancing consumer engagement, satisfaction, and potentially becoming a key business communication channel.	Van den Broeck et al. (2019), Tsai et al. (2021)
Impact of Chatbot Advertising Effectiveness	- Van den Broeck et al. (2019) studied chatbot advertising effectiveness. - Perceived intrusiveness is a determinant of effectiveness. - Perceived usefulness and helpfulness influence user experiences.	Van den Broeck et al. (2019)
Role of Chatbots in Consumer Engagement	- Tsai et al. (2021) highlighted rapid chatbot adoption across industries. - Chatbots engage consumers in social, intimate conversations. - Potential to enhance consumer satisfaction and act as a business communication channel.	Tsai et al. (2021)
Enhancing Social Presence Communication	- Anthropomorphic profiles in chatbot design amplify social presence communication. - Psychological mediators enhance favorable outcomes. - Integration of chatbots improves customer engagement and potential sales growth.	Tsai et al. (2021)
Impact on Integrated Marketing Communication	- Khoa (2021) studied chatbots' impact on integrated marketing communication. - Chatbots lead to impulsive buying behavior and subsequent purchases.	Khoa (2021)
Influence on Customer Trust and Engagement	- Mostafa & Kasamani (2022) explored chatbot initial trust and consequences. - Initial trust positively associates with customer engagement. - Trust drives revisits and influences purchasing decisions.	Mostafa & Kasamani (2022)
Role in Customer-Brand Relationships	- Chatbots gain popularity in building customer-brand relationships. - Cheng and Jiang (2022) studied AI-powered chatbot marketing's impact on relationships. - Positive association between relationship marketing and consumer intentions.	Cheng & Jiang (2022)
Pragmatic Applications in Marketing	- Ovuakporaye (2022) focused on chatbot applications in marketing. - Usage in employment, training, and promotional goals.	Ovuakporaye (2022)
Advancements and Possibilities in Different Sectors	Matic et al. (2021) highlighted technological advancements' impact on chatbot adoption. - Chatbots integrated in customer service, trade, and marketing. - Various studies underscore the necessity to explore chatbot implementation across sectors.	Matic et al. (2021), Kaczorowska-Spychalska (2019), Hildebrand & Bergner (2019), Sheehan et al. (2020)
Emergence as an Essential Marketing Tool	- Chatbots have gained popularity in various sectors. - They offer tailored messaging, amplify involvement, and provide continuous support. - Continual advancement of technology enhances chatbots' significance in marketing communication.	Lubbe & Ngoma (2021), Martinez et al. (2021)

psychological mediators. The integration of chatbots within the realm of marketing communication stands poised to usher in substantial improvements in customer engagement, thereby catalyzing the overarching objective of driving sales growth.

A distinct scholarly endeavor by Khoa (2021) delved into the influence of chatbots on integrated marketing communication practices within organizational settings. The findings of this study resonated with the notion that chatbots wield the potential to trigger impulsive purchasing behavior and cultivate a proclivity for subsequent purchases.

In tandem with their pronounced effects on marketing communication, chatbots have also been revealed to wield a substantial impact on customer trust and engagement. A study undertaken by Mostafa & Kasamani (2022) traversed the domain of chatbot-initiated trust and its subsequent ramifications. The researchers unearthed a compelling positive nexus between initial trust and customer engagement in the chatbot milieu, underlining the critical role that trust in virtual technologies assumes in heightening engagement levels in online undertakings. Furthermore, they accentuated that the bedrock of initial trust in chatbots propels customers to revisit the seller and actively advocate for them while making consequential purchasing determinations.

In sum, the ascendancy of chatbots within marketing communication has unfurled multifaceted dimensions that resonate across various academic explorations. These studies collectively underscore the transformative potential of chatbots in molding marketing communication dynamics, influencing consumer behaviors, fostering trust, and paving the way for enhanced customer engagement and ultimately bolstered sales outcomes.

Establishing robust connections between brands and their customers constitutes a pivotal facet of effective marketing communication. Recent years have witnessed the meteoric rise of chatbots in this arena, sparking a surge in studies delving into their role in nurturing customer-brand relationships. A case in point is the research conducted by Cheng and Jiang (2022), which delved into the impact of AI-powered chatbot marketing on fortifying these relationships. Their findings unveiled a positive correlation between relationship marketing and online consumer behavioral intentions, spotlighting chatbot marketing's potential to elevate customer-brand relationships and thereby foster heightened customer loyalty. Consequently, the integration of chatbots into marketing communication emerges as a potent instrument for enterprises to cultivate enduring customer connections and galvanize brand allegiance.

A study spearheaded by Ovuakporaye (2022) centered on the pragmatic applications of chatbots in marketing, casting a specific spotlight on their integration into areas like employment, training progression, and targeted promotional endeavors. Furthermore, insights from the study undertaken by Matic et al. (2021) underscore the transformative potential of communication and connectivity technologies, ushering in novel prospects for chatbot incorporation in domains spanning customer service, trade, and marketing.

In the realm of strategic marketing, chatbots play a pivotal role, harnessing sentiment analysis to enrich the customer experience (Massaro et al., 2022). Furthermore, the work of Lubbe and Ngoma (2021) accentuates the pivotal role of a positive chatbot experience in ensuring technological satisfaction, especially within burgeoning markets. The extensive reach of chatbots extends across an array of sectors encompassing customer service, marketing, sales, e-commerce, e-learning, travel, and education (Martinez et al., 2021).

As underscored by Matic et al. (2021), the march of communication and connectivity technologies has expanded the horizons for chatbot adoption in critical sectors including customer services, trade, and marketing. In a similar vein, Kaczorowska-Spychalska (2019) traversed the diverse landscape of chatbot integration across organizational activities. Precedent research (e.g., Hildebrand & Bergner, 2019; Sheehan et al., 2020) has incessantly emphasized the imperative of further probing into chatbot implementation within e-commerce across diverse spheres. The scholarly discourse underscores the significance of amassing insights into the pros and cons of chatbot utilization, all the while enriching the theoretical and methodological underpinnings of digital marketing and e-commerce. Consequently, chatbots have emerged as a cornerstone of marketing communication, adept at delivering tailored messages, elevating customer engagement, and furnishing uninterrupted customer support. In the backdrop of technology's relentless march, it becomes increasingly apparent that chatbots will embrace an ever-expanding role in marketing communication, particularly within the burgeoning realms of emerging markets.

Table 2. Chatbots in marketing communication: Definitions, purposes, and applications

Key point	Description and Applications	Key Authors
Chatbot Definition	Chatbots are AI-based software applications using text or voice interfaces to mimic human dialogue (Shumanov & Johnson, 2021; Nirala et al., 2022). They comprehend natural language, emotions, and provide purposeful responses (Shumanov & Johnson, 2021; Nirala et al., 2022).	Shumanov & Johnson (2021); Nirala et al. (2022)
Chatbot Purpose	Conversational AI, like chatbots enabling natural language communication (Arsenijevic & Jovic, 2019; Rese et al., 2020). They build relationships, provide answers, and influence decisions (Trofymenko et al., 2022).	Arsenijevic & Jovic (2019); Rese et al. (2020); Trofymenko et al. (2022)
	Chatbots engage in human-like conversations (Paliwal et al., 2020). They simulate conversations between devices and users (Rapp et al., 2021). They facilitate human-machine communication (Luo et al., 2022).	Paliwal et al. (2020); Rapp et al. (2021); Luo et al. (2022)
	Chatbots mimic human communication via natural language in text or auditory form (Sharma et al., 2017). They comprehend and deliver significant responses (Lubbe & Ngoma, 2021).	Sharma et al. (2017); Lubbe & Ngoma (2021)
Diverse Applications	Chatbots find applications in customer service, sales, and marketing (Ordemann et al., 2021). They integrate into digital platforms like websites, messaging apps, and social media (Smutny & Schreiberova, 2020). They offer 24/7 service, faster response times, and higher customer satisfaction (Nicolescu & Tudorache, 2022).	Ordemann et al. (2021); Smutny & Schreiberova (2020); Nicolescu & Tudorache (2022)

DECODING CHATBOTS: DEFINITION, APPLICATIONS, AND SIGNIFICANCE IN VARIOUS DOMAINS

Chatbots represent software applications that harness text or voice interfaces to replicate human conversation. These techniques, rooted in artificial intelligence (AI), enable chatbots to grasp natural language, decipher nuances and emotions, and formulate purposeful responses (Shumanov & Johnson, 2021; Nirala et al., 2022). The realm of conversational AI, embodied in chatbots, is a rapidly expanding domain (Arsenijevic & Jovic, 2019), with software applications adept at engaging in human-like language interactions (Rese et al., 2020). As highlighted by Trofymenko et al. (2022), chatbots facilitate relationship nurturing, offer solutions to queries, and bolster comprehension among employees within organizations, thereby influencing decision-making processes. Paliwal et al. (2020) assert that chatbots are automated software designed for authentic human-like discourse with users. According to Rapp et al. (2021), chatbots encompass a software category enabling simulated interactions between devices and users via conversational interfaces. Echoing this sentiment, Luo et al. (2022) describe chatbots as applications fostering human-machine communication.

Sharma et al. (2017) expound that chatbots are tailored to emulate human communication using natural language, expressed through textual or auditory means. As pointed out by Lubbe and Ngoma (2021), chatbots offer a conversational interface adept at comprehending natural language and furnishing pertinent responses. Fundamentally, chatbots are programmed to engage in human-like dialogues, mirroring interpersonal communication patterns. Their applications are diverse, spanning customer service, sales, and marketing (Ordemann et al., 2021). As noted by Smutny and Schreiberova (2020), chatbots can seamlessly integrate into various digital platforms, including websites, messaging apps, and social media channels. Likewise, Nicolescu and Tudorache (2022) underscore the escalating adoption of chatbots across myriad industries, driven by their ability to provide round-the-clock customer service, expedite response times, and elevate customer satisfaction.

Table 3. Impact and challenges of chatbots in various sectors

Sector	Impact and Challenge	Key Authors
Banking Sector	Scholars have examined determinants affecting chatbot adoption in banking (Alt & Ibolya, 2021). Chatbots manage inquiries, allowing focus on complex issues (Abdulquadri et al., 2021). Fubon Bank in Hong Kong adopted chatbots for continuous customer assistance (So, 2023). Benefits include improved customer experience, efficiency, and cost reduction (Gupta & Sharma, 2019). Trivedi's analysis emphasizes aligning chatbots with customer expectations (Trivedi, 2019). Challenges in design must be considered (Gupta & Sharma, 2019).	Alt & Ibolya (2021); Abdulquadri et al. (2021); So (2023); Gupta & Sharma (2019); Trivedi (2019).
Healthcare Sector	Chatbots in healthcare assist in patient scheduling, medication reminders, and inquiries (Agarwal et al., 2022). They enhance patient engagement, reduce expenses, and improve efficacy (Agarwal et al., 2022).	Agarwal et al. (2022)
E-commerce Sector	Chatbots in e-commerce offer recommendations, aid searches, and manage inquiries (Shafi et al., 2020). Benefits include enhanced experience, efficiency, and cost reduction (Shafi et al., 2020).	Shafi et al. (2020)
Retail Sector	Chatbots in retail enhance experience and processes, offering various customer services (Murugesan & Cherukuri, 2023). They lead to reduced response times and improved satisfaction (Murugesan & Cherukuri, 2023). They drive digital transformation, with challenges in natural language understanding (Mydyti & Kadriu, 2021).	Murugesan & Cherukuri (2023); Mydyti & Kadriu (2021)
Tourism Sector	Chatbots in tourism augment customer experience and efficiency, aiding travelers with various services (Pillai & Sivathanu, 2020). Benefits encompass customer satisfaction and cost reduction (Pillai & Sivathanu, 2020). Chatbot-based AI improves customer satisfaction and response times (Rafiq et al., 2022). Chiong et al. (2022) focused on smart tourism information chatbot in Mauritius, providing personalized recommendations and enhancing customer loyalty (Chiong et al., 2022). Design challenges, identified by Almutairi et al. (2023), include natural language understanding and precise responses, demanding meticulous chatbot development (Almutairi et al., 2023).	Pillai & Sivathanu (2020); Rafiq et al. (2022); Chiong et al. (2022); Almutairi et al. (2023)
Halal Tourism	Chatbots enhance halal tourism (Battour et al., 2023). They provide assistance, answer inquiries, suggest dining options, and facilitate product procurement (Battour et al., 2023). Challenges include recognizing and furnishing accurate halal information while respecting cultural and religious sensitivities (Battour et al., 2023).	Battour et al. (2023)

CHATBOTS: IMPACT AND CHALLENGES ACROSS VARIOUS SECTORS

Scholarly investigations have diligently examined the determinants influencing the adoption of chatbots in the banking sector. Alt and Ibolya (2021) embarked on a study aimed at delineating pertinent user segments for banking chatbots, basing their analysis on technology adoption behavior. Additionally, Abdulquadri et al. (2021) affirm that chatbots proficiently manage standard queries encompassing account balances, transaction histories, and bill payments, thereby freeing human agents to tackle more intricate matters.

In the realm of customer service, the integration of chatbots has found a pivotal role. Fubon Bank in Hong Kong stands as a pertinent example, deploying chatbots to provide uninterrupted customer support (So, 2023). The banking landscape has witnessed the proliferation of chatbots, driven by factors such as enriched customer experience, heightened efficiency, and cost reduction. Gupta and Sharma (2019) report a positive customer disposition towards banking chatbots, with their adoption gaining momentum. Trivedi's (2019) exploration into the consumer-brand rapport within the banking domain underscores the importance of aligning chatbot offerings with customer expectations. Their implementation holds promise for elevating both customer satisfaction and organizational productivity, though meticulous design and user-friendliness remain crucial considerations.

Turning to the healthcare sector, Agarwal et al. (2022) note the adoption of chatbots as virtual support for patients. These intelligent applications aid in appointment scheduling, medication reminders, and addressing common health queries. Such adoption in healthcare is fueled by benefits including heightened patient engagement, cost savings, and enhanced effectiveness.

The e-commerce landscape has embraced chatbots to furnish tailored recommendations, streamline product searches, and manage customer inquiries (Shafi et al., 2020). This integration stems from the desire to elevate customer experience, optimize efficiency, and curtail expenses. As chatbots continue to evolve, their presence is set to expand across sectors, offering virtual support and augmenting overall customer service quality.

In the retail domain, chatbots have become a cornerstone in enhancing customer experience and optimizing operations. They assist customers across various fronts, from product inquiries to order placement (Murugesan & Cherukuri, 2023). Mydyti and Kadriu's (2021) exploration of chatbot impact on digital transformation underscores their role in heightening customer engagement and reducing operational costs. However, challenges such as the need for natural language comprehension and precise responses must be acknowledged.

In sum, the strategic adoption of chatbots resonates across industries, redefining customer engagement and operational efficacy. Their application spans banking, healthcare, e-commerce, and retail, promising improved customer experiences and organizational efficiency while navigating design intricacies and evolving functionalities.

The tourism sector has swiftly embraced the adoption of chatbots, driven by the goal of enhancing the customer experience and streamlining operational efficiency. These AI-driven tools have been integrated to assist travelers in various capacities, such as providing information about tourist destinations, facilitating ticket reservations, and suggesting recreational activities. According to Pillai and Sivathanu (2020), the incorporation of chatbots into tourism can yield substantial advantages for enterprises, including heightened customer satisfaction and reduced operational costs.

Academic inquiries have delved into the ramifications of chatbot adoption within the tourism sector. For instance, Rafiq et al. (2022) explored consumers' intentions to adopt tourism chatbots, unveiling that AI-powered chatbots can significantly elevate customer satisfaction and trim response times. The study conducted by Chiong et al. (2022) centered on crafting a smart tourism information chatbot for Mauritius. Findings indicated that chatbots possess the potential to offer tailored recommendations based on travelers' preferences and past interactions, potentially fostering greater customer loyalty and transaction frequency. Nevertheless, the integration of chatbots in tourism does come with specific challenges. Authors like Almutairi et al. (2023) have pinpointed design challenges that could impact user behavior, including the need for chatbots to understand natural language and deliver precise responses. Therefore, meticulous design and evaluation are crucial for ensuring chatbots meet the demands and expectations of customers.

Halal tourism has also adopted chatbots as a means to enhance customer experience and offer information about halal travel (Battour et al., 2023). These chatbots provide diverse forms of assistance, ranging from addressing inquiries about halal destinations to suggesting halal dining establishments and facilitating the acquisition of halal products. However, the integration of chatbots within the halal sector is accompanied by specific challenges. It's imperative that chatbots accurately recognize and provide information about halal goods and services. Additionally, ensuring cultural and religious sensitivities are meticulously considered in the development of chatbots is crucial.

In summary, the tourism industry's embrace of chatbots for both general and halal-specific services underscores the potential to enrich customer experiences. Despite the benefits, challenges related to language comprehension, precision, and cultural nuances must be thoughtfully navigated to ensure the efficacy and appropriateness of chatbot interactions..

Table 4. Challenges, opportunities, and changing viewpoints in Halal marketing communication

Aspect	Description	Key Authors
Challenges in Halal Marketing Communication	Lack of exposure to Halal certification and brands, understanding Muslim consumer behavior are challenges (Rajagopal et al., 2011; Alserhan, 2010). Reframing perspectives on halal is essential (Rajagopal et al., 2011; Alserhan, 2010).	Rajagopal et al. (2011); Alserhan (2010)
Opportunities in Halal Marketing Communication	Opportunities include identified strategies from Halal tourism study enhancing visibility (Moshin et al., 2020). Factors like Islamic marketing, electronic word of mouth, and religious awareness impact halal product promotion (Musa et al., 2022). Effective distribution networks and trigger messages optimize marketing (Musa et al., 2022; Akın & Okumuş, 2021; Mustafa, 2021).	Moshin et al. (2020); Musa et al. (2022); Akın & Okumuş (2021); Mustafa (2021)
Changing Viewpoints in Halal Marketing Communication	Altering perspectives, implementing effective strategies leveraging Islamic marketing and religious consciousness is crucial for promoting Halal products and services (Musa et al., 2022).	Musa et al. (2022)

NAVIGATING CHALLENGES AND SEIZING OPPORTUNITIES: TRANSFORMATIVE STRATEGIES IN HALAL MARKETING COMMUNICATION

Marketing communication for Halal products and services presents a dynamic landscape with both challenges and opportunities. Among the challenges is the issue of limited exposure to Halal certification and brands through marketing efforts (Rajagopal et al., 2011). Marketers need to devise comprehensive strategies to enhance the visibility and distribution of Halal products and services. Another challenge involves understanding and catering to the behavior of Muslim consumers and Islamic brands (Alserhan, 2010). This necessitates a shift in marketers' perspectives on Halal.

However, the realm of marketing communication for Halal also offers promising opportunities. Recent research on developing a destination image for Halal tourism has unveiled potential marketing communication strategies (Moshin et al., 2020). Implementing these strategies can amplify the visibility and appeal of Halal products and services within the tourism sector. Moreover, the study conducted by Musa et al. (2022) underscores that Islamic marketing, electronic word of mouth, and religious awareness can serve as effective tools for promoting Halal consumption among Muslim consumers.

To optimize the marketing of Halal offerings, it's crucial for marketers to establish efficient distribution networks that foster proximity to consumers (Akın & Okumuş, 2021). Mustafa (2021) highlights the significance of trigger messages in marketing communication for promoting Halal food products. Addressing the challenge of insufficient awareness about Halal certification and brands requires robust marketing communication and branding strategies (Rajagopal et al., 2011).

In essence, the domain of marketing communication for Halal products and services presents a complex interplay of challenges and opportunities. Marketers must adapt their perceptions of Halal and employ strategic marketing and branding approaches to effectively promote these offerings. By leveraging Islamic marketing principles and religious awareness, marketers can successfully connect Halal products and services with Muslim consumers, thereby fostering engagement and loyalty.

Table 5. Roles and insights of marketing communication and chatbots in the Halal industry

Aspect	Role of Marketing Communication in Halal Industry	Role of Chatbots in Halal Marketing	Additional Insights from Academic Studies
Importance in Halal Marketing	Effective marketing communication crucial for gaining a competitive edge, differentiation, and adapting to evolving circumstances (Akın & Okumuş, 2021; Alserhan, 2010; Hidayat et al., 2022).	Chatbots enhance customer experience, offer personalized recommendations, address queries (Battour et al., 2023; Noor, 2022; Chung et al., 2020).	Chatbots influence impulse purchases, social presence communication (Khoa, 2021; Tsai et al., 2021).
Technological Advancements	Embracing technology, leveraging ICT, and strategic coordination essential for industry success (Rejeb et al., 2021; Hoque et al., 2018).	Chatbots leverage technology to provide accurate information and personalized experiences (Ovuakporaye, 2022; Nanda et al., 2021).	AI-based chatbots hold unprecedented business potential (Cheng et al., 2021).
Brand Loyalty and Trust	Building brand loyalty and trust through consistent and personalized interactions (Ovuakporaye, 2022; Hari et al., 2022).	Chatbots foster brand loyalty, enhance customer interactions (Mostafa & Kasamani, 2021).	Chatbots gather consumer information, facilitate marketing actions and sales (Illescas-Manzano, 2021).
Research Insights	Role of chatbots in analyzing competitors (Ovuakporaye, 2022).	Chatbots influence impulse purchases, repurchase intentions (Khoa, 2021).	Chatbots amplify social presence communication (Tsai et al., 2021).
Future Prospects	Chatbots have the potential to revolutionize Halal marketing, offer versatile and continuous improvement (Murugesan & Cherukuri, 2023).	AI-based chatbots present unprecedented business potential (Cheng et al., 2021).	Chatbots enhance customer interactions with the brand (Mostafa & Kasamani, 2021).

ENHANCING HALAL MARKETING COMMUNICATION THROUGH CHATBOTS: INSIGHTS, ADVANTAGES, AND FUTURE PROSPECTS

Marketing communication holds a pivotal role within the halal industry, driven by several compelling factors. The rapid expansion of the halal market underscores the necessity for businesses to deploy effective marketing communication strategies, thereby securing a competitive advantage and attracting a diverse customer base (Akın & Okumuş, 2021; Rajagopal et al., 2011). In a landscape where halal products contend with non-halal counterparts, adept marketing communication becomes instrumental in setting halal brands apart and showcasing their distinctive attributes (Alserhan, 2010; Ramzy & El-dahan, 2015; Yousaf, 2016). Moreover, the unprecedented challenges posed by the Covid-19 pandemic necessitate agile adaptation and robust customer engagement through strategic marketing communication tactics (Hidayat et al., 2022).

In the context of the halal industry's evolution, embracing technological advancements has garnered significant recognition as a means to bolster competitiveness (Rejeb et al., 2021; Hendayani & Fernando, 2022; Siraj et al., 2022). This involves harnessing information communication technology (ICT) to amplify marketing communication strategies and expand their reach across broader audiences. Furthermore, the success of the halal industry is intrinsically tied to effective collaboration and engagement among multiple stakeholders, underscored by the implementation of astute marketing approaches (Yunos et al., 2014; Hoque et al., 2018). The influential role of Islamic financial institutions in fostering the halal industry's growth and potential is notable, as they intertwine the industry with Islamic finance to cultivate a robust halal ecosystem (Hassan et al., 2021; Hoque et al., 2018).

Within this context, effective marketing communication becomes an imperative for halal industry businesses to establish a distinctive presence, adapt to dynamic circumstances, and differentiate themselves.

Amidst this landscape, chatbots have risen as indispensable assets within the realm of digital marketing communication, gaining widespread adoption by marketers to initiate, supervise, and nurture customer relationships (Herhausen et al., 2020; Yadav, 2022). In the realm of halal marketing, chatbots manifest considerable potential in elevating customer satisfaction and enriching the halal travel experience (Battour et al., 2023). Their foremost objective is to provide accurate and timely insights into halal offerings, empowering customers to make informed decisions by efficiently addressing their queries and concerns (Noor, 2022; Aziz & Chok, 2013).

Furthermore, chatbots contribute to an elevated customer experience by offering personalized recommendations grounded in individual preferences and past interactions (Chung et al., 2020). Particularly within halal travel, chatbots exhibit substantial promise in facilitating the discovery of halal dining options and places of worship, effectively aiding customers' journeys (Battour et al., 2022). Beyond their customer-facing role, chatbots yield valuable insights into customer behaviors and preferences (Aslam, 2023), thus enabling businesses to refine marketing strategies and tailor offerings. Moreover, they assume a role in identifying potential leads and opportunities for cross-selling and upselling (Nanda et al., 2021).

Critical to brand development, chatbots contribute to building customer loyalty and fostering trust by delivering a seamless and consistent experience across diverse channels, thereby instilling a sense of brand confidence (Hari et al., 2022). Additionally, chatbots nurture a sense of community among loyal customers through personalized recommendations and exclusive offerings, fostering enduring customer relationships (Ovuakporaye, 2022).

The integration of advanced technologies like chatbots not only enhances customer experiences but also augments brand loyalty and strategic insights. Another key aspects is that Chatbots stand poised to revolutionize the landscape of Halal marketing, ushering in a new era of personalized and interactive consumer experiences. Ovuakporaye (2022) underscores their potential to not only analyze competitors and brands effectively but also to shape consumers' purchasing behavior. Khoa's (2021) research underscores the transformative influence of chatbots on impulse buying and repeat purchase intentions. Moreover, Tsai et al.'s (2021) proposition that anthropomorphic chatbot profiles can enhance social presence communication through psychological mediation adds depth to their impact.

Rooted in advanced technology, chatbots possess a versatile character defined by their pervasiveness, inherent potential for continual enhancement, and innovative synergies (Murugesan & Cherukuri, 2023). Cheng et al. (2021) aptly highlight the unprecedented business prospects that AI-based chatbots bring forth. Approaching the matter from a user-centric stance, Chan & Leung (2021) contribute to an advanced understanding of chatbots, particularly their user interface and experiences, which are pivotal to successful integration. Mostafa and Kasamani (2021) delve into the crucial facet of fostering initial trust with chatbots, which serves as a catalyst for increased consumer engagement and interactions with brands.

Importantly, Illescas-Manzano (2021) propounds chatbots as a pivotal conduit for two-way communication, enabling businesses to glean invaluable consumer insights and facilitating marketing initiatives and sales strategies. In essence, chatbots hold the promise of reshaping Halal marketing paradigms by establishing dynamic and resonant interactions with consumers, fostering trust, and gathering critical data that underpins strategic decision-making.

Table 6. Emerging research areas

Research Area	Description	Key Authors
Optimizing Chatbot Adoption in Halal Marketing	Investigate the underexplored adoption of chatbots in Halal marketing. Assess their potential in enhancing customer experience and satisfaction, including the effectiveness of delivering accurate information, resolving queries, and aiding consumers in informed decision-making.	Trivedi (2019); Eren (2021); Aziz & Chok (2013)
Enhancing Certification Process with Chatbots	Address the theoretical gap in Halal studies related to certification processes. Study how chatbots can support and streamline Halal food certification by offering clear guidelines and addressing queries. Examine their role in boosting transparency and credibility in the certification process.	Ab Talib et al. (2016)
Elevating Customer Satisfaction in Apparel Retailing	Explore the impact of chatbots on customer satisfaction in Halal fashion retailing. Investigate their ability to provide personalized recommendations based on customer preferences, augmenting overall shopping experiences. Examine how chatbots can drive repeat purchases and foster brand loyalty.	Jansom et al. (2022); Aziz & Chok (2013)
Fortifying Halal Brand Equity through Chatbot Interaction	Investigate how chatbots can enhance Halal brand equity within the domain of hospitality and tourism. Study their role in meaningful dialogues with tourists, dissemination of Halal information, and reinforcing brand-customer relationships. Examine how chatbots can foster trust, loyalty, and positive brand perceptions.	Preko et al. (2021); Mostafa & Kasamani (2022)
Understanding Cross-Channel Trust and Loyalty	Examine the mechanisms through which chatbots can instill trust and loyalty among customers. Investigate their role in delivering consistent and responsive experiences across diverse communication channels. Study how these factors contribute to strengthening customer relationships and long-term brand loyalty.	Mostafa & Kasamani (2022)
Analyzing Consumer Behavior Patterns with Chatbots	Study the potential of chatbots in comprehending customer behavior in Halal food consumption. Investigate their effectiveness in gathering and evaluating customer preferences, as well as deciphering behavior patterns related to Halal food choices. Explore how chatbots can inform marketing strategies.	Iranmanesh et al. (2022)
Ethical Implications of Chatbot Adoption in Halal Marketing	Investigate the ethical considerations of employing chatbots in Halal marketing. Study the potential impacts on cultural sensitivity, trust, and consumer perceptions. Examine responsible and transparent deployment of chatbots in the context of Halal marketing communication.	A potential area for further research
Cultivating Inclusive Cross-Cultural Engagement	Explore the role of chatbots in facilitating inclusive cross-cultural engagement. Investigate their ability to adapt to diverse cultural preferences and effectively communicate with audiences across various cultural backgrounds. Study how chatbots can contribute to inclusive Halal marketing strategies.	A potential area for further research
Enhancing Halal Marketing Strategies with Chatbots	Synthesize research findings to formulate effective Halal marketing strategies with chatbots. Examine how optimizing chatbot capabilities, certification procedures, brand equity, trust-building, and consumer behavior insights can collectively drive successful Halal marketing campaigns.	Trivedi (2019); Eren (2021); Ab Talib et al. (2016); Jansom et al. (2022); Mostafa & Kasamani (2022); Iranmanesh et al. (2022)

CONCLUSION AND RESEARCH AGENDA

This synthesis of key research areas sheds light on the potential of chatbots in reshaping the Halal marketing paradigm. As researchers and practitioners delve deeper into this dynamic intersection, several insights and opportunities arise for future exploration.

The current body of research underscores the paramount importance of optimizing chatbot adoption within the realm of Halal marketing. Recognizing the untapped potential to elevate customer experiences, a deeper exploration into the intricacies of how chatbots adeptly deliver precise information, address inquiries, and facilitate informed decision-making promises a comprehensive grasp of their multifaceted impact.

Moreover, the pivotal role that chatbots can assume in the certification process of Halal products deserves special attention. Diving into the ways chatbots can streamline and augment transparency within the certification process not only amplifies regulatory efficiency but also bolsters consumer trust in the authenticity of Halal products and services.

The intriguing domain of Halal fashion retailing stands as a promising avenue for inquiry. Uncovering the nuanced influence of chatbots on customer satisfaction, the provision of personalized recommendations, stimulation of repeat purchases, and cultivation of brand loyalty within this context has the potential to illuminate their seamless integration.

Within the hospitality and tourism sector, delving into how chatbots interact with tourists, act as disseminators of Halal information, and serve as nurturers of brand-customer relationships offers a unique vantage point to enhance Halal brand equity and engender positive brand perceptions.

Furthermore, the intricate mechanisms by which chatbots contribute to cross-channel trust and loyalty present a fertile ground for exploration. By uncovering how these technologies bridge communication gaps and foster enduring customer connections, we gain insights into the very essence of fortified customer relationships.

A perceptive investigation into consumer behavior patterns associated with Halal food consumption unveils the potential of chatbots to efficiently collect and evaluate customer preferences, thus informing marketing strategies that resonate effectively.

Ethical considerations are crucial, and an in-depth analysis of the ethical implications of chatbot integration in Halal marketing is a necessary step toward responsible and transparent deployment. This entails addressing issues of cultural sensitivity, consumer perceptions, and building trust through ethical chatbot practices.

The arena of cultivating inclusive cross-cultural engagement through chatbots opens new horizons for exploration. A meticulous study of their adaptability to diverse cultural preferences and their efficacy in connecting with audiences of various cultural backgrounds promises a more inclusive approach to Halal marketing strategies.

In conclusion, the integration of chatbots in Halal marketing holds immense promise for enhancing customer experiences, fostering brand equity, and informing strategic marketing endeavors. By delving into the identified research areas, scholars and practitioners can contribute to the evolution of Halal marketing, ultimately benefiting businesses, consumers, and the broader Halal ecosystem. Through collaborative efforts, ongoing research can illuminate the transformative potential of chatbots and contribute to the advancement of Halal marketing strategies in the ever-evolving digital landscape.

REFERENCES

Ab Talib, M. S., Md. Sawari, S. S., Abdul Hamid, A. B., & Ai Chin, T. (2016). Emerging Halal food market: An Institutional Theory of Halal certificate implementation. *Management Research Review*, *39*(9), 987–997. doi:10.1108/MRR-06-2015-0147

Abdulquadri, A., Mogaji, E., Kieu, T. A., & Nguyen, N. P. (2021). Digital transformation in financial services provision: A Nigerian perspective to the adoption of chatbot. *Journal of Enterprising Communities: People and Places in the Global Economy*, *15*(2), 258–281. doi:10.1108/JEC-06-2020-0126

Adam, M., Wessel, M., & Benlian, A. (2021). AI-based chatbots in customer service and their effects on user compliance. *Electronic Markets, 31*(2), 427–445. doi:10.100712525-020-00414-7

Agarwal, P., Swami, S., & Malhotra, S. K. (2022). Artificial intelligence adoption in the post COVID-19 new-normal and role of smart technologies in transforming business: a review. *Journal of Science and Technology Policy Management*.

Ahmad Tarmizi, H., Kamarulzaman, N. H., Abd Rahman, A., & Atan, R. (2020). Adoption of internet of things among Malaysian halal agro-food SMEs and its challenges. *Food Research, 4*(S1), 256–265. doi:10.26656/fr.2017.4(S1).S26

Akın, M. S., & Okumuş, A. (2021). Shaping the consumers' attitudes towards Halal food products in Turkey. *Journal of Islamic Marketing, 12*(6), 1081–1096. doi:10.1108/JIMA-08-2019-0167

Ali, M. H., & Suleiman, N. (2016). Sustainable food production: Insights of Malaysian halal small and medium sized enterprises. *International Journal of Production Economics, 181*, 303–314. doi:10.1016/j.ijpe.2016.06.003

Alia, M. Q., & Ahmada, N. (2023). The Factors that affect Halal Food and Food Products Awareness and Different Challenges: An overview. *Journal of Agribusiness Marketing, 10*(1), 82–95. doi:10.56527/fama.jabm.10.1.6

Almutairi, S., Khan, S. A., Kuhail, M. A., & Taj, I. (2023). Chatbot Design Challenges and the Effect on User Behavior. *Trends, Applications, and Challenges of Chatbot Technology*, 24-35. doi:10.4018/978-1-6684-6234-8.ch002

Alserhan, B. A. (2010). Islamic branding: A conceptualization of related terms. *Journal of Brand Management, 18*(1), 34–49. doi:10.1057/bm.2010.18

Alt, M. A., & Ibolya, V. (2021). Identifying Relevant Segments of Potential Banking Chatbot Users Based on Technology Adoption Behavior. *Market-Tržište, 33*(2), 165–183. doi:10.22598/mt/2021.33.2.165

Arsenijevic, U., & Jovic, M. (2019, September). Artificial intelligence marketing: chatbots. In 2019 international conference on artificial intelligence: applications and innovations (IC-AIAI) (pp. 19-193). IEEE. doi:10.1109/IC-AIAI48757.2019.00010

Aslam, U. (2023). Understanding the usability of retail fashion brand chatbots: Evidence from customer expectations and experiences. *Journal of Retailing and Consumer Services, 74*, 103377. doi:10.1016/j.jretconser.2023.103377

Attar, R. W., Almusharraf, A., Alfawaz, A., & Hajli, N. (2022). New Trends in E-Commerce Research: Linking Social Commerce and Sharing Commerce: A Systematic Literature Review. *Sustainability (Basel), 14*(23), 16024. doi:10.3390u142316024

Aziz, Y. A., & Chok, N. V. (2013). The role of Halal awareness, Halal certification, and marketing components in determining Halal purchase intention among non-Muslims in Malaysia: A structural equation modeling approach. *Journal of International Food & Agribusiness Marketing, 25*(1), 1–23. doi:10.1080/08974438.2013.723997

Azmi, F. R., Musa, H., Sihombing, H., & Fen, F. S. (2018). Adoption factors of halal standards: The Malaysian perspectives. In *Proceedings of the 3rd International Halal Conference (INHAC 2016)* (pp. 315-329). Springer Singapore. 10.1007/978-981-10-7257-4_29

Battour, M., Mady, K., Elsotouhy, M., Salaheldeen, M., Elbendary, I., Marie, M., & Elhabony, I. (2022). Artificial intelligence applications in halal tourism to assist Muslim tourist journey. In *Proceedings of International Conference on Emerging Technologies and Intelligent Systems: ICETIS 2021* Volume 2 (pp. 861-872). Springer International Publishing. 10.1007/978-3-030-85990-9_68

Battour, M., Mady, K., Salaheldeen, M., Elsotouhy, M., Elbendary, I., & Boğan, E. (2023). AI-enabled technologies to assist Muslim tourists in Halal-friendly tourism. *Journal of Islamic Marketing*, *14*(5), 1291–1309. doi:10.1108/JIMA-01-2022-0001

Battour, M., Salaheldeen, M., & Mady, K. (2021). Exploring innovative marketing opportunities for Halal entrepreneurs in hospitality and tourism industry. In *SHS Web of Conferences* (*Vol. 124*, p. 10001). EDP Sciences. 10.1051hsconf/202112410001

Berakon, I., Wibowo, M. G., Nurdany, A., & Aji, H. M. (2023). An expansion of the technology acceptance model applied to the halal tourism sector. *Journal of Islamic Marketing*, *14*(1), 289–316. doi:10.1108/JIMA-03-2021-0064

Chan, W. T. Y., & Leung, C. H. (2021). Mind the gap: Discrepancy between customer expectation and perception on commercial chatbots usage. *Asian Journal of Empirical Research*, *11*(1), 1–10. doi:10.18488/journal.1007.2021.111.1.10

Cheng, X., Bao, Y., Zarifis, A., Gong, W., & Mou, J. (2021). Exploring consumers' response to text-based chatbots in e-commerce: The moderating role of task complexity and chatbot disclosure. *Internet Research*, *32*(2), 496–517. doi:10.1108/INTR-08-2020-0460

Cheng, Y., & Jiang, H. (2022). Customer–brand relationship in the era of artificial intelligence: Understanding the role of chatbot marketing efforts. *Journal of Product and Brand Management*, *31*(2), 252–264. doi:10.1108/JPBM-05-2020-2907

Chiong, P. S. S. C., Seeam, P., & Seeam, A. (2022). Development of a smart tourism information chatbot for Mauritius. *ICONIC*, 122-130. https://doi.org/ doi:10.59200/ICONIC.2022.013

Chung, M., Ko, E., Joung, H., & Kim, S. J. (2020). Chatbot e-service and customer satisfaction regarding luxury brands. *Journal of Business Research*, *117*, 587–595. doi:10.1016/j.jbusres.2018.10.004

ElasragH. (2016). Halal industry: Key challenges and opportunities. SSRN *Journal*. doi:10.2139/ssrn.2735417

Eren, B. A. (2021). Determinants of customer satisfaction in chatbot use: Evidence from a banking application in Turkey. *International Journal of Bank Marketing*, *39*(2), 294–311. doi:10.1108/IJBM-02-2020-0056

Gupta, A., & Sharma, D. (2019). Customers' Attitude towards Chatbots in Banking Industry of India. *International Journal of Innovative Technology and Exploring Engineering*, *8*(11), 1222–1225. doi:10.35940/ijitee.J9366.0981119

Hari, H., Iyer, R., & Sampat, B. (2022). Customer brand engagement through chatbots on bank websites–Examining the antecedents and consequences. *International Journal of Human-Computer Interaction, 38*(13), 1212–1227. doi:10.1080/10447318.2021.1988487

Hassan, M. K., Rabbani, M. R., & Chebab, D. (2021). Integrating Islamic finance and Halal industry: Current landscape and future forward. *International Journal of Islamic Marketing and Branding, 6*(1), 60–78. doi:10.1504/IJIMB.2021.117594

Hassan, S. H., Mohamed Haniba, N. M., & Ahmad, N. H. (2019). Social customer relationship management (s-CRM) among small-and medium-sized enterprises (SMEs) in Malaysia. *International Journal of Ethics and Systems, 35*(2), 284–302. doi:10.1108/IJOES-11-2017-0192

Hendayani, R., & Fernando, Y. (2022). Adoption of blockchain technology to improve Halal supply chain performance and competitiveness. *Journal of Islamic Marketing.*

Herhausen, D., Miočević, D., Morgan, R. E., & Kleijnen, M. H. (2020). The digital marketing capabilities gap. *Industrial Marketing Management, 90*, 276–290. doi:10.1016/j.indmarman.2020.07.022

Hidayat, S. E., Rafiki, A., & Nasution, M. D. T. P. (2022). Halal industry's response to a current and post-COVID-19 landscape and lessons from the past. *Journal of Islamic Marketing, 13*(9), 1843–1857. doi:10.1108/JIMA-06-2020-0180

Hildebrand, C., & Bergner, A. (2019). AI-driven sales automation: Using chatbots to boost sales. *NIM Marketing Intelligence Review, 11*(2), 36–41. doi:10.2478/nimmir-2019-0014

Hoque, M. E., Nik Hashim, N. M. H., & Azmi, M. H. B. (2018). Moderating effects of marketing communication and financial consideration on customer attitude and intention to purchase Islamic banking products: A conceptual framework. *Journal of Islamic Marketing, 9*(4), 799–822. doi:10.1108/JIMA-01-2017-0005

Illescas-Manzano, M. D., Vicente López, N., Afonso González, N., & Cristofol Rodríguez, C. (2021). Implementation of chatbot in online commerce, and open innovation. *Journal of Open Innovation, 7*(2), 125. doi:10.3390/joitmc7020125

Iranmanesh, M., Senali, M. G., Ghobakhloo, M., Nikbin, D., & Abbasi, G. A. (2022). Customer behaviour towards halal food: A systematic review and agenda for future research. *Journal of Islamic Marketing, 13*(9), 1901–1917. doi:10.1108/JIMA-01-2021-0031

Jansom, A., Srisangkhajorn, T., & Limarunothai, W. (2022). How chatbot e-services motivate communication credibility and lead to customer satisfaction: The perspective of Thai consumers in the apparel retailing context. *Innovative Marketing, 18*(3), 13–25. doi:10.21511/im.18(3).2022.02

Kaczorowska-Spychalska, D. (2019). How chatbots influence marketing. *Management, 23*(1), 251–270. doi:10.2478/manment-2019-0015

Kamarulzaman, N. H., Muhamad, N. A., & Mohd Nawi, N. (2022). An investigation of adoption intention of halal traceability system among food SMEs. *Journal of Islamic Marketing, 13*(9), 1872–1900. doi:10.1108/JIMA-11-2020-0349

Khoa, B. T. (2021). The Impact of Chatbots on the Relationship between Integrated Marketing Communication and Online Purchasing Behavior in The Frontier Market. *Jurnal The Messenger, 13*(1), 19–32. doi:10.26623/themessenger.v13i1.2439

Lo Presti, L., Maggiore, G., & Marino, V. (2021). The role of the chatbot on customer purchase intention: Towards digital relational sales. *Italian Journal of Marketing, 2021*(3), 165–188. doi:10.100743039-021-00029-6

Lubbe, I., & Ngoma, N. (2021). Useful chatbot experience provides technological satisfaction: An emerging market perspective. *South African Journal of Information Management, 23*(1), 1–8. doi:10.4102ajim.v23i1.1299

Luo, B., Lau, R. Y., Li, C., & Si, Y. W. (2022). A critical review of state-of-the-art chatbot designs and applications. *Wiley Interdisciplinary Reviews. Data Mining and Knowledge Discovery, 12*(1), e1434. doi:10.1002/widm.1434

Marković, J., & Stošić-Mihajlović, L. (2022). Halal product markets. *Ekonomski izazovi, 11*(22), 60-73. doi:10.5937/EkoIzazov2222060M

Martinez, M. E., López-Orozco, F., Olmos-Sánchez, K., & Sánchez-Solís, J. P. (2021). Mispronunciation Detection and Diagnosis Through a Chatbot. In *Handbook of Research on Natural Language Processing and Smart Service Systems* (pp. 31–45). IGI Global. doi:10.4018/978-1-7998-4730-4.ch002

MassaroA.MagalettiN.CosoliG.GiardinelliV.LeograndeA. (2022). Text Mining Approaches Oriented on Customer Care Efficiency. SSRN. doi:10.2139/ssrn.4026102

Masudin, I., Jie, F., Djajadikerta, H., & Widayat, W. (2021). The effect of halal retail and manufacturing technology readiness on halal meat logistics performance. *International Journal of Logistics Systems and Management, 40*(1), 1–27. doi:10.1504/IJLSM.2021.117688

Matic, R., Kabiljo, M., Zivkovic, M., & Cabarkapa, M. (2021). Extensible chatbot architecture using metamodels of natural language understanding. *Electronics (Basel), 10*(18), 2300. doi:10.3390/electronics10182300

Moshin, A., Brochado, A., & Rodrigues, H. (2020). Halal tourism is traveling fast: Community perceptions and implications. *Journal of Destination Marketing & Management, 18*, 100503. doi:10.1016/j.jdmm.2020.100503

Mostafa, M. M. (2021). Information diffusion in halal food social media: A social network approach. *Journal of International Consumer Marketing, 33*(4), 471–491. doi:10.1080/08961530.2020.1818158

Mostafa, R. B., & Kasamani, T. (2022). Antecedents and consequences of chatbot initial trust. *European Journal of Marketing, 56*(6), 1748–1771. doi:10.1108/EJM-02-2020-0084

Mukherjee, A., Rajendran, S. D., & Wahab, S. N. (2022). Technology Strategy in Boosting Halal Tourism Activities. In Technology Application in Aviation, Tourism and Hospitality: Recent Developments and Emerging Issues (pp. 41-56). Singapore: Springer Nature Singapore. doi:10.1007/978-981-19-6619-4_4

Murugesan, S., & Cherukuri, A. K. (2023). The Rise of Generative Artificial Intelligence and Its Impact on Education: The Promises and Perils. *Computer, 56*(5), 116–121. doi:10.1109/MC.2023.3253292

Musa, A. H., Baharuddin, F. N., Noh, S. N. S., & Asma'Rashidah Idris, S. M. S. (2022). Islamic Marketing, Electronic Word of Mouth (eWoM) and Religious Awareness Roles in Consuming Halal Food: A Conceptual Paper. *IJARBSS, 12*(12). doi:10.6007/IJARBSS/v12-i12/16038

Mydyti, H., & Kadriu, A. (2021). The impact of chatbots in driving digital transformation. [IJESMA]. *International Journal of E-Services and Mobile Applications, 13*(4), 88–104. doi:10.4018/IJESMA.2021100106

Nanda, P., Patnaik, D., & Patnaik, S. (2021). Computational Management—An Overview. *Computational Management: Applications of Computational Intelligence in Business Management*, 3-21. doi:10.1007/978-3-030-72929-5_1

Nazaruddin, L. O., Gyenge, B., Fekete-Farkas, M., & Lakner, Z. (2023). The Future Direction of Halal Food Additive and Ingredient Research in Economics and Business: A Bibliometric Analysis. *Sustainability (Basel), 15*(7), 5680. doi:10.3390u15075680

Nicolescu, L., & Tudorache, M. T. (2022). Human-Computer Interaction in Customer Service: The Experience with AI Chatbots—A Systematic Literature Review. *Electronics (Basel), 11*(10), 1579. doi:10.3390/electronics11101579

Nirala, K. K., Singh, N. K., & Purani, V. S. (2022). A survey on providing customer and public administration based services using AI: Chatbot. *Multimedia Tools and Applications, 81*(16), 22215–22246. doi:10.100711042-021-11458-y

Noor, N. (2022). Halal Service Marketing: A Strategic Perspective. In *Strategic Islamic Marketing: A Roadmap for Engaging Muslim Consumers* (pp. 11–29). Springer International Publishing. doi:10.1007/978-3-030-98160-0_3

Ordemann, S., Skjuve, M., Følstad, A., & Bjørkli, C. (2021). "Have a Nice Day:)": Social Interactions with Customer Service Chatbots. *Proceedings of the 19th International Conference on e-Society 2021*. Springer.

Ovuakporaye, K. (2022). The Impact, Comparison and Usefulness of Digital Marketing Communications Tools on Organizational Profit Maximization Using Facebook. *Asian Journal of Research in Computer Science, 13*(4), 46–64. doi:10.9734/ajrcos/2022/v13i430321

Paliwal, S., Bharti, V., & Mishra, A. K. (2020). Ai chatbots: Transforming the digital world. *Recent Trends and Advances in Artificial Intelligence and Internet of Things*, 455-482. doi:10.1007/978-3-030-32644-9_34

Pillai, R., & Sivathanu, B. (2020). Adoption of AI-based chatbots for hospitality and tourism. *International Journal of Contemporary Hospitality Management, 32*(10), 3199–3226. doi:10.1108/IJCHM-04-2020-0259

Preko, A., Mohammed, I., & Allaberganov, A. (2021). Antecedents of brand equity on halal tourism destination. *Journal of Islamic Marketing, 8*(13), 1685–1702. doi:10.1108/JIMA-09-2020-0283

Rafiq, F., Dogra, N., Adil, M., & Wu, J. Z. (2022). Examining consumer's intention to adopt AI-chatbots in tourism using partial least squares structural equation modeling method. *Mathematics, 10*(13), 2190. doi:10.3390/math10132190

Rajagopal, S., Ramanan, S., Visvanathan, R., & Satapathy, S. (2011). Halal certification: Implication for marketers in UAE. *Journal of Islamic Marketing*, *2*(2), 138–153. doi:10.1108/17590831111139857

Ramzy, O., & Eldahan, O. H. (2015). Marketing communications in the Islamic perspective: Communicating the halal branding. In Islamic Perspectives on Marketing and Consumer Behavior: Planning, Implementation, and Control (pp. 149-168). IGI Global. doi:10.4018/978-1-4666-8139-2.ch007

Rapp, A., Curti, L., & Boldi, A. (2021). The human side of human-chatbot interaction: A systematic literature review of ten years of research on text-based chatbots. *International Journal of Human-Computer Studies*, *151*, 102630. doi:10.1016/j.ijhcs.2021.102630

Rejeb, A., Rejeb, K., Zailani, S., Treiblmaier, H., & Hand, K. J. (2021). Integrating the Internet of Things in the halal food supply chain: A systematic literature review and research agenda. *Internet of Things*, *13*, 100361. doi:10.1016/j.iot.2021.100361

Rese, A., Ganster, L., & Baier, D. (2020). Chatbots in retailers' customer communication: How to measure their acceptance? *Journal of Retailing and Consumer Services*, *56*, 102176. doi:10.1016/j.jretconser.2020.102176

Ruiz-Bejarano, B. (2017). Islamophobia as a Deterrent to Halal Global Trade. *Islamophobia Studies Journal*, *1*(4). Advance online publication. doi:10.13169/islastudj.4.1.0129

Shafi, P. M., Jawalkar, G. S., Kadam, M. A., Ambawale, R. R., & Bankar, S. V. (2020). AI—Assisted Chatbot for E-Commerce to Address Selection of Products from Multiple Products. *Internet of Things, Smart Computing and Technology: A Roadmap Ahead*, 57-80. doi:10.1007/978-3-030-39047-1_3

Sharma, V., Goyal, M., & Malik, D. (2017). An intelligent behaviour shown by chatbot system. *International Journal of New Technology and Research*, *3*(4), 263312.

Sheehan, B., Jin, H. S., & Gottlieb, U. (2020). Customer service chatbots: Anthropomorphism and adoption. *Journal of Business Research*, *115*, 14–24. doi:10.1016/j.jbusres.2020.04.030

Shumanov, M., & Johnson, L. (2021). Making conversations with chatbots more personalized. *Computers in Human Behavior*, *117*, 106627. doi:10.1016/j.chb.2020.106627

Siraj, A., Shaikh, F. A., Shukla, V. K., Nanda, I., & Punhani, R. (2022). Impact of Mobile Applications and Internet of Things (IoT. In H. Tourism (Ed.), *Tourist Behavior* (pp. 239–261). Apple Academic Press. doi:10.1201/9781003282082-11

Smutny, P., & Schreiberova, P. (2020). Chatbots for learning: A review of educational chatbots for the Facebook Messenger. *Computers & Education*, *151*, 103862. doi:10.1016/j.compedu.2020.103862

So, S. (2023). An Analysis on the Adoption of Chatbots in the Banking Sector of Hong Kong: A Contemporary System for Improving Customer Experiences in E-Banking. In *Digital Entrepreneurship and Co-Creating Value Through Digital Encounters* (pp. 245–262). IGI Global. doi:10.4018/978-1-6684-7416-7.ch012

Sujata, J., Nikita, M., & Shubham, S. (2019). Applications of chatbots in marketing: use cases, impacts, challenges and drivers. *International Journal of Advanced Trends in Computer Science and Engineering*, *8*(1.6), 195-200.

Torres, A. I., & Delgado, C. J. (2023). Assessing Customer Interactions With Chatbots in Online Shopping Experiences: An Empirical Study. In Promoting Organizational Performance Through 5G and Agile Marketing (pp. 203-223). IGI Global. doi:10.4018/978-1-6684-5523-4.ch011

Trivedi, J. (2019). Examining the customer experience of using banking chatbots and its impact on brand love: The moderating role of perceived risk. *Journal of Internet Commerce*, *18*(1), 91–111. doi:10.1080/15332861.2019.1567188

Trofymenko, O., Prokop, Y., Zadereyko, O., & Loginova, N. (2022). Classification of chatbots. *System technologies, 2*(139), 147-159. https://doi.org/ doi:10.34185/1562-9945-2-139-2022-14

Tsai, W. H. S., Liu, Y., & Chuan, C. H. (2021). How chatbots' social presence communication enhances consumer engagement: The mediating role of parasocial interaction and dialogue. *Journal of Research in Interactive Marketing*, *15*(3), 460–482. doi:10.1108/JRIM-12-2019-0200

Van den Broeck, E., Zarouali, B., & Poels, K. (2019). Chatbot advertising effectiveness: When does the message get through? *Computers in Human Behavior*, *98*, 150–157. doi:10.1016/j.chb.2019.04.009

Yadav, R. (2022). Zero Customer Defection. In *Adoption and Implementation of AI in Customer Relationship Management* (pp. 139–153). IGI Global., doi:10.4018/978-1-7998-7959-6.ch009

Yousaf, S. (2016). Promotion mix management: A consumer focused Islamic perspective. *Journal of Marketing Communications*, *22*(2), 215–231. doi:10.1080/13527266.2014.888575

Yunos, R. M., Mahmood, C. F. C., & Abd Mansor, N. H. (2014). Understanding mechanisms to promote halal industry-the stakeholders' views. *Procedia: Social and Behavioral Sciences*, *130*, 160–166. doi:10.1016/j.sbspro.2014.04.020

Chapter 4
Islamic Entrepreneurship Nurturing New Ventures Through Islamic Principles

Juli Meliza
Sekolah Tinggi Ilmu Manajemen Sukma, Indonesia

Erwansyah Erwansyah
Universitas Pembangunan Panca Budi, Indonesia

Harianto Harianto
Universitas Pembangunan Panca Budi, Indonesia

Ku Halim Ku Ariffin
Universiti Malaysia Perlis, Malaysia

ABSTRACT

The chapter aims to explore factors, values, and education driving Islamic entrepreneurial initiatives, and their impact on economic development. It emphasizes integrating Islamic principles into new business creation. The study also examines roles of absorption capacity, financial development, Islamic debt financing, and family background in Islamic entrepreneurship. By linking Islamic teachings and entrepreneurial pursuits, the Initiative enhances understanding and promotes ethical, sustainable business. It values Islamic work ethics and management team insights to foster Islamic-based enterprises. The chapter guides entrepreneurs, policymakers, and researchers in nurturing Islamic entrepreneurship, contributing to knowledge and future research. Insights can fuel positive transformations in the evolving entrepreneurial landscape.

INTRODUCTION

The domain of studies centered on the Islamic Entrepreneurial Initiative, particularly in the context of establishing new businesses based on Islamic principles, is marked by certain limitations that warrant

DOI: 10.4018/978-1-6684-7519-5.ch004

recognition. These limitations stem from the scarcity of research that thoroughly delves into the intricate interplay of Islamic work ethics and their profound impact on the intentions and motivations of Muslim entrepreneurs in their business endeavors. While some studies, such as the one conducted by Suhariadi et al. in 2021, have explored the correlation between work ethics and entrepreneurial intentions, a more nuanced and specific exploration within the Islamic context remains a notable research gap.

Furthermore, the deficiency of research exploring the influence of management team experience on the initiation of new businesses within the realm of Islamic entrepreneurship is a salient point. Although the study conducted by Li & Dutta in 2018 has delved into the impact of diverse management team experiences on business outcomes, it has not ventured into the realm of Islamic perspectives with the requisite depth.

An area of particular significance lies in absorptive capacity—a concept elucidating an organization's ability to acquire, assimilate, and effectively apply external knowledge (Zahra & George, 2002). Despite absorptive capacity's prominence in the broader entrepreneurship literature, there remains a dearth of specific research investigating its role within the realm of Islamic entrepreneurship. Understanding how Islamic-oriented new businesses can optimally harness and apply external knowledge is pivotal for devising strategies and policies that foster the growth and success of such enterprises.

The variance in empirical findings regarding the Islamic Entrepreneurial Initiative, particularly in relation to the establishment of new Islamic businesses, can be attributed to several contributory factors. Notably, absorptive capacity stands as a critical factor. This pertains to the capacity of a company to effectively internalize external knowledge, playing a pivotal role in shaping competitive advantage (Zahra & George, 2002). However, differing interpretations and measurements of absorptive capacity across studies have led to incongruities in research outcomes.

Entrepreneurial Orientation (EO) also contributes to this variability. EO denotes a company's strategic disposition towards innovation, risk-taking, and proactivity (Lumpkin & Dess, 1996). Various dimensions of EO and their interplay with firm performance have undergone iterative discussions and refinements (Lumpkin & Dess, 1996). However, divergent definitions and metrics of EO utilized in different studies have resulted in incongruous findings.

The intermediary role of personal initiative and entrepreneurial alertness also contributes to these disparities. Personal initiative signifies proactive behaviors undertaken by individuals in pursuing opportunities and initiating action (Nsereko et al., 2021). In parallel, entrepreneurial alertness denotes an individual's ability to identify and comprehend entrepreneurial prospects (Nsereko et al., 2021).

Furthermore, cultural and situational factors cast a significant influence on research outcomes concerning Islamic entrepreneurial intentions. The confluence of Islamic values, practices, and cultural diversity within Muslim communities profoundly influences perceptions of entrepreneurship and the proclivity to engage in entrepreneurial activities (Wibowo et al., 2021; Basir & Musa, 2021). These factors exhibit variations across nations and within different Muslim communities, thus contributing to the heterogeneity in research findings.

In summary, the variability in empirical outcomes pertaining to the Islamic Entrepreneurial Initiative within the realm of establishing new Islamic businesses is a result of multifaceted factors. These encompass the concept of absorptive capacity, the nuances of Entrepreneurial Orientation, the mediating roles of personal initiative and entrepreneurial alertness, and the intricate interplay of cultural and situational elements.

Research pertaining to Shariah-compliant entrepreneurial initiatives holds paramount importance in the establishment and growth of new businesses aligned with Islamic principles. Islamic business constitutes a burgeoning field of study that resides at the juncture of Islamic tenets and business practices, seeking to unravel the intricate interplay between Islamic values and entrepreneurial conduct in the creation of novel enterprises within the Islamic paradigm.

A fundamental facet of this research domain revolves around the concept of absorptive capacity. This concept refers to an organization's adeptness in acquiring, assimilating, and operationalizing external knowledge and insights (Zahra & George, 2002). In the realm of forging new Islamic businesses, this receptivity becomes a linchpin, enabling entrepreneurs to adroitly adapt and integrate Islamic principles into their business frameworks. Through fostering responsiveness, entrepreneurs can adroitly harness external resources and knowledge to sculpt innovative and sustainable ventures in consonance with Islamic precepts.

Zahra and George (2002) have provided a comprehensive exegesis on absorptive capacity and its nuanced reinterpretation. Their model postulates the conditions under which a firm's latent and realized competencies can catalyze the genesis and sustenance of competitive advantage (Zahra & George, 2002). This model, suitably applied within the realm of Islamic business, offers a lens to fathom how assimilation can expedite the infusion of Islamic tenets into business dynamics, thereby amplifying the efficacy of Islamic enterprises.

Additionally, the study of Islamic social entrepreneurship constitutes another pivotal facet in comprehending the terrain of engendering new Islamic businesses. Islamic social entrepreneurship encapsulates endeavors that strive to tackle societal and environmental quandaries in consonance with Islamic principles (Asfiah, 2021). It champions ethical and socially responsible business practices, squarely embedded within the Islamic milieu.

Asfiah (2021) embarked on research elucidating the role of Islamic social entrepreneurship in mitigating the influence of Islamic management and emotional intelligence on business performance (Asfiah, 2021). This study accentuates the latent potential of Islamic social entrepreneurship in amplifying the efficiency and impact of Islamic enterprises, engendering ethical leadership and emotional intelligence among entrepreneurs.

Furthermore, investigations into Islamic work ethics and entrepreneurial intentions proffer insights into the motivational underpinnings driving individuals to embark on entrepreneurial journeys within the Islamic ethos (Abidin et al., 2021). The research sheds light on the affirmative role that Islamic values and religious practices play in fostering entrepreneurial intentions, underscoring the transformative impact of Islamic beliefs on shaping entrepreneurial proclivities (Abidin et al., 2021).

In synthesis, it is incontrovertible that research encapsulating the Islamic Entrepreneurship Initiative carries profound significance, particularly in the realm of forging new Islamic businesses. This research panorama delves into the realm of absorptive capacity, Islamic social entrepreneurship, and Islamic work ethics, unveiling their roles in shaping entrepreneurial behaviors and the emergence of new ventures within the Islamic framework. This holistic comprehension equips policymakers, educators, and entrepreneurs to champion the propagation of Islamic entrepreneurship, ushering in a trajectory of sustainable and ethically driven business expansion aligned with the tenets of Islam.

Therefore, the aim of this study is to offer valuable insights into the factors, values, and education that contribute to Islamic entrepreneurial initiatives and their consequential impact on economic development and performance.

ISLAMIC ENTREPRENEURIAL INITIATIVE FRAMEWORK

Research endeavors focused on the Islamic Entrepreneurial Initiative carry significant importance within the domain of establishing businesses that align with Sharia principles. Islamic-based businesses constitute a burgeoning field that spotlights the convergence of Islamic values and business practices. The objective is to grasp how Islamic beliefs influence entrepreneurial conduct and the process of establishing new enterprises within the purview of Islam.

A fundamental pillar of this research lies in the concept of absorptive capacity. Absorptive capacity denotes an organization's adeptness in acquiring, assimilating, and applying knowledge and information from external sources (Zahra and George, 2002). In the pursuit of creating businesses that resonate with Islamic principles, the capacity to respond effectively to the environment plays a pivotal role. This enables entrepreneurs to harmoniously integrate Islamic tenets into their business models. By cultivating this capability, entrepreneurs can optimally leverage external knowledge and resources to craft innovative and sustainable enterprises in consonance with Islamic values.

The work of Zahra and George (2002) provides an exhaustive panorama and reimagining of absorptive capacity (Zahra and George, 2002). They propose a model that delineates the circumstances under which a company's latent and realized capabilities impact the process of forging and sustaining competitive advantage (Zahra and George, 2002). This model can be aptly applied in the realm of Islamic business to elucidate how absorptive capacity can facilitate the infusion of Islamic principles into business practices, ultimately augmenting the efficacy of Islamic enterprises.

Furthermore, delving into Islamic social entrepreneurship is another pivotal facet in the exploration of crafting new businesses from an Islamic vantage point. Islamic social entrepreneurship pertains to entrepreneurial endeavors geared towards addressing social and environmental challenges in harmony with Islamic principles (Asfiah, 2021). This underscores the imperative of embracing ethical and socially responsible business conduct within the framework of Islam.

Asfiah's study (2021) unveils the role of Islamic social entrepreneurship in mitigating the impact of Islamic management and emotional intelligence on business performance (Asfiah, 2021). This research underscores the potential of Islamic social entrepreneurship to elevate the effectiveness and impact of Islamic businesses by fostering ethical leadership and emotional intelligence among entrepreneurs.

Moreover, inquiry into Islamic work ethics and entrepreneurial intentions provides insight into the impelling factors that propel individuals to engage in entrepreneurial pursuits within the Islamic context (Abidin et al., 2021). Islamic values and religious practices have demonstrated a positive influence on entrepreneurial intentions, underscoring the salience of Islamic beliefs in shaping entrepreneurial conduct (Abidin et al., 2021).

In summation, it is evident that studies centered on the Islamic Entrepreneurial Initiative bear substantial significance when it comes to shaping new businesses through an Islamic lens. These studies offer insight into the roles of absorptive capacity, Islamic social entrepreneurship, and Islamic work ethics in shaping entrepreneurial behavior and the genesis of new enterprises within the ambit of Islam

FOUNDATIONS OF THE ISLAMIC ENTREPRENEURIAL INITIATIVE: A PERSPECTIVE FROM PREMISES

The core of the Islamic Entrepreneurial Initiative revolves around the motivation and individual needs related to the utilization of media and technology. This premise posits that individuals actively seek and engage with media and technology to satisfy their personal requirements and fulfillments (Al-Debei & Avison, 2010). Within the context of establishing new businesses rooted in Islam, this principle extends to understanding the motivations and needs of Muslim entrepreneurs. Additionally, it delves into how these entrepreneurs leverage the principles of Islamic finance to address these needs.

Islamic finance, grounded in Sharia principles, forms the bedrock that fosters fair, equitable, and participatory alternatives within the realm of new ventures. Muslim entrepreneurs face an array of challenges when initiating their businesses, particularly in accessing funding (Fathonih et al., 2019). The tenets of Sharia financial principles offer solutions that align with Islamic teachings, allowing Muslim entrepreneurs to reconcile their financial resource needs with their religious convictions (Fathonih et al., 2019). By opting for Islamic finance, these entrepreneurs can fulfill their financial requirements while upholding their religious beliefs.

The practical essence of media and technology dimensions in satisfying individual needs is a paramount consideration. In the sphere of establishing new businesses rooted in Islam, the tangible role of Islamic finance becomes a pivotal factor driving economic growth and entrepreneurship. Extensive research highlights Islamic finance's role in propelling economic growth in nations like Malaysia (Ledhem & Moussaoui, 2021). By providing funding avenues for the entrepreneurship sector, particularly for small and medium-sized businesses, Islamic finance significantly contributes to economic advancement (Ledhem & Moussaoui, 2021). By facilitating access to funding, Islamic finance aids Muslim entrepreneurs in laying the foundations and nurturing the growth of their businesses, thereby addressing their business expansion needs and fostering economic prosperity.

Furthermore, it is imperative to affirm the integral role of individuals in the process of business creation. Comparable to other entrepreneurs, Muslim entrepreneurs hold a vital position in initiating and cultivating new businesses (Shook et al., 2003). Grasping the motivations and aspirations that propel Muslim entrepreneurs is pivotal in comprehending their rationale for embarking on the journey of creating new ventures. The motivations underpinning business initiation may vary among individuals and across nations (Shook et al., 2003). For instance, Muslim entrepreneurs may be driven by a commitment to adhere to Islamic teachings and contribute to the advancement of their communities.

The premises underlying the domain of Islamic entrepreneurship provide a robust foundation for comprehending the essence of the Islamic Entrepreneurial Initiative within the realm of establishing new businesses rooted in Islam. This theoretical framework underscores the motivations and individual needs of Muslim entrepreneurs and underscores the vital role played by Islamic finance in addressing those needs. Islamic finance, rooted in Sharia principles, presents an alternative financing avenue that aligns with Islamic values, thus surmounting the challenges faced by Muslim entrepreneurs. By harnessing Islamic finance, Muslim entrepreneurs can fulfill their financial requisites while upholding their religious convictions. Furthermore, Islamic finance assumes a practical role in driving economic growth and nurturing entrepreneurship. Understanding the motivations and aspirations of Muslim entrepreneurs holds paramount significance in analyzing their decisions to initiate new businesses and contribute to the progress of their communities.

PILLARS OF ISLAMIC ENTREPRENEURSHIP: INTEGRATION OF PRINCIPLES AND FACTORS IN NEW BUSINESS CREATION

The term "Islamic Entrepreneurial Initiative," within the context of Islamic new business creation, pertains to the examination of entrepreneurship guided by Islamic principles and values. This initiative delves into the incorporation of Islamic teachings and objectives, primarily guided by Maqasid Al-Shari'ah, throughout the process of establishing and maintaining new ventures (Shehu & Al-Aidaros, 2015). Islamic entrepreneurship encompasses both religious and economic Islamic aspirations, encompassing endeavors such as seizing opportunities, adhering to ethical conduct, fostering societal well-being, and advancing halal income (Muhammad et al., 2017; Kutsiyah, 2020).

The concept of "absorptive capacity" (Zahra & George, 2002), pertinent to the realm of the Islamic Entrepreneurial Initiative, denotes an organization's capacity to acquire, assimilate, and apply external knowledge and resources to bolster its competitive edge. Within the realm of Islamic entrepreneurship, absorptive capacity manifests as the ability of Islamic businesses to effectively integrate Islamic principles and teachings into their business practices and decision-making processes.

In the exploration of the Islamic Entrepreneurial Initiative, due consideration is granted to the role of "Islamic financial development" and "debt financing" in fostering entrepreneurship (Sohail & Arshed, 2022). Islamic finance proffers an alternative, equitable, and participatory avenue for funding new endeavors, displaying potential for augmenting growth (Sohail & Arshed, 2022). This examination delves into the intricate interplay between financial development, Islamic debt financing, and entrepreneurship, underscoring the capability of Islamic finance to bolster entrepreneurship, especially in nations characterized by underdeveloped financial sectors (Sohail & Arshed, 2022).

Moreover, the study encompassing the Islamic Entrepreneurial Initiative duly acknowledges the imprint of "family background" on the intentions of Muslimpreneurs (Juliana et al., 2020). Family background, encompassing upbringing, values, and cultural norms, possesses the potential to shape individuals' intentions and motivations to partake in Islamic entrepreneurship. A comprehensive grasp of the influence of family background offers insights into the factors that contribute to the emergence of Shariah entrepreneurs.

To encapsulate, the exploration of the Islamic Entrepreneurial Initiative focalizes on the amalgamation of Islamic principles and objectives in the voyage of establishing novel enterprises. This initiative contemplates the role of absorptive capacity, financial development, Islamic debt financing, and family background in shaping the landscape of Islamic entrepreneurship. By dissecting the nexus between Islamic teachings and entrepreneurship, the Islamic Entrepreneurial Initiative seeks to enrich the comprehension and advancement of Islamic entrepreneurship as a viable and ethical business approach..

DIMENSIONS OF ISLAMIC ENTREPRENEURIAL INITIATIVE: UNVEILING FACTORS IN NEW BUSINESS CREATION

Islamic entrepreneurship constitutes a multidimensional construct that encompasses both religious and economic facets (Rauf et al., 2022). It is rooted in Islamic teachings and principles, guided by the objectives of Maqasid Al-Syariah, which represent the highest aspirations of Islamic law (Shehu & Al-Aidaros, 2015). These objectives revolve around the promotion of social welfare, justice, and ethical conduct within business contexts (Shehu & Al-Aidaros, 2015).

The dimensions of the Islamic Entrepreneurial Initiative within the sphere of creating new Islamic businesses can be delineated by synthesizing existing references as follows:

1. **Absorptive Capacity**: This pertains to a company's capability to acquire, assimilate, and apply external knowledge (Zahra & George, 2002). It stands as a pivotal factor for establishing and sustaining competitive advantage within Islamic new ventures. The concept encapsulates firms' potential and realized capacity to harness external knowledge for fostering innovation and growth (Zahra & George, 2002).
2. **Entrepreneurial Orientation (EO)**: EO encompasses a firm's inclination to engage in entrepreneurial activities, such as innovation, risk-taking, and proactive behavior (Lumpkin & Dess, 1996). This multidimensional construct incorporates elements like innovativeness, proactiveness, and willingness to undertake risks (Lumpkin & Dess, 1996). Within the realm of Islamic entrepreneurship, EO is influenced by Islamic values and principles.
3. **Personality Traits**: Various traits, including initiative, excellence, honesty, patience, knowledge, ethics, social responsibility, and customer orientation, contribute to the manifestation of opportunities in Islamic entrepreneurship (Yaseen et al., 2022). These traits are shaped by adherence to Islamic values and the overarching Islamic value system.

In summation, the dimensions of the Islamic Entrepreneurial Initiative in the context of creating new Islamic businesses encompass absorptive capacity, entrepreneurial orientation, alignment with Islamic values and principles, and the integration of Maqasid Al-Syariah into decision-making (Zahra & George, 2002; Lumpkin & Dess, 1996; Janah & Subiyantoro, 2022; Rauf et al., 2022; Shehu & Al-Aidaros, 2015; Yaseen et al., 2022). These dimensions illuminate the distinct attributes and considerations of Islamic entrepreneurship, providing a comprehensive framework for comprehending and investigating this domain.

KEY INFLUENTIAL FACTORS IN THE STUDY OF ISLAMIC ENTREPRENEURIAL INITIATIVE FOR NEW BUSINESS CREATION

The investigation into the Islamic Entrepreneurial Initiative within the realm of creating new businesses aligned with Islamic principles unveils several pivotal factors. These factors, elucidated through the provided references, shed light on the multifaceted landscape of Islamic entrepreneurship:

Absorptive Capacity: The concept of absorptive capacity, denoting an organization's capability to acquire, assimilate, and apply external knowledge (Zahra & George, 2002), stands as a foundational element. This key dimension underpins the establishment and endurance of a firm's competitive advantage (Zahra & George, 2002). The research conducted by Zahra & George (2002) delves into the contours of absorptive capacity, offering a reconceptualization of the construct. This underscores the need to differentiate between a company's potential and realized capacity and discern the contextual factors that shape the impact of this capacity on competitive advantage.

Entrepreneurial Orientation (EO): EO embodies a firm's inclination towards entrepreneurial pursuits, encompassing innovation, risk-taking, and proactivity (Lumpkin & Dess, 1996). The scholarly work by Lumpkin & Dess (1996) further elucidates the nature of EO and introduces a contingency framework for investigating the interplay between EO and firm performance. This framework opens avenues for alternative models to explore the EO-performance relationship, encompassing moderation effects, mediation effects, independent effects, and interaction effects (Lumpkin & Dess, 1996).

Gender Dynamics: The role of gender finds its place within the narrative of entrepreneurial initiatives in the Islamic economy (Pita, 2021). This exploration uncovers that, under equitable circumstances, Islamic women exhibit a lower inclination towards initiating businesses in comparison to men (Pita, 2021). This revelation underscores the importance of acknowledging gender as a factor wielding influence over entrepreneurial endeavors within the Islamic context.

Influence of Islamic Values: Islamic values, a cornerstone of the Islamic Entrepreneurial Initiative, are pivotal forces shaping the landscape. The research by Wibowo et al. (2021) delves into the impact of Islamic values on the entrepreneurial intentions of Indonesian students. These findings accentuate the direct and indirect influence of Islamic values on students' entrepreneurial intentions through inspiration and motivation. This emphasizes the pivotal role of incorporating Islamic values in comprehending and advancing entrepreneurial endeavors within the Islamic milieu.

Entrepreneurial Characteristics from an Islamic Perspective: Entrepreneurial traits, when viewed through an Islamic lens, emerge as pivotal elements. The study conducted by Lisnawati & Ahman (2019) investigates the correlation between entrepreneurial characteristics rooted in Islamic values and the performance of small and medium-sized enterprises in Indonesia. Factors such as wisdom, trust, truth, and advocacy surface as potential influences shaping entrepreneurial characteristics from an Islamic perspective. This underscores the vital significance of integrating Islamic values and principles into the understanding and promotion of entrepreneurial initiatives in the Islamic realm.

In summation, the intricate fabric of factors guiding the exploration of the Islamic Entrepreneurial Initiative within the domain of new business creation resonates with absorptive capacity, entrepreneurial orientation, gender dynamics, the resonance of Islamic values, and the tenor of entrepreneurial characteristics from an Islamic vantage point. These factors illuminate diverse dimensions and influences shaping Islamic entrepreneurial endeavors, offering guidance for future research and practical ventures in this field.

CONSEQUENCES OF THE NEXUS BETWEEN ISLAMIC ENTREPRENEURIAL INITIATIVES AND NEW BUSINESS CREATION: INSIGHTS FROM ABSORPTIVE CAPACITY AND ENTREPRENEURIAL ORIENTATION

The interplay between Islamic entrepreneurial initiatives and the emergence of new businesses yields profound ramifications, illuminated through the prisms of absorptive capacity and entrepreneurial orientation.

Absorptive Capacity denotes an enterprise's prowess to assimilate, apply, and enrich itself with external knowledge to foster innovation and competitive prowess (Zahra & George, 2002). Within the realm of crafting Islamic new ventures, absorptive capacity ushers forth an array of outcomes. Primarily, heightened absorptive capacity empowers Islamic entrepreneurs to astutely identify and harness opportunities harmonizing with Islamic ethos. This catalyzes the creation of innovative, socially conscious businesses attuned to the requisites of the Muslim community (Rehan et al., 2019). Secondly, this capacity begets the fusion of Islamic values and practices into entrepreneurial processes, enabling the cultivation of distinctive value propositions that set entrepreneurs apart in the marketplace (Rehan et al., 2019). Lastly, absorptive capacity fortifies the aptitude of Islamic entrepreneurs to navigate the fluid, uncertain business landscape adeptly, priming them for agile responses to challenges and market fluxes (Cahyani & Siregar, 2022).

Entrepreneurial Orientation, an enterprise's strategic inclination toward innovation, proactiveness, and risk-taking (Lumpkin & Dess, 1996), ushers forth a constellation of effects in the context of Islamic new business germination. Firstly, heightened entrepreneurial orientation impels Islamic entrepreneurs to proactively seek and seize opportunities harmonizing with Islamic tenets. This catalyzes the emergence of enterprises fostering socio-economic advancement within the Muslim community, underpinned by ethical business conduct (Wibowo et al., 2021). Secondly, entrepreneurial orientation nurtures an ecosystem of ingenuity and originality within Islamic ventures, enabling the incubation of distinctive offerings tailored to the specific preferences and needs of Muslim consumers (Rehan et al., 2019). Lastly, this orientation amplifies the resilience and adaptability of Islamic enterprises, equipping them to navigate the labyrinthine currents of challenges and uncertainties endemic to the business milieu (Ilonen et al., 2017).

In summation, the intricate interrelationship between Islamic entrepreneurial initiatives and the birthing of nascent businesses heralds a cascade of affirmative outcomes. By harnessing absorptive capacity and entrepreneurial orientation, Islamic entrepreneurs forge ventures aligning with Islamic values, propelling innovation, bolstering social responsibility, and fortifying resilience in the Islamic business tapestry. This synergy culminates in the creation of enterprises that thrive within the dynamic, competitive vistas of the marketplace while remaining deeply rooted in the essence of Islamic principles and aspirations.

CONCLUSION AND RESEARCH AGENDA

The Islamic Entrepreneurial Initiative centers around the integration of Islamic principles and objectives into the process of creating new businesses. It encompasses the roles of absorptive capacity, financial development, Islamic debt financing, and family background in shaping the landscape of Islamic entrepreneurship. Through an exploration of the nexus between Islamic teachings and entrepreneurship, the Islamic Entrepreneurial Initiative aspires to enrich the comprehension and advocacy of Islamic entrepreneurship as a viable and morally upright business paradigm.

Comprehending Islamic work ethics and delving into the experiences of management teams can significantly impact the success of Islamic-oriented new business endeavors. Further research in this domain holds the potential to yield invaluable insights for entrepreneurs, policymakers, and scholars who are keen on fostering and bolstering the realm of Islamic entrepreneurship.

REFERENCES

Abidin, Z., Suhariadi, F., & Hadi, C. (2021). The Role of The Islamic Work Ethos Through the Motivation of Entrepreneurship and The Barriers of Entrepreneurship to Entrepreneurial Intention Santri In Pondok Pesantren Indonesia. *Ilkogretim Online*, *20*(3). doi:10.17051/ilkonline.2021.03.56

Al-Debei, M. M., & Avison, D. (2010). Developing a unified framework of the business model concept. *European Journal of Information Systems*, *19*(3), 359–376. doi:10.1057/ejis.2010.21

Amruloh, D. A. G. (2017). (the 3rd Icbess 2016-Proceeding Kartika Discovery Hotel Bali, August 10–11, 2016) Entrepreneur Orientation in Islamic Perspective. *Eqien-Jurnal Ekonomi dan Bisnis, 4*(1). 10.34308/eqien.v4i1.56

Asfiah, N. (2021). Do Islamic social entrepreneurship moderate Islamic leadership and emotional intelligence? Evidence from micro and small enterprises fostered by 'Aisyiyah. *Journal of Innovation in Business and Economics*, *5*(01), 23–34. doi:10.22219/jibe.v5i01.16221

Ashraf, M. A. (2021). Determinants of Islamic entrepreneurial intentions: An analysis using SEM. *Journal of Islamic Marketing*, *12*(1), 20–40. doi:10.1108/JIMA-05-2019-0116

Basir, K. H., & Musa, S. F. P. D. (2022). An Islamic perspective of agripreneurs motivation. *Journal of Enterprising Communities: People and Places in the Global Economy*, *16*(3), 402–420. doi:10.1108/JEC-08-2020-0147

Cahyani, U. E., Masruri, S., & Hanafi, S. M. (2022). Does Entrepreneurship Education Matter for Islamic Higher Education Students' Entrepreneurial Readiness. *Jurnal Ekonomi Bisnis Dan Kewirausahaan*, *11*(2), 258. doi:10.26418/jebik.v11i2.55092

Fathonih, A., Anggadwita, G., & Ibraimi, S. (2019). Sharia venture capital as financing alternative of Muslim entrepreneurs: Opportunities, challenges and future research directions. *Journal of Enterprising Communities: People and Places in the Global Economy*, *13*(3), 333–352. doi:10.1108/JEC-11-2018-0090

Janah, S., & Subiyantoro, S. (2022). Social responsibility on islamic spiritual entrepreneurs for blessing of life and successful entrepreneurship. *At-Tijaroh Jurnal Ilmu Manajemen Dan Bisnis Islam, 8*(2), 199-206. doi:10.24952/tijaroh.v8i2.5192

Juliana, J., Rahayu, A., & Wardhani, Y. (2020). Muslimpreneur intentions: Analysis of family background. *Jurnal Kajian Peradaban Islam*, *3*(1), 10–15. doi:10.47076/jkpis.v3i1.35

Kutsiyah, F. (2020). Social capital and its transformations in Sidogiri Islamic boarding school. Karsa: *Jurnal Sosial dan Budaya Keislaman, 28*(1), 57-94. doi:10.19105/karsa.v28i1.3058

Ledhem, M. A., & Moussaoui, W. (2021). Islamic finance for entrepreneurship activities and economic growth: a parametric and non-parametric analysis from Malaysia. *PSU Research Review*. doi:10.1108/PRR-02-2021-0012

Li, J., & Dutta, D. K. (2018). Founding team experience, industry context, and new venture creation. *New England Journal of Entrepreneurship*, *21*(1), 2–21. doi:10.1108/NEJE-04-2018-0008

Lisnawati, D., & Ahman, H. E. (2019). Relationship between Entrepreneurial Characteristics from Islamic Perspective and the Performance of Small and Medium-Sized Businesses (A Study of SMEs in Indonesia). *KnE Social Sciences*, (pp. 576-593). KNE Publishing. doi:10.18502/kss.v3i13.4232

Lumpkin, G. T., & Dess, G. G. (1996). Clarifying the entrepreneurial orientation construct and linking it to performance. *Academy of Management Review*, *21*(1), 135–172. doi:10.2307/258632

Muhammad, N., McElwee, G., & Dana, L. (2017). Barriers to the development and progress of entrepreneurship in rural pakistan. *International Journal of Entrepreneurial Behaviour & Research*, *23*(2), 279–295. doi:10.1108/IJEBR-08-2016-0246

Nsereko, I., Balunywa, J., Kyazze, L., Nsereko, H., & Nakato, J. (2021). Entrepreneurial alertness and social entrepreneurial venture creation: The mediating role of personal initiative. *Journal of Enterprising Communities People and Places in the Global Economy*, *16*(3), 361–383. doi:10.1108/JEC-05-2020-0099

Pita, M. (2021). Entrepreneurial initiative in islamic economics – the role of gender. a multi-country analysis. *Journal of Islamic Accounting and Business Research*, *12*(6), 793–813. doi:10.1108/JIABR-01-2020-0010

Rauf, A., Abubakar, Y., Abrar, A., Gohar, M., Slesman, L., & Mitra, J. (2022). Islam, entrepreneurship and economic development. *Journal of Entrepreneurship and Innovation in Emerging Economies*, *8*(2), 270–273. doi:10.1177/23939575211047022

Shehu, F. M., & Al-Aidaros, A. H. (2015). Islamic Entrepreneurship in the Light of Maqasid Al-Shariâ€™ ah: A Critical Review. *Journal of Social and Development Sciences*, *6*(4), 6–14. doi:10.22610/jsds.v6i4.854

Shook, C., Priem, R., & McGee, J. (2003). Venture creation and the enterprising individual: A review and synthesis. *Journal of Management*, *29*(3), 379–399. doi:10.1016/S0149-2063(03)00016-3

Sidek, F., Pavlovich, K., & Gibb, J. (2018). Entrepreneurship as worship: A malay muslim perspective. *Journal of Management & Organization*, *24*(5), 698–710. doi:10.1017/jmo.2018.13

Sohail, H., & Arshed, N. (2022). Contribution of Islamic debt financing in entrepreneurship promoting financial sector transformation. *International Journal of Management Research and Emerging Sciences*, *12*(2). Advance online publication. doi:10.56536/ijmres.v12i2.186

Wibowo, A., Widjaja, S., Utomo, S., Kusumojanto, D., Wardoyo, C., Wardana, L., & Narmaditya, B. (2021). Does islamic values matter for indonesian students' entrepreneurial intention? the mediating role of entrepreneurial inspiration and attitude. *Journal of Islamic Accounting and Business Research*, *13*(2), 242–263. doi:10.1108/JIABR-03-2021-0090

Yaseen, A., Mahmood, G., & Naheed, K. (2022). Who can practice islamic entrepreneurship: A review of recent literature on personality traits. *Journal of Law & Social Studies*, *4*(3), 429–440. doi:10.52279/jlss.04.03.429440

Zahra, S. A., & George, G. (2002). Absorptive capacity: A review, reconceptualization, and extension. *Academy of Management Review*, *27*(2), 185. doi:10.2307/4134351

Chapter 5

Islamic Quadruple Helix:
Social Finance Partnership for Developing Digital Financial Inclusion in Maghreb Region

Khairunnisa Musari
https://orcid.org/0000-0003-0525-9903
Kiai Haji Achmad Siddiq State Islamic University, Indonesia

Fatima Sayah
https://orcid.org/0000-0002-1333-3045
University Ahmed Zabana, Relizane, Algeria

ABSTRACT

Rooted in sharia values, Islamic finance should have the eligibility to lead microfinance in contributing to financial inclusion in Islamic countries in the Maghreb region. However, Islamic microfinance in this region has not been going well. At least when compared to the Southeast Asian region, Islamic microfinance in this region is still lagging behind. Through a literature study, this conceptual chapter promotes the Islamic Quadruple Helix approach, which integrates the Islamic social finance partnership model and digitalization to accelerate financial inclusion in this region. Therefore, this chapter focuses on three issues: (1) Describe the facts and figures of Islamic finance in the Maghreb region; (2) Explain the role of Islamic social finance partnership and digitalization in fulfilling the lack of Islamic microfinance in this region; and (3) Map the digital financial inclusion ecosystem in this region by illustrating the role of involvement from a number of parties.

INTRODUCTION

Financial inclusion nowadays is a global agenda in order to realize sustainable development goals (SDGs). As a target in eight of the seventeen goals in the SDGs, financial inclusion works obviously as an enabler for several developmental goals. Particularly at this time when the digital revolution works to accelerate

DOI: 10.4018/978-1-6684-7519-5.ch005

the world's experiences. Digitalization swiftly may fire enlarge and escalate access financial services. Digital financial inclusion will support actively the achievement of SDGs (United Nations Secretary-General's Special Advocate for Inclusive Finance for Development (UNSGSA), the Better Than Cash Alliance, the United Nations Capital Development (UNCDF), and the World Bank, 2018).

In Maghreb region, the financial inclusion level driven by Islamic microfinance in this region is lagging behind Southeast Asia. The market has not yet visible the full potential of the Islamic microfinance industry in driving socio-economic impacts at scale for people within the bottom of the pyramid (BoP) in the Maghreb as in the Southeast Asia (Aaminou, 2022). Southeast Asia region can be a representation of Asia regarding the financial inclusion agenda and Indonesia deserves to representative of the Southeast Asia region and Association of Southeast Asian Nations (ASEAN) in implementing the financial inclusion agenda (Musari, 2022). Besides the geographical factor that requires the presence of digital technology to reach its disperse, Indonesia delivers significant opportunities in the financial technology (fintech) sector based on its standing as the largest economy in Southeast Asia and the fourth-most populous nation in the world.

Furthermore, by taking lessons from Indonesia and ASEAN, this study would like to provide a proposed ecosystem for digital financial inclusion in the Maghreb region by integrating the Islamic social finance partnership model and digitalization to accelerate financial inclusion in this region. This ecosystem model is intended to map the positioning of Islamic social finance to the real sector which is reflected by micro, small, and medium enterprises (MSMEs) and nano enterprises (NEs), even pico enterprises (PEs). Also, to find out what components are needed in bringing digitalization that supports financial inclusion.

Overall, this paper believes Islamic microfinance, nanofinance, even picofinance are important tools for Maghreb MSMEs that can cater to their financial needs. With official support through cooperation and establishing a joint commitment from the government, financial authorities, and stakeholders in this region to create a digital financial inclusion ecosystem, it will make a significant contribution to easing MSMEs' access to finance and also supporting the industry to grow and develop, even for people who are in the BoP, excluded and unserved, underbanked and unbanked, as well as street vendors. An adequate regulatory and institutional framework supported by political stability is key to encouraging digital financial inclusion in the Maghreb region through the Islamic Quadruple Helix approach.

METHOD

This study is qualitative research with an explanation approach to exploring the integration of Islamic social finance as well as information and communications technology (ICT) or technologies toward Islamic Quadruple Helix to create the ecosystem of digital financial inclusion. Specifically, this study promotes Islamic nanofinance and picofinance to fill the lack of Islamic microfinance with digitally supported to accelerate financial inclusion in the Maghreb region.

This study also can be categorized as a Conceptual Paper with Models research design as a methodological approach. By focusing to propose a digital financial inclusion ecosystem model with an Islamic Quadruple Helix approach as a new insight, then developing a logical argument about this association rather than testing it empirically, the objective of this study is indeed to develop the rationality of the proposed ecosystem model. Model research design in Conceptual Paper offers a significant improvement in constructing valid theories in their scientific field. This method leads naturally to synthesizing previous research thus serving as an external validity check of research findings. This is critical to the sturdiness of academic fields, whether it is manifest in solely conceptual papers or in conceptual–empirical mixtures (Meredith, 1993; MacInnis, 2011).

Then, in establishing concepts and theories, this study uses a Narrative-based style. Narrative-based style is the specification of a process model that lays out a set of mechanisms explaining events and outcomes as the common style of theorizing in constructing a theoretical framework that predicts relationships between concepts in Conceptual Papers (Cornelissen, 2017). Therefore, by using the Islamic Helix approach, this study focuses on three issues: 1) Describe the facts and figures of Islamic finance in the Maghreb region; 2) Explain the role of Islamic social finance partnership and digitalization in fulfilling the lack of Islamic microfinance in this region; 3) Map the digital financial inclusion ecosystem based on Islamic Quadruple Helix.

RESULT AND DISCUSSIONS

The economic crisis of the mid-1980s gave rise to a worldwide tendency to form regional economic alliances. Similarly, a number of countries in North Africa formed the Arab Maghreb Union (AMU) on February 17, 1989, which consisted of Libya, Morocco, Tunisia, Algeria, and Mauritania which were referred to as Maghreb countries. Al Ghweel (2022) explained that the Maghreb actually is planned to become a political and economic confederation, concolidating a geographically neighboring and culturally unified part of the world into a superb pan-Arab block for mutual cooperation, interdependence, and free trade. The economic complementary among Maghreb State Members can be shown in Table 1.

In 2020, total inhabitants in all Maghreb countries counted about 102.87 million residents with the forecasted gross domestic product (GDP) as much as around US$328.74 billion (Statista, 2020a, 2020b). During 2017 until 2026, Table 2 shows the prediction of total population and GDP of the Maghreb countries. The countries with the most populations in the Maghreb are respectively Algeria, Morocco, Tunisia, Libya, and Mauritania. Meanwhile, countries with high GDP per capita respectively are Libya, Tunisia, Morocco, Algeria, and Mauritania.

The journey of the Maghreb today has not lived up to the expectations of its founders in the past. Maghreb is a flawless sample of an economic block whose member countries cannot be well integrated. This region is categorized as the lowest-performing trading block in the world. The cooperation that

Table 1. Economic complementary among Maghreb state members

Countries	Deficit	Comparative Advantage	Interaction's Outcomes
Libya	Labor; Foodstuff; Light industry.	Petro; Hydro; Capital.	More bargaining power; Political stability; Economic growth; Less dependency on external market.
Morocco	Hydro; Gas; Capital.	Labor; Agriculture products; Phosphates and its derivatives; Tourism.	
Tunisia	Gas; Iron; Capital.	Phosphor; Fertilizers; Olive oil; Light industry; Labor; Tourism.	
Algeria	Light industry; Foodstuff.	Labor; Heavy industry; Hydro; Petro; Liquified Natural Gas (LNG).	
Mauritania	Skilled labor; Petro; Hydro.	Fish; Cooper; Iron; Agriculture; Natural resources.	

Source: Messaoudi (1994), International Monetary Fund (IMF) (2018), Centre for Affordable Housing Finance (CAHF) in Africa (2021)

Table 2. Total population and GDP per capita in Maghreb region (2017-2026)

Maghreb	Country	2017	2018	2019	2020	2021*	2022*	2023*	2024*	2025*	2026*
Total Population (in million inhabitants)	Algeria	41.7	42.6	43.4	44.2	45.0	45.8	46.6	47.3	48.0	48.7
	Libya	6.5	6.5	6.6	6.6	6.7	6.8	6.9	6.9	7.0	7.1
	Mauritania	3.9	4.0	4.1	4.2	4.2	4.3	4.4	4.5	4.6	4.7
	Morocco	34.9	35.2	35.6	36.0	36.3	36.7	37.0	37.4	37.7	38.1
	Tunisia	11.5	11.7	11.8	11.9	12.0	12.1	12.2	12.3	12.4	12.5
GDP per Capita in current prices (in US$)	Algeria	4,080	4,119	3,940	3,337	3,638	3,672	3,697	3,674	3,633	3,596
	Libya	4,685	6,362	6,004	2,891	4,069	4,309	4,382	4,321	4,445	4,591
	Mauritania	1,759	1,852	1,944	1,956	2,161	2,154	2,212	2,255	2,277	2,337
	Morocco	3,147	3,353	3,368	3,188	3,471	3,617	3,801	3,992	4,196	4,380
	Tunisia	3,436	3,443	3,324	3,295	3,556	3,748	3,916	4,094	4,257	4,399

Source: Statista (2022a, 2022b)

is established is very basic. This is reflected in the trade between Maghreb members representing only 4.8% of their trading volume (Hamza, 2017). The incredibly low value of intra-regional trade in this region is mainly due to long-standing competition as well as unaccomplished tenseness between Algeria and Morocco as the two biggest economies in the Maghreb. Likewise trade protections and logistical restrictions cause it tough for industries to smoothly and continuously work within the region. Nevertheless, although the existence of Maghreb now is resulting in a disappointing and asleep status, this union remains solid even to this day (Al Ghweel, 2022).

In terms of Public Policy Economics, the existence of the Maghreb is still not generating the optimal economic outcomes for its members. The impact of public policies on resource allocation and income distribution in the economy in this region is still far from Pareto Optimum as well as Al-Ghazali/Al-Shatibi Optimum. The resources are not yet allocated in the most economically efficient manner. The economy does not reach its optimum because the economic change can not make one individual better off without making at least one other individual worse off. In other words, actually, there is still a way to rearrange things to make at least one person better off without making anyone worse off.

Regarding Al-Ghazali/Al-Shatibi Optimum, any policy would be recommendable if contributes to one of the *maqashid al sharia*'s components without undermining any of the other four. The Al-Ghazali/Al-Shatibi Optimum would be attained when it is no longer possible to make better any of the components without undermining one of the others (Çizakça, 2007, 2014). From Public Policy Economics perspective, the implementation of *maqashid al-sharia* can be interpreted as the obligations of the Maghreb to protect Islam, protect the reason or mind of people and have freedom of thought, protect human rights, protect property rights as well as protect future generations. All of them are important requirements for the Maghreb which has Islamic countries as members to realize the Islamic democracy and economic development. This is also the reason that Islamic finance should have eligibility to lead microfinance in contributing to financial inclusion in this region.

Fact and Figures of Islamic Finance in Maghreb

Islamic finance in the Maghreb, compared to other regions, can be considered relatively recent. In addition, laws and regulations related to Islamic finance have been put in place only a few years ago (Aaminou, 2022). Even there is no law governing Islamic finance in Libya and Mauritania, although the Muslims in Libya reach 97% and Mauritania reaches 100%. While Algeria, Morocco, and Tunisia already have laws that regulate Islamic finance (Daoud & Kammoun, 2020).

Figure 1 shows the milestones of Islamic banking in Morocco, Algeria, and Tunisia. Even though these Maghreb countries in North Africa are important contributors to the Islamic Development Bank (IsDB) and Islamic banking in two countries has existed since the 1980s and 1990s, the dynamics have been very slow. It was only in 2014-2018 that laws and regulations related to Islamic banking were approved (Aaminou, 2022).

Referring to IsDB Annual Report 2020 and 2021, Libya ranks second as the primary financial partner of the IsDB after Saudi Arabia in the first position of the 57 IsDB member countries. Then, followed by Algeria in the tenth rank, Morocco in the fifth rank, Tunisia and Mauritania in the thirty-fourth and thirty-fifth rank. Table 3 shows the share capital subscription of Maghreb member countries in IsDB as of 31 December 2020 and 31 December 2021.

Islamic finance in the Maghreb region is mostly driven by Islamic banking. Table 4 shows the statistic of Islamic finance institutions in Maghreb countries. Likewise in Indonesia, Islamic banking is the motor of the Islamic finance industry. However, the financing for MSMEs in Indonesia can be done not only by Islamic banking which includes Islamic Banks (BUS), Sharia Business Unit (UUS), and Sharia Rural Bank (BPRS). The micro financing can be done also by various Islamic microfinance institutions (IMFIs) such as *Baitul Maal Wa Tamwil* (BMT), Islamic Service Finance Cooperative (KJKS), and Bank Wakaf Mikro (BWM) as well as institutions such as *zakat infaq sadaqa waqf* (ZISWa) organizations, Islamic

Figure 1. Islamic banking milestones in Morocco, Algeria, and Tunisia
Source: Aaminou (2022)

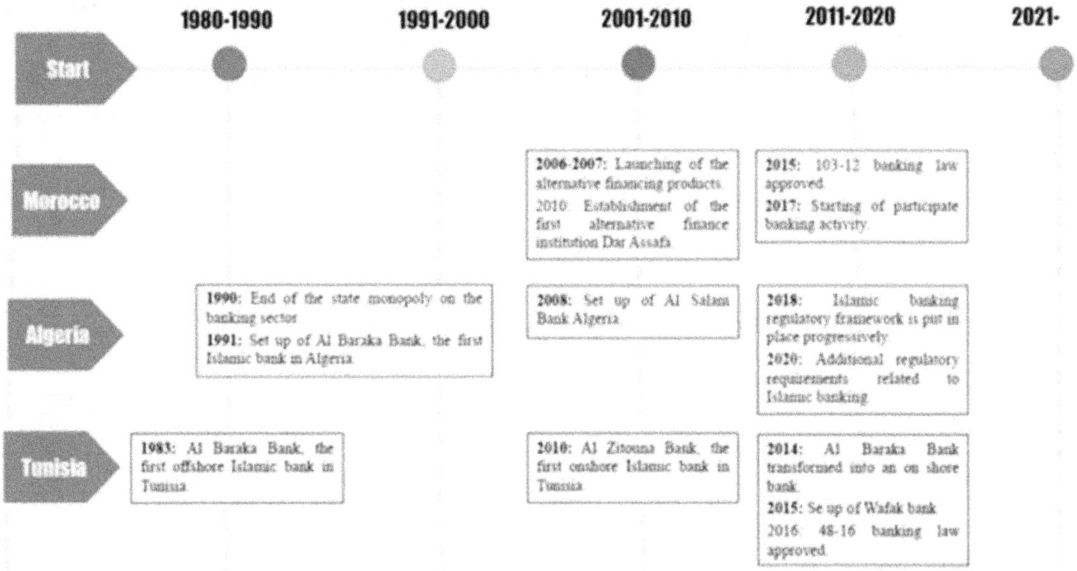

Table 3. Statement of IsDB share capital subscription as of 31 December 2020 and 2021

Rank	Country	No. of Shares (Units)	Consolidated Position of Subscribed Share Capital (% of Total Amount)
2	Libya	477,166	9.43
10	Algeria	128,559	2.54
15	Morocco	25,669	0.51
34	Tunisia	3,577	0.07
35	Mauritania	7,158	0.14

Source: IsDB Annual Report 2020, IsDB Annual Report 2021

philanthropy platforms, and also Islamic peer-to-peer (P2P) lending platform. Ismal (2012) confirmed that one of the unique features of the Islamic financial system in Indonesia that could not be perceived in another indeed is the variety of Islamic financial institutions (IFIs) to work for MSMEs.

Furthermore, referring to the Global Findex Database 2021, bank account ownership in the Maghreb countries is low compared to the countries in the other regions. This confirms that financial inclusion in Maghreb countries is relatively low compared to countries in other regions. Demirgüç-Kunt, Klapper, Singer, & Ansar (2022) reported that the ownership of adults with an account reached 44% in Morocco, 37% in Algeria, and 44% in Tunisia. While the poor adults with account reached 34% in Morocco, 32% in Algeria, and 32% in Tunisia. The significant gender gap is currently in Algeria and Tunisia, where women are more likely than men to mention that they do not have an account because a family member already has one. In Morocco, the borrowers who borrow only from family and friends dominated until 77%. Aaminou (2022) explained that the marginality of people within the "bottom of the pyramid (BOP)" in Maghreb countries also is due to Islamic finance-driven mostly by Islamic banking so the industry does not address the needs of those people.

In order to fill the lack of microfinance by Islamic banking or IMFIs for reaching the community groups like BoP, Musari (2016, 2020b, 2020c) promotes Islamic nanofinance and picofinance as new paradigms in Islamic finance which are descents of Islamic microfinance. Then, in order to innovate the micro-entrepreneurship, Musari & Fathorrazi (2021) and Musari & Sayah (2022) promoted Islamic Helix approach to develop the Islamic Social Finance Partnership Models. Islamic nanofinance and picofinance as well as the Islamic Helix approach target to reach the community groups that be categorized as the BoP, excluded and unserved, underbanked and unbanked as well as street vendors. These community groups which are often referred to as ultra-micro, super-poor, very poor, or PEs/NEs.

Table 4. A number of Islamic finance institutions in Maghreb

	Morocco	Algeria	Tunisia	Libya	Mauritania
Islamic Banks (Full-fledged and Windows)	9	3	4	9	7
Takaful Companies	0	0	3	1	2
Islamic Microfinance Institutions (IMFIs)	0	0	1	1	1

Source: Aaminou (2022), Abusloum, Ahmad, & Bello (2020), Khan & Sonko (Ed.) (2020), Daoud & Kammoun (2020), CAHF in Africa (2021).

Islamic Nanofinance, Digitalization, and Islamic Helix Approach

Many studies have proven that microfinance is a powerful poverty alleviation instrument. This instrument presents financial services to poor and low-income people whose economic status prevents them to access the formal financial system. However, it is undeniable that many studies have also found that microfinance does not work as expected. Musari (2016, 2021a, 2020b), Addai (2017), Rathiranee & Semasinghe (2016), Kato & Kratzer (2013), Owusu, Akanbasiam & Anyesepari (2013), Sinclair (2012), Hossain & Diaz (1997) found that microfinance institutions (MFIs) in Thailand, Cambodia, India, Ghana, Tanzania, Sri Lanka, Philippines, and Indonesia are not fully capable of making poor people better off. MFIs are also capitalizing money from the poor through very expensive interest rates just like the moneylender. They implicate a higher social tension, a never-ending debt spiral, and in some cases preside to domestic violence as well as hostile collection practices lead to child exploitation, suicide, forced prostitution, and a national uprising against microfinance authorities.

The facts that occur around the world show that the microfinance is indeed at a crossroads. The implication of this program in each region generates mixed results. Sample (2011) mentioned that microfinance is currently confronted with unprecedented problems and criticism. MFIs are dealed with two roads, one where the microfinance industry breaks into two opposing fortress and another where the industry runs with each other to terminate grave poverty. Study by Rosenberg, Gaul, Ford, & Tomilova (2013), Levin (2012), Bateman (2011), Mitra (2009), Rosenberg, Gonzalez, & Narain (2009), Rosenbreg (2002), Groen (2002), Meyer (2002), Rahman (1999) also confirmed some of the problems associated with the practice of MFIs, particulary about high interest rates. Transaction costs have a large fixed cost component so the unit costs for smaller loans are higher than the larger. Even Grameen Bank as the pioneer of microfinance ever charged annual interest rate until 20% or 8% higher than the commercial market rate in that country.

Nanofinance and picofinance are new paradigms in microfinance. Both are also new paradigms in Islamic finance which are descendants of Islamic microfinance. In Islamic finance, both are positioned as sustainable financing tools in providing very small loans without interest, without profit/loss sharing, and/or grants to community groups that can be categorized as BoP, excluded and unserved, underbanked and unbanked as well as street vendors. These groups of people are often referred to as ultra-micro, super-poor, very poor, very low-income or PEs/NEs.

There is no standard definition for the terms 'nanofinance' and 'picofinance'. Musari & Simanjuntak (2016), Musari (2016, 2020c) noted some countries in Asia and Africa–namely India, Thailand, Cambodia, Indonesia, Uganda– have practiced nanofinance, even picofinance, for these community groups. Each region or country has a different definition as well as its practice. However, they prove empirically that there are financial institutions in the world which serve them through nanofinance and picofinance. The similarity between nanofinance activities in those countries refer to (very) small loans from financial institutions with a simple procedure to avoid them from moneylenders. Even in Odisha, India, Musari (2020a) found the kind of loans for nano financing as alike as the *qardhul hassan* in Islamic finance, with no interest rate or any profit/loss sharing.

Furthermore, study by Musari & Fathorrazi (2021) and Musari & Sayah (2022) in Indonesia and Algeria found a generic scheme of institutional partnership models to empower the ZISWa as the engine of productive activities to realize financial inclusion was Islamic Triple Helix which consists of interactions '(Islamic) Government – (Islamic) Industry – (Islamic) Civil Society'. This is different from (Conventional) Triple Helix which so far has been known to consist of 'University-Industry-Government'. The institutional partnership models for micro-entrepreneurship in Indonesia and Algeria fulfill the assumption on Islamic Triple Helix: (1) At least one stakeholder involved must be a Shari'a-compliant; (2) At least two stakeholders are involved; (3) The performance of Islamic Triple Helix is the total performance of (Islamic) Government, (Islamic) Industry, and (Islamic) Civil Society.

A Triple Helix Model of knowledge production that emphasizes three interwoven 'helices' and produces an innovation system that includes: academia/universities, industries, and state governments are developed by Etzkowitz & Leydesdorff (1995, 1998, 2000). A Triple Helix concept came up from the double helix analysis (university-industry) which is then followed by the awareness that government is an important part of the equation of innovation (Etzkowitz, 2002, 2008; Etzkowitz, Dzisah, Ranga, & Zhou, 2007; Carayannis & Campbell, 2011; Carayannis, Barth, & Campbell, 2012; Carayannis, Grigoroudis, Campbell, Meissner, and Stamati, 2018). A Triple Helix Model can be considered as a core design for innovation gained from the interaction between university, industry, and government. In its progress, the Triple Helix is embodied into a broader model of innovation in the form of Quadruple Helix which consists of University, Industry, Government, and Civil Society; then Quintuple Helix with additional helix 'Natural Environments of Society'.

This study recommends Islamic Quadruple Helix which consist (Islamic) Government – (Islamic) Industry – (Islamic) Civil Society' and ICT Sector/Technologies to open the business innovation of MSMEs in Maghreb region. Islamic Quadruple Helix is a combination of Islamic Triple Helix with ICT/Technologies which the output of institutional arrangement will result a digitally-enabled society (Hidayat and Musari, 2023). As one of the phases in the Islamic Helix approach, this scheme also develops institutional partnership based on Islamic social finance institutions as an alternative source to

Figure 2. The nexus of Islamic finance and digitalization through Islamic Quadruple Helix approach
Source: Developed by Author

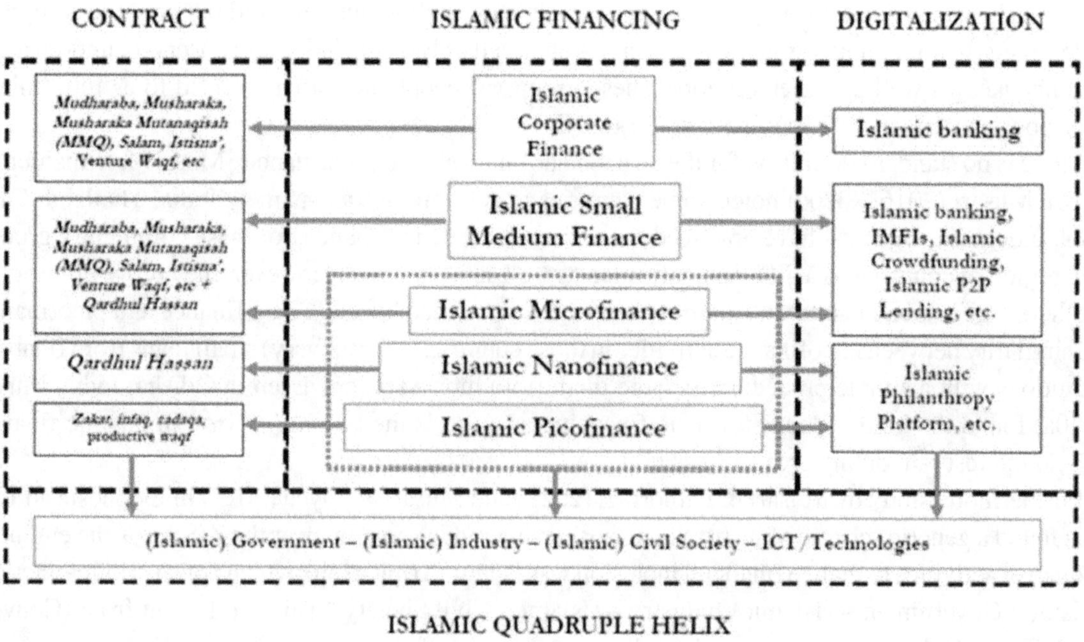

the socio-economic development. At a more complicated level, this Islamic Quadruple Helix may not be effective so it needs the existence 'University' or 'Environments' or other institutional entities towards Islamic Quintuple Helix, Islamic Sextuple Helix or another Islamic N-Tuple Helix.

Referring to Macchiavello (2016), the true microfinance should combine a social business structure with technological innovations to lower costs, through fintech, and merges with local traditions and structures, such as financial cooperatives, savings banks, Islamic banking, and other double-bottom line financial institutions as well as other experiences. Therefore, by developing the scheme from Musari (2016, 2019) and the study by Musari & Fathorrazi (2021), Musari & Sayah (2022), the nexus of Islamic finance and digitalization (based on fintech) through Islamic Quadruple Helix approach can be illustrated in Figure 2.

The Proposed Model of Digital Financial Inclusion Ecosystem

This study believes Islamic nanofinance and picofinance are important tools for reaching a better financial inclusion level. In addition, digitalization also become a requirement to accelerate the achievement. By targeting the BoP, excluded and unserved, underbanked and unbanked as well as street vendors which often referred to as ultra-micro, super-poor, very poor, very low-income or PEs/NEs, Islamic social finance which consist Islamic nanofinance and picofinance does not only need digitalization process to achieve a better financial inclusion level. With the official support through cooperation and building a joint commitment from the Islamic financial authorities and stakeholders to create a digital financial inclusion ecosystem, it will make a significant contribution to easing PEs, NEs, MSMEs to access the financing. An adequate regulatory and institutional framework supported by political stability as a form of (Islamic) government is key to encouraging digital financial inclusion in Maghreb Region.

Referring to Djeflat (2009a, 2009b), innovation systems in African countries need strong policy impulses from government for innovation to effectively take place. 'Innovation take off' is the prerequisite for innovation systems to work which characterized by the rise of a SMEs sector but with little experience in the fields of research, relatively weak industrial performances in terms of productivity, and high level of obsolescence both in terms of human resources and equipment. Unfortunately, very slight work has been done by African countries to engage in a real take off policy of their sustainable innovation system. In Maghreb, universities have strategic roles in facilitating and promoting integrated innovation system in this region. Regrettably, the political relations to power, both internally and in relation to central government, hampers to a large extent this integrative role, despite all the efforts invested to provide new impetus to research in the Maghreb. Decision-making decentralisation and power sharing are still difficult to bring about.

Therefore, particularly considering also the study by Musari & Sayah (2022), this study promotes Islamic Quadruple Helix as a framework of digital financial inclusion ecosystem. Empowering the ZISWa fund can be a low-cost fund to fuel the productive activities in real economy and for leading the economic growth to be higher and equitable. Islamic Quadruple Helix can be replicated for reaching financial inclusion by targeting the BoP, excluded and unserved, underbanked and unbanked as well as street vendors which often referred to as ultra-micro, super-poor, very poor, very low-income or PEs/NEs. Coupled with digitalization to embrace the Islamic finance stakeholders in this region, the basic ecosystem of digital financial inclusion in the Maghreb region can be mapped as shown in Table 5.

As digital transformation accelerates across financial ecosystems worldwide, Islamic philanthropy platforms and Islamic P2P lending are also taking part in the ecosystem. The pandemic has accelerated

Table 5. Proposed model of digital financial inclusion ecosystem

HELIX	ECOSYSTEM BUILDER AND ITS ROLE	
(Islamic) Industry	Target User	PEs/NEs (BoP, excluded and unserved, underbanked and unbanked, street vendors), MSMEs, business people, government, philanthropic institutions, non-profit groups.
	IFIs	Conventional / Islamic banks; Conventional / Islamic microfinance or nanofinance institutions; Cooperation / *baitul mal wat tamwil;* Venture capital firms; Sovereign wealth fund; Islamic financial industry associations.
	Financing Service	Islamic Picofinance; Islamic Nanofinance; Islamic Microfinance; Payments (digital payments, foreign exchange, remittance); Raising fund (Islamic crowdfunding; Islamic P2P lending); Capital market (investment, trading, sukuk, shares); Digital assets (token issuers, wallet & custodians, platform & exchange); Alternative finance.
	Investment & Saving Service	Transaction accounts; Saving accounts; Investment accounts; Deposit & lending; Wealth management.
	Protecting & Giving Service	Insurance; Philanthropy/Islamic social finance/donate.
	Business Intelligence Operation	Dashboards; Decision making tools; Market research.
	Middle Office Operation	Customer service; Supply chain; Risk; Treasury.
	Back Office Operation	Accounting; Human resources; Sharia compliance; Information technology.
(Islamic) Government	Legal and Regulatory Enablers	Regional sharia authorities/regulators; National sharia authorities/ regulators; International (sharia/industry organization/multilateral institutions).
(Islamic) Civil Society	Advisory	Regional/national sharia scholars communities/organization; Processors; Licensed nonbanks.
	Business assistance	Philanthropic institutions; Companion volunteers; Consultant / non governmental organizations (NGOs).
ICT/ Technologies	Artificial Intelligence	Big data; Data & analytics; Machine learning.
	Security	Biometrics; Cybersecurity; Indentify verification.
	Cloud	Cloud & software.
	Distributed Ledger Technology	Crypto; Blockchain; Tokenization.
	Technology Company	Fintech firms; Fintech associations.

Source: Developed from Musari (2022)

the process of financial digitalization and brings philanthropy platforms and P2P lending as a new face of digital financial inclusion. This is also because the PEs/NEs (BoP, excluded and unserved, underbanked and unbanked, street vendors) and MSMEs are the community groups that feel the most severe impacts. The existence of philanthropy platforms and P2P lending can fill the gap of microfinance in banks and MFIs by reaching the wider community groups. Likewise to MSMEs, the financing by Islamic philanthropy platforms based on Islamic social finance through Islamic picofinance and Islamic nanofince can help them to survive and revive again.

Absolutely, not all the financial inclusion gap can be faced with digital initiatives. But, it must be admitted, technology accelerates to the achievement of financial inclusion because of its ability to attain the wider community. UNSGSA, the Better Than Cash Alliance, UNCDF, and the World Bank (2018) mentioned that there is sufficient evidence how digital financial inclusion may boost the program progress towards the SDGs. Digital financial inclusion brings a resilient leverage on millions of people around the world economically and socially. Digital financial services help families save their liquidity, remain alive from shocks, lock assets over risk, permit pensions, wages, or government transfers to efficiently reach people, and agitate the grow business models for have occasions to access the low-cost financial services.

The last but not least, to succeed in establishing digital financial inclusion ecosystem for Islamic finance a more fruitful and deeper integration, the Maghreb countries should work closely together. By adopting the recommendations of Hamza (2017), at least there are two steps that must be done in the short term to realize them:

First, political economy integration. The Maghreb countries need to cooperate and produce a common social economy policy, especially in the areas of education, foreign affairs, trade economy, and common political institutions. This process should begin with the strengthening of the role of the Maghreb Union. This is a main requirement of Islamic Triple Helix to create (Islamic) government. All governments in Maghreb region must support each other. The first thing that must be implemented soon are the free movement of goods, people, services and capital. This starts with opening up borders between neighbours. The borders between Algeria and Morocco - the region's two largest countries - which have been closed since 1994. IMF (2018) confirmed that Maghreb countries should be more complementary with each other than with their main export partners. The complementarity value between them is much higher and offers a substantial source of untapped trade potential for Maghreb countries. All member states have substantial revealed comparative advantages to trade among themselves.

Second, cyber security and technology providers cooperation. The exchange of data and information at the highest level will create a safer region, thus attracting more foreign direct investment and tourism. When investment and tourism are active, they will automatically move the real economy which will automatically drive the economy of PEs/NEs and MSMEs. Likewise, management of IFIs in all areas of the Maghreb have the opportunity to digitize and digitalize their system towards digital transformation. This is a main requirement of Islamic Triple Helix to create (Islamic) industry as enabling technologies.

CONCLUSION

Rooted in sharia values, Islamic finance should have eligibility to lead microfinance in contributing the financial inclusion in Maghreb region which consist Islamic countries. This study shows how financial inclusion linked to faith and technology has potency to boost the better achievement. The existence of Islamic picofinance/nanofinance can fill the gap of Islamic microfinance of Islamic bank or IMFIs by reaching the community groups which can not be attained by Islamic microfinance. The existence of Islamic philanthropy platforms can fill the gap of microfinance program.of Islamic bank or IMFIs by utilizing technology to serve the PEs/NEs –the community groups which are often referred to as ultra-micro, super-poor, very poor– and MSMEs.

This study recommends Islamic Quadruple Helix as institutional partnership models based on Islamic social finance as low-cost fund to fuel the productive activities in real economy and for leading the economic growth to be higher and equitable. Coupled with ICT/techologies, Islamic Quadruple Helix can embrace IFIs and Islamic finance stakeholders in this region to develop innovation system of pico-nano-micro-entrepreneurship to the socio-economic development.

In the short term to realize the digital financial inclusion ecosystem for Islamic finance a more fruitful and deeper integration, the first step that must be implemented in the Maghreb region is to establish a new foundation for political integration. All state members, especially the two biggest economies, must end the long-standing competition as well as unaccomplished tenseness among them. All state members must wake up from their long deep sleep and must support each other to terminate grave poverty. This is the first requirement of the Islamic Triple Helix to create the (Islamic) government, also the basis for forming the Islamic quadruple helix This is also the key requirement of Public Policy Economics to generate optimal outcomes toward the Pareto Optimum and Al-Ghazali/Al-Shatibi Optimum. Then, do cooperation in developing cyber security and providing technologies.

REFERENCES

Aaminou, M. W. (2022). *Towards a better financial inclusion in Maghreb countries: Insights on the role of Islamic microfinance and fintech* (Research Report No. 22). İstanbul: Research Center for Islamic Economics (IKAM).

Abusloum, M. A. S., Ahmad, K., & Bello, N. (2020). Islamic banking in Libya: Emergence, growth, and prospects. In A. Rafay (Ed.), *Growth and emerging prospects of international Islamic banking*. IGI Global. doi:10.4018/978-1-7998-1611-9.ch002

Addai, B. (2017). Women empowerment through microfinance: Empirical evidence from Ghana. *Journal of Finance and Accounting*, *5*(1), 1–11. doi:10.11648/j.jfa.20170501.11

African Development Bank Group. (2021). *Note d'orientation politique: Impact de la crise COVID-19 sur l'emploi et les TPME au Maroc*. African Development Bank Group.

Al-Ghwell, H. (2022, May 28). Arab Maghreb Union needs a whole new foundation. *Arab News*. https://www.arabnews.com/node/2091501

Bateman, M. (2011). *Microfinance as a development and poverty reduction policy: is it everything it's cracked up to be?* Background Note of Overseas Development Institute (ODI) at 50: Advancing Knowledge, Shaping Policy, Inspiring Practice. March. www.odi.org.uk/50years

CAHF in Africa. (2021). 2021 yearbook: Housing finance in Africa. Johannesburg, South Africa: Centre for Affordable Housing Finance (CAHF) in Africa.

Carayannis, E. G., Barth, T. D., & Campbell, D. F. J. (2012). The quintuple helix innovation model: Global warming as a challenge and driver for innovation. *Journal of Innovation and Entrepreneurship*, *1*(2), 1–12. doi:10.1186/2192-5372-1-1

Carayannis, E. G., & Campbell, D. F. J. (2011). Open innovation diplomacy and a 21st century fractal research, education and innovation (FREIE) ecosystem: Building on the quadruple and quintuple helix innovation concepts and the "mode 3" knowledge production system. *Journal of the Knowledge Economy*, *2*(3), 327–372. doi:10.100713132-011-0058-3

Carayannis, E. G., Grigoroudis, E., Campbell, D. F. J., Meissner, D., & Stamati, D. (2018). The Ecosystem as helix: An exploratory theory-building study of regional co-opetitive entrepreneurial ecosystems as quadruple/quintuple helix innovation models. *R & D Management*, *48*(1), 148–162. doi:10.1111/radm.12300

Çizakça, M. (2007). Democracy, economic development and maqasid al-shari'ah. *Review of Islamic Economics*, *11*(1), 101–118.

Çizakça, M. (2014). *Can there be innovation in Islamic finance? Case study: Esham.* A paper was presented at the 11th IFSB Summit, New Markets and Frontiers for Islamic Finance: Innovation and the Regulatory Perimeter, Mauritius.

Cornelissen, J. (2017). Editor's comments: Developing propositions, a process model, or a typology? Addressing the challenges of writing theory without a boilerplate. *Academy of Management Review, 42*(1), 1–9. doi:10.5465/amr.2016.0196

Daoud, Y., & Kammoun, A. (2020). Islamic banking in North Africa: emergence, growth, and prospects. In A. Rafay, Growth and emerging prospects of international Islamic banking (pp. 78-98): IGI Global. doi:10.4018/978-1-7998-1611-9.ch005

Demirgüç-Kunt, A., Klapper, L., Singer, D., & Ansar, S. (2022). *The global findex database 2021: financial inclusion, digital payments, and resilience in the age of covid-19.* International Bank for Reconstruction and Development/The World Bank. doi:10.1596/978-1-4648-1897-4

Djeflat, A. (2009a). Building systems for innovation "take off" in African economies. *African Journal of Science, Technology, Innovation and Development, 1*(1), 53–75.

Djeflat, A. (2009b). Universities and scientific research in the Maghreb states: Power politics and innovation systems. *International Journal of Technology Management, 45*(1/2), 102–113. doi:10.1504/IJTM.2009.021522

Etkowitz, H. (2002). *The triple helix of university - industry - government implications for policy and evaluation.* (Working Paper 11). Institutet för Studier av Utbildning och Forskning.

Etzkowitz, H. (2008). *The triple helix: University-industry-government innovation in action.* Routledge. doi:10.4324/9780203929605

Etzkowitz, H., Dzisah, J., Ranga, M., & Zhou, C. (2007). The triple helix model of innovation: University-industry-government interaction. *Asia-Pacific Tech Monitor*, (Jan-Feb), 14–23.

Etzkowitz, H., & Leydesdorff, L. (1995). The triple helix---university-industry-government relations: A laboratory for knowledge based economic development. *European Association for the Study of Science and Technology (EASST). RE:view, 14*(1), 14–19.

Etzkowitz, H., & Leydesdorff, L. (1998). The endless transition: A "triple helix" of university-industry-government relations. *Minerva, 36*(3), 203–208. doi:10.1023/A:1004348123030

Etzkowitz, H., & Leydesdorff, L. (2000). The dynamics of innovation: From national systems and 'mode 2' to a triple helix of university-industry-government relations. *Research Policy, 29*(2), 109–123. doi:10.1016/S0048-7333(99)00055-4

Groen, R. P. G. (2002). *Making sense of microcredit interest rates.* The Consultative Group to Assist the Poor (CGAP) Donor Information Resource Centre (DIRECT).

Hamza, W. A. (2017, June 1). The Maghreb union is one of the world's worst-performing trading blocs. here are five ways to change that. *World Economic Forum.* https://www.weforum.org/agenda/2017/06/five-ways-to-make-maghreb-work/

Hassan, A., & Saleem, S. (2017). An Islamic microfinance business model in Bangladesh. *Humanomics, 33*(1), 15–37. doi:10.1108/H-08-2016-0066

Hidayat, S. E., & Musari, K. (2023, forthcoming). Towards the global halal MSMEs hub through the digitally-enabled society: an institutional arrangement with Islamic n-tuple helix. In A. Rafiki (Ed.), Digitalization in halal management. Springer.

Hossain, M., & Diaz, C. P. (1997). Reaching the poor eith effective microcredit: evaluation of a grameen bank replication in the Philippines. *Journal of Philippines Development, 44*, (2), 275-308.

IMF. (2018). Economic integration in the Maghreb – an untapped source of growth. Washington, DC: International Monetary Fund (IMF).

IsDB. (2020). IsDB annual report 2020 – Respond, restore, restart: post-covid resilience and prosperity for all. Jeddah: Islamic Development Bank (IsDB).

IsDB. (2021). IsDB annual report 2021 – Beyond recovery: resilience and sustainability. Jeddah: Islamic Development Bank (IsDB).

Ismal, R. (2012). *The Indonesian Islamic banking: performance and outlook.* Presentation for Panel Discussion held by Bakrie University in Jakarta.

Jabłoński, A., & Jabłoński, M. (2020). *Social business models in the digital economy new concepts and contemporary challenges.* Cham, Switzerland: Palgrave Macmillan, Springer Nature. doi:10.1007/978-3-030-29732-9

Kato, M. P., & Kratzer, J. (2013). Empowering women through microfinance: Evidence from Tanzania. The Academic Collaboration and Research Network, Austria, Cambridge UK (ACRN). *Journal of Entrepreneurship Perspectives, 2*(1), 31–59.

Khan, H., & Sonko, K. N. M. (Eds.). (2020). *Islamic finance as a complex system: new insights.* Lexington Books.

Levin, G. (2012). Critique of microcredit as a development model. *Pursuit - The Journal of Undergraduate Research at the University of Tennessee, 4*(1), 109–117.

Macchiavello, E. (2016). Microfinance and Financial inclusion: the challenge of regulating alternative forms of finance (introduction). *Microfinance and financial inclusion: the challenge of regulating alternative forms of finance.* Routledge.

MacInnis, D. J. (2011). A framework for conceptual contributions in marketing. *Journal of Marketing, 75*(4), 136–154. doi:10.1509/jmkg.75.4.136

Meredith, J. (1993). Theory building through conceptual methods. *International Journal of Operations & Production Management, 13*(5), 3–11. doi:10.1108/01443579310028120

Messaoudi, A. (1994). *Arab maghreb union: achievement and prospects.* [Thesis of Naval Postgraduate School, Monterey, California].

Meyer, R. L. (2002). *Track record of financial institutions in assisting the poor in Asia.* (Asian Development Bank (ADB) Institute Research Paper 49). Tokyo: ADB.

Mitra, S. K. (2009, May). Exploitative microfinance interest rates. *Asian Social Science*, *5*(5). doi:10.5539/ass.v5n5p87

Musari, K. (2016). *Redefining the Islamic nanofinance and its institutional strengthening: lesson learned from Asian countries.* 11th International Conference on Islamic Economics and Finance (ICIEF) Rethinking Islamic Economics and Finance: Paving The Way Forward for Inclusive and Sustainable Development. Institution Kulliyyah of Economics and Management Sciences International Islamic University Malaysia (IIUM).

Musari, K. (2019). Promoting qard al-hasan in nanofinance to counter the moneylender in southeast Asia. *Studia Islamica*, *26*(1), 1–16. doi:10.15408di.v26i1.5990

Musari, K. (2020a, January 17). Between Odisha, Jember, and Islamic Economy. *Jawa Pos Radar Jember Daily Newspaper*, 21 - 27.

Musari, K. (2020b). The loan shark in ASEAN: can nanofinance with qardhul hassan deal with it? lesson learned from bank wakaf mikro in Indonesia. In P. Ordoñez de Pablos, M. Almunawar, & M. Abduh (Eds.), *Economics, business, and Islamic finance in ASEAN Economics Community* (pp. 252–277). IGI Global. doi:10.4018/978-1-7998-2257-8.ch012

Musari, K. (2020c). Islamic nanofinance for the very poor by women, hopes for addressing the Islamic microfinance gap. In T. Azid & J. L. Ward-Batts (Eds.), *Economic empowerment of women in the Islamic world: theory and practice* (pp. 265–286). World Scientific Publishing. doi:10.1142/9789811212154_0013

Musari, K. (2022). P2P lending & philanthropy platform: a new face of Asian digital financial inclusion (evidence from Indonesia). In M. N. Almunawar, Z. Islam, and P. Ordóñez de Pablos (Eds.), Digital Transformation Management: Challenges and Futures in the Asian Digital Economy. New York, NY: Informa UK Limited, Taylor & Francis/Routledge.

Musari, K., & Fathorrazi, M. (2021). Islamic helix approach, the Islamic social finance partnership models for MSMEs: lesson learned from Indonesia. In T. Azid, M. Mukhlisin, N. Akbar, & M. Tahir (Eds.), *Monetary policy, Islamic finance, and Islamic corporate governance: an international overview* (pp. 303–322). Emerald Publishing Limited., doi:10.1108/978-1-80043-786-920211017

Musari, K., & Sayah, F. (2022). *Finding the Islamic social finance partnership models for micro entrepreneurship through Islamic helix approach: case study in Indonesia and Algeria.* A paper was presented at Entrepreneurship, Sustainable Development, and Halal Economy Conference: Concepts, Framework and Practice held by College of Islamic Studies (CIS), Hamad Bin Khalifa University (HBKU), Doha - Qatar.

Musari, K., & Simanjuntak, R. (2016). Nanofinance, redefinition of microfinance for the very micro society through philanthropy linkage program (case study in Indonesia, Cambodia, Thailand, India). [AARJSH]. *Asian Academic Research Journal of Social Sciences and Humanities*, *3*(4), 455–463.

O'Neill, A. (2021, Apr 22). *Maghreb region - Statistics & Facts.* Statista. https://www.statista.com/topics/4660/maghreb-region/#topicHeader__wrapper

Owusu, J., Akanbasiam, A. C., & Anyesepari, A. A. (2013). Microfinance schemes and poverty reduction among women in the northern region of Ghana. *International Journal of Humanities and Social Science*, *3*(19), 99–108.

Rahman, A. (1999). Micro-credit initiatives for equitable and sustainable development: Who pays? *World Development*, *27*(1), 67–82. doi:10.1016/S0305-750X(98)00105-3

Rathiranee, Y., & Semasinghe, S. D. (2016). The impact of micro finance factors on women entrepreneurs' performance in northern Sri Lanka. *International Journal of Social Science Studies*, *4*(3), 94–99.

Rosenberg, R. (2002). *Microcredit interest rates.* CGAP.

Rosenberg, R., Gaul, S., Ford, W., & Tomilova, O. (2013). *Microcredit interest rates and their determinants 2004–2011*. CGAP.

RosenbergR.GonzalezA.NarainS. (2009). The new moneylenders: are the poor being exploited by high microcredit interest rates? CGAP.

Sample, B. (2011). *Moving 100 million families out of severe poverty: how can we do it?*. 2011 Global Microcredit Summit, Auxiliary Session Paper, Valladolid, Spain.

Sinclair, H. (2012). *Confessions of a microfinance heretic, how microlending lost its way and betrayed the poor*. Berrett-Koehler Publishers, Inc.

Statista. (2022a). *Total population of the Maghreb countries from 2016 to 2026.* Statista. https://www.statista.com/statistics/796046/total-population-of-the-maghreb-countries/

Statista. (2022b). *Maghreb countries: Gross domestic product (GDP) per capita in current prices from 2016 to 2026.* Statista. https://www.statista.com/statistics/796087/gross-domestic-product-gdp-per-capita-in-the-maghreb-countries/

United Nations Secretary-General. (2018). *Igniting SDG progress through digital financial* inclusion. NY: UNSGSA.

World Bank. (2018). *Implementation completion and results report on a loan in the amount of euro 37.9 million (us$ 50 million equivalent) to the kingdom of Morocco for the MA MSMEs development project.* World Bank.

World Bank. (2021). *The global findex database 2021 financial inclusion, digital payments, and resilience in the age of covid-19*. World Bank.

ADDITIONAL READINGS

Hidayat, S. E., & Musari, K. (2023, forthcoming). Comparative analysis of digitally-enabled community in supporting the halal industry in muslim-majority countries in the ASEAN, central Asia, and Maghreb region. In A. Rafiki (Ed.), Digitalization in halal management. Springer Nature.

Sayah, F., & Musari, K. (2021). Reviving zakat for micro-financing and socio-economic development in Algeria. [IJAZ]. *International Journal of Zakat*, *6*(3), 23–40. doi:10.37706/ijaz.v6i3.356

Chapter 6
Exploring Factors Influencing International Muslim Tourists' Intentions Towards Homestays in Sabah, Malaysia

Azrin Jalasi
Politeknik Kota Kinabalu, Sabah, Malaysia

Sylvia Nabila Azwa Ambad
Universiti Teknologi MARA Sabah Branch, Kota Kinabalu Campus, Malaysia

Nor Irvoni Mohd Ishar
https://orcid.org/0000-0002-4461-3429
Universiti Teknologi MARA, Malaysia

Ahmad Rafiki
https://orcid.org/0000-0002-6360-8131
Universitas Medan Area, Indonesia

ABSTRACT

The rapid growth of the Muslim tourism market worldwide and its impact on global tourism development have led to the competition among countries to attract Muslim travelers. The study aims to address the lower number of international Muslim tourists visiting Sabah's homestays despite Malaysia's status as a top Muslim tourism destination. Based on the content analysis, the intention to visit homestays is influenced by halal image, halal awareness, and religiosity. The article underscores the significance of homestays in Sabah's tourism industry, its potential for rural socio-economic development, and the need to tap into the emerging market of Muslim tourists. The findings could provide insights for homestay marketers and operators to enhance halal image, increase halal awareness, and consider religiosity when targeting Muslim tourists, contributing to the growth of Sabah's tourism sector and rural economies. This study adds to the existing literature on Muslim tourists' intentions and sheds light on a less explored context of homestay tourism.

DOI: 10.4018/978-1-6684-7519-5.ch006

1. INTRODUCTION

In recent years, the fast-growing Muslim tourism market has urged many countries worldwide to compete to attract more tourists from Muslim-majority countries to visit their places. Many have realised that the Muslim travellers market significantly impacts global tourism development (Yusof et al., 2019). Moreover, worldwide Muslim travellers are expected to grow to over 230 million, representing more than 10 per cent of the world's tourists (Admin, 2019, April 9). Thus, tapping this lucrative market can strengthen any country's tourism industry. Evidently, in the highest expenditure per capita, Muslim-majority countries like Saudi Arabia have topped the list with MYR11, 376.90 in total and took the top spot for the highest average length of stay at 10.5 nights (TTRweekly.com, 2019). Meanwhile, other Muslim-majority countries such as Indonesia and Brunei were also listed as among Malaysia's top ten source markets for international tourist arrivals.

One of the important tourism products in Malaysia is the homestay programme. Of thirteen states in the country, Sabah has the most progressive business performance in the sector. As of 2019, there were 30 homestay associations in Sabah involving 51 villages, 406 active homestay operators, and 716 rooms (MOTAC, 2019). This number is expected to increase in the future. Hence, in this study, the state of Sabah was chosen because Sabah has the most progressive business performance in the homestay sector. Sabah has shown the most enlightened growth in the industry from thirteen states in Malaysia recently. As of 2019, Sabah's homestay programme was ranked as the highest-earning in the sector, with more than MYR6 million (Daily Express, 2020). In the same year, Sabah was also recognised as the leading tourists' destination for homestays in Malaysia and honoured as "Malaysia's Favourite Destination" at the 47th edition of the Malaysian Association of Tour and Travel Agents (MATTA) Fair in 2019. This recognition is essential since the tourism industry is the most significant economic contributor to the state (The Star, 2018).

As shown in Table 1, Sabah has received the highest number of international tourist arrivals for the homestay programme for three consecutive years since 2017 (MOTAC, 2019). It is also noted that the international tourist arrivals to homestays in Sabah increased tremendously to 93.7 per cent (2,999 in 2014 to 47,231 tourists in 2018). Meanwhile, the domestic tourist arrivals show an increase of 70.3 per cent from 17,131 in 2014 to 57,852 in 2018 (MOTAC, 2019). This growth is expected to continue rising in the future. On the other hand, the total receipts of Sabah's homestays also increased to 38.7 per cent in 2018. It started from RM3.8 million in 2017 and rose to RM6.2 million in 2018 (MOTAC, 2019). The rapid growth of tourist arrivals from domestic and international markets contributed to this remarkable increase.

However, according to MOTAC (2019), international Muslim tourists' arrivals to homestay in Sabah have remained lower since the state introduced the programme. As of 2019, 86 per cent of the international tourists visiting Sabah's homestays were from China and South Korea (see Table 2). Fewer international tourist arrivals from Muslim-majority countries to Sabah's homestay have sparked a debate, as Malaysia is one of the top Muslim tourism destinations globally (Yusof et al., 2016). Besides, Sabah was recognised as a vital tourism spot in Malaysia and the South Asian region (Khaled et al., 2013). Thus, two critical questions have arisen for further investigation in this study. Firstly, why does the number of international Muslim tourist arrivals at Sabah's homestay remain fewer? Secondly, what are the most critical factors influencing international Muslim tourists' intention to visit homestays in Sabah?

The importance of tourists' arrival from Muslim-majority countries to homestays in Sabah is indisputable. The Sabah's homestay programme is crucial in ensuring an equal share of economic prosperity,

Table 1. The number of international tourist arrivals to homestays in Malaysia from 2014 to 2020 (based on states' performances)

<table>
<tr><th rowspan="2">No</th><th rowspan="2">States</th><th colspan="7">Number of International Tourist Arrivals</th></tr>
<tr><th>2014</th><th>2015</th><th>2016</th><th>2017</th><th>2018</th><th>2019</th><th>2020</th></tr>
<tr><td>1</td><td>Sabah</td><td>2,999</td><td>4,143</td><td>5,219</td><td>23,129</td><td>47,231</td><td>55,600</td><td>14,804</td></tr>
<tr><td>2</td><td>Johor</td><td>32,551</td><td>27,208</td><td>22,668</td><td>15,094</td><td>12,788</td><td>7,335</td><td>314</td></tr>
<tr><td>3</td><td>Sarawak</td><td>6,891</td><td>5,610</td><td>4,648</td><td>3,372</td><td>5,637</td><td>7,195</td><td>2,509</td></tr>
<tr><td>4</td><td>Selangor</td><td>8,341</td><td>12,090</td><td>6,893</td><td>7,476</td><td>4,759</td><td>2,810</td><td>247</td></tr>
<tr><td>5</td><td>Melaka</td><td>13,417</td><td>15,025</td><td>12,355</td><td>6,143</td><td>4,440</td><td>7,170</td><td>280</td></tr>
<tr><td>6</td><td>Perak</td><td>421</td><td>127</td><td>98</td><td>1,470</td><td>3,109</td><td rowspan="8">6000</td><td>766</td></tr>
<tr><td>7</td><td>N. Sembilan</td><td>1,727</td><td>3,844</td><td>1,490</td><td>1,270</td><td>1,980</td><td>84</td></tr>
<tr><td>8</td><td>Pulau Pinang</td><td>738</td><td>827</td><td>926</td><td>1,222</td><td>849</td><td>53</td></tr>
<tr><td>9</td><td>Kedah</td><td>690</td><td>404</td><td>409</td><td>889</td><td>708</td><td>263</td></tr>
<tr><td>10</td><td>Pahang</td><td>2,428</td><td>1,805</td><td>1,711</td><td>1,434</td><td>571</td><td>6</td></tr>
<tr><td>11</td><td>Terengganu</td><td>291</td><td>203</td><td>263</td><td>90</td><td>99</td><td>25</td></tr>
<tr><td>12</td><td>Kelantan</td><td>224</td><td>185</td><td>238</td><td>231</td><td>98</td><td>25</td></tr>
<tr><td>13</td><td>Labuan</td><td>193</td><td>221</td><td>260</td><td>26</td><td>53</td><td>2</td></tr>
<tr><td>14</td><td>Perlis</td><td>95</td><td>138</td><td>0</td><td>0</td><td>0</td><td>0</td><td>0</td></tr>
<tr><td colspan="2">Total</td><td>62,847</td><td>71,034</td><td>57,178</td><td>61,846</td><td>82,322</td><td>85,341</td><td>19,378</td></tr>
</table>

Source: Statistik Programme Pengalaman Homestay Malaysia (October 2020)

Table 2. International visitors' arrival to Sabah by nationality in the year 2018-2019

Nationality / Years	2019	2018
Brunei	78,605	56,259
Indonesia	115,879	109,771
China	1,065,211	999,851
South Korea	396,660	337,100
Japan	24,435	19,357
Taiwan	45,550	49,771
United Kingdom	29,575	28,611
United States	16,294	16,043
Pakistan	1,748	1339
Middle East	1740	1503

Source: MASB, Sabah / Immigration Department Sabah / Airlines prepared by Research Division for Sabah Tourism.

not only in the city but also in the rural areas. This programme is an added support to the rural socio-economic development, social capital development, and contribution to conservation and enhancement of the rural areas by developing public understanding about to life in rural areas and environmental issues generally. The growth of the homestay programme in Sabah has provided considerable opportunities to rural communities.

As noted in the APEC Tourism Charter, Community-Based Tourism (CBT), such as homestay programmes has created direct employment opportunities and increased income levels in rural communities. This programme has created an opportunity for local communities in the rural area to contribute to the local economic development and reduce poverty (Kasim et al., 2016). Besides, the programme conserves and enhances rural areas by developing public understanding of life in rural areas and environmental issues (Ibrahim, 2004). On top of that, via homestay programme implementation, the villagers participating in the programme have enjoyed better infrastructure the government provides regarding road upgrading, electricity and water supply, and public amenities such as a multi-purpose hall, service centre, and computer centre.

The village participants also obtained other facilities for tourism purposes, such as a cultural stage and workshop. Apart from that, the arrivals of tourists from the Middle East countries such as Saudi Arabia, United Arab Emirates, Qatar, Morocco, Bahrain, and Oman can also significantly impact the Malaysian tourism industry (Yusof et al., 2019) since these tourists have a significant purchasing power (Isa et al., 2018). Thus, the ability to tap this new segment market will contribute to the development of Community-Based Tourism in Sabah. This market is still largely untapped, even with its tremendous potential. Hence, Sabah's Community-Based Tourism sector should seize this emerging market to strengthen the state's tourism sector.

Homestay Concept in Sabah

The homestay programme in Sabah is a combination of tourism and recreation. It has grown due to increasing demand for access to the countryside, better personal mobility, more leisure time, and the need for peaceful places (Ibrahim, 2004). Through this concept, the guests can interact, gain knowledge, and experience the lifestyle and culture of the host family and the local community. This element involves the guests eating, cooking, and engaging in many activities with their adopted families, thus allowing two parties with different cultural backgrounds to interact and learn from each other. In contrast to the traditional bed and breakfast accommodation concept, the Malaysian homestay programme allows guests to participate in the hosts' everyday activities.

The tourists will stay with the selected host's family and have a chance to experience the family's daily life in all manners (Ibrahim, 2004). This experiential element with the host families and communities become the uniqueness of the homestay programme in Sabah. Hence, the homestay programme in Sabah is not merely an accommodation but also a tourism experience of local people's lifestyle, culture, and economic activities. In particular, communities are the primary reason tourists travel and experience the way of life of others. The communities are essential in shaping the natural vistas that many visitors enjoy (Richards & Hall, 2000). It made the community realise that they are the object of tourism consumption and encouraged them to use this advantage to attract more tourists to come to their places.

Homestay programmes are one of the vital platforms for tourism activities. Through homestay programmes, tourists would be able to experience the daily life of the local people of a community. More importantly, the homestay programme in Sabah is in contrast to hotel and bed and breakfast accommodation services. Specifically, Sabah's homestay programs emphasised staying together with host families or adopted families. It is why Malaysia's definition of a homestay programme differs from other countries globally. The homestays are associated with farmhouses in most Western countries. Meanwhile, in Asian countries like Japan and South Korea, homestay is linked with educational stay and home visit activities. Conversely, in South Asian countries like the Philippines, Indonesia and Thailand, the homestay programme is more on cultural and leisure stays concept and urban stay concept in Singapore (Hamzah, 2010).

In Sabah, the homestay programme is a rural cultural Community-Based Tourism product. Hosts of the Sabah homestays have undergone the required training on the management of homestays so that host and visiting tourists will have an enjoyable guest and host relationship during their stay with host families. Sabah one of the thirteen states of Malaysia, offers various and unique cultural experiences. Henceforth, rural tourism in Sabah is the best in the country due to the diverse tourism products in this part of the country. Sabah is home to more than 33 ethnic groups living in different parts of Sabah. Each district offers their own unique culture, beliefs and way of life. These unique and diverse cultures, beliefs, as well as ways of life, allow the visitors to experience different lifestyles in each of the homestays where they stay.

For example, in the Long Pasia homestay, the ethnic group there are the Lundayehs while Kinabatangan, will be the Orang Sungai. In Tambunan, will be Kadazan Dusun people and in the North, Kudat will be the Rungus community, each having its own culture and traditions. Thus, Sabah's homestay programme has a lot of unique activities to offer tourists according to the culture and traditions of the various participating ethnic groups in this industry. Besides the highest mountain in Malaysia, the diversity in nature, beautiful beaches, islands and seas and, more importantly, the warmth of local hospitality make Sabah so unique for tourists. Also, the richness of the natural environment and diversity of landscapes have made Sabah one of Malaysia's most exciting places to visit in Malaysia. These stunning attractions have brought Sabah to the top of most important tourism spots in Malaysia and the South Asian region (Khaled et al., 2013).

2. LITERATURE REVIEW

Ajzen and Fishbein (2000) posited that the more robustly individual intends to perform a particular behaviour, the more likely the individual would perform the behaviour. In other words, the consumers' buying intent determines their actual purchasing behaviour (Ajzen and Fishbein, 1975; Ajzen, 1988). Therefore, it is unsurprising that the number of international Muslim tourists' arrivals to Sabah's homestays has remained fewer since the state introduced the programme. Weaker intents to visit homestays among international Muslim tourists, resulting in lower arrivals of international Muslim tourists to Sabah's homestays. The intention is considered an essential central component that immediately happens before the actual conduct occurs (Azjen, 1991). However, even though Muslim consumers' behavioural intentions have been studied widely, empirical research on Muslim's intention to visit homestays, particularly in the Sabah context, is still limited.

From the Islamic marketing scholars' perspective, adherence to religious principles is the essential determinant of Muslim consumers' behavioural intention. Muslim consumers who identify as obedient to the Islamic religion will prefer halal products (Arsil et al., 2018). They ought to follow the halal and haram guidelines in all facets of their everyday lives, even while travelling. Most of the scholars in the area of Islamic marketing found that constructs such as halal image (Salleh et al., 2020; Haque et al., 2019; Bashir, 2019), halal awareness (Pradana et al., 2020; Setyawati et al., 2019; Iranmanesh et al., 2019; Haque et al., 2019) and religiosity (Rizkitysha & Hananto, 2020; Hanafiah et al., 2020; Haque et al., 2019; Hosseini et., 2019; Iranmanesh et al., 2019) were found to be the stronger determinants of Muslim consumers' behavioural intention. Therefore, in this study halal image, halal awareness and religiosity are hypothesised as important determinants of Muslims' behavioural intention to visit homestays.

Muslim Behavioural Intention

Based on Ajzen and Fishbein (2002), the actual behaviour of an individual is determined by their intention (Ajzen & Fishbein, 2002). Further, it is considered that the motivational factors of a person influence intention. The intention is a concrete element that shows how much and how long efforts are exerted by an individual to perform a particular behaviour (Ajzen, 1991). As a rule of thumb, the higher the degree of intention, the higher the possibility of individuals performing a given behaviour (Ajzen, 1991). The intention is considered a critical antecedent that shapes consumers' purchase behaviour (Nguyen et al., 2010) and becomes a crucial determinant of actual buying behaviour. According to Ajzen and Fishbein (2000), intention is the central component of the Theory of Planned Behavior (TPB) model; occurs before the actual behaviour.

One of the most effective ways to understand the actual purchase behaviour of consumers is by examining what influences their intentions (Ghalandari & Norouzi, 2012). It will then lead to developing of appropriate strategies for business marketing services (Khaniwale, 2015). Earlier, intention was defined by Fishbein & Ajzen (1975) as a measure of the strength of one's intention to perform a specific behaviour. Their study, argued that a person commits actual conduct when an opportunity arises. The stronger the person's intention to perform a behaviour, the more likely an individual will perform the behaviour. The relationship between the individual's intention and actual performance has been empirically tested in a laboratory setting (Ajzen & Fishbein, 2000).

Actual behaviour results from a strong individual's intention to perform a specific action. It is a subjective probability to adopt or not adopt a particular behaviour (Correia, Santos and Barrwo, 2007). According to Yunus et al. (2014), intention is an essential key antecedent of actual conduct (Yunus et al., 2014), and it shapes consumers' purchase behaviour (Nguyen et al., 2010). Earlier, Fishbein and Ajzen (1975) defined the intention to measure the strength of one's intention to perform a specific behaviour. Later, in further studies, Ajzen (1985) expressed intention as the state where a person is willing to perform some behaviour. Meanwhile, other studies like Swan (1981) associated intention with an individual's expected or planned future behaviour. Similarly, Conner and Armitage (1998) defined intention as an individual's motivation in the sense of their conscious plan or decision to exert effort to enact the behaviour.

Other studies like Courneya (1994) extended the definition of intention by associating it with the frequency of achievement in physical activity participation. The intention is related to the brand selection tendency (Patwary & Rashid, 2016). It indicates of the possibility that consumers will be planning or willing to buy certain products or services in the future (Wu, Yeh & Hsiao, 2011). In the context of Muslim consumers, faith is part of the intention and purchase decision. For Muslims, the process of searching for products or services must be faith-based needs. Specifically, Muslims prefer to choose a destination where Islamic attributes are highly available in tourism. It may allow for tourism activities within their religious norms and practices comprising facilities for prayer and worship, no liquor, halal foods, and Islamic dress codes (Battour et al., 2014; Al-Ansi et al., 2019). Thus, in this study, intention refers to Muslims' readiness to visit homestays.

Halal Image

It is noted from previous studies that image influences the intention to visit a destination (Prayag et al., 2017). Lee and Back (2008) tested the effect of destination image on intention, and they found that it was the second most powerful variable on intention after past experiences. Another study that showed that destination image affected customers' visit intention was by Zhang et al. (2018). In the concept of halal image, the image concept is purely related to religious issues (Bonne et al., 2007). For religious Muslims, it is a prerequisite for any products or services to become halal before other purchase considerations such as price, quality, convenience, etc. (Ahmed, 2008). Thus, the halal image was asserted by many previous researchers as one of the crucial factors in determining Muslim consumers' behavioural intention (Salleh et al., 2020; Bashir, 2019; Haque et al., 2019). Halal symbolises permissibility concerning Islamic guidelines (Deuraseh, 2009), while haram symbolises all unlawful actions in Islam. Hence, the halal image refers to the symbol of permissibility concerning Islamic principles.

Halal Awareness

Halal awareness is another issue in the decision-making process of Muslim consumers. According to Wu et al. (2019), awareness is part of the buying process, and consumers will try to know as much as possible about the product or service. Meanwhile, halal represents the symbol of hygiene, quality and safety (Ambali & Bakar, 2014). For Muslims, their consumption awareness is associated with the halal term. It shows Muslim consumers' ability to understand a particular issue related to what is permitted (halal) and not permitted (haram) in Islam. Thus, halal awareness indicates Muslim consumers' commitment to halal consumption (Nusran et al., 2018). In the Islamic marketing literature, halal awareness was proven as the predictor of Muslim consumers' purchase intention (Pradana et al., 2020; Setyawati et al., 2019; Iranmanesh et al., 2019; Haque et al., 2019; Syukur & Nimsai, 2018; Patwary et al., 2018; Bashir et al., 2018; Mutmainah, 2018; and Zakaria et al., 2017).

In the recent research works of Pradana et al. (2020), Setyawati et al. (2019) and Mutmainah (2018), they have found that halal awareness has a significant and positive effect on Muslim consumers' purchase intention of halal foods. In other studies, Bashir et al. (2018) also noted in their investigations that awareness was a key factor in predicting Muslim consumers' purchase intentions for halal-certified products. They claimed that when Muslims buy a product or service, the most important factor determining their purchase intention is their knowledge of the product, whether it is halal or non-halal. Thus, they concluded that most Muslim consumers in South Africa know the importance of halal. The same findings were found in the studies of Muslim consumers' intention to buy services such as Sharia-compliant hotels. In other studies, Haque et al. (2019) investigated the vital aspects of understanding Muslim consumers' purchase behaviour towards Sharia-compliant hotels.

According to the findings, aspects of halal awareness play an integral role in Muslim consumers' purchase intention towards Sharia-compliant hotels. Other studies, such as Syukur and Nimsai (2018) and Zakaria et al. (2017), also provide empirical evidence to support the role of halal awareness in predicting Muslim consumers' behavioural intention. Studying the factors influencing the purchase intention of halal food among Muslim consumers in Thailand, Syukur and Nimsai (2018), found that halal awareness significantly influences the consumers' purchase intention. The data were collected from 480 Thailand Muslim consumers. On the other hand, Zakaria et al. (2017) revealed that the choice of Muslim consumers to bargain a particular product is highly affected by their awareness of that product. If the awareness is high, there will be high purchase intent.

Religiosity

Religiosity has also emerged as an essential factor in determining Muslims' behavioural intention. In Islamic definition, religiosity is the manifestation of committed religious life in an individual, which discerns from the depth of his belief (Manap et al., 2013). Religion is highly sensitive to Muslims in general, but to a certain extent, this depends on their level of devotedness or religiosity (Said et al., 2014). Many scholars in a different set of studies have found that Muslims' religiosity has a strong effect on their behavioural intentions. According to Ustaahmetoglu (2020), the influence of the level of religiosity on purchasing intention was significant. Ustaahmetoglu (2020) revealed that highly religious consumers' purchase intentions are differed as compared to the consumers with low levels of religiosity in Turkey.

In another research setting, Haque et al. (2019) have found that religiosity can influence Muslim consumers' intention to select Sharia-Compliant hotel in Malaysia. The researchers proposed the hotel operators develop marketing strategies and activities according to Islamic principles to attract Muslim customers. The rationale of this suggestion is to avoid anything that may offend the religious beliefs of Muslim consumers. Similarly, Johan et al. (2020) 's research results proved that religiosity's effect on Muslim consumers' purchase intention was significant. They have revealed that religiosity influences Muslim consumers' intention to hold Sharia-compliant credit card (SCCC) in Malaysia. Johan et al. (2020) further asserted that a strong Muslim usually has a positive attitude toward Islamic products.

Several other researchers support the religiosity influence on Muslim consumers' behavioural intention. For example, Ibrahim et al. (2017), in their studies of Muslim customers' intention to choose Islamic home financing products in Malaysia revealed that religiosity is the most important determinant of Muslim customers' behavioural intention. The study's results confirmed that religious beliefs are crucial for Muslim customers in choosing banks' services. Similarly, Hosseini et al. (2019) and Asnawi et al. (2018) have reported that Muslim consumers' religiosity positively affects their intention to select halal products. Investigating the religiosity influence on Muslim customers' willingness to pay for halal-certified meals in Malaysia, Hosseini et al. (2019) discovered that Muslim consumers' religious devotion influences their willingness to pay for halal meals. Therefore, Hoseini et al. (2019) suggest that firms highlight Islamic practices in their business operations because it is important for Muslim consumers with high religious commitment.

3. CONCLUSION

Previously, most studies focused on other sectors such as hotels (e.g. Haque et al., 2019; Patawary et al., 2018). This study's finding is expected to extend the understanding towards the driving forces that influence international Muslim tourists' intention to visit homestays. In this light, this study has focused on the effect of halal image, halal awareness and religiosity towards the international Muslim tourists' intention to visit homestays in Sabah. Consequently, the findings of this study are expected to enrich the current literature on Muslim tourists' intention to visit homestays, which has been largely focusing on other contexts of studies. Such information will be helpful for homestay marketers as it will help them to attract more tourists from Muslim-majority countries to visit the homestay programme in Sabah. This research tries to fill the gap and provides a new perspective on Muslim tourists' behavioural intentions from the standpoint of Muslims.

Understanding these factors provides essential insight to homestay marketers and operators, and guides researchers studying intention behaviour to Muslim tourists. Further studies on homestays are critical as this CBT's product is considered one of the rural economic mobilizers. It is recommended that homestay marketers should take the initiative of enhancing the halal image of their homestay by building positive perceptions in the minds of Muslim tourists. Additionally, homestay marketers should enhance Muslim tourists' awareness regarding the halal aspect of their homestays through various marketing activities. Besides, marketing strategies and activities should be developed according to Islamic principles to encourage Muslim tourists to visit homestays by avoiding anything that may offend Muslim's religious beliefs. The findings of this study is expected to assist homestay marketers in developing more effective strategies for homestays to cater to international Muslim tourists. As fewer international Muslim tourists visit homestays in Sabah, it is timely for homestays in Sabah to attract more international Muslim tourists.

REFERENCES

Admin. (2019, April 09). Halal Travel Holds Huge Potential, Remains Untapped. *Business Today*. https://www.businesstoday.com.my/2019/04/09/halal-travel-market remains-untapped-likely-to-grow-35/

Admin. (2020, January 13). Sabah's homestays among the highest earners in Malaysia. *Daily Express*. https://www.dailyexpress.com.my/news/146244/sabah-s-homestays-among-highest-earners-in-m-sia/

Ahmed, A. (2008). Marketing of halal meat in the United Kingdom – supermarkets versus local shops. *British Food Journal, 110*(7), 655–670. doi:10.1108/00070700810887149

Ajzen, I. (1988). *Attitudes, personality and behavior*. Open University Press.

Ajzen, I. (1991). The theory of planned behaviour. *Organizational Behavior and Human Decision Processes, 50*(2), 179–211. doi:10.1016/0749-5978(91)90020-T

Ajzen, I., & Fishbein, M. (2000). Attitudes and the Attitude-Behavior Relation: Reasoned and Automatic Processes. *European Review of Social Psychology, 11*(1), 1–33. doi:10.1080/14792779943000116

Ajzen, I., & Fishbein, M. (2002). *Understanding Attitudes and Predicting Social Behavior*. Prentice-Hall.

Al-Ansi, A., Olya, H., & Kim, W. (2019). Exploring halal-friendly destination attributes in South Korea: Perceptions and behaviors of Muslim travelers toward a non-Muslim destination. *Tourism Management, 71*, 151–164. doi:10.1016/j.tourman.2018.10.010

Ambali, A., & Bakar, A. N. (2014). People's Awareness on Halal Foods and Products: Potential Issues for Policy-makers. *Procedia: Social and Behavioral Sciences, 121*, 3–25. doi:10.1016/j.sbspro.2014.01.1104

Asnawi, N., Sukoco, B.M., & Fanani, M.A. (2018). Halal products consumption in international chain restaurants among global Moslem consumers. *International Journal of Emerging Markets, 13*.

Bashir, Abdalla. (2019). Effect of halal awareness, halal logo and attitude on foreign consumers' purchase intention. *British Food Journal*. . doi:10.1108/BFJ-01-2019-0011

Bashir, A. M., Bayat, A., Olutuase, S. O., & Abdul Latiff, Z. A. (2018). Factors affecting consumers' intention towards purchasing halal food in South Africa: A structural equation modelling. *Journal of Food Products Marketing*, *25*(1), 26–48. doi:10.1080/10454446.2018.1452813

Battour, M. M., Battor, M. M., & Bhatti, M. A. (2014). Islamic attributes of destination: Construct development and measurement validation, and their impact on tourist satisfaction. *International Journal of Tourism Research*, *16*(6), 556–564. doi:10.1002/jtr.1947

Bonne, K., Vermeir, I., Bergeaud-Blackler, F., & Verbeke, W. (2007). Determinants of halal meat consumption in France. *British Food Journal*, *9*(5), 367–386. doi:10.1108/0070700710746786

Conner, M., & Armitage, C. J. (1998). Extending the theory of planned behavior: Review and avenues for further research. *Journal of Applied Social Psychology*, *28*(15), 1429–1464. doi:10.1111/j.1559-1816.1998.tb01685.x

Correia, A., Santos, C. M., & Barros, C. P. (2007). Tourism in Latin America: A choice analysis. *Annals of Tourism Research*, *34*(3), 610–629. doi:10.1016/j.annals.2007.01.007

Courneya, K. S. (1994). Predicting repeated behavior from intention: The issue of scale correspondence. *Journal of Applied Social Psychology*, *24*(7), 580–594. doi:10.1111/j.1559-1816.1994.tb00601.x

Deuraseh, N. (2009). Lawful and unlawful foods in Islamic law focus on Islamic medical and ethical aspects. *International Food Research Journal*, *16*(4), 469–478.

Fishbein, M., & Ajzen, I. (1975). *Belief, Attitude, Intention, and Behaviour: An Introduction to Theory and Research*. Addison-Wesley.

Ghalandari, Kamal & Norouzi, A. (2012). The Effect of Country of Origin on Purchase Intention: The role of product knowledge. *Research Journal of Applied Sciences, Engineering and Technology*, *4*(9), 1166–1171.

Hamzah, A. (2010). Malaysian Homestays from the Perspective of Young Japanese Tourists. The Quest for Furusato. *Asian Tourism: Growth and Change, 2*. . doi:10.1016/B978-0-08-045356-9.50021-7

Hanafiah, M. H., & Hamdan, N. A. A. (2020). Determinants of Muslim travellers Halal food consumption attitude and behavioural intentions. *Journal of Islamic Marketing*.

Haque, N. A., Chowdhury, N. A., Yasmin, F., & Tarofder, A. K. (2019). Chowdhury, F. Yasmin, & A. K. Tarofder (2019). Muslim Consumers' Purchase Behavior Towards Shariah Compliant Hotels in Malaysia. *VJM*, *05*(1), 121–138. doi:10.31357/vjm.v5i1.3918

Hosseini, S. M. P., Mirzaei, M., & Iranmanesh, M. (2019). Determinants of Muslims' willingness to pay for halal certified food. *Journal of Islamic Marketing*.

Ibrahim, M. A., Fisol, W. N. M., & Haji-Othman, Y. (2017). Customer intention on Islamic home financing products: An application of theory of planned behavior (TPB). *Mediterranean Journal of Social Sciences*, *8*(2), 77–77. doi:10.5901/mjss.2017.v8n2p77

Ibrahim, Y. (2004). Homestay Programme in Malaysia. *ASEAN Journal on Hospitality and Tourism*, *3*(1), 65–75.

Iranmanesh, M., Mirzaei, M., Parvin Hosseini, S. M., & Zailani, S. (2019). Muslims' willingness to pay for certified halal food: An extension of the theory of planned behaviour. *Journal of Islamic Marketing*, *11*(1), 14–30. doi:10.1108/JIMA-03-2018-0049

Isa, S. M., Chin, P. N., & Mohammad, N. U. (2018). Muslim tourist perceived value: A study on Malaysia Halal tourism. *Journal of Islamic Marketing*, *9*(2), 402–420. doi:10.1108/JIMA-11-2016-0083

Johan, Z. J., Hussain, M. Z., Mohd, R., & Kamaruddin, B. H. (2020). Muslims and non-Muslims intention to hold Shariah-compliant credit cards: A SmartPLS approach. *Journal of Islamic Marketing*, *12*(9), 1751–1785. doi:10.1108/JIMA-12-2019-0270

Kasim, M. M., Kayat, K., Ramli, R., & Ramli, R. (2016). Sustainability Criteria for the Malaysia Homestay Programme. *International Review of Management and Marketing*, *6*, 1–7.

Khaled, Y., Eschweiler, S., & Gerhards-Padilla, E. (2013, October). REcompile: A decompilation framework for static analysis of binaries (Paper presentation). *8th International Conference on Malicious and Unwanted Software: The Americas (MALWARE),* IEEE.

Khaniwale, M. (2015). Consumer buying behaviour. *International Journal of Innovation and Scientific Research*, *14*(2), 278–286.

Lee, M. J., & Back, K. J. (2008). Association meeting participation: A test of competing models. *Journal of Travel Research*, *46*(3), 300–310. doi:10.1177/0047287507308320

Manap J.H., Hamzah A., Noah S.M., Kasan H., Krauss S.E., Mastor K.A, & Idris F., (2013). Prinsip pengukuran religiositi dan personaliti Muslim. *Jurnal Psikologi dan Pembangunan Manusia*, *1*(1), 36-43.

MOTAC. (2019). Statistik Program Pengalaman Homestay Malaysia tahun 2019. Kementerian Pelancongan, Seni dan Budaya, Kuala Lumpur.

Mutmainah, L. (2018). The role of religiosity, halal awareness, halal certification, and food ingredients on purchase intention of halal food. *Journal of Islamic Economics, Finance, and Banking*, *1*(1), 33–50. doi:10.12928/ijiefb.v1i1.284

Nguyen, T. D., Nguyen, T., & Barrett, N. J. (2010). Consumer ethnocentrism, cultural sensitivity, and intention to purchase local products evidence from Vietnam. *Journal of Consumer Behaviour*, *7*(1), 88–100. doi:10.1002/cb.238

Patwary, A. K., & Rashid, B. (2016). The impacts of hospitality services on visit experience and future visit intention of student travellers. *International Journal of Business and Technopreneurship*, *6*(8), 107–125.

Patwary, A. M., & Abdul, A., Hazbar, Abdulmalek S., N. Kamal, Mohammed, A., Azbar, H., & Kamal, N. (2018). Factors Influencing Consumers' Intentions towards Purchasing Islamic Hotel Service: Moderating Role of Religiosity. *International Journal of Management. Accounting and Economics*, *5*(7), 482–497.

Pradana, M., Garciac, R. H., & Marimon, F. (2020). Spanish Muslims' halal food purchase intention. *The International Food and Agribusiness Management Review, 9*(11), 434–461. doi:10.22434/IFAMR2019.0200

Prayag, G., Hosany, S., Muskat, B., & Del, C. G. (2017). Understanding the relationships between tourists' emotional experiences, perceived overall image, satisfaction, and intention to recommend. *Journal of Travel Research, 56*(1), 41–54. doi:10.1177/0047287515620567

Richards, G., & Hall, D. (2000). *The Community: A Sustainable Concept in Tourism Development*. Routledge. doi:10.4324/9780203464915_chapter_1

Rizkitysha, T. L., & Hananto, A. (2020). Do knowledge, perceived usefulness of halal label and religiosity affect attitude and intention to buy halal-labelled detergent? *Journal of Islamic Marketing*. . doi:10.1108/JIMA-03-2020-0070

Said, M., Hassan, F., Musa, R., & Rahman, N. A. (2014). Assessing Consumers' Perception, Knowledge and Religiosity on Malaysia's Halal Food Products. *Procedia: Social and Behavioral Sciences, 130*, 120–128. doi:10.1016/j.sbspro.2014.04.015

Salleh, A. S. A., Suki, N. M., Hashim, N., & Abang, A. S. (2020). Sobel Statistical Test on the Mediation Effect of Halal Image Toward Intention to Patronage Retail Stores. *ECON-Journal of Economics, Management & Business, 8*(3).

Setyawati, L. M., Chairy, S. J., & Syahrivar, J. (2019). Factors affecting intention to buy halal food by the millennial generation: The mediating role of attitude. *Jurnal Manajemen, 14*(2), 175–188. doi:10.1108/BFJ-10-2016-0455

Swan, J. (1981). Disconfirmation of expectations and satisfaction with a retail service. *Journal of Retailing, 57*(3), 49–66.

Syukur, M., & Nimsai, S. (2018). Factors influencing the purchase intention of halal packaged food in Thailand. *Int. J Sup. Chain. Mgt, 7*(4), 1–6.

The Star Online. (2018). Making Malaysia a top choice, no MATTA what. *The Star Online*. https://www.thestar.com.my/news/nation/2018/09/09/making-msia-a-top-choice-no-matta-what-minister-lauds-efforts-to-drive-tourism-industry-further

Ustaahmetoglu, E. (2020). The influence of different advertisement messages and levels of religiosity on attitude and purchase intention. *International Journal of Islamic and Middle Eastern Finance and Management*. . doi:10.1108/IMEFM-02-2019-0064

Wu, P. C., Yeh, G. Y. Y., & Hsiao, C. R. (2011). The effect of store image and service quality on brand image and purchase intention for private label brands. [AMJ]. *Australasian Marketing Journal, 19*(1), 30–39. doi:10.1016/j.ausmj.2010.11.001

Wu, W., Zhou, L., & Chien, H. (2019). Impact of Consumer Awareness, Knowledge, and Attitudes on Organic Rice Purchasing Behaviour in China. *Journal of Food Products Marketing, 25*(5), 549–565. doi:10.1080/10454446.2019.1611515

Yunus, N. S. N. M., Rashid, W. E. W., Ariffin, N. M., & Rashid, N. M. (2014). Muslim's Purchase Intention towards Non-Muslim's Halal Packaged Food Manufacturer. *Procedia: Social and Behavioral Sciences, 130*, 145–154. doi:10.1016/j.sbspro.2014.04.018

Yusof, N., Mohd Shariff, N., & Omar., H. (2019). Examining the importance of Muslim friendly facilities perceived by international Muslim tourists to Malaysia. *International Academic Journal of Social Sciences and Education, 2*(1), 262–274.

Yusof, N. S., Ramli, K. I., & Mohd Shariff, N. (2016). Image of Malaysia as a Halal destination (Paper presentation). *Prosiding Pengurusan Halal, Ekonomi dan Perniagaan 2016*, UUM.

Zakaria, N. B., Yunos, R. M., Mahmood, C. F. C., Anita, R., & Said, J. (2017). The effect of consumers' interest, information access and spending willingness on halal products trustworthiness. *Asia-Pacific Management Accounting Journal, 12*(2), 183–200.

Zhang, H., Wu, Y., & Buhalis, D. (2018). A model of perceived image, memorable tourism experiences and revisit intention. *Journal of Destination Marketing & Management, 8*, 326–336. doi:10.1016/j.jdmm.2017.06.004

Chapter 7
How Islamic Relational Capital Is Being Explored

Yusmazida Mohd Yusoff
https://orcid.org/0000-0002-6360-8131
Universiti Teknologi MARA, Malaysia

ABSTRACT

This study aims to develop a relational capital model from an Islamic perspective. This study uses qualitative research that involves three 3 focus group discussions including three zones. The data were then transcribed verbatim and analyzed using the Nvivo application. Empirical findings revealed that five sub-themes (conflict management, customer satisfaction as a priority, enhancing professional networking, mutual respect, practicing Islamic good governance, and produce halal toyyiban product) formed Islamic relational capital. The present study only includes Muslim SME organization in its determinant framework of Islamic relational in Malaysia. This study serves as guidelines to policymakers, and Muslim and non-Muslim organizations to improve SMEs' competitiveness. Academics and practitioners could also refer to this study to enhance the knowledge of relational capital from an Islamic perspective.

1. BACKGROUND

In a knowledge-based economy, the world focuses more on intangible assets rather than tangible assets to achieve better performance (Agostini, Nosella, & Filippini, 2017; Allameh et al., 2010). Intangible assets are believed to ensure the survival of the organisation (Obeng, Robson & Haugh, 2014), encourage value creation (Berezinets, Garanina & Ilina, 2016; Edvinsson & Malone, 1997; Firer, 2005; Sullivan, 1999) and improve competitive advantage (Bontis, 1996; Marr, Gray & Neely, 2003; Petty & Guthrie, 2000; Roos, 2017). All organisations are trying to improve their value whether monetary or nonmonetary.

The term "intangibles" or "intangible assets" also refers to intellectual capital (IC) (Alcaniz, Gomez-Bezares & Roslender, 2011; Petty and Guthrie, 2000). Organisations that have a higher IC will benefit more than those with a poor IC (Ahmad & Ahmed, 2016). According to Khalique et al. (2011) intellectual capital is an important resource for an organization to succeed in a competitive environment. Thus, organizations must competently control and stored knowledge (Bontis, 1998; Bontis et al., 2005). Besides

DOI: 10.4018/978-1-6684-7519-5.ch007

that, this topic has gained relevant attention among practitioners and academics (Berezinets, Garanina & Ilina, 2016; Cordazzo, 2005; Edvinsson & Malone, 1997; Firer, 2005; Keong Choong, 2008; Kujansivu & Lönnqvist, 2007; Secundo, Ndou, Vecchio & De Pascale, 2020; Starovic & Marr, 2004; Sullivan, 1999). Recently, Berezinets, Garanina and Ilina (2016) suggested IC as a weapon for overcoming the weakness of SMEs (Jordão & de Almeida, 2017; Verbano & Crema, 2016).

Relational capital (RC) is one dimension of the IC. Brooking (1996) view relational capital (RC) as market assets that refer to the potential an organisation has due to market related intangibles such as brands, customers and their loyalty, backlog, repeat business, distribution channels, various contracts and agreements such as licensing, franchises and so on. Market assets are important because they give companies a competitive market. Roos and Roos (1997) defines RC as "all the relationships that organisations have, such as customers, consumers, intermediaries, representatives, suppliers, partners, owners, lenders and the like." Roos et al. (1997) noted that RC could not be controlled and owned by the organisation. However, it may have an impact on the relationship. In other words, the organisation does not own its relationship, but enables it to influence it.

Edvinsson and Malone (1997) describe RC as a customer capital embedded in structural capital which focus to develop relationships with customers. Bontis (1998) also refer RC as "customer capital" or as all relationships between organizations and their customers, stakeholders, suppliers, community and government. In addition, Bontis (2001) stressed that RC is a knowledge embedded in external relationships. RC can also be defined as collective relationships that enable organisations to cooperate with other organisations Capello (2002) and individuals (Kostova & Roth, 2003; Shipilov & Danis, 2006) strong understanding, relationship, collaboration and trust among suppliers, alliance partners and channels (Capello & Faggian, 2005).

Currently, various resource management issues have closely related to religious roots such as how to pleasure employees appropriately and the influence of religion are of is at importance, but they are hardly studied because of the dominance of Western management solutions (Hashim, 2009). This means that they try to manage with theories and modify their relationships with employer and employer must base on Quran base Sunnah.

The reason behind that is Islam has the second highest second-highest lowers among all religions, with approximately 1.5 billion Muslims globally, and it is one of the fastest growing religions (Mellahi & Budhwar, 2010). Moreover, the study conducted in 2015 highlighted that Islam comprised of 23.9 percent of the population that have 1.8 billion believers (Lipka and Hackett, 2017). In addition, by 2050, Muslims are projected to increase until 2.6 billion believers worldwide (Alam & Sayuti, 2011). Currently, attempts have been made to study Islamic finance (Ledhem & Mekidiche, 2022) and Islamic leadership (Moghimi, 2018), Islamic marketing (S. A. Shah et al., 2022; Suandi et al., 2022). The search for Islamic management literature indicates the lack of sufficient content on Islamic RC. Furthermore, through literature survey, the researcher found, no such research focusing on RC from the Islamic perspective.

Thus, this study is a unique attempt to develop the features as well as a model of Islamic RC to help those business leaders, managers, and employees of today to ascertain a morally based competitiveness model namely Islamic Relational Capital (*Silah*). It is expected that this study will contribute to policy implications for Muslim countries, mainly in SMEs, as a backbone of national economic development and to share ideas across the academic fields. It is believed that this is the first study done on this concept that fills the big research gap in Islamic management literature.

1.1 Objectives of the Study

The objective of this study is to model relational capital (RC) from Islamic perspective as no inclusive study perspective has been undertaken. Only a few studies highlighting this issue, however, were not fully and critically throw lighted from Islamic viewpoint.

1.2 Practical Implications

The important practical implication for SME managers is that the guidelines provided from this study can be implemented within the organization. Managers must revise their current practice regarding human capital development based on Islamic perspective. Also, the policymakers can use these references to create new policies in the future. This study also intends to fill the gap in the existing literature by adapting Islamic values on the human capital concept. Moreover, the results showed the originality this is the first study that explored the components of relational capital based on Islamic point of view among Muslim SMEs in Malaysia that can be used globally.

2. LITERATURE REVIEW

2.1 Intellectual Capital

Previous researchers have their own intellectual capital (IC) classification regarding to research subjects and background, and there seems to be no consistent formulation. In their book, Intellectual Capital Core Asset for the Third Millennium Enterprise, Brooking (1996) sees IC as a broad term that can be split into four categories namely market assets, intellectual property assets, human-centred assets and infrastructure assets. Market assets are the potential an organisation has due to market related intangibles such as brands, customers and their loyalty, backlog, repeat business, distribution channels, various contracts, and agreements such as licensing, franchises and so on. Intellectual property (IP) assets include trade secret, know-how, copy-right, patent, and various design rights. Human-centred assets comprise the collective expertise, creative and problem-solving capability, leadership, entrepreneurial and managerial skills embodied by the employees of the organisation. Infrastructure assets are those technologies, methodologies, and processes, that enable the organisation to function.

Roos and Roos (1997) assert that the three common classification of IC by many authors is based on their economic behaviour, which are relational capital, organisational capital and human capital. Edvinsson and Malone (1997) categorized IC into human capital and structural capital. Rezende (2001) suggests three categories of IC namely individual competence assets, structure assets and market assets. This classification proposed by Rezende (2001) is similar to Lev (2001), Rocha (2012), Rodrigues, Dorrego, Fernández and Fernández (2009). Subramaniam and Youndt (2005) present IC as comprising human, organisational and social capital. Reed et al. (2006) create a similar distinction state that IC comprised of human, organisational and social capital. Zerenler, Hasiloglu and Sezgin (2008) categorised IC into three elements namely employee capital, customer capital and structural capital.

Hayton (2005) maintains that the different definitions of IC are due to the lack of a converging approach in terms of their classification due to scholars, which generally classifies IC between two or four dimensions of IC. Therefore, Kujansivu and Lönnqvist (2007) acknowledge that the classification of IC is difficult to establish. However, from the review of past literatures, this study concludes that the wide agreement of IC categories have three constituents namely human capital, structural capital and relational capital. Structural capital is one dimension of the IC and can be considered as main components that give more advantages within an organisation and that require bigger consideration by top management (Bontis et al., 2018; Zahra et al., 2018).

2.2 Islamic Relational Capital

Youndt, Subramaniam and Snell (2004) define social capital as "relationships that are not limited to internal knowledge among employees, but also extend to linkages with customers, suppliers, alliance partners and the like". Cabrita and Bontis (2008) assert RC can also mean the knowledge that embedded in networking with suppliers, customers, competitors or stakeholders. One of the contributors in this field, Allameh (2018) defines RC as the total assets that organize relationships with the environment. This includes the relationship between the organization and its customers, suppliers, competitors, shareholders, government, society and public institutions (Chahal & Bakshi, 2015; Han & Li, 2015; Hsu & Fang, 2009). RC also is described as the ability of an organisation in creating relational value with its external shareholders such as customers, resource providers and shareholders (Bontis, 2001; Jardon & Martos, 2012; Joshi et al., 2010).

Bontis (1998) notes that RC is the attitude of an organisation to accept the knowledge received from the interaction with the external stakeholders such as customers, suppliers, community and associated network. The same agreements with other contributors asserted that RC is the knowledge obtained from the establishment of relationship with business stakeholders (Johnson, 1999) (Kweh & Wang, 2014; Yu, Wang, & Chang, 2015). Collaboration accelerates the transfer of knowledge and technology between the parties (Nieto & Santamaría, 2007). Joshi et al. (2010) argues that retaining RC is more important than just creating RC. Investment in RC is essential to enhance the organisation's relationship with stakeholders, including customers and suppliers, in order to enhance their image (Esther et al., 2011). They note that the image of the organisation is linked to the trust of the customer and the supplier. In other words, there is a significant positive relationship between SC and business success.

Like the other two dimensions of IC, only few studies discussed on Islamic relational capital concept. This study will explore other dimensions of RC that was missing in the field involving Muslim SMEs and proposed new novel concept which is called Islamic RC (*Silah*).

3. METHODOLOGY

3.1 Research Design

To answer the research questions as explained above, this study used a basic qualitative approach to collect and analyze data. The researcher is the key instrument in qualitative research. Also, an interview guide was developed to conducting focus group discussion (FGD), which to discover the structural capital in Islamic perspectives among Muslim SMEs in Malaysia. The discussions were recorded using a voice recorder to guarantee that rich data were attained. The data then then transcribed verbatim and analyzed to produce themes.

Figure 1. Model of Islamic relational capital (Silah)

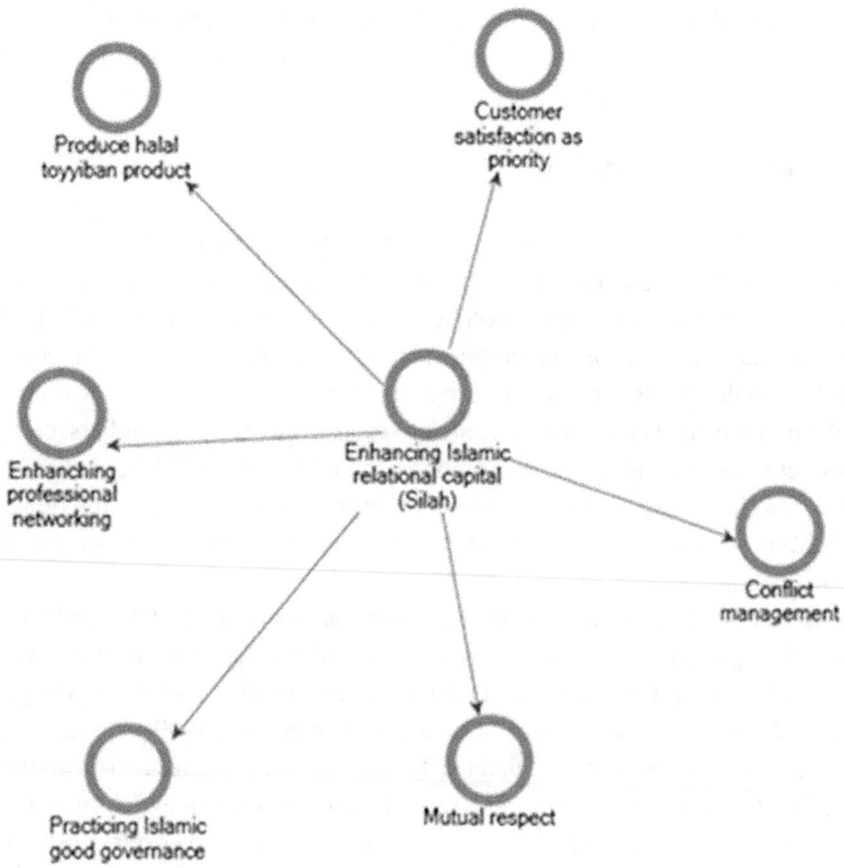

3.2 Sampling

Informants were chosen among Muslim SMEs who holds the position as owners, founders or even managers from three zones (Central, East and North). Information about the participants was obtained through the list of SMEs registered with the Malay Chamber of Commerce in Malaysia. The informants were selected from different sectors, such as food, health, beauty and saloon, hardware, printing, property, and retail. This study also appointed five religious people that give guidance and advise on Quran and Hadith. Purposive sampling was used where the informants must fill the specific criteria include hold the top position in management, at least one year business operation, be easily contacted and be ready to join in this study. Various approach to contact informants thru WhatsApp, telephone and Email. After an informant's consent had been confirmed, a date, time and venue were provided for data collection. The objective of the study, the procedure of data collection and the sign of informant's consent were briefly explained before the discussion began.

3.3 Data Collection and Analysis

The informants were from three zones include central, north, and east zone. Before the actual discussion session, the researcher contacted the informants to introduce researcher and the purpose of the study and how the discussions would be conducted. This was done to ensure the informants feel comfortable to share information in the actual discussion sessions. At the discussions themselves, the same things were explained to the informants. The session starts with basic questions about their background. The discussions used structured questions that were provided before the discussion sessions by the researcher. Each discussion was transcribed verbatim and then analyzed to recognize codes, categories and theme. Nvivo application was used to help in managing and analyzing data during the data analysis process.

4. FINDINGS AND DISCUSSION

Section below describes respondent profiles and findings of this study.

4.1 Profile of Respondents

In this study, three Focus Group Discussion (FGD) were involved. The list of informants shown in Table 1.

4.2 Dimension of Islamic Relational Capital

Based on the FGD sessions, five themes were identified to answer the research question: (1) Conflict management; (2) Customer satisfaction as priority; (3) Enhancing professional networking; (4) Mutual respect; (5) Practicing Islamic good governance; (6) Produce halal toyyiban product, Sub-theme and category illustrated in Table 2.

4.2.1 Conflict Management

Based on this study, there are two sub-theme found in conflict management include good communication skills and good in managing conflict.

4.2.1.1 Good Communication Skills

Communication is generally understanding as the spread, sharing, or discuss of the ideas, thoughts, information, perceptions between two or more people (K. Shah & D'Souza, 2008). The Quran postulates "The most gracious (Allah SWT)! It is he who taught the Quran: he has created man: he taught him speech (Surah Al-Rahman:1-4)." This study was extended for examining an opinion based on Muslim SMEs's perspective. Central Zone 1 highlighted that:

"Younger generation should learn more on communication skills. They used unproper word to treat people. For example, the word "*akak*" and "*sis*". They don't know to differentiate between these two words based on the right setting. Same goes to student nowadays. Most of them have lack of communication skills which is very important in working environment."

Table 1. Demographic profile

Zone	FGD	Informant	Years of operation	Sector
Central	Central Zone 1	Religious Expert		
		Owner 1	10	Food Supplement
		Owner 2	3	Hardware
		Owner 3	2	Food
	Central Zone 2	Owner 1	2	Supplement
	Central Zone 3	Owner 1	5	Retail
North	North Zone 1	Religious Expert		
		Owner 1	20	Printing
		Owner 2	20	Printing
		Owner 3	3	Interior design
		Owner 4	3	Interior design
		Owner 5	5	Online Business
	North Zone 2	Religious Expert		
		Owner 1	6	Online Trader
		Owner 2	2	Printing
		Owner 3	8	Fresh Mart
		Owner 4	7	Hardware
		Owner 5	6	Printing
East	East Zone 1	Religious Expert	3	Property
		Owner 1	3	Property
		Owner 2	2	Food
		Owner 3	5	Hardware
		Owner 4	7	Construction
	East Zone 2	Religious Expert		
		Owner 1	5	Retail
		Owner 2	16	Beauty & Spa
		Owner 3	4	Online Business
		Owner 4	5	Food

The finding also found that the employees must equipped with unformal training like how to great people. In light of this, individuals should deliver the message well and communicate in manner that it pleases Allah SWT. Islam teach kindness and politeness in communication towards others. On the contrary, Allah SWT abhorred disrespect towards people, backbiting, liar and two-faced personality. Communication in Islam goes beyond to teach Muslims what, when, how and to whom we speak and why.

4.2.1.2 Good in Managing Conflict

Conflicts describes to disagreement, struggle or incompatibility between individuals or teams or within organizations (Rahim, 2010). Conflicts is negative perception of individual's behavior or action that

Table 2. Theme and categories

Islamic structural capital (*Baniah*)	**Theme 1**
Conflict management	**Sub-Theme**
Good communication skills	
Good in managing conflict	
Customer satisfaction as priority	**Sub-Theme**
Customer feedback from social media	
Customer needs	
Customer-friendly	
Effort to get customer feedback	
Good communication with customer	
Implement *akad* with customer	
Managing after sales issues	
Enhancing professional networking	**Sub-Theme**
Attending seminar for networking	
Mutual respect	**Sub-Theme**
Consult staff personally	
Create greetings as norm in workplace	
Maintaining relationship employer-employee	
Take care for the staff	
Use right words when talking to the staff	
Practicing Islamic good governance	
Auditing	
Belief in business is about worship	
Business plan based on KPI	
Empowering Integrity Department	
Ethical in business	
Get middle management brief about task	
Good in time management	
Good reporting flow	
Shariah advisor position in organization	
Produce halal toyyiban product	
Clean and hygiene product	
Halalan toyyiban product	
Produce Islamic product	
Sell only quality product	
Use halal gelatin in product	

causes harm (Trudel & Reio, 2011). Increasing diversity in the workplace brings various advantages to organization, also raises the chance of conflicts.

Islam views conflicts as normal scenario in organization. Allah SWT says: "And if your Lord had willed, He could have made mankind one community; but they will not cease to differ (Surah Hud 11: 118). These verses proved that Allah SWT purposely create discrepancies among mankind. From that, they can think and solve problem in creative ways according to Islamic guidelines. The principle of conflict management has been reviewed in the Quran both in specific and general contexts (49:9-13, 5:8, 2:213, 10:19, 43:65, 3:105, 45:17, 16:64, 8:55). Similarly, the Prophet Muhammad trained his followers by example on how to cope with conflicts in many situations. Conflict management is observed throughout the life of the Prophet Muhammad (Abu-Nimer, 2001; Monjur, 2011; Sarif et al., 2004). Central Zone 1 highlighted that: "It is very difficult to handle 30 female staffs. In this case, we must get help from our religious advisor in our company to solve any conflict occur. The solution is very important because it will affect our packaging production process."

East Zone 2 mentioned:

"The Prophet used gentleness. It will always adorn the deeds. Gentle here means, not shimmering, not bouncy. It's kind of a Prophet, gentle but firm. It has been said that the Prophet was not a critic. But when A was said by the Prophet, it was A."

North Zone 2:

نوفلتخي هيف اميف مهنيب يضقل كبر نم تقبس ةملك الولوءاوفلتخاف ةدحاو ةمأ الإ سانلا ناك امو

And mankind was not but one community [united in religion], but [then] they differed. And if not for a word that preceded from your Lord, it would have been judged between them [immediately] concerning that over which they differ. (Surah Yunus: 19)

مالس اولاق نولهاجلا مهبطاخ اذإو انوه ضرألا ىلع نوشمى نىذلا نمحرلا دابعو

The ⌜true⌝ servants of the Most Compassionate are those who walk on the earth humbly, and when the foolish address them ⌜improperly⌝, they only respond with peace.

4.2.2 Customer Satisfaction as Priority

Customer satisfaction is an essential construct in the marketing literature, owing to its ability to generate customer loyalty and sustainable long-term profit for the organization (Liu and Jang, 2009). Holbrook (2012) suggested satisfaction as one of the significant goals of marketing and related activities. Some researchers assert that customer satisfaction is the fundamental concern of marketing (Cronin et al., 2000; Brady and Cronin, 2001). Existing literature identifies customer satisfaction to affect customer retention (Cronin et al., 2000; Jin et al., 2012). Anderson and Sullivan (1993) identified customer satisfaction as an effective way of maintaining a long-term relationship with the firm.

4.2.2.1 Customer Feedback From Social Media

To ensure customer satisfaction, the study found that giving feedback to customer thru social media is very important. East Zone 2 mentioned that the comment in social media is setting to public. It allows their customers to give comments and recommendations openly. For product that wrongly posted, they will give back it to the customer.

4.2.2.2 Customer Needs

This study found that to achieve customer satisfaction, a company must understand the customer's need. East Zone 1 highlighted: "My employee as a driver received complaints from customers where he is a talkative person. Some customers dislike the behavior. In this situation, I advised my employee to focus on their job without too friendly with the customer. Consequently, no comments received from them."

Other opinion also raised by respondent from construction service where it is not directly involved the customer. However, there have an issue among contractor in which they give advanced payment. This is malpractice in this industry. In terms of food industry, Central Zone 3 ensures all products in good quality and not exceed expired date. There are two reasons for the importance of customer needs. First, it shows whether a company is doing the right things for the customer and second the customer they will repeat buying. Besides, any mistakes by company starts with apologies to the customer and provide feedback.

4.2.2.3 Customer-Friendly

Constomer-friendly is another elusive concept. It makes absolute business sense to reach customer-friendly that covers the entire customer experience in terms of products, services, and user interfaces. Central Zone 3 noted that conversational greeting is an essential which adds a human touch to the whole experience. "We assume our customers are all Muslims. So, always greet customer with religious greeting. So does to other celebration like Hari Raya Aidilfitri or AidilAdha."

This statement also agreed by East Zone 1 noted: "In my organisation, culture is simple, customer-friendly, easy to deal with." As for East Zone 2: "For staff that work in counter, if they give wrong balance that exceeds the actual, I asked them to give it back. Instead, advise them to accept responsibility for their mistake ensure not repeat the same mistake."

4.2.2.4 Effort to Get Customer Feedback

Customer feedback is very important to measure complaints (Bosch and Enrıquez, 2005) and satisfaction (Hallencreutz & Parmler, 2021). For example, customer feedback collected from criticism submitted to customer service employees is a standard channel producing activation triggers for providers (Gremyr et al., 2022). Central Zone 1 reported: "We use phone and WhatsApp to get feedback from our customer. We are asking for permission to take screenshot as our testimony. We don't have a formal CRM (Customer Relationship Management). We still use manual. But we decide to use it later as database keep increasing." Other respondents highlighted the same approach to get customer feedback which is using social media platform. For example, Central Zone 2 using Facebook. That example captures the importance of customer feedback.

Another example of getting customer feedback is through religious person where only them can claim this product halal. They also can try the products to take a testimony. Central Zone 3 stressed the importance to treat customer well even the customer is too arrogant to lodge their complaints. In this case, business must investigate the root caused and provide a longer answer for such inquiries. Other views from East Zone 1:"We access from sales, attitude, and behaviour. The way he talks to us, customers, manager, and also to his family in which we also care about. Not in the written form through WhatsApp, speak and eat."

East Zone 2 believed customer feedback is essential component for service enhancements as suggested by (Caemmerer & Alan, 2010). The respondents logged in the customer complaints through a formal complaint system which is form and compulsory for them to answer. From the above responses, it can be concluded that an important factor is the ability to take necessary actions instantly for improvements (Lervik Olsen et al., 2014; Nagati and Rebolledo, 2012; Sony et al., 2020).

4.2.2.5 Good Communication With Customer

The ability to communicate well is the most essential requirement of employee's personality. There are certain qualities to ensure success in communication from both in oral and written forms. Moreover, a single message is strong enough to achieve customer engagement. Currently, business is struggling to meet customer expectations. To success in communication not only depends on putting your opinions but expressing them in a way that would get the attention of the receiver at the same time (Beattie & Ellis, 2014). Central Zone 1 stressed the importance of word used when communicate to customer: "If the customer is a girl, please call Sis and sir for male. Don't call "brother" that is not appropriate in our business setting. This must apply to written communication through WhatsApp. Make it a formal. If the customer requests a picture, we will respond quickly. Because if you are doing business online, if it's slow, 5 or 10 minutes, people will be looking for someone else."

Some respondents also attend training course to learn copywriting and applied it to their posting in social media platform. Central Zone 1: "I have gone to the training. Do copywriting anyhow. Copywriting, we didn't learn things like that. Technology, so I have got to learn. Kind of copywriting, kind of verse. So, that's what I implemented in my posting." This statement agreed by East Zone 1: "We have template in communicating with customer. The template is written from experience, searching through the internet, and we are always going to the courses. And we are also extracting from there. We also get information sharing from competitors."

North Zone 3: "Okay, an example of communication between employees and customers, we have SOP on how to talk to customers. How prudent is the way. We have got scripts that make SOP scripts, the way we want to talk. The script we did was a good one. The findings also show that majority of the respondents were using business number." However, Central Zone 2 have their own reason in selecting personal phone number. The mentioned, "People like personal ones. People like human touch, even on the phone. Well, he knows that number. If it was a business, there would be an automatic reply. But if we follow the real, we ourselves, the people, we can know how to respond. This is a really tiring start. That's why we are trying to develop team.

East Zone 1 posited: "We ask the customer directly what the problem is. If there is a problem, we are going to give the fast response. While East Zone 2 have their own approach "We have a feedback form, and if the customer isn't happy, we will call him to talk face to face about how we can improve our operations. When it comes to speaking, I always remind staff to use good language with customers. If I want to give the customer the balance, I tell him to place it on the customer's hand, not to put anywhere else. I just want to express my gratitude. I have a google form for appointments during the PKP season. Usually, my customers are from high level income."

North Zone 2:

إن أحسنتم أحسنتم لأنفسكم وإن أسأتم فلها فإذا جاء وعد الآخرة ليسوءوا وجوهكم وليدخلوا المسجد كما دخلوه أول مرة وليتبروا
ما علوا تتبيرا

[And said], "If you do good, you do good for yourselves; and if you do evil, [you do it] to yourselves." Then when the final promise came, [We sent your enemies] to sadden your faces and to enter the temple in Jerusalem, as they entered it the first time, and to destroy what they had taken over with [total] destruction.

4.2.2.6 Implement Akad With Customer

In SMEs business setting, the business transaction complete with "akad" which is purchase agreement from both seller and customer. North Zone 3: "It is like one declaration. I sell to you, you sign. The most important thing is, my intention to sell." According to Mazhab Shafie', the legal conditions for sale and purchasing in Islam is the purchase agreement (*akad*). The findings also found that *akad* is flexible. In certain case, the customer orders the goods and seller will post it later. The payment will make after that. This is we called a reservation.

4.2.2.7 Managing After Sales Issues

Managing after sales service has a great impact on customer loyalty. It is a big part of business to create close relationships with customers so that they can trust. Generally, customer who satisfied with product or service offers, tends to come back. Majority of respondents believed that excellent customer sales service is a source of profit and business improvement. However, the findings found several challenges to manage after sales issues for SMEs business.

Central Zone 2: "My customer faced a negative effect after consuming the supplement. Some of them decided to stop eating. To settle this issue, we go live to explain to all customers. During that time, very lucky other customer also agreed that the have negative effect for a while. And become normal after that. Normally, the customer is going to believe what other customers say." As for Central Zone 3:"Sometimes, we overlooked on customer complaints. We encourage them to share it quickly. That's the way we want to monitor customer feedback." East Zone 2 noted: "My staff also posted the wrong item to customer. For example, they order the day cream, but my staff posted the night cream. We contact the customer immediately and talk nicely explaining what was happening. Next, I asked my staff to cover the postage cost so that she could me more careful. So, I will make sure my staff no repeat the same mistake. I have a briefing every day once a week in my place. We are going to focus on such things. We share the mistake during the session. Other than that, is, we provide feedback form. If the customer isn't happy, we will call them to talk face to face about how we can improve our operations."

4.2.3 Enhancing Professional Networking

The importance of close long-term relationships in business has long been studied in marketing research that focus on supply chain (Kozlenkova, Hult, Lund, Mena & Kekec, 2015; Wathne & Heide, 2004) and also distribution channels (Anderson & Narus, 1990; Krafft et al., 2015). In fact, long-term relationships differentiate business markets from consumer markets (Keep et al., 1998).

4.2.3.1 Attending Seminar for Networking

From a personal standpoint, learning value is an important value from seminars and events (Sheth et al., 1991) as highlighted by Central Zone 2: "I attend to a lot of seminars. A lot of people I meet offline and can gain my knowledge."

This demonstrates organizational learning value which has been associated to absorptive capacity include recognition, assimilation, knowledge exploitation (Berghman, L., Matthyssens, P. Vandenbempt, 2011) and increased from the ability of manipulating existing competencies through sharing and effective knowledge transformation (Möller & Rajala, 2007).

4.2.4 Mutual Respect

In Islamic perspective, there should have mutual respect among Muslims. Prophet (pbuh) highlights in his last speech: Hurt no one so that no one may hurt you. Remember that you will indeed meet your LORD, and that HE will indeed reckon your deeds. All mankind is from Adam and Eve, an Arab has no superiority over a non-Arab nor a non-Arab has any superiority over an Arab; also, a white has no superiority over black nor does a black have any superiority over white except by piety and good action.

Allah SWT says: "O Mankind! We have created you from a male and a female, and made you into nations and tribes, that you may know one another. Verily, the most honourable of you in the Sight of Allah is the believer who has Taqwa (faithfulness and righteousness). Verily, Allah is All-Knowing, All Aware (Quran, 49:13)." Developing mutual respecting culture in business it would be easier to create cohesiveness and unity among organisational members.

4.2.4.1 Consult Staff Personally

Central Zone 1: "We always call our staff and sit down. We are giving them advice." While East Zone 1:"I am very strict when it comes to work. If you want 2 o'clock, 1.30 is already on my desk. But even if it's a personal matter, my staff will meet me and talk. We had lunch together. She's going to talk about personal problems. But, she knows, when it comes to work. No compromise."

For business that hire village people, they have another method: "Usually, I meet my staff directly. If I need to give them advice, I will advise when salary time. I'm using cash because they from village that prefer cash rather than bank in. East Zone 2: "I told my staff to work hard and sincere. Some of them have family problems and bring them to work. They feel lazy and depressed. To cater this issue, I always discuss personally with them asking what was happening and provide suggestions based on Islamic guideline."

4.2.4.2 Create Greetings as Norm in Workplace

One the important element of mutual respect including create greetings as norm in workplace in Islam is that social groups should communicate nicely which offer happiness and peace of mind of the employees. The Prophet (SAW) encourages that to give greetings and smiling in front of colleagues displaying them respect. Prophet Muhammad said: "You shall not enter Paradise until you believe; and you will not believe until you love one another. Shall I not guide you to a thing? Which when done, will make you love one another: Spread the greeting of Salam among you (Muslim)."

East Zone 2: "First, I share the positive through smile. It follows the Islamic standpoints; individual should communicate nicely that it pleases Allah. Islam encourages kindness and politeness in conversation while communicating."

4.2.4.3 Maintaining Relationship Employer-Employee

The goal of a business is to maintaining good relationship which will increase profits for the business as a whole result in higher returns for the company as a whole. Central Zone 1:"Business might look like in production. But also need to give full attention on employee welfare. One of my employees is Chinese. We are making good friends and always talk to him to reduce insecure in himself."

4.2.5 Practicing Islamic Good Governance

Governance is a process and practices that help organization to make important decision ((IOG), 2003). In Islam viewpoint, the objectives of good governance principles is based one Tawheed concept (Al-Faruqi, 1986). SMEs business is no exception. Good governance can guide the decision-making process of management. Nevertheless, like larger organizations, SMEs business have also experienced financial scandals that received less public exposure. Moreover, good governance would require SMEs manager to responsible to Allah and people anywhere and anytime. Muslims would account for their actions in the hereafter.

In brief, there are nine domains of good governance conceptualized in this study include belief in business is about worship, business plan based on KPI, empowering Integrity Department, ethical in business, get middle management brief about task, good in time management, good reporting flow and shariah advisor position in organization

4.2.5.1 Auditing

Central Zone 1: "Audit is required for certification, as it is compulsory. You must truly open everything like accounts, factory, among other things. Every day, we check the sales. Every year, we hire an accountant to audit our income taxes."

4.2.5.2 Belief in Business is About Worship

Central Zone 1 also mentioned: "The 9/10 sustenance comes from a business. We are sitting, the longest near the surau is an hour or two, but we cannot make our business an act of worship."

4.2.5.3 Business Plan Based on KPI

East Zone 2: "I can say, my business plan is excellent. I started from small business to large and can grow. So, this business cn go larger when the product is nationalized and use machine. The manpower will be decreased. The manufacture of this paste can therefore go to a large extent when the product is nationalized. That's one of the reasons for that. I don't need a lot of workers because I have a huge number of machines."

4.2.5.4 Empowering Integrity Department

Central Zone 1: "We don't have a integrity department. But we have been supervised by shariah advisor. If we want to make a drop of our own, we will find advice from him."

4.2.5.5 Ethical in Business

North Zone 2:

هللا نإضرألا يف داسفلا غبت الوكيلإ هللا نسحأ امك نسحأوايندلا نم كبيصن سنت الوةرخآلا رادلا هللا كاتآ اميف غتباو
نيدسفملا بحي ال

But seek, through that which Allah has given you, the home of the Hereafter; and [yet], do not forget your share of the world. And do good as Allah has done good to you. And desire not corruption in the land. Indeed, Allah does not like corrupters."

4.2.5.6 Get Middle Management Brief About Task

East Zone 1: "I pay attention to the low-level staff. If anything happen, I am going to call the project manager who's going to give advice to them, not me." The same response to other informant: "Me too. First, I am going to talk to some senior staff. After that, look at their suggestions on what to do."

4.2.5.7 Good in Time Management

East Zone 1: "Let's say, for example, there's a chef, he's always ordering a hotel in bulk. So we need to focus on them. Focus on this production. That's why we always remind the staff, we want to break, we want to break in half an hour, we want to pray, and we want to eat. Okay, so come back, we usually don't let him out of here."

4.2.5.8 Good Reporting Flow

Central Zone 1: "Like near Minsyam, we have meetings for production every day, every morning. Okay, today we have a job, 300 thousand, 2 productions, 600 thousand right. This is what I want, this is how you are going to do it and make it happen. Managers need to report back to me."

4.2.5.9 Shariah Advisor Position in Organization

One of the most differentiate features Central Zone 1 is that they have their own Shariah advisor. The role of Shariah advisor is to give advice regarding to all matter in business to follow Islamic guidelines including product, marketing and other business process. It is essential for SMEs to have this kind of position in their business. Not all SMEs implemented it.

4.2.6. Produce Halal Toyyiban Product

This study identified factors which related to produce halal toyyiban product include clean and hygiene product, halalan toyyiban product, produce Islamic product, sell only quality product and use halal gelatin in product.

4.2.6.1 Clean and Hygiene Product

East Zone 3:

We are looking at hygiene product. I have a food truck and provide internship for students. There were two Chinese students. But I do have to concern things like that. Wear gloves and other hygiene in Islam.

4.2.7 Halalan Toyyiban Product

The informants were concern over all halal matters. Muslims will be eager to look at halal-certified food labeled in particularly Islamic countries. According to Central Zone 2, halalan toyyiban product must clean and hygiene. Informants also mentioned the Prophet s.a.w. emphasizes halal include clean products. If they have these both criteria, it is good enough and can sell our product. Another interesting feedback is related to cheating about product ingredients:

Considering the cheating of halal-certified products, they can refer to MOH (Ministry of Health) to secure the halal integrity of the products sold. Some informant believed that credible halal certification is very important to influence the international trade of halal commodities as mentioned by East Zone 1, an international trader. "If it's halal, we are going to ask for a certificate. If you don't have a certificate, we will google even on the website. So, if there have no Halal certificate, we are not going to take his product."

"It's a halal indication. Need to give a description. When we give quotations to Muslims, we know the contents of 'Halal' and 'Toyyiba; It's Japan, the Chinese asked me, so we put 'Halal Toyyiba' there. We are explaining the contents to him. After that, if it benefits, we are doing charity work."

Other informant, claimed that, in addition to religious concern, the companies should only sell the good product without using unethical marketing technique: "We don't place any more promotional verses in our field. There is emphasis on the aspect of honesty in business. We explain what kind of clothes, how many specifications, after the printing process, enter the machine, there's a pair of them, how many percent cut, the mockup is likely to cut 10-15%. So, it means that when the goods are delivered, it's easy to understand. What we want to convey is a product, like printing, tone colour isn't always the same."

Moreover, some Muslim consumers are careful and selective about food quality as their religious knowledge improves. Halal label works to persuade the target Muslim customers that the companies' services and products fulfil with halal and Shariah.

4.2.6.3 Produce Islamic Product

Central Zone 1: "Being a company that promotes Islamic products, morality is very important to us. It's useless if we say the Islamic product, and our distributor wears short tshirt/pant. It's very difficult to please the customer's demand. If you can't handle this situation, please pass it on to me. If the customer is talking to the higher ranking's staff, we can do it now. Okay, we have said, feedback from this user satisfaction, they can expand their point of view. We had to reply almost immediately."

4.2.6.4 Sell Only Quality Products

East Zone 1:" We need to feel love to our product. Furthermore, it must abide by the SOP so that what is produced is of real quality and will bring benefits to consumers. If it has expired we will change it." Meanwhile for printing service, East Zone 3 highlighted the quality of product is very important: "We don't place any more promotional verses in our field. There is emphasis on the aspect of honesty in business. We explain what kind of clothes, how many specifications, after the printing process, enter the machine, there's a pair of them, how many percent cut, the mockup is likely to cut 10-15%. So, it means that when the goods are delivered, it's easy to understand. What we want to convey is a product, like printing, tone colour isn't always the same."

5. PRACTICAL CONTRIBUTION

The important practical implication for SMEs managers is that the guidelines provided from this study can be implemented within the organisation. Managers must revise their current practice regarding to intellectual capital development based on Islamic perspective. Likewise, the policy makers can use this recommendation as reference to establish new policies in the organisation to achieve competitiveness. This present study intends to fill the gap in the existing literature by adapting Islamic values on human capital concept. Moreover, the results showed the originality where this is the first study that explored the components of human capital based on Islamic point of view among Muslim SMEs in Malaysia that can be used globally.

6. CONCLUSION

It can be concluded that there are five essential dimensions in modelling Islamic Relational Capital that is believed will have positive consequences in the organisation to achieve competitiveness. Most of the informants stated the same arguments. That is, a very important element that needs to focus on. This study also proves that there is a strong relationship between each criteria discussed aligned with Quran and Hadith. On a conclusive note, Islam teaches good values embedded in a human being. As Muslims should practice their religion in workplace.

Moreover, this paper was conceived to contribute to the creating of a comprehensive Islamic RC framework due to the importance of the Islamic concepts that need to be adopted to achieve competitiveness. The need for adapting these theoretical models to the new comprehensive model based on Islamic perspective justifies an effort in improving previous conventional models. This study shall, therefore, help the Muslim and non-Muslim organizations as well as policymakers to improve SMEs competitiveness. Academics and practitioners also could make a reference from this study to enhance the relational capital using Islamic perspective.

Funding Statement

This study is funded by the Fundamental Research Grant Scheme (600-IRMI/FRGS 5/3 (014/2019) from Universiti Teknologi MARA, Bandar Puncak Alam, Selangor, Malaysia.

Ethical Compliance

All procedures performed in studies involving human participants were in accordance with the ethical standards of the institutional and/or national research committee.

REFERENCES

Abu-Nimer, M. (2001). Conflict resolution, culture, and religion: Toward a training model of interreligious peace-building. *Journal of Peace Research*, *38*(6), 685–704. doi:10.1177/0022343301038006003

Agostini, L., Nosella, A., & Filippini, R. (2017). Does intellectual capital allow improving innovation performance? A quantitative analysis in the SME context. *Journal of Intellectual Capital*, *18*(2), 400–418. doi:10.1108/JIC-05-2016-0056

Ahmad, M., & Ahmed, N. (2016). Testing the relationship between intellectual capital and a firm's performance: An empirical investigation regarding financial industries of Pakistan. *International Journal of Learning and Intellectual Capital*, *13*(2–3), 250–272. doi:10.1504/IJLIC.2016.075691

Alam, S. S., & Sayuti, N. M. (2011). Applying the Theory of Planned Behaviour (TPB) in Halal Food Purchasing. *International Journal of Commerce and Management*, *21*(1), 8–20. doi:10.1108/10569211111111676

Alcaniz, L., Gomez-Bezares, F., & Roslender, R. (2011). Theoretical perspectives on intellectual capital: A backward look and a proposal for going forward. *Accounting Forum*, *35*(2), 104–117. doi:10.1016/j.accfor.2011.03.004

Allameh, S. M. (2018). Antecedents and consequences of intellectual capital: The role of social capital, knowledge sharing and innovation. *Journal of Intellectual Capital*, *19*(5), 858–874. doi:10.1108/JIC-05-2017-0068

Allameh, S. M., Abbasi, S., & Shokrani, S. A. R. (2010). The mediating role of organizational learning capability between intellectual capital and job satisfaction. *European Journal of Soil Science*, *17*(1), 125–136.

Anderson, J. C., & Narus, J. A. (1990). A model of distributor firm and manufacturer firm working partnerships. *Journal of Marketing*, *54*(1), 42–58. doi:10.1177/002224299005400103

Beattie, G., & Ellis, A. (2014). *The psychology of language and communication*. Psychology Press. doi:10.4324/9781315804767

Berezinets, I., Garanina, T., & Ilina, Y. (2016). Intellectual capital of a board of directors and its elements: Introduction to the concepts. *Journal of Intellectual Capital*, *17*(4), 632–653. doi:10.1108/JIC-01-2016-0003

Berghman, L., Matthyssens, P., & Vandenbempt, K. (2011). Value innovation, deliberate learning mechanisms and information from supply chain partners. *Industrial Marketing Management*, *41*(1), 27–39. doi:10.1016/j.indmarman.2011.11.014

Bontis, N. (1996). There's a price on your head: Managing intellectual capital strategically. *Business Quarterly*, *60*(4), 40–47.

Bontis, N. (1998). Intellectual capital: An exploratory study that develops measures and models. *Management Decision*, *36*(2), 63–76. doi:10.1108/00251749810204142

Bontis, N. (2001). Assessing knowledge assets: A review of the models used to measure intellectual capital. *International Journal of Management Reviews*, *3*(1), 41–60. doi:10.1111/1468-2370.00053

Bontis, N., Wu, S., Wang, W.-Y., & Chang, C. (2005). Intellectual capital and performance in causal models: Evidence from the information technology industry in Taiwan. *Journal of Intellectual Capital*, *6*(2), 222–236. doi:10.1108/14691930510592816

Brooking, A. (1996). *Intellectual Capital – Core Asset for the Third Millennium Enterprise*. International Thomson Business Press.

Cabrita, M. R., & Bontis, N. (2008). Intellectual capital and business performance in the Portuguese banking industry. *International Journal of Technology Management, 43*(1–3), 212–237. doi:10.1504/IJTM.2008.019416

Caemmerer, B., & Alan, W. (2010). No Title. *Journal of Operations & Production Management, 30*(3), 288–311. doi:10.1108/01443571011024638

Capello, R. (2002). Spatial and Sectoral Characteristics of Relational Capital in Innovation Activity. *European Planning Studies, 10*(2), 177–200. doi:10.1080/09654310120114481

Capello, R., & Faggian, A. (2005). Collective learning and relational capital in local innovation processes. *Regional Studies, 39*(1), 75–87. doi:10.1080/0034340052000320851

Chahal, H., & Bakshi, P. (2015). Examining intellectual capital and competitive advantage relationship: Role of innovation and organizational learning. *International Journal of Bank Marketing, 33*(3), 376–399. doi:10.1108/IJBM-07-2013-0069

Cordazzo, M. (2005). IC statement vs environmental and social reports: An empirical analysis of their convergences in the Italian context. *Journal of Intellectual Capital, 6*(3), 441–464. doi:10.1108/14691930510611166

Edvinsson, L., & Malone, M. S. (1997). *Intellectual Capital: Realizing your Company's true value by finding its hidden brainpower*. Harper Business.

Esther, H., Canino, B. R., Sánchez, B. R., & Agustín, M. (2011). The Impact of relational capital on the success of new business start-ups. *Journal of Small Business Management, 49*(4), 617–638. doi:10.1111/j.1540-627X.2011.00339.x

Firer, S. (2005). Using intellectual capital as a success strategy in South Africa. *Southern African Business Review, 9*(1), 1–20.

Gremyr, I., Birch-Jensen, A., Kumar, M., & Lofberg, N. (2022). Quality function's use of customer feedback as activation triggers for absorptive capacity and value co-creation. *International Journal of Operations & Production Management, 42*(13), 218–242. doi:10.1108/IJOPM-11-2021-0692

Hallencreutz, J., & Parmler, J. (2021). Important drivers for customer satisfaction–from product focus to image and service quality. *Total Quality Management & Business Excellence, 32*(5–6), 501–510. do i:10.1080/14783363.2019.1594756

Han, Y., & Li, D. (2015). Effects of intellectual capital on innovative performance: The role of knowledge-based dynamic capability. *Management Decision, 53*(1), 40–56. doi:10.1108/MD-08-2013-0411

Hayton, J. C. (2005). Competing in the new economy: The effect of intellectual capital on corporate entrepreneurship in high-technology new ventures. *R & D Management, 35*(2), 137–155. doi:10.1111/j.1467-9310.2005.00379.x

Hsu, Y. Y., & Fang, W. (2009). Intellectual capital and new product development performance: The mediating role of organizational learning capability. *Technological Forecasting and Social Change*, *76*(5), 664–677. doi:10.1016/j.techfore.2008.03.012

IOG. (2003). *Governance Principles for Protected Areas in the 21st Century: Prepared for the Fifth World* (J. Graham, B. Amos, & T. Plumptre (eds.)). Parks Congress Durban, Ottawa.

Jardon, C. M., & Martos, M. S. (2012). Intellectual capital as a competitive advantage in emerging clusters in Latin America. *Journal of Intellectual Capital*, *13*(4), 462–481. doi:10.1108/14691931211276098

Johnson, W. H. A. (1999). An Integrative Taxonomy of Intellectual Capital: Measuring the Stock and Flow of Intellectual Capital Components in the Firm. *International Journal of Technology Management*, *18*(5–8), 562–575. doi:10.1504/IJTM.1999.002788

Jordão, R. V. D., & de Almeida, V. R. (2017). Performance measurement, intellectual capital and financial sustainability. *Journal of Intellectual Capital*, *18*(3), 643–666. doi:10.1108/JIC-11-2016-0115

Joshi, M., Cahill, D., & Sidhu, J. (2010). Intellectual capital performance in the banking sector: An assessment of Australian owned banks. *Journal of Human Resource Costing and Accounting*, *14*(2), 151–170. doi:10.1108/14013381011062649

Keep, W. W., Hollander, S. C., & Dickinson, R. (1998). Forces impinging on long-term business-to- business relationships in the United States: An historical perspective. *Journal of Marketing*, *62*(2), 31–45. doi:10.1177/002224299806200203

Keong Choong, K. (2008). Intellectual capital: Definitions, categorization and reporting models. *Journal of Intellectual Capital*, *9*(4), 609–638. doi:10.1108/14691930810913186

Khalique, M., & Isa, A., Shaari, Abdul, J., & Ageel, A. (2011). Challenges faced by the small and medium enterprises (SMEs) in Malaysia: An intellectual capital perspective. *International Journal of Current Research*, *3*(6), 398–401.

Kostova, T., & Roth, K. (2003). Social capital in multinational corporations and a micro-macro model of its formation. *Academy of Management Review*, *28*(2), 297–317. doi:10.2307/30040714

Kozlenkova, I. V., Hult, G. T. M., Lund, D. J., Mena, J. A., & Kekec, P. (2015). The role of marketing channels in supply chain management. *Journal of Retailing*, *91*(4), 586–609. doi:10.1016/j.jretai.2015.03.003

Krafft, M., Goetz, O., Mantrala, M., Sotgiu, F., & Tillmanns, S. (2015). ion of marketing channel research domains and methodologies: An integrative review and future directions. *Journal of Retailing*, *91*(4), 569–585. doi:10.1016/j.jretai.2015.05.001

Kujansivu, P., & Lönnqvist, A. (2007). Investigating the value and efficiency of intellectual capital. *Journal of Intellectual Capital*, *8*(2), 272–287. doi:10.1108/14691930710742844

Kweh, Q. L., Lu, W.-M., & Wang, W.-K. (2014). Dynamic efficiency: Intellectual capital in the Chinese non-life insurance firms. *Journal of Knowledge Management*, *18*(5), 937–951. doi:10.1108/JKM-06-2014-0240

Ledhem, M. A., & Mekidiche, M. (2022). Islamic finance and economic growth: The Turkish experiment. *ISRA International Journal of Islamic Finance, 14*(1), 4–19. doi:10.1108/IJIF-12-2020-0255

Lev, B. (2001). *Intangibles: Management, Measurement and Reporting*. Brookings Institution Press.

Marr, B., Gray, B. D., & Neely, A. (2003). Why do firms measure their intellectual capital? *Journal of Intellectual Capital, 4*(4), 441–464. doi:10.1108/14691930310504509

Mellahi, K., & Budhwar, P. S. (2010). Introduction: Islam and human resource management. *Personnel Review, 39*(6), 685–691. doi:10.1108/00483481011075558

Moghimi, S. M. (2018). Leadership Styles in Islamic Management. *Organizational Behavior Management*, 159–220. doi:10.1108/978-1-78769-677-820181009

Möller, K., & Rajala, A. (2007). Rise of strategic nets — New modes of value creation. *Industrial Marketing Management, 36*(7), 895–908. doi:10.1016/j.indmarman.2007.05.016

Monjur, M. (2011). An analysis of the practices of Muhammad (pbuh) on resolving conflicts. *Journal of the Bangladesh Association of Young Researchers, 1*(1), 109–125. doi:10.3329/jbayr.v1i1.6840

Nieto, M. J., & Santamaría, L. (2007). The importance of diverse collaborative networks for the novelty of product innovation. *Technovation, 27*(6), 367–377. doi:10.1016/j.technovation.2006.10.001

Obeng, B. A., Robson, P., & Haugh, H. (2014). Strategic entrepreneurship and small firm growth in Ghana. *International Small Business Journal, 32*(5), 501–524. doi:10.1177/0266242612463946

Petty, R., & Guthrie, J. (2000). Intellectual capital literature review: Measurement, reporting and management. *Journal of Intellectual Capital, 1*(2), 155–176. doi:10.1108/14691930010348731

Rahim, R. (2010). *Managing Conflict in Organizations*. Transaction Publishers.

Reed, K. K., Lubatkin, M., & Srinivasun, N. (2006). Proposing and testing an intellectual capital-based view of the firm. *Journal of Management Studies, 43*(4), 867–893. doi:10.1111/j.1467-6486.2006.00614.x

Rezende, Y. (2001). Informação para negócios: Os novos agentes do conhecimento e a gestão do capital intelectua. *El Profesional de la Información, 8*(1), 75–83. doi:10.1076/epri.10.5.21.6523

Rocha, P. R. Z. (2012). *Métodos de avaliação de ativos intangíveis e capital intelectual: análise das competências individuais*. Dissertação (Mestrado) – Universidade Federal de Santa Catarina].

Rodrigues, H. M. S. S., Dorrego, P. F. F., Fernández, C. M., & Fernández, J. (2009). La influencia del capital intelectual en la capacidad de innovación de las empresas del sector de automoción de la Eurorregión Galicia Norte de Portugal. Tese (Doutorado) – Universidade de Vigo, Vigo, 1–221.

Roos, G. (2017). Knowledge management, intellectual capital, structural holes, economic complexity and national prosperity. *Journal of Intellectual Capital, 18*(4), 745–770. doi:10.1108/JIC-07-2016-0072

Roos, G., & Roos, J. (1997). Measuring your company's intellectual performance. *Long Range Planning, 30*(3), 413–426. doi:10.1016/S0024-6301(97)90260-0

Roos, J., Roos, G., Dragonetti, N. C., & Edvinsson, L. (1997). *Intellectual Capital: Navigating in the New Business Landscape*. Macmillan. doi:10.1007/978-1-349-14494-5

Sarif, S., Noordin, K., & Abdullah, A. (2004). Managing organizational Conflict from Islamic perspective. *Jurnal Syariah, 12*(2), 107–222.

Secundo, G., Ndou, V., Del Vecchio, P., & De Pascale, G. (2020). Sustainable development, intellectual capital and technology policies: A structured literature review and future research agenda. *Technological Forecasting and Social Change, 153*(January), 119917. doi:10.1016/j.techfore.2020.119917

Shah, K., & D'Souza, A. (2008). *Advertising and Promotions – An IMC Perspective*. Tata McGraw-Hill.

Shah, S. A., Bhutto, M. H., & Azhar, S. M. (2022). Integrative review of Islamic marketing. *Journal of Islamic Marketing, 13*(6), 1264–1287. doi:10.1108/JIMA-07-2020-0216

Sheth, J. N., Newman, B. I., & Gross, B. I. (1991). Why we buy what we buy: A theory of consumption values. *Journal of Business Research, 22*(2), 159–170. doi:10.1016/0148-2963(91)90050-8

Shipilov, A., & Danis, W. (2006). TMG social capital, strategic choice and firm performance. *European Management Journal, 24*(1), 16–27. doi:10.1016/j.emj.2005.12.004

Starovic, D., & Marr, B. (2004). *Understanding Corporate Value: Managing and Reporting Intellectual Capital.* The Chartered Institute of Management Accountants (CIMA) and Cranfield University, London. www.cimaglobal.com/Documents/ImportedDocuments/ intellectual capital.pdf

Suandi, H., Herri, H., Yulihasri, Y., & Syafrizal, S. (2023, May 11). H., Yulihasri, Y., & Syafrizal, S. (2022). An empirical investigation of Islamic marketing ethics and convergence marketing as key factors in the improvement of Islamic banks performance. *Journal of Islamic Marketing, 14*(6), 1438–1462. doi:10.1108/JIMA-07-2021-0225

Subramaniam, M., & Youndt, M. A. (2005). The influence of intellectual capital on the types of innovative capabilities. *Academy of Management Journal, 48*(3), 450–463. doi:10.5465/amj.2005.17407911

Sullivan, P. H. (1999). Profiting from intellectual capital. Journal of Knowledge Management. *Journal of Knowledge Management, 3*(2), 132–142. doi:10.1108/13673279910275585

Trudel, J., & Reio, T. Jr. (2011). Managing workplace incivility: The role of conflict management styles—antecedent or antidote? *Human Resource Development Quarterly, 22*(4), 395–423. doi:10.1002/hrdq.20081

Verbano, C., & Crema, M. (2016). Linking technology innovation strategy, intellectual capital and technology innovation performance in manufacturing SMEs. *Technology Analysis and Strategic Management, 28*(5), 524–540. doi:10.1080/09537325.2015.1117066

Wathne, K. H., & Heide, J. B. (2004). Relationship governance in a supply chain network. *Journal of Marketing, 68*(1), 73–89. doi:10.1509/jmkg.68.1.73.24037

Youndt, M. A., Subramaniam, M., & Snell, S. A. (2004). Intellectual capital profiles: An examination of investments and returns. *Journal of Management Studies, 41*(2), 335–361. doi:10.1111/j.1467-6486.2004.00435.x

Yu, H.-C., Wang, W.-Y., & Chang, C. (2015). The stock market valuation of intellectual capital in the IT industry. *Review of Quantitative Finance and Accounting, 45*(2), 279–304. doi:10.100711156-014-0437-5

Zerenler, M., Hasiloglu, S. B., & Sezgin, M. (2008). Intellectual capital and innovation performance: Empirical evidence in the Turkish automotive supplier. *Journal of Technology Management & Innovation, 3*(4), 31–40. doi:10.4067/S0718-27242008000200003

Chapter 8
Harnessing Islamic Entrepreneurship for the Belt and Road Initiative:
Opportunities, Challenges, and Future Directions

Mohamad Zreik
https://orcid.org/0000-0002-6812-6529
Independent Researcher, Lebanon

ABSTRACT

This chapter delves at how Islamic business practices and the belt and road initiative (BRI) can complement one another. It evaluates the potential synergy between Islamic business principles and the sustainability aims of the BRI. As the BRI expands into nations with a mainly Muslim population, it will create new markets, halal industries, and Islamic internet platforms. The chapter also talks about how Islamic financing might help support BRI projects, creating a more equitable economic system overall. The difficulties of adapting digital processes to Sharia law in various markets are discussed. The chapter concludes with suggestions for where future research may go to help BRI's stakeholders better tap into Islamic entrepreneurship and tap into the transformative force that it has for global economic policies.

1. INTRODUCTION

Entrepreneurship is crucial to driving economic expansion, technological advancement, and social progress in today's interconnected world (Whittaker et al., 2020). The concept of Islamic entrepreneurship, which is based on Islamic ideals, has become increasingly popular in this setting. Beyond the pursuit of financial gain, the principles of Islam encourage entrepreneurs to act in a way that benefits society as a whole. It offers something no other financial system does, making it a standout in the international business world (Ramadani et al., 2015).

DOI: 10.4018/978-1-6684-7519-5.ch008

Meanwhile, Belt and Road Initiative (BRI) has emerged as one of the most massive infrastructure projects ever envisaged as part of China's drive of economic globalization. The BRI intends to improve economic cooperation and promote mutual development among participating states by establishing a globally integrated trade route spanning Asia, Europe, and Africa (Zreik, 2022a). Due to the fact that several of these countries have Muslim-majority populations, an interesting intersection between the Islamic entrepreneurship paradigm and the BRI has emerged.

Insight into untapped avenues for promoting long-term economic growth can be gained at the crossroads of Islamic entrepreneurship and the BRI. Bringing together the ideals of Islamic entrepreneurship and the development aims of the BRI could result in a more ethical, inclusive, and well-balanced economic system. This chapter's central focus is on examining this interface, which represents a novel area for research into international economic tactics.

This chapter explores the relationship between Islamic entrepreneurship and the BRI in an effort to better understand how the two might work together for everyone's benefit. Given the importance of Islamic entrepreneurship to the success of the Belt and Road Initiative, this topic is relevant to a wide range of stakeholders, including practitioners, academics, students, businessmen, entrepreneurs, and policymakers.

The unique intersection of Islamic entrepreneurship with China's BRI is the subject of this chapter's in-depth analysis. The chapter begins with a comprehensive introduction to the BRI, covering its background, relevance, and massive scope, with a special emphasis on the role of Muslim-majority countries.

Then, it goes into the tenets of Islamic entrepreneurship, explaining the Islamic ideas behind business, the ethics that guide them, and how they relate to the Maqasid Shariah. It also sheds light on the ways in which these tenets complement the BRI's development objectives.

Next, the chapter looks at the BRI through the lens of Islamic entrepreneurship and the possibilities it presents. Prospects for growth in halal industries and the development of Islamic digital platforms are among the topics that could arise in such a conversation. It will also explore Islamic financing mechanisms and how they might be utilized to finance BRI-related projects.

The chapter also deals with the difficulties of incorporating Islamic entrepreneurship into the BRI's framework. This includes issues like adjusting to the increasing digitalization of enterprises in BRI countries, the importance of intercultural awareness, and the use of Sharia-compliant procedures in a variety of sectors.

Finally, it looks forward into the future, suggesting areas for future research and outlining prospective methods based on best practices. The goal is to offer useful information and guidance to people interested in the relationship between Islamic business and the BRI. The chapter seeks to highlight the crucial role that Islamic entrepreneurship may play in global economic policies generally and the BRI in particular by providing a context for the transformative potential of this convergence.

2. OVERVIEW OF THE BELT AND ROAD INITIATIVE

2.1. Historical Context and Rationale

China's President Xi Jinping announced the Belt and Road Initiative (BRI), also known as the One Belt One Road (OBOR), in 2013 as a major initiative to promote economic growth and connectivity. It is modeled after the historic Silk Road, a network of ancient trade routes that joined Asia and Europe and promoted cultural and economic exchange between the two regions.

The idea behind the BRI is to strengthen international trade and investment relationships in order to boost economic growth for all parties involved. It strives to promote regional connectivity by creating railways, highways, ports, and energy facilities between countries, thereby lowering the cost and time required for trade and encouraging a more connected global economy (Liu & Dunford, 2016). This ideal represents the Chinese ideology of "a community with a shared future for mankind," which stresses cooperation, acceptance, and long-term survival (Nathan & Zhang, 2022).

The Silk Road Economic Belt, representing land linkages, and the 21st Century Maritime Silk Road, representing maritime lines, are the two key components of the BRI. Over 70 nations in Asia, Europe, and Africa are linked together by these corridors; together they account for roughly 2/3 of the world's population and 1/3 of global GDP (Rana & Ji, 2020).

Central Asian, Middle Eastern, and North African countries with Muslim majorities are among the many targeted by the BRI. Many of these nations play crucial supporting roles in this global endeavor as strategic partners. Due to Islam's pervasive influence in the economies of these countries, this outreach provides a rare chance for synergies with Islamic business. With its shared commitment to ethics, social responsibility, and long-term growth, the BRI and the Islamic business model offer a fertile ground for collaboration and mutual prosperity.

2.2. Significance and Objectives of BRI

The Belt and Road Initiative is one of the largest infrastructure projects ever undertaken. In fostering more connection, promoting sustainable development, and driving shared prosperity among participating nations, it has the potential to profoundly alter the global economic landscape (Zhang, 2018).

The BRI aims to strengthen connections between many forms of infrastructure. Creating a "belt" of land-based corridors and a "road" of waterborne shipping lanes necessitates the construction of extensive networks of roads, railroads, airports, seaports, pipelines, and digital infrastructure. The result should be unhindered trade and investment between Asia, Europe, and Africa (Zreik, 2021a).

Economic integration is another primary focus of the BRI. The goal of the effort is to create a global economic cooperation platform through promoting policy coordination, unrestricted trade, and financial cooperation among participating countries (Sun & Hou, 2019). This not only promotes cultural interaction and mutual understanding, but also opens up new markets and business prospects.

The BRI also incorporates social, economic, and environmental factors into its projects to promote sustainable development. It is designed to help developing nations combat poverty, adapt to climate change, and develop economically and socially in line with the UN's 2030 Agenda for Sustainable Development (Dong, Yang, & Li, 2018).

The BRI is not just about business; it also aims to strengthen ties between people. It seeks to foster better understanding and camaraderie between people of other countries by encouraging cultural and intellectual exchanges, tourism, and cooperation in research, health, and technology (Carrai, 2018).

The BRI's inclusion of numerous countries with a mainly Muslim population highlights Islamic business concepts. Islamic entrepreneurship's emphasis on ethics, social responsibility, and sustainable development is consonant with the aims of the BRI. Therefore, it is not only significant, but could have revolutionary effects on the global economic landscape, to investigate how these concepts can be harnessed inside the BRI's framework.

2.3. BRI's Reach Into Muslim-Majority Countries

A major aspect of China's agenda, the Belt and Road Initiative reaches out to many nations with Muslim majorities. Countries in Central Asia, the Middle East, North Africa, and Southeast Asia are all vital cogs in the BRI network as strategic partners.

Kazakhstan, Kyrgyzstan, Tajikistan, Turkmenistan, and Uzbekistan are just some of the countries that make up the Silk Road Economic Belt in Central Asia. The BRI's focus in these areas is on building infrastructure including roads, railways, and power plants. The goals of these endeavors are to improve communications, increase economic activity, and foster regional cohesion (Vakulchuk & Overland, 2018).

Countries like Saudi Arabia, the United Arab Emirates, Iran, and Egypt all play important roles in the BRI framework, and all are located in the Middle East. These countries' strategic locations make them key nodes for the BRI's land and sea routes. With the goal of fostering economic and trade relations and serving as a gateway to Africa, many projects here center on port development, energy, and partnership in commerce (Zreik, 2022b).

Indonesia and Malaysia, both of which have Muslim majorities, are important players in the BRI because of their location in Southeast Asia. They play a crucial role in the 21st century Maritime Silk Road because to their strategic positioning along important global shipping routes (Clarke, 2018). Ports, railroads, and industrial parks are all examples of essential infrastructure developments that would greatly improve the region's ability to engage in maritime trade and economic cooperation.

The BRI's expansion to include countries with a mainly Muslim population creates opportunities for cooperation with Islamic business practices (Vakulchuk & Overland, 2018). Islam's strong emphasis on morality, equality, and the common good shapes the political and economic structures of these countries. By adopting Islamic business practices, the BRI can better reflect local customs and values, leading to a more equitable and long-lasting economic model.

3. CONCEPT OF ISLAMIC ENTREPRENEURSHIP

3.1. Introduction to Islamic Business Concepts

An all-encompassing concept, Islamic business seeks to reconcile Islam's moral principles with the realities of the corporate world. It goes beyond the traditional profit-maximizing strategy by including a holistic perspective that considers not just financial but also spiritual, social, and environmental concerns.

Islamic law, or Sharia, is the basis for the Islamic business model. Sharia is based on the Quran, the Hadiths, and the consensus of Islamic scholars. Fundamentally, it is based on principles of honesty, equity, openness, and social justice (Kamali, 2008). Islamic principles for a fair and equitable economic climate include a ban on interest (Riba), uncertainty (Gharar), and gambling (Maysir) (Iqbal, 2005).

Islamic corporations have larger social and ethical duties than just making a profit. They have an obligation to serve the common good, safeguard the environment, and operate in accordance with the tenets of Islamic ethics. Tazkiyah, a notion central to Islam, embodies this ideal by calling for not only individual spiritual growth but also societal progress and ecological responsibility (Brammer, Williams, & Zinkin, 2007).

Within the Islamic ethical framework, Islamic entrepreneurship places a premium on experimentation, risk-taking, and the creation of new value. It views the business owner as a 'Khalifah' (steward) who has been entrusted with resources for the common good (Abuhmaira, 2006). Islamic enterprises have a special ethical, social, and sustainable character because of this perspective, and they play a crucial role in fostering inclusive growth and development.

Given the BRI's focus on sustainable and equitable development and its expansive reach into Muslim-majority nations, the Islamic business model provides vital insights. Its tenets are congruent with the BRI's aims and can resound with the cultural fabric of the Muslim-majority countries that are part of the initiative.

3.2. Principles of Islamic Entrepreneurship

Islamic entrepreneurship is characterized by a unique synthesis of conventional economic practices and the moral standards championed by Islam. It promotes a novel method of conducting business by emphasizing values like equality, accountability, and long-term growth. Several unique characteristics set this model apart even further.

Islamic business practices, such as the 'Adl wal Ihsan' code of ethics, are essential to the religion's economic and social ideals. In accordance with this idea, business owners must always act fairly, justly, and charitably. Business owners in the Islamic faith are held to a higher standard of ethics, which they must uphold at all times (Haniffa, & Hudaib, 2002).

Interest, or "Riba," is forbidden in all forms of Islamic business. According to this rule, companies can neither charge nor receive interest payments. Instead, they need to adopt financial structures based on partnerships or profit-sharing agreements like Musharaka and Mudarabah (Farooq, 2007).

Another distinguishing feature of Islamic entrepreneurship is its emphasis on shared risk. Islamic entrepreneurship, in contrast to risk-averse traditional approaches, promotes joint responsibility for business outcomes. This guiding principle encourages stakeholders to work together and take responsibility for their actions.

According to Islamic economic theory, the business owner is a 'Khalifah' who manages Allah's property on Earth (Iqbal & Mirakhor, 2004). Entrepreneurs have the responsibility of safeguarding these assets, making sure they are used for the greater good of society and not causing any unnecessary harm to the environment.

Muslims also demand business owners to contribute to society. They should make a constructive impact for the greater good of their neighborhood. Many other kinds of charitable actions, including as the distribution of alms (Zakat) and the production of high-quality goods and services, can help accomplish this goal.

Furthermore, sustainable development is given a lot of weight in Islamic entrepreneurship. Entrepreneurs are asked to promote sustainable development by balancing economic expansion with protection of natural resources (Hoque, Mamun, & Mamun, 2014).

These values, with their roots in Islamic teachings, give business owners a moral compass that helps them balance financial success with their obligations to society and the environment. As the BRI strives to achieve sustainable and equitable development across its vast network of partner nations, this values-based approach can bring enormous benefits.

3.3. Maqasid Shariah in Business

One of the most important tenets of Islamic economics is adherence to the Maqasid Shariah, or Shariah's goals. It serves as an example of Islamic law's overarching goals by giving a values-based framework for conducting business in a way that promotes individual and societal well-being.

Hifz al-Din, or the Protection of Religion, is crucial in this setting. It indicates that enterprises must act in a way that is consistent with Islamic principles and values (Kamali, 2015). Companies should steer clear of policies that could make it harder for Muslims to follow their faith or directly contradict Islamic principles.

Hifz al-Nafs, or the safeguarding of souls, is another important goal. It's the practice of making sure everyone involved in a business venture stays healthy and safe (Al-Munshi, 2021). It is the responsibility of businesses to ensure their employees' safety, provide superior goods and services, and not engage in activities that could endanger the public.

Hifz al-'Aql, which translates to "Protection of Intellect," is a notion that advocates for the defense and development of intellectual property and other forms of knowledge (Moten, 2021). In doing so, it promotes an environment where employees feel valued for their ideas and efforts to improve the company.

Hifz al-Nasl, or the Protection of Progeny, entails looking out for the interests of the next generation (Nurjanah et al., 2022). This takes the form of encouraging businesses to adopt policies and methods that are family-friendly and sustainable so as not to put future generations at risk.

Hifz al-Mal, or "Protection of Wealth," highlights the value of lawful income, wealth growth, and property rights (Lateef et al., 2017). Businesses must ensure honest dealings, shun dishonest tactics like fraud and corruption, and treat their customers' money and possessions with due regard.

Maqasid Shariah seeks to strike a balance between material progress and spiritual fulfillment for the sake of the well-being of individuals and society as a whole. These goals can help firms within the BRI make constructive contributions to the economies, societies, and environments of the countries involved. Sustainable regional connectivity is improved, and mutual economic development and cultural exchange are encouraged, all of which are core goals of the BRI.

3.4. Intersection of Islamic Entrepreneurship and BRI's Developmental Goals

There is a rare opportunity for synergy between Islamic entrepreneurship and the goals of the BRI. Both ideas place a premium on ethical behavior, social responsibility, and sustainable development, which serve as the cornerstones of mutually beneficial collaboration.

The goal of the BRI is to create a system of economic cooperation based on mutual trust and benefit, which is a cornerstone of ethical business practices. This objective echoes the Islamic tenet of ethical conduct, which places a premium on openness, honesty, and justice in economic transactions. The BRI may foster a more trustworthy atmosphere by incorporating Islamic values into its design. Having more people join in can make the cooperative effort that much more powerful.

The BRI's aim of strengthening ties between communities is consistent with the notion of social responsibility embedded in Islamic entrepreneurship. Islamic companies can play a crucial role in fortifying ties between BRI countries. They can improve cross-cultural understanding and harmony by aiding the common good and fostering local growth.

The BRI and Islamic business both place a premium on long-term viability. Both the BRI and Islamic entrepreneurship stress the importance of striking a balance between economic development and environmental protection. This balance is central to the UN's 2030 Agenda for Sustainable Development. Development that is economically viable, environmentally sustainable, and socially inclusive is possible thanks to BRI initiatives that include the principles of Islamic entrepreneurship (Yakovlev & Nikulina, 2019).

The BRI's goal of fostering greater monetary cooperation among its member states is consistent with the notion of mutual benefit at the heart of Islamic banking. Islamic finance schemes, with their emphasis on risk-sharing and interest restriction, present novel funding mechanisms that can be applied to BRI initiatives. This would guarantee a fair allocation of advantages.

Incorporating Islamic business concepts into the BRI will make it more ethical, inclusive, and sustainable while also increasing its appeal in Muslim-majority countries. This method would help bring about the BRI's ideal of a "community with a shared future for mankind," fostering economic growth and diplomatic understanding among the countries involved.

4. OPPORTUNITIES FOR ISLAMIC ENTREPRENEURSHIP IN THE BRI

4.1 New Market Prospects and Expansion Opportunities

Given the BRI's emphasis on infrastructure development and connection enhancement, it provides Islamic business owners with a plenty of new market prospects and expansion options. Numerous industries have room to expand and innovate, which could lead to a sea change in the Islamic economy.

The BRI's focus on infrastructure development offers significant opportunity for Islamic businesspeople to enter traditionally male-dominated fields like construction and logistics. These enterprises can be made more economically successful, ethically congruent, and socially useful by applying the concepts of Islamic entrepreneurship to their development and execution.

Furthermore, the BRI's emphasis on facilitating free commerce provides Islamic business owners with an opportunity to expand into new markets. Many of these developing economies are located in Muslim-majority regions, making them ideal for Islamic businesses due to a shared cultural background and an understanding of Islamic economic concepts (Rabeya & Hossain, 2019).

Muslim business owners can make a killing catering to the growing market for Halal goods and services in BRI countries. The Halal market is not limited to the food industry; it also includes the cosmetics and pharmaceuticals industries as well as the travel and hospitality industry, providing several opportunities for growth (El Bernoussi, 2021).

In addition, the widespread digital transformation in BRI countries offers substantial opportunities for Islamic business owners. From e-commerce to fintech, Islamic digital platforms have enormous room to grow. Sharia-compliant digital finance platforms that may meet the financial demands of millions in the BRI region are possible thanks to the inherent compatibility between Islamic finance concepts and digital finance (Alam, Gupta, & Zameni, 2019).

The notion of environmental stewardship in Islamic business aligns with the BRI's focus on green development. Opportunities abound for Islamic businesspeople committed to eco-friendly practices in fields including renewable energy, sustainable agriculture, and eco-tourism.

4.2. Access to and Development of Halal Industries

If Islamic businesspeople are interested in entering or expanding Halal markets, they can use the BRI as a launching pad. The BRI connects a large number of Muslim-majority nations, so the Halal market is an attractive place to grow a company.

When discussing business from an Islamic perspective, the Halal industry encompasses far more than just food and drink. Everything from Halal medicine and cosmetics to Halal travel and fashion is available to meet the needs of the world's Muslim population. The Islamic business community can benefit greatly from such a varied environment (Azam & Abdullah, 2020).

The BRI's ability to connect the Halal industry to new consumers and businesses across the globe is a win for the industry as a whole. Higher-quality and more varied Halal goods and services are possible thanks to the sharing of knowledge, technology, and best practices. In addition, the BRI's emphasis on free commerce makes international transactions less cumbersome, making it simpler to ship Halal goods to other nations.

The prospects for the Halal business are improved by the BRI's focus on infrastructure development. If logistics and transportation systems could be upgraded, more Halal items would be more widely available. Also, progress in IT infrastructure will help Halal e-commerce grow, bringing Halal goods to more people (Siswadi & Soemitra, 2022).

The BRI framework can help the Halal business grow, which can have positive effects on the economies of nations that adopt it. It has the potential to increase economic growth, diversity, and job creation. Furthermore, the Halal industry naturally encourages a knowledge of Islamic culture and lifestyle, which is consistent with the BRI's aim of fostering cultural interchange and mutual learning among civilizations.

4.3. Potential Creation of Islamic Digital Platforms

Opportunities abound for the development of Islamic digital platforms thanks to the proliferation of digital technology and connectivity along the BRI routes. The unique requirements of the Muslim people in the BRI region may be met by these platforms since they combine Islamic entrepreneurship concepts with cutting-edge digital advancements.

Islamic digital platforms may cause a paradigm shift in a number of industries. There is a huge market for Islamic digital financial platforms that include banking, insurance, and investing options that adhere to Sharia law. The digital banking sector is ripe for innovation since Islamic finance concepts are compatible with peer-to-peer transactions and risk-sharing arrangements (Hasan, Hassan, & Aliyu, 2020).

In addition, Islamic digital platforms have enormous potential in the e-commerce market. The increasing demand for Halal goods in BRI countries can be satisfied by creating a dedicated online marketplace that sells everything from food and drink to cosmetics and clothing. Features like Halal certification verification can be built onto these systems to increase reliability and confidence among customers.

Islamic digital platforms also have applications in the field of education. To help boost the abilities and knowledge of entrepreneurs in the BRI region, online learning platforms that offer courses on Islamic entrepreneurship, Islamic finance, and related areas can be invaluable. These kinds of online communities can play a crucial role in promoting Islamic entrepreneurship and fueling long-term growth.

The development of Islamic internet platforms has both economic and societal implications. They can help underprivileged groups gain economic and social mobility by expanding access to basic necessities.

In addition, they can help Islamic business owners from all across the BRI countries connect with one another and share knowledge and experiences.

Developing an original ecosystem of Islamic digital platforms is possible through the combination of Islamic entrepreneurship concepts and digital technology (Saba, Kouser, & Chaudhry, 2019). This ecosystem, which is part of the BRI framework, has the potential to increase productivity, fuel innovation, and make the global economy more equitable and sustainable.

4.4. Islamic Financing Schemes for BRI Projects

Within the context of the BRI, Islamic finance schemes present a considerable opportunity, both for supporting the projects themselves and for fitting with the initiative's broader goals of encouraging sustainable and inclusive growth.

Risk-sharing, the abolition of interest (Riba), and a focus on ethical investing are just a few of the Islamic finance concepts that set it apart from more traditional forms of funding (Anas & Mounira, 2009). The goals of the BRI to create a more just and inclusive economic system are consistent with these guiding principles.

Sukuk, or Islamic bonds, could be a useful tool for financing BRI projects. It is possible that BRI infrastructure projects might be financed by the issuance of Sukuk, which is based on the principles of asset backing and profit and loss sharing (Chu & Muneeza, 2019). Sukuk issuance frequently finances projects with a beneficial social or environmental impact, making them appealing not only to investors looking for Sharia-compliant options but also to those seeking ethical investments.

Mudarabah (profit-sharing agreement), Musharakah (joint venture), and Ijarah (lease agreement) are all examples of Islamic modes of financing that can provide firms along the BRI route with flexible and ethical financing options (Al-Ali, 2019). These types of finance, based on sharing both risks and rewards, encourage fair distribution of economic gains and losses.

In addition, Islamic microfinance in the BRI region has a lot of untapped potential. Since many people in BRI nations may not have easy access to traditional banking, Islamic microfinance could help them meet their financial obligations in a way that is consistent with their religious beliefs. In line with the BRI's developmental aims, this can encourage local entrepreneurship and help bring about poverty reduction.

Because of the ethical and all-inclusive nature of Islamic financing, it can make a big contribution to the BRI. By incorporating various forms of finance into the BRI framework, a more stable and equitable financial system in the area can be established.

5. CHALLENGES IN INTEGRATING ISLAMIC ENTREPRENEURSHIP IN THE BRI

5.1. Necessity of Intercultural Understanding and Cooperation

Due to the BRI's cross-cultural scope, proficiency in other languages and the ability to work across cultural boundaries are of the utmost importance (Zreik, 2021b). Given the unique ethical and values-based orientation of Islamic business, this becomes even more crucial when exploring the incorporation of Islamic entrepreneurship within the BRI framework (Balog, Baker, & Walker, 2014).

In order to create marketing campaigns that connect with local customers, it is essential to have a firm grasp of cultural subtleties. Muslim-majority countries contain a wide variety of cultures and peoples, and Islamic businesspeople working in BRI countries need to be aware of this. Despite their religious affinity, these nations have quite different customs and traditions, requiring localized strategies for each market. Islamic firms can benefit from a deeper understanding of these cultural nuances by making themselves more appealing to customers in these varied marketplaces.

The success of the BRI framework also depends on the cooperation of Islamic businesspeople from diverse nations. The worldwide competitiveness of Islamic enterprises can be improved through the exchange of knowledge, experiences, and best practices (Ali & Al-Owaihan, 2008). The needs of Muslim customers can be met with higher-quality goods and services, which will boost Islamic entrepreneurship across the BRI region.

Islamic enterprises can benefit from intercultural understanding and collaboration as they face the challenges of varying regulatory frameworks in BRI nations. For instance, to promote trade in Halal products, cooperative communication and mutual recognition agreements are necessary due to differences in Halal certification criteria among nations.

The BRI's overarching goal is to facilitate new social and cultural connections between people all around the world (Yilmaz & Li, 2020). Muslim business owners can serve as cultural ambassadors by building relationships with people from different backgrounds in other nations.

5.2. Implementation of Sharia-Compliant Practices in Diverse Markets

It's a special difficulty to implement Sharia-compliant procedures in the many markets along the BRI routes. These markets require a context-specific approach to implementation due to the wide variety in regulatory climate, social conventions, and business practices.

The difficulty stems from the lack of a common, agreed-upon interpretation of Sharia law as it relates to commercial transactions. Entrepreneurs who follow Islamic principles in business should also be familiar with the laws and regulations of the nations in which they do business (Cerimagic, 2010). To accomplish this, one needs an extensive body of information and the expertise to decipher intricate legal systems.

Implementing procedures that are in line with Islamic law, or Sharia, also requires striking a balance with the customs and mores of the target market. This calls for an in-depth familiarity with regional norms and a clear comprehension of how Islamic precepts can be applied with grace and respect.

The Halal market is an important part of this problem. Islamic business owners face a unique challenge in today's global economy due to the wide variety of Halal certification requirements in different countries (Al-shami & Abdullah, 2023). Therefore, it is crucial to establish close working relationships with Halal certification agencies in one's area and to learn their special needs. Concurrently, work must be done to unify Halal requirements across BRI countries to make it simpler to trade Halal items across borders.

Also important is maintaining an open line of communication and working closely with local communities, commercial partners, and government agencies. Facilitating the adoption of Sharia-compliant procedures, such participation might increase familiarity with and support for such measures.

5.3. Adaptation to Digitalization in the BRI Countries

Muslim business owners can benefit from and learn from the BRI's rapid digitalization of economies along the path. While this provides exciting new opportunities for business, it also requires the development of novel competencies and approaches if companies are to succeed in the Internet Age.

The process of adapting a company's business model to digitization is complex and time-consuming (Almeida, Santos, & Monteiro, 2020). Technology must be incorporated into every stage of an Islamic company's operations, from research and design to sales and customer service. To attract more customers, they should strengthen their online identity and ramp up their use of digital channels. They must also verify that their online activities are consistent with Islamic business principles including openness, honesty, and fairness.

The client experience is another area that needs to be rethought in light of digitalization. More and more people are shopping online because of its convenience, thus it's important for Islamic businesses to provide a positive and stress-free digital shopping experience. The digital platforms must have user-friendly interfaces, safe payment options, and helpful customer service (El Junusi, 2020). They should also adjust their digital strategy to the specific needs and tastes of their target audience in each BRI country.

In addition, learning the ins and outs of the digital business regulatory framework in various BRI countries is an important part of responding to digitization. It's crucial to be aware of data privacy laws, e-commerce rules, and digital tax restrictions. To remain true to Islamic ethical norms, Islamic enterprises must ensure compliance with these rules.

Islamic businesspeople also have to adjust to the new realities of the digital financial sector. There is a growing demand for Islamic firms to become proficient in digital financial instruments and platforms due to the increasing digitization of financial services (Umar & Danlami, 2022). They should research the potential benefits of e-waqf and other forms of Islamic digital money for their operations and expansion.

6. FUTURE DIRECTIONS FOR ISLAMIC ENTREPRENEURSHIP IN THE BRI

6.1 Potential Areas for Further Research

Given the relative obscurity of the topic, there are a plethora of interesting directions that research on the BRI's incorporation of Islamic entrepreneurship could go. The effect of Islamic entrepreneurship on BRI countries' societal and economic growth is one possible field for research. Ample empirical research is required to measure the impact and comprehend the underlying mechanisms, despite the fact that anecdotal data supports a good influence. Jobs, poverty, and local innovation and entrepreneurship are all areas that could benefit from research into the effects of Islamic business models.

Research on the obstacles and potential solutions for introducing Sharia-compliant practices in various markets is another promising subject. Islamic firms operating in a variety of cultural and regulatory environments have unique obstacles that could be better understood through case studies that also reveal effective methods for addressing those challenges. Practitioners and policymakers alike may benefit from the information gleaned from such research.

Research into the incorporation of Islamic financing into the BRI framework is also required. This might incorporate research on the effects of various Islamic financial instruments on the long-term viability and broad participation of the BRI as a whole. Research on how to harmonize Islamic finance legislation among BRI countries should also be performed to improve the efficiency of international financial transactions.

Studying the effects of digitization on Islamic commercial enterprises is equally important. Research might be done to learn more about the potential and obstacles faced by Islamic businesses in the BRI region as they attempt to adopt digital technology, as well as the efficacy of various methods aimed at improving their digital competitiveness. This kind of study can be useful in directing the BRI region's Islamic business community toward a successful digital transformation.

6.2. Strategies and Best Practices for Success

Implementing Islamic entrepreneurship within the context of the BRI requires using proven methods and procedures. One effective tactic is to put a premium on both market research and cultural awareness. Islamic business owners in the BRI region need a thorough familiarity with consumer behavior, preferences, and cultural nuances in order to succeed in those markets. With this information, Islamic companies will be better able to tailor their offerings to the preferences of local consumers and strengthen their position in the market.

Building solid relationships on the ground can also help a lot. Partners on the ground can help businesses with things like understanding the regulatory landscape, making contacts with key players, and more. Islamic enterprises can benefit from market access and credibility in BRI nations by forming joint ventures or strategic collaborations with local industries (Chin, 2021).

Another important component is a commitment to Islamic business ethics. In all their dealings, businesses should be open, honest, and socially responsible. Also, they need to make sure everything is in line with Sharia law, especially when it comes to things like Halal certification. Consumer trust and loyalty can be boosted by a firm's dedication to ethics and compliance, which in turn can boost the company's bottom line.

It's also important to focus on the needs of your customers. In order to succeed, Islamic companies must learn to identify and meet the specific wants and demands of their target demographic. This could include adapting products and services to regional preferences, providing unparalleled support, and interacting with customers in a variety of ways (Alserhan, 2010).

In addition, in the current digital world, it is crucial to embrace digital transformation. Technology should be used by Islamic businesses to improve efficiency, expand their consumer base, and provide better service. If they want to conduct business and expand financially, they should look into Islamic digital finance solutions (Temporal, 2011).

Islamic business practices should be founded on a foundation of constant growth and innovation. A company's products and services should evolve in response to shifting customer demands, new technologies, and government regulations. To fuel the expansion and success of the company, management should also put money into training and education for the staff.

6.3. Implications for Practitioners, Academicians, Students, Businessmen, Entrepreneurs, and Policymakers

There are many parties who stand to benefit from the BRI's incorporation of Islamic entrepreneurship. This crossroads provides professionals with a broader corporate landscape rich with new development and innovation prospects. To be competitive, they'll need to learn how to tailor their strategy to new cultural and legal environments and take advantage of technological advancements. They are strongly encouraged to adhere to Islamic business ethics in all that they do, underscoring the importance of ethics-driven corporate culture for long-term success.

This field of inquiry presents a wealth of possibilities for academics. The dynamics, difficulties, and effects of Islamic entrepreneurship in the BRI setting require in-depth empirical research. Such studies can aid in the expansion of entrepreneurship, international business, and Islamic business philosophy.

Islamic entrepreneurship and the BRI have come together to create a fertile field of study for students. They gain knowledge of the intricacies of Islamic business principles, the promise of digital technology, and the realities of doing business in multiple marketplaces. It may encourage individuals to work in or start businesses related to this growing industry.

This hub provides fresh opportunities for businesspeople to work together and make investments. It encourages them to look out ways to collaborate with Islamic businesses in the BRI region or to put their money into Islamic startups. It also highlights the possibilities of ethical, values-based company in creating growth and social impact, encouraging them to think about incorporating Islamic business ideas into their own activities.

The incorporation of Islamic business into the BRI framework highlights the necessity for enabling rules and regulations among policymakers. It stresses the significance of creating a hospitable atmosphere for digital commerce and reducing the complexity of Halal certification processes in order to encourage the expansion of Islamic enterprises. The importance of policymakers in fostering intercultural understanding and collaboration among BRI countries is also highlighted.

7. CONCLUSION

The growing convergence of Islamic entrepreneurship with China's grand BRI ushers in a new era of considerable prospects and risks. As this chapter has shown, there is great potential for strengthening the inclusiveness and sustainability of global economic strategy by combining the ethical, values-based framework of Islamic entrepreneurship with the vast opportunities presented by the BRI. In addition, it creates a brand-new setting for study, application, and policy development in the international business and entrepreneurship communities.

Many of the BRI's most important hubs are located in Muslim-majority nations, creating an ideal environment for the growth of Islamic business. There is tremendous potential for synergy because the tenets of Islamic business and the BRI's developmental goals are so naturally aligned. Islamic firms that follow the maqasid shariah can make substantial contributions to the BRI's goals of sustainable, inclusive development. At the same time, they can take use of the BRI's many advantages, such as the opening of new markets, the development of halal sectors, and the potential for the emergence of Islamic digital platforms.

However, there are obstacles to overcome while attempting to include Islamic entrepreneurship within the BRI framework. Among the most significant challenges to be surmounted are the need for intercultural understanding and cooperation, the implementation of Sharia-compliant procedures in varied marketplaces, and the adaptation to rapidly developing digitization in the BRI countries. To successfully face these issues, Islamic businesses need to use tactics such as strengthening local relationships, emphasizing customer focus, and embracing digital transformation.

The ramifications of this expanding junction for different parties have also been discussed in this chapter. The effects, dynamics, and best practices of Islamic entrepreneurship within the BRI environment require additional study. The success of the BRI depends on the collective efforts of practitioners, academics, students, businessmen, entrepreneurs, and policymakers. A more moral and inclusive economic landscape along the Belt and Road might be realized with their combined efforts.

The intersection of Islamic entrepreneurship and the BRI framework presents a promising way ahead as we approach a new era of global economic cooperation. We may work toward building an economic ecosystem that is prosperous economically, socially, and environmentally by combining the BRI with Islamic entrepreneurship. For this mission to succeed, there must be an unwavering dedication to moral, value-driven business processes; constant creativity; and widespread collaboration. A better, more equitable future awaits us all, making this an adventure worth taking.

REFERENCES

Abuhmaira, M. A. (2006). *The Impact of" AAOIFI" Standards on the Financial Reporting of Islamic Banks: Evidence from Bahrain.* University of South Wales.

Al-Ali, S. (2019). *Raising capital on ṣukūk markets: structural, legal and regulatory issues.* Springer. doi:10.1007/978-3-030-14536-1

Al-Munshi, M. Y. A. H. (2021). *Islamic Ethics on Environmental Sustainability versus Economic Development: Dam Construction as an Applied Case Study* [Doctoral dissertation, Hamad Bin Khalifa University (Qatar)].

Al-shami, H. A., & Abdullah, S. (2023). Halal food industry certification and operation challenges and manufacturing execution system opportunities. A review study from Malaysia. *Materials Today: Proceedings, 80*, 3607–3614. doi:10.1016/j.matpr.2021.07.331

Alam, N., Gupta, L., & Zameni, A. (2019). Fintech and Islamic finance. Springer International Publishing. doi:10.1007/978-3-030-24666-2

Ali, A. J., & Al-Owaihan, A. (2008). Islamic work ethic: A critical review. *Cross Cultural Management, 15*(1), 5–19. doi:10.1108/13527600810848791

Almeida, F., Santos, J. D., & Monteiro, J. A. (2020). The challenges and opportunities in the digitalization of companies in a post-COVID-19 World. *IEEE Engineering Management Review, 48*(3), 97–103. doi:10.1109/EMR.2020.3013206

Alserhan, B. A. (2010). Islamic branding: A conceptualization of related terms. *Journal of Brand Management, 18*(1), 34–49. doi:10.1057/bm.2010.18

Anas, E. L. M. E. L. K. I., & Mounira, B. A. (2009). Ethical investment and the social responsibilities of the Islamic banks. *International Business Research, 2*(2), 123–130. doi:10.5539/ibr.v2n2p123

Azam, M. S. E., & Abdullah, M. A. (2020). Global halal industry: Realities and opportunities. [International Journal of Islamic Business Ethics]. *IJIBE, 5*(1), 47–59. doi:10.30659/ijibe.5.1.47-59

Balog, A. M., Baker, L. T., & Walker, A. G. (2014). Religiosity and spirituality in entrepreneurship: A review and research agenda. *Journal of Management, Spirituality & Religion, 11*(2), 159–186. doi:10.1080/14766086.2013.836127

Brammer, S., Williams, G., & Zinkin, J. (2007). Religion and attitudes to corporate social responsibility in a large cross-country sample. *Journal of Business Ethics, 71*(3), 229–243. doi:10.100710551-006-9136-z

Carrai, M. A. (2018). It is not the end of history: The financing institutions of the belt and road initiative and the Bretton Woods system. In *The Belt and Road Initiative* (pp. 107–145). Brill Nijhoff. doi:10.1163/9789004373792_006

Cerimagic, S. (2010). The effects of Islamic law on business practices. *Education, Business and Society, 3*(1), 40–47. doi:10.1108/17537981011022805

Chin, K. F. (2021). Malaysia's perception and strategy toward China's BRI expansion: Continuity or change? *Chinese Economy, 54*(1), 9–19. doi:10.1080/10971475.2020.1809814

Chu, J., & Muneeza, A. (2019). Belt and road initiative and Islamic financing: The case in public private partnership infrastructure financing. *International Journal of Management and Applied Research, 6*(1), 24–40. doi:10.18646/2056.61.19-002

Clarke, M. (2018). The belt and road initiative: Exploring Beijing's motivations and challenges for its new silk road. *Strategic Analysis, 42*(2), 84–102. doi:10.1080/09700161.2018.1439326

Dong, L., Yang, X., & Li, H. (2018). The Belt and Road Initiative and the 2030 Agenda for Sustainable Development: Seeking linkages for global environmental governance. *Zhongguo Renkou Ziyuan Yu Huanjing, 16*(3), 203–210. doi:10.1080/10042857.2018.1487745

El Bernoussi, Z. (2021). Developing the halal market: China's opportunity to strengthen MENA ties and address Uighur/hui issues. In *Rethinking Halal* (pp. 108–127). Brill. doi:10.1163/9789004459236_006

El Junusi, R. (2020). Digital marketing during the pandemic period; A study of islamic perspective. *Journal of Digital Marketing and Halal Industry, 2*(1), 15–28. doi:10.21580/jdmhi.2020.2.1.5717

Farooq, M. O. (2007). Partnership, equity-financing and Islamic finance: Whither profit-loss sharing? *Review of Islamic Economics, 11*(Special Issue), 67–88.

Haniffa, R., & Hudaib, M. A. (2002). A theoretical framework for the development of the Islamic perspective of accounting. *Accounting. Commerce and Finance: The Islamic Perspective Journal, 6*(1/2), 1–71.

Hasan, R., Hassan, M. K., & Aliyu, S. (2020). Fintech and Islamic finance: Literature review and research agenda. [IJIEF]. *International Journal of Islamic Economics and Finance, 3*(1), 75–94. doi:10.18196/ijief.2122

Hoque, N., Mamun, A., & Mamun, A. M. A. (2014). Dynamics and traits of entrepreneurship: An Islamic approach. *World Journal of Entrepreneurship, Management and Sustainable Development, 10*(2), 128–142. doi:10.1108/WJEMSD-04-2013-0027

Iqbal, M. (2005). *General Takaful Practice: Technical Approach to Eliminate Gharar (uncertainty), Maisir (gambling), and Riba'(usury)*. Gema Insani.

Iqbal, Z., & Mirakhor, A. (2004). Stakeholders model of governance in Islamic economic system. *Islamic Economic Studies, 11*(2).

Kamali, M. H. (2008). *Shari'ah law: an introduction*. Simon and Schuster.

Kamali, M. H. (2015). *The middle path of moderation in Islam: The Qur'anic principle of wasatiyyah*. Oxford University Press. doi:10.1093/acprof:oso/9780190226831.001.0001

Lateef, A. W., Abdurrazzaq, A. A., Shukor, S. A., & Tajudin, A. A. (2017). Maqasid Al-Shari'ah in Ijarah (Leasing) Contract of Islamic Banking System. *Journal of Islamic Finance, 6*(2), 038-044.

Liu, W., & Dunford, M. (2016). Inclusive globalization: Unpacking China's belt and road initiative. *Area Development and Policy, 1*(3), 323–340. doi:10.1080/23792949.2016.1232598

Moten, A. R. (2021). *Humanising Education Maqasid al-Shari'ah and Sustainable Development*. IIUM PRESS.

Nathan, A. J., & Zhang, B. (2022). 'A shared future for mankind': Rhetoric and reality in Chinese foreign policy under Xi Jinping. *Journal of Contemporary China, 31*(133), 57–71. doi:10.1080/10670564.2021.1926091

Nurjanah, S., Santoso, D., Fatarib, H., Jalil, M., & Murdiana, E. (2022). Lessons Learned From Child Protection Rights in Religion Paradigm and National Law. *Journal of Social Studies Education Research, 13*(1), 237–258.

Rabeya, S., & Hossain, I. (2019). China's One Belt One Road (OBOR) Initiative and the Muslim World. *The Journal of Social, Political, and Economic Studies, 44*(1/2), 3–38.

Ramadani, V., Dana, L. P., Ratten, V., & Tahiri, S. (2015). The context of Islamic entrepreneurship and business: Concept, principles and perspectives. *International Journal of Business and Globalisation, 15*(3), 244–261. doi:10.1504/IJBG.2015.071906

Rana, P. B., & Ji, X. (2020). *China's Belt and Road Initiative*. Springer Singapore. doi:10.1007/978-981-15-5171-0

Saba, I., Kouser, R., & Chaudhry, I. S. (2019). FinTech and Islamic finance-challenges and opportunities. *Review of Economics and Development Studies, 5*(4), 581–890. doi:10.26710/reads.v5i4.887

Siswadi, Y., & Soemitra, A. (2022). Literature Study on Fiqh Muamalah Digital Business Transactions (e-commerce). *International Journal of Economics, Social Science* [IJESET]. *Entrepreneurship and Technology, 1*(3), 220–236.

Sun, J., & Hou, J. W. (2019). Monetary and financial cooperation between China and the One Belt One Road countries. *Emerging Markets Finance & Trade, 55*(11), 2609–2627. doi:10.1080/1540496X.2018.1540976

Temporal, P. (2011). *Islamic branding and marketing: Creating a global Islamic business*. John Wiley & Sons.

Umar, U. H., & Danlami, M. R. (2022). The need for revitalization of Islamic social finance instruments in the Covid-19 period in Nigeria: The role of digitalization. In *Artificial Intelligence for Sustainable Finance and Sustainable Technology: Proceedings of ICGER 2021 1* (pp. 177-187). Springer International Publishing.

Vakulchuk, R., & Overland, I. (2018). China's Belt and Road Initiative through the lens of Central Asia. In *Regional Connection under the Belt and Road Initiative* (pp. 115–133). Routledge. doi:10.4324/9780429467172-5

Whittaker, D. H., Sturgeon, T., Okita, T., & Zhu, T. (2020). *Compressed development: time and timing in economic and social development*. Oxford University Press. doi:10.1093/oso/9780198744948.001.0001

Yakovlev, I. A., & Nikulina, S. I. (2019). Indonesia's Strategy for Sustainable Finance. *Finansovyj žhurnal—Financial Journal*, (6), 83-95.

Yilmaz, S., & Li, B. (2020). The BRI-led globalization and its implications for east Asian regionalization. *Chinese Political Science Review*, *5*(3), 395–416. doi:10.100741111-020-00145-2

Zhang, Z. (2018). The belt and road initiative: China's new geopolitical strategy? *China Quarterly of International Strategic Studies*, *4*(03), 327–343. doi:10.1142/S2377740018500240

Zreik, M. (2021a). China and Europe in Africa: Competition or Cooperation?. *MJIR| Malaysian Journal of International Relations, 9*(1), 51-67.

Zreik, M. (2021b). Academic Exchange Programs between China and the Arab Region: A Means of Cultural Harmony or Indirect Chinese Influence? *Arab Studies Quarterly*, *43*(2). doi:10.13169/arabstudquar.43.2.0172

Zreik, M. (2022a). Contemporary geopolitics of Eurasia and the Belt and Road Initiative. *Eurasian Research Journal*, *4*(1), 7–26. doi:10.53277/2519-2442-2022.1-01

Zreik, M. (2022b). The Chinese presence in the Arab region: Lebanon at the heart of the Belt and Road Initiative. *International Journal of Business and Systems Research*, *16*(5-6), 644–662. doi:10.1504/IJBSR.2022.125477

Chapter 9
Involvement of Women in Islamic Finance in Pakistan:
Challenges and Prospects

Nazia Nasir
Minhaj University, Lahore, Pakistan

Muhammad Bilal Zafar
https://orcid.org/0000-0001-6329-303X
Minhaj University, Lahore, Pakistan

Muhammad Nawaz
Iqra University, Pakistan

ABSTRACT

The purpose of the study is to explore challenges facing by women and avenues of future prospects available for women in Islamic finance in Pakistan. To achieve the purpose of the study, in-depth interviews from women working in academia and industry associated with Islamic finance were conducted through purposive and snowball sampling. The findings revealed that women prefer to earn HALAL money as a source of income and they have an opportunity to work in Islamic bank rather than traditional bank. Unfortunately, due to male-dominated society, women face inequalities at the workplace as well. Along with having challenges, obstacles and gender stereotype issues, women are trying to overcome the barriers. The findings of this study may motivate women to get education in order to assess their future potential in both academics and industry of Islamic finance in Pakistan. Moreover, this study draws the attention of government and regulatory agencies to develop policies that support women, and increasing the proportion of women in the Islamic finance sector.

1. INTRODUCTION

Islamic finance has now become an increasingly important part of the global financial market. It is based on the values of Shariah law, rules and Islamic jurisprudence. Islamic banking is growing all around the

DOI: 10.4018/978-1-6684-7519-5.ch009

world including Muslim and Non-Muslim countries and states as well. In relation to business innovation and corporate strategies, women are indeed a more dominant force (Gait & Worthington, 2015). Women are playing a significant role in the growth of Islamic banking and finance in different capacities including Islamic banking and industry (Shah,Che & Mohd, 2012).

Women must excel and shine in Islamic norms and business enterprises, that raise their position and status as well as their role and contribution must be appreciated along with their abilities (Mittal & Bhakar, 2018). Financial independence has a positive influence on the development of women as it effects the job and work opportunities (Azid & Ward-Batts, 2020). Women are always recognised as equal to men, with some important and core responsibilities relating to their decisions and the ability to resolve concerns and problems. (Arnez, 2010). It is well-evident that Muslim women perform a major role in the economic and social growth of their countries (Azid & Ward-Batts, 2020).

The advancement of women in Islamic finance is fueled by a number of factors, including business expansion, venture capital experience, and the business market. In Muslim societies, when women engage in economic activities, the community becomes uncomfortable. As a result, women are not encouraged to engage in economic activities. This misperception runs counter to Islamic beliefs. The educated women are increasing and involving in various aspects of life. Subsequently, getting a lot of coverage from intellectuals and academics in recent years (Maria, Raquel & Carlos, 2020). Women are becoming more informed, competent, and aware of investing opportunities (Aziz & Kassim, 2021). Women have skills and potential, but a few have progressed and got senior positions (Aziz & Kassim, 2021). (Nabi, 2019) also agreed that the role of women in Islamic finance is gradually increasing across the globe, as well as well-known roles within Islamic financial firms' supportive infrastructure. Mostly women in Islamic finance are strong, intelligent, talented and hardworking.

Women can play a crucial role in Islamic finance and trade in a slightly different manner. The wife of Prophet Muhammad (PBUH), Hazrat Khadijah, a wealthy, powerful, famous and esteemed business executive. It is noticeable that economic independence of women in Muslim societies should be reconsidered (Azmi, 2017). Today, Muslim women are expected to perform a momentous and significant share in the Islamic financial business, which will eventually need to respond to their needs (Gulzar & Munir, 2019). Few research have been performed on the role of women in Islamic business and their socioeconomic decision-making abilities (Shkodra, Ymeri & Ibishi, 2021). Women have been observed to be more capable in managing and dealing finance. Financial inclusion has been indicated to have a positive impact on motivation of women to obtain professional goals as well as get economic opportunities and benefits (Alam & Azad, 2021). However, there is a scarcity of research that examines the role of women in Islamic business and finance from a comprehensive perspective, taking into consideration many possibilities and difficulties that women face. This study aims to explore the women's involvement in Islamic finance by coping the challenge and opportunities in Pakistan.

2. LITERATURE REVIEW

The stupendous growth of Islamic banking operations demonstrates the huge turnover and revenue that occurs. As a result, some governments have started the developments and procedures in order to become prominent Islamic financial hubs. Likewise, Hong Kong, New York, and Singapore are doing momentous and outclass progress in cooperative Islamic finance. Bahrain and Dubai are famous for Islamic finance. These cities have strong powerful and comprehensive Islamic financial system. Islamic finance is swiftly escalating throughout whole financial spectrum, from trade investment to insurance and capital market operations. The most visible thing in Islamic finance is undoubtedly the fast rise of Islamic bonds and the most widely used kind of securitized credit finance (Jobst, Kunzel, Mills & Sy, 2008). Mansori, Kim and Safari (2015) stated that Islamic financing is an upward and rising business in numerous Muslim states such as Bangladesh, Nigeria, and Malaysia. The concept of microfinance and financial inclusion are key components of the rapidly expanding Islamic finance trade. Islamic finance guidelines address not just for the working people and professionals, but also thoughtful for the less lucky and deserving persons (Mansori et al 2015).

The original objective of Islamic financial system is to facilitate interest-free transactions that is based on Shariah principles and only on Halal trades. Risk sharing and loss distribution among investors, banks, and borrowers is the most significant element in Islamic banking (Ahmad & Humayoun, 2011). Prior to the coming of Islam, Arabs employed interest-free financing, which Muslims eventually embraced as a legitimate kind of capital works (Ahmad & Humayoun, 2011).

Religion is an important characteristic that influences the values and perceptions of individuals and their decision- making controls. Broadly, religious values directly effects on future lives (Alazzani, Wan-Hussain & Jones, 2019). One of the foremost religions in world is Islam and the concept of Islamic finance is widely evolving around the world. Such firms as working under certain rules and adhering to the tenets of Islam are called Shariah compliant firms. Somehow, there are rare firms that are fully Shariah compliants. On the other way it is difficult to explore firms which are not connecting with traditional banks. As a result, investors are looking for Shariah-compliant enterprise activities. To determine Shariah compliant firms, there is no clear strategy. Although the aspect of earning is important and any income that is getting from non Shariah complaint firms would be impure (Hooy & Ali, 2017).

Ahmad and Humayoun (2011) described that Islamic banking is practicing in conformity with Shariah ethics. The twenty-first century brought a combination of challenges and opportunities due to the global growth of Islamic banking practices. It is conceivable that fairness and risk sharing are actively involved to quarantine Islamic banking from traditional banking. As a centrally governed and individually managed system, Islamic banking emphasizes on impartiality and freedom in accordance with commands of Allah. The purpose of an Islamic financial institution is to conduct potable banking activities and avoid banned happenings which is not regarded in Islam.

2.1 Women, Islam and Gender Equality

According to Saifee, Baloach and Sultan (2012) explained and analyzed the status of women. In a male-dominated society, the West has frequently labeled Islamic women as backward. On the contrary, Islam appears to be the first religion to formally offer women a position that had never been known before. A famous Muhibbu-Din (2019) scholar has explained the same thing that Muslim women in the Islamic world were depicted by the West as dehumanized and wicked. Women have the duty of educating and guiding future generations and she is often the first one to initiate his or her to the faith. Women have a special place in Islam and granted the right to own property (Azmi, 2017). Tariq and Umar (2012) defined that dignified position of women in some Muslim societies, depending on how Islamic religion and law are viewed in such countries. In Islam, it is believed that GOD has the highest power and reigns supreme over the enormous cosmos, the earth and the heavens.

Patoari (2019) stated that Islam is a faith that accords women are equal as males. Gender equality and rights of women are retained by Islam in all aspects of their lives. Islam makes sure equal rights to men and women, and there is no disparity between men and women. The primary goal of this research is to determine how rights of women are protected in Islam. This research indicates that women are not submissive to males and the point is to correctly identify women in the context of Islam. The findings revealed that Islam does not rob right of the women as well as their dignity, sufficient rights, and position. Proper Islamic knowledge and teaching is essential for women.

Tariq and Umar (2012) erected that the Islamic ethnicity based on revelations to Muhammad (PBUH), who was involved, engaged and constantly active about equal treatment of men and women around the year 610 C.E. Okon (2013) also agreed that in Islam, gender roles are based on scriptures, traditional practices, and regulations. While it is widely acknowledged that Islam has significantly improved the equality of women in comparison to pre-Islamic Arabia. The study showed that the Islam has been the most conscientious of all religions in safeguarding rights and equality of women. Islam has paid much attention to literate and liberate women because it is vital to involve women in future prospects and rights of women must be unfettered and uncontrolled in terms of taking an active role in society (Okon, 2013).

2.2 Women Education and Empowerment

Naeem and Mahvish (2021) elaborated that Muslims are encouraged to get an education and to work in order to live a good life. In terms of education, Islam makes no explicit distinction between males and women. It does, however, insist on retaining women in professions that empower them to live a sustainable life. Prophet Muhammad (peace be upon him) sayings and deeds give clear instruction on to treat women decently and nicely. Ahmed (2021) clearly demonstrated that the actual significance of women in Islam, as well as the fact that Islam provided the best answer and suggests that as Muslims, it is our responsibility to create awareness and educate women. If the teachings of Islam are followed all around the globe, there is no doubt that the world will be a more peaceful place, and women will get more rights and freedom as well.

Shaikh and Ali (2020) defined that Women empowerment can be realized through education, which develops strategic controls, expertise, and awareness in women, enabling them to explore economic opportunities. Empowerment may help in behavioral change, to manage their lives and enhance the mind of the society towards women and their issues. They also endorsed that women of Pakistan has talents and if more chances are given to join Islamic financial institutions, empowerment of women can be proficient. This will optimise the upended self-esteem, salary, working output and financial status of women. Ramadani, Hisrich and Gërguri-Rashit (2015) explicated that working woman and their practical activities are important like scholars and investigators. Women can contribute by encouraging individuals to promote actively the women empowerment. Women devote their time and energy for institutions and organizations in order to overcome hurdles and difficulties, and they also take the initiative to develop skill programs, trainings and workshops.

2.3 Women in Islamic Banking & Finance

Ayub (2013) explored Islamic banking has skyrocketed and became one of the extremely fastest growing business and finance sector in the entire globe. According to a magazine article, Stella (2018) described that hundreds of Muslim women have performed and achieved pivotal roles and get positions in governing, politics, academics, and business throughout Islamic history, beginning with Khadija Bint Khuwailad, the first and greatest woman entrepreneur. A modern phenomenon about active participation and constructive engagement of women in business and finance which may be linked in great part to Western commerce and economic influence. However, throughout the years, researchers have observed and noticed an increasing number of women breaking through the glass ceiling in the sector over the years. A new and fresh wave of female talent has been inspired and driven by these remarkable women executives and industry pioneers.

Corcoran-nantes (2016) illustrated that Islamic banks tried to attract, develop and promote their female number of clients in the late 1990s. Tariq and Umar (2012) remarked that Eoncap Islamic Bank offered savings product for women called An-Nisa, as well as other privileges such as health coverage, in Malaysia. While in the Middle East, a financial services firm-initiated Wealth Management Division for women in Saudi Arabia in 2010. The Cayman Islands–based wealth management firm announced the Ameerah fund in the Middle East in 2009 that gave women Shariah-compliant investing guidance and expert advices. Islamic banks treat women with pride, honor and dignity. Corcoran-nantes (2016) demonstrated that two women were CEOs, one Fozia Amanulla, was the first female CEO of any Islamic bank and second, Zeti Akhtar Aziz, was the governor of the central bank in Malaysia. According to Corcoran-nantes (2016), Indonesia performed outstanding where women have started their careers and left their mark in business and finance.

Presence of women on boards may help the organization to assess the diversification and related choices in a better way as women are known to be more considerable and environmentally conscious than males (Jaffee & Hyde, 2000). Women can increase their board expertise for two reasons firstly if they get advanced degrees. Secondly, women are mostly more oriented towards environmental and social issues. Professional and talented women can have a big impact and influence on concerned parties. (Kirsch, 2018). Hashmi and Gulzar (2020) elaborated that the relationship between women on board of Shariah compliant firms and corporate choices is an under researched area. Diversification has always been an area of interest for strategy makers and researchers. Women directors on boards can do perform better and provide useful information. Because women may bring a great change with different collections of experiences and expertise that can help to enhance the level of environmental awareness in boards.

3. METHODOLOGY

In this study qualitative approach was used to explore the perspectives of involvement of women in Islamic finance. Crick (2021) reported the qualitative research is compelling because of the depth of information and penetrations into participants' involvement and knowledge, as well as their comprehensive outline.

In-depth interviews are the most extensively adopted interviewing method for qualitative research, and they can take place with associate members (DiCicco-Bloom & Crabtree, 2006). By keeping in view, the purpose of the study, the semi-structured in-depth interview method was thought to be most appropriate as a research tool. Hence, this study was directed by conducting in-depth interviews with individual women to unfold different aspects including material, data and information beyond initial and surface level answers regarding the involvement of women in Islamic finance. The selected women were erecting on their experiences, attitudes, perceptions and beliefs about the research topic. They were also having the capability to deliver an inclusive perception showcasing about the connection of women in Islamic finance.

3.1 Sampling Techniques and Sample Size

Purposive and snowball sampling technique was used to identify the respondents and conduct interviews. As per Tongco (2007) purposive sampling in this type of research is certainly focused, determined and aimed towards predetermined integrated characteristics. Marshall (1996) mentioned that one of the most common purposive sampling approach which refers to finding the most fruitful results for achieving the goal of the study. Timmons and Park (2008) described that snowball sampling relies on ongoing study participants to support in the recruitment of major potential individuals.

Malterud, Siersma and Guassora (2016) argued that in qualitative research, the most broader recognized essence of sample is saturation. The perception of saturation is the most significant aspect which occurs when the data collecting process no longer provides any fresh or useful data (Dworkin, 2012). Divergence of opinions from respondents required to produce data saturation for themes. It is also discovered that conducting 16 or fewer interviews are adequate for identifying common themes from places with relatively populations (Hagaman & Wutich, 2017). By keeping in consideration these arguments, the qualitative study was based on in-depth interviews with 14 women bankers and academicians. The 18 interviews were conducted, but 14 were considered and rest of the 4 were cancelled due to the poor recording and repetitions. The replies of the respondents were depending on the up taken questions of the interviews.

3.2 Pilot Test

Before moving ahead on deep studies, it is quite beneficial to conduct some interviews as pilot testing to incorporate the type of questions properly (Majid et al., 2017). Therefore, pilot testing was conducted as a part of qualitative research design that observed the contribution of women in Islamic finance. It encouraged the refinement of research protocols, the identification of significant challenges faced by women, working opportunity, and the expansion of knowledge and abilities. The duration of interviews was remained between 15 to 30 minutes and the questions of interview had been designed, updated, and altered to be more transparent with additional questions arising from the interviewer and interviewee's conversation. The pilot testing was done to evaluate the potential of the techniques, methods, and interviews, as well as how they had interacted in a specific situation. After conducting 3 interviews as pilot testing, few questions were arisen. The understanding of the relevant concerns and issues that might impede the main study were also disclosed.

The following questions were matured based on the pilot study:

1. What is the motivation of a female to work in Islamic finance industry?
2. How a female plays a role in the establishment and development of Islamic finance?
3. What are the challenges that women in Islamic finance confront as a result of religious conservatism, prohibitions on mixed gender working environments, and gender stereotypes?
4. How can Islamic finance put a spotlight on successful and capable women in order to promote female empowerment?
5. What makes Islamic financing appealing to women?
6. Why has there been a few women participate in Islamic finance Sector?
7. What opportunities do women have in Islamic finance?
8. What's next for the women in Islamic Finance and business?
9. How pretty difficult or convenient is it for women to join Islamic financial institution boards?

3.3 Data Analysis

Through in-depth interview, the primary data was collected from women working in academics and banks. After recorded the interviews, they were transcribed and translated

After the interview, a complete transcription was brought on paper through notes and audio recording. The interviews were bilingual, such that in English and Urdu, the Urdu portion of interview was translated into English. Further, the inductive data coding was applied to the executed interviews, and data was aligned with crucial aspects. Hence, several themes were identified during the transcription and different categories were created and connected, as well as recurrences were eliminated by lowering the level of unprocessed data. This allowed to organize data in a consistent manner and categories were labelled before detailing the links among them.

3.5 Profile of the Respondents

All of the participants of the interviews were female bankers and academicians of Islamic finance. The profiles of the interviewees are given as:

4. RESULTS AND DISCUSSIONS

Using an interview method and a qualitative approach, this research uncovers the women involvement in Islamic finance, as well as its opportunities and challenges. This research focuses on: (1) what motivation for a woman to join Islamic bank / Islamic finance Industry, (2) how they contribute in growth of

Table 1. Profile of the respondents

Sr.	Education	Age	Experience	Job Designation
Respondents 1	PhD in Islamic Banking	38-40	7-9	Assistant Professor (Islamic Finance)
Respondents 2	Master in Finance	35-40	6-8	Product Manager (Islamic Banking)
Respondents 3	Master in HR & Finance	38-40	6-5	Branch Manager (Islamic Banking)
Respondents 4	Master in Islamic Banking & Finance	35-37	5-7	Finance Analyst (Islamic Finance Industry)
Respondents 5	MPhil in Islamic Banking & Finance	35-37	7-8	Relationship Manager (Islamic Banking)
Respondents 6	MPhil in Finance	35-40	6-8	Branch Manager (Islamic Banking)
Respondents 7	MPhil in Finance	36-39	6-8	Operation Manager (Islamic Banking)
Respondents 8	PhD in Islamic Banking	35-40	6-8	Assistant Professor (Islamic Finance)
Respondents 9	MPhil in Finance	40-42	9-11	International Sales Executive (Islamic Finance Industry)
Respondents 10	MPhil in Islamic Banking & Finance	40-42	9-10	Assistant Professor (Islamic Finance)
Respondents 11	MPhil in Islamic Banking & Finance	38-42	8-10	Branch Manager (Islamic Banking)
Respondents 12	MS Accounting & Finance (Islamic Banking)	40-42	10-11	Lecturer (Islamic Finance)
Respondents 13	MPhil in Finance	40-42	10-11	Branch Manager (Islamic Banking)
Respondents 14	MPhil in Finance	40-42	10-12	Branch Manager (Islamic Banking)

this sector, (3) what challenges they have to face at working place, (4) what are the future for women in this emerging and new field. The results and analysis of the interviews have been presented with themes and along with thoughtful facts, acuity and experiences.

Theme 1: Motivation for Women

The motivation for women to work in Islamic finance is Shariah compliance. Subsequently, their motivation in relating to Islamic finance is to earn Halal income from Halal sources. As growing industry, women get knowledge and learn as well as explore new things. Women are certain and confident in their profession. Knowledge along with expertise are supportive to increase the growth of Islamic finance. Women who have knowledge and higher education get encouragement and inspiration from Hazrat Khadija. Her contribution made a mark in Islamic history. She has set examples for the rest of the coming generations. A momentous portion of respondents agreed that motivation for women is an ultimate fact to join Islamic finance industry is based on Shariah. Though Shariah based banking system not only bring motivation but also women get dignity and confidence as well. Specifically, shariah compliance relates to Islamic finance. Islamic finance is an understood ethical approach for borrowing and lending. It is genuinely and truly based on Islamic religious belief. (M. R. A. Aziz et al., 2021). So, Islamic finance welcomes women in this Islamic banking and finance industry\sector. Azmi (2017) elaborated that women have knowledge and their expertise may really helpful in increasing the performance and productivity of Islamic finance . Though, motivated women are confidently effective in their profession and career. Women have professional attributes to achieve the target. They are also good in multi-tasking and performing their duties with full determination.

Theme 2: Role of Women in Development

Women play a vitol role in development and establishment of this Islamic finance sector. Involvement of women in Islamic finance Industry has been remarkable and noteworthy. Females and males are cooperative and supportive. Their collaboration creates a radical revolution in the realm of Islamic finance. Women on the other hand, are comfortably satisfy to communicate with women boss\ workers \customers. So, women inspire, feel motivation and encourage their families. But women employees are diligent and meticulous in helping female customers. Respondents 7, 9,10,11, 12 and 13 remarked that women are seasoned and have courage to develop and grow Islamic finance industry. Women as entrepreneurs are assumed to be as competent and proficient. Effectiveness in women leads them to an

Table 2. Theme identification

Theme 1	**Motivation for Women**
Theme 2	**Role of Women in development**
Theme 3	**Gender Diversity**
Theme 4	**Bright Future**
Theme 5	**Female Empowerment**
Theme 6	**Islamic Finance as an Opportunity**
Theme 7	**Women Constraints**

organized approach. Women have strength in articulating new ideas and push them forward. Respondent 8 said that contributions of women may bring incredible efforts, work and corporations. We will make progress if we expand the number of women entrepreneurs.

"If we neglect or disregard 50% of the population you may not expand the banking business in foreign markets. You will notice progress if you bring more female entrepreneur. I attended a seminar (xxx) where a world report (xxx) presented and showed that they eliminated gender concerns and presented the true picture of the rapid growth and highlighted the perks of the employment of women in the Islamic financial system"

Theme 3: Gender Diversity

Women has to face many things at working place on daily basis due to male dominant society or culture. This brings a huge hurdle in life of working women. Gender diversity has a positive effect on any organization or banking or business industry. Gender inequality is a factor which creates the pay gap or pay disparities. It has been observed for decades, but still exists. When a woman begins to work, she is subjected to such differences. Women receive less salaries over men. Pay gap has been narrowing for many reasons but it is a slow process. Respondent13 said that there are issues regarding pay disparities. Men get higher salaries than women. Respondent 13 stated:

"I would say that any organization or sector must accept this problem of gender impartiality and gender pay gaps go well beyond. As a woman I faced such things and there is no doubt about this. It still exists in this modern age".

Inequality ingredients creates unequal opportunity and pay gaps. Unequal opportunity narrates injustice and instability. Inequality generates displeasure and uncomfortable environment that women face at working place. Women are always confronted with enormous impediments to achievement. Respondents 3,4,9,10,12 and 14 clearly defined that consideration is must and essential in gender diversity.

Theme 4: Bright Future

Islamic finance enables women to develop knowledge and set an example for coming youth. Women are encouraged and promoted in many areas and segments. So, there is a bright future for women in Islamic finance and banking industry. Bright future for women in Islamic Finance is venerable and admirable. Talented and educated women are always welcome in this industry. Many respondents said that women are better in managing financial matters and problems. Islamic finance helps poor, needy and lower income persons as microfinance lays the groundwork for women's collective action capacity to grow. Microfinance provides services to low-income individuals or customers who are usually separated from conventional banking. Fintech is a limitless innovation as open doors for coming generation. Males are filled with their leadership positions but there is need for upgrading and classifying the criteria for women that bring them under one net of Islamic finance Industry. High caliber women are eligible for leadership\CEOs position.

Theme 5: Women Empowerment

Women are empowered with many rights and protections under Islamic law and are honored with a dignified stature in societies. Women empowerment is a thoughtful subject and is an important goal in achieving sustainable development globally. Respondents said that women empowerment focuses not only on encouraging women, but also on educating women building a sense of appreciation and devotion to women as equals. Women are the most important figure in societies and cannot be developed without the contribution of women. The sense of empowerment rises with the contribution and involvement of women. The crucial support in Islamic finance is women empowerment that is a significant belief based on social notion and confidence. Women empowerment comes with the concept of equality. One of the most important measures to overcome poverty is to empower women to reach their full potential. So, women empowerment and equality contribute to poverty eradication. Women empowerment leads to economic prosperity. Rights of equality is given to women by Islam.

1.1 Theme 6: Islamic finance as an Opportunity

Islamic finance is considered to be a good platform for increasing job opportunities. As it develops and grows the finance industry faces challenges as well. Islamic finance is an opportunity for women who want to work in Islamic finance industry. Opportunities bring challenges and obstacles as well. Respondents said that opportunities come with a difference those women who are working in conventional banks are now switching to Islamic banks. The alternative choice for women to work in Islamic bank appears to be having a significant impact on Islamic finance.

Theme: 7 Women Constraints

Women are financially dependent on others and do not have the freedom to use money for their own purpose. Women do not have the same degree of independence and authority as males. Women are frequently facing problems to find a balance between social expectations and their personal objectives. Due to lack of financial freedom and less education they mostly depend on family like brothers, husbands and fathers.

5. CONCLUSION AND RECOMMENDATION

This study focuses on women involvement in Islamic finance along with opportunities and challenges. Islamic finance has gained acceptance and recognition globally. The main objective of this study is to demonstrate that women are playing their important role in the development and establishment of Islamic finance. For this study, women who work in banks and in academics have been chosen. Women avail opportunity with devotion and achieve their goals despite the numerous hurdles they face. They also maintain their dignity from an Islamic perspective. Islamic finance gives opportunities to raise speedily and the participation of women is highly admirable and honourable. The most appealing thing in women is to earn Halal money as a source of income.

A majority of respondents clearly defined that women empowerment brings the notion of equality and this belief comes from Islam. Islam has given equal rights to women. Women who have higher education tending towards Islamic finance, is a dynamic mark. Women empowerment supports in reduction of poverty and gender equality. The increasing availability of the fintech has enabled women to empower themselves. Some respondents explained that Fintech and microfinance are easily accessible components of Islamic banking and finance that provide low-cost services to the needy. The cause for a few numbers of women in Islamic finance sector is that lacking of back support from institutions, regulatory and family. Some women have insufficient knowledge regarding financial system and they do not know how it really works. Due to male dominant society, women have been challenged for inequality at workplace. Most women with higher education have less or no chance to get senior position\post. Along with having challenges, obstacles and gender stereotype issues, women try to overcome the barriers. This thing develops more motivation and inspiration in women.

Women have many opportunities in Islamic finance like to earn money under Islamic laws and regulations. They, also have an opportunity to switch from traditional banks to Islamic banks. Women have become more empowered and support in reduction of poverty and gender equality. The increasing availability of the fintech has enabled women to empower themselves. Some respondents explained that Fintech and microfinance are easily accessible components of Islamic banking and finance that provide low-cost services to the needy.

Due to male dominant society, women face challenges like unequal opportunities and unequal pay at workplace. Most of women with higher education have less or no chance to get senior position\post. A few numbers of women in Islamic finance sector having back support from institutions and family. Some women do not have much financial freedom because they have insufficient knowledge regarding Islamic finance and financial system and do not know how they really works. Along with having challenges, obstacles and gender stereotype issues, women try to overcome the barriers. This thing develops more motivation and inspiration in women

Policies should be developed to encourage women and make them possible to engage in financial activities and the proportion of women should be increased in any sector or industry. Educated women's workforce should be recognized as one of the most crucial responses for the long-term expansion of Islamic banking and finance. Women empowerment and creating opportunities for girls and underprivileged societies should be prioritized. Unequal disparities concept should be eliminated. Consideration should be initiated to fostering professional degree as well as opportunities for lifelong learning for women. Educated and competent women's workforce should be recognized as one of the most crucial responses for the long-term expansion of Islamic banking and finance. Women empowerment and creating opportunities for girls and underprivileged societies should be prioritized. Unequal opportunity, unequal pay and unequal attention concept should be eliminated. Consideration should be initiated to fostering professional degree as well as opportunities for lifelong learning for women.

Knowledge and expertise can lead to new innovative development as well as giving a basis for future generations. Islamic finance is considered as an alternative source of funds for companies especially as the industry incorporates FinTech. Women should be given opportunities, and their contributions will be an asset. However, professional and experience women may come onward for senior post either in CEOs or shariah supervisory board. To be very hopeful, women are getting motivate to join Islamic finance Industry but support from institution and regulatory authority is must and essential. Education is essential and helpful to women empowerment. Families should be supportive and give them independence to make their own financial decisions.

This study raises additional questions that will need to be explored in future studies, for instance, (a) how can various aspects including administrative, family environments, high technology, and cultural environments influence women's economic activities? (b) how can regulatory bodies and policymakers contribute to recognise and support women's leadership in Islamic finance? (c) how should women's corporations be developed in terms of realizing the richness, prosperities and growth features in Islamic business establishment?

REFERENCES

Abdallah, J., & Jibai, S. (2020). Women in Leadership: Gender Personality Traits and Skills. *Business Excellence and Management, 10*(1), 5–15. doi:10.24818/beman/2020.10.1-01

Ahmad, A., & Humayoun, A. A. (2011). Islamic banking and prohibition of Riba/interest. *African Journal of Business Management, 5*(5), 1763–1767. doi:10.5897/AJBM10.723

Ahmed, F. (2021). The Real Feminism. *The International Journal of Islamic Business. Administration and Social Sciences, 1*(1), 29–36.

Alam, P., & Azad, I. (2021). Impact of Microfinance on Income and Employment of Women in Jigjiga, Ethiopia. *International Journal of Economics and Business Administration, 9*(1), 373–381. doi:10.35808/ijeba/679

Alam, S., Senik, Z. C., & Jani, F. M. (2012). An Exploratory Study of Women Entrepreneurs in Malaysia: Motivation and Problems. *Journal of Management Research, 4*(4), 282–297. doi:10.5296/jmr.v4i4.2377

Alam, S. S., Jani, M. F. M., & Omar, N. A. (2011). An Empirical Study of Success Factors of Women Entrepreneurs in Southern Region in Malaysia. *International Journal of Economics and Finance, 3*(2), 166–175. doi:10.5539/ijef.v3n2p166

Alazzani, A., Wan-Hussin, W. N., & Jones, M. (2019). Journal of Islamic Accounting and Business Research Article information. *Journal of Islamic Accounting and Business Research, 10*(2), 274–296. https://doi.org/https://doi.org/10.1108/JIABR-01-2017-0002. doi:10.1108/JIABR-01-2017-0002

Ali, H., Bajwa, R., & Hussain, U. (2015). Women ' s Empowerment and Human Development in Pakistan : An Elaborative Study. *Asian Journal of Management Sciences & Education, 4*(4), 23–30.

Ambert, A. M., Adler, P. A., Adler, P., & Detzner, D. F. (1995). Understanding and Evaluating Qualitative Research. *Journal of Marriage and Family, 57*(4), 879–893. doi:10.2307/353409

Anjum, G. (2020). Women's Activism in Pakistan: Role of Religious Nationalism and Feminist Ideology among Self-Identified Conservatives and Liberals. *Open Cultural Studies, 4*(1), 36–49. doi:10.1515/culture-2020-0004

Arnez, M. (2010). Empowering women through Islam: Fatayat NU between tradition and change. *Journal of Islamic Studies, 21*(1), 59–88. doi:10.1093/jis/etp025

Ayub, R. (2013). Perception Of Working Women Towards Islamic Banking In Pakistan. *RADS Journal of Social Sciencess & Business Management, 1*(1), 7–12.

Azid, T., & Ward-Batts, J. L. (2020). Economic Empowerment of Women in the Islamic World []. World Scientific.]. *Theory into Practice, 1*, •••.

Aziz, M. R. A., Khalid, N. S. B., Firdaus, M. H. B. A., Yatim, A. F. B. M., Navamohan, F. A. B. M. A., & Omar, M. N. W. Bin. (2021). A Review on Literatures of Islamic Financial Institutions And Market Between 2010 – 2020. *Library Philosophy and Practice*, 1–35. doi:10.5281/zenodo.5012446

Aziz, N. I. M., & Kassim, S. (2021). Investment decision making towards investing in Islamic unit trusts amongst women. *International Journal of Banking and Finance*, *16*(1), 43–54.

Azmi, I. A. G. (2014). The Implementation of Islamic Business Practices of Women Traders: A Study in An Islamic State in a Developing Country. *Global Journal Al-Thaqafah*, *4*(2), 17–28. doi:10.7187/GJAT632014.04.02

Azmi, I. A. G. (2017). Muslim Women Entrepreneurs Motivation in SMEs: A Quantitative Study in Asia Pacific Countries. *Asian Economic and Financial Review*, *7*(1), 27–42. doi:10.18488/journal.aefr/2017.7.1/102.1.27.42

Bahri, S., & Batoebara, M. U. (1981). *The Position and Participation of Khadijah in Developing Da ' wah in Islam at the First Period. 3*, 287–295.

Cardella, G. M., Hernández-Sánchez, B. R., & Sánchez-García, J. C. (2020). Women entrepreneurship: A systematic review to outline the boundaries of scientific literature. *Frontiers in Psychology*, *11*, 1557. doi:10.3389/fpsyg.2020.01557 PMID:32765357

Corcoran-nantes, Y. (2016). Oxford Reference The Oxford Encyclopedia of Islam and Women Financial Institutions. January 2013, 1–8. https://doi.org/ doi:10.1093/acref

Crick, J. M. (2021). Qualitative research in marketing: What can academics do better? *Journal of Strategic Marketing*, *29*(5), 390–429. doi:10.1080/0965254X.2020.1743738

Cuba, R., Decenzo, D., & Anish, A. (1983). Management Practices of Successful Female Business Owners. *American Journal of Small Business*, *8*(2), 40–46. doi:10.1177/104225878300800208

Dang, T. T., & Vu, H. Q.DANG. (2020). Fintech in Microfinance: A new direction for Microfinance institutions in Vietnam. *Journal of Business Economics and Environmental Studies*, *10*(3), 13–22. doi:10.13106/jbees.2020.vol10.no3.13

DiCicco-Bloom, B., & Crabtree, B. F. (2006). The qualitative research interview. *Medical Education*, *40*(4), 314–321. doi:10.1111/j.1365-2929.2006.02418.x PMID:16573666

Dutta, P., & Bose, S. (2006). *MP. 34*(6), 70–74.

Dworkin, S. L. (2012). Sample size policy for qualitative studies using in-depth interviews. *Archives of Sexual Behavior*, *41*(6), 1319–1320. doi:10.100710508-012-0016-6 PMID:22968493

Ethnology, S., & Summer, N. (2013). Muslim Women Traders of Northern Nigeria: Perspectives from the City of Yola. *Ethnology*, *32*(3), 217–236.

Gait, A., & Worthington, A. C. (2015). Attitudes of Libyan retail consumers toward Islamic methods of finance. *International Journal of Islamic and Middle Eastern Finance and Management*, *8*(4), 439–454. doi:10.1108/IMEFM-04-2013-0056

Gastmans, C., Bryon, E., Denier, Y., & De Casterle, B. D. (2012). QUAGOL : A guide for qualitative data analysis. *International Journal of Nursing Studies, 49*(3), 360–371. doi:10.1016/j.ijnurstu.2011.09.012 PMID:21996649

Gulzar, S., & Munir, M. (2019). Economic Empowerment of Women and Challenges in Pakistan: An Analytical Study in Islamic Perspective. *Al-Aẓvā, 34*(52).

Hagaman, A. K., & Wutich, A. (2017). How Many Interviews Are Enough to Identify Metathemes in Multisited and Cross-cultural Research? Another Perspective on Guest, Bunce, and Johnson's (2006) Landmark Study. *Field Methods, 29*(1), 23–41. doi:10.1177/1525822X16640447

Hakim, A., & Razak, A. (2015). the Fundamentals of Islamic Banking and Finance: A Prologue. *European Journal of Islamic Finance, 0*(2), 1–11. doi:10.13135/2421-2172/790

Hashmi, S. D., & Gulzar, S. (2020). Does Diversity Matter for Religious Firms Too? Board Gender Diversity and Corporate Choices of Shar̄ı'ah Compliant Firms. [JIBM]. *Journal of Islamic Business and Management, 10*(01), 170–187. doi:10.26501/jibm/2020.1001-011

Hooy, C. W., & Ali, R. (2017). Does a Muslim CEO matter in Shariah-compliant companies? Evidence from Malaysia. *Pacific-Basin Finance Journal, 42*, 126–141. doi:10.1016/j.pacfin.2016.08.010

Hunter, M. G. (2012). Creating qualitative interview protocols. *International Journal of Sociotechnology and Knowledge Development, 4*(3), 1–16. doi:10.4018/jskd.2012070101

Jaffee, S., & Hyde, J. S. (2000). Gender differences in moral orientation: A meta-analysis. *Psychological Bulletin, 126*(5), 703–726. doi:10.1037/0033-2909.126.5.703 PMID:10989620

Jobst, A., Kunzel, P., Mills, P., & Sy, A. (2008). Islamic bond issuance: What sovereign debt managers need to know. *International Journal of Islamic and Middle Eastern Finance and Management, 1*(4), 330–344. doi:10.1108/17538390810919637

Kammer, A., Norat, M., Pinon, M., Prasad, A., Towe, C., & Zeidane, Z. (2015). Islamic Finance: Opportunities, Challenges, and Policy Options. In Staff Discussion Notes (Vol. 15, Issue 5). doi:10.5089/9781498325035.006

Kirsch, A. (2018). The gender composition of corporate boards: A review and research agenda. *The Leadership Quarterly, 29*(2), 346–364. doi:10.1016/j.leaqua.2017.06.001

Kmeid, R. (2015). Islamic Finance vs Ethical Finance. *Islamic Finance Today*, 18–20. https://pdfs.semanticscholar.org/d986/ba2251648577b3c3e96ab4397c9ffaa7bd92.pdf

Majid, M. A. A., Othman, M., Mohamad, S. F., Lim, S. A. H., & Yusof, A. (2017). Piloting for Interviews in Qualitative Research: Operationalization and Lessons Learnt. *International Journal of Academic Research in Business & Social Sciences, 7*(4). Advance online publication. doi:10.6007/IJARBSS/v7-i4/2916

Malterud, K., Siersma, V. D., & Guassora, A. D. (2016). Sample Size in Qualitative Interview Studies: Guided by Information Power. *Qualitative Health Research, 26*(13), 1753–1760. doi:10.1177/1049732315617444 PMID:26613970

Mansoor, M., Ellahi, N., Hassan, A., Malik, Q. A., Waheed, A., & Ullah, N. (2020). Corporate governance, Shariah governance, and credit rating: A cross-country analysis from asian islamic banks. *Journal of Open Innovation*, *6*(4), 1–15. doi:10.3390/joitmc6040170

Mansori, S., Kim, C. S., & Safari, M. (2015). A Shariah perspective review on islamic microfinance. *Asian Social Science*, *11*(9), 273–280. doi:10.5539/ass.v11n9p273

Marshall, M. N. (1996). Sampling for qualitative research. *Family Practice*, *13*(6), 522–526. doi:10.1093/fampra/13.6.522 PMID:9023528

Miles, D. A. (2019). Let's Stop the Madness Part 2: Understanding the Difference Between Limitations vs. Delimitations. *5th Annual 2017 Black Doctoral Network Conference in Atlanta, August*, 1–17.

Mittal, M., & Bhakar, S. S. (2018). Examining the impact of role overload on job stress, job satisfaction and job performance-a study among married working women in banking sector. *International Journal of Management Studies*, *2*(7), 1. doi:10.18843/ijms/v5i2(7)/01

Muhibbu-Din, M. O. (2019). Feminism and modern Islamic politics: The fact and the fallacy. *International Journal of Islamic Thought*, *15*(1), 44–59. doi:10.24035/ijit.15.2019.005

Mukherjee, R. R., & Patel, S. (2020). Critical Analysis of the Factors Affecting Gender Pay Gap. Gender Sensitive Education: A necessity to eradicate Gender Discrimination in India.". *Journal on 8th February*.

Nabi, N. (2019). Women in Islamic Economics: A Study of Some Prominent Muslim Women Scholars. *Insight Islamicus*, *19*, 33–46.

Naeem, G., & Mahvish, S. (2021). The honor and respect of Women: A comparative study based on Quran o Sunnah and current practices in Pakistan. *Rahatulquloob*, *5*(1), 40–46. doi:10.51411/rahat.5.1.2021/192

Nguyen, Q. K. (2021). Oversight of bank risk-taking by audit committees and Sharia committees: Conventional vs Islamic banks. *Heliyon*, *7*(8), e07798. doi:10.1016/j.heliyon.2021.e07798 PMID:34458627

Nielsen, S., & Huse, M. (2010). Women directors' contribution to board decision-making and strategic involvement: The role of equality perception. *European Management Review*, *7*(1), 16–29. doi:10.1057/emr.2009.27

Okafor, C., & Amalu, R. (2010). Entrepreneurial Motivations as Determinants of Women Entrepreneurship Challenges. *Petroleum-Gas University of Ploiesti Bulletin*, (2), 67–77.

Okon, E. E. (2013). The Status of Woman in Islam. *IOSR Journal of Humanities and Social Science*, *10*(2), 21–27. doi:10.9790/0837-01022127

Panda, S. (2018). Constraints faced by women entrepreneurs in developing countries: Review and ranking. *Gender in Management*, *33*(4), 315–331. doi:10.1108/GM-01-2017-0003

Patoari, M. H. (2019). The Rights of Women in Islam and Some Misconceptions: An Analysis from Bangladesh Perspective. *Beijing Law Review*, *10*(05), 1211–1224. doi:10.4236/blr.2019.105065

Qu, S. Q., & Dumay, J. (2011). The qualitative research interview. *Qualitative Research in Accounting & Management*, *8*(3), 238–264. doi:10.1108/11766091111162070

Rabiee, F. (2004). Focus-group interview and data analysis. *The Proceedings of the Nutrition Society, 63*(4), 655–660. doi:10.1079/PNS2004399 PMID:15831139

Rahbari, L. (2020). Women's Ijtihad and Lady Amin's islamic ethics on womanhood and motherhood. *Religions, 11*(2), 1–13. doi:10.3390/rel11020088

Ramadani, V., Hisrich, R. D., & Gërguri-Rashiti, S. (2015). Female entrepreneurs in transition economies: Insights from Albania, Macedonia and Kosovo. *World Review of Entrepreneurship, Management and Sustainable Development, 11*(4), 391–413. doi:10.1504/WREMSD.2015.072066

Report. (2019). *Celebrating Women in Islamic Business and Finance in Islamic Business and Finance who are leading.*

Saifee, A. U. R., Baloach, A. G., Sultan, S., & Khalid, I. (2012). Status, identity, and privileges of women in Islam. *European Journal of Soil Science, 30*(1), 146–154.

Sandelowski, M. (1995). Sample size in qualitative research. *Research in Nursing & Health, 18*(2), 179–183. doi:10.1002/nur.4770180211 PMID:7899572

Self, S., & Grabowski, R. (2012). Opportunities for women and Islam: Variations upon variations. *Applied Economics, 44*(1), 65–79. doi:10.1080/00036846.2010.498370

Shaikh, S. N., & Ali, A. (2020). Islamic Finance and Empowerment of Women: A Case Study of Pakistan. *Asian Journal of Economics, Business and Accounting*. doi:10.9734/ajeba/2020/v16i430243

Shkodra, J., Ymeri, P., & Ibishi, L. (2021). Role of microfinance institutions for developing women entrepreneurship – The case study of Kosovo. *Economics & Sociology (Ternopil), 14*(1), 120–129. doi:10.14254/2071-789X.2021/14-1/8

Sidani, Y. (2005). Women, work, and Islam in Arab societies. *Women in Management Review, 20*(7), 498–512. doi:10.1108/09649420510624738

Sinha, N., Raju, D., & Morrison, A. (2007). Gender equality and economic growth. In *Women and Girls Rising*. Issue September., doi:10.4324/9781315708379-17

Stella. (2018). The Most Powerful Women in Islamic Finance Women. *Islamic Finance Review*, 12–43.

Tariq, F., & Umar, S. (2012). Arming the other half: Attaining sustainability through women with microfinance. *WIT Transactions on Ecology and the Environment, 155*, 811–819. doi:10.2495/SC120682

Timmons, S., & Park, J. (2008). A qualitative study of the factors influencing the submission for publication of research undertaken by students. *Nurse Education Today, 28*(6), 744–750. doi:10.1016/j.nedt.2007.12.002 PMID:18226843

Tongco, M. D. C. (2007). Purposive Sampling as a Tool for Informant Selection. *Ethnobotany Research and Applications, 5*, 147–158. doi:10.17348/era.5.0.147-158

Vaismoradi, M., & Snelgrove, S. (2019). Theme in qualitative content analysis and thematic analysis. *Forum Qualitative Social Research, 20*(3). Advance online publication. doi:10.17169/fqs-20.3.3376

Van Es, M. A. (2019). Muslim women as 'ambassadors' of Islam: Breaking stereotypes in everyday life. *Identities (Yverdon)*, *26*(4), 375–392. doi:10.1080/1070289X.2017.1346985

Williams-Mcbean, C. T. (2019). The value of a qualitative pilot study in a multi-phase mixed methods research. *Qualitative Report*, *24*(5), 1055–1064. doi:10.46743/2160-3715/2019.3833

Yaumidin, U. K., Suhodo, D. S., Yuniarti, P. I., & Hidayatina, A. (2017). Financial Inclusion for Women: Impact Evaluation on Islamic Microfinance to Women's Empowerment in Indonesia. In Financial Inclusion and Poverty Alleviation. doi:10.1007/978-3-319-69799-4_3

Younis Khan, M., Jamil, A., Ali Khan, U., Kareem, U., & Imran, G. (2012). Female Students Opinion about Women's Participation in Sports. *International Journal of Academic Research in Business & Social Sciences*, *2*(9), 275–283.

Chapter 10
Islamic Marketing for Small Firms Value

Onan Marakali Siregar
Universitas Sumatera Utara, North Sumatera, Indonesia

Andriansyah Andriansyah
Universitas Sumatera Utara, North Sumatera, Indonesia

ABSTRACT

This study examines how Islamic marketing influences the value of small enterprises. It analyzes strategies aligned with Islamic principles that engage Muslim consumers and differentiate small businesses in competitive markets. The research synthesizes insights from various sources, emphasizing empirical research and theoretical frameworks that reveal the interaction between Islamic marketing, small business value, and related factors. This chapter dissects the complex relationship between Islamic marketing, small business value, and relevant factors. It highlights the importance of aligning marketing strategies with Islamic principles to cater to Muslim consumers and address diverse client challenges. This chapter lays a foundation for further research, providing guidance to small enterprises thriving in Islamic markets with ethical, value-driven marketing strategies.

INTRODUCTION

The research focused on Islamic marketing holds undeniable significance for small enterprises. It introduces distinct strategies that resonate with the principles of Islam, inherently appealing to Muslim consumers. This resonance is particularly critical for small businesses grappling with resource constraints and aiming to carve a unique niche within the market.

An empirical study by Santosa, (2020) significantly advances our comprehension by revealing the positive and substantial influence of profitability on the valuation of Islamic firms. This seminal research underscores that small enterprises prioritizing profitability while embracing Islamic marketing methodologies can effectively bolster their market valuation. Intriguingly, the study also highlights the moderating role of firm size, illustrating how the interplay between profitability and firm size can synergistically enhance market value.

DOI: 10.4018/978-1-6684-7519-5.ch010

The relevance of Islamic marketing principles extends beyond Muslim-majority contexts, as suggested by Tournois & Aoun, (2012). These principles serve as a compass for non-Muslim firms navigating the complexities of decision-making aligned with Islamic marketing ethos. For Western firms, assimilating the core tenets of Islamic marketing and branding offers invaluable insights to attract Muslim consumers while preserving appeal to a broader demographic.

Another facet of Islamic marketing, pertinent to small businesses, is the concept of Zakah. This framework can be harnessed for both social cause marketing and corporate philanthropy, providing a unique avenue for small enterprises to cultivate a benevolent corporate image. Integrating Zakah into social responsibility initiatives allows small businesses to manifest commitment to Islamic values, resonating deeply with conscientious Muslim consumers.

A study by Guizani, (2020) delving into capital structure choices among firms adhering to Islamic principles underscores the ramifications of these principles on financial strategies. This insight is particularly salient for small enterprises. A comprehensive understanding of financial avenues within the Islamic framework empowers these businesses to make judicious decisions aligned with their values, appealing to investors with a preference for Islamic financial modalities.

In summary, the body of research on Islamic marketing serves as an indispensable guide for small businesses. Strategic adoption of Islamic marketing practices enables these entities to differentiate themselves and effectively engage Muslim consumers. Simultaneously, an informed comprehension of the interplay between Islamic principles and financial choices enhances decision-making coherence while attracting like-minded investors. Ultimately, this research guides small enterprises toward success in the intricate landscape of the Islamic market.

Islamic Marketing

The interpretations of Islamic marketing, as presented by scholars and researchers, exhibit notable variation. Experts describe it as a multi-layered, dynamic, and multifaceted engagement involving Muslim and non-Muslim stakeholders. This engagement entails the creation of explicit or implicit cultural cues, facilitated through marketing strategies (Wilson, 2012). In this perspective, Islamic marketing transcends the traditional notions of commerce, encompassing a wide range of consumer segments and sub-cultures, spanning areas like fashion, entertainment, cosmetics, and vacations.

An alternative definition offered by Alharbi, Yahya, & Kassim, (2022) portrays Islamic marketing as a distinctive domain that challenges conventional marketing norms. It places emphasis on values intrinsic to Islamic culture, including modesty, nobility, sacrifice, and struggle. This definition underscores the potential disparities between Islamic marketing and the Western marketing paradigm.

Sulasih et al., (2023) articulate Islamic marketing as a faith-based marketing approach guided by principles from Islamic Sharia (Islamic Law). This approach extends to both Muslim and non-Muslim companies catering to Muslim consumers. Notably, sustainability principles deeply rooted in Islam align Islamic marketing with sustainable practices. Ahmad, (2018) offers a fresh perspective, highlighting the intersections of Islam and marketing. This viewpoint delves into Islam's tenets and activities and advocates for a more comprehensive approach to Islamic marketing discussions. It proposes treating consumers as individuals rather than mere target markets, exploring how Islam can propel marketing theory and application.

In the context of Islamic branding, Ismail et al., (2022) present diverse definitions gleaned from prior studies. These definitions encompass the Islamic brand via adherence, the Islamic brand by origin, the

Islamic brand from a consumer standpoint, and Sharia-compliant offerings carrying halal certifications. Therefore, the array of definitions surrounding Islamic marketing underscores its multi-dimensional essence, its adherence to Islamic principles, and its potential deviations from conventional marketing paradigms. This all-encompassing concept spans various sectors and consumer segments, presenting companies with opportunities to cater to the needs and preferences of Muslim consumers while remaining aligned with Islamic values.

In a broader perspective, the progression towards Islamic marketing's full potential is marked by four distinct stages forming a logical sequence (Alserhan et al., 2022). These stages are (Fig. 1) as follows:

Islamic Marketing 1.0 (IM 1.0)—awareness

Islamic Marketing 2.0 (IM 2.0)—Islamization of existing theory

Islamic Marketing 3.0 (IM 3.0)—theory making

Islamic Marketing 4.0 (IM 4.0)—thought leadership

In the period spanning from 1997 to 2022, a comprehensive inquiry into the Scopus database, widely acclaimed for its credibility and stature, yielded a substantial compilation of 200 documents singularly centered on the keyword "Islamic Marketing." This ample reservoir of literature bears testament to a robust and sustained research engagement with this subject matter. Notably, this scholarly curiosity reveals discernible focal points, with the years 2018 and 2020 emerging as particularly pivotal epochs of heightened academic exploration.

The sheer volume of results underscores the palpable interest and scholarly dedication channeled toward the multifaceted domain of Islamic Marketing. It is evident that this specialized field has garnered substantive attention, solidifying its significance within the academic realm. The concentration of research output in specific years, especially the notable peaks in 2018 and 2020, potentially signifies distinct phases of evolution within the discipline, characterized by intensified scholarly activity and burgeoning insights.

Figure 1. Development stages in Islamic marketing thought
Source: Alserhan et al. (2022)

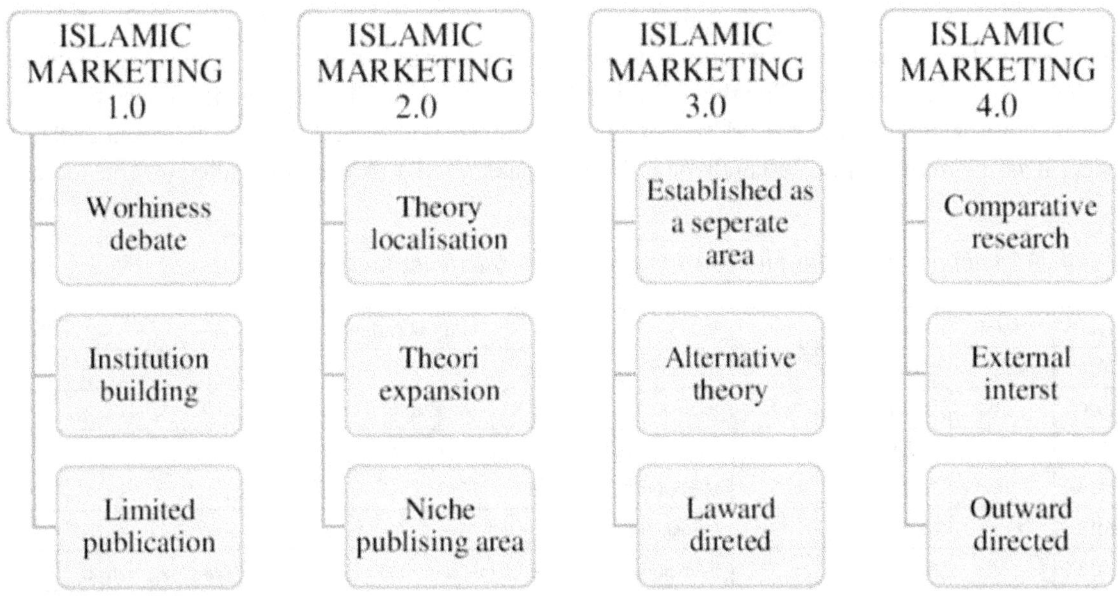

These observations collectively accentuate the vibrant scholarly discourse enveloping Islamic Marketing over the past twenty-five years. The discernible spikes in research productivity serve as indicators of dynamic shifts in thematic focus and scholarly investigation, prompting further inquiry into the drivers underpinning these temporal patterns. This diverse array of research undoubtedly enriches and nuances our comprehension of Islamic Marketing's intricacies, firmly establishing it as an emerging and vital domain within the broader marketing landscape.

Small Firm and Value

The delineation of a small firm can exhibit variability contingent upon the context and jurisdiction. In the investigation conducted by Delmar & Wiklund, (2008), the characterization of small firms entailed enterprises with a specified level of investment in plant and machinery, notably ranging between INR 25 lakh and INR 5 crore for Indian firms (Kumar, 2015). Similarly, within the Ghanaian framework, small-scale enterprises were defined on the basis of employee count, marked by a delineating threshold of 30 employees (Peprah et al., 2022). Expanding upon this, Peprah et al., (2022) introduced a classification encompassing micro, small, medium, and large enterprises, predicated on criteria such as turnover and employee count.

The contours of defining small firms also exhibit malleability when contextualized within tax parameters and firm performance. In an inquiry spearheaded by Dabla-Norris et al., (2017), a definition anchored in normalized employment was adopted, designating a firm as 'small' if its normalized employment remained below the 25th percentile across firms and countries. Remarkably, their findings unveiled that adept tax administration could temper the productivity chasm between small and large firms, thereby accentuating the pertinence of refining tax administration for bolstering their performance.

It is pertinent to note that the very definition of small firms wields substantial ramifications for research and policy domains, as elucidated by Steeger & Hoffmann, (2016). They highlighted that studies on family firms often disproportionately pivot towards sizeable listed entities, inadvertently neglecting the reverberations of familial influence upon smaller enterprises.

Marom (2021) further propounded that the conventional size-centric classifications of small businesses might fall short in encapsulating the growth potential of individual firms. He advocated a dynamic-oriented classification methodology aimed at identifying enterprises manifesting high growth potential.

In essence, the contours framing the definition of a small firm manifest divergence hinged upon variables encompassing investment, workforce magnitude, financial turnover, and the contextual backdrop. Hence, it is incumbent upon researchers and policymakers alike to exercise judicious consideration

Table 1. A summary of articles published in Scopus on Islamic marketing

Year	Total	Author	Total	Publication	Total
2018	22	J. Wilson	6	Journal of Islamic Marketing	104
2020	21	O. Sandikci	4	International Journal of Bank Marketing	9
2016	20	A. Jafari	3	International Journal of Tourism Research	5
2019	16	J.A.J. Wilson	3	Marketing Theory	4
2013	15	M. Battour	3	Journal of Business Research	4
2012	14	M. Tieman	3	International Journal of Islamic and Middle Eastern Finance and Management	3

Figure 2. Model small firm
Source: fourweekmba.com

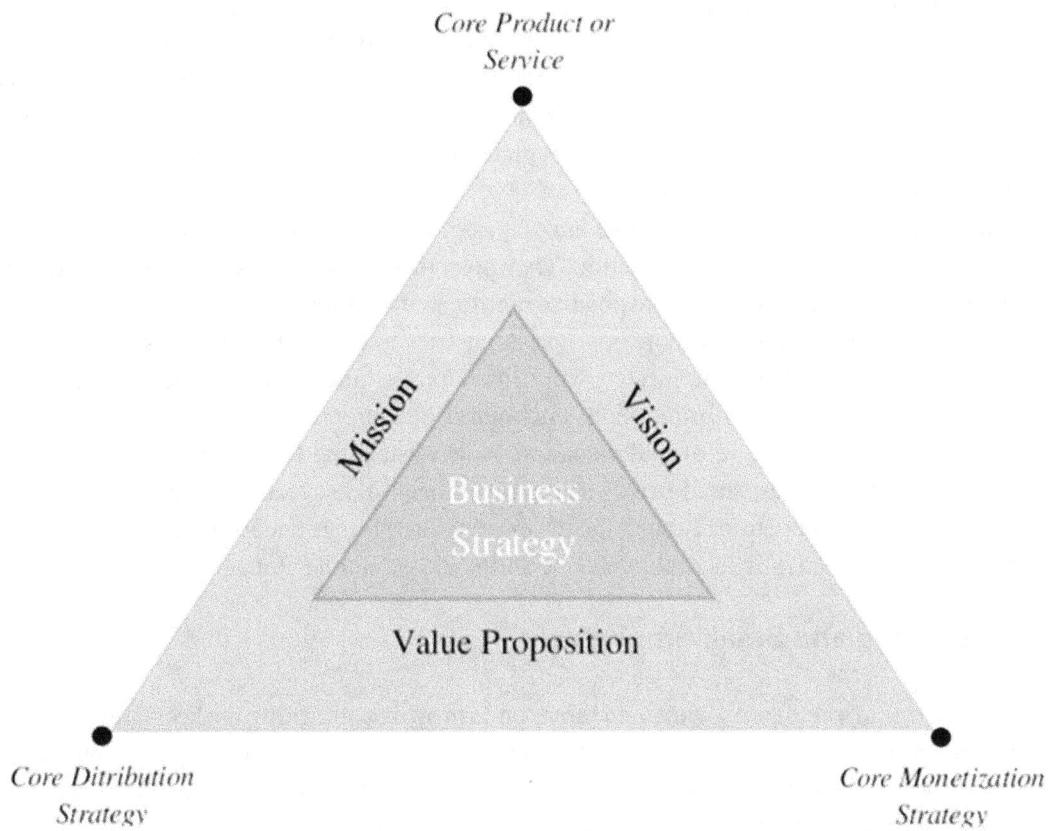

when selecting the definitions underpinning their studies or directives. This diligence ensures precision, relevance, and effective support tailored for the diverse realm of small businesses.

The perceptions concerning the value of small firms are heavily influenced by contextual factors and the perspectives of researchers. In the insightful framework proposed by Lumpkin & Dess, (1996), small firm value finds articulation as Entrepreneurial Orientation (EO), denoting the proclivity of the firm towards entrepreneurial pursuits. They posit EO as a multidimensional construct, fostering avenues for probing its interplay with firm performance through diverse models like moderation, mediation, independence, and interaction effects. Conversely, Kumar, (2015) offers a distinct contour, grounding small firms within the domain of green marketing innovations in India. As per the Ministry of MSME (2008), a small firm is characterized by an investment in plant and machinery ranging from INR 25 lakh to INR 5 crore, a prevalent definition in seminal Indian studies.

In the realm of Adelekan et al., (2021), small firms are encapsulated as entities harboring 10-49 employees and a total value ranging between $10,000 to $100,000, in accordance with the Small and Medium Firms Development Agency (SMEDAN, 2019). These enterprises play a pivotal role in fostering job creation, spurring economic advancement, alleviating poverty, and elevating living standards. However, they grapple with an array of challenges encompassing limited access to credit, restricted marketing and technical resources, and formidable operational costs. Adelekan et al., (2021) underscore the significance of small firms in driving wealth distribution and realizing sustainable objectives. The discourse extends into alliance strategies with larger entities as per Yang et al. (2013), who dissect the potential gains and obstacles confronting small firms. Their perspective sheds light on alliances with larger counterparts, a conduit offering legitimacy, reputation, and complementary resources for harnessing their technologies. Yet, there looms the risk of larger firms exploiting the value engendered within alliances. The efficacy of alliance governance becomes pivotal in enhancing value accrual for small firms within exploration-based alliances.

Furthermore, Adelekan et al., (2021) delve into the essence of competition among small businesses and its consequential impact on value generation. They posit that small businesses forge value through a unidirectional process that holds substantial positive ramifications for society. Furthermore, they critique existing literature for its exigency for more appropriate metrics to gauge small business value creation.

In summation, the contours that delineate small firm value are inherently contextual and researcher-centric. Definitions manifest across dimensions encompassing entrepreneurial orientation, investment profiles, workforce magnitude, and overall valuation. Notwithstanding the challenges stemming from competition with larger entities, small firms can augment their value spectrum through adept alliance governance and strategic coopetition. Critically, the existing literature is underscored for its necessity to refine metrics and systematically incorporate value shifts and economic dynamics.

Islamic Marketing and Small firm Velue

The realm of Islamic marketing has witnessed remarkable growth, captivating the keen attention of both scholars and practitioners in recent times (Abdullah et al., 2017). Positioned as a strategic business discipline, it steadfastly adheres to Islamic principles in the orchestration of product creation, promotion, and delivery (Yusfiarto & Pambekti, 2019). Central to Islamic marketing's ethos is the harmonization of marketing strategies with Islamic values, tenets, and benchmarks (Zakaria & Abdul-Talib, 2010). This resonance assumes particular significance for small enterprises operating within Muslim regions or serving Muslim clienteles.

A cornerstone of Islamic marketing is the marketing mix, encompassing product, price, promotion, and place (Abdullah et al., 2017). For small entities, the pivotal consideration lies in aligning these facets with Islamic principles. For instance, the development of halal offerings adhering to Islamic dietary laws might be requisite (Zakaria & Abdul-Talib, 2010). Pricing strategies must echo fairness and transparency, precluding any unethical undercurrents (Abdullah et al., 2017). Pertaining to promotion, small firms can harness marketing communication channels that resonate with Islamic values, eschewing explicit or misleading overtures (Abdullah et al., 2017). The final strand of the marketing mix, 'place,' could entail distribution channels aligned with Islamic tenets, avoiding entanglements with businesses engaged in haram activities (Abdullah et al., 2017).

Parallel to the marketing mix, small businesses stand to gain by embracing a market-oriented cultural paradigm attuned to the needs and proclivities of Muslim consumers (Zakaria & Abdul-Talib, 2010). This entails an astute comprehension of the diverse exigencies of Muslim clientele, paving the way for bespoke strategies catering to their distinct needs (Zakaria & Abdul-Talib, 2010). Such an approach not only bolsters the competitive edge of small firms but also nurtures robust customer relationships (Zakaria & Abdul-Talib, 2010).

However, the path to implementing Islamic marketing strategies isn't devoid of challenges for small businesses. One such challenge resides in the delicate equilibrium required between Muslim customers' requisites and the preferences of non-Muslim counterparts. Navigating this terrain necessitates a nuanced approach to resonate with both segments without estranging either (Abdullah et al., 2017). Furthermore, the empirical landscape and research underpinning Islamic marketing, particularly within the purview of small businesses, remain relatively scarce (Abdullah et al., 2017). A compelling case emerges for more research to furnish pragmatic insights and tangible directions for small firms aspiring to integrate Islamic marketing strategies.

In summation, Islamic marketing assumes heightened relevance for small firms entrenched in Muslim domains or catering to Muslim clienteles. The synchronization of marketing strategies with Islamic principles, particularly through the marketing mix and market orientation, can greatly benefit these enterprises.

Nevertheless, the journey isn't devoid of challenges, urging the expansion of empirical evidence and scholarly investigation to equip small businesses with actionable insights in this realm.

Figure 3. Marketing mix in Islamic marketing
Source: Hashim & Hamzah, (2014)

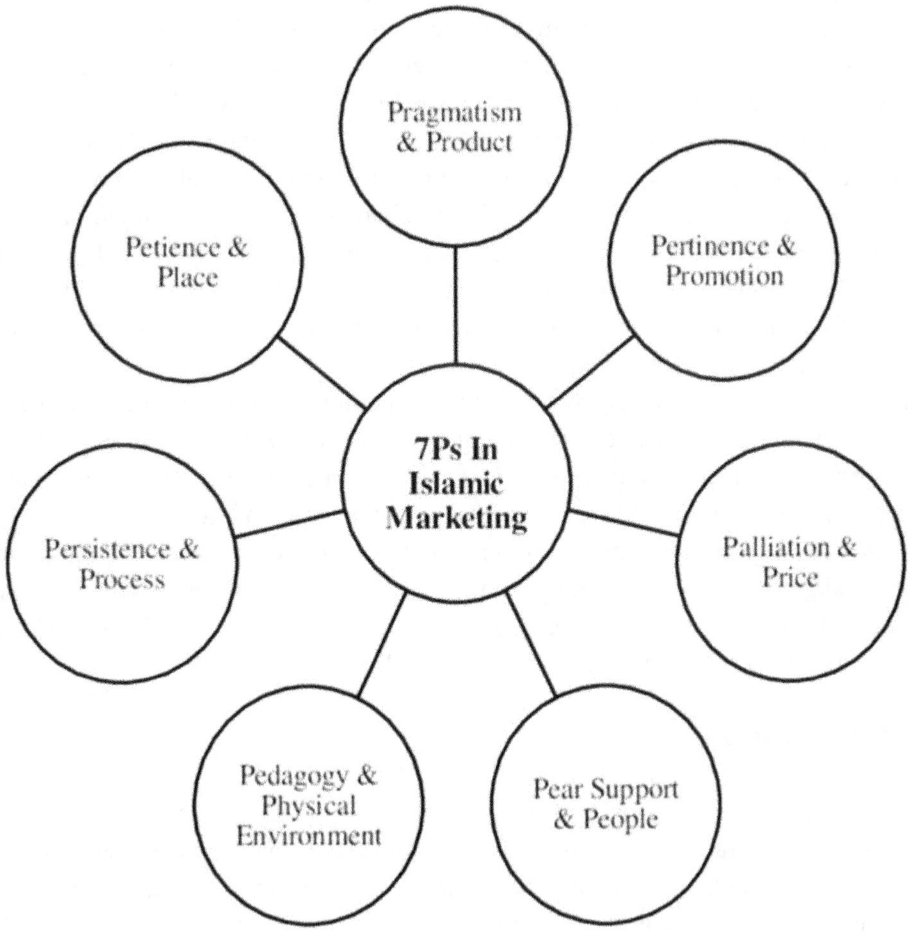

IMPACT ISLAMIC MARKETING AND SMALL FIRM VELUE

Financial Characteristics

The investigation delves into the ramifications of Islamic marketing on the financial dynamics of small businesses. Within the Islamic financial ecosystem, adherence to Islamic principles permeates financial operations, branding, and marketing strategies of Islamic financial institutions, effectively setting them apart from their conventional counterparts. The discourse unpacks pertinent Islamic marketing attributes that enable the positioning and provision of products congruent with Islamic values. This holds notable import due to the limited expanse of literature encompassing pragmatic Islamic marketing approaches tailored for Islamic financial institutions. Moreover, a pivotal nexus emerges between Islamic financial literacy and the inclination to establish micro, small, and medium-sized enterprises (MSMEs). Acquiring a grasp of Islamic finance principles proves indispensable for business stakeholders, including MSMEs, with Islamic legal financial literacy forming an extension of financial acumen. This, in turn, impacts the decision to embark on a small business venture.

While the assessment of small business success often rests upon financial benchmarks, a multifaceted panorama unfolds. Notably, many small business proprietors are impelled to initiate ventures grounded in personal or lifestyle considerations (Walker & Brown, 2004). This introduces non-financial aspirations and metrics, encompassing personal contentment, achievement, professional pride, and a flexible lifestyle, as pivotal gauges of success for small business proprietors (Walker & Brown, 2004). Personal attributes such as age and business characteristics interplay with perceptions of the import attributed to both financial and non-financial markers of success (Walker & Brown, 2004). These non-financial dimensions, colloquially referred to as psychic rewards or psychic income, resonate with individuals who may not have attained substantial financial achievements but derive personal fulfillment and alternative rewards from their entrepreneurial endeavors (Walker & Brown, 2004). The study's findings resonate: Islamic financial literacy underpins 13.8% of the impetus driving interest in establishing MSMEs, while the remaining 86.2% is entwined with extrinsic variables outside the study's purview. These encompass self-motivation, familial milieu, capital inflow dynamics, technological dimensions, educational variables, and knowledge garnered through formal education.

In summation, the symbiotic interplay of Islamic marketing and financial literacy emerges as pivotal for the triumph of small businesses. Islamic financial institutions are compelled to align marketing strategies in harmony with Islamic principles to carve a distinct niche from conventional entities. A nuanced grasp of Islamic financial tenets augments the predilection to initiate small business ventures. While financial yardsticks don't encapsulate the entirety of small business success, non-financial factors, including personal gratification and accomplishment, significantly contribute. Moreover, the echelons of Islamic financial literacy bear marked influence on the aspiration to establish MSMEs, although a consortium of external factors also holds sway in this realm.

Firm Size Moderation

The exploration of Islamic marketing's influence on the value of small businesses unfolds within the prism of firm size moderation. Islamic marketing, championing ethical and socially responsible business conduct, garners mounting recognition as an indispensable facet of business strategy, particularly within saturated markets or during periods of sluggish customer growth (Floren et al., 2020). In the realm of relationship marketing, preserving existing clientele emerges as a pivotal objective, touted for its cost-effectiveness compared to acquiring new patrons (Ahmad & Buttle, 2002). Consequently, comprehending the nexus between Islamic marketing and small business value bears paramount significance for enterprises navigating Islamic markets.

The intricate interplay of firm size on the interrelationship between financial characteristics and Islamic firm value has undergone scrutiny within the Indonesian equity milieu (Santosa, 2020). This inquiry uncovered that profitability exercises a positive and substantial impact on Islamic firm value, with the moderating effect of firm size amplifying the influence of profitability on firm value. Moreover, the magnitude of a firm's assets correlates with the magnitude of its liquidity's sway over Islamic firm value. These findings underscore firm size's pivotal role in molding the connection between financial traits and Islamic firm value. Additionally, the study accentuates the pivotal import of incorporating firm size and corporate governance attributes into the purview of Islamic firm investors within the equity sphere. Consequentially, managers and relevant entities are prompted to integrate firm size and corporate governance mechanisms to enrich the financial market discourse concerning firm value.

Within the realm of Islamic marketing, the crux lies in formulating marketing strategies harmonizing with Islamic principles (Abdullah et al., 2017). This underpins the necessity to uphold Islamic tenets in business activities, especially within marketing, guaranteeing promotional endeavors align with Islamic precepts (Abdullah et al., 2017). Such an endeavor is acutely pertinent in Islamic markets, where consumers' purchasing determinations are profoundly shaped by their religious convictions (Floren et al., 2020).

In summation, the ripples of Islamic marketing's impact upon small business value are inflected by the mediating influence of firm size. Parsing the intricate fabric interlinking financial attributes, Islamic firm value, and size is imperative for enterprises navigating Islamic markets. Crafting sagacious marketing strategies that sync with Islamic principles while factoring in firm size moderation stands poised to amplify business value and adeptly address the requisites of Muslim consumers.

Corporate Governance

Numerous studies have delved into the intricate interplay between Islamic marketing, small business value, and corporate governance, with notable insights emerging from diverse perspectives. For instance, Alnasser & Muhammed, (2012) underscore the imperative to scrutinize corporate governance within the realm of Islamic banks. Their work accentuates the significance of comprehending governance through an Islamic lens, particularly the functioning of the Shariah Supervisory Board and its interrelation with the Islamic banking landscape.

Mamatzakis et al., (2023) embarked on an investigation to unveil the repercussions of corporate governance practices on the performance and stability of Islamic banks. Their meticulous study discloses that Islamic and conventional banks exhibit divergent implications of corporate governance practices on cost efficiency and financial stability. The authors sound a note of caution against blindly adopting additional layers of binding practices, beyond those mandated by the Sharia Board and the Board of Directors. Such hasty adoption, they contend, could lead to cumbersome operational dynamics and a depreciation in value for Islamic banks. The practical ramifications of their findings extend to regulators, policymakers, and managerial cadres within Islamic banks, advocating for a judicious selection of international corporate governance practices grounded in empirical findings. Additionally, their research underscores the role of Sharia risk as a facet of corporate governance within Islamic banks, shaping the dynamics of these institutions and impacting their stakeholders.

In a parallel vein, Lidyah, (2018) delves into the implementation of Islamic corporate governance and its reverberations on the performance of Islamic banks. The study posits that Islamic corporate governance wields a substantial sway on the performance metrics of these banks. Complementary research by Prativi et al., (2021) corroborates this notion, affirming the influence of Islamic corporate governance on fostering sustainable business practices—a concordant sentiment with prior scholarly discourse. Further augmenting this landscape, an exploration of corporate governance's impact on sustainability endeavors within Islamic financial institutions comes to the fore. The study "Sustainability Factors of Sharia Banks in Indonesia" (Aisjah et al., 2022) illuminates a significant and affirmative correlation between corporate governance and sustainability initiatives within Islamic financial entities.

Collectively, this confluence of studies spotlights the intricate interrelationship among Islamic marketing, small business value, and corporate governance in the precincts of Islamic banks. The research resonates with the imperative of comprehending governance from an Islamic vantage point and prudently selecting corporate governance paradigms tailored for Islamic banks. Furthermore, the cumulative findings postulate that Islamic corporate governance's ramifications traverse the domains of performance, stability, and sustainability, furnishing actionable insights for regulators, policymakers, and managerial stewards of Islamic banks. The clarion call for the integration of Islamic corporate governance within decision-making processes resounds with undeniable significance.

Islamic Business Ethics

The exploration of the ramifications of Islamic marketing and the underpinning significance of small business value within the realm of Islamic ethics has been a focal point of numerous scholarly inquiries. A clarion call for the adoption of Islamic business ethics rings out, as evidenced by the formulation of novel frameworks and approaches (Ismaeel & Blaim, 2012). The pivotal role of Islamic ethics in shaping the contours of marketing principles and exerting influence over consumer behaviors emerges as a salient theme (Floren et al., 2020). Extensive research substantiates the assertion that Islamic marketing exerts a pronounced impact on the inclinations and preferences of Muslim consumers, sculpting their choices of services and products in consonance with Islamic Shariah law (Floren et al., 2020).

The vista of inquiry expands to encompass the influence of Islamic business ethics on the modus operandi of small micro enterprises (SMEs). A corpus of research underscores that Islamic business ethics resonates with a positive and robust influence on the performance and expansion trajectory of SMEs (Najmudin et al., 2022). This ethical stance further spills over into the realm of sales and customer satisfaction, evoking affirmative effects across varying contexts (Fakhrurozi et al., 2022). It is, however, imperative to acknowledge that the digital sphere doesn't uniformly conform to the contours of Islamic business ethics; therein lies a propensity to neglect Islamic law in online commercial transactions (Saputra et al., 2022).

The annals of scholarship on Islamic marketing and consumer behavior yield invaluable insights for the seamless integration of Islamic practices into consumer behavior analysis. A cogent recommendation emerges—namely, the incorporation of Islamic practices pertaining to consumer consumption patterns within studies concentrated on the analysis of consumer behavior (Floren et al., 2020). The adoption of Islamic marketing within the precincts of Islamic banks hasn't escaped scrutiny either, with findings underscoring the wholehearted embrace of the concept of Islamic ethics among the marketing personnel within Islamic banks (Abdullah et al., 2017).

In summation, the compendium of scrutinized studies underscores the resounding impact of Islamic marketing and business ethics on multifarious facets of small businesses and consumer behaviors. Charting a course for further inquiry becomes imperative, with a keen eye on aligning online business practices with the tenets of Islamic ethics. The call to weave Islamic practices intricately into the tapestry of consumer behavior analysis resonates as a clarion imperative, promising a more comprehensive understanding of the dynamic interplay between Islamic marketing and consumer behavior (Rahmayati, 2021).

Social Cause Marketing

The discourse surrounding the interplay of Islamic marketing and the value of small businesses within the realm of social cause marketing has garnered remarkable traction in recent times. Recognized as a distinctive marketing approach rooted in Islamic principles and values, Islamic marketing has emerged as a nuanced strategy (Hasan, 2020). A notable facet under scrutiny is the role of Zakah, an obligatory form of charity in Islam, within the domain of social cause marketing (Abdullahi, 2019).

Zakah has emerged as a potent instrument for propelling social causes and corporate benevolence, wielding the potential to bolster Halal enterprises, alleviate poverty, and galvanize sustainable progress (Abdullahi, 2019). By crafting offerings that cater to the needs of Zakah beneficiaries, Islamic firms stand not only to alleviate destitution but also to amplify their market share and contribute to industry growth and broader economic vitality (Abdullahi, 2019). Implicit in this is the notion that Zakah can exert substantial influence on the social, promotional, and cause-centric marketing endeavors of businesses operating within Islamic societies (Abdullahi, 2019).

Furthermore, a burgeoning paradigm advocates for the fusion of Islamic marketing principles with conventional social marketing, constituting a novel avenue in the realm of Islamic marketing (Hasan, 2020). This convergence holds the potential to steer the formulation of social marketing interventions in societies with a substantial Muslim populace, offering guidance to practitioners aligning with Islamic values (Hasan, 2020). It is posited that enterprises targeting Muslim consumers could devise marketing strategies that seamlessly weave in religious elements, while simultaneously addressing socio-psychological undercurrents to advocate Islamic products (Syahrivar et al., 2022). The peril of marketing myopia looms if businesses overlook the socio-psychological incentives underlying Islamic consumption (Syahrivar et al., 2022). Further research by Syafitri, (2022) unveils that beyond Zakah, service quality and Islamic business ethics also exert an impact on social values through the mediation of religious values. Small businesses adhering to Islamic business ethics and furnishing top-notch services stand to enrich their communities by fostering social values.

In essence, the nexus between Islamic marketing, small business value, and social cause marketing represents a tapestry of intricate dimensions. This panorama encompasses delving into the role of Zakah, harmonizing Islamic marketing tenets with social marketing, and deciphering the interplay of socio-psychological motivations and religious values in marketing stratagems. A further voyage into these realms, underpinned by rigorous research, holds the promise of furnishing pragmatic directives for Islamic firms and social marketing practitioners navigating the complex terrains of Muslim-dominated societies.

CONCLUSION

The realm of Islamic marketing emerges as a promising domain for small businesses aiming to fortify their standing in the market. The distinctive underpinning of Islamic marketing, firmly rooted in Islamic principles and values, unfurls vistas for differentiation and resonance among Muslim consumers. This acquires heightened relevance for small enterprises grappling with resource constraints and the struggle to carve out distinct identities amidst saturated markets.

Scholarly inquiry attests to the affirmative impact that the adoption of Islamic marketing strategies can wield on the value of small businesses. The confluence of profitability pursuits and fidelity to Islamic tenets equips these enterprises to augment their market valuation. Furthermore, the discernment of Islamic marketing's nuances equips non-Muslim enterprises to deftly navigate the intricacies of engaging Muslim consumers while upholding inclusivity. A pivotal Islamic pillar, Zakah, bequeaths a unique avenue for small businesses to orchestrate social cause marketing and corporate benevolence. The integration of Zakah within the gamut of social responsibility initiatives not only forges a sanguine corporate image but also magnetizes Muslim consumers and aligns seamlessly with Islamic precepts.

The facets of firm dimensions, corporate governance, Islamic business ethics, and social cause marketing interweave with intricate synchrony, delineating the course of Islamic marketing's influence on the value of small businesses. This symbiotic interplay accentuates the indispensable nature of comprehensive strategies, seamlessly interlacing Islamic principles into the very tapestry of diverse business realms.

Notwithstanding the evident advantages poised by Islamic marketing for small enterprises, the landscape is studded with challenges. The delicate equilibrium between the preferences of Muslim and non-Muslim consumers poses a conundrum, necessitating deft navigation. Moreover, the call for augmented empirical research resounds across the field. This research lacuna beckons further exploration, unearthing pragmatic insights, stratagems, and compasses for small businesses to adroitly harness Islamic marketing's prowess and amplify their market value in the sphere of Islamic consumerism.

Collectively, this research engenders a richer comprehension of Islamic marketing's potential as an invaluable asset for small enterprises, enroute to differentiation, expansion, and triumph within the crucible of cutthroat business rivalry.

REFERENCES

Abdullah, J., Haji Hamali, J., & Abdullah, F. (2017). Success Strategies In Islamic Marketing MIX. *International Journal of Business and Society*, *16*(3). doi:10.33736/ijbs.581.2015

Abdullahi, S. I. (2019). Zakah as tool for social cause marketing and corporate charity: A conceptual study. *Journal of Islamic Marketing*, *10*(1), 191–207. doi:10.1108/JIMA-03-2017-0025

Adelekan, A. S., Ojo, J. O., & Worimegbe, P. M. (2021). Coopetition and Small Firms Value Creation. *European Journal of Business Science and Technology*, *133*.

Ahmad, N. (2018). Toward advancing debates on Islamic marketing: A renewed perspective. *Journal of Islamic Marketing*, *9*(1), 152–166. doi:10.1108/JIMA-08-2016-0064

Ahmad, R., & Buttle, F. (2002). Customer retention management: A reflection of theory and practice. *Marketing Intelligence & Planning*, *20*(3), 149–161. doi:10.1108/02634500210428003

Aisjah, S., Prabandari, S. P., & Hamid, W. (2022). Sustainability Factors of Sharia Banks in Indonesia. *Quality - Access to Success, 23*(190).

Alharbi, R. K., Yahya, S., & Kassim, S. (2022). Impact of religiosity and branding on SMEs performance: Does financial literacy play a role? *Journal of Islamic Marketing, 13*(12), 2717–2741. doi:10.1108/JIMA-08-2019-0162

Alnasser, S. A. S., & Muhammed, J. (2012). Introduction to corporate governance from Islamic perspective. *Humanomics, 28*(3), 220–231. doi:10.1108/08288661211258110

Alserhan, B. A., Zeqiri, J., Ramadani, V., & Dana, L.-P. (2022). An Introduction to Strategic Islamic Marketing. In *Strategic Islamic Marketing: A Roadmap for Engaging Muslim Consumers* (pp. 1–5). Springer. doi:10.1007/978-3-030-98160-0_1

Dabla-Norris, M. E., Misch, F., Cleary, M. D., & Khwaja, M. (2017). *Tax administration and firm performance: New data and evidence for emerging market and developing economies*. International Monetary Fund.

Delmar, F., & Wiklund, J. (2008). The effect of small business managers' growth motivation on firm growth: A longitudinal study. *Entrepreneurship Theory and Practice, 32*(3), 437–457. doi:10.1111/j.1540-6520.2008.00235.x

Fakhrurozi, F., Najmudin, N., & Maelani, P. (2022). Do Islamic Business Ethics Have An Effect on Indonesian Citizens' Interest in Saving At The Faisal Islamic Bank of Egypt? A Case in Cairo, Egypt. *MUAMALATUNA, 14*(2), 147–163. doi:10.37035/mua.v14i2.7093

Floren, J., Rasul, T., & Gani, A. (2020). Islamic marketing and consumer behaviour: A systematic literature review. *Journal of Islamic Marketing, 11*(6), 1557–1578. doi:10.1108/JIMA-05-2019-0100

Guizani, M. (2020). Testing the pecking order theory of capital structure: The case of Islamic financing modes. *Future Business Journal, 6*(1), 1–12. doi:10.118643093-020-00042-9

Hasan, M. (2020). Social marketing: An Islamic perspective. *Journal of Islamic Marketing, 11*(4), 863–881. doi:10.1108/JIMA-12-2016-0105

Hashim, N., & Hamzah, M. I. (2014). 7P's: A literature Review of Islamic marketing and Contemporary Marketing MIx. *Procedia: Social and Behavioral Sciences, 130*, 155–159. doi:10.1016/j.sbspro.2014.04.019

Ismaeel, M., & Blaim, K. (2012). Toward applied Islamic business ethics: Responsible halal business. *Journal of Management Development, 31*(10), 1090–1100. doi:10.1108/02621711211281889

Ismail, M. S. I., Harun, T. W. R., Ismail, S., Aziz, A., & Ibrahim, M. A. (2022). *Definition of Islamic Brand: A Study From Islamic Conjuction and its Findings*.

Kumar, P. (2015). Green marketing innovations in small Indian firms. *World Journal of Entrepreneurship, Management and Sustainable Development, 11*(3), 176–190. doi:10.1108/WJEMSD-01-2015-0003

Lidyah, R. (2018). Islamic corporate governance, islamicityfinancial performance index and fraudat Islamic bank. *Jurnal Akuntansi, 22*(3), 437–453. doi:10.24912/ja.v22i3.398

Lumpkin, G. T., & Dess, G. G. (1996). Clarifying the entrepreneurial orientation construct and linking it to performance. *Academy of Management Review*, *21*(1), 135–172. doi:10.2307/258632

Mamatzakis, E., Alexakis, C., Al Yahyaee, K., Pappas, V., Mobarek, A., & Mollah, S. (2023). Does corporate governance affect the performance and stability of Islamic banks? *Corporate Governance (Bradford)*, *23*(4), 888–919. doi:10.1108/CG-05-2022-0217

Marom, S. (2021). Toward Dynamic-Based Classification of SMEs. *International Journal of Business Administration*, *12*(3), 25. doi:10.5430/ijba.v12n3p25

Peprah, J. A., Andoh, F. K., Avorkpo, E. A., Dafor, K. N., Afful, B. Jr, & Obeng, C. K. (2022). Compliance Burden and Tax gap among micro and small businesses: Evidence from Ghana. *SAGE Open*, *12*(4), 21582440221126984. doi:10.1177/21582440221126985

Prativi, Y. P., Sukmadilaga, C., & Cupian, C. (2021). The Impact of Islamic Corporate Governance Disclosure, Islamic Intellectual Capital, Zakat, Financial Performance (SCnP Model) & Islamic Ethical Identity to Sustainable Business. *Jurnal Ekonomi Syariah Teori Dan Terapan*, *8*(2), 171. doi:10.20473/vol8iss20212pp171-182

Rahmayati, R. (2021). Competition Strategy In The Islamic Banking Industry: An Empirical Review. *International Journal Of Business, Economics, and Social Development*, *2*(2), 65–71.

Santosa, P. W. (2020). The moderating role of firm size on financial characteristics and Islamic firm value at Indonesian equity market. *Business: Theory and Practice*, *21*(1), 391–401. doi:10.3846/btp.2020.12197

Saputra, A. D., Rahmatia, A., Wahyuningsih, S. H., & Azhar, A. (2022). Online Business Practices: A Study of Islamic Business Ethics Perspective in Indonesia. *Jurnal Penelitian*, 97–108.

Steeger, J. H., & Hoffmann, M. (2016). Innovation and family firms: Ability and willingness and German SMEs. *Journal of Family Business Management*, *6*(3), 251–269. doi:10.1108/JFBM-09-2015-0036

Sulasih, Pramono Hari Adi, Weni Novandari, & Suliyanto. (2023). Islamic Perspective on Marketing Strategy Through Quantitative Strategic Planning Matrix (QSPM). *Ijtimā Iyya Journal of Muslim Society Research*, *8*(1 SE-Articles), 11–32. doi:10.24090/ijtimaiyya.v8i1.6242

Syafitri, I. N. A. (2022). The Meaning of Profit for Krempyeng Market Gresik's Merchants through the Cultural Perspective. *Interdisciplinary Social Studies*, *1*(6), 793–808. doi:10.55324/iss.v1i6.145

Syahrivar, J., Hermawan, S. A., Gyulavári, T., & Chairy, C. (2022). Religious compensatory consumption in the Islamic context: The mediating roles of religious social control and religious guilt. *Asia Pacific Journal of Marketing and Logistics*, *34*(4), 739–758. doi:10.1108/APJML-02-2021-0104

Tournois, L., & Aoun, I. (2012). From traditional to Islamic marketing strategies: Conceptual issues and implications for an exploratory study in Lebanon. *Education, Business and Society*, *5*(2), 134–140. doi:10.1108/17537981211251179

Walker, E., & Brown, A. (2004). What success factors are important to small business owners? *International Small Business Journal*, *22*(6), 577–594. doi:10.1177/0266242604047411

Wilson, J. A. J. (2012). The new wave of transformational Islamic marketing. *Journal of Islamic Marketing, 3*(1), 5–11. doi:10.1108/17590831211225436

Yusfiarto, R., & Pambekti, G. T. (2019). Do internet marketing factors with islamic values improve sme performance? *Journal of Islamic Monetary Economics and Finance, 5*(4), 807–828. doi:10.21098/jimf.v5i4.1101

Zakaria, N., & Abdul-Talib, A. (2010). Applying Islamic market-oriented cultural model to sensitize strategies towards global customers, competitors, and environment. *Journal of Islamic Marketing, 1*(1), 51–62. doi:10.1108/17590831011026222

Chapter 11
Entrepreneurial Intentions From an Islamic Perspective:
A Case Study of Muslim Entrepreneurs in Pakistan

Zahid Hussain
Shaheed Benazir Bhutto University, Pakistan

Asadullah Mari
Shaheed Benazir Bhutto University, Pakistan

Muhammad Arif
Shaheed Benazir Bhutto University, Pakistan

ABSTRACT

In Islam, with its own method of doing business as stated in the Quran and Hadith, entrepreneurship is part of everyday life. In Islam, determining a person's intentions and personality traits when starting a business largely depends on his intentions. This study attempts to cast an Islamic perspective on Muslim business owners in Pakistan regarding the concept and element of business intent. A survey of over 250 Muslim business owners in Pakistan was conducted to collect primary data on the motivations and characteristics of Pakistani Muslim entrepreneurs, such as their reasons for deciding to pursue a career. According to previous studies, the two main characteristics of business intentions in Islam are honesty and worship of Allah (functions of a spiritual, personal, and socio-economic nature). This research shows that all human behavior, especially that related to entrepreneurship, has been consistently driven by the effects of five key traits on entrepreneurial personalities: amanah, tabligh, fathonah, istiqomah, and saddiq.

1. INTRODUCTION

Entrepreneurship is widely recognized as the engine of economic growth. It may have contributed to development by opening employment opportunities, increasing income and wealth, and linking economic

DOI: 10.4018/978-1-6684-7519-5.ch011

growth to the global market (Davis et al., 2013). Essentially, religion is defined as a set of guidelines governing how people should relate to God, others, and the world around them. According to (Gümüsay et al., 2015), religion may have contributed to the economy. Although the advancement of technology, investment, and environmental assets were considerations that influenced the community's economic growth, religion was seen as a crucial element in shaping the community's work rate. Furthermore, it has been claimed that religion plays an important role in influencing a country's economy. According to (Hassan et al., 2014), Protestant morality has a significant impact on the economic development of many regions of Asia and the United States under the capitalist system. A further study by (Muhammad et al., 2020), which also noted that Tokugawa's religious ideology was a crucial pillar for the growth of Japanese capitalism, also found evidence of the importance of perseverance in achieving success. Furthermore, he believes that Chinese entrepreneurs have grown and thrived within the Chinese Confucian faith. A person's choice to become an entrepreneur, his entrepreneurial skills, the style of running his business and his network with other entrepreneurs are all factors that religion can have an impact on (Anggadwita et al., 2015).

Islam in general and in particular is a religion that supports entrepreneurship (Fozia et al., 2016). In Islam, the primary intention is a crucial element in determining a person's qualities and driving forces in starting a business. Ambition is therefore very important in Islam. According to the Prophet Muhammad, every action and every deed is influenced by a specific intention. Furthermore, Prophet Muhammad said: "The reward for actions should be based on the specific intention and each person will receive the reward in accordance with what he has willed" (Hadith Bukhari), while Allah SWT said in the Quran: "That, whoever does justice, male or female, as one who believes We will grant him a comfortable life." We will encourage them according to their better knowledge of what they have done before. "[Quran: Al-Nahl 16:97]. Despite this, Muslims currently have a low level of motivation and commitment to start their own business and implement business ethics in line with Islamic principles.

Among the benefits of entrepreneurship is the creation of jobs that increase the well-being of Muslims in particular, as well as all individuals in general. In recent years, questions about corporate intent have swirled among many legislators, academics, and professionals. According to (Ahmed et al., 2008), an intention is a driving force that influences behavioral patterns and shows how preparatory efforts are made to accomplish a task. In fact, behind any human behavior, there is always at least one intention. An important approach that considers additional internal, external and contextual variables is primarily responsible for influences on entrepreneurial intention (Ratten et al., 2017). Internal influences on an individual's entrepreneurial behavior include socio-demographic variables, personal characteristics, and many more, such as age, gender, work history, and marital status (Harizan et al., 2020). Environmental components and the environmental context are examples of external influences. According to (Adham et al., 2012), one of the most important predictors of becoming an entrepreneur is an individual's intention to start their own business. In summary, entrepreneurial behavior is a commitment to actively participate in generating new ideas and achieving something new or unique, with the ultimate goal of generating income for people and strengthening the community (Àbras et al., 2022).

However, little research has been done on Islamic entrepreneurship. Consequently, this research will contribute to the literature on Islam focused on entrepreneurial goals. Islamic religious restrictions are explored to contribute to the literature, particularly those relating to the goals of entrepreneurs and the characteristics of individuals who have run businesses with the wonderful gift of Allah SWT in mind. From an Islamic perspective, this research aims to provide a general overview of the ideas and measures of entrepreneurial intent from an Islamic perspective. The goal is achieved by considering the possibility that, in accordance with Islamic religious law, a mixture of moral, sociocultural and economic conditions may have contributed to the completion of Islamic industries (Machmud et al., 2020).

This article is organized as follows to provide a solid explanatory framework: the probable links between Islam and entrepreneurship are developed in section 2, while the research approach is attempted to be elaborated in section 3, the Study results are covered and discussed in Section 4, and Conclusion of the study research findings are presented in Section 5.

1.1 LITERATURE REVIEW

1.1.1 The Islamic View of Entrepreneurship

Islam and entrepreneurship, two highly controversial ideas, are combined to form the concept of entrepreneurship from an Islamic perspective. The basic tenets of Islam are that there is only one God, but Muhammad (peace be upon him) is his messenger. In a well-known Hadith narrated by Al-Bukhari, the Prophet is questioned by the angel Gabriel about Islam, Iman and Ihsan. The Prophet replies that Islam is a witness to the absence of any god other than Allah, but also that Muhammad is his messenger and that one must pray, give alms, pay zakat, observe the Ramadan fast and continue the pilgrimage when you are able. do it. Iman is the acceptance of Allah, His miracles, His written and spoken word, His prophets, the last day and the spiritual plane. Ihsan is the act of worshiping Allah as if you see Him, even if you do not see Him and He has seen you. This belief and submission to God is associated with the Islamic characteristics of EIP.

The French and German words "entrepreneur" and "unternehmen" are the origin of the term "entrepreneurship". Both of these phrases mean "behaviour". In a way, the entrepreneur sees tasks that no one else would have. In the multitude of characters that make up the subject of the financial balance sheet, the entrepreneur is "among the most fascinating and at the same time the most ethereal" (Haque et al., 2014). ((As a classification of business models of entrepreneurship, combine the Austrian, Chicago and German schools - three dominant intellectual traditions. Entrepreneurs should seize opportunities, according to proponents of the so-called Austrian school, e.g. B. (Kayed, 2015). The Chicago School emphasizes the value of taking calculated risks and embracing unpredictability. The German school emphasizes the importance of different formations and imaginative losses and is particularly known for its works by Schumpeter (1934). An entrepreneur is someone who seizes opportunities, often by combining the reserves they already have while accepting the risk inherent in the business.

EIP is more than a brief overview of Islam; it is also a bargain. It is supported by three intertwined cornerstones. According to the definition of entrepreneurship, the search for possibilities is the first pillar. The socio-economic status or moral component is the second. In reality, EIP is governed by a set of rules, ideals and suggestions. The cornerstone that connects people to God with the ultimate goal of making Allah happy is not only religious but also spiritual. Such foundations connect to each other. The second and third foundations are not actually added. The cornerstones influence each other. These foundations have specific religious textual references, organizations and interpretative procedures. Consequently, EIP uses its own technique to arrive at understanding. It needs to be understood and explored holistically, taking into account entrepreneurial endeavors, principles shaped by religion, specific Islamic commitments, sufficient to convey scriptural input, as well as an ecosystem of individuals and organizations that serve as the interpretative framework for that religion prism of doctrine.

The EIP is occasionally challenged or evaluated by comparing it with ethically questionable Western entrepreneurship. In response, it could be argued that entrepreneurship in general, but also culture-based or social entrepreneurship in particular, is moral and probably includes the aforementioned foundations of entrepreneurship and ethics. To allow for evaluation, comparison and integration, specific Western initiatives in the fields of social responsibility and morality could be effectively linked to the intrinsic moral goals implanted in Islamic religious teachings. The Skoll Center, other recently established scientific institutes, research initiatives and courses on social entrepreneurship have institutionalized the growing interest of research in social entrepreneurship. The mix of entrepreneurship and interpersonal task is typically used to define social entrepreneurship (Ramadani et al., 2015). "Entrepreneurship integrated with a social cause," Austin said, "is what social entrepreneurship is." Some academics have also explored how morality and entrepreneurship interact.

In moral, interpersonal and social entrepreneurship, however, there is no religious doctrine or specific procedures that serve as a moral basis or specific procedures on which they focus. Therefore, despite incorporating ethical principles and applying Islamic ethics to the economic system, EIP is more than just an ethical stance on entrepreneurship (). It differs from moral, interpersonal, or social entrepreneurship because it involves certain practices, biblical references, a spiritual purpose, or a connection with God. EIP can be mistaken for entrepreneurship in Muslim-majority or Muslim-majority countries. Despite the existence of an educational element in support of EIP and above all of the entrepreneurial spirit, the country does not need to have a Muslim majority. Furthermore, the articles and services must not be aimed at Muslims. Since EIP involves a religious and spiritual perspective, the entrepreneur, or at least part of the business, must be Muslim. While any entrepreneur's practice may be consistent with Islamic principles, EIP also involves a belief or practice of God that requires some degree of religious commitment. This is not to say that non-Muslims are excluded from the perspectives of EIP. The EIP, on the other hand, offers a strategy for critical reflection on entrepreneurship, such as B. Shift the discussion from person-centered and self-interested entrepreneurship to family or community entrepreneurship. It is possible to replace some belief systems with others and implement the norms and beliefs of IPE. EIP could and should allow us to think more broadly about the role of religion in business and how a particular scripture reference and a spiritual being provide guidance and advice. Furthermore, knowledge of EIP could improve interaction with religious entrepreneurs.

The EIP focused on implementing and adapting entrepreneurship for Muslim majority countries rather than reintegrating into entrepreneurship. The movement to Islamize understanding in the late 1970s and early 1980s, particularly through the International Center for Islamic Ideas, is directly related to the growth of an Islamic perspective on economic principles, business and services financial. The fundamental principle was that a significant number of studies and ideas are theoretically and empirically based on the West and may not be relevant to some other regions of the world. Islamic notions of finance and economics provided a contextualized perspective and were integrated into a strong, values-based global curriculum. Academics should join EIP to re-evaluate and advocate the long-term nature of EIP and make it more relevant to the principles of entrepreneurship and their application in general. This includes both educational and religious references.

We also need to review the conditions and how they occurred. In the context of Islamic economics, but also Islamic finance, the word "Islamic entrepreneurship" is often used today to denote an Islamic-based method for certain financial and business practices. The phrase "entrepreneurship from such an Islamic point of view" might be more appropriate. It can be argued that Islam does not represent a specific concept of entrepreneurship, financial services or economics, but rather provides a structure and basis for the development of a variety of entrepreneurship modeling techniques, financial services and economy. As such, it serves more as a point of view or base. Therefore, concepts such as Islamic entrepreneurship, Islamic finance and Islamic economics could be misleading. It is a long and difficult road to move from religious texts through their analysis to a religious conception of entrepreneurship or perhaps to more precise terms that could be used from an Islamic perspective, entrepreneurship, economics and financial services. However, the Islamic business is undoubtedly more memorable and easier to market. Rather than being a strictly pedagogical and theologically relevant concept, Islamic entrepreneurship seems more marketing-based. Therefore, we must engage in an indicative and productive discussion of the word, both with restraint and with a better analysis of what it encompasses and is not yet. One might well advise using the extra-precise alternative when it comes to Islamic entrepreneurship, at least in educated circles.

1.1.2 An Islamic Perspective on Entrepreneurship

The relationship between texts or perspectives informs Islam's importance in entrepreneurship. The Quran and Sunnah are also the primary contributors. For Muslims, the Quran is a collection of 114 surahs (chapters) and more than 6,000 verses (plural: yah) that were progressively disclosed over the course of 23 years, roughly 600 AD. The Sunnah is a collection of the Prophet Muhammad's acts and sayings, as well as implicit endorsements (pbuh). Ijma's (Consensus) as well as Qiy's is secondary research and methods (Analogy). According to the Madhhab, which is the particular school of jurisprudence, ijma is the unanimity of a group of individuals, such as religious scholars or the whole Muslim community. These factors could have a significant impact on how the entrepreneur, the organization, or its surrounding conditions are shaped at multiple stages of entrepreneurship. So at the micro-level, the specific entrepreneur might be driven by religion (Abd Muin et al., 2014), and they might have a different entrepreneurial goal than a person who is more homophobic in trade links. Even though entrepreneurship is a crucial component, this type of entrepreneur's accomplishments also includes socio-economic as well as spiritual accomplishments that apply to both the present world and the afterlife. This accomplishment is more often than not referred to as falah, and it denotes a situation of both substance and spiritual growth (Ramadani et al., 2017).

The entrepreneur is impacted by integrating work into all aspects of his religious practice, including fasting as well as prayer. He views work as a kind of worship in which he seeks Allah's blessings, as stated in the Quran in paragraph 62, verse 10. His view of the world might alter underlying principles like how risk is perceived with God acting as a savior or how work is rewarded in three ways: materially, socioeconomically, and spiritually. In addition to moral factors in the terms and conditions of employment and interactions with partners, social and economic factors in the larger society also influence how people act. For instance, the Quran declares: "O you who believe! Avoid misusing your assets by trading against one another instead (Quran, 4.29). "Nothing at all of you has finished Iman till he appreciates for his brother that which he loves for him," the Prophet Muhammad (pbuh) stated in a Hadith (Bukhari, Muslim).

He quoted the Hadith, "Consider giving the employee his salary until his sweat begins to dry," in another instance (Tirmidhi; Ibn Majah). God provides clear instructions on trading activities in section 11 verse 85, including providing just an indicator and mass. Numerous Hadiths support what can be summed up as environmentally friendly practices for both the environment and animals. The Quran makes numerous references to essence. According to one hadith, the prophet remarked to Sa'd ibn Abi Waqqas, "O Sa'd, how inefficient users are," as he took ablution. Sa'd questioned whether ritual cleansing might waste water. "Yeah, sure, even if you utilise a river's flowing water," the prophet retorted (Ahmad). In a different hadith (Al-Bukhari, Muslim), the prophet narrates how Allah praised a person and pardoned his sins since the person descended down a well, packed his shoe with water, but then descended again when going to hold his shoe in his teeth to provide a desperate dog with certain water.

Allah (Qur'an 24:33) is the ultimate owner of EIP, with people serving as caliphs, officials, or deputy governors (Quran 2:30; 57:7). The entrepreneurs do not even possess instant control. They must also purify their capital by paying Zakat (Quran 9:103), because it is correct for the homeless and the poor in their income, and wealth is forbidden (Quran 3:180; 9:34). (Quran 51:19). Wealth involves responsibilities. Principled Muslims who have the basic necessities necessary to pay zakat (Nisb) in addition to their liabilities and urgent needs are required to do so annually. The majority of products as well as assets have a 2.5% zakat percentage. As the Prophet said, "Zakat doesn't really minimize property." Muslims believe that offering doesn't quite lead to a reduction in income but rather a boost (Muslim).

So at mesa stage, Islam influences the organization in a variety of ways because it affects most parts of the business, including strategic planning, organization, HR, financial management, and advertising. The plan is anticipated to promote both spiritual development and global social economic wellbeing, in addition to financial success. The Quran forbids the consumption of some goods, including pork (2:173), alcohol, and gambling (5:90). False measurements and telling a lie are prohibited by the Qur'an (6:152; 33:70; 17:36), while other behaviors', like carrying out agreements, are required (Quran 5:1). The organization might well be shaped by religious practices such as the daily five prayers or fasting, for example, through the creation of a prayer hall, assigned job times during Holy month, or celebrations.

The firm's financial aspect is crucial to entrepreneurship. Islam specifically forbids financial support and investing in business activities. Allah steadily emphasized that riba, or the having taken of interest, is prohibited over the course of four stages. "Something which you consider giving in usury [riba] in sequence that it might raise on people's things seems to have no rise with Allah," God declared in the first verse of the Quran (30:39). "And (because of) their taking usury when they were forbidden," the second verse (4:161) says. "O users, who believe, need not continue living on usury, expanding your interest numerous times too much," says the third disclosure (3:130). Verse 2:275 concluded by stating:"...Allah has allowed business as well as forbade usury." There is also a declaration of battle in the Quran. Gharar as well as maisir and qimr are additional restrictions. Gharar is the Arabic word for unpredictability or uncertainty brought on by a lack of understanding regarding the terms of a deal or transfer. Sports of chance like gambling are related to the terms "maisir" or "qimr." Islam supports specific (commercial) financial alliances like Mudrabah and Mushrakah. In Mudrabah collaboration, the rabb-ul-ml, each party, offers the investment, as well as the mudrib, or other in, the labour of the entrepreneur. In a Mushrakah, different parties contribute capital, while others take on management responsibilities. The investor bears the loss of money in accordance with additional funds, whereas the entrepreneur inadvertently ends up losing time and resources put into the venture. Profits are allocated based on previously determined percentages. Microfinance seems to be a comparatively recent method of delivering financial products. The requirements of the banking system, such as short-term loans to relatively underprivileged micro-enterprises, are known as micro-finance (Abdullah et al., 2015). Team lending to customers who are equally responsible is an important component, as is civic engagement on the part of the lender. Microfinance, which is associated with micro lending, became especially popular in Southeast Asia and Latin America starting in the 1970s. As of Dec. 31, 2010, it reaches over 200 million individuals, over 80 million of whom are women. It has gained popularity in the last ten years. However, because microfinance relies on debt paid back with interest, researchers and practitioners have worked to develop an Islamic method for the field. The inclusion of Islamic financial intermediaries, a focus on households, and the inclusion of religious entitlements are just a few of the distinctive features that distinguish Islamic microfinance from traditional microfinance (Ramadani et al., 2021). Therefore, it might alter the allocation of financial equity well within the confines of religion, focusing especially on Muslim micro-enterprises. Islam has a large-scale impact on a number of organizations, including the market and the government. There is intellectual discussion surrounding the particular functions of these organizations from an Islamic perspective, and this discussion has a lengthy tradition (Mebroui et al., 2021). During the last 1400 years, researchers like Ghazali, Ibn Khaldun, Shah Wali Allah, Muhammad Iqbal, Chapra, as well as Siddiqi contributed to the development of Islamic economics in different stages or tides (Siddiqi, 1992). Through the establishment of institutions like the Hisbah, a type of industry watchdog, in addition to specific ethical and moral impacts like inherited wealth or welfare policy, Islam offers comprehensive rules for an economic structure and regulatory environment. Islamic economies could be "described inside the bounds of each nation's ethical framework". The organizational environment of entrepreneurship is therefore shaped by the marketplace and the state.

1.1.3 Islam as a Religion for Entrepreneurs

Islam itself can be described as an "entrepreneurial religious practice" in the context in which it supports and promotes commercial activities such as the pursuit of equal opportunity, calculated risk-taking and innovation. The search for this world is emphasized in the Qur'an and the Sunnah. But pursue the abode of the Farthest in all that Allah must have provided for you, but also neglect your part of the world and be compassionate, even though Allah has always been very kind to you, and actively seeks corrupt practices in the ground; for Allah claims to love the corrupters, "he says in verse 77 of section 28. Work on your present life as you were expected to live forever and only on your future life as if you were to die soon, as the Prophet once said (considered a weak hadith.) According to a statement by Ahmad of the Prophet, "Even if the Day of Judgment approaches, if anyone has a plant in his hand, he should plant it quickly," advises the Prophet. Richard Cantillon, who invented the word "entrepreneur" for economic principles in 1931, saw an entrepreneur as an expert in taking great risks. The employer somehow makes a profit or a loss when he closes the trading company, while the employee receives an insured salary. Not only in alphabetical terms, the concepts of risk and rizq (life or income) are strongly linked. Eventually Rizq is given to a Muslim by Allah. Therefore, a businessman must have tawakkul or faith in Allah. In this way, the risk "is about to be saved" and it is easy to exceed the limits. Due to the interest ban, it also qualifies as an obligation on the economic site. Wealth alone cannot create more wealth. Investments must involve risks, so by financing business ventures, the shareholder would become both a personal entrepreneur who would support entrepreneurs.

But "Islam is also unfavorable associated with entrepreneurial success within the dominant intellectual context of entrepreneurship" (Ramadani et al., 2021). Laws influenced by Islam are easily blamed for the lack of economic growth. (Abdullah et al., 2013) argues that some Islamic institutional structures have an anti-development character. "[T]his task continues to repeat well-known ethnocentric tropes and implicit operational elements associated with stagnation, underdevelopment, lack of democratic governance, lack of honesty, dysfunctional principles, and the inability to modernize", writes (Ahmed et al., 2015). For (Abd Muin et al., 2014), transformation is perceived as a Western influence in some respects. According to scholars such as (Ramadani et al., 2017), Islam does not hinder trade. The reverse can be supported by empirical information on Muslim practices, including rulings on fatwas and business practices. This is, of course, categorically partial, as it would make Islam recognize as something could also be related to geographic location, society or world affairs. According to (Mebroui et al., 2021), it was actually the absence of the working class, cities, individual freedoms and reforms that held back progress. It is sometimes noted that entrepreneurship and innovation should be discouraged based on an often misunderstood hadith. Any technology (bid'ah), according to the Hadith narrated by Abu Dawud, is unbelief. Rather than business innovation practices, this hadith refers to a deviation from the Bible and religious matters, as it is believed to have occurred in some other religious beliefs. More broadly, Imam Al-Shfi and others distinguish between good or praiseworthy bid'ah and negative or blameworthy bid'ah, classifying progress according to the five groups of Muslim law (akm): required advancement, suggested, authorized, censored and prohibited.

It is important to remember that a religion is by definition based on a certain immutable core and suggests certain immutable norms and beliefs. Whether this is true is less important than how many and whether there are procedures that allow for the integration of innovation and transformation into religious practice. Positive and negative developments are distinguished through the Ijtihad procedure. Ijtihad integrates background and message and enables "entrepreneurial" communication. The closure of the entrances to the Ijtihad will instead cause a kind of slowness. Even Islamic law may not be static; something more, the double method and the subject can be described as entrepreneurial, empowering, but also stimulating for the business.

2. FINDINGS

2.1 Respondents' Backgrounds

53.6% of survey participants were female, compared with 46.4% of all male participants. According to the results, 54% of Muslim entrepreneurs in Pakistan are responsible for micro-enterprises (annual turnover less than $ 300 million), 26% are still responsible for smaller companies (from $ 300 million to $ 2.50 billion.), 16% are responsible for midsize companies ($ 2.5 billion to $ 50 billion) and only 4% are responsible for large companies ($ 50 billion or more). In terms of time spent in the corporate environment, 15% of Muslim entrepreneurs started their business just under a year ago, 25% in one and three years, 30% in four and six years, 15% in seven and ten years and 15% have also been in business for at least 10 years.

Furthermore, it appears that Muslim entrepreneurs in Pakistan usually start their business between the ages of 25 and 35. 28.8% of respondents say they started their business before the age of 25. In addition, 41.6% of people who started their own business did so between the ages of 25 and 35; 17.6% did so between the ages of 36 and 45; and 12% did so after age 45. The vast majority of Muslim businessmen have advanced degrees in their fields of study. About 48% hold a bachelor's, master's or doctoral degree; 8% have an associate degree; 36% have a high school diploma; but only 8% have only completed primary school.

Next, Pakistani Muslims who own businesses are involved in a variety of industries. Of these, 44.8% work in the food industry, followed by 7.2% in crafts, 2.4% in application technologies (such as telephone services and applications), 33, 6% in clothing, 2.4% in fittings and 9.6% in other industries. In other words, most of the Muslim entrepreneurs in Pakistan have managed to establish their own businesses in the food sector.

On the contrary, the reasons why Muslim entrepreneurs choose to start their own businesses are a crucial question. Compared to continuing to work for other people in organizations, around 48% of respondents said their main motivation is the fulfillment of individual interests, such as profit-seeking, appreciation and social standing, as well as a willingness to manage your business. To the percentage is added 30% of the participants, driven by the desire to improve social well-being, while 10% of the participants are motivated by the desire to reduce poverty by creating job opportunities for someone else. The ability to meet the financial needs of one's family drives the remaining 12% of the population.

Enterprise goals from an Islamic perspective:

Entrepreneurial Intentions:

2.1.1 Intentions Are Important

An intention is the desire, strategy, or goal to perform a task. According to the survey, each participant believes it is vital to have a plan before embarking on any business. In fact, there are many different ways in which participants perceive what an intention is.

Participants' views on the meaning of intention are presented in Figure 1. Furthermore, the results show that 74.4% of participants define intention as an obligation or ambition to participate in activities. 11.2% of the participants on average believe that the truthfulness in the action is determined by the intention. Similar to Islamic law, it also states that a person's intention is an act of worship that is meant to bring him closer to Allah SWT. Intent, according to the concept, refers to honesty. The remaining 14.4%

Table 1. Respondents' personal characteristics

No	Profiles	Categories	Frequencies	Percentages
1	Gender	Male	132	53.6
		Female	116	44.4
2	Age	Less than 25 years	72	28.8
		25-35 years	104	41.6
		36-45 years	44	17.6
		More than 45 years	30	12
3	Qualifications	High school level	20	8
		Bachelors	90	36
		Masters	120	48
		M.Phil. or Ph.D.	20	8
4	Business	Super stores	112	44.8
		Information Technology	84	33.6
		Hospitality	30	12
		Others	24	9.6
5	Motives	Family needs	30	12
		Improve social welfare	25	10
		Creating jobs	75	30
		Personal ambition	120	48

is evenly divided between two groups, each of which argues that intention refers to both the sincerity and the condition of the goals. From a religious perspective, the following points of view emphasize the importance of intention at the beginning of a task. "The basis of our actions is intention. Without such an intention, people would not take our responsibilities seriously.

A different participant stated:

"Intent is a description of an event's standards, such as its inspiration and purpose." A statement is a form of worship to achieve a goal, even if everything that is said aloud is a form of worship. It also implies that there are signs that must be achieved in order to achieve the goals, such as methods for achieving the goals.

For a Muslim, running a business would be a form of worship that should begin with a specific sacred intent or intended purpose. If someone has the best priorities, Allah SWT will ensure their success. Islam pays special attention to this due to the life force that moves our body. Only those who intend to perform acts for Allah will receive rewards. According to Imam Ibn Hajar Al-'Asqalani, "No doubt reasons, he returned to truthfulness and honesty had no partner for Him."

2.1.2 Entrepreneurial Goals From an Islamic Perspective

From an Islamic perspective, entrepreneurship is a fact of life covered by the Mu'amalah dealing with issues related to interpersonal relationships and responsibility in the hereafter. The entrepreneurial spirit of the Quran writings Hud: 61, Al-Mulk:15, as well as Al-Jumuh:10, show that human beings are commanded to seek happiness and promote the welfare of the earth, but also of progressive movement. The Quran describes entrepreneurship as follows:

But also to Saleh, Thamood's brother. "O my people, worship God; there is no god but oneself," he ordered. He put you on earth after having also initiated you from this place. So ask him for forgiveness and turn to him in repentance. My Lord is accessible and near. Hud 11:61 from Quran.

Figure 1. Intentions as perceived by participants

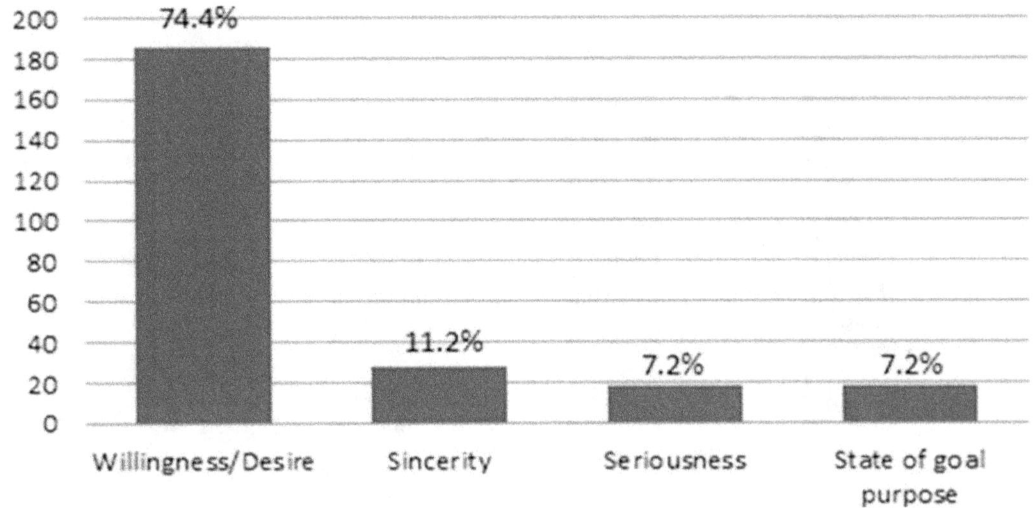

"He made the world controllable for himself; so explore him and eat of his offerings." He is the resurrection. Al-Mulk 16:97 from the Quran. "Trade is like interest." However, God approved trade while prohibiting interest-based transactions. Al-Baqarah 2:275 of the Quran.

Figure 2 presents the outcomes of an investigation into the business goals of Pakistani Muslim businesspeople.

According to the study, 36% of the participants intend to start a business to receive the blessings of Allah SWT, while 30% of the participants intend to start a business to worship Allah SWT. In addition, 18% of people plan to start their own business to pursue personal goals such as improving their social position. The remaining 16% are enterprising and want to make money. According to Islam, the intention is more important than the result (Syed and Ali, 2010). Several participants, in light of research on the importance of corporate intentions from an Islamic perspective, say:

"Good intentions would then undoubtedly guide action and produce positive business results."

Good deeds are motivated by positive motives, and good deeds produce positive results. Every intention must also be accompanied by honesty, but honesty in itself does not guarantee that our actions will be approved by Allah SWT if they do not follow the Islamic rules established in the Quran and Hadiths. The study also shows that collective intentions are a way of worshiping God. Some respondents admitted.

"But if our intentions were not good, the agreement could still be a beneficial decision, particularly beneficial for everyone and of course a thank you."

"In worship, real intention is what matters most. Entrepreneurship is a way of worshiping Allah SWT, but we need to put real effort into our businesses in addition to good intentions. Muslims who run their own businesses are completely subordinate to Allah (SWT) but also seek His grace in doing so. This is one of the indications of prayer. Adh-Dhariyat 51:56 of the Quran says, "I created the spirits of the dead and of the living beings only to worship Me." Available research also concludes that Islamic business guidance provides basic guidelines for Muslim businesses. owners that they must follow when acting in accordance with Islamic law. Muslim businessmen adhere to a number of rules, including refraining from harming others, following Islamic laws when buying or selling, and maintaining good interpersonal relations.

Figure 2. Participants' intentions and aspirations in terms of entrepreneurship

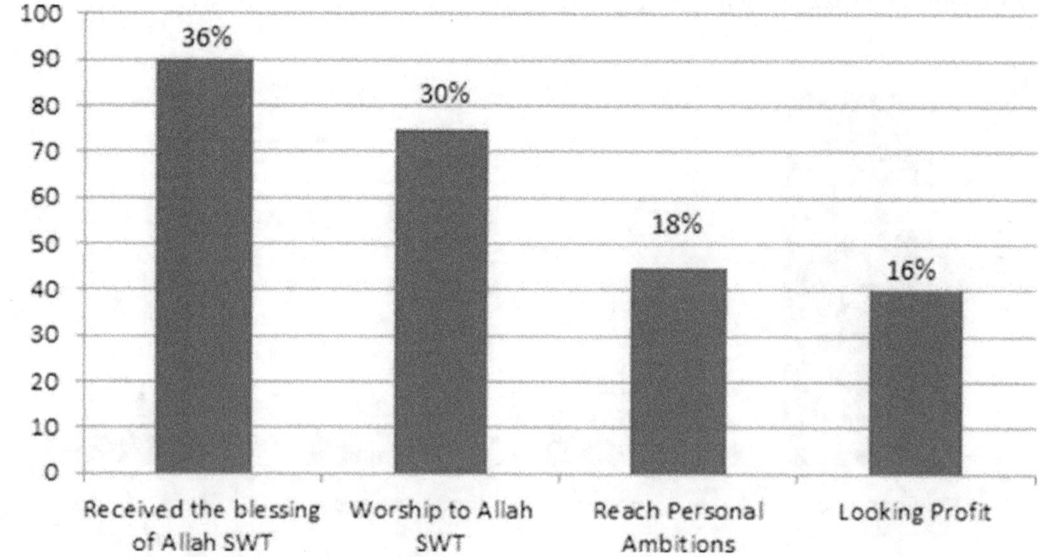

2.2 Characteristics of Entrepreneurs

Previous studies have shown that an entrepreneur's traits are related to the effectiveness with which they behave in determining the success or failure of their ventures, which is determined by examining the maintenance or expansion of their business or organization (Bailey, 1986). A profitable business requires quality training, adequate experience and expertise, and a commitment to take a constructive approach to behavior and entertainment. This included experience, determination and trust, all of which are considered essential to the effective expansion of any business. Furthermore, on the basis of their intention to engage in economic ventures, this study evaluated the characteristics of Muslim entrepreneurs from the point of view of Islam. According to the questionnaire, traits include being intelligent, trustworthy, and capable of effective communication, as well as being consistent and courageous. Some respondents claim.

Entrepreneurs need to be trustworthy, truthful and skilled in effective communication.

Entrepreneurs "must have the qualities of courage, consistency and sincerity".

Entrepreneurs must be trustworthy and transparent.

Entrepreneurs must possess the qualities of intelligence, honesty, reliability, effective communication skills, consistency and courage.

(1) The qualities mentioned are comparable to those of the Prophet Mohammed SAW. (1) The word "Fathonah" means "wise and able". The Prophet Muhammad demonstrated Fathonah's identity in business through her aptitude for commerce.

(2) Amanah is Arabic for "reliable." To inspire confidence in both himself and the company he is establishing, an entrepreneur should be truthful in all business dealings. A willingness to obtain monetary benefit (wealth) through unethical means, such as manipulation, corrupt practices, complicity, bribery, etc., is one reason why someone might not be amanah. The quality of amanah, which denotes dependability and obligation, is necessary for a competent Muslim. A Muslim businessperson must fully own their amanah identity in order to refrain from any actions that might be harmful to others. Additionally, the trait of reliability might well be owned if one maintains the conviction that God is almost always conscious of their actions, including when they start taking a job, and they are going to be held to account.

(3) Siddiq means "one who possesses a good moral character," which means intellectually honest. To gain the respect of others, such as staff and customers, an entrepreneur should consistently uphold his or her promises. In the Prophet himself, in addition to his sayings, and also his actions, that are consistent with his sayings. The Quran's An-Najm 53:4-5 mentions the Siddiq persona as saying, "It is only a disclosure revealed." The Highly Strong did teach him."

(4) "Tabligh" is an expression (communicative). "That he might understand that they've transmitted the communications of their Lord," says Tabligh, a character mentioned inside the Quran. He must have counted all of it and incorporated how much they possessed (Quran Al-Jin 72:28).

(5) The final word, istiqomah, is Arabic for "personality" (Continuity of bravery).

3. DISCUSSIONS

At every stage of a person's life, Islam demonstrates the important relevance of attitude and behavioural intention. It is suggested that one's motives for performing something now heavily influence how highly the morals of their work are valued. One must move forward with the simple understanding that Allah SWT is watching everything they do. As a result, a Muslim should practice gratitude, make the proper regulations, and understand that everything they receive should be held to account by Allah SWT. In essence, honesty could lessen the utilization or manipulation of everyone else for one's own gain.

Additionally, from an Islamic perspective, the idea of entrepreneurialism could make a significant contribution in terms of legal, interpersonal, or economic considerations. Entrepreneurship would be an encouraging action to increase human wellbeing from either a religious or secular standpoint. Entrepreneurship might have a positive impact on society by generating job positions and stimulating the economy. On the financial front, entrepreneurship might have an effect on a nation's tax income and rate of economic expansion. In specific, the intention to start a lengthy enterprise is considered to be the first step in the procedure (Lee and Wong, 2004). According to Krueger (1993), a core problem to take into account in comprehending the entrepreneurship of establishing a brand-new company is someone's dedication to starting a new venture, which can be reflected in one's entrepreneurial intention. In conclusion, any entrepreneur must begin with the goal of running a business and ultimately being successful.

Following that, the theory of planned behaviour (TPB) has focused on motives as a primary driver of human nature, which would be influenced by three crucial factors: mindset forward into actions, normative beliefs, and perceived control over behavior's (). Acknowledging one's actual intent to become an entrepreneur could thus reveal the propensity for individuals to launch enterprises in reality (Jenkins and Johnson, 1997). Spirituality, according to Mokhlis (2009), is one of the most pervasive and significant influencing factors on mindsets, beliefs, and actions, whether at the personal or communal level.

According to the Islamic viewpoint, business endeavors should be devoted to God's prayer. This research defines praying as a Muslim action in undertaking religious teachings that also incorporate religious, interpersonal, and economic tasks. The term "religious" describes actions that involve a person's connection to God in order to obtain benefits through prayer, something that Muslims should perform in accordance with God's instructions. The Quran's Al-Hujurat 49:10, that states that "The people of faith are brothers, so rectify among your brothers, as well as stay conscious of God, even though you might obtain compassion," refers to social interactions between people. As a result, Muslims should appreciate one another. Humans engage in economic output as a form of worship in order to fulfill their needs and live prosperous lives. According to Al-'Aadiyat 100:8, "And because he is intense in his adoration of income," humans were originally made with the goal of loving wealth. The capital includes elements produced by people to meet their own and their households' daily needs. Individuals have been urged to discuss their profits with others in order to benefit the community while also creating income for their personal benefit. Islam places a strong emphasis on the advancement of the community as a whole. Next, as a caliph, Muslims have an obligation to perform charitable acts through their economic endeavors (leader).

Dana (2009) asserts that although any entrepreneurship effect is heavily reliant on the question of moral social behaviour, spirituality is a notable fundamental basis of entrepreneurialism. Dana (2009, 2010) has highlighted the fact that religion is impartial and doesn't forbid entrepreneurship, wherein business practices could help an entrepreneur become a good human according to ethical and societal rules that are relevant inside the community. Islam bases its entrepreneurial traits on precepts found in the Quran and Hadith that serve as a manual for conducting business (Oukil, 2013). Islam embraces entrepreneurship, as evidenced by the Prophet Muhammad and also his accomplices. Islam has often encouraged all Muslims to be inventive and engaged businesspeople.

On the other hand, an effective entrepreneur is typically seen as having a few specific traits that contribute to their success. According to Hisrich (2014), these distinctive qualities should include self-control, a drive for success, being goal-but also action-oriented, and a powerful enthusiasm. Muslim businesspeople should generally possess qualities like integrity, equality, humility, devotion to God as their first prime concern, avoidance of corrupt practices, generosity, and a desire to assist everyone else (Mushtaq, 2001). Muslim business owners should be able to run a firm with good, straightforward, and equitable intentions and behaviors while avoiding whatever forbidden situations they may encounter because they're subject to Islamic statutes and regulations when engaging in whatever economic ventures.

According to the latest research, Muslim businesspeople in Pakistan can be classified as fathonah, ibadah, siddiq, a feature of Islam, and Istiqomah. Similarly, Trim (2009) confirmed that the Prophet Muhammad's integrity as well as capacity are encapsulated in four outstanding actors, namely FAST (fathonah, ibadah, siddiq, and feature of Islamic) and, furthermore, "I," backs up the results (istiqomah). From an Islamic perspective, having entrepreneurial behavior is the first step in taking action, which contributes to having entrepreneurial traits. Fathonah elaborates on the traits of a smart businessperson in relation to a specific intent about how businesspeople try to keep learning and comprehending the notion of entrepreneurship and could then enhance their qualifications. Additionally, almost any entrepreneur needs to adopt the traits of siddiq but also ibadah, who believe that whatever intention should arrive from the soul in order to be judged as trustful, having honesty, or even being truthful—all of which rely heavily here on specific intent. The actor of Tabligh also suggests that a business owner ought to be capable of communicating with other people and communicating ideas. Finally, istiqomah suggests that every initiative must be in line with the original intentions. Therefore, Muslim business owners who exhibit these traits have contributed to the achievement of their enterprises, thereby establishing themselves as productive Muslim business owners.

4. CONCLUSION

In our community, the influence of religion on business has become increasingly common. Researchers shouldn't avoid the spiritual because it is now an interpersonal reality; instead, they must view it as a significant phenomenon, including both management principles and practices. Entrepreneurship, socio-economic status, and religious-spiritual principles form the foundation of EIP, a controversial and complicated idea. It differs from moral entrepreneurship in that it involves specific guidelines, biblical support, and a unique metaphysical goal. We prefer to relate to entrepreneurship from such an Islamic perspective, but although prevalent, the use and functional advertising attention favour the combination of Islamic entrepreneurship since the actual facts of EIP must be derived and understood from the religious texts and implemented to sense.

EIP shapes the individual, the organization, and a wide range of entities, including the counties and marketplaces, in a number of ways that have an impact here on medium enterprises, mesa, as well as macro levels of evaluation. It is essential to include this sophistication into effective measures that produce informational fullness without sacrificing the importance of formalism. In fact, the entrepreneurial nature of Islam itself could be studied. Its interpretive methods and content both fit the definition of entrepreneurial. Ijtihad enables elaboration and critical thought. For instance, the focus on diligence and also the ban on interest support entrepreneurial endeavors.

EIP calls for a lot of extra academic involvement as it expands both empirical evidence and cognitively. Islam is both underestimated and slightly inaccurately portrayed in Western literary works. It is necessary to integrate the scant and specialized studies on EIP into conventional management and business literature by, among other things, connecting it to organizational, financial, personnel management, and strategic planning theories. While an ethical perspective is necessary, and research on EIP can be highly beneficial at times, we must remain theoretically strict and distinguish between explanation and medication. Awareness must be carefully contextualized instead of being Islamized in certain ways. EIP is a major element in the worldwide entrepreneurial environment, and not just a side effect. Furthermore, it is a multi-dynamic idea that changes as circumstances change, our understanding of entrepreneurship evolves, and our understanding of how to perceive doctrinal source material evolves. Multidisciplinary research is essential for EIP, which is an extremely entrepreneurial endeavour.

REFERENCES:

Abd Muin, M. A., Abdullah, S., & Bahari, A. (2014, November). Model on social entrepreneurship: Identify the research gap based on islamic perspective. In *International Conference on Social Entrepreneurship* (pp. 7-9). Research Gate.

Abdullah, S., & Mikail, S. A. (2013). Entrepreneurship and Islam: An expository study on characteristics of Muslim entrepreneur. In *5th Islamic Economics System Conference: Sustainable Development Through The Islamic Economics System, Faculty Economics And Muamalat, Universiti Sains Islam Malaysia*, Kuala Lumpur.

Abras, A., & Al Mahameed, M. (2022, March). The rise and fall of institutional entrepreneurship in Islamic financial reporting standardisation projects. In *Accounting Forum* (pp. 1-26). Routledge. 10.1080/01559982.2022.2051684

Adham, K. A., Said, M. F., Saâ, N., & Yaakub, N. I. (2012). Technological innovation and entrepreneurship from the western and Islamic perspectives. *International Journal of Economics, Management and Accounting, 20*(2).

Ahmed, M. (2008). *The role of RDS in the development of women entrepreneurship under Islamic micro finance: A case study of Bangladesh. Islamic Finance for Micro and Medium Enterprises*, 211. Research Gate.

Anggadwita, G., Mulyaningsih, H. D., Ramadani, V., & Arwiyah, M. Y. (2015). Women entrepreneurship in Islamic perspective: A driver for social change. *International Journal of Business and Globalisation, 15*(3), 389–404. doi:10.1504/IJBG.2015.071914

Davis, M. K. (2013). Entrepreneurship: An Islamic perspective. *International Journal of Entrepreneurship and Small Business, 20*(1), 63–69. doi:10.1504/IJESB.2013.055693

Fozia, M., Rehman, A., & Farooq, A. (2016). Entrepreneurship and leadership: An Islamic perspective. International Journal of Economics. *Management and Accounting, 24*(1), 15–47.

Gümüsay, A. A. (2015). Entrepreneurship from an Islamic perspective. *Journal of Business Ethics, 130*(1), 199–208. doi:10.100710551-014-2223-7

Harizan, S. H. M., & Mustafa, M. S. (2020). Islamic Entrepreneurship: Analysis of Research Trend. *Islamiyyat, 42*(2), 71–84. doi:10.17576/islamiyyat-2020-4202-07

HassanM. K.HipplerW. (2014). Entrepreneurship and Islam: an overview. Available at SSRN 3263110.

Hoque, M. J., Rahman, M. A., & Razia, S. (2014). Women Entrepreneurship Development under Islamic Perspective-A Study on Some Selected Muslim Women Entrepreneurs of Bangladesh. *World Review of Business Research, 4*(3), 45–63.

Kayed, R. N., & Hassan, M. K. (2013). *Islamic entrepreneurship*. Routledge. doi:10.4324/9780203840801

Machmud, A., & Hidayat, Y. M. (2020). Characteristics of Islamic entrepreneurship and the business success of SMEs in Indonesia. *Journal of Entrepreneurship Education, 23*(2), 1–16.

Mebroui, T., & Mosbah, A. (2020). Islamic entrepreneurship: Issues and debates. *International Journal of Management and Commerce Innovations, 7*(2), 461–468.

Muhammad, S., Ximei, K., Sharif, I., & Haq, Z. (2020). An overview of women entrepreneurship from islamic perspective. *Review of Economics and Development Studies, 6*(4), 857–866. doi:10.47067/reads.v6i4.285

Ramadani, V. (2021). Islamic entrepreneurship. In *World Encyclopedia of Entrepreneurship* (pp. 457–470). Edward Elgar Publishing. doi:10.4337/9781839104145.00059

Ramadani, V., Dana, L. P., Gërguri-Rashiti, S., & Ratten, V. (2017). An introduction to entrepreneurship and management in an Islamic context. In *Entrepreneurship and management in an Islamic context* (pp. 1–5). Springer. doi:10.1007/978-3-319-39679-8_1

Ramadani, V., Dana, L. P., Ratten, V., & Tahiri, S. (2015). The context of Islamic entrepreneurship and business: Concept, principles and perspectives. *International Journal of Business and Globalisation, 15*(3), 244–261. doi:10.1504/IJBG.2015.071906

Ratten, V., Ramadani, V., Dana, L. P., & Gerguri-Rashiti, S. (2017). Islamic entrepreneurship and management: Culture, religion and society. In *Entrepreneurship and management in an Islamic context* (pp. 7–17). Springer. doi:10.1007/978-3-319-39679-8_2

Chapter 12
Exploring the Multifaceted Landscape of Halal Branding Challenges, Opportunities, and Cross-Cultural Dynamics

Pipit Buana Sari
Universitas Pembangunan Panca Budi, Indonesia

Megasari Gusandra Saragih
Universitas Pembangunan Panca Budi, Indonesia

Slamet Widodo
Universitas Pembangunan Panca Budi, Indonesia

Firman Ario
Universitas Pembangunan Panca Budi, Indonesia

Thorique Akbar Maulana Nasution
Universiti Kebangsaan Malaysia, Malaysia

ABSTRACT

The primary goal of this research is to thoroughly explore challenges and opportunities in Halal branding. This covers disciplines like marketing, consumer behavior, culture, and religion, offering a multidimensional perspective. The study delves into subthemes including the global Halal market appeal, complex Halal branding-consumer behavior link, and strategic business implications. There's a need to further investigate Halal branding's impact on decision-making and loyalty. Future research should develop branding frameworks for the Halal market nuances. Understanding the interplay between Halal branding and cultural identity is vital. This study significantly contributes to Halal branding's evolving field, shedding light on its multifaceted aspects. It benefits academics, marketers, and businesses in this dynamic landscape.

DOI: 10.4018/978-1-6684-7519-5.ch012

INTRODUCTION

Halal branding has gained significant attention in recent years, primarily driven by the expanding Muslim population and the increasing demand for products aligned with Islamic principles and guidelines (Ali et al., 2018). This dynamic landscape presents a unique and promising avenue for researchers to delve into a plethora of disciplines, including marketing, consumer behavior, cultural studies, and religious exploration (Fernando et al., 2022; Ali et al., 2018; Ahmad, 2015).

A robust case for exploration emerges from a report by DinarStandard (2019), which posits the global Halal market at a staggering value in the trillions of dollars, with the food and beverage sector commanding a significant share. This financial allure underscores the imperative for researchers to dissect the intricacies of Halal branding strategies and their attendant challenges. Beyond mere financial implications, Halal branding unfurls opportunities for businesses to expand into new markets, command premium pricing, and thereby enhance profitability (Fernando et al., 2022). These strategic dimensions necessitate in-depth investigations into the implications and potential benefits of Halal branding for businesses.

The arena of Halal branding provides an intriguing vantage point to explore the nexus of religion and consumer behavior (Ali et al., 2018). Embedded in Islamic principles, the notion of ethical consumption and adherence to Halal tenets resonates across domains like food, cosmetics, pharmaceuticals, and beyond. Deciphering the manner in which these religious underpinnings shape consumer decisions and brand preferences can yield invaluable insights for marketers and scholars immersed in the realm of consumer behavior.

Crucially, the realm of Halal branding transcends the confines of the Muslim demographic. Both Muslim and non-Muslim consumers gravitate towards Halal branded products, drawn by the association with quality, hygiene, safety, sustainability, and ethical business practices (Fernando et al., 2022). In navigating the challenges inherent in Halal brands, the establishment of effective branding frameworks assumes paramount significance (Ahmad, 2015). The conceptual dichotomy of Halal and Haram extends its discourse beyond business into broader life aspects, forming a subject of scholarly debate (Ahmad, 2015).

Furthermore, the contours of Halal branding invite scrutiny into the realm of cultural authenticity and identity (Wilson & Liu, 2011). As Halal products and services permeate mainstream markets, the art of harmonizing the dual pursuit of catering to the Muslim consumer base while resonating with a wider audience becomes paramount. This delicate equilibrium mandates a nuanced understanding of cultural sensitivities, religious symbolism, and the nuanced effects of Halal certification on brand perception.

In summation, the universe of Halal branding beckons academicians with its intricate dynamics. The allure of the Halal market's potential, the intricate interplay between Halal branding and consumer behavior, the strategic implications for businesses, and the underlying cultural context beckon for comprehensive exploration. By illuminating these dimensions, academicians are poised to delve into a captivating field of study, enriching our comprehension of the multifaceted world of Halal branding. In this light, the aims of this study encompass a comprehensive review of the challenges and opportunities inherent in the realm of Halal branding.

HALAL BRANDS

Halal brands are those that have acquired Halal certification and strictly adhere to Islamic dietary laws and regulations (Fuseini et al., 2020). These brands ensure that their products are manufactured, processed, and packaged in strict accordance with Halal guidelines, rendering them permissible for consumption among Muslims (Shahid et al., 2018). The practice of Halal branding enables businesses to explore new markets, secure a competitive edge, and bolster profitability by pricing their products higher and enjoying improved profit margins (Ali et al., 2018). To distinguish a Halal brand from conventional ones, companies pursue Halal certifications and employ distinct labels to apprise potential consumers of the Halal attributes embedded within their brand (Jaiyeoba et al., 2020; Ali et al., 2018). This branding strategy holds particular significance for Muslim customers who prioritize their religious convictions in their purchasing decisions (Shah et al., 2020).

Traditional branding constructs, such as brand image, satisfaction, trust, and loyalty, can be extrapolated to the realm of Halal brands to discern consumer behavior and purchasing intentions (Ali et al., 2018; Garg & Joshi, 2018; Ali et al., 2020). The perceived quality of a brand significantly and positively influences aspects like brand image, satisfaction, trust, loyalty, and the intention to purchase Halal products (Ali et al., 2018). Halal brands act as symbols of religious association, thereby sparking cognitive decision-making processes among consumers (Joshi & Garg, 2022; Qurniawati et al., 2023). Notably, projecting a Halal image emerges as pivotal for Halal brands to resonate with Muslim consumers, often serving as their initial impression before evaluating other attributes (Ali et al., 2018). Religious convictions wield a positive and substantial impact on brand affection and loyalty, with brand affection serving as a mediator between brand experience and brand loyalty (Qurniawati et al., 2023). Halal brands offer a valuable lens to investigate the consumption patterns of Muslim consumers, given that Islamic Sharia governs various facets of life, including consumption practices (Rodrigo & Turnbull, 2019). In sum, the significance of Halal brands is underscored by their pivotal role in catering to the requisites and inclinations of Muslim consumers who actively seek products aligned with their religious beliefs and dietary preferences.

HALAL BRANDS AND ISLAMIC BRANDS

Halal brands and Islamic brands are frequently used interchangeably; however, distinctions between the two exist. Halal brands pertain to products or services adhering to Islamic dietary regulations, permissible for consumption by Muslims (Hidayat et al., 2021). They undergo a stringent certification process ensuring alignment with Islamic standards set by authorities (Muhammad et al., 2020). This involves scrutinizing ingredient origins, manufacturing, and handling (Ali et al., 2018). Halal labels, obtained through this process, assure Muslim consumers of the products' permissibility (Alam & Maknun, 2021). The label is pivotal for devout Muslims who prioritize adherence to dietary laws and seek reassurance in their consumption choices (Ahmad, 2015).

In contrast, Islamic brands encompass a wider spectrum of products and services in line with Islamic principles, extending beyond the Halal facet (Wilson & Liu, 2011). These brands span sectors like finance, fashion, cosmetics, and tourism (Yusup et al., 2022). While not mandatorily Halal-certified, these products align with Islamic ethics (Ahmad & Syed, 2020). Focus on ethical sourcing, fair trade, sustainability, and social responsibility is common (Ali et al., 2018). They frequently emphasize Islamic values, like equity, integrity, and social responsibility (Ahmad, 2015). Islamic brands cater to Muslim consumers seeking products resonating with their religious convictions, harmonizing brand values with Islamic principles (Alserhan, 2010; Bukhari & Isa, 2019; Jumani & Sukhabot, 2021).

HALAL BRANDS AND HALAL BRANDING

Halal brands and Halal branding are interconnected yet distinct concepts within the realm of Islamic products. A Halal brand signifies a brand that secures Halal certification and employs Halal symbols to assure consumers, particularly Muslims, of adherence to Islamic Shariah in ingredient sourcing and production (Ali et al., 2018). These brands align with Shariah requisites, establishing themselves as dedicated Halal entities, thus carving a niche in the market (Yusof et al., 2021).

Conversely, Halal branding encompasses the process of conceiving and promoting a brand embodying Halal attributes (Ali et al., 2018). This entails securing Halal certifications and deploying specific labels to signal conformity with Halal benchmarks to potential consumers (Fernando et al., 2022). Halal branding extends opportunities to penetrate fresh markets, attain competitive edges, and potentially enhance profitability by commanding higher prices and profit margins (Ali et al., 2018).

The pivotal contrast between Halal brands and Halal branding resides in their essence. Halal brands denote the physical products endowed with Halal certification, whereas Halal branding encapsulates the strategic orchestration of marketing to position and distinguish these Halal products for the target audience (Jaiyeoba et al., 2020; Awan et al., 2015; Ali et al., 2018). In essence, Halal brands denote tangible products adhering to Halal norms, while Halal branding embodies the tactical maneuvers to spotlight and set apart these products in the market.

THE UNIVERSE OF HALAL BRANDING

The realm of Halal branding has emerged as a compelling sphere of interest for both academics and marketing practitioners. Halal branding, characterized by the marketing of products and services aligned

Table 1. Distinction between Halal brands and Halal branding

Concept	Definition
Halal Brands	Brands that have obtained Halal certification and use Halal logos or symbols to assure consumers, especially Muslims, that their products adhere to Islamic Shariah and are suitable for consumption (Ali et al., 2018).
	These brands comply with Shariah requirements and carve out their niche in the market by projecting themselves as Halal brands (Ali et al., 2018).
Halal Branding	The process of creating and promoting a brand with Halal features, including obtaining certifications and using labels to communicate that the brand adheres to Halal standards (Ali et al., 2018).
	This strategy enables businesses to access new markets, gain a competitive edge, and potentially increase profitability (Ali et al., 2018).
Difference	Halal Brands are actual certified products adhering to Halal standards. Halal Branding is the strategic marketing process to position and market those products as Halal to target consumers (Ali et al., 2018).
	Halal Brands focus on product compliance, while Halal Branding encompasses broader marketing strategies to appeal to the Muslim consumer market (Ali et al., 2018).

with Shariah principles, has garnered significant attention (Khan et al., 2021). Over time, Muslim consumer decision-making has evolved, urging marketers to transcend mere quality and hygiene attributes in their communication efforts (Joshi & Garg, 2022).

Scholarly exploration in the arena of Islamic marketing and branding has gained momentum, with researchers honing their focus on comprehending this burgeoning discipline (Khan et al., 2021). The nuanced concept of Halal introduces challenges in decoding consumer behavior and sustaining an authentic brand proposition that resonates emotionally (Wilson & Liu, 2011). Halal-conscious consumers tend to be risk-averse, leading to heightened discernment and engagement levels (Suki & Salleh, 2018). Yet, brand managers grapple with ascertaining the optimal extent of emotionally driven brand messaging (Wilson & Liu, 2011).

Defining Halal is both a dynamic and sensitive undertaking, and academic literature continues to grapple with forging a comprehensive connection between branding and Islam (Kok, 2021). Notably, efforts have been made to classify Islamic branding, although the ever-evolving importance of Halal is perpetuated within the Muslim consciousness through an intricate and cyclical process (Wilson & Liu, 2011).

Halal branding holds promises of expanded market horizons, competitive advantages, and amplified profitability for businesses (Ali et al., 2018). This approach facilitates the potential to command elevated prices and profit margins. Previous research has duly explored facets like brand image, satisfaction, trust, and loyalty within the precincts of Halal products, uncharted realms, however, still exist within the domain of traditional constructs in relation to Halal products (Ali et al., 2018).

In summation, the universe of Halal branding beckons the scholarly and practitioner community in the marketing arena. Embracing Islamic marketing, also known as Halal branding, is tantamount to an evolving subject of interest. It revolves around marketing commodities and services that align with Shariah, while simultaneously unveiling the intricacies of understanding consumer behavior, authentic branding, and the enigmatic connection between branding and Islam in the context of Halal products.

THE ALLURE OF THE HALAL MARKET

The allure of the Halal market's immense potential is underpinned by a confluence of compelling factors. Foremost, the rapid proliferation of the global Muslim population stands as a pivotal driver. This demographic surge, coupled with escalating economic development and amplified purchasing power within the Muslim community, synergistically fuels the expansive trajectory of the Halal market (Azam & Abdullah, 2020). Notably, the Halal market's horizon is not circumscribed by Muslim-majority countries; it is burgeoning even in non-Muslim nations, unfurling novel avenues for growth (Azam, 2016).

Furthermore, the purview of the Halal market has transcended its traditional confines of food and related products. Its ambit now extends across multifarious sectors, encompassing cosmetics, personal care, pharmaceuticals, health products, and beyond (Azam & Abdullah, 2020). This strategic diversification caters comprehensively to the preferences and requisites of the discerning Muslim consumer base.

Eminent within the allure of the Halal market is the resounding echo of consumer demand. Studies underscore that Muslim consumers evince a distinct predilection for Halal products, spanning categories like cosmetics and personal care (Aisyah, 2016). Anchored in factors like attitude, subjective norms, perceived behavioral control, and purchase intent, the proclivity of Muslim consumers to embrace Halal products is palpable (Amalia et al., 2020). This burgeoning demand cascades into a wealth of prospects for businesses to tap into, allowing them to cater adeptly to this evolving market and address the unique needs and desires of their Muslim clientele.

Moreover, the concept of Halal resonates beyond its religious underpinnings; it encompasses dimensions of quality and ethical consumption that resonate universally. This appeal extends not only to Muslim consumers but also encompasses a broader spectrum, encapsulating non-Muslims (Shahid et al., 2023). The potential for Halal market growth reverberates not only within the confines of the Muslim demographic but also holds sway over penetration and advancement among non-Muslim segments (Iranmanesh et al., 2022). This expansion into uncharted consumer realms further amplifies the allure of the Halal market, broadening its appeal and scope.

In summation, the Halal market's allure emanates from a potent amalgamation of factors. The rapid ascent of the global Muslim population, burgeoning economic potential, cross-boundary market emergence, sectoral diversification, and cross-cultural demand dynamics all converge to present a compelling landscape for businesses. This landscape beckons them to delve into the vibrant Halal market, offering tailored products and services that resonate with the multifaceted preferences of a diverse clientele.

HALAL BRANDING AND CONSUMER BEHAVIOR

The intricate interplay between Halal branding and consumer behavior constitutes a multifaceted phenomenon characterized by a multitude of factors and intricate relationships. Halal branding, at its core, involves the process of certifying products and services in alignment with Islamic dietary laws and regulations. Within this landscape, it wields a formidable influence over consumer behavior and the consequential purchase decisions that ensue.

A pivotal facet of Halal branding revolves around the cultivation of a positive brand image. Analogous to conventional products, the brand image of Halal offerings bestows value upon a company by facilitating consumer access to Halal product information and engendering favorable associations that cascade to other offerings within the same brand portfolio (Ali et al., 2018). Notably, perceived brand quality occupies a pivotal role in shaping consumers' impressions of the Halal brand image and subsequently, their purchase intentions (Ali et al., 2018). In instances where an organization commits to delivering Halal products, the preexisting perceptions of quality etched in consumers' consciousness positively reverberate to elevate the Halal brand image and galvanize purchase intentions (Ali et al., 2018).

The tapestry of consumer behavior concerning Halal products is interwoven with myriad factors, including brand satisfaction, trust, and loyalty. These elements wield substantial sway over consumers' intentions to purchase Halal brands (Ali et al., 2018). The intricate interplay among the constructs of Halal brand image, satisfaction, trust, and loyalty collectively orchestrate consumer behavior and ultimately, guide purchasing decisions (Ali et al., 2018; Ali et al., 2020).

Halal branding's ramifications reverberate beyond individual transactions, opening gateways to novel markets, fostering competitive advantages, and enhancing profitability. Enterprises embracing Halal branding often find themselves empowered to proffer their products at premium prices, accompanied by heightened profit margins (Ali et al., 2018). The Halal brand, in consumers' eyes, conveys principles of fairness, ethics, and integrity in business dealings, significantly shaping their proclivity towards opting for Halal products (Fernando et al., 2022).

Crucially, the symbiotic interplay between Halal branding and consumer behavior is not circumscribed solely within Muslim-majority territories. Extensive research probes the response of consumers to Halal products across diverse contexts, spanning Pakistan, China, Southeast Asian nations, and beyond (Ali et al., 2018; Ali et al., 2020; Septiarini et al., 2023). These studies delve into the intricate relationships, spanning traditional branding dimensions (like brand image, perceived quality, satisfaction, trust, and loyalty) and the unique contours of Halal branding constructs (comprising Halal brand image, satisfaction, trust, and loyalty), in forecasting consumers' intentions to embrace Halal brands (Ali et al., 2018; Ali et al., 2020; Septiarini et al., 2023).

Religion, too, emerges as a pivotal determinant shaping consumer behavior towards Halal products. Within Muslim-majority domains like Pakistan and Indonesia, religion assumes a pronounced role in shaping consumers' purchasing propensities (Sabbar et al., 2023). The moral fabric and societal norms inherent in Islamic teachings, alongside the consumption of Halal goods, stand as pivotal considerations steering consumer preferences within these regions.

In sum, the nuanced symbiosis between Halal branding and consumer behavior paints a multifaceted canvas. It's a landscape where perceived brand image, satisfaction, trust, and loyalty coalesce to choreograph purchasing decisions. An arena where Halal branding's influences stretch far beyond financial transactions, rippling into realms of market penetration, competitive edge, and profitability. It's a realm where research transcends geographical boundaries, unraveling the intricate threads of consumer behavior towards Halal products. Religion, too, emerges as a powerful force sculpting purchasing proclivities within Muslim-majority contexts.

HALAL BRANDING AND THE STRATEGIC IMPLICATIONS FOR BUSINESSES

The intricate interplay between Halal branding and its strategic implications for businesses has emerged as a compelling topic within the realm of marketing. Halal branding, at its essence, encompasses the process of certifying products and services in alignment with Islamic dietary laws and regulations—a certification that serves to reassure Muslim consumers of the products' adherence to their religious tenets and requirements (Garg & Joshi, 2018).

Within this paradigm, one of the paramount strategic implications of Halal branding lies in the avenue it opens to new markets. As the global Muslim population burgeons, an expansive market potential for Halal goods and services emerges. Through the acquisition of Halal certification, businesses can effectively tap into this burgeoning market segment, casting a wider net over an extended customer base (Katuk et al., 2021). The ensuing consequence may translate into augmented sales volumes and heightened profitability for these enterprises (Ali et al., 2018).

Moreover, Halal branding unfurls a unique opportunity for businesses to cultivate a competitive edge. The escalating demand for Halal products among Muslim consumers is paralleled by their willingness to allocate a premium budget for these offerings. By embracing the mantle of Halal certification, businesses can effectively distinguish themselves from competitors, garnering the loyalty of a discerning customer cohort (Ali et al., 2018). This cultivation of loyalty can, in turn, cascade into fortified brand equity, bolstering the foundation for lasting customer relationships.

The strategic implications of Halal branding also extend to the domains of brand image and trust. Within the perspective of Muslim consumers, the imprimatur of Halal certification epitomizes quality and authenticity. As businesses secure Halal certification, the resultant augmentation of brand image is complemented by the cultivation of trust among Muslim consumers (Hidayati & Sunaryo, 2021). This catalytic interplay can engender augmented purchase intentions and foster the recurrence of patronage.

Notably, Halal branding's footprint can be traced to supply chain management as well. The exigency here lies in the alignment of the entire supply chain—spanning sourcing, production, and distribution—with Halal prerequisites. This might necessitate the integration of traceability technologies and the provisioning of Halal training to logistics service providers (Fernando et al., 2022). By threading the tenets of Halal integrity throughout the supply chain, businesses are primed to augment their Halal brand value and burnish their reputation.

In summation, the symphony of Halal branding and its strategic ramifications for businesses is a composition replete with harmonious complexities. This paradigm furnishes enterprises with key avenues to embrace novel markets, wield competitive advantages, cultivate brand image and trust, and orchestrate seamless supply chain management. The astute assimilation of the strategic implications inherent in Halal branding equips businesses to navigate and thrive within the burgeoning expanse of the Halal market.

HALAL BRANDING AND THE UNDERLYING CULTURAL CONTEXT

The intricate interplay between Halal branding and the underlying cultural context embodies a relationship of complexity and multifaceted dynamics. This context encompasses the intricate tapestry of beliefs, values, norms, and practices woven into the fabric of a specific society or community.

At the heart of this interplay lies the profound impact of religious beliefs and societal norms on consumers' intent to purchase Halal-branded products. Research underscores that consumers' inclination to opt for Halal-branded products is profoundly shaped by their religious convictions and adherence to the tenets of Islamic dietary laws (Garg & Joshi, 2018). The cultural context, particularly pronounced in regions with substantial Muslim populations, serves as a pivot in shaping consumers' attitudes and predilections towards Halal offerings (Garg & Joshi, 2018). For instance, in a nation like India characterized by a significant Muslim demographic, a keen comprehension of the cultural milieu and consumers' dispositions towards Halal brands can inform marketers in their quest to harmonize demand for these products while assuaging any discordance (Garg & Joshi, 2018).

Another dimension of the interplay lies in the nexus of brand image, trust, and loyalty that, in tandem, influence consumers' purchasing inclinations. Evidential studies highlight the predictive prowess of Halal branding constructs—namely, Halal brand image, trust, and loyalty—in shaping consumers' proclivity towards Halal-branded products (Ali et al., 2018). Here, the cultural backdrop, rife with factors like religious affiliations, cultural identities, and intrinsic values, exerts a discernible influence over how consumers perceive Halal brands and the degree of allegiance they bestow upon them (Qurniawati et al., 2023). Consider, for instance, the scenario of consumers forging enduring brand loyalty to Halal skincare products, wherein this loyalty emanates from an alignment with their religious beliefs and adherence to Sharia principles (Qurniawati et al., 2023).

Moreover, the synergy between Halal branding and cultural context extends its embrace beyond commodities and into domains such as tourism. In the context of halal tourism, the branding strategies of travel destinations are informed by an amalgam of elements spanning halal sustenance, hygiene facilities, and the embodiment of Islamic culture (Preko et al., 2021). The cultural backdrop acts as a rudder, steering the branding maneuvers of halal tourism destinations, effectively beckoning to Muslim tourists.

In summation, the interplay between Halal branding and the intricate tapestry of cultural context is a nexus underpinned by intricate dynamics—where religious convictions, societal norms, brand perceptions, trust, and loyalty converge. Profoundly understanding and assimilating the cultural milieu is the keystone for marketers seeking to adeptly address the call for Halal products while crafting branding narratives that resonate harmoniously with the religious and cultural tapestry of consumers.

CHALLENGES FOR HALAL BRANDING

Navigating the challenges of Halal branding is a multifaceted endeavor entwined with several pivotal factors. One of these challenges stems from the absence of a unified global definition of Halal, a void that casts a shadow on the Halal market's expansion (Fuseini et al., 2020). The variations in interpretations of Islamic dietary laws originating from the Quran and Hadith have engendered disparities and disharmony in standards, constraining the Halal market from achieving its full potential (Fuseini et al., 2020). This lack of standardization gives rise to complexities in ensuring the fidelity of Halal products throughout the intricacies of the supply chain (Soon et al., 2017).

The intricate nature of communicating the Halal attributes of a brand to consumers presents another challenge. The essence of Halal as a product attribute lies in the intrinsic nature, origin, and processing techniques of the food—elements that may not be readily apparent or easily validated by consumers (Ali et al., 2018). This opacity can breed uncertainty in quality during the purchase phase, as consumers grapple with an inability to comprehensively gauge the Halal facets of a product.

The challenge of brand consciousness emerges when venturing into domains dominated by Western or conventional brands (Hosain, 2021). Fostering brand awareness and recognition for Halal brands can prove arduous, particularly in the face of entrenched brands that have already secured significant market shares. Likewise, there's the challenge of cultivating consumer education and awareness about Halal brands. A dearth of understanding regarding the concept of Halal or its significance in consumption can breed misconceptions and resistance towards embracing Halal brands. In response, marketers need to channel resources into potent marketing strategies that extol the virtues of Halal brands and enlighten consumers about their merits (Ali et al., 2018).

Maintaining the quality and consistency of Halal products poses yet another challenge. Consumers harbor expectations of Halal brands meeting stringent quality benchmarks, with any deviation jeopardizing trust and loyalty (Ali et al., 2020). Safeguarding the sanctity of the Halal food supply chain emerges as a pivotal task in maintaining product Halal integrity (Soon et al., 2017). This necessitates orchestrated coordination among diverse entities involved in production, processing, and logistics.

The tapestry of cultural and religious diversity among Muslim consumers across various nations presents a formidable challenge to Halal branding. The influences of brand perceived quality, Halal brand image, satisfaction, and trust may not hold uniform validity across diverse countries and product types (Ali et al., 2018). Herein lies the imperative for businesses to meticulously account for the specific religious and migration dynamics of their target market while fashioning Halal branding strategies.

It is paramount to acknowledge that the challenges within the realm of Halal branding are not one-size-fits-all; they morph across countries and consumer segments. As the Muslim populace burgeons even in non-Muslim territories (Ali et al., 2018), the factors governing Halal brand purchase intent may exhibit disparate validity for Muslims in distinct nations and in the context of diverse product categories (Ali et al., 2018). In this intricate tapestry, marketers must intricately weave the specifics of cultural and religious landscapes into their Halal branding endeavors.

In sum, the journey through the challenges of Halal branding navigates a labyrinth replete with multifaceted hurdles. The absence of global consensus on Halal's definition, the intricacies of communicating Halal attributes, grappling with established Western brands, consumer education, quality assurance, and the mosaic of cultural and religious diversity—all converge as pivotal chapters in the tale of Halal branding.

OPPORTUNITIES FOR HALAL BRANDING

Halal branding unfurls a tapestry of opportunities for businesses to weave into their strategic fabric. Primarily, it serves as a gateway to novel markets. The crescendo of the Muslim population resounds not only in traditional enclaves but also resonates in non-Muslim terrains (Ali et al., 2018). Through the embrace of Halal branding, businesses can enkindle connections with this burgeoning demographic, adroitly addressing the unique inclinations and proclivities of Muslim consumers.

Furthermore, Halal branding imparts a competitive edge, a shimmering allure that sets Halal products apart. The aegis of Halal ushers in connotations of quality, safety, and ethical sanctity (Ali et al., 2018). Amidst the cacophony of options, this differentiation transforms businesses into beacons that beckon to discerning customers who prize the essence of Halal. The symphony of Halal branding harmonizes with the crescendo of profitability. A symposium of research attests that businesses can orchestrate the sale of Halal products at a premium, thereby embellishing profit margins (Ali et al., 2018). The auras of exclusivity and value embellish these offerings, culminating in an orchestra of heightened profitability.

Moreover, Halal branding sews the seeds of loyalty and trust. Within the hearts of those who prioritize Halal products, an affinity burgeons for brands that mirror their values and convictions (Ali et al., 2018). The careful cultivation of a Halal brand image, coupled with the steadfast delivery of quality and reliability, nurtures enduring relationships with customers. In this symphony of opportunity, customer satisfaction emerges as a resonating note. The acquisition of Halal certifications, coupled with explicit labels signaling Halal attributes, fosters transparency and reassurance (Ali et al., 2018). This transparency breeds contentment, amplifying the likelihood of recurring purchases and casting a spotlight on customer satisfaction.

In summation, the world of Halal branding is awash with an orchestra of prospects for businesses to compose their narratives. It forges avenues to new markets, crafts a competitive symphony, enriches profitability's melody, sews the fabric of trust, and orchestrates crescendos of customer satisfaction. By unveiling Halal branding's potential, businesses can harness the harmony of growth and prosperity.

CONCLUSION AND FUTURE RESEARCH AGENDA

Firstly, the distinction between Halal brands and Islamic brands highlights their distinct characteristics within the realm of Islamic consumer behavior and branding strategies. While Halal brands undergo specific certification to adhere to Islamic dietary laws and offer assurance to Muslim consumers, Islamic brands encompass a wider spectrum by aligning with Islamic principles beyond dietary considerations. The interplay between these two branding types reflects the diverse preferences and values of Muslim consumers, presenting businesses with opportunities to genuinely connect with this demographic.

For future research in this field, several avenues warrant deeper exploration. Firstly, delving into consumer perceptions and preferences towards Islamic brands that emphasize ethical sourcing, sustainability, and social responsibility could offer insights into how these values influence purchase decisions.

Secondly, investigating the strategies that businesses employ to effectively communicate their alignment with Islamic principles in their branding efforts could unveil successful approaches. Additionally, comprehending the intricacies of consumer behavior towards non-Halal Islamic brands and the role of cultural variations can enhance our understanding of the market's dynamics. Ultimately, further research can equip businesses with strategies resonating with Muslim consumers' values, while also uncovering growth potential and meaningful connections in this evolving landscape.

Secondly, the differentiation between Halal brands and Halal branding underscores their intertwined yet distinct roles in the realm of Islamic products. While Halal brands pertain to products that have undergone stringent Halal certification and comply with Shariah requirements, Halal branding entails strategic endeavors to position and market these certified products as Halal to the intended audience. This distinction is pivotal for businesses aiming to effectively engage with Muslim consumers and tap into the escalating demand for Halal products.

In terms of future research in this domain, several facets merit in-depth investigation. Firstly, scrutinizing the efficacy of diverse Halal branding strategies and their impact on consumer perception, loyalty, and market share could yield valuable insights for businesses. Secondly, probing the influence of cultural and regional variations on the reception of Halal brands and branding could lead to customized approaches for various markets. Additionally, comprehending the evolving preferences of Muslim consumers and their inclination to pay a premium for Halal products could foster a deeper grasp of market dynamics. Overall, advancing research in this field can guide businesses in optimizing their Halal branding strategies to resonate with the varied values and preferences of Muslim consumers while nurturing sustainable market growth.

Thirdly, the domain of Halal branding has captured the attention of both scholars and marketing practitioners alike, as it navigates the intersection of Islamic principles and consumer behavior. The shifting preferences of Muslim consumers towards comprehensive decision-making have prompted marketers to explore the communication of attributes that go beyond conventional quality and hygiene factors. The academic landscape of Islamic marketing and branding is currently experiencing growth, characterized by efforts to comprehend the intricate interplay between Halal concepts and consumer dynamics. Challenges persist in unraveling the complex relationship between Halal branding and consumer behavior, particularly in conveying emotionally-driven brand messages and understanding the boundaries of Islamic branding. The evolving and delicate nature of the Halal concept further adds to the intricacies of this domain.

For future research in this arena, several avenues warrant deeper exploration. Firstly, a more comprehensive and precise definition of Halal branding that encompasses its dynamic and evolving nature is necessary. Further studies could shed light on the typologies of Islamic branding, providing insights into the multiple facets and dimensions shaping consumer perceptions and choices. Secondly, delving into the process by which the significance of Halal is instilled in the consciousness of Muslim consumers can offer valuable insights into the driving forces behind their preferences and behaviors. Exploring the role of cultural context and regional variations in Halal branding strategies and consumer responses can also contribute to a nuanced understanding of this field. Lastly, investigating how traditional branding constructs such as brand image, satisfaction, trust, and loyalty manifest in the context of Halal products can offer a comprehensive view of consumer behavior and its implications for businesses. By addressing these research directions, scholars can provide strategic insights for businesses looking to effectively navigate the intricate landscape of Halal branding while maintaining authenticity and establishing profound connections with their target audience.

Fourthly, the allure of the Halal market's potential emanates from a convergence of factors that collectively shape a captivating landscape for both businesses and researchers. The substantial and continually growing global Muslim population, accompanied by their increasing economic empowerment, lays the foundation for the market's expansion. This growth trajectory transcends traditional boundaries, as the Halal market gains traction even in non-Muslim nations, creating new avenues for development. The diversification of the market to encompass various industries beyond food – including cosmetics, pharmaceuticals, and services – contributes to its dynamic nature.

Consumer demand acts as a potent driver, with Muslim consumers exhibiting a strong preference for Halal products driven by various psychological factors. This demand not only resonates with their religious values but also provides businesses with opportunities to tailor offerings. Furthermore, the concept of Halal extends beyond religious requirements, resonating with ethical consumption and quality, thus appealing to a broader consumer base, including non-Muslims. This inclusivity presents the potential for market growth across diverse segments.

For future research in this realm, a few directions deserve focus. Firstly, understanding the intricacies of consumer behavior within both Muslim-majority and non-Muslim contexts can yield insights for effective customization of strategies. Secondly, delving into the drivers compelling non-Muslim consumers to engage with the Halal market and their perceptions of Halal as an indicator of quality can inform marketing endeavors. Additionally, investigating cross-cultural marketing strategies and their impact on distinct consumer groups can guide businesses seeking to tap into this multifaceted market. Lastly, exploring the intersections of Halal with sustainability and ethical considerations presents a promising avenue for enhancing the market's appeal. By delving deeper into these dimensions, researchers can provide invaluable insights for businesses aiming to navigate the dynamic Halal market and unlock its full potential across diverse consumer segments.

Fifth, the interplay between Halal branding and consumer behavior is a complex phenomenon encompassing intricate factors. Halal branding wields significant influence over consumer purchase decisions through the creation of a positive brand image and perceived quality. Factors like brand satisfaction, trust, and loyalty shape consumer behavior towards Halal products, underpinned by a holistic framework guiding their purchasing intentions. Beyond offering access to new markets and competitive advantages, Halal branding aligns with consumers' perception of fair and ethical business practices.

In terms of future research, this domain holds promise for further enriching our understanding. Investigating the dynamics of Halal branding beyond Muslim-majority countries, particularly in non-Muslim contexts, can illuminate how Halal attributes resonate with diverse consumer segments. Further exploration into the intricate relationships between traditional branding constructs and Halal branding constructs can provide nuanced insights into the mechanisms propelling consumer behavior and purchase intentions. Additionally, delving into the role of religion in influencing consumer attitudes towards Halal products and how these dynamics vary across regions and cultures can yield valuable insights for businesses aiming to engage effectively with this market. By delving deeper into these dimensions, researchers can contribute to a more comprehensive understanding of the interplay between Halal branding and consumer behavior, providing strategic insights for businesses seeking to tap into the burgeoning potential of the Halal market.

Sixth, the intricate interplay between Halal branding and the underlying cultural context underscores the complexity of consumer behavior and preferences within the realm of Halal products and services. Religious beliefs and social norms wield significant influence over consumers' purchase intentions, particularly among those adhering to Islamic dietary laws. The cultural context, especially in regions with substantial Muslim populations, shapes attitudes and preferences, necessitating a nuanced understanding for effective marketing strategies.

Brand image, trust, and loyalty emerge as critical factors influencing consumers' purchase decisions. Halal branding constructs, such as brand image and trust, exert substantial impact on consumers' perceptions and intentions. The cultural context further magnifies this effect by linking religious associations, cultural identity, and values to consumer loyalty. This connection drives the development of lasting brand connections that transcend mere product attributes.

Moreover, the interplay between Halal branding and cultural context extends its reach to various domains, including the burgeoning landscape of halal tourism. In this sphere, the cultural context shapes branding strategies by integrating elements like halal amenities and Islamic culture, catering to the preferences of Muslim tourists and delivering a holistic travel experience.

In terms of future research, delving deeper into cross-cultural variations in the impact of Halal branding, both within Muslim-majority and non-Muslim contexts, could yield valuable insights. Investigating the relationship between Halal branding and emotions, as well as exploring the interplay of these constructs in the digital realm, presents a promising avenue. Additionally, examining how Halal branding strategies intersect with sustainability and ethical considerations could open new dimensions for businesses in this ever-evolving landscape. By unraveling these dimensions, researchers can equip businesses with the knowledge needed to effectively navigate the intricate interplay between Halal branding and cultural context, ultimately enhancing consumer satisfaction and brand success.

Seventh, successfully navigating the challenges posed by Halal branding demands a thorough comprehension of the multifaceted factors that influence consumer perceptions and behaviors within the Halal market. The absence of a standardized global definition for Halal constitutes a significant hurdle, leading to inconsistencies in standards and a lack of clarity in the market. Communicating the Halal attributes of a brand to consumers is a formidable challenge due to the inherent nature of these characteristics, often hidden from plain view. Moreover, establishing brand recognition and awareness within a competitive landscape dominated by conventional brands necessitates strategic endeavors.

The imperative of educating and raising consumer awareness about Halal brands cannot be overstated as a means to dispel misconceptions and foster consumer trust. Guaranteeing the quality and integrity of Halal products across the supply chain is pivotal for maintaining consumers' confidence in the authenticity of these brands. The diversity of Muslim consumers across various countries and cultural contexts underscores the importance of tailored branding strategies that take these nuances into account.

In terms of future research, delving into the establishment of standardized Halal definitions that reconcile Islamic dietary laws on a global scale holds the potential to mitigate market uncertainties. Exploring innovative approaches to effectively communicate the Halal attributes of products to consumers, possibly through technology and packaging, warrants exploration. Addressing the challenges of brand consciousness and market entry within a competitive landscape could benefit from insights into successful brand positioning strategies. Furthermore, understanding the intricacies of consumer education and awareness campaigns, along with their impact on consumer perceptions, remains a promising avenue of research. Studies unraveling the complexities of maintaining the quality and integrity of Halal products throughout the supply chain could provide practical insights for businesses. Moreover, a more profound exploration of the cultural and religious diversity among Muslim consumers and its influence on the effectiveness of Halal branding can offer valuable insights for crafting targeted strategies.

Eight, the realm of Halal branding presents businesses with a range of opportunities that can drive growth, differentiation, and enhanced consumer relationships. The expanding Muslim population in various parts of the world, coupled with the increasing demand for Halal products, provides an untapped market for businesses to explore and cater to. By aligning their offerings with Halal principles, companies can effectively penetrate both Muslim-majority and non-Muslim markets, expanding their reach and customer base.

Halal branding serves as a potent tool for businesses to gain a competitive edge. The association of Halal products with quality, safety, and ethical standards enables brands to stand out in competitive markets, resonating with consumers who prioritize Halal attributes. This differentiation not only attracts new customers but also cultivates a brand identity that can foster enduring loyalty.

The financial implications of Halal branding are also substantial. Businesses that venture into the Halal market can potentially command higher prices and profit margins due to the perceived premium nature of Halal products. This financial advantage, coupled with strategic marketing efforts, can contribute significantly to a company's bottom line.

As businesses adopt Halal branding, they also have the opportunity to cultivate trust and loyalty among consumers. By upholding the promises associated with Halal attributes and delivering on consumer expectations, brands can forge lasting relationships, leading to increased brand loyalty and advocacy.

Future research in this field could delve deeper into understanding the mechanisms that drive consumer loyalty and trust within the context of Halal branding. Exploring effective strategies for communicating Halal attributes to consumers and measuring the impact of such communication on brand perception could provide valuable insights. Furthermore, investigations into the role of cultural context in shaping consumer responses to Halal branding, particularly in non-Muslim markets, could uncover novel avenues for market expansion and engagement.

REFERENCES

Ahmad, M. F. (2015). Antecedents of halal brand personality. *Journal of Islamic Marketing*, *6*(2), 209–223. doi:10.1108/JIMA-03-2014-0023

Ahmad, M. G., & Syed, J. (2021). Meta-characteristics of Islamic ethics and moral consistency in Islamic banking. *Business & Society*, *60*(8), 2026–2059. doi:10.1177/0007650320928470

Aisyah, M. (2016). Consumer demand on halal cosmetics and personal care products in Indonesia. Al-Iqtishad. *Jurnal Ilmu Ekonomi Syariah*, *9*(1), 125–142.

Alam, A., & Maknun, L. (2021, February). *Impact of Islamic branding on purchasing decisions on facial wash product.* In First International Conference on Economics, Business and Social Humanities, Madiun, Indonesia. 10.4108/eai.4-11-2020.2304556

Ali, A., Sherwani, M., Ali, A., Ali, Z., & Sherwani, M. (2021). Investigating the antecedents of halal brand product purchase intention: An empirical investigation. *Journal of Islamic Marketing*, *12*(7), 1339–1362. doi:10.1108/JIMA-03-2019-0063

Ali, A., Xiaoling, G., Sherwani, M., & Ali, A. (2018). Antecedents of consumers' Halal brand purchase intention: An integrated approach. *Management Decision*, *56*(4), 715–735. doi:10.1108/MD-11-2016-0785

Alserhan, B. (2010). On islamic branding: Brands as good deeds. *Journal of Islamic Marketing*, *1*(2), 101–106. doi:10.1108/17590831011055842

Amalia, F., Sosianika, A., & Suhartanto, D. (2020). Indonesian millennials' halal food purchasing: Merely a habit? *British Food Journal, 122*(4), 1185–1198. doi:10.1108/BFJ-10-2019-0748

Azam, A. (2016). An empirical study on non-Muslim's packaged halal food manufacturers: Saudi Arabian consumers' purchase intention. *Journal of Islamic Marketing, 7*(4), 441–460. doi:10.1108/JIMA-12-2014-0084

Azam, M. S. E., & Abdullah, M. A. (2020). Global halal industry: Realities and opportunities. *IJIBE, 5*(1), 47–59. doi:10.30659/ijibe.5.1.47-59

Bukhari, S. N. Z., & Isa, S. M. (2020). Islamic branding: Insights from a conceptual perspective. *Journal of Islamic Marketing, 11*(6), 1743–1760. doi:10.1108/JIMA-02-2018-0035

DinarStandard. (2019). *State of the Global Islamic Economy Report 2019/20*. DinarStandard. https://www.dinarstandard.com/state-of-the-global-islamic-economy-report-2019-20/

Fernando, Y., Wahyuni-TD, I. S., Zainul Abideen, A., & Mergeresa, F. (2023). Traceability technology, halal logistics brand and logistics performance: Religious beliefs and beyond. *Journal of Islamic Marketing, 14*(4), 1007–1031. doi:10.1108/JIMA-06-2020-0183

Fuseini, A., Hadley, P., & Knowles, T. (2021). Halal food marketing: An evaluation of UK halal standards. *Journal of Islamic Marketing, 12*(5), 977–991. doi:10.1108/JIMA-02-2020-0037

Garg, P., & Joshi, R. (2018). Purchase intention of "Halal" brands in India: The mediating effect of attitude. *Journal of Islamic Marketing, 9*(3), 683–694. doi:10.1108/JIMA-11-2017-0125

Hidayat, S. E., Rafiki, A., & Nasution, M. D. T. P. (2022). Halal industry's response to a current and post-COVID-19 landscape and lessons from the past. *Journal of Islamic Marketing, 13*(9), 1843–1857. doi:10.1108/JIMA-06-2020-0180

Hidayati, N., & Sunaryo, H. (2021). The role of halal label to increase the effect of attitude toward halal product on brand image and purchase intention. [International Journal of Entrepreneurship and Business Development]. *IJEBD, 4*(5), 744–752. doi:10.29138/ijebd.v4i5.1496

Hosain, M. S. (2021). Branding "Halal": Application of a certain religious emotion to attract a specific customer segment. *PSU Research Review, 5*(3), 195–200. doi:10.1108/PRR-12-2020-0043

Iranmanesh, M., Senali, M. G., Ghobakhloo, M., Nikbin, D., & Abbasi, G. A. (2022). Customer behaviour towards halal food: A systematic review and agenda for future research. *Journal of Islamic Marketing, 13*(9), 1901–1917. doi:10.1108/JIMA-01-2021-0031

Jaiyeoba, H. B., Abdullah, M. A., & Dzuljastri, A. R. (2020). Halal certification mark, brand quality, and awareness: Do they influence buying decisions of Nigerian consumers? *Journal of Islamic Marketing, 11*(6), 1657–1670. doi:10.1108/JIMA-07-2019-0155

Joshi, R., & Garg, P. (2022). Assessing brand love, brand sacredness and brand fidelity towards halal brands. *Journal of Islamic Marketing, 13*(4), 807–823. doi:10.1108/JIMA-04-2020-0104

Jumani, Z. A., & Sukhabot, S. (2021). Identifying the important attitude of Islamic brands and its effect on buying behavioural intentions among Malaysian Muslims: A quantitative study using smart-PLS. *Journal of Islamic Marketing*, *12*(2), 408–426. doi:10.1108/JIMA-09-2019-0196

Katuk, N., Ku-Mahamud, K. R., Kayat, K., Abdul Hamid, M. N., Zakaria, N. H., & Purbasari, A. (2021). Halal certification for tourism marketing: The attributes and attitudes of food operators in Indonesia. *Journal of Islamic Marketing*, *12*(5), 1043–1062. doi:10.1108/JIMA-03-2020-0068

Khan, A., Mohammad, A. S., & Muhammad, S. (2021). An integrated model of brand experience and brand love for halal brands: Survey of halal fast food consumers in Malaysia. *Journal of Islamic Marketing*, *12*(8), 1492–1520. doi:10.1108/JIMA-11-2019-0236

Kok, S. K. (2021). The branding of religious financial institutions in the UK: Conversations with market actors within the Islamic financial sector. *Journal of Islamic Marketing*, *12*(4), 900–917. doi:10.1108/JIMA-01-2020-0016

Mohd Suki, N., & Abang Salleh, A. S. (2018). Mediating effect of Halal image on Muslim consumers' intention to patronize retail stores: Some insights from Malaysia. *Journal of Islamic Marketing*, *9*(2), 338–355. doi:10.1108/JIMA-02-2017-0014

Mohd Yusof, Y. L., Wan Jusoh, W. J., & Maulan, S. (2021). Perceived quality association as determinant to re-patronise Shariah-compliant brand restaurants. *Journal of Islamic Marketing*, *12*(2), 302–315. doi:10.1108/JIMA-10-2018-0190

Muhammad, M. A., Elistina, A. B., & Ahmad, S. O. (2020). The challenges faced by halal certification authorities in managing the halal certification process in Malaysia. *Food Research*, *4*(1), 170–178. doi:10.26656/fr.2017.4(S1).S17

Preko, A., Mohammed, I., & Allaberganov, A. (2021). Antecedents of brand equity on halal tourism destination. *Journal of Islamic Marketing*, *13*(8), 1685–1702. doi:10.1108/JIMA-09-2020-0283

Qurniawati, R. S., Sakinah, A. N., & Nurohman, Y. A. (2023). The Impact of Religious Beliefs on Halal Skincare Brand Loyalty in Central Java Indonesia: The Mediating Role of Brand Love. *Jurnal Ekonomi Syariah Teori dan Terapan, 10*(2).

Rodrigo, P., & Turnbull, S. (2019). Halal holidays: How is value perceived by Muslim tourists? *International Journal of Tourism Research*, *21*(5), 675–692. doi:10.1002/jtr.2290

Sabbar, S. D., Kara, M. H., Said, S., Ahmed, S., & Asad, M. (2023). Awareness of Halal Branding and Marketing: Consumer Perception in Makassar, Indonesia. *Journal of Advances in Humanities Research*, *2*(2), 98–124. doi:10.56868/jadhur.v2i2.128

Septiarini, D. F., Ratnasari, R. T., Salleh, M. C. M., Herianingrum, S., & Sedianingsih, S. (2023). Drivers of behavioral intention among non-Muslims toward halal cosmetics: Evidence from Indonesia, Malaysia, and Singapore. *Journal of Islamic Accounting and Business Research*, *14*(2), 230–248. doi:10.1108/JIABR-02-2021-0064

Shah, S. A. A., Sukmana, R., Fianto, B. A., Ahmad, M. A., Usman, I. U., & Mallah, W. A. (2020). Effects of Halal social media and customer engagement on brand satisfaction of Muslim customer: Exploring the moderation of religiosity. *Journal of Islamic Marketing*, *11*(6), 1671–1689. doi:10.1108/JIMA-06-2019-0119

Shahid, S., Ahmed, F., & Hasan, U. (2018). A qualitative investigation into consumption of halal cosmetic products: The evidence from India. *Journal of Islamic Marketing*, *9*(3), 484–503. doi:10.1108/JIMA-01-2017-0009

Shahid, S., Parray, M. A., Thomas, G., Farooqi, R., & Islam, J. U. (2023). Determinants of Muslim consumers' halal cosmetics repurchase intention: An emerging market's perspective. *Journal of Islamic Marketing*, *14*(3), 826–850. doi:10.1108/JIMA-08-2021-0265

Soon, J. M., Chandia, M., & Mac Regenstein, J. (2017). Halal integrity in the food supply chain. *British Food Journal*, *119*(1), 39–51. doi:10.1108/BFJ-04-2016-0150

Wilson, J. A., & Liu, J. (2011). The challenges of Islamic branding: Navigating emotions and halal. *Journal of Islamic Marketing*, *2*(1), 28–42. doi:10.1108/17590831111115222

Yusup, M., Mas'ud, R., & Johari, M. (2022). Brand Value and Tourists' Satisfaction in Lombok Indonesia as a Halal Tourism Destination. *Shirkah: Journal of Economics and Business*, *7*(1), 1–16. doi:10.22515hirkah.v7i1.403

Chapter 13
Strategizing Islamic Medicine Marketing Through Social Media:
The Case of Northern Nigeria

Nasir Yahaya
https://orcid.org/0009-0006-2238-4852
Indonesian International Islamic University, Indonesia

ABSTRACT

This chapter explored the role of social media in marketing Islamic medicine. The chapter utilized qualitative case study approach through interviews and participant observation. Using purposive sampling, a sample of ten respondents were interviewed in Kano and Kaduna. The author found that social media has strategic positive implications for the marketing of Islamic medicines in Northern Nigeria. In addition, Islamic medicine practitioners use content creation and influencer marketing to create awareness and increase visibility of their products. The prospects of social media adoption lie in the promotion and customization of advertising strategies such as influencer marketing and content creation, which draw attention and aid in promoting a product. Despite its prospect in expanding market share, lack of regulation and the spread of fake news pose serious challenges. Therefore, the chapter suggested that the Nigerian government should support and encourage the business of Islamic medicine through regulations on health standards, fair marketing policies and sound digital innovation.

INTRODUCTION

The global adoption of Islamic medicine products, commonly referred to as prophetic medicines, has experienced a rapid and substantial expansion in recent time. Moreover, Alrawi & Fetters, (2012) sees Islamic medicine as a healing method used within the framework of Islamic religious influences. In addition, it consists of herbal medicine, nutritional habits, mental-physical therapies, and spiritual healing. The medication process is crucial in treating several diseases such as HIV, COVID-19, sexual and

DOI: 10.4018/978-1-6684-7519-5.ch013

spiritual-related problems (Tocco, 2011; Maideen, 2020; Muhammad, 2022; Bello & Isah, 2015; Aliyu Gobir et al., 2018). However, the practice is very common in Northern Nigeria – a Muslim dominated region. It is a lucrative business providing employment opportunities to many. With the evolution of the digital era, the Islamic pharmacist adopts the use of social media for marketing Islamic Medicine, besides the traditional marketing strategies. Interestingly, social media has influenced how people interact and communicate with one another. Accordingly, people can communicate virtually using social media, particularly those socially connected on the Internet. In addition, social media's unique features and popularity have influenced traditional marketing strategies. It has a significant impact on dissemination of information across to the target audiences be it marketing, sermon, and related issues.

Cheung et al., (2021) maintain that social media marketing is currently the most essential element of a marketing strategy due to its interactive nature. Also, Assaad & Gomez, (2013) argue that Social media platforms offer the opportunity to interact personally with clients, which is frequently hard or challenging to do via traditional means. Thus, it should be understood that Marketing on social media does not take over the role of traditional marketing strategies. Rather, it should be viewed as an additional medium with unique capabilities that support more marketing activities. Therefore, strategizing social media to promote its marketing will have many benefits in upgrading the business. First, it is expected to foster market penetration by increasing market share, thereby improving revenue and increasing production. Second, modernizing Islamic medicine marketing is necessary due to intense competition between Islamic medicine and conventional (modern) medicine. Through a well- coordinated social media marketing, the entrepreneurs could increase consumer awareness about the effectiveness of their products. This is important because there are many people who perceive Islamic medicine as ineffective and inferior to modern medications. However, many Islamic medicinal products have been tested and trusted but such vital information is not widely circulated to the potential customers. Third, social media would be instrumental in promoting cooperation among the business stakeholders. Due to proliferation of sub-standard Islamic medicines and incompetent practitioners, the business owners may lean on social media as a platform to educate the masses on how to differentiate between original and sub-standard products, and between competence and incompetence. This would help in sanitizing the business and boost consumer confidence to patronizing the products.

Against the above background, the aim of this study is to discuss Islamic medicine entrepreneurship in the context of northern Nigeria by investigating how social media is used as a strategy to promote Islamic medicine marketing and exploring how Islamic medicine, social media, and marketing interact. The study will examine the potential benefits as well as the challenges that arise when Islamic medication processes adopt the use of social media for marketing. To achieve this goal, the study raised the following questions:

1- To what extent does successful social media marketing promote Islamic medicine in Northern Nigeria?
2- What variables contributed to the success of an effective social media Islamic medicine marketing campaign?

The current study contributes to the literature and practice in the following ways:

1- It offers policy suggestion to the authorities on the importance of regulating and monitoring the practice of Islamic medicine both online and offline so as to guarantee the safety, quality, and efficacy of the products.

2- By exploring the growing trends, techniques, and guidelines, the chapter provides a crucial insights and motivations to Islamic medicine entrepreneurs regarding the use of social media platforms for the advertisement of their products.
3- The chapter adds to the existing body of knowledge on Islamic medicine entrepreneurship and online marketing particularly in Nigerian context.

The remaining sections of the chapter are thematically outlined as follows: the first section contains an overview of Islamic medicine business; section two provides details about Islamic medicine and entrepreneurship; section three presents the role of social media in promoting entrepreneurship; section four explores the contribution of social media to marketing Islamic medicine products; and the challenges and prospects of using social media for Islamic medicine marketing are discussed in section five. Finally, conclusions and recommendations are discussed in the last section.

An Overview of Islamic Medicine

Medication through the use of Islamic medicine products, popularly known as prophetic medicines, has grown rapidly across the globe, specifically in most Muslim majority countries, including Nigeria. Alrawi and Fetters (2012) define Islamic medicine as a healing method used within the framework of Islamic religious influences. The medication process takes place in various forms, which consist of using herbal medicine, nutritional habits, mental-physical therapies, and spiritual healing. Additionally, Azaizeh, et al. (2010) claims that Islamic medicine practitioners offer treatments through inhaling a solution of oily substances, infusions that consist of either water or oil, or a normal mixture generated from boiling components of plants in water. Furthermore, it can be consumed in form of a juice, sweetener, fried food, raw fruit, berries, veggies, soaking plant parts, dietary fat, creamy liquid, poultice, or powder.

Nevertheless, from a medical historiographical perspective, Ebrahimnejad (2011) argues that the term "Islamic medicine" was first used by modern historians from the west in order to demonstrate that it was developed within the framework of Islam, in addition to the contribution made by future Islamic scholars in the development of a substantial medical manuscript translated into Arabic from Greek. Similarly, Nagamia (2003) claims that in the 16th and 17th centuries, the division between Islamic and modern medicine first emerged. As a result, it had a significant impact on society. However, many Muslim societies have solidly relied on Islamic Medicine as their primary form of medication for centuries. This is done due to the fact that many hadiths are associated with how to treat medical issues or treatments prescribed by the noble prophet. Islamic scholars therefore developed interpretations in order to have an extensive understanding of these hadiths. In this regard, Ismail, et al. (2021) claim that Islamic scholars had two different perspectives on the subject matter. From the first perspective, many Islamic scholars, like Ghazali (d. 505 AH), believe that prophetic medicines are divine and supported by revelation. While other Islamic scholars, like Abu Jafar At-Tahawy (d. 321 AH), believe that these hadiths are ijtihad from the Noble Prophet as a human being and therefore not supported by revelation.

Considering the opinion of these proponents, many studies were carried out on multiple variables from a scientific perspective, which prove the efficiency of the prophetic or Islamic medicines. For example, studies conducted by (Mohamed El Sayed et al., 2014), (Omar, et al (2015), (Musharraf & Arman, 2018), and (Maideen, 2020) indicate that cupping (Hijama), vinegar, and black seeds (Habbatus sauda) are critical to several health issues.

According to Ojo, (2019), religion is more than just a collection of beliefs for an African; it is an aspect of life and an essential component of identity, culture, and ethical values. In a nutshell, religion plays a significant role in tradition and encourages both social peace and creativity. In Nigeria, specifically the northern region where Muslims are predominant, religious and cultural practices shape the lives of the people and impact their daily activities (Ojo, 2019). For many years, the culture of the region has relied heavily on traditional healing methods due to several factors, including a lack of access to modern hospitals, the high rate of poverty in the region, and the inherited tradition of using herbal remedies for physical and spiritual health issues. Also, (Ajala, et al. 2019) argue that diseases related to piles, infertility, mental illnesses, black magic, witchcraft, and many more are treated traditionally in Nigeria because modern hospitals only offer temporary solutions to the diseases. However, malaria, typhoid fever, and many others are common diseases many people are suffering from In northern Nigerian societies. (Okunlola & Oyeyemi, 2019), argues that with an estimated 53.7 million cases and 79,900 deaths, Nigeria is considered to be one of the most malaria-affected countries in the world. Interestingly, northern Nigeria holds more cases of malaria than other parts of the nation. In addition, (Akinyemi et al., 2018) claim that due to antibiotic resistance, typhoid fever continues to remain a considerable health risk to Nigerians, making it a major threat to the nation's health security.

Furthermore, Gobir and Sani (2018) explore how spiritually related health issues are treated through the Girka and Bori rituals within the Hausa communities of northern Nigeria. So, scholars recently identified with regard to the abovementioned illnesses have supported the claim that these diseases are a common problem in northern Nigerian communities. Apparently, (Ojo, 2019) believes that when they are ill, Africans, including Nigerians, frequently apply modern and traditional forms of treatment. In this regard, I am definitely aware of the ongoing struggle that northern Nigerian societies are having to find a cure for physical and spiritual health problems. As a result, they experience various stages in their approaches to illness, taking into consideration the accessibility, affordability, and availability of the medication process. Among the various forms of medication utilized are Islamic medicines. This is done due to the fact that Islamic medicine products are critical for many diseases for which modern hospitals mostly provide temporary solutions, as well as their compatibility with the socio-religious backgrounds and beliefs of the patient and their anticipated safety and efficacy.

Adapting Islamic medicine as a form of medication has grown rapidly within the last two decades in northern Nigeria (Tocco, 2011). The practice is considered to be an increasingly important profession because it emphasizes the physical and spiritual aspects of illness through the efficacy of spiritualities in the form of Qur'anic recitation, prayers, and the use of herbs and remedies within the Islamic framework either prescribed by the noble prophet or classic Islamic scholars, such as Zamzam water, ajwa dates, black seed, vinegar, olive oil, and many more. Many Muslims in northern Nigeria are attracted to Islamic medicine because they believe that the products are compounded and manufactured within the framework of Islamic tradition. In addition, an increase in healthcare expenses and possible side effects of modern medicine are among the other reasons identified. Moreover, the extensive variety of natural-based therapies, remedies, herbs, and services offered by Islamic medicine practitioners are considered safe and efficient. Based on the arguments of (Tocco, 2011), the warm, friendly, confidential, and often ritualistic approach of the Islamic pharmacists, impersonal environments and usually hurried treatments offered at the government health care centres are among the factors that contribute to the acceptance of Islamic medicine products within northern Nigerian society. Moreover, (Ajala et al., 2019) believes that the products are considered harmless because they are mostly natural made. This trend has shaped the demand in the region for products that are associated with Islamic medicine, which has allowed businesses that engage in such products to expand significantly. These claims are in line with the argument of (Ojo, 2019) which maintains that religions are a source of knowledge and ideals that are wrapped in cultural norms in order to impact different types of businesses. In a nutshell, it is argued that religious beliefs have a significant impact on economic growth at the individual, group, state, and national levels within a given society.

In conclusion, medication through Islamic medicine in northern Nigeria is crucial in treating several physical health issues such as HIV, COVID-19, sexual-related problems, and others (Bello & Isah, 2015; Maideen, 2020; Muhammad, 2022; Tocco, 2011). Also, Gobir and Sani (2018) suggest that the practice is found to be vital for various spiritual health issues. For example, the medicines are critical for Rukyah (exorcism), particularly for the patients possessed by Jins. Consequently, many entrepreneurs seized the chance to set up businesses in this area after observing the opportunity for Islamic medicine products. However, while some of these entrepreneurs often have in-depth knowledge of Islamic medical practices, they utilize this expertise to identify, develop, and produce remedies from natural herbs that are critical to physical and spiritual health issues. As a result, Tocco (2011) argues that many Islamic medicine centres have been established with full-time employees, a consultation room, and an Islamic pharmacy. Based on the authors experience and observation, the business has expanded significantly as a result of the efforts of entrepreneurs, which were also important in satisfying the rising demand of society for products related to Islamic medicine. On the other hand, individuals with inadequate knowledge and experience are involved in the process due to the lucrative nature of the practice. This casts doubt on the credibility of genuine people who have the knowledge, potential, skills, and ability to serve humanity through Islamic medicine.

Islamic Medicine and Entrepreneurship

Greve and Salaff (2003) maintains that a common definition of an entrepreneur is an individual who owns, starts, controls, and takes over the risks of an economic venture. However, despite an increase in entrepreneurship studies across religious and socio-cultural fields, there is still much to learn and understand regarding how these factors impact the development of entrepreneurship. Nevertheless, extant literatures (Ahen, et al. 2023; Torri, 2010; Yazdi, et al. 2021) identify and evaluate the connection between entrepreneurship and traditional herbal medicine in the context of Tamil Nadu, Iran and Ghana. In the case of Nigeria, based on the authors knowledge, Islamic medicine and entrepreneurship interact in mutually beneficial ways that impact, influence and benefit each other. This is due to the fact that entrepreneurship provides an extensive range of opportunities in the field of Islamic medicine, resulting in the development and growth of the sector. The paragraphs below will highlight the lucrative nature of the business and the potential benefits that might arise when these concepts interact.

The lucrative nature of the Islamic medicine business attracts entrepreneurs due to the growing demand for Islamic medicine products in society and the opportunities available in the market. Therefore, entrepreneurs utilize this advantage by investigating more about the business before investing in it. Based on Greve and Salaff (2003), data, knowledge, capital, labour, skills, and expertise are required in order to start a business activity. Therefore, before engaging into the business, most people that are interested in the field consult experts or invest in an ongoing business so as to share the profit. This really help the financial performance and growth of the business that are directly linked to Islamic medicine. Modern advertising techniques, branding strategies, innovation, and expertise are used by entrepreneurs in order to develop an environment that promotes the business to prosper, and grow. Additionally, entrepreneurship enables the sector of Islamic medicine to become more standard and professional. This is due to the fact that the entrepreneurs understand the importance and value of licenses, certifications, guarantees of quality, and compliance with laws and regulations. They work tirelessly together to make sure that their goods meet the appropriate rules and regulations. In this regard, some of the Islamic medicine practitioners collaborate with traditional healers to get an additional in-depth knowledge in the subject matter.

Furthermore, attending seminars, conferences related to the subject matter, and learning classical Arabic books of medicine from Islamic scholars are among other activities utilized by the Islamic medicine practitioners. This dedication to high standards and professionalism raises the credibility and image of Islamic medicine in the northern Nigerian societies, resulting in more consumers and establishing trust in the market. Ajala, et al. (2019) claims that most of Islamic medicine practitioners are Islamic scholars. The abovementioned strategies help the entrepreneurs to produce Islamic medicinal products that will attract and satisfied the potential customers. These techniques help expand the customer base as well as promote sales. The drive to succeed makes sure that the business remains competitive within Islamic medicine practitioners as well as in the intense competition between Islamic medicine and conventional (modern) medicine.

In summary, there is a positive relationship between entrepreneurship and Islamic medicine. Entrepreneurs benefit from the significant economic potential offered by Islamic medicine, and entrepreneurship also helps the sector of Islamic medicine expand and prosper. Through creative thinking, business expertise, and professionalism, entrepreneurs improve the sector by raising the quality of products, customer base, and business standards. At the same time, the demand for Islamic medical products provides entrepreneurs with more potential customers motivated by bonds with their respective cultures and religions. Integrating Islamic medicine and entrepreneurship shows the positive aspects of one another and raises the value and profitability of the business.

The Role of Social Media in Promoting Entrepreneurship

Dwivedi, et al. (2015) maintain that social media has demonstrated itself to be an affordable communication system available for everyone, including consumers, entrepreneurs, associations, governments, and anyone else who wants to learn, contribute, create, and advertise the main idea being circulated. In the current 21st century, the trend of utilizing social media is a well-known phenomenon. This is because social media has brought many innovative changes in our daily lives, including our business activities. On one hand, Bajpai, et al. (2012) claim that the process of increasing internet traffic or gaining attention through the use of social media platforms is known as social media marketing. The primary objective of social media marketing campaigns usually depends on efforts toward creating content that attracts readers' interest and motivates them to share it with other people on social media. Moreover, social media helps people connect virtually through several platforms, and shapes the consumers decision on the goods and services they are interested in, how they make their purchases, and how they give feedback on those purchases. In contrast, Assaad and Gomez (2013) maintain that entrepreneurs can benefit from utilizing social media in their marketing by gaining a deeper knowledge of consumer demands and developing customer relationships. Therefore, businesses have to organize their activities on social media platforms for greater control and evaluation if they want to achieve measurable profits. This is because proper behaviour has the power to influence how businesses view their clients. When social networking and marketing are integrated, entrepreneurs may be able to track their customers, fulfil their needs, and manage and evaluate their behaviours. Moreover, (Shah, et al.

(2020) maintain that the information flow in traditional marketing strategies has changed as a result of social media. Due to advances in consumer feedback capabilities for marketers, today's consumers are more in control than they were a decade ago.

Furthermore, Vinerean (2017) argues that all businesses attempt to develop significant relationships with all of their stakeholders, including their customers, at all levels. In light of this, one of the primary objectives of social media and modern technology has been the ability to interact, communicate, and gain a deeper understanding of a business's main target consumers. This is important in order to create a competitive environment for every kind of interaction or targeted audience within an enterprise. However, Dwivedi, et al. (2015) claim that social media continues to be recognized as a significant and crucial marketing component that determines the success of a certain good, service, or business. According to Vinerean (2017), researchers and practitioners have both been interested in the topic of social media in internet marketing. Many studies have explored social media marketing from several angles, and different perspectives in order to highlight the various roles that these platforms fulfil. For example, Cheung, et al. (2021) analyse the impacts of social media marketing and the outcomes it provides in China. Similarly, Mason, et al. (2021) focus on post COVID- 19 evolution of social media marketing. Moreover, Vinerean (2017) discussed about the significance of strategic social media marketing. Additionally, Dwivedi, et al. (2015) maintain social media marketing and advertisement. Furthermore, Vinerean, et al. (2013) analyse the impacts of social media marketing on online consumer behaviour. Finally, Nakara, et al. (2012) explore social media marketing and entrepreneurship in the context of France.

To Shah, et al. (2020), religion and culture are like two sides of the same coin. This is the reason why the status of Muslims is regulated by Shariah law in the Muslim world. However, this is necessary because of shariah-compliant social media marketing has increased, just as it has for all other economic endeavours. (Pratiwi, et al. (2022) opine that the goal is to fulfil the financial success of society within the framework of Islamic ethical behaviour, which stands simply in the way of healthy business competition. Besides, Wilson and Grant (2013) claims that Islamic marketing is a unique development in marketing operations and consumer behaviours that is currently being led by both Muslims and non-Muslims, despite the fact that it has its roots in the Islamic faith, tradition, and culture. In relation to this, it is possible to compare it to other innovations in the marketing industry. Considering this, it is useful to explore the halal and non-halal aspects of social media marketing From the Islamic entrepreneurship perspective. In the view of Shah et al. (2020), the halal meaning of Halal social media marketing includes goods and services related to many aspects of life, not just about food or tourism. This is due to the fact that "Halal social media" marketing significantly boosts brand satisfaction among Muslim consumers. So, Islamic medicine business owners in northern Nigeria are experiencing recognition outside of their own region. Entrepreneurs explored the possibility of exporting their products to other regions of the nation, especially states with significant Muslim populations like Lagos and Oyo. Since these markets are more open to penetration due to shared cultural and religious beliefs, businesses can reach potential consumers and boost revenue. Additionally, there is significant interest in Islamic medicine products from neighbouring countries with related cultural and religious traditions, especially from the Hausa-Fulani tribes that are in Niger, Chad, and Cameroon, and Entrepreneurs are utilizing this opportunity to expand their businesses from local to international standards. Therefore, they brand their products as halal to attract and boost the satisfaction of many Muslim consumers within and outside the country.

Data and Methods

The main objective of this study is to explore Islamic medicine entrepreneurship in the context of northern Nigeria by investigating the strategy of Islamic Medicine Marketing through social media, as well as the potential benefits and challenges that arise within the process. In order to analyse this issue, the study uses a qualitative case study approach. Before proceeding, it is important to point out that the definitions of the terms "qualitative" and "case study" are presented separately. Creswell and David, (2011) define qualitative research as a method used for explaining, describing, evaluating, and interpreting shared habits of behaviours, opinions, beliefs, and language conversations that change over a period of time in groups that share a culture. In order to clarify, explain, and interpret the habits, beliefs, traditions, and values of a group of people, this approach employs several forms of data collection, which include interviews and observation. This method is suitable for the study because it enables an extensive evaluation of a particular phenomenon.

In this case, I explore the strategies of Islamic medicine marketing through social media, using two northern Nigerian states as a case study: Kano and Kaduna states. According to (Mustafa, et al. 2020), with a population of more than 15 million and a 95% Muslim majority, Kano is the most populous state in Nigeria. As well, the state's industrial and business sectors have historically prospered, making it the commercial centre of the Northern region and even sub-Saharan Africa at large. Similarly, Okeshola and Sadiq (2015), explores that Kaduna State has an ethnically diverse community of more than 6 million, but the majority ethnic group is made up of Hausas, and the dominant religion is Islam. The states mentioned were chosen for numerous reasons, including their commercial impacts, large consumers of Islamic medicine products, and connections to other major cities in northern Nigeria. These factors were determined based on the author's three years of experience as an Islamic pharmacist and the observations made while residing and conducting business in the chosen states. Based on Sofaer (1999), case study research is a recognized set of qualitative techniques that deals with a single case, multiple cases, or even a summary of an event that is chosen on purpose or at random in order to meet the requirements of particular types of data.

The research data are collected through personal experience and interviews. Creswell and Creswell (2018) maintain that data, strong evidence, and logical reasoning shape knowledge. Therefore, the researcher collects data based on evaluations completed by individuals or through personal observation. In addition, Creswell (2015) claims that interviews provide more opportunity for the researcher to obtain specific details that cannot be gathered via observation, making this method so essential. Therefore, the combination of these data collection techniques is crucial because it enables the researcher to gain an in-depth understanding of the context from different perspectives aside from one's own and to explore extensively through the insights, motives, and viewpoints of others.

However, in order to identify the study participants, the research adapts the purposive sampling method. According to Van Eeuwijk and Angehrn (2017), purposive sampling is a qualitative method of sampling where participants are selected by considering a number of criteria, such as expertise, status, and knowledge within a group or community. The researcher believes that using this method is crucial to the study because all the participants selected ought to fulfil certain criteria to be recruited, including being knowledgeable about the subject matter, having experience in Islamic Medicine entrepreneurship, and using social media for marketing the products.

According to Creswell and David (2011), individuals with an in-depth understanding of issues related to the research's topic can be selected for purposeful sampling. Similarly, Akyildiz (2021) claims that in qualitative studies, people are questioned in an effort to obtain deeper information and relevant justifications. Therefore, in order to learn from their viewpoints and experiences, a sample of 10 Islamic pharmacists were interviewed; five from Kano and the remaining five from Kaduna State. The objective of the initial contact with the participants was to obtain their formal acceptance to take part in the study. Likewise, the study is carried out with full confidentiality. Before interviews, participants are asked for approval to take notes on the conversations. These notes are transcribed, translated, coded, displayed. Finally, the data are interpreted using Miles and Huberman (1994) thematic analysis framework in order to have a full data set, which refers to the data that was reduced and purified from the entire range of individuals, events, and procedures that are being studied. They suggested the application of four methods for analysing qualitative data: First, the data collected through interviews is interpreted in Hausa language, which is then transcribed and translated into English. The data was reduced through coding by selecting the key points deemed important to the study. Consequently, general themes from the data are presented, and conclusions are drawn, which are later presented in the findings.

Findings: Social media Marketing and Islamic Medicine Products

The marketing strategies utilized by entrepreneurs have been completely transformed by social media (Li, et al. 2021). This is also applicable for the business of Islamic medicinal products in Nigeria. Islamic medicine has become more popular as people look for alternative healthcare solutions for physical and spiritual health issues. In northern Nigeria, social media platforms have served as a primary key to promoting Islamic medicine products in the last few decades, creating connections between manufacturers and consumers and creating a sense of community around Islamic medical treatment. The following paragraphs explore the important role social media has played in the marketing of products related to Islamic medicine, highlighting their usefulness, audience, challenges, and future prospects.

Κάγιας (2020) observes that the capacity of social media to connect with a global audience is one of its significant contributions to marketing. However, when it comes to marketing Islamic medicinal products in northern Nigeria, social media platforms like Facebook, TikTok, Instagram, WhatsApp, and YouTube serve as a home for marketing because the abovementioned platforms have massive user bases with people from different backgrounds. Therefore, Islamic medicine practitioners and potential customers utilize this opportunity to connect and have access to each other virtually for different purposes, which was previously unavailable in traditional marketing strategies that had a narrow audience.

Questions related to the role of social media in promoting Islamic medicine marketing are asked to an Islamic medicine practitioner, and the answers are quoted below:

"Our business has benefited significantly from social media, and it is really rare to find someone in the marketplace who isn't using social media for marketing purposes. This is because social media makes it easier to connect with and engage with individuals from all parts of Nigeria as well as from nearby nations like Niger, Chad, and Cameroon. People can simply consult you digitally, and you get paid for your services either through your bank accounts, PayPal and even through your crypto wallet addresses. Furthermore, the buyer can simply receive all acquired products through cargo channels. In summary, social media has simplified and made life easier for both Islamic medicine practitioners and our customers". (Ahmad Yusuf, Kaduna state).

Based on the above statements, it is clearly understood that social media has a positive impact on marketing Islamic medicinal products, not only in Nigeria but across neighbouring countries as well. Also, the availability of several modes of payment makes it easier to attract more customers. In nutshell, this strategy is crucial in order to have access to a global audience.

Moreover, Islamic medicine practitioners utilize social media to create a virtual community. This strategy is essential because social media platforms have made it easier for communities on the internet focused on Islamic medicine to develop. In these communities, there are practitioners and experts who offer their knowledge, as well as individuals seeking advice and solutions for certain health-related issues. Hence, creating such kinds of virtual communities' fosters credibility, trust, and loyalty for the products and practitioners. User reviews, testimonials, and interactive information enhance the credibility of Islamic medicine by creating a sense of authenticity. According to Bajpai, et al. (2012), social networking platforms serve as a channel for word of mouth. So, more people are approaching the product and/or business as a result of the knowledge about it being shared and repeated. This kind of one-on-one communication can cultivate a sense of loyalty among followers and future clients. Also, Vinerean (2017) suggests that Facebook alone is a home to about 1.18 billion active social media users, creating marketing opportunities for both international and local businesses that may target this sizable audience based on different demographics and interests. This shows that high profit might be gain if the strategy of cultivating a digital community is utilized.

Questions related to this are asked to an Islamic medicine practitioner, and the answers are quoted below:

"I'm an Islamic medicine practitioner and a content creator at the same time. Through my social media accounts on Facebook, TikTok, YouTube, and Instagram, I share my knowledge about several health issues and respond to the questions asked in the comment section. I also teach people how to make remedies for several health issues and, at the same time, promote and advertise my products to my virtual community. With the strategy of this method, your videos can easily go viral, which will help you attract more viewers and followers. As a result, you make money through your social media platforms, particularly YouTube, TikTok, Instagram, and Facebook, in addition to the sale of your products. In a nutshell, proper selection of social media platforms based on the preferences of the target audience is very important when it comes to marketing Islamic medicinal products.". (Aminu Musa, Kano State)

It is clearly understood from the above statements that some Islamic medicine practitioners utilize the strategy of content creation in addition to selling their respective products. (Cheung et al., 2021) maintain that consumers are motivated to buy through creative events created by interesting things on social media brand pages. These experiences include enjoyment, fun, and pleasure. In addition, (Vinerean, 2017) claims that existing consumers can share their brand experiences with other potential customers, influencing them. Meanwhile, businesses may track these open comments and adjust their social media marketing strategy as required. The utilization of this technique by business owners in order to gain insight into consumer demand is crucial for both business owners and consumers. The possibility of convincing others or conducting price comparisons, on the other hand, is determined by how satisfied consumers are with the products they have used.

Another strategy utilized in marketing Islamic medicinal products is influencer marketing, which has become an effective tool on social media. Influential people can affect the beliefs of their followers, especially those who are connected to Islamic health and practices. The reliability and visibility of Islamic medicinal products are increased by the useful insights, testimonials, and recommendations that these influencers frequently offer. Questions related to this are asked, and an Islamic practitioner responded the following:

"In this modern world of technology, we are trying to upgrade our business to a global standard. Therefore, adapting new skills and strategies in marketing is necessary, especially in this digital era. This is the reason why we used to pay social media influencers to advertise our products on their social media handles in order to attract more customers, and the outcome is appreciating positively because many customers used to tell us that they heard about our products on such a person's social media handle, although family and friends do recommend them in many situations". (Kabiru Balarabe, Kaduna State)

According to the above statements, some Islamic medicine practitioners are into influencer marketing. (Vinerean, 2017) argues that influencer marketing refers to the advertising and sale of goods and services through individuals (influencers) who have a large number of followers on social media. However, anyone with a large number of followers across a variety of social media platforms can work as an influencer for a company or product. Besides, the fundamental goal is to identify specific behavioural outcomes, such as followers' purchases or purchase intentions.

Another form of influencer marketing utilized by Islamic medicine practitioners is advertising their respective products through celebrities or local movie producers. Questions related to this are asked, and the responses are as follows:

"Many people are approaching our products as a result of the knowledge about them being shared or advertised by a celebrity in a respected local movie, series, or TV and Radio program. In order to influence their fans to buy or promote our products, we frequently pay singers or celebrities a lot of money to sing for our company or products". (Nazifi Ahmad, Kano State)

Based on the following statements, we understand that social media platforms serve as an effective medium for educational content related to Islamic medicine. Islamic medicine practitioners, in collaboration with celebrities such as singers, Musicians, actors, etc., utilize social media in order to share informative posts, videos, and articles explaining the principles and benefits of various products. (Yahya & Kamalul Ariffin, 2020) maintain that a celebrity draws attention and aids in promoting a product, and a celebrity that is well-liked by the general public might draw a better recall. The fundamental goal is to effectively associate oneself with a product being advertised in order to influence consumers' behaviour in the desired manner. Moreover, Li, et al. (2021) maintains that the creation and spread of educational or compelling content in various formats aims to draw in customers and/or keep them. As a result, rather than emphasizing product promotion, this kind of strategy tries to produce and provide important, useful content based on customer needs. Consequently, this approach offers two-way communication where businesses take the initiative to provide helpful material and customers respond favourably to this content. The basic principles of this strategy are to promote consumer interactions, increase brand exposure and popularity through content spread through social media. Therefore, this approach not only assists potential customers in making informed decisions but also raises awareness about Islamic medicine in general.

Prospects and Challenges of Using Social Media for Islamic Medicine Marketing

Utilizing social media for marketing Islamic medicinal products has tremendous prospects since it allows the customization of advertising strategies such as influencer marketing and content creation, which draw attention and aid in promoting a product. Also, it has made it possible for Islamic medicine practitioners and marketers to quickly, effectively, and easily reach their target consumers. Κάγιας (2020) maintains that cost reductions and increased reach are the two primary benefits of social media marketing. In general, the cost of a social media platform is lower than the cost of other marketing platforms like in-person salespeople, middlemen, or distributors. Similarly, marketing Islamic medicinal products through social media offers a unique opportunity for both consumers and practitioners to engage digitally with people around the globe. Through virtual communities, consumers can ask for a remedy for a specific illness, and via connections with experts in the field, knowledge about a cure for a specific disease will be shared, which leads to an increase in consumer awareness about the effectiveness of Islamic medicinal products. This is important because there are many people who perceive Islamic medicine as ineffective and inferior to modern medications.

Moreover, the potential for using social media to advertise Islamic medicinal products creates job opportunities that help eradicate unemployment in the country. For example, Islamic clerics are paid to educate the masses on the importance of leaning on Islamic medicinal products, while social media influencers, singers, musicians, actors, and actresses are paid to advertise Islamic medicinal products on their social media handles. (Κάγιας, 2020) claims that studies on consumer behaviour show that people pay more attention to advice and information given online and spend more time on websites that offer third-party evaluations. Additionally, social media helps encourage collaboration among business owners due to the proliferation of substandard Islamic medicines and incompetent practitioners. The union of the Islamic medicine practitioners frequently organized seminars, workshop, public speech both online and offline in order to sanitize the business and boost consumer confidence to patronize the products. Also, to educate potential consumers on how to distinguish between original and substandard products and between competence and incompetence. Furthermore, using social media to advertise Islamic medicinal products fosters market penetration due to the intense competition between Islamic medicine, traditional medicine, and conventional (modern) medicine by increasing market share, thereby improving revenue and increasing production.

Though social media platforms can assist businesses in quickly disseminating good news, they can do the opposite considering its global scope. Yet, false claims and information about Islamic medicinal products may spread easily in northern Nigeria due to the impact of religious and cultural beliefs in the region. Through their various social media handles, customers can express their anger towards the products or services offered because social media is less heavily regulated or censored compared to traditional media. So, users are free to express their opinions, positively or negatively about any business, product, or brand. Thus, practitioners need to manage ethical difficulties if they want to give accurate, research-based information and must be able to react instantly and effectively to these situations.

Correspondingly, many Islamic medicinal products have been tested and trusted, but such vital information is not widely circulated to potential customers due to ineffective social media coordination or personal security concerns. Interestingly, many people avoid approaching Islamic medicine practitioners on social media because they are unnecessarily worried about their safety, either due to the widespread use of substandard Islamic medicines or due to the involvement of unqualified practitioners in the field due to the lucrative nature of the business. Assaad and Gomez (2013) argue that privacy and personal security concerns are potential issues that businesses using social media may experience. Besides, it takes time, effort, and consistency to build credibility online. Thus, developing a virtual audience's trust can be difficult since some people are suspicious in nature.

Finally, the legal and regulatory framework in Nigeria makes it easy to effectively market Islamic medicinal products on social media. Therefore, it is essential to monitor and regulate the practice so as to comply with the rules and regulations of the health sector as well as legal advertising standards in order to avoid legal issues.

CONCLUSION

The strategy of marketing Islamic medicinal products on social media in northern Nigeria is effective depending on a number of variables that interact to engage the audience, spread the message, and provide the intended and desired outcomes. This includes the proper selection of social media platforms based on the preferences of the target audience. Also, the target audience's lifestyles, preferences, behaviors, and demands must be properly understood because if you are familiar with their interests, cultural values, and beliefs, it will be easier to provide messages and content that will attract them. This is because a clear content that includes a mix of motivating, educational, informative, and entertaining elements is essential to maintaining the audience's interest. Besides, an engaged audience is developed by successfully engaging with the audience through comments, live streaming, and direct messages, along with demonstrating dedication and concern by providing quick responses to inquiries and addressing problems. Moreover, in order to establish credibility, trust, and confidence in marketing Islamic medicinal products online, one must demonstrate expertise, share knowledge, and provide reliable facts supported by reputable sources. Furthermore, working together with social media influencers or reputable members of the community can increase this strategy's exposure and give it more legitimacy. The impact can be increased if combined with offline activities like workshops and seminars and promoted on other social media platforms.

However, Islamic medicine practitioners also have to deal with issues like disseminating bad news quickly, ineffective social media coordination, challenges to trust and credibility either due to the widespread use of substandard Islamic medicinal products or due to the involvement of unqualified practitioners in the field, and the overwhelming amount of online content. So, with adequate preparation, ethical considerations, and a commitment to providing accurate information, the addition of social media to Islamic medicine marketing may ultimately lead to meaningful relationships and the promotion of handling health-related issues based on Islamic traditions since the products are consumed massively due to its efficiency, cheap and affordability.

The study suggests the following measures based on the findings:

First, to minimize the unemployment rate and generate tax and revenue for the nation, it is suggested that the Nigerian government support, encourage, and promote the business of Islamic medicine. Also, they ought to collaborate with organizations such as the National Agency for Food and Drug Administration and Council (NAFDAC), the National Drug Law Enforcement Agency (NDLEA), and the Pharmacists Council of Nigeria (PCN) to regulate and supervise the practice in order to ensure the involvement of expertise in the field and to ensure the products' safety, quality, efficacy, accurate identification, and treatment. Also, they should be organizing online-offline awareness and sensitization campaigns on the matter for the benefit of the society.

Secondly, Islamic medicinal products should be produced, branded, compounded, stored, sold, consumed, and dispensed utilizing innovative methods and techniques in order to meet both marketing and therapeutic goals.

Thirdly, the use of social media for marketing Islamic medicinal products is rising in Northern Nigeria. Therefore, entrepreneurs should take advantage of these opportunities to expand their consumer base and spread their brand and products.

REFERENCES

Ahen, F., Buabeng, K. O., & Salo-Ahen, O. M. H. (2023). Market violence through destructive entrepreneurship: Assessing institutional responses to the proliferation of counterfeit traditional and alternative medicines in Ghana. *Heliyon*, *9*(3), e13881. doi:10.1016/j.heliyon.2023.e13881 PMID:36895339

Ajala, A. O., Kolawole, E. A., Adefolaju, T., Owolabi, A. O., Ajiboye, B. O., Adeyonu, A. G., Akangbe, J. A., Obaniyi, K. S., Adebimpe, A. T., & Adeniyi, V. (2019). Traditional medicine practices in Nigeria: A SWOT analysis. *International Journal of Mechanical Engineering and Technology*, *10*(2), 117–126.

Akinyemi, K. O., Oyefolu, A. O. B., Mutiu, W. B., Iwalokun, B. A., Ayeni, E. S., Ajose, S. O., & Obaro, S. K. (2018). Typhoid fever: Tracking the trend in Nigeria. *The American Journal of Tropical Medicine and Hygiene*, *99*(3), 41–47. doi:10.4269/ajtmh.18-0045 PMID:30047362

Akyildiz, S. T. (2021). An Overview of Qualitative Research and Focus Group Discussion. *International Journal of Academic Research in Education*. doi:10.17985/ijare.866762

Alrawi, S. N., & Fetters, M. D. (2012). Traditional arabic & islamic medicine: A conceptual model for clinicians and researchers. *Global Journal of Health Science*, *4*(3), 164–169. doi:10.5539/gjhs.v4n3p164 PMID:22980243

Assaad, W., & Gomez, J. (2013). Social Network in Marketing (Social Media Marketing) Opportunities and Risk. *International Journal of Managing Public Sector Information and Communication Technologies*, *2*(1), 13–22.

Azaizeh, H., Saad, B., Cooper, E., & Said, O. (2010). Traditional Arabic and Islamic medicine, a re-emerging health aid. *Evidence-Based Complementary and Alternative Medicine*, *7*(4), 419–424. doi:10.1093/ecam/nen039 PMID:18955344

Bajpai, V., Pandey, D. S., & Shriwas, M. S. (2012). Social Media Marketing: Strategies & Its Impact. *IRJC International Journal of Social Science & Interdisciplinary Research*, *1*(7), 214–223.

Bello, U. L., & Isah, J. (2015). Use of Herbal Medicines and Aphrodisiac Substances among Women in Kano State, Nigeria Article in Nursing and Health Sciences. *Journal of Nursing and Health Science*, *4*, 41–50. doi:10.9790/1959-04434150

Cheung, M. L., Pires, G. D., Rosenberger, P. J. III, & De Oliveira, M. J. (2021). Driving COBRAs: The power of social media marketing. *Marketing Intelligence & Planning*, *39*(3), 361–376. doi:10.1108/MIP-11-2019-0583

Creswell, J. W., & David Creswell, J. (n.d.). *Research Design: Qualitative*. Quantitative, and Mixed Methods Approaches.

Dwivedi, Y. K., Kapoor, K. K., & Chen, H. (2015). Social media marketing and advertising. *The Marketing Review*, *15*(3), 289–309. doi:10.1362/146934715X14441363377999

Ebrahimnejad, H. (2011). What is 'Islamic' in Islamic Medicine? An Overview. In *Boston Studies in the Philosophy and History of Science* (Vol. 275, pp. 259–270). Springer Nature., doi:10.1007/978-90-481-9968-6_17

Gobir, A. Y. & Sani, A. (2018). The Jinn, Women Vulnerabilities and the Act of Healings in The Hausa Communities Of 21 st Century. *IOSR Journal Of Humanities And Social Science (IOSR-JHSS, 23*(1), 67. https://doi.org/ doi:10.9790/0837-2301056773

Greve, A., & Salaff, J. W. (2003). Theory: Entrepreneurs and Network Activities Social Capital and Social Network. *Entrepreneurship Theory and Practice*, *28*(1), 1–22. https://onlinelibrary.wiley.com/store/10.1111/1540-8520.00029/asset/1540-8520.00029.pdf?v=1&t=j9ywa8bj&s=c1a6cb2ad31d88b1d8e8614619fb76a49c584751. doi:10.1111/1540-8520.00029

Ismail, A. T. B., & Asnawi, A. R. (2021). Issues in Scientific Approach to Ḥadīth Commentary A Critical Study of Selected Hadiths on Prophetic Medicine. *Al-Burhān Journal of Qur'an and Sunnah Studies,* *5*(Special Issue 1), 1-.

Κάγιας, K. (2020). Social media marketing σε ξενοδοχειακές μονάδες. *Фундаментальные Исследования, 2016*(2), 1–10. https://anaktisis.uowm.gr/10491/

Li, F., Larimo, J., & Leonidou, L. C. (2021). Social media marketing strategy: Definition, conceptualization, taxonomy, validation, and future agenda. *Journal of the Academy of Marketing Science*, *49*(1), 51–70. doi:10.100711747-020-00733-3

Maideen, N. M. P. (2020). Prophetic Medicine-Nigella Sativa (Black Cumin Seeds) – Potential Herb for COVID-19? In Journal of Pharmacopuncture, 23(2), 62–70. Korean Pharmacopuncture Institute. doi:10.3831/KPI.2020.23.010

Mason, A. N., Narcum, J., & Mason, K. (2021). Social media marketing gains importance after Covid-19. *Cogent Business and Management*, *8*(1), 1870797. Advance online publication. doi:10.1080/23311975.2020.1870797

Miles, M. B., & Huberman, A. M. (1994). Qualitative Data Analysis: An Expanded Sourcebook (2nd ed.). Thousand Oaks, California

El Sayed, S., Al-quliti, A.-S., Salah Mahmoud, H., Baghdadi, H., Maria, A. R., Helmy Nabo, M., & Hefny, A. (2014). Therapeutic Benefits of Al-hijamah: in Light of Modern Medicine and Prophetic Medicine. American Journal of Medical and Biological Research, 2(2), 46–71. doi:10.12691/ajmbr-2-2-3

Muhammad, D. G. (2022). Kayan mata: A silent and emerging form of female genital mutilatiin Nigeria. In Rwanda Medical Journal, 79(1). Bioline International. doi:10.4314/rmj.v79i2.2

Musharraf, H. M., & Saiful Islam Arman, M. (2018). Prophetic medicine is the cheapest, safest and the best remedy in the prevention and treatment of hypertension (high blood pressure) – a mini review. *International Journal of Molecular Biology (Edmond, Okla.), 3*(6). doi:10.15406/ijmboa.2018.03.00084

Mustafa, D., Baita, A. J., & Adhama, H. D. (2020). Quantitative Economic Evaluation of Zakah-Poverty Nexus in Kano State, Nigeria. [IJIEF]. *International Journal of Islamic Economics and Finance, 3*(1), 21–50. doi:10.18196/ijief.2120

Nakara, W. A., Gabriel, D., Street, M., & Cedex, T. (2012). Entrepreneurship and social media marketing: Evidence from French small business Fatim-Zohra Benmoussa Annabelle Jaouen. *International Journal of Entrepreneurship and Small Business, 16*(4), 386–405. doi:10.1504/IJESB.2012.047608

Ojo, S. (2019). Navigating ethnic entrepreneurship in religion and culture meld. *Journal of Enterprising Communities, 13*(5), 625–646. doi:10.1108/JEC-11-2018-0089

Okeshola, F. B., & Sadiq, I. T. (2015). Determinants of Home Delivery among Hausa in Kaduna South Local Government Area of Kaduna State, Nigeria. *American International Journal of Contemporary Research, 3*(5), 78–85.

Okunlola, O. A., & Oyeyemi, O. T. (2019). Spatio-temporal analysis of association between incidence of malaria and environmental predictors of malaria transmission in Nigeria. *Scientific Reports, 9*(1), 17500. Advance online publication. doi:10.103841598-019-53814-x PMID:31767899

Pratiwi, A., Aidid, H., Uin, M., & Makassar, A. (n.d.). The Holy Quran perspective of business competition. *JISHIM, 2*(4).

Shah, S. A. A., Sukmana, R., Fianto, B. A., Ahmad, M. A., Usman, I. U., & Mallah, W. A. (2020). Effects of Halal social media and customer engagement on brand satisfaction of Muslim customer: Exploring the moderation of religiosity. *Journal of Islamic Marketing, 11*(6), 1671–1689. doi:10.1108/JIMA-06-2019-0119

Sofaer, S. (2010, December). *Articles Qualitative Methods: What Are They and Why Use Them?* Tocco, J. U. (2011). Every disease has its cure: Faith and HIV therapies in Islamic northern Nigeria. *African Journal of AIDS Research, 9*(4), 385–395. doi:10.2989/16085906.2010.545646

Torri, M. C. (2010). Increasing knowledge and traditional use of medicinal plants by local communities in tamil nadu: Promoting self-reliance at the grassroots level through a community-based entrepreneurship initiative. *Complementary Health Practice Review, 15*(1), 40–51. doi:10.1177/1533210110379938

Van EeuwijkP.AngehrnZ. (2017). *How to Conduct a Focus Group Discussion (FGD). Methodological Manual.* doi:10.5167/uzh-150640

Vinerean, S. (2017). Importance of Strategic Social Media Marketing. *Expert Journal of Marketing, 5*(1), 28–35.

Vinerean, S., Cetina, I., Dumitrescu, L., & Tichindelean, M. (2013). The Effects of Social Media Marketing on Online Consumer Behavior. *International Journal of Business and Management*, *8*(14). doi:10.5539/ijbm.v8n14p66

Wilson, J. A., & Grant, J. (2013). Islamic marketing – a challenger to the classical marketing canon? *Journal of Islamic Marketing*, *4*(1), 7–21. doi:10.1108/17590831311306327

Yahya, S., & Kamalul Ariffin, S. (2020). Determinants of Consumer Purchase Intention of Halal Meat in Kano-Nigeria: a Conceptual Paper. *International Journal of Industrial Management*, *6*(2015), 40–48. doi:10.15282/ijim.6.0.2020.5628

Yazdi, N. S., Shokoh, Z., Amiri, A., Nikpour, A., & Kamali, M. J. (2021). Identifying and examining the status of mental health and entrepreneurial organizational motivation components based on Islamic medicine culture. *International Journal of Hospital Research*, *10*(4), 1–10. https://ijhr.iums.ac.ir/article_133543.html

KEY TERMS AND DEFINITIONS

Islamic Medicinal Products: Products manufactured by Islamic medicine practitioners in different forms and formats aimed at curing physical, spiritual, and other health-related issues.

Islamic Medicine Consumers: Customers that promote Islamic medicine products by relying on them either as a primary or secondary form of medication.

Islamic Medicine Entrepreneurship: The ability to take advantage of the opportunities available and run the business of Islamic medicinal products in order to make a profit.

Islamic Medicine Marketing: The process of advertising Islamic medicinal products to a targeted audience, either online or offline.

Islamic Medicine Practitioners: These are people popularly known as Islamic pharmacists who offer medication to people with health-related issues.

Islamic Medicine: Islamic medicine is an alternative way of medication within the framework of Islam practiced by many Muslims in Northern Nigeria.

Marketing Strategy: The technique utilized in order to promote or sell products and services so that a business can grow and prosper.

Social Media Marketing: The process of advertising, buying, and selling products through virtual means with the help of social media platforms.

Chapter 14
Value-Based Intermediation:
The Islamic Social Capital Perspective in Baitul Maal Wat Tamwil Institutions (BMTIs) in Indonesia

Rahmawati Rahmawati
Syarif Hidayatullah State Islamic University, Jakarta, Indonesia

ABSTRACT

This study investigated the implementation of value intermediation by strengthening the Islamic social capital (ISC) information in Indonesia's Baitul Maal Wat Tamwil institution (BMTI) activities. ISC dimensions are considered an intangible resource that reinforces BMTI and plays a crucial role in its development in Indonesia. ISC consisted of four categories: networking, norms, trust, and spirituality. Thus, this chapter aimed to examine the stakeholder's perception of the importance of ISC as value intermediation in Indonesia's BMT. The study found that the respondents perceived ISC as valuable information for decision-making in BMT activities. Additionally, the mean for the importance of spiritual information is higher than that of networking, norms, and trust. The findings of the ANOVA revealed that the perceptions of spiritual, networking, norms, and trust confirmed the significance in the importance perception of the four categories.

1. INTRODUCTION

The economic crisis, i.e., in 1998 and 2008, impacted corporations and small institutions, including groups such as employees, customers, and communities, where the company is located or conduct operations. The economic crisis calls for social participation to handle the economic downturn (Zizumbo-Colunga et al., 2010). Accordingly, increasing intermediation capital may incentivise community social participation (Meyer, 2004). Social capital is the value of intermediating social and financial mitigation (Kamukama & Natamba, 2013). Value intermediation may reduce the risk of losses from unethical behaviours by other parties (Meyer, 2004).

DOI: 10.4018/978-1-6684-7519-5.ch014

Meanwhile, social capital is the method of building trust, networking, and norms that force operating nations to erode (Bridger & Luloff, 2001). It is a moral element with social relationship value, presenting the ability to generate positive outcomes (Ayios et al., 2014). The concept has strong links with the family business ethics territory such as reciprocity, stakeholder relationships, community engagement, trust development, and social cohesion (Ayios et al., 2014). An established Islamic microfinance institution (IMF) in Indonesia is the *Baitul Maal Wat Tamwil* (BMT). The *Baitul Maal* (*Bait* = House, *al Maal* = Wealth) collects and distributes charity funds (e.g., *Zakat, Infaq, Shadaqah*). Meanwhile, the *Baitul Tamwil* (*Bait* = house, *at Tamwil* = finance) operates based on commercial or economic activities and the deposits are mobilised to productive investments (Holloh, 2001).

BMTI, also known as Islamic cooperative, are based on ownership as they are a cooperative institution owned by members who are shareholders and associated members (Nasution, 2013). Sustainability is recognised as a pillar of the International Co-operative Alliance's (ICA) (Birchall, 2004; Deng & Hendrikse, 2014). The Least Development Countries (LCDs) aims for sustainable development, designed to assist the international community, decreasing poverty and oppression in the planning action for triple P: people, planet, and prosperity (Gicheru, 2016). There are seventeen sustainable development (SDGs) goals in Indonesia that are expected to be achieved by 2030. These goals focus on increasing the level of people (no-poor people) and enhancing the sustainability of communities, quality of education, and partnerships for goals.

In terms of the economic recession and crisis may further erode social and environmental values that impacts society because of behavioral, moral, and cultural, which could be solved by social capital (Correa-Ruiz & Abadia, 2011). (Zizumbo-Colunga et al., 2010) highlighted that financial crises are linked to attitudes and behaviours. Furthermore, the networks of trusting people are critical to a healthy democracy and politics. Therefore, organisations must emphasise the role of the social context to enhance sustainable development activity (Bebbington et al., 2009). Hence, strengthening social capital is critical in achieving sustainable development objectives providing financial and non-financial services to stakeholders.

Social capital is a valued intermediary that confers advantages, reduces costs, monitoring malfeasant behaviour, and enforces sanctions that allow them to operate and cooperate with ventures efficiently (Meyer, 2004). Social capital is essential for landscape management and the provision of environmental services since, in many situations, the area concerned surpasses the parcel or farm, and the players present in the landscape must coordinate to ensure proper management (Meyer, 2004). Few Islamic Microfinance Institutions (IMFIs) focus on creating social capital aspects in their activities (Dieter & Seibel, 2000), and thus most well-established institutions collapse due to the insufficient social capital function (Dowla, 2006). Social capital presents a significant relationship with MFIs (Dieter & Seibel, 2000). In line with Dowla (2006), (Abdullah & Ismail, 2014) asserted that social capital strengthens these institutions.

A study examined the activities to enhance social capital values such as regular meetings, group meetings among members, management and members followed by regular attendance (Dowla, 2006). Thus, staggered and accelerated lending appears, creating the norm of transparency in financial transactions in the meeting. In this process, the group chairperson, a position that regularly rotates to prevent distrust, collect repayment from members and staff. The group chairperson participated in the development process and was in charge of expanding the organization's capacity through the employment, management, and training of technical and community consultants (Gittell & Vidal, 1998).

Islamic principles should be enhanced in Islamic financial institutions to achieve the holistic objective of sharia (Mahadi et al., 2019). (Ascarya, 2017) highlighted that BMTI should integrate social and financial purposes by complying with Islamic principles and values. However, existing studies on social capital in microfinance only centred on increasing trust, network, and social activities(Deng & Hendrikse, 2014; Postelnicu et al., 2014). Most studies neglected the spiritual dimension, unsuitable for the characteristics and nature of BMTIs in Indonesia. Thus, this study proposes a spiritual dimension not tailored to BMTI activities (Aw Dusuki, 2006; A. Hassan, 2015).

Spiritual capital is the value intermediation in BMTIs activities (Jahar, 2018), where spirituality is the actual conduct in BMTI's operations (Rokhman, 2013). Spiritual capital is the internal resources that create value and increase human and supports organizational performance (Ariawan et al., 2016). Spirituality offers employees with well-being and quality of life, purpose and meaning at work, and a sense of interconnectedness and community (Karakas, 2010). However, this non-financial information is difficult to disclose in annual reports (Cormier et al., 2009; Millen & Patterson, 2003). In essence, spirituality is embedded in individuals and influence them in organisations, maintaining and producing the act with honour, strength, commitment, teamwork, determination, passion, moral, and ethics (Ariawan et al., 2016).

Stakeholders expect relevant information that is suitable for their capacity. Frequently, most preparers and investors focus on providing financial information than social information (Lev & Zarowin, 1999). Hence, social information is yet to be thoroughly examined compared to financial information. This finding aligns with (Sarea & Hanefah, 2013) 's study, which asserted the stakeholder theory. This theory is based on explaining the need for financial, non-financial information, and accounting standards and determining the need for users' financial reports.

Social capital potentially creates bonds through organisations and associations, in which members are expected to establish several factors. These factors include internal controls, supervision, and governance that minimises error while monitoring the employees' behaviours who could place the firm's capital at risk (Meyer, 2004). Social capital information is non-financial information (Zeller et al., 2003). The stakeholders use this information for decision-making, allocate resources (Deegan & Blomquist, 2006), and expect preparers to disclose their financial and non-information (Sridhar, 2012). However, most BMTIs' preparers disclose financial information rather than non-financial information (Wahyuni, 2008).

The telecommunication technology might make possible exchanges of capital from the dispersed sites of employees (Steinfield et al., 2009). Therefore, it is essential to enhance the ISC in this country by increasing its transparency level. From the above explanation, it is crucial to explore the stakeholders' perception of the importance of ISC information as value-intermediation to be disclosed in BMTIs annual reports. Hence, in this study, the stakeholder's perceptions on the usefulness of financial and ISC information were explored.

This study is expected to contribute to the theoretical perspective by the ISC information's inclusion into the accountability theory. This idea will be regarded as additional non-financial information towards the social accountability of BMTIs operation. Furthermore, one of the social capital dimensions is to measure the spirituality intelligence of BMTIs activities. Therefore, a new scale measuring the spiritual dimension will be developed, and the existing functional dimension scale, based on the conventional context, will be amended to suit the Islamic business nature.

From the practical point of view, this study's findings will provide valuable inputs for policymakers, regulators, the respective ministries, and users (shareholders). These parties may benefit from the study in different ways. Additionally, this study proposes that each of them disclose sufficient information that will enhance the transparency and accountability of BMTs. Given these points, this study will benefit BMTs to present a better financial reporting framework, which they may use as guidelines when preparing their reports.

2. VALUE INTERMEDIATION (VBI) IN BMTIS

In 2017, the Central bank of Malaysia's value intermediation (VBI) initiative for Islamic financial institutions offered it as a strategy and guideline. VBIs reorient the Islamic finance business, aligning with the Islamic principles, which positively impact the economy, community, and environment through practices and processes (Mahadi et al., 2019). Furthermore, it acts as a guideline for Islamic banking to assess the impact-based risk management system, following Islamic principles and objectives. They are expected to increase the growth of Islamic financial institutions in Malaysia (Mahadi et al., 2019) and play a crucial role in delivering the objectives of sharia principles through various strategies (Hassan & Nor, 2019).

Social capital is a critical value to mediate increasing the growth of BMTs (Dariah, 2012). Principally, Islamic microfinance must increase the social capital value by creating activities, such as trust, norms, and networking activities (Dowla, 2006). (Jahar, 2018) emphasises that the fundamental value of social capital in BMTI is spirituality, in which the spirituality dimension increases the social capital value (Dusuki, 2006; Hassan, 2014). Therefore, a new scale for measuring the spiritual dimension will be developed, and the existing functional dimension scale, which is based on the conventional context, will be amended to suit the Islamic business nature.

Social capital influences the initiation of organisational activities, and therefore it is vital to determine the social capital information in annual reports of entities. Moreover, organisations must publish information concerning their activities to the public (Lee & Tweedie, 1975). It is vital to construct and implement the social capital in the entities' mobilisation in their decision making. Furthermore, it is imperative to disclose social capital information (Cormier, Aerts, Ledoux, & Magnan, 2009) as it is an intangible resource (Dodd, 2016). Accordingly, this information can be used as a based decision maker's perspective.

The use of social capital information for decision-making is a critical prerequisite for driving value for both business and society (Li et al., 2014). Social capital also strengthens weak relationships by facilitating the effective information flow that results in an efficient cooperative organization (Spence & Schmidpeter, 2003). Providing these decision-makers with precise information is essential to integrate relevant social considerations into business thinking and action (Li et al., 2014). Therefore, in organization action should consider the business ethics as a tool of social capital (Spence et al., 2003).

The Islamic financial industry should disclose its financial and non-financial information to increase the intermediation value (Roshayani et al., 2018). Disclosure of non-financial information is used to measure the effectiveness of MFI (Adnan & Ajija, 2015). In essence, financial information alone is not sufficient, though it is challenging to disclose non-financial information. Therefore, additional non-financial information is critical and a complementary element (Adnan and Ajija, 2015).

The relationship between social capital and implementation will be defined not just by the strength of social capital, but also by the degree to which the environment of social capital encourages the implementation of certain programmes, policies, or practises (Smylie & Evans, 2006). It must also acknowledge that the substance of social relations is never neutral; rather, it is value-laden and serves to mould thinking and behaviour in particular ways and for certain purposes (Smylie & Evans, 2006).

2.1 ISC

2.1.1 Creating Networking Information

Networks are defined as linking or relationships among individuals, organisations, and communities (Putnam, 1993). The essence of establishing social structure relationships in the community enables individuals to coordinate actions and achieve desired goals (Woolcock & Narayan, 2000). Social capital has been examined in a broad scope of social activities by establishing excellent relationships inside and outside the family, followed by relations within and beyond the firm. Mutual trust, responsibility, and cooperation exist among members of a social network. Notably, it is an efficient instrument that reduces transaction costs and exposes numerous financial risks, i.e., offering credit to the rural poor (Dusuki, 2008).

A qualitative method establishes small institutions to consider networking with large institutions, reaping the available resources (Machado, 2013). This idea is specific to traditional marketing, fading out in the global competition. Therefore, they should actively engage in communication, strengthen their connection among members and non-members, and improve organisational learning and relationships. Similarly, (Okem, 2015) suggested that the South African government educate cooperative members regarding the importance of social literacy and appreciate the values of networking. He highlighted several networking benefits: production cost reduction via transaction process, sharing of innovation experience, marketing strategies coordination, and developing financial and social services.

2.1.2 Creating Spirituality Information

Social capital is related to spiritual capital (Maselko et al., 2011), which moderate the social capital value(Adhariani, 2017). The findings are consistent with (Coleman, 1988), in which religious affiliation enhances social capital. Karakas (2010) reviews 140 articles and confirmed that organisations need spiritual values to enhance the institutions' performance significantly. Furthermore, he highlighted that spirituality benefits employees, i.e., increased quality of life and well-being. The employees were also delivered a sense of commitment in their work, ultimately increasing the awareness and interconnectedness and community. However, most organisations with the spiritual orientation improve organizational effectiveness (Karakas, 2010).

Studies have reported that managers combine spirituality in their administration (Dehaghi et al., 2012). This idea significantly impacts employee behaviour in organisations, such as creating employee commitment. Additionally, the factor enhances their relationship via mutual support, making them feel more connected to the organisation's objective. Ultimately, the impact may increase their loyalty, resulting in a less materially committed employee.

Scarce studies explain social capital based on faith (Farooqi, 2006). Among the available studies, ISC may be owned jointly by the community since Islamic financial institutions are based on universal brotherhood principles, with no exclusive ownership rights for individuals. Thus, it is essential to develop social capital studies from Islamic principles, specifically in trust, norms, networking, and spirituality. According to (Wediawati et al., 2018). There are three aspects social capital that should be considered in building the sustainability of BMTIs in Indonesia which aspects include financial, social, and spiritual intermediaries.

2.1.3 Creating Norms Information

Norms are the accepted rule or ways of executing matters approved by most individuals. Institutions with norms can be more focused and deviate from unnecessary activities (Coleman, 1988b). Principally, norms enrich the activities of an institution and reduce its weaknesses. Organisations with a well-established norm may achieve their goal through communal support and share the benefits with stakeholders. Notably, practical norms may reduce unsecured environmental and mitigate risks. Hence, practical norms will create awareness that the significant interest is greater than personal interests, namely the interests of groups or organisations.

2.1.4 Creating Norms Information

Trust is a crucial dimension and a primary element in social capital (Bourdieu, 1989; Fukuyama, 1995). It is a necessary form of confidence that requires the passage of time before it can be built (Nahapiet, 2011). Furthermore, this element is the basis for establishing relationships that originate from knowing each other based on the frequency of the interaction. The level of trust depends on the mutual behaviour during the interaction, and thus the more interaction among members, the closer their relationship is to each other (Li, Ye, & Sheu, 2014). However, acquiring trust from others, especially building the poor's trust, has been one of the most significant challenges involving a long and arduous process (Dowla, 2006).

Significantly, trust begins when people possess similar goals and objectives. Through proper disclosure, the members may understand whether the members' common interest is protected. Thus, this process develops their trust in the BMTs' management (Tsai & Ghoshal, 1998). Moreover, an individual trust may be strengthened by religious participation and their transparency level (Nahapiet, 2011). The finding is consistent with Fukuyama, 1995's study that reports trust transferability from family and religious affiliations into work applications.

Since microfinance institutions are not-for-profit, ethical norms and values are essential in their decision-making process (Hudon, 2008). Ethical norms should be applied in every aspect for practical application and meaningful results. Often, the ethical norms and values depend on the member's agreement. In cooperative decision-making, ethical norm is significant (Hudon, 2008), where its emphasis in the philosophy of cooperative is encompassing from, for, and by the members. Hence, the role members in the management process are stated in the ethical norms. Based on the above explanation, this study develops the hypotheses as follows:

Test of hypothesis H1: There is a significant difference in perceptions among stakeholder groups regarding the vital networking activities disclosed in annual reports of BMTIs.

Test of hypothesis H2: There is a significant difference in perceptions among stakeholder groups regarding the important spiritual activities disclosed in annual reports of BMTIs.

Test of hypothesis H3: There is a significant difference in perceptions among stakeholder groups regarding the important norms disclosed in annual reports of BMTIs.

Test of hypothesis H4: There is a significant difference in perceptions among stakeholder groups regarding the vital trust activities disclosed in annual reports of BMTIs.

3. RESEARCH DESIGN

The research design employed in this study is the survey method. The study population includes preparers (General manager and managers), regulators, members, experts, and BMT's Sharia Supervisory Board (SSB). The General manager and manager represent the preparers based on their responsibility to handle the management of BMTIs. Meanwhile, the members are the primary users of BMTIs but lack the knowledge and capacity of members. Additionally, they did not fill out the questionnaire and believed in the management of BMTIs.

The stakeholders' perception of the importance of the information item required to be disclosed was rated using a five-point Likert scale. The scale ranged between not important for scale one and extremely important for scale five. Additionally, the stakeholders were asked to suggest additional information items worth considering for the importance of disclosure. Finally, a sample size of 64 respondents comprised members of BMTIs 4, SSB 3, experts 3, Manager of BMTIs 43, and regulators 11 chosen from the Ministry of cooperative.

The primary data for the study were obtained through a questionnaire divided into two sections. Section one deals with the respondents' biographic information, while part two consists of questions that capture respondents' opinions on the ISC information's importance in BMTIs' annual reports. The respondents were asked to answer the questions on a five-point Likert scale, where (5) strongly agreed and (1) strongly disagreed. The variables' reliability was then tested using Cronbach alpha, and unreliable items were dropped before computing the scores of the constructed variable. Subsequently, descriptive and inferential statistics were employed in analysing the data. The hypotheses formulated from the study were tested using the analysis of variance (ANOVA).

ANOVA is a collection of statistical models and their associated procedures, in which the observed variance is partitioned into components due to different explanatory variables. As a significant type of ANOVA, two-way ANOVA is used to test for differences among two or more independent groups. The null hypothesis states that all population means associated with each group or condition under investigation are similar in a two-way ANOVA. Furthermore, if the null hypothesis is true, the difference (comparison value) between any complex or straightforward comparison of population means must be zero.

4. DISCUSSION

4.1 Demographic Characteristics

Sixty-four (64) usable copies were returned and analyzed from 117 copies of the administered questionnaires. Table 4.1 shows a total response rate of 55 per cent for all the respondent groups. This section presents the respondents' demographic characteristics, including gender, profession, income, and age. Notably, there is an unequal number of respondents from the professions. In terms of genders, 70.3 per cent of respondents were male, and 29.7 per cent were female. For the profession of respondents, 43.8 per cent were managers, 23.4 per cent were general managers, 17.2 per cent were regulators, 6.3 per cent were members of BMTIs, followed by SSB and experts at 1.7 per cent. Most respondents have more than Rp.10 million income followed by 5.1 million - $\leq$ 10 million, 3.1 million - $\leq$ 5 million, 1 million, and - $\leq$ 3 million.

In terms of the number of years in the organisation, 59.4 per cent had more than 40 years, 34.4 per cent had between 29-39 years, 4.7 per cent between 19-28 years and 1.6 per cent possessed less than 18 years. A small number of respondents were not interested in filling out the form because they did not comprehend the ISC meaning. Accordingly, this observation is consistent with previous studies, stating the low level of skills and knowledge exhibited by the members of BMTI (Kassim & Wulandari, 2016; Muttaqin, 2012).

4.2 Descriptive Results

This paper uses a two-way ANOVA approach to analyse whether the different stakeholders exhibit similar opinions on the importance of each dimension. This paper designed a questionnaire to accomplish this idea by including four dimensions based on the Likert scale.

In Table 2, descriptive statistics are shown, indicating the mean value and standard deviation obtained by different stakeholders vis-à-vis the importance to disclose ISC information in the annual reports of BMTIs. The table analysis suggests that the regulators present the most significant mean value of 4.406 on a five-point scale with a standard deviation of 0.165 on the perception of importance to disclose networking activities. Meanwhile, BMT managers exhibit the most substantial mean value, 4.411, with a

Table 1. The demographic details and categories of respondents

		Frequency	Per cent	Valid Per cent	Cumulative Per cent
Gender	Male	45	70.3	70.3	70.3
	Female	19	29.7	29.7	100.0
	Total	64	100.0	100.0	
Profession	SSBs	3	4.7	4.7	4.7
	General Managers	15	23.4	23.4	28.1
	Managers	28	43.8	43.8	71.9
	Regulators	11	17.2	17.2	89.1
	Members of BMTIs	4	6.3	6.3	95.3
	Experts	3	4.7	4.7	100.0
	Total	64	100.0	100.0	
Income	≥ 10 million	26	40.6	40.6	40.6
	1 - 3 million	1	1.6	1.6	42.2
	1 - ≤ 3 million	6	9.4	9.4	51.6
	3.1 - ≤ 5 million	14	21.9	21.9	73.4
	5.1 - ≤ 10 million	17	26.6	26.6	100.0
	Total	64	100.0	100.0	
Experience	≤ 18 years	1	1.6	1.6	1.6
	≥ 40 years	38	59.4	59.4	60.9
	19-28 year	3	4.7	4.7	65.6
	29-39 year	22	34.4	34.4	100.0
	Total	64	100.0	100.0	

Source: Researchers' computation, 2020

Table 2. The descriptive results on the perceptions of stakeholders regarding the importance of ISC

Dimension	Group	Mean	Std. Error
Networking	SSBs	4.0513	0.224
	General Managers	4.0308	0.110
	Managers	3.9698	0.096
	Regulators	**4.406**	0.165
	Members of BMTIs	4.385	0.157
	Experts	3.846	0.666
Spiritual	SSBs	4.333	0.273
	General Managers	4.350	0.129
	Managers	**4.411**	0.071
	Regulators	**2.750**	0.299
	Members of BMTIs	4.406	0.187
	Experts	4.375	0.361
Norms	SSBs	4.482	0.161
	General Managers	4.304	0.111
	Managers	4.357	0.072
	Regulators	4.333	0.118
	Members of BMTIs	4.333	0.120
	Experts	**4.741**	0.133
Trust	SSBs	**4.611**	0.222
	General Managers	4.322	0.099
	Managers	4.185	0,066
	Regulators	4.242	0,122
	Members of BMTIs	4.375	0,239
	Experts	4.167	0,600

standard deviation of 0.071. Experts' perception is the most significant importance of dimension norms activities at 4.741 and a standard deviation of 0.133. Moreover, the perception of SSB on the importance of trust activities presented the highest mean at 4.611 and standard deviation 0.222 on the perception of dimension spiritual activities.

This result indicates that the ISC dimension has a more positive perception concerning the information disclosure in BMTIs' annual reports. The most significant perception on the importance of dimension of norms activities is expert at 4.741. Meanwhile, the lowest perception on the importance of dimension of spirituality activities is regulators at 2.750. The results indicate the stakeholders had a strong preference for information items on the importance of ISC information.

Based on the normality test in Table 3, it was found that Kolmogorov-Smirnov and Shapiro-Wilk's hypotheses 2 and 3 are not normal as certain variables are above the cut-point. Therefore, the distribution is considered non-normal. Hypotheses 2 and 3 are tested using the Kruskal-Wallis test as both hypotheses test the possibility of different perceptions among stakeholders, comprising six groups of respondents.

Table 3. The normality test

Hypothesis Testing	Group	Kolmogorov-Smirnov[a]	Shapiro-Wilk	Distribution	Statistical Test
Hypothesis 1	Networking	0.200	0.189	Normal	Two-way ANOVA
Hypothesis 2	Spirituality	0.200	0.001	Not Normal	Non-Parametric (Kruskal-Wallis Test)
Hypothesis 3	Norms	0.002	0.004	Not Normal	Non-Parametric (Kruskal-Wallis Test)
Hypothesis 4	Trust	0.200	0.109	Normal	Two-way ANOVA

Before conducting the ANOVA, Table 4 shows the assumption of homogeneity of variance that must be met. Thus, the scores in each group should have homogeneous variances. Levene's test is used to determine whether variances are equal or unequal. The results of Levene's test for the four dimensions are given in Table 4, potentially indicating that the homogeneity assumptions were not violated. Levene's test for homogeneity of variances is not significant (P > 0.05). Therefore, this study can ensure that the population variances for each group are approximately equal, and the ANOVA can be carried out.

The ANOVA results in Table 5 show that the p-value for networking and trust dimensions is more significant than 0.05, suggesting that the null hypothesis is rejected. Furthermore, the alternative hypothesis state that different stakeholders have the same opinion regarding the importance of networking and trust dimensions disclosed in the annual reporting of BMTI.

Table 6 show the results of ANOVA testing and Kruskal-Wallis. The result shows that norms and trust hold the same opinion regarding its importance in networking. At the same time, the spirituality dimension holds different opinions regarding its importance, which were marked with underlines.

5. DISCUSSION

The results show that the stakeholders' perceptions are essential to disclose information about Islamic social capital information in the annual reports of BMTIs. Four aspects of Islamic social capital information, creating trust, network, norms, and spiritualties activities, strengthen and enhance the value-added

Table 4. Test of homogeneity of variances

Dimensions	Levene Statistic	df1	df2	Sig
Networking	1.458	5	58	0.217
Spirituality	3.698	5	58	0.06
Norms	1.282	5	58	0.284
Trust	2.673	5	58	0.357

Table 5. ANOVA

Dimensions	df	Mean Square	F	Sig.	Testing Result
Networking	5	0.416	1.532	0.194	Rejected, P>0.05
Trust	5	0.134	0.764	0.579	Rejected, P>0.05

Table 6. The Kruskal-Wallis test results

Group		N	Mean Rank
Spiritual	SSBs	3	35.17
	General Managers	15	36.13
	Managers	28	37.34
	Regulators	11	11.68
	Members of BMTIs	4	37.13
	Experts	3	36.67
Norms	SSBs	3	40.33
	General Managers	15	29.83
	Managers	28	31.79
	Regulators	11	31.14
	Members of BMTIs	4	31.75
	Experts	3	50.67
Spirituality	Kruskal-Wallis	16.867	
	df	5	
	Asymp. Sig.	0.005	
	Testing results	Accepted	
Norms	Kruskal-Wallis	3.854	
	df	5	
	Asymp. Sig.	0.571	
	Testing results	Rejected	

service of the BMTIs. Stakeholders could use the Islamic social information to making synergies through linkages that support BMTIs from outside and inside of BMTIs used empowerment approach through in-depth professional knowledge, organizational learning, protection, and reduce risk; information security can contribute to BMTIs activities.

The result obtained from the survey indicates that social accountability for Islamic social capital items is required, but it has not yet emerged. Overall, social accountability in BMTIs was recognized as an essential component and the responsibility that BMTIs (defined and implied) should discharge to the community. Therefore, this study suggests that law enforcement discloses Islamic social capital information mandatory information to be disclosed in the annual report of BMTIs. Through this, obstacles facing the BMTIs may be resolved as the stakeholders will be confident of increasing their support for the BMTIs and motivating potential investors to contribute without fear of insecurity. This result shows that BMTIs need to reflect a benefit-oriented environment to meet their stakeholders' expectations. The extent of social accountability disclosure catches the stakeholders' interest as it is considered significant and value-added to their community.

Due to the absence, as mentioned above, detailed reporting requirements of social information in the BMTIs guidelines found that BMTIs need to provide Islamic social capital information in their annual reports. The findings from this study also support that Islamic social capital information must be well disclosed, which implies that the theory supports this finding. However, excluding such important information in the annual report of BMTIs indicates that BMTIs are not disclosing sufficient information. The fact that BMTIs is not a new industry that is expected to provide the necessary information by the stakeholders and the communities for more transparency in their operation. In this respect, the BMTIs should consistently focus on the disclosure of Islamic social capital information. The social concern of the BMTIs should be their priority, and their focus on their stakeholders, both internally and externally, is highly essential.

6. CONCLUSION

There is a positive response to the importance of ISC dimensions such as networking, norms, and trust in the annual reports of BMTI. The ANOVA method showed that different stakeholders exhibit similar opinions regarding these dimensions in the reports. Meanwhile, from the Kruskal-Wallis test, there is a different response on the importance of spirituality activities, which should be critically focused on while making relevant policies to strengthen the BMTI's capacity from applied skills and spiritual knowledge. Based on the statistical analysis, the perception of regulators presented the least significant score. Most regulators do not know the importance of spirituality in BMTI activities, and thus a more profound exploration is needed on spiritual matters.

This research has various expected determinations on the ISC term. Accordingly, future work could be pursued in the following dimensions. Firstly, comparative stakeholder analysis could be conducted using different methods such as structural equation modelling (SEM) and ANOVA. This method can be delivered for different grouping samples of varying income, social statuses, education levels, and age. Finally, the policy-making study must be delivered according to the results obtained from this research.

The authors acknowledge with thanks the helpful comments of conference participants at the 12th International Conference on Islamic Economics and Finance held at IZU from 14-20 June 2020.

REFERENCES

Abdullah, R., & Ismail, A. G. (2014). Al-Tawhid in Relation to the Economic Order of Microfinance Institutions. *Humanomics, 30*(4), 325–348. doi:10.1108/H-01-2014-0006

Adhariani, D. (2017). *Social Capital, Broken Trust, and Social Accountability: Exploring the Role of Religion in Microfinance Context.*

Adnan, M. A., & Ajija, S. R. (2015). The Effectiveness of Baitul Maal Wat Tamwil in Reducing Poverty: The Case of Indonesian Islamic Microfinance Institution. *Humanomics, 31*(2), 160–182. doi:10.1108/H-03-2012-0003

Ariawan, Sudarma, Djumahir, & Ghozali. (2016). The Role of Spiritual Capital, Human Capital, Structural Capital, and Relational Capital of SMES To Improving on Performance: Study Literature. *South East Journal of Contemporary Business. Economics and Law, 11*(2), 87–94.

Ascarya. (2017). *Baitul Maal Wat Tamwil (BMT): An Integrated Islamic Social and Comercial Financial Institutions in Indonesia.*

Ayios, A., Jeurissen, R., Manning, P., & Spence, L. J. (2014). Social capital: A review from an ethics perspective. *Business Ethics (Oxford, England)*, *23*(1), 108–124. doi:10.1111/beer.12040

Bebbington, J., Higgins, C., & Frame, B. (2009). Initiating sustainable development reporting: Evidence from New Zealand. *Accounting, Auditing & Accountability Journal*, *22*(4), 588–625. doi:10.1108/09513570910955452

Birchall, J. (2004). *Cooperatives and the Millennium Development Goals*.

Bourdieu, P. (1989). Social space and symbolic power. *Sociological Theory*, *7*(1), 14–25. doi:10.2307/202060

Bridger, S., & Luloff, A. (2001). Building the Sustainable Community: Is Social Capital the Answer? *Sociological Inquiry*, *71*(4), 458–472. doi:10.1111/j.1475-682X.2001.tb01127.x

Coleman, J. S. (1988). Social Capital in the Creation of Human Capital. *American Journal of Sociology*, *94*, 95–120. doi:10.1086/228943

Cormier, D., Aerts, W., Ledoux, M. J., & Magnan, M. (2009). Attributes of Social and Human Capital Disclosure and Information Asymmetry. *Canadian Journal of Administrative Sciences-Revue Canadienne Des Sciences De L Administration*, *88*(1), 71–88.

Correa-Ruiz, C., & Abadia, J. M. (2011). Special issue on"social responsibility accounting and reporting in times of 'sustainability Downturn/crisis. *Revista de Contabilidad*, *14*(1), 1–25. doi:10.1016/S1138-4891(11)70032-2

Dariah, A. R. (2012). Improving Social Capital of BMT (Baitul Mal Wat Tamwil): An Experience From BMT Lathifah, Sumedang Indonesia. *The International Journal of Social Sciences (Islamabad)*, *4*(1), 64–70.

Deegan, C., & Blomquist, C. (2006). Stakeholder influence on corporate reporting: An exploration of the interaction between WWF-Australia and the Australian minerals industry. *Accounting, Organizations and Society*, *31*(4–5), 343–372. doi:10.1016/j.aos.2005.04.001

Dehaghi, M., Goodarzi, M., & Arazi, Z. (2012). The effect of spiritual values on employees' organizational commitment and its models. *Procedia: Social and Behavioral Sciences*, *62*, 159–166. doi:10.1016/j.sbspro.2012.09.025

Deng, W., & Hendrikse, G. (2014). *Cooperative Social Capital Towards a Lifecycle Perspective*. 1–6.

Dieter, H., & Seibel, H. D. (2000). How values create value: social capital in microfinance-the case of the Philippines. In *Working Paper in Economics and Development Studies*.

Dodd, M. (2016). Intangible resource management: Social capital theory development for public relations. *Journal of Communication Management (London)*, *20*(4), 1–41. doi:10.1108/JCOM-12-2015-0095

Dowla, A. (2006). In credit we trust: Building social capital by Grameen Bank in Bangladesh. *Journal of Socio-Economics*, *35*(1), 102–122. doi:10.1016/j.socec.2005.12.006

Dusuki, Aw. (2006). *Empowering Islamic Microfinance: Lesson from Group-Based Lending Scheme and Ibn Khaldun's Concept of 'Asabiyah*. Monash University.

Dusuki, A.W. (2008). Banking for the poor: the role of Islamic banking in microfinance initiatives. *Humanomics, 24*(24), 49–66.

Farooqi, A. H. (2006). Islamic social capital and networking. *Humanomics, 22*(4), 113–125. doi:10.1108/08288660610669400

Fukuyama, F. (1995). Social capital and the global economy. *Foreign Affairs, 74*(5), 89–103. doi:10.2307/20047302

Gicheru, E. (2016). *The role of the cooperative enterprise model in implementating the Sustainable Development Goals (SDGs) in Least Developed Countries (LDCs).*

Gittell, R., & Vidal, A. (1998). *Community organizing: Building social capital as a development strategy.* Sage publications. doi:10.4135/9781452220567

Hassan, A. (2015). Financial inclusion of the poor: From microcredit to Islamic microfinancial services. *Humanomics, 3112*(11), 354–371. doi:10.1108/H-07-2014-0051

Hassan, R., & Nor, F. M. (2019). Value-based Intermediation: The Shari'ah Perspective. [IJFUS]. *International Journal of Fiqh and Usul Al-Fiqh Studies, 3*(1), 81–89.

Holloh, D. (2001). *Microfinance Institutions Study.* FinDev.

Hudon, M. (2008). Norms and values of the various microfinance institutions. *International Journal of Social Economics, 35*(1/2), 35–48. doi:10.1108/03068290810843828

Jahar, A. (2018). *Managing social capital in developing Islamic Microfinance enterprises BMT in Muslim countries: case study in Indonesia and Pakistan.* Research Gate.

Kamukama, N., & Natamba, B. (2013). Social intermediation and financial services access in Uganda's microfinance industry. *African Journal of Economic and Management Studies, 4*(3), 358–371. doi:10.1108/AJEMS-10-2011-0077

Karakas, F. (2010). Spirituality and Performance in Organizations: A Literature Review. *Journal of Business Ethics, 94*(1), 94–106. doi:10.100710551-009-0251-5

Lee, T. A., & Tweedie, D. P. (1975). Accounting information: An investigation of private shareholder usage. *Accounting and Business Research, 5*(20), 280–291. doi:10.1080/00014788.1975.9728653

Lev, B., & Zarowin, P. (1999). The Boundaries of Financial Reporting and How to Extend Them. *Journal of Accounting Research, 37*(2), 353–385. doi:10.2307/2491413

Li, Y., Ye, F., & Sheu, C. (2014). Social capital, information sharing and performance: Evidence from China. *International Journal of Operations & Production Management, 34*(11), 1440–1462. doi:10.1108/IJOPM-03-2013-0132

Machado, C. (2013). *The Importance of Social Capital for Small Business Owners: An Entrepreneurial Marketing Approach for Decision Making.* 1–15.

Mahadi, N. F., Zain, N. R. M., & Ali, E. R. A. E. (2019). *Leading Towards Impactful Islamic Social Finance: Malaysian Experience with The Value-Based Intermediation Approach. Al-Shajarah: Journal of the International Institute of Islamic Thought and Civilization.*

Maselko, J., Hughes, C., & Cheney, R. (2011). Religious social capital : Its measurement an dutility in the study of social determinants of health. *Social Science & Medicine*, *73*(5), 759–769. doi:10.1016/j.socscimed.2011.06.019 PMID:21802182

Meyer, D. (2004). *Hong Kong as a Global Metropolis*. Cambridge University Press.

Millen, D. R., & Patterson, J. F. (2003). Identity Disclosure and the Creation of Social Capital. *Proceedings of the SIGCHI Conference on Human Factors in Computing Systems*, (pp. 720–721). ACM. 10.1145/765891.765950

Nahapiet, J. (2011). *Social Capital, Intellectual Capital, and the Organizational Advantage, 23*(2), 242–266.

Nasution, A. C. (2013). A framework to analyse the efficiency of Baitul Maal wa Tamwil (BMT) As Islamic Microfinance Institutions in Indonesia. *Proceeding of Sharia Economic Conference, February*, 81–86.

Okem, A. (2015). Exploring the Opportunities and Challenges of Network Formation for Cooperatives in South Africa. *KJBM*, *5*(1), 16–33.

Postelnicu, L., Hermes, N., & Szafarz, A. (2014). Defining social collateral in microfinance group lending. *Microfinance Institutions*, 187–207.

Putnam, R. (1993). The prosperous community; Social capital and public life. *The American Prospect*, *13*, 35–42.

Rokhman, W. (2013). Baitul mal wat tamwil (bmt) and poverty empowerment. *Qudus International Journal of Islamic Studies*, *1*(2), 181–196.

Roshayani, A., Ruhaini, M., Ramesh, N., & Idora, B. (2018). Value-based intermediation for islamic banking institutions directed towards sustainable development goals. *He International Revue of Entrepreneurial Finance, 1*(1).

Sarea, A. M., & Hanefah, M. M. (2013). The Need of Accounting Standards for Islamic Financial Institutions: Evidence from AAOIFI. *Journal of Islamic Accounting and Business Research*, *4*(1), 64–76. doi:10.1108/17590811311314294

Smylie, M. A., & Evans, A. E. (2006). Social Capital and Problem of Implementation. In M. Honig (Ed.), *Social capital and the problem of implementation. New directions in education policy implementation: Confronting complexity* (pp. 187–208). State University of New York Press.

Spence, L. J., & Schmidpeter, R. (2003). SMEs, social capital and the common good. *Journal of Business Ethics*, *45*(1), 93–108. doi:10.1023/A:1024176613469

Spence, L. J., Schmidpeter, R., & Habisch, A. (2003). Assessing social capital: Small and medium sized enterprises in Germany and the UK. *Journal of Business Ethics*, *47*(1), 17–29. doi:10.1023/A:1026284727037

Sridhar, K. (2012). Is the Triple Bottom Line a restrictive framework for non-financial reporting? In Asian Journal of Business Ethics, 1(2). doi:10.100713520-011-0010-4

Steinfield, C., DiMicco, J. M., Ellison, N. B., & Lampe, C. (2009). Bowling online: social networking and social capital within the organization. *In Proceedings of the Fourth International Conference on Communities and Technologies*, (pp. 245–254). ACM. 10.1145/1556460.1556496

Tsai, W., & Ghoshal, S. (1998). Social capital and value creation: The role of intrafirm networks. *Academy of Management Journal*, *41*(4), 464–476. doi:10.2307/257085

Wahyuni, E. T. (2008). The Accountability of Islamic Microfinance Institution: Evidence From Indonesia. *The Winners*, *9*(1), 22–34. doi:10.21512/tw.v9i1.728

Wediawati, B., Effendi, N., Herwany, D., & Mashita, D. (2018). Sustainability of Islamic Microfinance in Indonesia: A Holistic Approach. *Academy of Strategic Management Journal*, *17*(3), 1–15.

Woolcock, M., & Narayan, D. (2000). Social Capital: Implications for Development Theory, Research, and Policy What Is Social Capital? *The World Bank Research Observer*, *15*(2), 225–249. doi:10.1093/wbro/15.2.225

Zeller, M., Greeley, M., & Lapenu, C. (2003). *Measuring social performance of microfinance institutions.* CGAP Printer, Washington DC, USA. www.cerise-microfinance.org

Zizumbo-Colunga, D., Zechmeister, E., & Mitchell, S. (2010). Social capital and economic crisis in the United States. *Americas Barometer Insights*, *43*, 1–9.

APPENDIX

Table 7.

No	Dimension	Items	Description	sig	Cronbach Alpha (N)
1	**Networking**	NW6	Information about cooperation /link with *Waqf* Institutions.	0.000	0.929/13
2		NW 3	Information about cooperation – link activities with Islamic communities such as *Muhammadiyah Nathadatul* Ulama.		
3		NW 1	Information about cooperation with formal, informal education institutions.		
4		NW 5	Information about cooperation/link with *Zakat* Institutions.		
5		NW 8	Information about cooperation-link with the cooperative department.		
6		NW 9	Information about cooperation/link with the health department.		
7		NW 4	Information about cooperation/link with Islamic Banking.		
8		NW 7	Information about cooperation with Not profit organisations.		
9		NW 2	Information about cooperation with other Islamic cooperatives, microfinance, or BMTs.		
10		N 11	For the very poor borrower Using Islamic instruments in the increasing *Qordhu Hasan* financing and ZIS (*Zakat, Infaq* and *Sodaqah*) against the default		
11		N 10	Information about pension fund		
12		N 20	Information BMTs have created the norm of group lending		
13		N 19	Information about creating norms of transparency in financial transactions by providing audited annual reports.		
14	**Spirituality**	SPI 3	Organizing *Jamaah* Prayer.	0.000	0.959/8
15		SPI 2	Charity activities between management and members in their society.		
16		SPI 4	Reciting Holy Al-Quran (*Tahsin* and Memories Al Quran).		
17		SPI 1	Organizing morning prayers (*Dhuha* prayer).		
18		SPI 7	Obligation wearing hijab for women staff.		
19		NW 11	Information about activities involves the communities surrounding the BMTs (neighbour/area of BMT).		
20		SPI 5	Socialises and Organising among members in Mosque.		
21		NW 10	Information about the productive partnership with the market, such as manufacturing and services companies.		
22	**Norms**	N 9	Information about financing program	0.000	0.865/9
23		N 8	Information in creating the norm of credit discipline by Pick-Up service program to insistence on timely repayment		
24		T14	Information the percentage of distribution Sisa Hasil Usaha (sharing for cooperative institutions).		
25		T 15	Information of BMTs in monitoring and supervision group lending.		
26		T 13	Information about Sisa Hasil Usaha of BMTs (sharing for cooperative institutions).		
27		T 4	Information about a regular meeting- group meeting among members, management and members, regular attendance (doing *Sillaturrahim*).		

continued on following page

Table 7. Continued

No	Dimension	Items	Description	sig	Cronbach Alpha (N)
28		T 7	Information about regular meetings and attendance of management and *Shariah* Supervisory Board.		
29		N 18	Information about the monitoring program.		
30		N 12	Information about representative of *Shariah* board supervision responsibilities.		
31	Trust	T 11	Information about Salary structure (and benefit) in line with comparable sectors.	0.000	0.827/6
32		T 3	Information about the training program for the Board of directors and supervision (leaders)		
33		T 1	Information about the training program for staff		
34		T 9	Information about choosing board members from outside of their establishments.		
35		T 12	Information about Fairness and transparency of incentive systems as perceived by staff.		
36		T 2	Information about the training program for members		

Chapter 15
Using the Unified Theory of Acceptance and Use of Technology to Explore the Factors Influencing Muslim Consumers in Purchasing Halal Products

Nilam Sari
Universitas Islam Negeri Ar-Raniry, Banda Aceh, Indonesia

Ima Dwitawati
Universitas Islam Negeri Ar-Raniry, Banda Aceh, Indonesia

Khairunnisak Khairunnisak
Universitas Islam Negeri Ar-Raniry, Banda Aceh, Indonesia

ABSTRACT

The purpose of this study is to explore the factors that influence Muslim Consumers in purchasing halal products through the digital marketplace, using the unified theory of acceptance and use of technology (UTAUT). The approach of this study was based on the UTAUT's constructs such as performance expectancy, effort expectancy, social influence, and facilitating conditions toward behavioral intention and use behavior. There were 296 data collected through an online questionnaire from Muslim consumers in Indonesia by using the purposive sampling method. The structural equation modeling (SEM) Amos application was used to analyze the data of this study. The results of this study indicated that performance expectancy and social influence significantly affected the behavioral intention of Muslim consumers in purchasing halal products through the digital marketplace. On the other hand, effort expectancy had no significant effect on behavioral intention.

DOI: 10.4018/978-1-6684-7519-5.ch015

INTRODUCTION

Indonesia is a country with the largest Muslim population in the world. There are 229 million Muslims in Indonesia or around 87.2% out of its total population. This number of the population become an important global economic opportunity that attracts the attention of many parties. Besides that, Indonesia is the largest online trade market in Southeast Asia. In 2025, Indonesia's Gross Domestic Product (GDP) is predicted to reach US$ 150 billion or around Rp 2,000 trillion from the digital economy sector only. Based on the Indonesian digital data, 93% of internet users in Indonesia search then purchase products (goods or services) online and 90% of internet users visit online retail stores on the website through various devices While, 86% of them purchase the product online, and 76% of internet users make online transactions through the mobile devices. The market value of goods purchased by e-commerce consumers' based on the total annual sales revenue is US$ 9,536 billion and has increased 23% year by year.

The pattern of e-commerce in Indonesia shows that there are 49 active marketplaces at moment. The five marketplaces with the most visitors are *Tokopedia, Bukalapak, Shopee, Lazada*, and *Bibli*. Each marketplace makes various efforts to attract consumers such as the efforts to improve their performance, offer diverse and innovative products and provide services that make consumers happy. However, it is found that something is still missing here, namely the lack of offers, product innovations and services that offered specifically for Muslim consumers.

Whereas, Islamic culture is one of the largest and the most unique cultures in the world (Hassan et al., 2013). Although the demand for the Muslim lifestyle (*halal* lifestyle) is increasing, it has not been identified what is needed by Muslim consumers in their economic activities. In reality, Muslims need products and services that are in line with their lifestyle and the principles of Islamic rules. Thus the term of Muslim lifestyle now becomes significant and is distinguished from a non-Muslim lifestyle. So, this trend should be interpreted properly by economic actors to create new opportunities for the growth of the Islamic economic itself.

Nowadays, it cannot be denied that the phenomenon of an online transaction has widely spread in the community and has become an alternative on daily bases such as buying food, clothes, tickets and cosmetics. Besides being easy and do not require a lot of time, buying and selling online is also cheaper and more efficient. One of the media for online transaction is the digital marketplace. So, what are the factors that influence consumers in buying products both goods and services through the digital marketplace? One of the factors that influence Muslim consumers' online shopping intentions is website design.

Another factor that could be identified is the effort of the digital marketplaces to provide features that can make/offer the differentiation of products or services needed and intended for Muslim consumers. So the technology created or offered should be suitable with the needs and necessities that must be fulfilled by Muslim consumers in their economic activities. To create these features, an analysis of Muslim consumer interest in utilizing a digital marketplace is required through four factors, namely: 1) Performance expectancy, 2) Effort expectancy, 3) Social influence, and 4) Facilitating Conditions of the digital technological facilities owned by the marketplace itself.

As explained in the model of Unified Theory of Acceptance and Use of Technology (UTAUT) that the acceptance of information technology will be influenced by performance expectations, effort expectancy, social influence, facilitating conditions. Thus this study aims to explore "the

Factors Affecting Muslim Consumers in Purchasing Products through Digital Marketplace Facilities" using UTAUT.

THEORETICAL REVIEW

Consumers, according to Article 1 Number 8 of Constitution 1999 about Consumer Protection, are all users of goods and /or services that available in the community to be used for their interests, family, others, and other living things and not for trading (Nugrahaningsih and Erlinawati, 2017).

Muslim consumers are Muslim who carry out consumption activities based on the principles of Islamic law. In Islam, not all goods and services can be consumed, because a Muslim consumer is only allowed to consume *halal* goods and services (Ashraf, 2019). Thus Muslim must pay attention to the consumption principles that accord to Islamic rules (Suki and Abang Sulaiman Abang Salleh, 2018).

On the other hand, a marketplace is an e-commerce technology that is an online intermediary media that designed to build relationships between sellers and buyers, promote the products, facilitate trading activities of various products from different sellers. (Sfenrianto et al., 2018). The marketplace is an online trading site that offers a complete sales service. It means that the promotion activities till the bargaining transactions are all served with a credible system.

Indonesia is the largest online trading market in Southeast Asia. In 2025, Indonesia's Gross Domestic Product (GDP) is predicted to grow up to US$ 150 billion or around Rp 2,000 trillion from the digital economy sector (Usman, 2017). The digital marketplace business in Indonesia has experienced rapid development since the last decade as the expansion of internet services reach every corner of the country (Laras, 2018). One factor that supports Indonesia's e-commerce industry is the increase in internet penetration (McKinsey, 2018).

Based on the e-commerce pattern in 2019, there are 49 active marketplaces at the moment in Indonesia. The five marketplaces with the highest visitors are Tokopedia, Bukalapak, Shopee, Lazada, and Bibli (Tan, 2019) . Each marketplace makes efforts to attract consumers with various and innovative offers and better service. But, there is still something missing in the Indonesian online trading market, which is a special offer for Muslim consumers. Among the 49 marketplaces, it was found that there are no facilities that have a specific differentiation for Muslim needs. Thus, experts suggested developing the appropriate strategy for managing a business, because understanding the behavior of actual and potential customers is very important, especially in Indonesian as a Muslim-majority country (Suhartanto, 2019).

One effort that could be done to find out the factors that influence Muslim consumers in buying products through digital marketplace facilities is through the identification of digital technology features that can make/offer differentiation of products or services intended for Muslim consumers. So, the technology created or offered must be truly accorded with the needs and necessities that should be known by Muslim consumers in purchasing *halal* products through digital marketplaces.

Unified Theory of Acceptance and Use of Technology (UTAUT)

Unified Theory of Acceptance and Use of Technology (UTAUT) is a model of technology acceptance and use invented by Venkatesh (Venkatesh et al., 2003). UTAUT is a model developed by Venkatesh to

Table 1. Ten marketplaces based on the most visitors in 2019

No.	*Marketplace*	Monthly Web Visitors	Ranking	
			Appstore	Playstore
1.	Tokopedia	141,414,500	2	2
2.	Shoope	90,705,300	1	1
3.	Buka Lapak	89,765,800	4	4
4.	Lazada	49,620,200	3	3
5.	Blibli	38,453,000	6	6
6.	Orami	9,813,100	27	26
7.	Bhinneka	7,678,900	23	21
8.	JD ID	7,102,300	8	7
9.	Blanja	5,511,600	19	12
10.	Zalora	5,218,300	5	8

Source: (Indonesia, 2019)

explore the factors that influence the interest of the technology use or information system. Venkatesh combined the best characteristics of eight famous technology acceptance theories, then developed them into one new theory called UTAUT,

UTAUT has been proved to be more successful than the eight previous theories in explaining up to 70% of the intention variance in exploring the factors that affect the acceptance and utilization of a system or technology (Venkatesh et al., 2003) UTAUT model can be seen in Figure 1.

Figure 1. UTAUT model
Source: Venkatesh (2003)

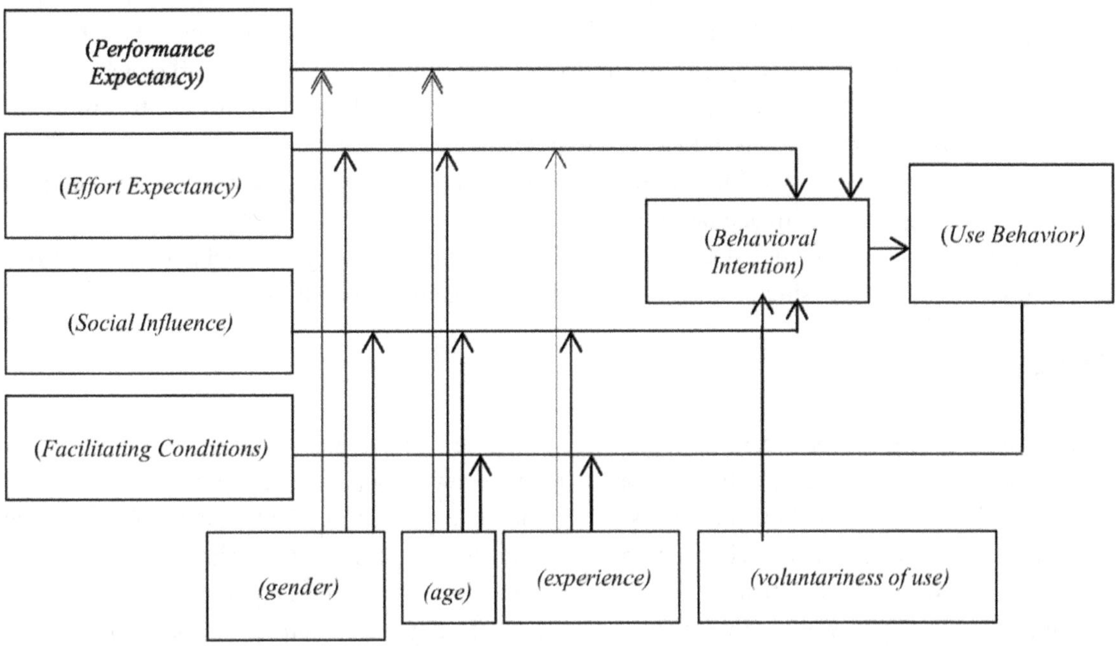

Performance Expectancy

Performance Expectancy is the individual's belief in the use of the system that will help his performance become better or someone's expectation on the use of a system that can assist his work (Lawan and Dahalin, 2011). It means that the extent to which the use of technology will avail consumers in carrying out certain activities.

Performance expectation affects the intention of how to behave in using a system or technology (Venkatesh et al., 2012). In the previous studies, performance expectancy had a significant effect on behavioral intentions in purchasing goods or services through the marketplace or on use behavior in the marketplace (Yu and Lee, 2019)

It was argued that the better technology in satisfying consumer performance expectations, the greater the interest in using technology. From a business standpoint, consumers' understanding of the marketplace system is also used to improve consumer satisfaction in transactions. It is because the main purpose of the benefits of a system will affect consumers' perceptions of buying interest. Besides, the suitability and utilization of technology performance are factors that also have a significant and positive relationship to the improvement of individual performance (Angelova and Zekiri, 2011).

In Islam, performance is a form of self-actualization or a way for individuals to actualize themselves. Performance is the evidence of values, beliefs, and understandings that are held, based on strong moral principles and can become a motivation to produce quality work (Ud Din et al., 2019). Performance appraisal must be done as a servant or as a worker. Because Allah tells Muslim to do that. As Allah says in the Qur'an Surat At taubah verse 105 which means *"And Say: Do [as you will], for Allah will see your deeds, and [so, will] His Messenger and the believers. And you will be returned to the Knower of the unseen and the witnessed, and He will inform you of what you used to do."* (QS. At-taubah [9]: 105).

The expectation of Muslim consumers in using the digital marketplace will provide benefits for consumers in finding and buying products according to their needs. Muslims search and buy *halal*-certified products that according to Islamic practices and beliefs. Every Muslim must consume *halal* products. For example, a product must be identified as *halal* or haram and the transaction does not contain *riba, maysir*, and *gharar*, there is no fraud, does not violate both consumers (buyers) and marketplace (sellers). Thus, the marketplace's ability to track online product compliance with *halal* requirements is useful and important for Muslim consumers in Indonesia (Ayuniyyah et al., 2017).

H_1 : Performance expectancy influence the behavioral intention of Muslim consumers in purchasing products through digital marketplace facilities.

$H0a_1$: Performance expectancy does not affect the use behavior through the behavioral intention of Muslim consumers in purchasing products using digital marketplace facilities.

Effort Expectancy

Effort Expectancy is the level of ease of usage that a person feels about using a technology system or the level of thought and effort required by someone in using technology (Venkatesh et al., 2003). It means that the use of a system can reduce the efforts in term of someone's energy and time in doing activities. Effort Expectancy affects the behavioral intention of consumers to utilize the digital system.

Venkatesh (2003) suggested that the ease of use will give an insight into a person that the system is useful and user friendly to work with. Consumers will use the digital marketplace for shopping because its shopping system is simple and easy to operate, so the term called the ease of use will emerge from what is perceived to be beneficial by the consumers.

Effort Expectancy is the second factor that influences behavioral intention in using technology. Consumers consider the time and effort to perceive the overall effort in receiving and using technology. It means that, before deciding to buy or to shop using the marketplace, consumers will take the time to evaluate what efforts are needed to receive and use the marketplace's technology. Based on that evaluation, their likelihood of adopting technology is increasing or decreasing. This means that two factors play a role in this regard. Those are, how much they require the effort and the benefits they get from using such technology. The effort expectancy referred to in this research is how much the level of effort is given by Muslim consumers and whether they consider it could facilitate them in buying or shopping the products according to their needs (*halal* goods and services) through the *digital marketplace.*

From some of the explanations above, it can be concluded that a marketplace that is easy to understand and easy to operate will generate consumer's interest in using the technology and the marketplace. Conversely, the marketplace technology that is relatively difficult to understand and operate will harm the interest in using the marketplace itself..

H_2 : Efforts expectancy affects the behavioral intention of Muslim consumers in purchasing products through digital marketplace facilities.

Ha_2 : Performance expectancy) affects the use behavior through behavioral intention of Muslim consumers in purchasing products using digital marketplace facilities.

Social Influence

Social influence is the extent to which an individual considers others opinions are important thus he believes that he must use a system. Social influence is an effort made by an individual to change the beliefs, perceptions and behavior of potential users of technology. Social influence affects someone's intention of using the digital marketplace.

The greater the influence caused by the surrounding environment on potential marketplace users to shop, the higher the interest that arises from an individual to use the technology because of the influence of their surrounding environment. The social influence in this study is the social environment that influences consumers to buy through the marketplace that comes from those the closest people to the consumers, such as family and friends.

H_3 : Social influence affects the intention (behavioral intention) of Muslim consumers in purchasing products through *digital marketplace* facilities.

Ha_3 : Social influence affects the consumers' use behavior through the behavioral intention of Muslim consumers in purchasing products through *digital marketplace* facilities.

Facilitating Conditions

Facilitating conditions refer to consumers' perceptions about the resources and supports available to use in a system, or the level of supports that individuals feel are available in the facilities of a system and equipment so it will relevant to use (Venkatesh et al., 2012). Facilitating conditions are defined as the extent to which an individual believes that the existing organizational and technical infrastructure can support the use of the system. According to Venkatesh (2003), the condition of the facility directly influenced the use behavior. In previous study, the condition of the facility had a significant positive effect on the behavior of using a system (Putra and Ariyanti, 2013).

In this research facilitating conditions is described as something that can facilitate the use of digital marketplaces so that it can support someone in purchasing goods on the site, such as internet connections, devices or gadgets that provide information and skills needed by consumers to buy products in the marketplace.

H_4 : *Facilitating Conditions* affect the Use behavior of Muslim consumers in purchasing a product through a digital marketplace facility.

Behavioral Intention and Use Behavior

Behavioral intention is a consideration of how strong the customer's interest to behave (Venkatesh et al., 2012). The intention is the best predictor, where the intention is a cognitive representation of one's readiness to perform a certain behavior. In this study behavioral intention is used to describe how much interest Muslim consumers to use the marketplace in purchasing goods or services. While use behavior is used to explain the intensity or frequency of consumers in using the marketplace to shop or buy goods or services online. Venkatesh (2012) illustrated that the behavioral intention influenced the use behavior. The behavioral intention is positively and significantly related to the use behavior (Chao, 2019).

The intention is a very important consideration for Muslim consumers in carrying out every activity. As mentioned in a *hadith* narrated by Imam Bukhari *rahimahullah* in the *Sahih* book, the Prophet *sallallaahu 'alayhi wa sallam* said as follows (Al-Bukhari, 2003vol 1, Book 1, Hadith 1): Narrated 'Umar bin Al-Khattab: I heard Allah's Messenger shallahu 'alaihi wa sallam saying, "The reward of deeds depends upon the intentions and every person will get the reward according to what he has intended. So whoever emigrated for worldly benefits or for a woman to marry, his emigration was for what he emigrated for." [HR. Bukhari].

H_5 : Behavioral intention influences the use behavior of Muslim consumers in purchasing a product through digital marketplace facilities.

RESEARCH METHODOLOGY

The method used in this research was quantitative research. The quantitative research method is used to the answer research problems related to data in the form of numbers and statistical programs. The approach used in this research was causality research. Causality research aims to investigate the probable cause and effect of an event or phenomenon (Kadri, 2018). This approach is suitable to be used to explain the pattern of relationships between variables.

The Population and Sampling Technique

The population in this study were all Muslim students who had bought an unidentified amount of products included in the four sectors of Global Islamic Economy Indicators (GIEI), namely *halal* food, Islamic clothing, *halal* cosmetics, and *halal* medicines through digital marketplace facilities, and domiciled in Banda Aceh. The characteristics that represented the population were 1) respondents are Muslim;

2) experienced buyers or had ever purchased a product through a digital marketplace; 3) the products purchased are included in the GIEI sector (*halal* food, Islamic clothing, *halal* cosmetics, *halal* medicines); and 4) respondents are students and domiciled in Banda Aceh. Given the numbers of Muslim students who purchase products through the digital marketplace could not be certainly identified and were always increasing every time. Thus the selected samples in this study were 296 respondents. The determined samples were considered could be representative of the Muslim student population in Banda Aceh who had ever purchased *halal* products through the digital marketplace. This was supported by the opinion that the recommended minimum sample size of SEM analysis ranged from 100 to 300 (Kock and Hadaya, 2016).

Data Analysis Method

The data analysis method used in this study was the Structural Equation Model (SEM) method. Structural Equation Model (SEM) is a multivariate statistical technique that is the combination of factor analysis and regression analysis (correlation). It aims to examine the relationship between variables that exist in a model, both the relationship between indicators with their constructs or inter-construct relationships that allows testing a complex or relatively complex set of relationships. The estimation method used in this study was Maximum Likelihood Estimation. This method is effective for sample sizes between 150 till 400 (Kock and Hadaya, 2016). The software used is Amos 22 application. Amos (Analysis of moment structures) is one of the application for conducting the structural analysis. Besides this study also used SPSS (*Statistical Product and Service Solutions*) applications for data description purposes (Fan et al., 2016)

RESULT

Validity Testing

The validity was tested by the CFA test (Construct Validity Test) which measures whether or not the indicator reflects the latent variable. The critical ratio and probability could be read in the estimate column, and it is determined as significant and meet the criteria if the critical ratio is > 1.96 and probability is < 0.05 so it could be marked by three stars sign (***)as in Table 4.10.

Then, the validity testing was tested by the convergence test of validity, to know whether the constructs have a high proportion of variants or not. Validity testing was done by analyzing the value of the loading factor seen from the standardized loading estimate which has been standardized. An indicator is said to be valid if the loading factor value is bigger than 0.5 (Hair et al., 2014).

Based on the test results were shown in Table 4.11, all standardized loading estimates are bigger than 0.5. It showed that all indicators used met the validity testing criteria.

Reliability Testing

Reliability testing was carried out by testing the construct reliability of each variable. Reliability testing is used to test the reliability and consistency of data. It is considered meeting the criteria if the rehabilitation construct is > 0.7. The formula used to calculate construct reliability is as follows:

Table 2. Regression weights (Group number 1: Default model)

No	Variables	Indicators	Estimate	S.E.	C.R.	P
1.	*Performance Expectanc)*	x1.1 <--- x1	1.000			
		x1.2 <--- x1	1.058	.062	16.985	***
		x1.3 <--- x1	.989	.057	17.359	***
		x1.4 <--- x1	1.115	.065	17.143	***
2.	*Effort Expectancy*	x2.1 <--- x2	1.000			
		x2.2 <--- x2	1.077	.059	18.323	***
		x2.3 <--- x2	1.077	.061	17.554	***
		x2.4 <--- x2	1.079	.062	17.323	***
3.	*Social Influence*	x3.1 <--- x3	1.000			
		x3.2 <--- x3	1.046	.086	12.218	***
		x3.3 <--- x3	1.114	.083	13.385	***
		x3.4 <--- x3	1.172	.094	12.454	***
		x3.5 <--- x3	1.065	.088	12.114	***
4.	*Facilitating Conditions*	x4.1 <--- x4	1.000			
		x4.3 <--- x4	.902	.056	16.075	***
5.	*Behavioral Intention*	y1 <--- y	1.000			
		y2 <--- y	1.017	.041	24.739	***
6.	*Use Behavior*	z1 <--- z	1.000			
		z2 <--- z	.994	.069	14.398	***
		z3 <--- z	1.098	.076	14.385	***
		z4 <--- z	1.083	.080	13.555	***

Source: Data Processed, 2019
Note: *** = 0,001

$$ConstructReliability = \frac{(\sum StdLoading)^2}{(\sum StdLoading)^2 + \sum \epsilon_j}$$

where:

Std. Loading: obtained directly from standardized loading for each indicator.

Î: is *measurement error* from each indicator.

Measurement error is equal to 1.

Table 4.12 showed that all indicators are reliable and could be continued to the next stage. This was indicated by the construct reliability value of each indicator was bigger than 0.7.

Table 3. Standardized regression weights (Group number 1: Default model)

No.	Variables	Indicators	Estimate	Decision
1.	*Performance Expectancy*	x1.1 <--- x1	.811	Valid
		x1.2 <--- x1	.847	Valid
		x1.3 <--- x1	.859	Valid
		x1.4 <--- x1	.859	Valid
2.	*Effort Expectanc)*	x2.1 <--- x2	.791	Valid
		x2.2 <--- x2	.904	Valid
		x2.3 <--- x2	.883	Valid
		x2.4 <--- x2	.881	Valid
3.	*Social Influence*	x3.1 <--- x3	.705	Valid
		x3.2 <--- x3	.751	Valid
		x3.3 <--- x3	.842	Valid
		x3.4 <--- x3	.806	Valid
		x3.5 <--- x3	.787	Valid
4.	*Facilitating Conditions*	x4.1 <--- x4	.870	Valid
		x4.3 <--- x4	.805	Valid
5.	*Behavioral Intention*	y1 <--- y	.909	Valid
		y2 <--- y	.919	Valid
6.	*Use Behavior*	z1 <--- z	.756	Valid
		z2 <--- z	.843	Valid
		z3 <--- z	.824	Valid
		z4 <--- z	.784	Valid

Source: Test Result, 2019

Table 4. Construct reliability

Variables	Constructs Reliability	Alpha	Decision
X1	0,900738	0,7	Reliable
X2	0,913078	0,7	Reliable
X3	0,877629	0,7	Reliable
X4	0,800778	0,7	Reliable
Y	0,902744	0,7	Reliable
Z	0,861028	0,7	Reliable

Source: Data Analysis, 2019

Test Result

Figure 2. SEM test result
Source: Test Result, 2019

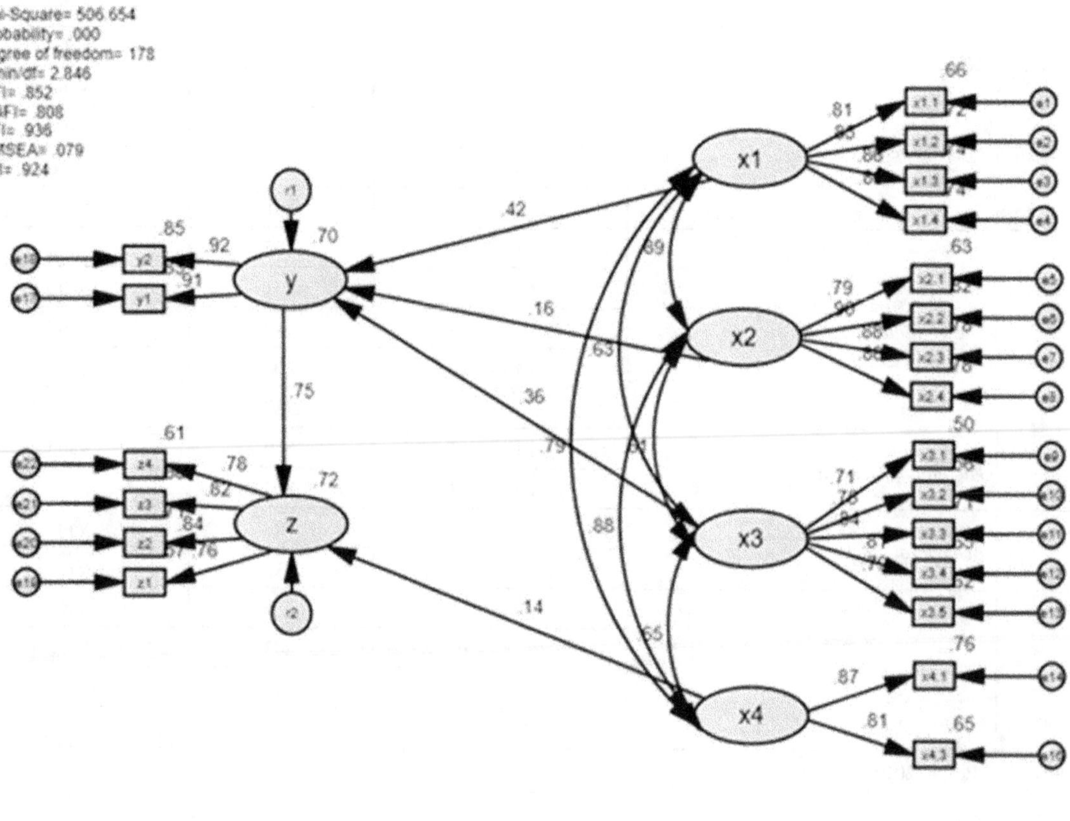

HYPOTHESIS TEST

The Analysis of SEM Test Results

The result of the regression analysis was used to analyze the significance of influence between constructs. The direct effects between exogenous and endogenous variables were seen from the probability value. It is considered to meet the criteria if the critical ratio is > 1.96. While the probability (p-value) should be < 0.05. then it could be determined as significant. The three stars symbol in the table below is equal to p-value < 0.001 which marked as significant (Santoso, 2010).

Performance Expectancy (X1) had a significant effect on behavioral intention (Y). This was indicated by the p-value marked with *** so H1 was accepted H01 was rejected. Moreover, Social Influence (X3) had a significant effect on behavioral intention (Y). This was also indicated by the p-value marked with *** so that H3 was accepted H03 was rejected. On the other hand, effort expectancy (X2) had no significant effect on behavioral intention (Y). It was shown by the value of p-value 0.16 3 > 0.05, which meant H02 was accepted H2 was rejected. In addition, facilitating conditions (X4) also did not significantly influence the behavioral intention (Y), which marked by the p-value 0.102 > 0.05, so that

Table 5. Regression weights (Group number 1: Default model)

			Estimate	S.E.	C.R.	p-value
Y	<---	X1	0.469	0.132	3.562	***
Y	<---	X2	0.173	0.124	1.393	**0.163**
Y	<---	X3	0.457	0.077	5.932	***
Z	<---	X4	0.119	0.073	1.635	**0.102**
Z	<---	Y	0.646	0.082	7.928	***

Source: Data Analysis, 2019
where: *** = significant

H04 was accepted H4 was rejected. Lastly, behavioral intention (Y) significantly influenced use behavior (Z). This is indicated by the p-value of the behavioral intention variable (Y)was marked by ***, so that H5 was accepted H05 was rejected.

Sobel Test

The Sobel test aims to analyze the significance of the indirect effect of the independent variable on the dependent variable through mediator variables (intervening). In this study, the t-test was used to see the significance of the indirect effect between the variables of performance expectancy, effort expectancy, and social influence on use behavior through the variable of behavioral intention. The testing was carried out using the Microsoft Excel application. In this study, the test was done by comparing the value of t-calculation with t-table. The result was partially categorized as significant affecting if the value of t-calculation > t table. The test results were carried out by using the Sobel formula as follows:

$$Sab = \sqrt{\left(b^2 Sa^2\right) + a^2 \left[Sb\right]^2 + \left[Sa\right]^2 \left[Sb\right]^2}$$

where:

a = raw (unstandardized) regression coefficient for the association between the independent variable and the mediator variable

b = raw coefficient for the association between the mediator and the dependent variable (when the independent is also a predictor of the dependent variable).

Sa = standard error of *a*

Sb = standard error of *b*

a. The Significant Effect of Performance Expectation on Use Behavior through Behavioral Intention

Sab = 0.417316 x 0.01744 + 0.2191 x 0.0064 + 0.0174 x 0.0064

= 0.007271 + 0.001472 + 0.0007

$= 0.008867$

$$t_{cal} = \frac{axb}{sab}$$

$$= \frac{0.469x0.646}{0.008867}$$

$t_{cal} = 34.16682$

$t_{tab} = 1.968235$

From the calculation above, it can be seen that performance expectancy had a significant effect on use behavior through behavioral intention. This could be seen from the value of Sab is 0.008867 with t-cal value is bigger than t-table (t-cal = 34.16682 > 1.968235), so H0a1 was rejected and Ha1 was accepted.

b. The Significant Effect of Effort Expectation on Use Behavior through Behavioral Intention

Sab = 0.4176 x 0.015376 + 0.02999 x 0.00674 + 0.01536 x 0.0064

= 0.0067 + 0.000204 + 0.00013

= 0.006721

$$t_{cal} = \frac{axb}{sab}$$

$$= \frac{0.173x0.646}{0.006721}$$

$t_{cal} = 16.62748$

$t_{tab} = 1.968235$

From the calculation above, it could be determined that effort expectancy had a significant effect on use behavior through behavioral intention. It was shown from the value of Sab was 0.006721 with t-cal value 16.62748 > 1.968235 (t-table), thus H0a2 was rejected and Ha2 was accepted.

c. The Significance of Social Influence on Use Behavior through Behavioral Intention

Sab = 0.41736 x 0.005929 + 0.20889 x 0.00674 + 0.00599 x 0.00674

= 0.00244 + 0.001403 + 0.00674

= 0.01063

$$t_{cal} = \frac{axb}{sab}$$

$$= \frac{0.457x0.646}{0.010603}$$

$$t_{cal} = 27.84439$$

$$t_{tab} = 1.968235$$

From the calculation of the Sobel test before, it can be determined that social influence had a significant effect on use behavior through behavioral intention, because the value of Sab (0.010603) with the t-cal value of 27.84439 > 1.968235 (t-table), so, it could be concluded that H0a3 was rejected and Ha3 was accepted.

The result of the Sobel test analysis showed that the t-value is calculated to see the indirect significant effect between the independent variables and the dependent variables, thus the results can be summarized in the table below:

The significance of the indirect effect is seen from the comparison between the value of t-calculation and t-table, if t-calculation > t-table, it means the effect is significant. From the table above it was determined that performance expectancy (X1), effort expectancy (X2), and social influence (X3) had significant effects on use behavior (Z) through behavioral intention (Y). This was indicated from the calculation of the three variables of t-calculation > t-table.

Direct Effect Analysis and Indirect Effect Analysis

Direct effect, indirect effect, and total effect analysis were performed to analyze the relationship or influence between exogenous variables on endogenous variables. The direct effect is the coefficient of a line with one end of an arrow and occurs in two constructs directed by a line of one-way arrows. The indirect effect is the effect that arises through an intermediate variable and occurs in two constructs that are not addressed by a line of the one-way arrow. While the total effect is the effect of various relationships, the total effect is the combination of direct effect and indirect effect.

To find out the value of direct effect, the value of Standardized Direct Effect must be squared. To find out the magnitude of the indirect effect, the output value of Standardized Indirect Effect needs to be squared (Group number 1 - Default model).

Table 6. Indirect significant effect

	t-calculation	*t*-table	Decision
Performance Expectancy (X_1)	34.16682	1.968235	Significant
Effort Expectancy (X_2)	16.62748	1.968235	Significant
Social Influence (X_3)	27.84439	1.968235	Significant

The results of the analysis of direct and indirect effects between the independent variables and the dependent variables in this study can be summarized in the table below:

DISCUSSION

The Effects of Performance Expectancy on Behavioral Intention

The results of this study indicated that performance expectancy had a positive significant effect on Muslims' intentions in purchasing goods and services through digital marketplaces. This was indicated by the significant value obtained from the SEM regression using Amos application that fulfilled the criteria and the probability value which was smaller than the predetermined significant value. Thus, it could be concluded that the higher the perception of Muslim consumers toward the usefulness of a digital marketplacc for their activities the higher their intention to make online purchases through a digital marketplace. The faster digital market place in increasing productivity, then the greater opportunities for the trading activities of *halal* products,

The results of this study were in line with research conducted by Sair and Danish(2018) "*Effect of Performance Expectancy and Effort Expectancy on the Mobile Commerce Adoption Intention through Personal Innovativeness among Pakistani Consumers*" and research (Kamal and Azis, 2015) entitled "*Internet Technology Adoption by Consumer MSMEs to Online Shopping (Study at Tokopedia in 2015)*". Both of these studies showed that performance expectancy had a significant effect on behavioral intention.

Performance is a form or way for individuals to actualize themselves. Performance is a tangible form of values, beliefs, and understandings that are believed and based on strong moral principles and can be a motivation to produce quality work. (Din et al., 2019). In Islam, performance appraisal must be done as a servant or as a worker. Because God tells us to do that. As Allah says in the Qur'an Surah At taubah verse 105, which means: "And say, "*Do [as you will], for Allah will see your deeds, and [so, will] His Messenger and the believers. And you will be returned to the Knower of the unseen and the witnessed, and He will inform you of what you used to do.*" (QS. At-taubah [9]: 105).

The Effects of Performance Expectancy on Use Behavior Through the Behavioral Intention as an Intervening Variable

The behavioral intention of Muslim consumers in this study successfully mediated the relationship between performance expectancy and Muslim's use behavior in the digital marketplace. Indirectly, the performance expectancy variable had a significant effect on use behavior through the digital marketplace

Table 7. Results of direct and indirect effects

			Direct effect	Indirect effect	Decision
Z	<---	x1	0.174724	0.091809	Direct Effect > Indirect Effect
Z	<---	x2	0.024649	0.012544	Direct Effect > Indirect Effect
Z	<---	x3	0.128164	0.087025	Direct Effect > Indirect Effect

Source: Data Analysis, 2019

with behavioral intention as an intervening variable based on the Sobel test. But the value of the direct effect was greater than the value of the indirect effect of the performance expectancy variable on use behavior through the intention to make a purchase.

The results of this study were inversely proportional to the research conducted by Priyadi, (Priyadi et al., 2017) entitled *"Behavior of using e-office portals at XYZ banks using the UTAUT model approach"*. This study showed that performance expectancy had a significant effect on use behavior through the mediation of behavioral intention.

The Effects of Effort Expectancy on Behavioral Intention

The results of this study indicate that effort expectancy did not have a significant effect on Muslims' intentions to make purchases through the digital marketplace. This was determined by the significant value obtained from the SEM regression using Amos application that did not meet the criteria and the probability value, where the t-calculation was bigger than the predetermined significant value. Thus it could be concluded that the more a person feels the digital marketplace is user friendly, and accessible easily, it did not affect Muslims costumers' behavioral intention to purchase products through a digital marketplace.

The results of this study were supported by the research conducted by Mustaqim et al. (2018) entitled "Analysis of Factors Influencing the Intention of Using XYZ E-Commerce Using the UTAUT Model (Unified Theory Acceptance and Use Of Technology)" which stated effort expectancy did not affect the behavioral intention. But it was contradicted to the research conducted by Kiat and Samadi (2017) entitled *"Consumer Behavior towards Acceptance of Mobile Marketing"* and research (Ramantoko et al., 2015) entitled *"Early Adoption Characteristic of Consumers': A Behavioral Intention to Use Home Digital Services in Indonesia"*. Both of these studies argued that effort expectancy had a significant effect on behavioral intention.

The Effects of Effort Expectancy on Use Behavior With Behavioral Intention as an Intervening Variable

Muslim's behavioral intention in this study succeeded in mediating the relationship between effort expectancy and Muslim's use behavior through the digital marketplace. Indirectly, the effort expectancy variable has a significant effect on use behavior variable through a digital marketplace with the behavioral intention as an intervening variable based on the Sobel test. However, the value of the direct effect was bigger than the value of the indirect effect of effort expectancy variables on use behavior through the behavioral intention.

The results of this study were in line with research that has been conducted by Sedana and Wijaya (2012) entitled *"Application of UTAUT Model to Understand the Acceptance and Use of Learning Management System Case Study: Experimental E-Learning Of Sanata Dharma University"*. This study showed that effort expectancy had a significant effect on use behavior through behavioral intention. But it was contradicted to the research (Priyadi et al., 2017) entitled *"behavior of using e-office portals at XYZ banks using the UTAUT model approach"*. This study showed that effort expectancy did not have a significant effect on use behavior through the mediating variable of behavioral intention.

The Effects of Social Influence on Behavioral Intention

The results of this study found that social influence had a significant positive effect on Muslims' behavioral intention to purchases goods and services through the digital marketplace. This was indicated by the significant value obtained from the SEM regression using Amos application fulfilled the criteria and the probability value which were smaller than the predetermined significant value. Thus it could be concluded that the greater encouragement, support and advice from the social environment, family, and friends to purchase *halal* products, the higher the intention of Muslims to have online transactions through the digital marketplace.

This result was coherence with research conducted by Alshehri and Meziane (2015) entitled "*The Impact of Social Influence and Third-Party Endorsement on Online Shopping in Saudi Arabia*" and the research (Kamal and Azis, 2015) entitled "*Internet Technology Adoption by Consumer MSMEs to Online Shopping (Study at Tokopedia in 2015)*". Both of these studies showed that social influence had a significant effect on behavioral intention.

SOCIAL INFLUENCE

Social Influence Effects on Use Behavior through the Behavioral Intention as an Intervening Variable

Muslim's behavioral intention to make online purchases in this study succeeded in mediating the relationship between social influence and Muslims' use behavior through the digital marketplace. Indirectly, the social influence variable had a significant effect on use behavior through the digital marketplace with the behavioral intention to purchase goods and services online as an intervening variable based on the Sobel test. But the value of the direct effect was bigger than the value of the indirect effect of social influence variable on use behavior through the behavioral intention.

The result of this study was supported by research conducted by Sedana and Wijaya (2012) entitled "*The Application UTAUT model in Understanding the Acceptance and Utilization of Leaning Management, a Case Study: Experimental E-Learning of Sanata Dharma University*". This study showed that the social influence variable had a significant effect on use behavior through behavioral intention. However, the research conducted by Priyadi et al., (2017) entitled "*Behavior of Using E-Office Portals at XYZ Banks Using the UTAUT Model Approach*" was in contrast with the result of this study. It argued that social influence did not significantly influence use behavior through behavioral intention as the mediating variable.

The Effects of Facilitating Conditions Toward Use Behavior

The result of this study indicated that the facilitating conditions variable had no significant effect on Muslims' behavioral intention in the digital marketplace. It showed from the significant value obtained from the SEM regression using Amos application that did not meet the criteria and the probability value, which was bigger than the predetermined significant value. Thus it could be concluded that having resources such as cellphones/laptops, internet networks, and the knowledge on how to technical use the digital marketplaces, did not influence Muslims in purchasing products online through the digital marketplaces.

This result was supported by Kiat and Samadi (2017) in their research entitled *"Consumer Behavior towards Acceptance of Mobile Marketing"*. The study showed that effort expectancy had a significant effect on behavioral intention. In contrast, the research conducted by Christina et al. (2018) entitled *"Analysis of Acceptance and Use of Ojek Online Technology with TAM"* mentioned that the facilitating conditions had a significant effect on use behavior.

The Effects of Behavioral Intention on Use Behavior

This study found that behavioral intention had a significant positive effect on Muslims' intentions in making online purchases using the digital marketplace. It could be seen from the significant value obtained from the SEM regression using Amos application fulfilled the criteria and the probability value, where the obtained value was smaller than the predetermined significant value. In short, the higher the Muslims' perception toward the use of a digital marketplace that will be beneficial for trading activities, will increase online purchasing activity in a digital marketplace. A faster digital marketplace would also increase productivity, and give greater opportunities for trading activities of *halal* products.

This finding was in line with some previous researches. For instance, research conducted by Christina et al. (2018) entitled *"Analysis of Acceptance and Use of Ojek Online Technology with TAM* " and Kamal and Aziz's (2015) study entitled *"Internet Technology Adoption by Consumer MSMEs to Online Shopping (Study at Tokopedia in 2015)"*, that argued the behavioral intention significantly affected the use behavior.

The intention itself is a crucial point for Muslim consumers in carrying out every activity. As mentioned in a hadith narrated by Imam Bukhari rahimahullah in the book of the Saheeh of the Prophet sallallaahu 'alaihi wa sallam said (Al-Bukhari, 2003: vol 1, Book 1, Hadith 1): Narrated 'Umar bin Al-Khattab: I heard Allah's Messenger shallahu 'alaihi wa sallam saying, "*The reward of deeds depends upon the intentions and every person will get the reward according to what he has intended. So whoever emigrated for worldly benefits or for a woman to marry, his emigration was for what he emigrated for.*" [HR. Bukhari].

Research Implications

Performance expectancy, social influence had direct significant positive effects on the intention to purchase *halal* products through a digital marketplace (behavioral intention). Whereas effort expectancy did not significantly influence the intention to make a purchase (behavioral intention). Facilitating conditions also did not significantly influence the buying behavior of *halal* products using digital marketplaces (use behavior). Lastly, behavioral intention significantly affected the buying behavior of *halal* products through a digital marketplace (use behavior).

Indirectly, performance expectancy, effort expectancy and social influence had no significant effect on the use behaviour in purchasing *halal* products in the digital marketplaces.

The results of this research are useful for marketplace companies and digital businesses to evaluate special offers for Muslim consumers. Thus Muslims could cater to their needs for *halal* products which fulfill the requirements of the Islamic religion. As in his study, Alam (2019) said that financial services companies that want to achieve prosperity must be able to innovate in services by increasing Muslim customers in developing countries.

Limitations and Future Research

The limitation of this research was that it only focused on discussing Muslims' behavior in using the digital marketplace to purchase *halal* products using the Unified Theory of Acceptance and Use of Technology (UTAUT) model. Besides, this research also used modified simpler models of UTAUT that only involved ten digital marketplaces with the highest number of visitors in 2019. It is expected that future researchers can engage the UTAUT 2 model to investigate Muslim consumers' behavior in using the digital marketplace by employing different approaches and focuses. Thus it will have more significant variables that affected the digital marketplaces used by Muslim consumers to purchase *halal* products.

REFERENCES

Alam, I. (2019). Interacting with Muslim customers for new service development in a non-Muslim majority country. *Journal of Islamic Marketing. Emerald Group Publishing Ltd., 10*(4), 1017–1036.

Alshehri, H. & Meziane, F. (2015). The Impact of Social Influence and Third Party Endorsement on Online Shopping in Saudi Arabia. *Journal of Internet and E-Business Studies*, 1–9.

Angelova, B., & Zekiri, J. (2011). Measuring Customer Satisfaction with Service Quality Using American Customer Satisfaction Model (ACSI Model). *International Journal of Academic Research in Business & Social Sciences, 1*(3), 232–257. doi:10.6007/ijarbss.v1i2.35

Ashraf, M. A. (2019). Islamic marketing and consumer behavior toward *halal* food purchase in Bangladesh An analysis using SEM. *Journal of Islamic Marketing, 10*(3), 893–910. doi:10.1108/JIMA-03-2018-0051

Ayuniyyah, Q., Hafidhuddin, D., & Hambari, H. (2017). Factors Affecting Consumers' Decision in Purchasing MUI *Halal*-Certified Food Products. *Tazkia Islamic Finance and Business Review, 10*(2), 122–141. doi:10.30993/tifbr.v10i2.111

Chao, C. M. (2019). Factors determining the behavioral intention to use mobile learning: An application and extension of the UTAUT model. *Frontiers in Psychology, 10*, 1–14. doi:10.3389/fpsyg.2019.01652 PMID:31379679

Christina, H., Suhud, U., & Rizan, M. (2018). Analisis Penerimaan dan Penggunaan Teknologi Ojek Online dengan TAM [JPEB]. *Jurnal Pendidikan Ekonomi Dan Bisnis, 6*(1), 34–44. doi:10.21009/JPEB.006.1.4

Din, M. U., Khan, F., Khan, U., Kadarningsih, A., & Astuti, S. D. (2019). Effect Of Islamic Work Ethics On Job Performance: Mediating Role Of Intrinsic Motivation *IJBE, 4*(2), 676–688.

Fan, Y., Chen, J., Shirkey, G., John, R., Wu, S.R. & Shao, H. (2016). Applications of structural equation modeling (SEM) in ecological studies: an updated review. *Springer Open*. https://ecologicalprocesses.springeropen.com/articles/10.1186/s13717-016-0063-3

Hair, J., Sarstedt, M., Hopkins, L., & Kuppelwieser, V. (2014). Partial Least Squares Structural Equation Modeling (PLS-SEM): An Emerging Tool for Business Research. *European Business Review, 26*(2), 106–121. doi:10.1108/EBR-10-2013-0128

Hassan, S., Marimuthu, M., & de Run, E. (2013). Conceptualizing Convergence and Divergence of Muslim Consumption behaviour in Malaysia. *Indian Journal of Management Science*, *3*(4), 1–7.

Indonesia, Ip. (2019). *Bandingkan Harga, Promo, Kode Kupon & Diskon*. IPrice Indonesia. https://iprice.co.id/

Kadri, T. (2018), *Rancangan Penelitian*. Deepublisheer, Yogyakarya. https://books.google.co.id/books?id=_-tmDwAAQBAJ&pg=PR5&lpg=PR5&dq=Kadri,+Trihono.+2018.+Rancangan+Penelitian.+Yogyakarta:+Deepublish.&source=bl&ots=7LrPeP4J8i&sig=ACfU3U23xBOkVHiWqJ6p-dZcxETul_LkOsg&hl=en&sa=X&ved=2ahUKEwjb48nric_oAhURXn0KHZACAwwQ6AEwAXoE (accessed 4 April 2020).

Kamal, R. M., & Azis, E. (2015). Internet Technology Adoption by Consumer MSMEs to Online Shopping (Study at Tokopedia.com in 2015). In M. Se (Ed.), *Dr.Maya Ariyanti* (pp. 147–152). Managing Business for Smart Economy.

Kock, N., & Hadaya, P. (2016). Minimum sample size estimation in PLS-SEM: The inverse square root and gamma-exponential methods. *Information Systems Journal*, *28*(1), 227–261. doi:10.1111/isj.12131

Laras, A. A. (2018). Tiga Celah Pengembangan E-Commerce di Indonesia - Analisis Data. *Katadata.Co.Id*, https://katadata.co.id/analisisdata/2018/10/23/tiga-celah-pengembangan-e-commerce-di-indonesia

Lawan, A. & Dahalin, Z.M. (2011). Conceptual Model of the Unified Theory of Acceptance and Use of Technology (UTAUT). *Journal of Information Systems : New Pardigms*, *1*(1), 43–46.

McKinsey. (2018). McKinsey Expects Great Growth for Indonesia's E-Commerce Market. *Indonesia Investments*. https://www.indonesia-investments.com/id/news/todays-headlines/mckinsey-expects-great-growth-for-indonesia-s-e-commerce-market/item8959

Mustaqim, R., Kusyanti, A., & Aryadita, H. (2018). Analisis Faktor-Faktor yang Memengaruhi Niat Penggunaan E-Commerce XYZ Menggunakan Model UTAUT (Unified Theory Acceptance and Use Of Technology). *Jurnal Pengembangan Teknologi Informasi Dan Ilmu Komputer*, *2*(7), 2584–2593.

Nugrahaningsih, W., & Erlinawati, M. (2017). Implementasi Undang-Undang Nomor 8 Tahun 1999 Tentang Perlindungan Konsumen Terhadap Bisnis Online. *Jurnal Serambi Hukum*, *11*(1), 27–40.

Priyadi, R., Daryanto, A., & Hermandi, I. (2017). View of Perilaku Penggunaan Portal E-office di Bank XYZ Dengan Pendekatan Model UTAUT. *Aplikasi Bisnis Dan Manajemen*, *3*(2), 186–193.

Putra, G., & Ariyanti, M. (2013). Pengaruh Faktor-Faktor Dalam Modified Unified Theory of Acceptance and Use of Technology 2 (Utaut 2) Terhadap Niat Prospective Users Untuk Mengadopsi Home Digital Services Pt. Telkom Di Surabaya. *Jurnal Manajemen Indonesia*, *12*(4), 59–76.

Ramantoko, G., Putra, G., Ariyanti, M., & Sianturi, N. (2015). Early Adoption Characteristic of Consumers' Behavioral Intention to Use Home Digital Services in Indonesia. In *Advances in Social Science Education and Humanities Reasearch* (pp. 1–8). Atlanta Press.

Sair, S. A., & Danish, R. Q. (2018). Effect of Performance Expectancy and Effort Expectancy on the Mobile Commerce Adoption Intention through Personal Innovativeness among Pakistani Consumers. *Pakistan Journal of Commerce and Social Sciences*, *12*(2), 501–520.

Santoso, S. (2010), Statistik Multivariat. *PT Elex Media Compotindo*, Jakarta. https://books.google.co.id/books?hl=en&lr=&id=E5Dli6puzYUC&oi=fnd&pg=PR5&ots=cRyAe8KFm3&sig=2CI2sF4IQySFjvkgzcOIs1fSa-g&redir_esc=y#v=onepage&q&f=false

Sedana, I. G. N., & Wijaya, S. W. (2012). Penerapan Model Utaut Untuk Memahami Penerimaan Dan Penggunaan Learning Management System Studi Kasus: Experential E-Learning of Sanata Dharma University. *Jurnal Sistem Informasi*, *5*(2), 114–120. doi:10.21609/jsi.v5i2.271

Sfenrianto, S., Wijaya, T., & Wang, G. (2018). Assessing the buyer trust and satisfaction factors in the E-marketplace. *Journal of Theoretical and Applied Electronic Commerce Research*, *13*(2), 43–57. doi:10.4067/S0718-18762018000200105

Suhartanto, D. (2019). Predicting behavioural intention toward Islamic bank : A multi-group analysis approach. *Journal of Islamic Marketing*, *10*(4), 1091–1103. doi:10.1108/JIMA-02-2018-0041

Suki, N. M. (2018). Mediating effect of *Halal* image on Muslim consumers' intention to patronize retail stores: Some insights from Malaysia. *Journal of Islamic Marketing*, *9*(2), 338–355. doi:10.1108/JIMA-02-2017-0014

Tan, H. S. (2019). Overview of Indonesia's Online Consumers in Q4. *Janio*. https://janio.asia/sea/indonesia/indonesia-q4-consumer-overview/

Ud Din, M., Khan, F., Khan, U., Kadarningsih, A., & Astuti, S. D. VI. (2019). Effect of Islamic Work Ethics on Job Performance: Mediating Role of Intrinsic Motivation. *International Journal of Islamic Business Ethics*, *4*(2), 676–686. doi:10.30659/ijibe.4.2.676-688

Usman, S. (2017). Kesamaan dan perbedaan pasar e-Commerce Indonesia dengan Tiongkok. *Merdeka.Com*, https://www.merdeka.com/teknologi/kesamaan-dan-perbedaan-pasar-e-commerce-indonesia-dengan-tiongkok.html

Venkatesh, V., Morris, G., Davis, & Davis. (2003). User Acceptance of Information Technology: Toward A Unified View. *Management Information Systems Quarterly*, *27*(3), 425–478. doi:10.2307/30036540

Venkatesh, V., Thong, J. Y., & Xin, X. U. (2012). Consumer Acceptance and Use of Information Technology: Extending the Unified Theory of Acceptance and Use of Technology. *Management Information Systems Quarterly*, *36*(1), 157–178. doi:10.2307/41410412

Yu, S., & Lee, J. (2019). The effects of consumers' perceived values on intention to purchase upcycled products. *Sustainability (Basel)*, *11*(4), 1034. doi:10.3390u11041034

Chapter 16
Islamic Entrepreneurship Application and Its Strategies: A Case Study of Bangladesh

AlFatih Gessan Pananjung
Bahrain Institute of Banking and Finance, Bahrain

Ammar Ibna Ala
https://orcid.org/0000-0002-4671-0230
University of Bangor, UK

Ahmad Rafiki
https://orcid.org/0000-0002-6360-8131
Universitas Medan Area, Indonesia

ABSTRACT

This study aims to explore various facets of entrepreneurship, particularly Islamic entrepreneurship, from a religious perspective, with a focus on its practice within the context of Bangladesh. In Bangladesh, diverse social enterprises, some profit-driven and rooted in Islamic principles like Zakat and Waqf, exemplify Islamic entrepreneurship. Examples include the Baitul Mukarram complex and the Islamic Bank Hospital, which generate income, promote Islamic culture, and address social needs. Social Islamic Bank Ltd. employs Cash Waqf, while organizations like Muslim Aid Bangladesh focus on economic empowerment. These approaches showcase the blend of profit motives, social impact, and religious values in Bangladeshi Islamic entrepreneurship.

1. INTRODUCTION

The revolution of industry led to both an increase in prosperity and wealth but also led to greater disparities in income and wealth distribution (Piketty, 2014). Recently, the global financial crisis has led to the rise of "social enterprise" business models that focus on addressing social issues rather than maximizing

DOI: 10.4018/978-1-6684-7519-5.ch016

profits as Muhammad Yunus propagated which received enormous courtesy. Social enterprise initiatives prioritize addressing social issues such as affordable healthcare, affordable housing, drug abuse and environmental hazards over maximizing profits through the use of corporate and business strategies. Simultaneously, the Islamic banking and finance industry is growing and becoming a new rival to the existing economic system.

Entrepreneurial activity has been shown to be a valuable way to create more wealth and build a better society. However, many poor countries are lacking entrepreneurs which can lead to economic decline. Entrepreneurship refers to the process of starting and managing a new business venture with the goal of making a profit by providing valuable products or services and accepting financial risks. Despite the high risk, entrepreneurship is highly valued for its potential to contribute to a sustainable economy, create employment opportunities, and generate innovative business ideas. This study aims to investigate various aspects of entrepreneurship, specifically Islamic entrepreneurship, from a religious perspective, and to examine how it is practiced in the context of Bangladesh.

2. LITERATURE REVIEW

2.1 Conventional Entrepreneurship

Entrepreneurship is a vital force in economic growth, job creation and innovation. According to a study by the Global Entrepreneurship Monitor (GEM) "Entrepreneurial activity is positively related to economic growth and development" (Acs et al., 2008). The study also found that countries with higher levels of entrepreneurial activity tend to have higher levels of GDP per capita and higher rates of job creation.

The GEM report also points out that Entrepreneurship is not only important for economic growth but also for innovation, which is a key driver of productivity and competitiveness. Entrepreneurs are known to be risk-takers and they are often the ones who come up with new ideas and find ways to commercialize them. This is important because it leads to new products, services and revenue to the market. Additionally, new businesses provide employment opportunities and contribute to the diversification of the economy.

Economic is spurred by entrepreneurs as they contribute to society by introducing new and innovative production methods (Leibenstine, 1978; Juliana, 2018). Azim (2011) also stated that strategic entrepreneurs also play a vital role in making sound business decisions and leveraging opportunities such as technology and globalization to gain a competitive advantage.

Traditional entrepreneurship is often viewed as an individual trait that is considered desirable rather than a tangible reality. Defining entrepreneurship can be difficult and there can be conflicting opinions on what it means. However, comprehensive, and consensual definition of entrepreneurship that portrays it as a holistic and moral effort by individuals or corporations to act as "economic heroes."

2.2 The Interrelationship Between Entrepreneurship and Religion

The relationship between entrepreneurship and religion is a complex one, with various religious beliefs and practices influencing the attitudes and actions of entrepreneurs. Religion can have a major impact on the values and actions of entrepreneurs, particularly in terms of their ethical decision-making and their approach to risk-taking. For example, a study by Chrisman et al. (1998) found that Protestant religious beliefs were positively associated with entrepreneurial activity, as Protestants tend to value hard work, self-discipline, and the pursuit of wealth, which are all traits that are conducive to entrepreneurship.

On the other hand, some religious traditions discourage the pursuit of wealth and material success, instead emphasizing spiritual pursuits and the sharing of resources among community members. This means religion can have both positive and negative effects on entrepreneurship. While some religious beliefs and practices may encourage entrepreneurial activity, others may discourage it. Additionally, cultural and religious values of a society can play a role in shaping the entrepreneurial ecosystem, by influencing the level of support and resources available to entrepreneurs.

As noted by sociologist Max Weber, religious beliefs can play a role in shaping an individual's attitude towards wealth creation and entrepreneurial ventures. He argued that Protestantism specifically can foster an inclination towards innovation and taking on risks, influencing the creation of wealth through new and ambitious ideas. It has been acknowledged that religious beliefs have a direct influence on the actions and outcomes of entrepreneurs, as argued by Weber. The role of faith in shaping financial and organizational structures by religious entrepreneurs is becoming more widely acknowledged. The religiosity of an entrepreneur can drive their success and motivations in business, and it is commonly believed that religious entrepreneurs make business decisions based on ethical and religious principles.

2.3 An Islamic Perspective of Entrepreneurship

In the Islamic perspective, entrepreneurial success is not only measured by material accomplishments but also by success in the afterlife. Only through the lens of Maqasid al-Shariah the principles of Islamic entrepreneurship can be evaluated (Yaacob and Azmi, 2012).

Islamic entrepreneurship is the art of innovating and venturing into the unknown while adhering to the principles of Shariah. It prioritizes ethical practices such as opposing fraud, greed, and exploitation in the accumulation of wealth. A Muslim entrepreneur must abide by religious laws and conduct their business with the moral compass of the Quran and the teachings of Prophet Muhammad PBUH.

The primary distinction between conventional and Islamic entrepreneurship is that the latter is guided by religious principles, while the former is guided by non-religious principles. While conventional models rely on reason and evidence, Islamic entrepreneurs must base their decisions on the principles laid out in the Quran and the Sunnah. This means that Islamic entrepreneurs must conduct their business and financial activities within the guidelines of Shariah, while conventional models may lack ethical and moral considerations (Abdullah et al.,2019).

Islam considers entrepreneurship to be vital for the progress of human societies and requires that economic endeavors benefit the community rather than just the individual. Furthermore, unlike the mainstream economic philosophy, Islamic entrepreneurship prioritizes improving society and the economy over personal gain. Entrepreneurial activities in Islam are focused on addressing social issues and boosting the economy, rather than solely maximizing profits. Additionally, for an enterprise to be considered socially responsible from an Islamic perspective, it must abide by moral principles and scriptural guidelines (Islamic Shariah) in its operations within the community.

2.4 Islamic and Conventional Entrepreneurship Model Study

Measuring the effect of micro-credit on conventional micro-credit, and also on IMF can be done in two ways. One way is to use the "Welfarist" approach, which concentrates on the data of the well-being of microfinance members and is commonly used by field researchers. The second approach is the "institutionist" strategy, which evaluates the financial practicality and ensures the distribution of funds in Islamic microfinance projects..

On the other hand, Muslim scholars and practitioners have studied various models of Islamic entrepreneurship which are based on the principles outlined in the Qur'an and Sunnah and are considered an integral part of Muslim culture. It is encouraged for Muslims to engage in business activities that are innovative and avoid charging interest, in order to better their own lives and contribute to the well-being of their communities.

Similarly, Prophet Muhammad PBUH and his followers during the 6th century did apply the business practices that are the root of Islamic entrepreneurship principles and techniques. Guidance and practices for entrepreneurship can be derived from the Sunnah and the teachings of the Quran.

2.5 Principles of Islamic Entrepreneurship

Islamic social enterprise emphasizes various ethical, moral and social ideals, including viewing business operations as forms of devotion by entrepreneurs. Secondly, it emphasizes on the importance of God-consciousness (Taqwa) in shaping models of business, interactions, and dealing with customers. Thirdly, it promotes taking on difficult business endeavors as stated by Prophet Muhammad PBUH that most of livelihoods are to be found in trade activities. In addition to that, Islamic entrepreneurship must conform to Islamic economy and the motivations for its operation should be in line with the way Prophet Muhammad PBUH conducted himself (Ullah,2013).

Similarly, Abdullah et al. (2019) in his paper argues that following fundamental ethical principles in Islamic entrepreneurship is mandatory, including avoiding interest based or Riba transactions, implementing fair trade policies, and refraining from prohibited or Haram products.

3. DISCUSSION

3.1 Islamic Entrepreneurship: The Context of Bangladesh

In terms of operations of social enterprise, there are various types, such as "non-profit", "profit-form", "merchant-style" or "social mission-style." In addition, various activities that are based on traditional religious practices (e.g. Zakat) and others that are more novel, such as cash Waqf or charitable services (e.g. non-profit organizations) do exist. In Bangladesh, Islamic entrepreneurship employs the profit-driven social enterprise model, as demonstrated by the Baitul Mukarram complex which was constructed on Waqf land and generates income from the revenue generated by the shopping mall operations, which is later used for the maintenance of the mosque.

Furthermore, it promotes the promotion of Islamic beliefs and culture, creating job opportunities for fellow Muslims. A portion of the revenue is also allocated to Islamic foundations for social welfare programs (an independent organization under the ministry of religious affairs). The Baitul Mukarram project not only relies on the profits they create but also receives funding from foreign sources and the government aid (Mohiuddin, 2017). The Baitul Mukarram Islamic Foundation can be seen as an example of the model of Islamic social enterprise in action, indirectly or directly.

In Bangladesh, Social Islami Bank Ltd. has adopted an Islamic entrepreneurship strategy by utilizing Cash Waqf, in which funds are set aside for the benefit of those in need. Additionally, Muslim Aid Bangladesh, a non-governmental organization and other similar organizations focusing on economy have introduced new methods for distributing Zakat, such as training to underprivileged individuals to engage in profitable ventures, rather than just providing them with food and clothing, and providing financial grants. Furthermore, an outstanding example of Islamic entrepreneurship as it offers affordable medical services to the needy and operates according to Islamic principles is The Islami Bank Hospital which is under the management of the Islami Bank Foundation. (Islami Bank Foundation, 2014)

3.2 Islamic Microfinance as a Tool of Entrepreneurship: Bangladesh

The method of providing goods and services in Islamic microfinance differs from that of conventional financing as it follows Islamic ethical and rational principles. Recently, there has been a rising interest in poverty reduction strategies that adopt the Islamic entrepreneurial model. The NGO programs aimed at reducing poverty and inequality among rural populations who lack access to financial institutions enabled Bangladesh to gain a global recognition (Noble Prize Winner).

Following the recognition of Grameen Bank for its interest-based financial programs, plenty of microfinance institutions have emerged to provide interest-free loans to needy farmers, particularly. Research has demonstrated that microfinance initiatives in Bangladesh have been successful in raising the living standards of lower-income families and that 90% of female entrepreneurs have received direct benefits from a microfinance institution or small and medium-sized enterprise (Nabi et al., 2017).

Islamic microfinance was introduced in Bangladesh to address poverty by offering financial services and access to unprivileged clients through a shared risk and equitable distribution system. This framework is not present in conventional microfinance models. Islamic Microfinance plays a significant role in promoting economic growth, improving the lives of poor communities, and reducing poverty through its ethical framework of interest-free financing, creating a bridge between lower and middle classes. Islami Bank Bangladesh Limited (IBBL) has implemented the Rural Development Scheme (RDS) to provide financial freedom and socio-economic welfare, targeting women entrepreneurs specifically. Studies have shown that IBBL has been effective in fighting poverty through the RDS program, with 520,000 clients benefitting, 80% of which were women entrepreneurs. Thus, the engagement of women entrepreneurs in building an Islamic socio-economic society has significantly contributed to the success of the Islamic Microfinance system in Bangladesh.

3.3 Muslim Women Entrepreneurship in Bangladesh

Parvin et al. (2012) found that a significant portion of Bangladeshi women, 66%, have chosen to become entrepreneurs, with 16% of them becoming self-employed over time. According to research conducted by Parvin et al. (2012), a significant percentage of Bangladeshi women have taken on entrepreneurial careers, specifically in rural areas. Opportunities for women's financial independence are more prevalent in these areas as non-governmental organizations provide microfinance for rural women's financial activities. This has led to an increase in women becoming engaged and independent in entrepreneurship, particularly in the agricultural and non-agricultural sectors, such as plant cultivation, handmade product manufacturing, and seasonal food preparation.

Bangladeshi Muslim women entrepreneurs are not only making an impact on their families and communities, but also on the country's economy as a whole by actively participating in the business sector. Bangladeshi Muslim women entrepreneurs are increasingly participating in the business sector and contributing to socio-economic development with the aid of Islamic microcredit, small and medium-sized enterprises (SMEs), and government initiatives (Al-Hossienie and Abdullah, 2011).

Entrepreneurship among Muslim women in Bangladesh has indeed been on the rise in recent years, as more and more women are starting their own businesses and becoming self-sufficient. However, there are still many challenges that Muslim women entrepreneurs in Bangladesh face, including limited access to education, lack of access to financial resources, and social and cultural barriers.

One of the main challenges facing Muslim women entrepreneurs in Bangladesh is limited access to education. Many Muslim women in Bangladesh do not have access to formal education, which makes it difficult for them to acquire the skills and knowledge necessary to start and run a successful business. This lack of education also makes it difficult for Muslim women to access business training and support programs, which can provide them with the tools they need to succeed as entrepreneurs.

Another major challenge facing Muslim women entrepreneurs in Bangladesh is lack of access to financial resources. Many Muslim women in Bangladesh do not have access to traditional forms of financing, such as bank loans, due to their lack of collateral or credit history. This makes it difficult for them to start and grow their businesses, as they are unable to secure the funding they need to purchase equipment, hire employees, and expand their operations.

Social and cultural barriers also play a significant role in hindering the development of Muslim women entrepreneurship in Bangladesh. Bangladeshi society is traditionally patriarchal and women are often not seen as capable of running a business, which can make it difficult for Muslim women to gain the support and recognition they need to succeed as entrepreneurs. In addition, there is a lack of female role models in the business world, which can make it difficult for Muslim women to envision themselves as successful entrepreneurs.

Despite these challenges, there have been some efforts made to support Muslim women entrepreneurship in Bangladesh. For example, some organizations have started to provide business training and support programs specifically for Muslim women entrepreneurs. These programs can help Muslim women acquire the skills and knowledge they need to start and run successful businesses. In addition, some microfinance institutions have started to offer Islamic microfinance products, which provide Muslim women with access to financing that is consistent with their religious beliefs.

3.4 The Role of Islamic Microfinance in the Islamic Economy System

The encouragement of entrepreneurship and Islamic microfinancing is crucial in order for Islamic communities to experience economic growth. Zapalska et al. (2013) argue that creating a prosperous and long-term entrepreneurial environment is vital for the advancement of Muslim countries and their economic growth. One effective method to achieve this is through Islamic micro-investments, which are based on the Islamic financial framework. These investments can greatly benefit the socio-economic welfare of the community and Muslim women entrepreneurs. The authors recommend promoting Islamic micro-investment schemes rather than just micro-loans to drive economic development.

Islamic microfinance is an essential component of the Islamic economic system, as it allows for the provision of financial services to individuals and small businesses who might not otherwise have access to them. This is achieved by providing small loans and other forms of financing to individuals and businesses that are not served by traditional financial institutions, such as banks.

In the Islamic economic system, the principles of risk sharing and prohibition of interest-based transactions are central. Islamic microfinance addresses these principles by offering financing through the concept of mudharabah which is a profit and loss sharing partnership between the financier and the entrepreneur. This ensures that both parties share in the risks and rewards of the business, rather than the financier simply charging interest on a loan.

Islamic microfinance also promotes social and economic development by providing small businesses with the resources they need to grow and create jobs. This is especially important in developing countries, where small businesses often struggle to access the capital they need to expand and succeed.

Furthermore, Islamic microfinance can also play an important role in reducing poverty and income inequality. By providing small loans and other forms of financing to individuals and businesses in low-income communities, Islamic microfinance can help to improve the economic opportunities available to these individuals, thereby reducing poverty and income inequality.

Despite the benefits of Islamic microfinance, there are also some challenges that must be addressed. One of the biggest challenges is the lack of awareness and understanding of the principles of Islamic finance among potential clients and financial institutions. This can make it difficult to implement Islamic microfinance programs and attract potential clients. Additionally, Islamic microfinance institutions often face operational challenges, such as high transaction costs and limited staff capacity. Therefore, efforts should be made to raise awareness and understanding of Islamic microfinance, and to develop effective strategies to address the operational challenges faced by Islamic microfinance institutions

3.5 Limitations in the Application of Islamic Microfinance

The implementation of Islamic microfinance can face challenges in countries where the economic system is not aligned with Shariah principles. Establishing a proper Islamic economic system is crucial for the development of Muslim nations, as it will promote socio-economic growth and prevent the need for Muslims to engage in interest-based lending transactions which can be problematic. Additionally, it will help to prevent accusations that Islamic financial institutions are supporting extremist activities as seen in some cases where conventional NGOs and MFIs dominate.

Islamic microfinance is designed to provide financial services to low-income individuals and small businesses who may not have access to traditional banking services. The following are limitations of Islamic microfinance that must be considered, not just in existence in Bangladesh but globally.

Firstly, one of the main limitations of Islamic microfinance is the lack of awareness and understanding of the concept among potential borrowers. Many individuals and small businesses in the target market may not be familiar with the principles of Islamic finance and may not understand how it differs from traditional microfinance. This lack of understanding can make it difficult for Islamic microfinance institutions to attract and retain customers.

Secondly, the absence of a full-grown regulatory framework for Islamic microfinance can also be a limitation. Islamic microfinance institutions are not always subject to the same regulations as traditional microfinance institutions, which can lead to inconsistencies and inefficiencies in the sector. Additionally, the lack of a regulatory framework can make it difficult for Islamic microfinance institutions to access funding from traditional sources.

Thirdly, the high cost of providing Islamic microfinance services can also be a limitation. The complex nature of Islamic finance and the need for specialized expertise can make it more expensive for Islamic microfinance institutions to provide services. This can make it difficult for them to compete with traditional microfinance institutions and may limit their ability to serve low-income individuals and small businesses.

Lastly, the lack of standardization in the Islamic microfinance sector can also be a limitation. Different Islamic microfinance institutions may use different contracts and products, which can make it difficult for customers to compare products and make informed decisions. Additionally, the lack of standardization can make it difficult for Islamic microfinance institutions to share information and collaborate with other institutions.

While there is a potential for Islamic microfinance to provide financial services to low-income individuals and small businesses who may not have access to traditional banking services, there are several limitations that must be considered. These include lack of awareness and understanding, lack of a well-developed regulatory framework, high cost of providing services, and lack of standardization in the sector. Addressing these limitations will be essential for the successful development and growth of the Islamic microfinance sector.

4. CONCLUSION

In summary, both conventional and Islamic entrepreneurship models aim to create goods and services for the market, however, the Islamic model follows the principles of Shariah, which includes avoiding Riba and prohibited products. Additionally, this essay discussed various models for poverty alleviation, income generation, and socio-economic welfare. Both conventional and Islamic models share a similar strategy, with the added aspect of an ethical framework in the Islamic model. Furthermore, Islamic finance and entrepreneurship are closely connected in the development of an interest-free economic system. Overall, Islamic entrepreneurship is focused on serving the community and society rather than solely pursuing material gain, with the ultimate goal of achieving success in the afterlife.

Last of all, as a conclusion after conducting a thorough appraisal of strategic entrepreneurship implementation in Bangladesh, with the help of the government through the induction of Shariah-compliance-based enterprises, to enhance the development of Islamic social enterprise, researchers and foundations must actively participate in the process in Bangladesh.

REFERENCES

Abdullah, A., Abdullah, S., & Ramli, A. J. (2019). Entrepreneurship according to the hadeeth. *International Journal of Business and Management, 3*(4), 1–5. doi:10.26666/rmp.ijbm.2019.1.1

Acs, Z., Audretsch, D., Braunerhjelm, P., Carlsson, B., & Karlsson, C. (2008). *Global Entrepreneurship Monitor 2007 Global Report.* Global Entrepreneurship Research Association.

Al-Hossienie. & Abdullah, C. (2011). *Socio-Economic Impact of Women Entrepreneurship in Sylhet City, Bangladesh.* Bangladesh Development Research Working Paper Series.

Azim, M. (2011). *Entrepreneurship Development in Bangladesh* (1st ed.). UGC.

Chrisman, J. J., Bauerschmidt, A., & Hofer, C. W. (1998). The role of personal religious faith in the development of entrepreneurial intent and ability. *Entrepreneurship Theory and Practice.*

Juliana, J., Ropi, M., Udin, S., & Husnul, K. (2017). Syariapreneur: The New Paradigm Of Islamic-Based Entrepreneurship. In *1st International Conference On Islamic Economics, Business, And Philanthropy (Iciebp 2017)* (pp. 668-672). ScitePress. 10.5220/0007087706680672

Leibenstine, H. (1978). *General X-Efficiency Theory and Economic Deployment.* Oxford University Press.

Mohiuddin, M. F. (2017). Islamic social enterprises in Bangladesh: Conceptual and institutional challenges. *Cogent Business & Management*, *4*(1), 1305674. doi:10.1080/23311975.2017.1305674

Nabi, G., Islam, A., Bakar, R., & Nabi, R. (2017). Islamic microfinance as a tool of financial inclusion in Bangladesh. *Journal of Islamic Economics, Banking, and Finance*, *113*(6218), 1–28. doi:10.12816/0051154

Parvin. (2012). Women entrepreneurship development in Bangladesh: What are the challenges ahead? *African Journal of Business Management*, *6*(11), 3862–3871.

Piketty, T. (2014). Capital in the twenty-first century. In Mohiuddin, M.F. (ed.) Islamic social enterprises in Bangladesh: Conceptual and institutional challenges. The Belknap Press of Harvard University Press. doi:10.4159/9780674369542

Ullah, M. M., Mahmud, T. B., & Yousuf, F. (2013). Women entrepreneurship: Islamic perspective. *European Journal of Business and Management*, *5*(11), 44–52.

Yaacob, Y., & Azmi, I. A. G. (2012). Entrepreneur's Social Responsibilities From Islamic Perspective: A Study of Muslim Entrepreneurs In Malaysia. *Procedia: Social and Behavioral Sciences*, *58*, 1131–1138. doi:10.1016/j.sbspro.2012.09.1094

Zapalska, A., & Wingrove-Haugland, E. (2013). Micro-Entrepreneurship And Islamic Economic System. *Business Journal for Entrepreneurs*, (1).

Compilation of References

Aaminou, M. W. (2022). *Towards a better financial inclusion in Maghreb countries: Insights on the role of Islamic microfinance and fintech (Research Report No. 22).* İstanbul: Research Center for Islamic Economics (IKAM).

Ab Talib, M. S., Md. Sawari, S. S., Abdul Hamid, A. B., & Ai Chin, T. (2016). Emerging Halal food market: An Institutional Theory of Halal certificate implementation. *Management Research Review, 39*(9), 987–997. doi:10.1108/MRR-06-2015-0147

Abd Muin, M. A., Abdullah, S., & Bahari, A. (2014, November). Model on social entrepreneurship: Identify the research gap based on islamic perspective. In *International Conference on Social Entrepreneurship* (pp. 7-9). Research Gate.

Abdallah, J., & Jibai, S. (2020). Women in Leadership: Gender Personality Traits and Skills. *Business Excellence and Management, 10*(1), 5–15. doi:10.24818/beman/2020.10.1-01

Abdullah, A., Abdullah, S., & Ramli, A. J. (2019). Entrepreneurship according to the hadeeth. *International Journal of Business and Management, 3*(4), 1–5. doi:10.26666/rmp.ijbm.2019.1.1

Abdullahi, S. I. (2019). Zakah as tool for social cause marketing and corporate charity: A conceptual study. *Journal of Islamic Marketing, 10*(1), 191–207. doi:10.1108/JIMA-03-2017-0025

Abdullah, J., Haji Hamali, J., & Abdullah, F. (2017). Success Strategies In Islamic Marketing MIX. *International Journal of Business and Society, 16*(3). doi:10.33736/ijbs.581.2015

Abdullah, R., & Ismail, A. G. (2014). Al-Tawhid in Relation to the Economic Order of Microfinance Institutions. *Humanomics, 30*(4), 325–348. doi:10.1108/H-01-2014-0006

Abdullah, S., & Mikail, S. A. (2013). Entrepreneurship and Islam: An expository study on characteristics of Muslim entrepreneur. In *5th Islamic Economics System Conference: Sustainable Development Through The Islamic Economics System, Faculty Economics And Muamalat, Universiti Sains Islam Malaysia*, Kuala Lumpur.

Abdulquadri, A., Mogaji, E., Kieu, T. A., & Nguyen, N. P. (2021). Digital transformation in financial services provision: A Nigerian perspective to the adoption of chatbot. *Journal of Enterprising Communities: People and Places in the Global Economy, 15*(2), 258–281. doi:10.1108/JEC-06-2020-0126

Abidin, C. (2016). Visibility labour: Engaging with Influencers' fashion brands and# OOTD advertorial campaigns on Instagram. *Media International Australia, Incorporating Culture & Policy, 161*(1), 86–100. doi:10.1177/1329878X16665177

Abidin, Z., Suhariadi, F., & Hadi, C. (2021). The Role of The Islamic Work Ethos Through the Motivation of Entrepreneurship and The Barriers of Entrepreneurship to Entrepreneurial Intention Santri In Pondok Pesantren Indonesia. *Ilkogretim Online, 20*(3). doi:10.17051/ilkonline.2021.03.56

Abras, A., & Al Mahameed, M. (2022, March). The rise and fall of institutional entrepreneurship in Islamic financial reporting standardisation projects. In *Accounting Forum* (pp. 1-26). Routledge. 10.1080/01559982.2022.2051684

Abuhmaira, M. A. (2006). *The Impact of" AAOIFI" Standards on the Financial Reporting of Islamic Banks: Evidence from Bahrain*. University of South Wales.

Abu-Nimer, M. (2001). Conflict resolution, culture, and religion: Toward a training model of interreligious peace-building. *Journal of Peace Research, 38*(6), 685–704. doi:10.1177/0022343301038006003

Abusloum, M. A. S., Ahmad, K., & Bello, N. (2020). Islamic banking in Libya: Emergence, growth, and prospects. In A. Rafay (Ed.), *Growth and emerging prospects of international Islamic banking*. IGI Global. doi:10.4018/978-1-7998-1611-9.ch002

Acs, Z., Audretsch, D., Braunerhjelm, P., Carlsson, B., & Karlsson, C. (2008). *Global Entrepreneurship Monitor 2007 Global Report*. Global Entrepreneurship Research Association.

Adam, M., Wessel, M., & Benlian, A. (2021). AI-based chatbots in customer service and their effects on user compliance. *Electronic Markets, 31*(2), 427–445. doi:10.100712525-020-00414-7

ADB. (2000). *Finance for the poor: microfinance development strategy.* Asian Development Bank (ADB).

Addai, B. (2017). Women empowerment through microfinance: Empirical evidence from Ghana. *Journal of Finance and Accounting, 5*(1), 1–11. doi:10.11648/j.jfa.20170501.11

Adelekan, A. S., Ojo, J. O., & Worimegbe, P. M. (2021). Coopetition and Small Firms Value Creation. *European Journal of Business Science and Technology, 133.*

Adham, K. A., Said, M. F., Saâ, N., & Yaakub, N. I. (2012). Technological innovation and entrepreneurship from the western and Islamic perspectives. *International Journal of Economics, Management and Accounting, 20*(2).

Adhariani, D. (2017). *Social Capital, Broken Trust, and Social Accountability: Exploring the Role of Religion in Microfinance Context.*

Admin. (2019, April 09). Halal Travel Holds Huge Potential, Remains Untapped. *Business Today*. https://www.businesstoday.com.my/2019/04/09/halal-travel-market remains-untapped-likely-to-grow-35/

Admin. (2020, January 13). Sabah's homestays among the highest earners in Malaysia. *Daily Express*. https://www.dailyexpress.com.my/news/146244/sabah-s-homestays-among-highest-earners-in-m-sia/

Adnan, M. A., & Ajija, S. R. (2015). The Effectiveness of Baitul Maal Wat Tamwil in Reducing Poverty: The Case of Indonesian Islamic Microfinance Institution. *Humanomics, 31*(2), 160–182. doi:10.1108/H-03-2012-0003

African Development Bank Group. (2021). *Note d'orientation politique: Impact de la crise COVID-19 sur l'emploi et les TPME au Maroc*. African Development Bank Group.

Agarwal, P., Swami, S., & Malhotra, S. K. (2022). Artificial intelligence adoption in the post COVID-19 new-normal and role of smart technologies in transforming business: a review. *Journal of Science and Technology Policy Management.*

Agostini, L., Nosella, A., & Filippini, R. (2017). Does intellectual capital allow improving innovation performance? A quantitative analysis in the SME context. *Journal of Intellectual Capital, 18*(2), 400–418. doi:10.1108/JIC-05-2016-0056

Ahen, F., Buabeng, K. O., & Salo-Ahen, O. M. H. (2023). Market violence through destructive entrepreneurship: Assessing institutional responses to the proliferation of counterfeit traditional and alternative medicines in Ghana. *Heliyon, 9*(3), e13881. doi:10.1016/j.heliyon.2023.e13881 PMID:36895339

Ahmad Tarmizi, H., Kamarulzaman, N. H., Abd Rahman, A., & Atan, R. (2020). Adoption of internet of things among Malaysian halal agro-food SMEs and its challenges. *Food Research*, *4*(S1), 256–265. doi:10.26656/fr.2017.4(S1).S26

Ahmad, A., & Humayoun, A. A. (2011). Islamic banking and prohibition of Riba/interest. *African Journal of Business Management*, *5*(5), 1763–1767. doi:10.5897/AJBM10.723

Ahmad, M. F. (2015). Antecedents of halal brand personality. *Journal of Islamic Marketing*, *6*(2), 209–223. doi:10.1108/JIMA-03-2014-0023

Ahmad, M. G., & Syed, J. (2021). Meta-characteristics of Islamic ethics and moral consistency in Islamic banking. *Business & Society*, *60*(8), 2026–2059. doi:10.1177/0007650320928470

Ahmad, M., & Ahmed, N. (2016). Testing the relationship between intellectual capital and a firm's performance: An empirical investigation regarding financial industries of Pakistan. *International Journal of Learning and Intellectual Capital*, *13*(2–3), 250–272. doi:10.1504/IJLIC.2016.075691

Ahmad, N. (2018). Toward advancing debates on Islamic marketing: A renewed perspective. *Journal of Islamic Marketing*, *9*(1), 152–166. doi:10.1108/JIMA-08-2016-0064

Ahmad, R., & Buttle, F. (2002). Customer retention management: A reflection of theory and practice. *Marketing Intelligence & Planning*, *20*(3), 149–161. doi:10.1108/02634500210428003

Ahmed, M. (2008). *The role of RDS in the development of women entrepreneurship under Islamic micro finance: A case study of Bangladesh. Islamic Finance for Micro and Medium Enterprises*, 211. Research Gate.

Ahmed, A. (2008). Marketing of halal meat in the United Kingdom – supermarkets versus local shops. *British Food Journal*, *110*(7), 655–670. doi:10.1108/00070700810887149

Ahmed, F. (2021). The Real Feminism. *The International Journal of Islamic Business. Administration and Social Sciences*, *1*(1), 29–36.

Aisjah, S., Prabandari, S. P., & Hamid, W. (2022). Sustainability Factors of Sharia Banks in Indonesia. *Quality - Access to Success*, *23*(190).

Aisyah, M. (2016). Consumer demand on halal cosmetics and personal care products in Indonesia. Al-Iqtishad. *Jurnal Ilmu Ekonomi Syariah*, *9*(1), 125–142.

Ajala, A. O., Kolawole, E. A., Adefolaju, T., Owolabi, A. O., Ajiboye, B. O., Adeyonu, A. G., Akangbe, J. A., Obaniyi, K. S., Adebimpe, A. T., & Adeniyi, V. (2019). Traditional medicine practices in Nigeria: A SWOT analysis. *International Journal of Mechanical Engineering and Technology*, *10*(2), 117–126.

Ajzen, I. (1988). *Attitudes, personality and behavior*. Open University Press.

Ajzen, I. (1991). The theory of planned behaviour. *Organizational Behavior and Human Decision Processes*, *50*(2), 179–211. doi:10.1016/0749-5978(91)90020-T

Ajzen, I., & Fishbein, M. (2000). Attitudes and the Attitude-Behavior Relation: Reasoned and Automatic Processes. *European Review of Social Psychology*, *11*(1), 1–33. doi:10.1080/14792779943000116

Ajzen, I., & Fishbein, M. (2002). *Understanding Attitudes and Predicting Social Behavior*. Prentice-Hall.

Akın, M. S., & Okumuş, A. (2021). Shaping the consumers' attitudes towards Halal food products in Turkey. *Journal of Islamic Marketing*, *12*(6), 1081–1096. doi:10.1108/JIMA-08-2019-0167

Akinyemi, K. O., Oyefolu, A. O. B., Mutiu, W. B., Iwalokun, B. A., Ayeni, E. S., Ajose, S. O., & Obaro, S. K. (2018). Typhoid fever: Tracking the trend in Nigeria. *The American Journal of Tropical Medicine and Hygiene*, *99*(3), 41–47. doi:10.4269/ajtmh.18-0045 PMID:30047362

Akyildiz, S. T. (2021). An Overview of Qualitative Research and Focus Group Discussion. *International Journal of Academic Research in Education*. doi:10.17985/ijare.866762

Al-Ali, S. (2019). *Raising capital on ṣukūk markets: structural, legal and regulatory issues*. Springer. doi:10.1007/978-3-030-14536-1

Alalwan, A. A., Rana, N. P., Dwivedi, Y. K., & Algharabat, R. (2017). Social media in marketing: A review and analysis of the existing literature. *Telematics and Informatics*, *34*(7), 1177–1190. doi:10.1016/j.tele.2017.05.008

Alam, A., & Maknun, L. (2021, February). *Impact of Islamic branding on purchasing decisions on facial wash product.* In First International Conference on Economics, Business and Social Humanities, Madiun, Indonesia. 10.4108/eai.4-11-2020.2304556

Alam, N., Gupta, L., & Zameni, A. (2019). Fintech and Islamic finance. Springer International Publishing. doi:10.1007/978-3-030-24666-2

Alam, I. (2019). Interacting with Muslim customers for new service development in a non-Muslim majority country. *Journal of Islamic Marketing. Emerald Group Publishing Ltd.*, *10*(4), 1017–1036.

Alam, P., & Azad, I. (2021). Impact of Microfinance on Income and Employment of Women in Jigjiga, Ethiopia. *International Journal of Economics and Business Administration*, *9*(1), 373–381. doi:10.35808/ijeba/679

Alam, S. S., Jani, M. F. M., & Omar, N. A. (2011). An Empirical Study of Success Factors of Women Entrepreneurs in Southern Region in Malaysia. *International Journal of Economics and Finance*, *3*(2), 166–175. doi:10.5539/ijef.v3n2p166

Alam, S. S., & Sayuti, N. M. (2011). Applying the Theory of Planned Behaviour (TPB) in Halal Food Purchasing. *International Journal of Commerce and Management*, *21*(1), 8–20. doi:10.1108/10569211111111676

Alam, S., Senik, Z. C., & Jani, F. M. (2012). An Exploratory Study of Women Entrepreneurs in Malaysia: Motivation and Problems. *Journal of Management Research*, *4*(4), 282–297. doi:10.5296/jmr.v4i4.2377

Al-Ansi, A., Olya, H., & Kim, W. (2019). Exploring halal-friendly destination attributes in South Korea: Perceptions and behaviors of Muslim travelers toward a non-Muslim destination. *Tourism Management*, *71*, 151–164. doi:10.1016/j.tourman.2018.10.010

Alazzani, A., Wan-Hussin, W. N., & Jones, M. (2019). Journal of Islamic Accounting and Business Research Article information. *Journal of Islamic Accounting and Business Research*, *10*(2), 274–296. https://doi.org/https://doi.org/10.1108/JIABR-01-2017-0002. doi:10.1108/JIABR-01-2017-0002

Alcaniz, L., Gomez-Bezares, F., & Roslender, R. (2011). Theoretical perspectives on intellectual capital: A backward look and a proposal for going forward. *Accounting Forum*, *35*(2), 104–117. doi:10.1016/j.accfor.2011.03.004

Al-Debei, M. M., & Avison, D. (2010). Developing a unified framework of the business model concept. *European Journal of Information Systems*, *19*(3), 359–376. doi:10.1057/ejis.2010.21

Al-Ghwell, H. (2022, May 28). Arab Maghreb Union needs a whole new foundation. *Arab News*. https://www.arabnews.com/node/2091501

Alharbi, R. K., Yahya, S., & Kassim, S. (2022). Impact of religiosity and branding on SMEs performance: Does financial literacy play a role? *Journal of Islamic Marketing*, *13*(12), 2717–2741. doi:10.1108/JIMA-08-2019-0162

Al-Hossienie. & Abdullah, C. (2011). *Socio-Economic Impact of Women Entrepreneurship in Sylhet City, Bangladesh.* Bangladesh Development Research Working Paper Series.

Ali, A. J., & Al-Owaihan, A. (2008). Islamic work ethic: A critical review. *Cross Cultural Management, 15*(1), 5–19. doi:10.1108/13527600810848791

Ali, A., Sherwani, M., Ali, A., Ali, Z., & Sherwani, M. (2021). Investigating the antecedents of halal brand product purchase intention: An empirical investigation. *Journal of Islamic Marketing, 12*(7), 1339–1362. doi:10.1108/JIMA-03-2019-0063

Ali, A., Xiaoling, G., Sherwani, M., & Ali, A. (2018). Antecedents of consumers' Halal brand purchase intention: An integrated approach. *Management Decision, 56*(4), 715–735. doi:10.1108/MD-11-2016-0785

Alia, M. Q., & Ahmada, N. (2023). The Factors that affect Halal Food and Food Products Awareness and Different Challenges: An overview. *Journal of Agribusiness Marketing, 10*(1), 82–95. doi:10.56527/fama.jabm.10.1.6

Ali, H., Bajwa, R., & Hussain, U. (2015). Women ' s Empowerment and Human Development in Pakistan : An Elaborative Study. *Asian Journal of Management Sciences & Education, 4*(4), 23–30.

Ali, M. H., & Suleiman, N. (2016). Sustainable food production: Insights of Malaysian halal small and medium sized enterprises. *International Journal of Production Economics, 181*, 303–314. doi:10.1016/j.ijpe.2016.06.003

Allameh, S. M. (2018). Antecedents and consequences of intellectual capital: The role of social capital, knowledge sharing and innovation. *Journal of Intellectual Capital, 19*(5), 858–874. doi:10.1108/JIC-05-2017-0068

Allameh, S. M., Abbasi, S., & Shokrani, S. A. R. (2010). The mediating role of organizational learning capability between intellectual capital and job satisfaction. *European Journal of Soil Science, 17*(1), 125–136.

Almeida, F., Santos, J. D., & Monteiro, J. A. (2020). The challenges and opportunities in the digitalization of companies in a post-COVID-19 World. *IEEE Engineering Management Review, 48*(3), 97–103. doi:10.1109/EMR.2020.3013206

Al-Munshi, M. Y. A. H. (2021). *Islamic Ethics on Environmental Sustainability versus Economic Development: Dam Construction as an Applied Case Study* [Doctoral dissertation, Hamad Bin Khalifa University (Qatar)].

Almutairi, S., Khan, S. A., Kuhail, M. A., & Taj, I. (2023). Chatbot Design Challenges and the Effect on User Behavior. *Trends, Applications, and Challenges of Chatbot Technology*, 24-35. doi:10.4018/978-1-6684-6234-8.ch002

Alnasser, S. A. S., & Muhammed, J. (2012). Introduction to corporate governance from Islamic perspective. *Humanomics, 28*(3), 220–231. doi:10.1108/08288661211258110

Alrawi, S. N., & Fetters, M. D. (2012). Traditional arabic & islamic medicine: A conceptual model for clinicians and researchers. *Global Journal of Health Science, 4*(3), 164–169. doi:10.5539/gjhs.v4n3p164 PMID:22980243

Alserhan, B. (2010). On islamic branding: Brands as good deeds. *Journal of Islamic Marketing, 1*(2), 101–106. doi:10.1108/17590831011055842

Alserhan, B. A. (2010). Islamic branding: A conceptualization of related terms. *Journal of Brand Management, 18*(1), 34–49. doi:10.1057/bm.2010.18

Alserhan, B. A., Zeqiri, J., Ramadani, V., & Dana, L.-P. (2022). An Introduction to Strategic Islamic Marketing. In *Strategic Islamic Marketing: A Roadmap for Engaging Muslim Consumers* (pp. 1–5). Springer. doi:10.1007/978-3-030-98160-0_1

Al-shami, H. A., & Abdullah, S. (2023). Halal food industry certification and operation challenges and manufacturing execution system opportunities. A review study from Malaysia. *Materials Today: Proceedings, 80*, 3607–3614. doi:10.1016/j.matpr.2021.07.331

Alshehri, H. & Meziane, F. (2015). The Impact of Social Influence and Third Party Endorsement on Online Shopping in Saudi Arabia. *Journal of Internet and E-Business Studies*, 1–9.

Alt, M. A., & Ibolya, V. (2021). Identifying Relevant Segments of Potential Banking Chatbot Users Based on Technology Adoption Behavior. *Market-Tržište, 33*(2), 165–183. doi:10.22598/mt/2021.33.2.165

Amalia, F., Sosianika, A., & Suhartanto, D. (2020). Indonesian millennials' halal food purchasing: Merely a habit? *British Food Journal, 122*(4), 1185–1198. doi:10.1108/BFJ-10-2019-0748

Ambali, A., & Bakar, A. N. (2014). People's Awareness on Halal Foods and Products: Potential Issues for Policy-makers. *Procedia: Social and Behavioral Sciences, 121*, 3–25. doi:10.1016/j.sbspro.2014.01.1104

Ambert, A. M., Adler, P. A., Adler, P., & Detzner, D. F. (1995). Understanding and Evaluating Qualitative Research. *Journal of Marriage and Family, 57*(4), 879–893. doi:10.2307/353409

Amruloh, D. A. G. (2017). (the 3rd Icbess 2016-Proceeding Kartika Discovery Hotel Bali, August 10–11, 2016) Entrepreneur Orientation in Islamic Perspective. *Eqien-Jurnal Ekonomi dan Bisnis, 4*(1). 10.34308/eqien.v4i1.56

Anas, E. L. M. E. L. K. I., & Mounira, B. A. (2009). Ethical investment and the social responsibilities of the Islamic banks. *International Business Research, 2*(2), 123–130. doi:10.5539/ibr.v2n2p123

Anderson, J. C., & Narus, J. A. (1990). A model of distributor firm and manufacturer firm working partnerships. *Journal of Marketing, 54*(1), 42–58. doi:10.1177/002224299005400103

Angelova, B., & Zekiri, J. (2011). Measuring Customer Satisfaction with Service Quality Using American Customer Satisfaction Model (ACSI Model). *International Journal of Academic Research in Business & Social Sciences, 1*(3), 232–257. doi:10.6007/ijarbss.v1i2.35

Anggadwita, G., Mulyaningsih, H. D., Ramadani, V., & Arwiyah, M. Y. (2015). Women entrepreneurship in Islamic perspective: A driver for social change. *International Journal of Business and Globalisation, 15*(3), 389–404. doi:10.1504/IJBG.2015.071914

Anjum, G. (2020). Women's Activism in Pakistan: Role of Religious Nationalism and Feminist Ideology among Self-Identified Conservatives and Liberals. *Open Cultural Studies, 4*(1), 36–49. doi:10.1515/culture-2020-0004

Ariawan, Sudarma, Djumahir, & Ghozali. (2016). The Role of Spiritual Capital, Human Capital, Structural Capital, and Relational Capital of SMES To Improving on Performance: Study Literature. *South East Journal of Contemporary Business. Economics and Law, 11*(2), 87–94.

Arnez, M. (2010). Empowering women through Islam: Fatayat NU between tradition and change. *Journal of Islamic Studies, 21*(1), 59–88. doi:10.1093/jis/etp025

Arsenijevic, U., & Jovic, M. (2019, September). Artificial intelligence marketing: chatbots. In 2019 international conference on artificial intelligence: applications and innovations (IC-AIAI) (pp. 19-193). IEEE. doi:10.1109/IC-AIAI48757.2019.00010

Ascarya & Sanrego. Y. D. (2007). *Redefine micro, small, and medium enterprises classification and the potency of baitul maal wa tamwiel as intermediary institutions in Indonesia.* Paper was presented at UBD-IRTI International Conference on Inclusive Islamic Financial Sector Development "Enhancing Islamic Financial Services for Micro and Medium Sized Enterprises (MMEs)", Empire Hotel and Country Club, Negara Brunei Darussalam.

Ascarya. (2017). *Baitul Maal Wat Tamwil (BMT): An Integrated Islamic Social and Comercial Financial Institutions in Indonesia.*

Asfiah, N. (2021). Do Islamic social entrepreneurship moderate Islamic leadership and emotional intelligence? Evidence from micro and small enterprises fostered by 'Aisyiyah. *Journal of Innovation in Business and Economics, 5*(01), 23–34. doi:10.22219/jibe.v5i01.16221

Ashraf, M. A. (2019). Islamic marketing and consumer behavior toward *halal* food purchase in Bangladesh An analysis using SEM. *Journal of Islamic Marketing, 10*(3), 893–910. doi:10.1108/JIMA-03-2018-0051

Ashraf, M. A. (2021). Determinants of Islamic entrepreneurial intentions: An analysis using SEM. *Journal of Islamic Marketing, 12*(1), 20–40. doi:10.1108/JIMA-05-2019-0116

Aslam, U. (2023). Understanding the usability of retail fashion brand chatbots: Evidence from customer expectations and experiences. *Journal of Retailing and Consumer Services, 74*, 103377. doi:10.1016/j.jretconser.2023.103377

Asnawi, N., Sukoco, B.M., & Fanani, M.A. (2018). Halal products consumption in international chain restaurants among global Moslem consumers. *International Journal of Emerging Markets, 13*.

Assaad, W., & Gomez, J. (2013). Social Network in Marketing (Social Media Marketing) Opportunities and Risk. *International Journal of Managing Public Sector Information and Communication Technologies, 2*(1), 13–22.

Attar, R. W., Almusharraf, A., Alfawaz, A., & Hajli, N. (2022). New Trends in E-Commerce Research: Linking Social Commerce and Sharing Commerce: A Systematic Literature Review. *Sustainability (Basel), 14*(23), 16024. doi:10.3390u142316024

Awan, H. M., Siddiquei, A. N., & Haider, Z. (2015). Factors affecting Halal purchase intention–evidence from Pakistan's Halal food sector. *Management Research Review, 38*(6), 640–660. doi:10.1108/MRR-01-2014-0022

Ayios, A., Jeurissen, R., Manning, P., & Spence, L. J. (2014). Social capital: A review from an ethics perspective. *Business Ethics (Oxford, England), 23*(1), 108–124. doi:10.1111/beer.12040

Ayub, R. (2013). Perception Of Working Women Towards Islamic Banking In Pakistan. *RADS Journal of Social Sciencess & Business Management, 1*(1), 7–12.

Ayuniyyah, Q., Hafidhuddin, D., & Hambari, H. (2017). Factors Affecting Consumers' Decision in Purchasing MUI *Halal*-Certified Food Products. *Tazkia Islamic Finance and Business Review, 10*(2), 122–141. doi:10.30993/tifbr.v10i2.111

Azaizeh, H., Saad, B., Cooper, E., & Said, O. (2010). Traditional Arabic and Islamic medicine, a re-emerging health aid. *Evidence-Based Complementary and Alternative Medicine, 7*(4), 419–424. doi:10.1093/ecam/nen039 PMID:18955344

Azam, A. (2016). An empirical study on non-Muslim's packaged halal food manufacturers: Saudi Arabian consumers' purchase intention. *Journal of Islamic Marketing, 7*(4), 441–460. doi:10.1108/JIMA-12-2014-0084

Azam, M. S. E., & Abdullah, M. A. (2020). Global halal industry: Realities and opportunities. [International Journal of Islamic Business Ethics]. *IJIBE, 5*(1), 47–59. doi:10.30659/ijibe.5.1.47-59

Azid, T., & Ward-Batts, J. L. (2020). Economic Empowerment of Women in the Islamic World [). World Scientific.]. *Theory into Practice, 1*, •••.

Azim, M. (2011). *Entrepreneurship Development in Bangladesh* (1st ed.). UGC.

Aziz, M. R. A., Khalid, N. S. B., Firdaus, M. H. B. A., Yatim, A. F. B. M., Navamohan, F. A. B. M. A., & Omar, M. N. W. Bin. (2021). A Review on Literatures of Islamic Financial Institutions And Market Between 2010 – 2020. *Library Philosophy and Practice*, 1–35. doi:10.5281/zenodo.5012446

Aziz, N. I. M., & Kassim, S. (2021). Investment decision making towards investing in Islamic unit trusts amongst women. *International Journal of Banking and Finance, 16*(1), 43–54.

Aziz, Y. A., & Chok, N. V. (2013). The role of Halal awareness, Halal certification, and marketing components in determining Halal purchase intention among non-Muslims in Malaysia: A structural equation modeling approach. *Journal of International Food & Agribusiness Marketing*, *25*(1), 1–23. doi:10.1080/08974438.2013.723997

Azmi, F. R., Musa, H., Sihombing, H., & Fen, F. S. (2018). Adoption factors of halal standards: The Malaysian perspectives. In *Proceedings of the 3rd International Halal Conference (INHAC 2016)* (pp. 315-329). Springer Singapore. 10.1007/978-981-10-7257-4_29

Azmi, I. A. G. (2014). The Implementation of Islamic Business Practices of Women Traders: A Study in An Islamic State in a Developing Country. *Global Journal Al-Thaqafah*, *4*(2), 17–28. doi:10.7187/GJAT632014.04.02

Azmi, I. A. G. (2017). Muslim Women Entrepreneurs Motivation in SMEs: A Quantitative Study in Asia Pacific Countries. *Asian Economic and Financial Review*, *7*(1), 27–42. doi:10.18488/journal.aefr/2017.7.1/102.1.27.42

Bahri, S., & Batoebara, M. U. (1981). *The Position and Participation of Khadijah in Developing Da ' wah in Islam at the First Period. 3*, 287–295.

Bajpai, V., Pandey, D. S., & Shriwas, M. S. (2012). Social Media Marketing: Strategies & Its Impact. *IRJC International Journal of Social Science & Interdisciplinary Research*, *1*(7), 214–223.

Balci, E. V., Tiryaki, S., & Karakuş, M. (2022). Exploring the transformation of opinion leaders from a traditional to a digital mindset. *International Journal of Organizational Leadership, 11*(Special Issue 2022), 36-50.

Balog, A. M., Baker, L. T., & Walker, A. G. (2014). Religiosity and spirituality in entrepreneurship: A review and research agenda. *Journal of Management, Spirituality & Religion*, *11*(2), 159–186. doi:10.1080/14766086.2013.836127

Bashir, Abdalla. (2019). Effect of halal awareness, halal logo and attitude on foreign consumers' purchase intention. *British Food Journal*. . doi:10.1108/BFJ-01-2019-0011

Bashir, A. M., Bayat, A., Olutuase, S. O., & Abdul Latiff, Z. A. (2018). Factors affecting consumers' intention towards purchasing halal food in South Africa: A structural equation modelling. *Journal of Food Products Marketing*, *25*(1), 26–48. doi:10.1080/10454446.2018.1452813

Basir, K. H., & Musa, S. F. P. D. (2022). An Islamic perspective of agripreneurs motivation. *Journal of Enterprising Communities: People and Places in the Global Economy*, *16*(3), 402–420. doi:10.1108/JEC-08-2020-0147

Bateman, M. (2011). *Microfinance as a development and poverty reduction policy: is it everything it's cracked up to be?* Background Note of Overseas Development Institute (ODI) at 50: Advancing Knowledge, Shaping Policy, Inspiring Practice. March. www.odi.org.uk/50years

Bateman, M. (2011). *Microfinance as a development and poverty reduction policy: is it everything it's cracked up to be?* Overseas Development Institute (ODI). www.odi.org.uk/50years

Battour, M., Salaheldeen, M., & Mady, K. (2021). Exploring innovative marketing opportunities for Halal entrepreneurs in hospitality and tourism industry. In *SHS Web of Conferences* (*Vol. 124*, p. 10001). EDP Sciences. 10.1051hsconf/202112410001

Battour, M. M., Battor, M. M., & Bhatti, M. A. (2014). Islamic attributes of destination: Construct development and measurement validation, and their impact on tourist satisfaction. *International Journal of Tourism Research*, *16*(6), 556–564. doi:10.1002/jtr.1947

Battour, M., Mady, K., Elsotouhy, M., Salaheldeen, M., Elbendary, I., Marie, M., & Elhabony, I. (2022). Artificial intelligence applications in halal tourism to assist Muslim tourist journey. In *Proceedings of International Conference on Emerging Technologies and Intelligent Systems: ICETIS 2021* Volume 2 (pp. 861-872). Springer International Publishing. 10.1007/978-3-030-85990-9_68

Battour, M., Mady, K., Salaheldeen, M., Elsotouhy, M., Elbendary, I., & Boğan, E. (2023). AI-enabled technologies to assist Muslim tourists in Halal-friendly tourism. *Journal of Islamic Marketing*, *14*(5), 1291–1309. doi:10.1108/JIMA-01-2022-0001

Beattie, G., & Ellis, A. (2014). *The psychology of language and communication.* Psychology Press. doi:10.4324/9781315804767

Bebbington, J., Higgins, C., & Frame, B. (2009). Initiating sustainable development reporting: Evidence from New Zealand. *Accounting, Auditing & Accountability Journal*, *22*(4), 588–625. doi:10.1108/09513570910955452

Bello, U. L., & Isah, J. (2015). Use of Herbal Medicines and Aphrodisiac Substances among Women in Kano State, Nigeria Article in Nursing and Health Sciences. *Journal of Nursing and Health Science*, *4*, 41–50. doi:10.9790/1959-04434150

Berakon, I., Wibowo, M. G., Nurdany, A., & Aji, H. M. (2023). An expansion of the technology acceptance model applied to the halal tourism sector. *Journal of Islamic Marketing*, *14*(1), 289–316. doi:10.1108/JIMA-03-2021-0064

Berezinets, I., Garanina, T., & Ilina, Y. (2016). Intellectual capital of a board of directors and its elements: Introduction to the concepts. *Journal of Intellectual Capital*, *17*(4), 632–653. doi:10.1108/JIC-01-2016-0003

Berghman, L., Matthyssens, P., & Vandenbempt, K. (2011). Value innovation, deliberate learning mechanisms and information from supply chain partners. *Industrial Marketing Management*, *41*(1), 27–39. doi:10.1016/j.indmarman.2011.11.014

Birchall, J. (2004). *Cooperatives and the Millennium Development Goals.*

Bonne, K., Vermeir, I., Bergeaud-Blackler, F., & Verbeke, W. (2007). Determinants of halal meat consumption in France. *British Food Journal*, *9*(5), 367–386. doi:10.1108/0070700710746786

Bontis, N. (1996). There's a price on your head: Managing intellectual capital strategically. *Business Quarterly*, *60*(4), 40–47.

Bontis, N. (1998). Intellectual capital: An exploratory study that develops measures and models. *Management Decision*, *36*(2), 63–76. doi:10.1108/00251749810204142

Bontis, N. (2001). Assessing knowledge assets: A review of the models used to measure intellectual capital. *International Journal of Management Reviews*, *3*(1), 41–60. doi:10.1111/1468-2370.00053

Bontis, N., Wu, S., Wang, W.-Y., & Chang, C. (2005). Intellectual capital and performance in causal models: Evidence from the information technology industry in Taiwan. *Journal of Intellectual Capital*, *6*(2), 222–236. doi:10.1108/14691930510592816

Bourdieu, P. (1989). Social space and symbolic power. *Sociological Theory*, *7*(1), 14–25. doi:10.2307/202060

Brammer, S., Williams, G., & Zinkin, J. (2007). Religion and attitudes to corporate social responsibility in a large cross-country sample. *Journal of Business Ethics*, *71*(3), 229–243. doi:10.100710551-006-9136-z

Bridger, S., & Luloff, A. (2001). Building the Sustainable Community: Is Social Capital the Answer? *Sociological Inquiry*, *71*(4), 458–472. doi:10.1111/j.1475-682X.2001.tb01127.x

Brooking, A. (1996). *Intellectual Capital – Core Asset for the Third Millennium Enterprise*. International Thomson Business Press.

Bukhari, S. N. Z., & Isa, S. M. (2020). Islamic branding: Insights from a conceptual perspective. *Journal of Islamic Marketing, 11*(6), 1743–1760. doi:10.1108/JIMA-02-2018-0035

Cabrita, M. R., & Bontis, N. (2008). Intellectual capital and business performance in the Portuguese banking industry. *International Journal of Technology Management, 43*(1–3), 212–237. doi:10.1504/IJTM.2008.019416

Caemmerer, B., & Alan, W. (2010). No Title. *Journal of Operations & Production Management, 30*(3), 288–311. doi:10.1108/01443571011024638

CAHF in Africa. (2021). 2021 yearbook: Housing finance in Africa. Johannesburg, South Africa: Centre for Affordable Housing Finance (CAHF) in Africa.

Cahyani, U. E., Masruri, S., & Hanafi, S. M. (2022). Does Entrepreneurship Education Matter for Islamic Higher Education Students' Entrepreneurial Readiness. *Jurnal Ekonomi Bisnis Dan Kewirausahaan, 11*(2), 258. doi:10.26418/jebik.v11i2.55092

Capello, R. (2002). Spatial and Sectoral Characteristics of Relational Capital in Innovation Activity. *European Planning Studies, 10*(2), 177–200. doi:10.1080/09654310120114481

Capello, R., & Faggian, A. (2005). Collective learning and relational capital in local innovation processes. *Regional Studies, 39*(1), 75–87. doi:10.1080/0034340052000320851

Carayannis, E. G., Barth, T. D., & Campbell, D. F. J. (2012). The quintuple helix innovation model: Global warming as a challenge and driver for innovation. *Journal of Innovation and Entrepreneurship, 1*(2), 1–12. doi:10.1186/2192-5372-1-1

Carayannis, E. G., & Campbell, D. F. J. (2011). Open innovation diplomacy and a 21st century fractal research, education and innovation (FREIE) ecosystem: Building on the quadruple and quintuple helix innovation concepts and the "mode 3" knowledge production system. *Journal of the Knowledge Economy, 2*(3), 327–372. doi:10.100713132-011-0058-3

Carayannis, E. G., Grigoroudis, E., Campbell, D. F. J., Meissner, D., & Stamati, D. (2018). The Ecosystem as helix: An exploratory theory-building study of regional co-opetitive entrepreneurial ecosystems as quadruple/quintuple helix innovation models. *R & D Management, 48*(1), 148–162. doi:10.1111/radm.12300

Cardella, G. M., Hernández-Sánchez, B. R., & Sánchez-García, J. C. (2020). Women entrepreneurship: A systematic review to outline the boundaries of scientific literature. *Frontiers in Psychology, 11*, 1557. doi:10.3389/fpsyg.2020.01557 PMID:32765357

Carrai, M. A. (2018). It is not the end of history: The financing institutions of the belt and road initiative and the Bretton Woods system. In *The Belt and Road Initiative* (pp. 107–145). Brill Nijhoff. doi:10.1163/9789004373792_006

Cerimagic, S. (2010). The effects of Islamic law on business practices. *Education, Business and Society, 3*(1), 40–47. doi:10.1108/17537981011022805

Chahal, H., & Bakshi, P. (2015). Examining intellectual capital and competitive advantage relationship: Role of innovation and organizational learning. *International Journal of Bank Marketing, 33*(3), 376–399. doi:10.1108/IJBM-07-2013-0069

Cha, M., Haddadi, H., Benevenuto, F., & Gummadi, K. (2010, May). Measuring user influence in twitter: The million follower fallacy. In *Proceedings of the international AAAI conference on web and social media* (Vol. 4, No. 1, pp. 10-17). 10.1609/icwsm.v4i1.14033

Chan, W. T. Y., & Leung, C. H. (2021). Mind the gap: Discrepancy between customer expectation and perception on commercial chatbots usage. *Asian Journal of Empirical Research, 11*(1), 1–10. doi:10.18488/journal.1007.2021.111.1.10

Chao, C. M. (2019). Factors determining the behavioral intention to use mobile learning: An application and extension of the UTAUT model. *Frontiers in Psychology, 10*, 1–14. doi:10.3389/fpsyg.2019.01652 PMID:31379679

Chapra, M. U. (2008). *The Islamic vision of development in the light of maqasid al-shari'ah.* (Occasional Paper No. 15). The International Institute of Islamic Thought (IIIT)

Cheng, X., Bao, Y., Zarifis, A., Gong, W., & Mou, J. (2021). Exploring consumers' response to text-based chatbots in e-commerce: The moderating role of task complexity and chatbot disclosure. *Internet Research, 32*(2), 496–517. doi:10.1108/INTR-08-2020-0460

Cheng, Y., & Jiang, H. (2022). Customer–brand relationship in the era of artificial intelligence: Understanding the role of chatbot marketing efforts. *Journal of Product and Brand Management, 31*(2), 252–264. doi:10.1108/JPBM-05-2020-2907

Chen, J., Wang, H., & Chao, X. (2022). Cross-platform opinion dynamics in competitive travel advertising: A coupled networks' insight. *Frontiers in Psychology, 13*, 1003242. doi:10.3389/fpsyg.2022.1003242 PMID:36389514

Cheung, M. L., Pires, G. D., Rosenberger, P. J. III, & De Oliveira, M. J. (2021). Driving COBRAs: The power of social media marketing. *Marketing Intelligence & Planning, 39*(3), 361–376. doi:10.1108/MIP-11-2019-0583

Chin, K. F. (2021). Malaysia's perception and strategy toward China's BRI expansion: Continuity or change? *Chinese Economy, 54*(1), 9–19. doi:10.1080/10971475.2020.1809814

Chiong, P. S. S. C., Seeam, P., & Seeam, A. (2022). Development of a smart tourism information chatbot for Mauritius. *ICONIC*, 122-130. https://doi.org/ doi:10.59200/ICONIC.2022.013

Chrisman, J. J., Bauerschmidt, A., & Hofer, C. W. (1998). The role of personal religious faith in the development of entrepreneurial intent and ability. *Entrepreneurship Theory and Practice.*

Christina, H., Suhud, U., & Rizan, M. (2018). Analisis Penerimaan dan Penggunaan Teknologi Ojek Online dengan TAM [JPEB]. *Jurnal Pendidikan Ekonomi Dan Bisnis, 6*(1), 34–44. doi:10.21009/JPEB.006.1.4

Chu, J., & Muneeza, A. (2019). Belt and road initiative and Islamic financing: The case in public private partnership infrastructure financing. *International Journal of Management and Applied Research, 6*(1), 24–40. doi:10.18646/2056.61.19-002

Chung, M., Ko, E., Joung, H., & Kim, S. J. (2020). Chatbot e-service and customer satisfaction regarding luxury brands. *Journal of Business Research, 117*, 587–595. doi:10.1016/j.jbusres.2018.10.004

Çizakça, M. (2014). *Can there be innovation in Islamic finance? Case study: Esham.* A paper was presented at the 11th IFSB Summit, New Markets and Frontiers for Islamic Finance: Innovation and the Regulatory Perimeter, Mauritius.

Çizakça, M. (2007). Democracy, economic development and maqasid al-shari'ah. *Review of Islamic Economics, 11*(1), 101–118.

Clarke, M. (2018). The belt and road initiative: Exploring Beijing's motivations and challenges for its new silk road. *Strategic Analysis, 42*(2), 84–102. doi:10.1080/09700161.2018.1439326

Coleman, J. S. (1988). Social Capital in the Creation of Human Capital. *American Journal of Sociology, 94*, 95–120. doi:10.1086/228943

Conner, M., & Armitage, C. J. (1998). Extending the theory of planned behavior: Review and avenues for further research. *Journal of Applied Social Psychology, 28*(15), 1429–1464. doi:10.1111/j.1559-1816.1998.tb01685.x

Corcoran-nantes, Y. (2016). Oxford Reference The Oxford Encyclopedia of Islam and Women Financial Institutions. January 2013, 1–8. https://doi.org/ doi:10.1093/acref

Cordazzo, M. (2005). IC statement vs environmental and social reports: An empirical analysis of their convergences in the Italian context. *Journal of Intellectual Capital*, *6*(3), 441–464. doi:10.1108/14691930510611166

Cormier, D., Aerts, W., Ledoux, M. J., & Magnan, M. (2009). Attributes of Social and Human Capital Disclosure and Information Asymmetry. *Canadian Journal of Administrative Sciences-Revue Canadienne Des Sciences De L Administration, 88*(1), 71–88.

Cornelissen, J. (2017). Editor's comments: Developing propositions, a process model, or a typology? Addressing the challenges of writing theory without a boilerplate. *Academy of Management Review*, *42*(1), 1–9. doi:10.5465/amr.2016.0196

Correa-Ruiz, C., & Abadia, J. M. (2011). Special issue on"social responsibility accounting and reporting in times of 'sustainability Downturn/crisis. *Revista de Contabilidad*, *14*(1), 1–25. doi:10.1016/S1138-4891(11)70032-2

Correia, A., Santos, C. M., & Barros, C. P. (2007). Tourism in Latin America: A choice analysis. *Annals of Tourism Research*, *34*(3), 610–629. doi:10.1016/j.annals.2007.01.007

Courneya, K. S. (1994). Predicting repeated behavior from intention: The issue of scale correspondence. *Journal of Applied Social Psychology*, *24*(7), 580–594. doi:10.1111/j.1559-1816.1994.tb00601.x

Creswell, J. W., & David Creswell, J. (n.d.). *Research Design: Qualitative*. Quantitative, and Mixed Methods Approaches.

Crick, J. M. (2021). Qualitative research in marketing: What can academics do better? *Journal of Strategic Marketing*, *29*(5), 390–429. doi:10.1080/0965254X.2020.1743738

Cuba, R., Decenzo, D., & Anish, A. (1983). Management Practices of Successful Female Business Owners. *American Journal of Small Business*, *8*(2), 40–46. doi:10.1177/104225878300800208

Dabla-Norris, M. E., Misch, F., Cleary, M. D., & Khwaja, M. (2017). *Tax administration and firm performance: New data and evidence for emerging market and developing economies*. International Monetary Fund.

Dang, T. T., & Vu, H. Q.DANG. (2020). Fintech in Microfinance: A new direction for Microfinance institutions in Vietnam. *Journal of Business Economics and Environmental Studies*, *10*(3), 13–22. doi:10.13106/jbees.2020.vol10.no3.13

Daoud, Y., & Kammoun, A. (2020). Islamic banking in North Africa: emergence, growth, and prospects. In A. Rafay, Growth and emerging prospects of international Islamic banking (pp. 78-98): IGI Global. doi:10.4018/978-1-7998-1611-9.ch005

Dariah, A. R. (2012). Improving Social Capital of BMT (Baitul Mal Wat Tamwil): An Experience From BMT Lathifah, Sumedang Indonesia. *The International Journal of Social Sciences (Islamabad)*, *4*(1), 64–70.

Davis, M. K. (2013). Entrepreneurship: An Islamic perspective. *International Journal of Entrepreneurship and Small Business*, *20*(1), 63–69. doi:10.1504/IJESB.2013.055693

Deegan, C., & Blomquist, C. (2006). Stakeholder influence on corporate reporting: An exploration of the interaction between WWF-Australia and the Australian minerals industry. *Accounting, Organizations and Society*, *31*(4–5), 343–372. doi:10.1016/j.aos.2005.04.001

Dehaghi, M., Goodarzi, M., & Arazi, Z. (2012). The effect of spiritual values on employees' organizational commitment and its models. *Procedia: Social and Behavioral Sciences*, *62*, 159–166. doi:10.1016/j.sbspro.2012.09.025

Delmar, F., & Wiklund, J. (2008). The effect of small business managers' growth motivation on firm growth: A longitudinal study. *Entrepreneurship Theory and Practice*, *32*(3), 437–457. doi:10.1111/j.1540-6520.2008.00235.x

Demirgüç-Kunt, A., Klapper, L., Singer, D., & Ansar, S. (2022). *The global findex database 2021: financial inclusion, digital payments, and resilience in the age of covid-19.* International Bank for Reconstruction and Development/The World Bank. doi:10.1596/978-1-4648-1897-4

Deng, W., & Hendrikse, G. (2014). *Cooperative Social Capital Towards a Lifecycle Perspective.* 1–6.

Deuraseh, N. (2009). Lawful and unlawful foods in Islamic law focus on Islamic medical and ethical aspects. *International Food Research Journal, 16*(4), 469–478.

DiCicco-Bloom, B., & Crabtree, B. F. (2006). The qualitative research interview. *Medical Education, 40*(4), 314–321. doi:10.1111/j.1365-2929.2006.02418.x PMID:16573666

Dieter, H., & Seibel, H. D. (2000). How values create value: social capital in microfinance-the case of the Philippines. In *Working Paper in Economics and Development Studies.*

DinarStandard. (2019). *State of the Global Islamic Economy Report 2019/20.* DinarStandard. https://www.dinarstandard.com/state-of-the-global-islamic-economy-report-2019-20/

Din, M. U., Khan, F., Khan, U., Kadarningsih, A., & Astuti, S. D. (2019). Effect Of Islamic Work Ethics On Job Performance: Mediating Role Of Intrinsic Motivation *IJBE, 4*(2), 676–688.

Ditlmann, R., & Paluck, E. L. (2015). Field experiments. In J. D. Wright (Ed.), *International encyclopedia of the social & behavioral sciences* (2nd ed., Vol. 9, pp. 128–134). Elsevier. doi:10.1016/B978-0-08-097086-8.10542-2

Djeflat, A. (2009a). Building systems for innovation "take off" in African economies. *African Journal of Science, Technology, Innovation and Development, 1*(1), 53–75.

Djeflat, A. (2009b). Universities and scientific research in the Maghreb states: Power politics and innovation systems. *International Journal of Technology Management, 45*(1/2), 102–113. doi:10.1504/IJTM.2009.021522

Dodd, M. (2016). Intangible resource management: Social capital theory development for public relations. *Journal of Communication Management (London), 20*(4), 1–41. doi:10.1108/JCOM-12-2015-0095

Dong, L., Yang, X., & Li, H. (2018). The Belt and Road Initiative and the 2030 Agenda for Sustainable Development: Seeking linkages for global environmental governance. *Zhongguo Renkou Ziyuan Yu Huanjing, 16*(3), 203–210. doi:10.1080/10042857.2018.1487745

Dowla, A. (2006). In credit we trust: Building social capital by Grameen Bank in Bangladesh. *Journal of Socio-Economics, 35*(1), 102–122. doi:10.1016/j.socec.2005.12.006

Dusuki, A.W. (2008). Banking for the poor: the role of Islamic banking in microfinance initiatives. *Humanomics, 24*(24), 49–66.

Dusuki, Aw. (2006). *Empowering Islamic Microfinance: Lesson from Group-Based Lending Scheme and Ibn Khaldun's Concept of 'Asabiyah.* Monash University.

Dutta, P., & Bose, S. (2006). *MP. 34*(6), 70–74.

Dwivedi, Y. K., Kapoor, K. K., & Chen, H. (2015). Social media marketing and advertising. *The Marketing Review, 15*(3), 289–309. doi:10.1362/146934715X14441363377999

Dworkin, S. L. (2012). Sample size policy for qualitative studies using in-depth interviews. *Archives of Sexual Behavior, 41*(6), 1319–1320. doi:10.100710508-012-0016-6 PMID:22968493

Ebrahimnejad, H. (2011). What is 'Islamic' in Islamic Medicine? An Overview. In *Boston Studies in the Philosophy and History of Science* (Vol. 275, pp. 259–270). Springer Nature., doi:10.1007/978-90-481-9968-6_17

Edvinsson, L., & Malone, M. S. (1997). *Intellectual Capital: Realizing your Company's true value by finding its hidden brainpower*. Harper Business.

El Bernoussi, Z. (2021). Developing the halal market: China's opportunity to strengthen MENA ties and address Uighur/hui issues. In *Rethinking Halal* (pp. 108–127). Brill. doi:10.1163/9789004459236_006

El Junusi, R. (2020). Digital marketing during the pandemic period; A study of islamic perspective. *Journal of Digital Marketing and Halal Industry*, *2*(1), 15–28. doi:10.21580/jdmhi.2020.2.1.5717

El Sayed, S., Al-quliti, A.-S., Salah Mahmoud, H., Baghdadi, H., Maria, A. R., Helmy Nabo, M., & Hefny, A. (2014). Therapeutic Benefits of Al-hijamah: in Light of Modern Medicine and Prophetic Medicine. American Journal of Medical and Biological Research, 2(2), 46–71. doi:10.12691/ajmbr-2-2-3

ElasragH. (2016). Halal industry: Key challenges and opportunities. SSRN *Journal*. doi:10.2139/ssrn.2735417

Eren, B. A. (2021). Determinants of customer satisfaction in chatbot use: Evidence from a banking application in Turkey. *International Journal of Bank Marketing*, *39*(2), 294–311. doi:10.1108/IJBM-02-2020-0056

Esther, H., Canino, B. R., Sánchez, B. R., & Agustín, M. (2011). The Impact of relational capital on the success of new business start-ups. *Journal of Small Business Management*, *49*(4), 617–638. doi:10.1111/j.1540-627X.2011.00339.x

Ethnology, S., & Summer, N. (2013). Muslim Women Traders of Northern Nigeria: Perspectives from the City of Yola. *Ethnology*, *32*(3), 217–236.

Etkowitz, H. (2002). *The triple helix of university - industry - government implications for policy and evaluation.* (Working Paper 11). Institutet för Studier av Utbildning och Forskning.

Etzkowitz, H. (2008). *The triple helix: University-industry-government innovation in action*. Routledge. doi:10.4324/9780203929605

Etzkowitz, H., Dzisah, J., Ranga, M., & Zhou, C. (2007). The triple helix model of innovation: University-industry-government interaction. *Asia-Pacific Tech Monitor*, (Jan-Feb), 14–23.

Etzkowitz, H., & Leydesdorff, L. (1995). The triple helix---university-industry-government relations: A laboratory for knowledge based economic development. *European Association for the Study of Science and Technology (EASST). RE:view*, *14*(1), 14–19.

Etzkowitz, H., & Leydesdorff, L. (1998). The endless transition: A "triple helix" of university-industry-government relations. *Minerva*, *36*(3), 203–208. doi:10.1023/A:1004348123030

Etzkowitz, H., & Leydesdorff, L. (2000). The dynamics of innovation: From national systems and 'mode 2' to a triple helix of university-industry-government relations. *Research Policy*, *29*(2), 109–123. doi:10.1016/S0048-7333(99)00055-4

Fakhrurozi, F., Najmudin, N., & Maelani, P. (2022). Do Islamic Business Ethics Have An Effect on Indonesian Citizens' Interest in Saving At The Faisal Islamic Bank of Egypt? A Case in Cairo, Egypt. *MUAMALATUNA*, *14*(2), 147–163. doi:10.37035/mua.v14i2.7093

Fan, Y., Chen, J., Shirkey, G., John, R., Wu, S.R. & Shao, H. (2016). Applications of structural equation modeling (SEM) in ecological studies: an updated review. *Springer Open*. https://ecologicalprocesses.springeropen.com/articles/10.1186/s13717-016-0063-3

Farooqi, A. H. (2006). Islamic social capital and networking. *Humanomics*, *22*(4), 113–125. doi:10.1108/08288660610669400

Farooq, M. O. (2007). Partnership, equity-financing and Islamic finance: Whither profit-loss sharing? *Review of Islamic Economics, 11*(Special Issue), 67–88.

Fathonih, A., Anggadwita, G., & Ibraimi, S. (2019). Sharia venture capital as financing alternative of Muslim entrepreneurs: Opportunities, challenges and future research directions. *Journal of Enterprising Communities: People and Places in the Global Economy, 13*(3), 333–352. doi:10.1108/JEC-11-2018-0090

Fernando, Y., Wahyuni-TD, I. S., Zainul Abideen, A., & Mergeresa, F. (2023). Traceability technology, halal logistics brand and logistics performance: Religious beliefs and beyond. *Journal of Islamic Marketing, 14*(4), 1007–1031. doi:10.1108/JIMA-06-2020-0183

Firer, S. (2005). Using intellectual capital as a success strategy in South Africa. *Southern African Business Review, 9*(1), 1–20.

Fishbein, M., & Ajzen, I. (1975). *Belief, Attitude, Intention, and Behaviour: An Introduction to Theory and Research.* Addison-Wesley.

Floren, J., Rasul, T., & Gani, A. (2020). Islamic marketing and consumer behaviour: A systematic literature review. *Journal of Islamic Marketing, 11*(6), 1557–1578. doi:10.1108/JIMA-05-2019-0100

Fozia, M., Rehman, A., & Farooq, A. (2016). Entrepreneurship and leadership: An Islamic perspective. International Journal of Economics. *Management and Accounting, 24*(1), 15–47.

Frangi, L., Zhang, T., & Hebdon, R. (2020). Tweeting and retweeting for fight for $15: Unions as dinosaur opinion leaders? *British Journal of Industrial Relations, 58*(2), 301–335. doi:10.1111/bjir.12482

Fukuyama, F. (1995). Social capital and the global economy. *Foreign Affairs, 74*(5), 89–103. doi:10.2307/20047302

Fuseini, A., Hadley, P., & Knowles, T. (2021). Halal food marketing: An evaluation of UK halal standards. *Journal of Islamic Marketing, 12*(5), 977–991. doi:10.1108/JIMA-02-2020-0037

Gait, A., & Worthington, A. C. (2015). Attitudes of Libyan retail consumers toward Islamic methods of finance. *International Journal of Islamic and Middle Eastern Finance and Management, 8*(4), 439–454. doi:10.1108/IMEFM-04-2013-0056

Garg, P., & Joshi, R. (2018). Purchase intention of "Halal" brands in India: The mediating effect of attitude. *Journal of Islamic Marketing, 9*(3), 683–694. doi:10.1108/JIMA-11-2017-0125

Gastmans, C., Bryon, E., Denier, Y., & De Casterle, B. D. (2012). QUAGOL : A guide for qualitative data analysis. *International Journal of Nursing Studies, 49*(3), 360–371. doi:10.1016/j.ijnurstu.2011.09.012 PMID:21996649

Ghalandari, Kamal & Norouzi, A. (2012). The Effect of Country of Origin on Purchase Intention: The role of product knowledge. *Research Journal of Applied Sciences, Engineering and Technology, 4*(9), 1166–1171.

Gicheru, E. (2016). *The role of the cooperative enterprise model in implementating the Sustainable Development Goals (SDGs) in Least Developed Countries (LDCs).*

Gittell, R., & Vidal, A. (1998). *Community organizing: Building social capital as a development strategy.* Sage publications. doi:10.4135/9781452220567

Gobir, A. Y. & Sani, A. (2018). The Jinn, Women Vulnerabilities and the Act of Healings in The Hausa Communities Of 21 st Century. *IOSR Journal Of Humanities And Social Science (IOSR-JHSS, 23*(1), 67. https://doi.org/ doi:10.9790/0837-2301056773

Gremyr, I., Birch-Jensen, A., Kumar, M., & Lofberg, N. (2022). Quality function's use of customer feedback as activation triggers for absorptive capacity and value co-creation. *International Journal of Operations & Production Management, 42*(13), 218–242. doi:10.1108/IJOPM-11-2021-0692

Greve, A., & Salaff, J. W. (2003). Theory: Entrepreneurs and Network Activities Social Capital and Social Network. *Entrepreneurship Theory and Practice, 28*(1), 1–22. https://onlinelibrary.wiley.com/store/10.1111/1540-8520.00029/asset/1540-8520.00029.pdf?v=1&t=j9ywa8bj&s=c1a6cb2ad31d88b1d8e8614619fb76a49c584751. doi:10.1111/1540-8520.00029

Groen, R. P. G. (2002). *Making sense of microcredit interest rates.* The Consultative Group to Assist the Poor (CGAP) Donor Information Resource Centre (DIRECT).

Guizani, M. (2020). Testing the pecking order theory of capital structure: The case of Islamic financing modes. *Future Business Journal, 6*(1), 1–12. doi:10.118643093-020-00042-9

Gulzar, S., & Munir, M. (2019). Economic Empowerment of Women and Challenges in Pakistan: An Analytical Study in Islamic Perspective. *Al-Aẕvā, 34*(52).

Gümüsay, A. A. (2015). Entrepreneurship from an Islamic perspective. *Journal of Business Ethics, 130*(1), 199–208. doi:10.100710551-014-2223-7

Gümüş, N., & Onurlubas, E. (2023). Investigation of Factors Affecting Generation Z's Halal Cosmetics Adoption. *Marketing and Management of Innovations, 14*(1), 1–11. doi:10.21272/mmi.2023.1-01

Gupta, A., & Sharma, D. (2019). Customers' Attitude towards Chatbots in Banking Industry of India. *International Journal of Innovative Technology and Exploring Engineering, 8*(11), 1222–1225. doi:10.35940/ijitee.J9366.0981119

Hagaman, A. K., & Wutich, A. (2017). How Many Interviews Are Enough to Identify Metathemes in Multisited and Cross-cultural Research? Another Perspective on Guest, Bunce, and Johnson's (2006) Landmark Study. *Field Methods, 29*(1), 23–41. doi:10.1177/1525822X16640447

Hair, J., Sarstedt, M., Hopkins, L., & Kuppelwieser, V. (2014). Partial Least Squares Structural Equation Modeling (PLS-SEM): An Emerging Tool for Business Research. *European Business Review, 26*(2), 106–121. doi:10.1108/EBR-10-2013-0128

Hakim, A., & Razak, A. (2015). the Fundamentals of Islamic Banking and Finance: A Prologue. *European Journal of Islamic Finance, 0*(2), 1–11. doi:10.13135/2421-2172/790

Hallencreutz, J., & Parmler, J. (2021). Important drivers for customer satisfaction–from product focus to image and service quality. *Total Quality Management & Business Excellence, 32*(5–6), 501–510. doi:10.1080/14783363.2019.1594756

Hamza, W. A. (2017, June 1). The Maghreb union is one of the world's worst-performing trading blocs. here are five ways to change that. *World Economic Forum.* https://www.weforum.org/agenda/2017/06/five-ways-to-make-maghreb-work/

Hamzah, A. (2010). Malaysian Homestays from the Perspective of Young Japanese Tourists. The Quest for Furusato. *Asian Tourism: Growth and Change, 2.* . doi:10.1016/B978-0-08-045356-9.50021-7

Hanafiah, M. H., & Hamdan, N. A. A. (2020). Determinants of Muslim travellers Halal food consumption attitude and behavioural intentions. *Journal of Islamic Marketing.*

Handayani, S. A. (2016). Money and the culture of debt in the ex-cresidence of Besuki in cross history. *Paramita: Historical Studies Journal, 26*(2), 203–216.

Handriana, T., Yulianti, P., Kurniawati, M., Arina, N. A., Aisyah, R. A., Ayu Aryani, M. G., & Wandira, R. K. (2021). Purchase behavior of millennial female generation on Halal cosmetic products. *Journal of Islamic Marketing, 12*(7), 1295–1315. doi:10.1108/JIMA-11-2019-0235

Haniffa, R., & Hudaib, M. A. (2002). A theoretical framework for the development of the Islamic perspective of accounting. *Accounting. Commerce and Finance: The Islamic Perspective Journal, 6*(1/2), 1–71.

Han, Y., & Li, D. (2015). Effects of intellectual capital on innovative performance: The role of knowledge-based dynamic capability. *Management Decision, 53*(1), 40–56. doi:10.1108/MD-08-2013-0411

Haque, N. A., Chowdhury, N. A., Yasmin, F., & Tarofder, A. K. (2019). Chowdhury, F. Yasmin, & A. K. Tarofder (2019). Muslim Consumers' Purchase Behavior Towards Shariah Compliant Hotels in Malaysia. *VJM, 05*(1), 121–138. doi:10.31357/vjm.v5i1.3918

Hari, H., Iyer, R., & Sampat, B. (2022). Customer brand engagement through chatbots on bank websites–Examining the antecedents and consequences. *International Journal of Human-Computer Interaction, 38*(13), 1212–1227. doi:10.1080/10447318.2021.1988487

Harizan, S. H. M., & Mustafa, M. S. (2020). Islamic Entrepreneurship: Analysis of Research Trend. *Islamiyyat, 42*(2), 71–84. doi:10.17576/islamiyyat-2020-4202-07

Hasan, M. (2020). Social marketing: An Islamic perspective. *Journal of Islamic Marketing, 11*(4), 863–881. doi:10.1108/JIMA-12-2016-0105

Hasan, R., Hassan, M. K., & Aliyu, S. (2020). Fintech and Islamic finance: Literature review and research agenda. [IJIEF]. *International Journal of Islamic Economics and Finance, 3*(1), 75–94. doi:10.18196/ijief.2122

Hashim, N., & Hamzah, M. I. (2014). 7P's: A literature Review of Islamic marketing and Contemporary Marketing MIx. *Procedia: Social and Behavioral Sciences, 130*, 155–159. doi:10.1016/j.sbspro.2014.04.019

Hashmi, S. D., & Gulzar, S. (2020). Does Diversity Matter for Religious Firms Too? Board Gender Diversity and Corporate Choices of Shar¯ı'ah Compliant Firms. [JIBM]. *Journal of Islamic Business and Management, 10*(01), 170–187. doi:10.26501/jibm/2020.1001-011

Hassan, A. (2015). Financial inclusion of the poor: From microcredit to Islamic microfinancial services. *Humanomics, 3112*(11), 354–371. doi:10.1108/H-07-2014-0051

Hassan, A., & Saleem, S. (2017). An Islamic microfinance business model in Bangladesh. *Humanomics, 33*(1), 15–37. doi:10.1108/H-08-2016-0066

HassanM. K.HipplerW. (2014). Entrepreneurship and Islam: an overview. Available at SSRN 3263110.

Hassan, M. K., Rabbani, M. R., & Chebab, D. (2021). Integrating Islamic finance and Halal industry: Current landscape and future forward. *International Journal of Islamic Marketing and Branding, 6*(1), 60–78. doi:10.1504/IJIMB.2021.117594

Hassan, R., & Nor, F. M. (2019). Value-based Intermediation: The Shari'ah Perspective. [IJFUS]. *International Journal of Fiqh and Usul Al-Fiqh Studies, 3*(1), 81–89.

Hassan, S. H., Mohamed Haniba, N. M., & Ahmad, N. H. (2019). Social customer relationship management (s-CRM) among small-and medium-sized enterprises (SMEs) in Malaysia. *International Journal of Ethics and Systems, 35*(2), 284–302. doi:10.1108/IJOES-11-2017-0192

Hassan, S., Marimuthu, M., & de Run, E. (2013). Conceptualizing Convergence and Divergence of Muslim Consumption behaviour in Malaysia. *Indian Journal of Management Science, 3*(4), 1–7.

Hayton, J. C. (2005). Competing in the new economy: The effect of intellectual capital on corporate entrepreneurship in high-technology new ventures. *R & D Management, 35*(2), 137–155. doi:10.1111/j.1467-9310.2005.00379.x

Hendayani, R., & Fernando, Y. (2022). Adoption of blockchain technology to improve Halal supply chain performance and competitiveness. *Journal of Islamic Marketing.*

Herhausen, D., Miočević, D., Morgan, R. E., & Kleijnen, M. H. (2020). The digital marketing capabilities gap. *Industrial Marketing Management, 90*, 276–290. doi:10.1016/j.indmarman.2020.07.022

Hidayat, S. E., & Musari, K. (2023, forthcoming). Towards the global halal MSMEs hub through the digitally-enabled society: an institutional arrangement with Islamic n-tuple helix. In A. Rafiki (Ed.), Digitalization in halal management. Springer.

Hidayati, N., & Sunaryo, H. (2021). The role of halal label to increase the effect of attitude toward halal product on brand image and purchase intention. [International Journal of Entrepreneurship and Business Development]. *IJEBD, 4*(5), 744–752. doi:10.29138/ijebd.v4i5.1496

Hidayat, S. E., Rafiki, A., & Nasution, M. D. T. P. (2022). Halal industry's response to a current and post-COVID-19 landscape and lessons from the past. *Journal of Islamic Marketing, 13*(9), 1843–1857. doi:10.1108/JIMA-06-2020-0180

Hildebrand, C., & Bergner, A. (2019). AI-driven sales automation: Using chatbots to boost sales. *NIM Marketing Intelligence Review, 11*(2), 36–41. doi:10.2478/nimmir-2019-0014

Holloh, D. (2001). *Microfinance Institutions Study.* FinDev.

Hooy, C. W., & Ali, R. (2017). Does a Muslim CEO matter in Shariah-compliant companies? Evidence from Malaysia. *Pacific-Basin Finance Journal, 42*, 126–141. doi:10.1016/j.pacfin.2016.08.010

Hoque, M. E., Nik Hashim, N. M. H., & Azmi, M. H. B. (2018). Moderating effects of marketing communication and financial consideration on customer attitude and intention to purchase Islamic banking products: A conceptual framework. *Journal of Islamic Marketing, 9*(4), 799–822. doi:10.1108/JIMA-01-2017-0005

Hoque, M. J., Rahman, M. A., & Razia, S. (2014). Women Entrepreneurship Development under Islamic Perspective-A Study on Some Selected Muslim Women Entrepreneurs of Bangladesh. *World Review of Business Research, 4*(3), 45–63.

Hoque, N., Mamun, A., & Mamun, A. M. A. (2014). Dynamics and traits of entrepreneurship: An Islamic approach. *World Journal of Entrepreneurship, Management and Sustainable Development, 10*(2), 128–142. doi:10.1108/WJEMSD-04-2013-0027

Hosain, M. S. (2021). Branding "Halal": Application of a certain religious emotion to attract a specific customer segment. *PSU Research Review, 5*(3), 195–200. doi:10.1108/PRR-12-2020-0043

Hossain, M., & Diaz, C. P. (1997). Reaching the poor eith effective microcredit: evaluation of a grameen bank replication in the Philippines. *Journal of Philippines Development, 44*, (2), 275-308.

Hosseini, S. M. P., Mirzaei, M., & Iranmanesh, M. (2019). Determinants of Muslims' willingness to pay for halal certified food. *Journal of Islamic Marketing.*

Hsu, Y. Y., & Fang, W. (2009). Intellectual capital and new product development performance: The mediating role of organizational learning capability. *Technological Forecasting and Social Change, 76*(5), 664–677. doi:10.1016/j.techfore.2008.03.012

Hudon, M. (2008). Norms and values of the various microfinance institutions. *International Journal of Social Economics, 35*(1/2), 35–48. doi:10.1108/03068290810843828

Hunter, M. G. (2012). Creating qualitative interview protocols. *International Journal of Sociotechnology and Knowledge Development*, *4*(3), 1–16. doi:10.4018/jskd.2012070101

Ibrahim, M. A., Fisol, W. N. M., & Haji-Othman, Y. (2017). Customer intention on Islamic home financing products: An application of theory of planned behavior (TPB). *Mediterranean Journal of Social Sciences*, *8*(2), 77–77. doi:10.5901/mjss.2017.v8n2p77

Ibrahim, Y. (2004). Homestay Programme in Malaysia. *ASEAN Journal on Hospitality and Tourism*, *3*(1), 65–75.

Illescas-Manzano, M. D., Vicente López, N., Afonso González, N., & Cristofol Rodríguez, C. (2021). Implementation of chatbot in online commerce, and open innovation. *Journal of Open Innovation*, *7*(2), 125. doi:10.3390/joitmc7020125

IMF. (2018). Economic integration in the Maghreb – an untapped source of growth. Washington, DC: International Monetary Fund (IMF).

Indonesia, Ip. (2019). *Bandingkan Harga, Promo, Kode Kupon & Diskon*. IPrice Indonesia. https://iprice.co.id/

Indriani, S. S., Limilia, P., & Alam, P. W. (2022). Opinion Leaders and Health Information: A Systematic Literature Review in Indonesia. In *Proceedings of International Conference on Communication Science*, (pp. 737-744). IEEE. 10.29303/iccsproceeding.v2i1.110

IOG. (2003). *Governance Principles for Protected Areas in the 21st Century: Prepared for the Fifth World* (J. Graham, B. Amos, & T. Plumptre (eds.)). Parks Congress Durban, Ottawa.

Iqbal, M. (2005). *General Takaful Practice: Technical Approach to Eliminate Gharar (uncertainty), Maisir (gambling), and Riba'(usury)*. Gema Insani.

Iqbal, Z., & Mirakhor, A. (2004). Stakeholders model of governance in Islamic economic system. *Islamic Economic Studies*, *11*(2).

Iranmanesh, M., Mirzaei, M., Parvin Hosseini, S. M., & Zailani, S. (2019). Muslims' willingness to pay for certified halal food: An extension of the theory of planned behaviour. *Journal of Islamic Marketing*, *11*(1), 14–30. doi:10.1108/JIMA-03-2018-0049

Iranmanesh, M., Senali, M. G., Ghobakhloo, M., Nikbin, D., & Abbasi, G. A. (2022). Customer behaviour towards halal food: A systematic review and agenda for future research. *Journal of Islamic Marketing*, *13*(9), 1901–1917. doi:10.1108/JIMA-01-2021-0031

Isa, S. M., Chin, P. N., & Mohammad, N. U. (2018). Muslim tourist perceived value: A study on Malaysia Halal tourism. *Journal of Islamic Marketing*, *9*(2), 402–420. doi:10.1108/JIMA-11-2016-0083

IsDB. (2020). IsDB annual report 2020 – Respond, restore, restart: post-covid resilience and prosperity for all. Jeddah: Islamic Development Bank (IsDB).

IsDB. (2021). IsDB annual report 2021 – Beyond recovery: resilience and sustainability. Jeddah: Islamic Development Bank (IsDB).

Ismaeel, M., & Blaim, K. (2012). Toward applied Islamic business ethics: Responsible halal business. *Journal of Management Development*, *31*(10), 1090–1100. doi:10.1108/02621711211281889

Ismail, A. T. B., & Asnawi, A. R. (2021). Issues in Scientific Approach to Ḥadīth Commentary A Critical Study of Selected Hadiths on Prophetic Medicine. *Al-Burhān Journal of Qur'an and Sunnah Studies, 5*(Special Issue 1), 1-.

Ismail, M. S. I., Harun, T. W. R., Ismail, S., Aziz, A., & Ibrahim, M. A. (2022). *Definition of Islamic Brand: A Study From Islamic Conjuction and its Findings.*

Ismal, R. (2012). *The Indonesian Islamic banking: performance and outlook.* Presentation for Panel Discussion held by Bakrie University in Jakarta.

Jabłoński, A., & Jabłoński, M. (2020). *Social business models in the digital economy new concepts and contemporary challenges.* Cham, Switzerland: Palgrave Macmillan, Springer Nature. doi:10.1007/978-3-030-29732-9

Jaffee, S., & Hyde, J. S. (2000). Gender differences in moral orientation: A meta-analysis. *Psychological Bulletin, 126*(5), 703–726. doi:10.1037/0033-2909.126.5.703 PMID:10989620

Jahar, A. (2018). *Managing social capital in developing Islamic Microfinance enterprises BMT in Muslim countries: case study in Indonesia and Pakistan.* Research Gate.

Jaiyeoba, H. B., Abdullah, M. A., & Dzuljastri, A. R. (2020). Halal certification mark, brand quality, and awareness: Do they influence buying decisions of Nigerian consumers? *Journal of Islamic Marketing, 11*(6), 1657–1670. doi:10.1108/JIMA-07-2019-0155

Janah, S., & Subiyantoro, S. (2022). Social responsibility on islamic spiritual entrepreneurs for blessing of life and successful entrepreneurship. *At-Tijaroh Jurnal Ilmu Manajemen Dan Bisnis Islam, 8*(2), 199-206. doi:10.24952/tijaroh.v8i2.5192

Jansom, A., Srisangkhajorn, T., & Limarunothai, W. (2022). How chatbot e-services motivate communication credibility and lead to customer satisfaction: The perspective of Thai consumers in the apparel retailing context. *Innovative Marketing, 18*(3), 13–25. doi:10.21511/im.18(3).2022.02

Jardon, C. M., & Martos, M. S. (2012). Intellectual capital as a competitive advantage in emerging clusters in Latin America. *Journal of Intellectual Capital, 13*(4), 462–481. doi:10.1108/14691931211276098

Jobst, A., Kunzel, P., Mills, P., & Sy, A. (2008). Islamic bond issuance: What sovereign debt managers need to know. *International Journal of Islamic and Middle Eastern Finance and Management, 1*(4), 330–344. doi:10.1108/17538390810919637

Johan, Z. J., Hussain, M. Z., Mohd, R., & Kamaruddin, B. H. (2020). Muslims and non-Muslims intention to hold Shariah-compliant credit cards: A SmartPLS approach. *Journal of Islamic Marketing, 12*(9), 1751–1785. doi:10.1108/JIMA-12-2019-0270

Johnson, W. H. A. (1999). An Integrative Taxonomy of Intellectual Capital: Measuring the Stock and Flow of Intellectual Capital Components in the Firm. *International Journal of Technology Management, 18*(5–8), 562–575. doi:10.1504/IJTM.1999.002788

Jordão, R. V. D., & de Almeida, V. R. (2017). Performance measurement, intellectual capital and financial sustainability. *Journal of Intellectual Capital, 18*(3), 643–666. doi:10.1108/JIC-11-2016-0115

Joshi, M., Cahill, D., & Sidhu, J. (2010). Intellectual capital performance in the banking sector: An assessment of Australian owned banks. *Journal of Human Resource Costing and Accounting, 14*(2), 151–170. doi:10.1108/14013381011062649

Joshi, R., & Garg, P. (2022). Assessing brand love, brand sacredness and brand fidelity towards halal brands. *Journal of Islamic Marketing, 13*(4), 807–823. doi:10.1108/JIMA-04-2020-0104

Juliana, J., Rahayu, A., & Wardhani, Y. (2020). Muslimpreneur intentions: Analysis of family background. *Jurnal Kajian Peradaban Islam, 3*(1), 10–15. doi:10.47076/jkpis.v3i1.35

Juliana, J., Ropi, M., Udin, S., & Husnul, K. (2017). Syariapreneur: The New Paradigm Of Islamic-Based Entrepreneurship. In *1st International Conference On Islamic Economics, Business, And Philanthropy (Iciebp 2017)* (pp. 668-672). ScitePress. 10.5220/0007087706680672

Jumani, Z. A., & Sukhabot, S. (2021). Identifying the important attitude of Islamic brands and its effect on buying behavioural intentions among Malaysian Muslims: A quantitative study using smart-PLS. *Journal of Islamic Marketing, 12*(2), 408–426. doi:10.1108/JIMA-09-2019-0196

Kaczorowska-Spychalska, D. (2019). How chatbots influence marketing. *Management, 23*(1), 251–270. doi:10.2478/manment-2019-0015

Kadri, T. (2018), *Rancangan Penelitian.* Deepublisheer, Yogyakarya. https://books.google.co.id/books?id=_-tmDwAAQBAJ&pg=PR5&lpg=PR5&dq=Kadri,+Trihono.+2018.+Rancangan+Penelitian.+Yogyakarta:+Deepublish.&source=bl&ots=7LrPeP4J8i&sig=ACfU3U23xBOkVHiWqJ6pdZcxETul_LkOsg&hl=en&sa=X&ved=2ahUKEwjb48nric_oAhURXn0KHZACAwwQ6AEwAXoE (accessed 4 April 2020).

Kamali, M. H. (2008). *Shari'ah law: an introduction.* Simon and Schuster.

Kamali, M. H. (2015). *The middle path of moderation in Islam: The Qur'anic principle of wasatiyyah.* Oxford University Press. doi:10.1093/acprof:oso/9780190226831.001.0001

Kamal, R. M., & Azis, E. (2015). Internet Technology Adoption by Consumer MSMEs to Online Shopping (Study at Tokopedia.com in 2015). In M. Se (Ed.), *Dr.Maya Ariyanti* (pp. 147–152). Managing Business for Smart Economy.

Kamarulzaman, N. H., Muhamad, N. A., & Mohd Nawi, N. (2022). An investigation of adoption intention of halal traceability system among food SMEs. *Journal of Islamic Marketing, 13*(9), 1872–1900. doi:10.1108/JIMA-11-2020-0349

Kammer, A., Norat, M., Pinon, M., Prasad, A., Towe, C., & Zeidane, Z. (2015). Islamic Finance: Opportunities, Challenges, and Policy Options. In Staff Discussion Notes (Vol. 15, Issue 5). doi:10.5089/9781498325035.006

Kamukama, N., & Natamba, B. (2013). Social intermediation and financial services access in Uganda's microfinance industry. *African Journal of Economic and Management Studies, 4*(3), 358–371. doi:10.1108/AJEMS-10-2011-0077

Kapitan, S., & Silvera, D. H. (2016). From digital media influencers to celebrity endorsers: Attributions drive endorser effectiveness. *Marketing Letters, 27*(2), 553–567. doi:10.100711002-015-9363-0

Karakas, F. (2010). Spirituality and Performance in Organizations: A Literature Review. *Journal of Business Ethics, 94*(1), 94–106. doi:10.100710551-009-0251-5

Kasim, M. M., Kayat, K., Ramli, R., & Ramli, R. (2016). Sustainability Criteria for the Malaysia Homestay Programme. *International Review of Management and Marketing, 6*, 1–7.

Kato, M. P., & Kratzer, J. (2013). Empowering women through microfinance: Evidence from Tanzania. The Academic Collaboration and Research Network, Austria, Cambridge UK (ACRN). *Journal of Entrepreneurship Perspectives, 2*(1), 31–59.

Katuk, N., Ku-Mahamud, K. R., Kayat, K., Abdul Hamid, M. N., Zakaria, N. H., & Purbasari, A. (2021). Halal certification for tourism marketing: The attributes and attitudes of food operators in Indonesia. *Journal of Islamic Marketing, 12*(5), 1043–1062. doi:10.1108/JIMA-03-2020-0068

Katz, E., Lazarsfeld, P. F., & Roper, E. (2017). Personal influence: The part played by people in the flow of mass communications. *The American Journal of Psychology, 70*(1), 157.

Kayed, R. N., & Hassan, M. K. (2013). *Islamic entrepreneurship.* Routledge. doi:10.4324/9780203840801

Kazkaz, L. (2020). Role of New Opinion Leaders on Social Media in Political and Religious Polarization (Jordanian case study). *Lebanese Science Journal, 21*(2), 211–229. doi:10.22453/LSJ-021.2.211-229

Keep, W. W., Hollander, S. C., & Dickinson, R. (1998). Forces impinging on long-term business-to- business relationships in the United States: An historical perspective. *Journal of Marketing*, *62*(2), 31–45. doi:10.1177/002224299806200203

Keong Choong, K. (2008). Intellectual capital: Definitions, categorization and reporting models. *Journal of Intellectual Capital*, *9*(4), 609–638. doi:10.1108/14691930810913186

Khaled, Y., Eschweiler, S., & Gerhards-Padilla, E. (2013, October). REcompile: A decompilation framework for static analysis of binaries (Paper presentation). *8th International Conference on Malicious and Unwanted Software: The Americas (MALWARE)*, IEEE.

Khalique, M., & Isa, A., Shaari, Abdul, J., & Ageel, A. (2011). Challenges faced by the small and medium enterprises (SMEs) in Malaysia: An intellectual capital perspective. *International Journal of Current Research*, *3*(6), 398–401.

Khan, A., Mohammad, A. S., & Muhammad, S. (2021). An integrated model of brand experience and brand love for halal brands: Survey of halal fast food consumers in Malaysia. *Journal of Islamic Marketing*, *12*(8), 1492–1520. doi:10.1108/JIMA-11-2019-0236

Khan, H., & Sonko, K. N. M. (Eds.). (2020). *Islamic finance as a complex system: new insights*. Lexington Books.

Khaniwale, M. (2015). Consumer buying behaviour. *International Journal of Innovation and Scientific Research*, *14*(2), 278–286.

Khan, S., Zaman, I., Khan, M. I., & Musleha, Z. (2022). Role of Influencers in Digital Marketing: The moderating impact of follower's interaction. *Gmjacs*, *12*(1), 15–43. doi:10.59263/gmjacs.12.01.2022.218

Khoa, B. T. (2021). The Impact of Chatbots on the Relationship between Integrated Marketing Communication and Online Purchasing Behavior in The Frontier Market. *Jurnal The Messenger*, *13*(1), 19–32. doi:10.26623/themessenger.v13i1.2439

Kirsch, A. (2018). The gender composition of corporate boards: A review and research agenda. *The Leadership Quarterly*, *29*(2), 346–364. doi:10.1016/j.leaqua.2017.06.001

Kmeid, R. (2015). Islamic Finance vs Ethical Finance. *Islamic Finance Today*, 18–20. https://pdfs.semanticscholar.org/d986/ba2251648577b3c3e96ab4397c9ffaa7bd92.pdf

Kock, N., & Hadaya, P. (2016). Minimum sample size estimation in PLS-SEM: The inverse square root and gamma-exponential methods. *Information Systems Journal*, *28*(1), 227–261. doi:10.1111/isj.12131

Kok, S. K. (2021). The branding of religious financial institutions in the UK: Conversations with market actors within the Islamic financial sector. *Journal of Islamic Marketing*, *12*(4), 900–917. doi:10.1108/JIMA-01-2020-0016

Kostova, T., & Roth, K. (2003). Social capital in multinational corporations and a micro-macro model of its formation. *Academy of Management Review*, *28*(2), 297–317. doi:10.2307/30040714

Kozlenkova, I. V., Hult, G. T. M., Lund, D. J., Mena, J. A., & Kekec, P. (2015). The role of marketing channels in supply chain management. *Journal of Retailing*, *91*(4), 586–609. doi:10.1016/j.jretai.2015.03.003

Krafft, M., Goetz, O., Mantrala, M., Sotgiu, F., & Tillmanns, S. (2015). ion of marketing channel research domains and methodologies: An integrative review and future directions. *Journal of Retailing*, *91*(4), 569–585. doi:10.1016/j.jretai.2015.05.001

Kühn, J., & Riesmeyer, C. (2021). Brand Endorsers with Role Model Function. MedienPädagogik. *Zeitschrift Für Theorie Und Praxis der Medienbildung*, *43*(43), 67–96. doi:10.21240/mpaed/43/2021.07.25.X

Kujansivu, P., & Lönnqvist, A. (2007). Investigating the value and efficiency of intellectual capital. *Journal of Intellectual Capital*, *8*(2), 272–287. doi:10.1108/14691930710742844

Kumar, P. (2015). Green marketing innovations in small Indian firms. *World Journal of Entrepreneurship, Management and Sustainable Development, 11*(3), 176–190. doi:10.1108/WJEMSD-01-2015-0003

Kutsiyah, F. (2020). Social capital and its transformations in Sidogiri Islamic boarding school. Karsa: *Jurnal Sosial dan Budaya Keislaman, 28*(1), 57-94. doi:10.19105/karsa.v28i1.3058

Kweh, Q. L., Lu, W.-M., & Wang, W.-K. (2014). Dynamic efficiency: Intellectual capital in the Chinese non-life insurance firms. *Journal of Knowledge Management, 18*(5), 937–951. doi:10.1108/JKM-06-2014-0240

Κάγιας, Κ. (2020). Social media marketing σε ξενοδοχειακές μονάδες. *Фундаментальные Исследования, 2016*(2), 1–10. https://anaktisis.uowm.gr/10491/

Laras, A. A. (2018). Tiga Celah Pengembangan E-Commerce di Indonesia - Analisis Data. *Katadata.Co.Id*, https://katadata.co.id/analisisdata/2018/10/23/tiga-celah-pengembangan-e-commerce-di-indonesia

Lateef, A. W., Abdurrazzaq, A. A., Shukor, S. A., & Tajudin, A. A. (2017). Maqasid Al-Shari'ah in Ijarah (Leasing) Contract of Islamic Banking System. *Journal of Islamic Finance, 6*(2), 038-044.

Lawan, A. & Dahalin, Z.M. (2011). Conceptual Model of the Unified Theory of Acceptance and Use of Technology (UTAUT). *Journal of Information Systems : New Pardigms, 1*(1), 43–46.

Ledhem, M. A., & Moussaoui, W. (2021). Islamic finance for entrepreneurship activities and economic growth: a parametric and non-parametric analysis from Malaysia. *PSU Research Review*. doi:10.1108/PRR-02-2021-0012

Ledhem, M. A., & Mekidiche, M. (2022). Islamic finance and economic growth: The Turkish experiment. *ISRA International Journal of Islamic Finance, 14*(1), 4–19. doi:10.1108/IJIF-12-2020-0255

Lee, M. J., & Back, K. J. (2008). Association meeting participation: A test of competing models. *Journal of Travel Research, 46*(3), 300–310. doi:10.1177/0047287507308320

Lee, T. A., & Tweedie, D. P. (1975). Accounting information: An investigation of private shareholder usage. *Accounting and Business Research, 5*(20), 280–291. doi:10.1080/00014788.1975.9728653

Leibenstine, H. (1978). *General X-Efficiency Theory and Economic Deployment*. Oxford University Press.

Leikem, K. (2012). Microfinance: a tool for poverty reduction? *Senior Honors Projects*. Digital Commons. https://digitalcommons.uri.edu/srhonorsprog/300

Lev, B. (2001). *Intangibles: Management, Measurement and Reporting*. Brookings Institution Press.

Lev, B., & Zarowin, P. (1999). The Boundaries of Financial Reporting and How to Extend Them. *Journal of Accounting Research, 37*(2), 353–385. doi:10.2307/2491413

Levin, G. (2012). Critique of microcredit as a development model. *Pursuit - The Journal of Undergraduate Research at the University of Tennessee, 4*(1), 109–117.

Lidyah, R. (2018). Islamic corporate governance, islamicityfinancial performance index and fraudat Islamic bank. *Jurnal Akuntansi, 22*(3), 437–453. doi:10.24912/ja.v22i3.398

Li, F., Larimo, J., & Leonidou, L. C. (2021). Social media marketing strategy: Definition, conceptualization, taxonomy, validation, and future agenda. *Journal of the Academy of Marketing Science, 49*(1), 51–70. doi:10.100711747-020-00733-3

Li, J., & Dutta, D. K. (2018). Founding team experience, industry context, and new venture creation. *New England Journal of Entrepreneurship, 21*(1), 2–21. doi:10.1108/NEJE-04-2018-0008

Lisnawati, D., & Ahman, H. E. (2019). Relationship between Entrepreneurial Characteristics from Islamic Perspective and the Performance of Small and Medium-Sized Businesses (A Study of SMEs in Indonesia). *KnE Social Sciences*, (pp. 576-593). KNE Publishing. doi:10.18502/kss.v3i13.4232

Liu, W., & Dunford, M. (2016). Inclusive globalization: Unpacking China's belt and road initiative. *Area Development and Policy*, *1*(3), 323–340. doi:10.1080/23792949.2016.1232598

Li, Y., Ye, F., & Sheu, C. (2014). Social capital, information sharing and performance: Evidence from China. *International Journal of Operations & Production Management*, *34*(11), 1440–1462. doi:10.1108/IJOPM-03-2013-0132

Lo Presti, L., Maggiore, G., & Marino, V. (2021). The role of the chatbot on customer purchase intention: Towards digital relational sales. *Italian Journal of Marketing*, *2021*(3), 165–188. doi:10.100743039-021-00029-6

Lubbe, I., & Ngoma, N. (2021). Useful chatbot experience provides technological satisfaction: An emerging market perspective. *South African Journal of Information Management*, *23*(1), 1–8. doi:10.4102ajim.v23i1.1299

Lumpkin, G. T., & Dess, G. G. (1996). Clarifying the entrepreneurial orientation construct and linking it to performance. *Academy of Management Review*, *21*(1), 135–172. doi:10.2307/258632

Luo, B., Lau, R. Y., Li, C., & Si, Y. W. (2022). A critical review of state-of-the-art chatbot designs and applications. *Wiley Interdisciplinary Reviews. Data Mining and Knowledge Discovery*, *12*(1), e1434. doi:10.1002/widm.1434

Macchiavello, E. (2016). Microfinance and Financial inclusion: the challenge of regulating alternative forms of finance (introduction). *Microfinance andfinancial inclusion: the challenge of regulating alternative forms offinance*. Routledge.

Machado, C. (2013). *The Importance of Social Capital for Small Business Owners: An Entrepreneurial Marketing Approach for Decision Making*. 1–15.

Machmud, A., & Hidayat, Y. M. (2020). Characteristics of Islamic entrepreneurship and the business success of SMEs in Indonesia. *Journal of Entrepreneurship Education*, *23*(2), 1–16.

MacInnis, D. J. (2011). A framework for conceptual contributions in marketing. *Journal of Marketing*, *75*(4), 136–154. doi:10.1509/jmkg.75.4.136

Magnini, V. P., Garcia, C., & Honeycutt, E. D. Jr. (2010). Identifying the attributes of an effective restaurant chain endorser. *Cornell Hospitality Quarterly*, *51*(2), 238–250. doi:10.1177/1938965510363669

Mahadi, N. F., Zain, N. R. M., & Ali, E. R. A. E. (2019). *Leading Towards Impactful Islamic Social Finance: Malaysian Experience with The Value-Based Intermediation Approach. Al-Shajarah: Journal of the International Institute of Islamic Thought and Civilization.*

Mahanti, J. (2008). Women helping women through nano finance institution. *Ashanet.* http://www.ashanet.org/detroit/Projects/BISWA/Nano_Finance_Report_ Jan2008.pdf

Maideen, N. M. P. (2020). Prophetic Medicine-Nigella Sativa (Black Cumin Seeds) – Potential Herb for COVID-19? In Journal of Pharmacopuncture, 23(2), 62–70. Korean Pharmacopuncture Institute. doi:10.3831/KPI.2020.23.010

Majid, M. A. A., Othman, M., Mohamad, S. F., Lim, S. A. H., & Yusof, A. (2017). Piloting for Interviews in Qualitative Research: Operationalization and Lessons Learnt. *International Journal of Academic Research in Business & Social Sciences*, *7*(4). Advance online publication. doi:10.6007/IJARBSS/v7-i4/2916

Malterud, K., Siersma, V. D., & Guassora, A. D. (2016). Sample Size in Qualitative Interview Studies: Guided by Information Power. *Qualitative Health Research*, *26*(13), 1753–1760. doi:10.1177/1049732315617444 PMID:26613970

Mamatzakis, E., Alexakis, C., Al Yahyaee, K., Pappas, V., Mobarek, A., & Mollah, S. (2023). Does corporate governance affect the performance and stability of Islamic banks? *Corporate Governance (Bradford), 23*(4), 888–919. doi:10.1108/CG-05-2022-0217

Manap J.H., Hamzah A., Noah S.M., Kasan H., Krauss S.E., Mastor K.A, & Idris F., (2013). Prinsip pengukuran religiositi dan personaliti Muslim. *Jurnal Psikologi dan Pembangunan Manusia, 1*(1), 36-43.

Mansoor, M., Ellahi, N., Hassan, A., Malik, Q. A., Waheed, A., & Ullah, N. (2020). Corporate governance, Shariah governance, and credit rating: A cross-country analysis from asian islamic banks. *Journal of Open Innovation, 6*(4), 1–15. doi:10.3390/joitmc6040170

Mansori, S., Kim, C. S., & Safari, M. (2015). A Shariah perspective review on islamic microfinance. *Asian Social Science, 11*(9), 273–280. doi:10.5539/ass.v11n9p273

Marković, J., & Stošić-Mihajlović, L. (2022). Halal product markets. *Ekonomski izazovi, 11*(22), 60-73. doi:10.5937/EkoIzazov2222060M

Marom, S. (2021). Toward Dynamic-Based Classification of SMEs. *International Journal of Business Administration, 12*(3), 25. doi:10.5430/ijba.v12n3p25

Marr, B., Gray, B. D., & Neely, A. (2003). Why do firms measure their intellectual capital? *Journal of Intellectual Capital, 4*(4), 441–464. doi:10.1108/14691930310504509

Marshall, M. N. (1996). Sampling for qualitative research. *Family Practice, 13*(6), 522–526. doi:10.1093/fampra/13.6.522 PMID:9023528

Martinez, M. E., López-Orozco, F., Olmos-Sánchez, K., & Sánchez-Solís, J. P. (2021). Mispronunciation Detection and Diagnosis Through a Chatbot. In *Handbook of Research on Natural Language Processing and Smart Service Systems* (pp. 31–45). IGI Global. doi:10.4018/978-1-7998-4730-4.ch002

Maselko, J., Hughes, C., & Cheney, R. (2011). Religious social capital : Its measurement an dutility in the study of social determinants of health. *Social Science & Medicine, 73*(5), 759–769. doi:10.1016/j.socscimed.2011.06.019 PMID:21802182

Maslow, A. H. (1943). A theory of human motivation. *Psychological Review, 50*(4), 370–396. doi:10.1037/h0054346

Mason, A. N., Narcum, J., & Mason, K. (2021). Social media marketing gains importance after Covid-19. *Cogent Business and Management, 8*(1), 1870797. Advance online publication. doi:10.1080/23311975.2020.1870797

MassaroA.MagalettiN.CosoliG.GiardinelliV.LeograndeA. (2022). Text Mining Approaches Oriented on Customer Care Efficiency. SSRN. doi:10.2139/ssrn.4026102

Masudin, I., Jie, F., Djajadikerta, H., & Widayat, W. (2021). The effect of halal retail and manufacturing technology readiness on halal meat logistics performance. *International Journal of Logistics Systems and Management, 40*(1), 1–27. doi:10.1504/IJLSM.2021.117688

Matic, R., Kabiljo, M., Zivkovic, M., & Cabarkapa, M. (2021). Extensible chatbot architecture using metamodels of natural language understanding. *Electronics (Basel), 10*(18), 2300. doi:10.3390/electronics10182300

McKinsey. (2018). McKinsey Expects Great Growth for Indonesia's E-Commerce Market. *Indonesia Investments.* https://www.indonesia-investments.com/id/news/todays-headlines/mckinsey-expects-great-growth-for-indonesia-s-e-commerce-market/item8959

Mebroui, T., & Mosbah, A. (2020). Islamic entrepreneurship: Issues and debates. *International Journal of Management and Commerce Innovations, 7*(2), 461–468.

Mellahi, K., & Budhwar, P. S. (2010). Introduction: Islam and human resource management. *Personnel Review*, *39*(6), 685–691. doi:10.1108/00483481011075558

Meredith, J. (1993). Theory building through conceptual methods. *International Journal of Operations & Production Management*, *13*(5), 3–11. doi:10.1108/01443579310028120

Messaoudi, A. (1994). *Arab maghreb union: achievement and prospects.* [Thesis of Naval Postgraduate School, Monterey, California].

Meyer, R. L. (2002). *Track record of financial institutions in assisting the poor in Asia.* (Asian Development Bank (ADB) Institute Research Paper 49). Tokyo: ADB.

Meyer, D. (2004). *Hong Kong as a Global Metropolis.* Cambridge University Press.

Miles, D. A. (2019). Let's Stop the Madness Part 2: Understanding the Difference Between Limitations vs. Delimitations. *5th Annual 2017 Black Doctoral Network Conference in Atlanta, August*, 1–17.

Miles, M. B., & Huberman, A. M. (1994). Qualitative Data Analysis: An Expanded Sourcebook (2nd ed.). Thousand Oaks, California

Millen, D. R., & Patterson, J. F. (2003). Identity Disclosure and the Creation of Social Capital. *Proceedings of the SIGCHI Conference on Human Factors in Computing Systems*, (pp. 720–721). ACM. 10.1145/765891.765950

Mitra, S. K. (2009, May). Exploitative microfinance interest rates. *Asian Social Science*, *5*(5). doi:10.5539/ass.v5n5p87

Mittal, M., & Bhakar, S. S. (2018). Examining the impact of role overload on job stress, job satisfaction and job performance-a study among married working women in banking sector. *International Journal of Management Studies*, *2*(7), 1. doi:10.18843/ijms/v5i2(7)/01

Modigliani, F., & Miller, M. H. (1958). The cost of capital, corporation finance and the theory of investment. *The American Economic Review*, *48*(3), 261–297.

Moghimi, S. M. (2018). Leadership Styles in Islamic Management. *Organizational Behavior Management*, 159–220. doi:10.1108/978-1-78769-677-820181009

Mohd Suki, N., & Abang Salleh, A. S. (2018). Mediating effect of Halal image on Muslim consumers' intention to patronize retail stores: Some insights from Malaysia. *Journal of Islamic Marketing*, *9*(2), 338–355. doi:10.1108/JIMA-02-2017-0014

Mohd Yusof, Y. L., Wan Jusoh, W. J., & Maulan, S. (2021). Perceived quality association as determinant to re-patronise Shariah-compliant brand restaurants. *Journal of Islamic Marketing*, *12*(2), 302–315. doi:10.1108/JIMA-10-2018-0190

Mohiuddin, M. F. (2017). Islamic social enterprises in Bangladesh: Conceptual and institutional challenges. *Cogent Business & Management*, *4*(1), 1305674. doi:10.1080/23311975.2017.1305674

Möller, K., & Rajala, A. (2007). Rise of strategic nets — New modes of value creation. *Industrial Marketing Management*, *36*(7), 895–908. doi:10.1016/j.indmarman.2007.05.016

Monjur, M. (2011). An analysis of the practices of Muhammad (pbuh) on resolving conflicts. *Journal of the Bangladesh Association of Young Researchers*, *1*(1), 109–125. doi:10.3329/jbayr.v1i1.6840

Morduch, J., & Haley, B. (2002). *Analysis of the effects of microfinance on poverty reduction.* (NYU Wagner Working Paper No. 1014). New York University. https://www.nyu.edu/wagner/workingpapers.html

Moshin, A., Brochado, A., & Rodrigues, H. (2020). Halal tourism is traveling fast: Community perceptions and implications. *Journal of Destination Marketing & Management, 18*, 100503. doi:10.1016/j.jdmm.2020.100503

Mostafa, M. M. (2021). Information diffusion in halal food social media: A social network approach. *Journal of International Consumer Marketing, 33*(4), 471–491. doi:10.1080/08961530.2020.1818158

Mostafa, R. B., & Kasamani, T. (2022). Antecedents and consequences of chatbot initial trust. *European Journal of Marketing, 56*(6), 1748–1771. doi:10.1108/EJM-02-2020-0084

MOTAC. (2019). Statistik Program Pengalaman Homestay Malaysia tahun 2019. Kementerian Pelancongan, Seni dan Budaya, Kuala Lumpur.

Moten, A. R. (2021). *Humanising Education Maqasid al-Shari'ah and Sustainable Development*. IIUM PRESS.

Muhammad, D. G. (2022). Kayan mata: A silent and emerging form of female genital mutilatiin Nigeria. In Rwanda Medical Journal, 79(1). Bioline International. doi:10.4314/rmj.v79i2.2

Muhammad, M. A., Elistina, A. B., & Ahmad, S. O. (2020). The challenges faced by halal certification authorities in managing the halal certification process in Malaysia. *Food Research, 4*(1), 170–178. doi:10.26656/fr.2017.4(S1).S17

Muhammad, N., McElwee, G., & Dana, L. (2017). Barriers to the development and progress of entrepreneurship in rural pakistan. *International Journal of Entrepreneurial Behaviour & Research, 23*(2), 279–295. doi:10.1108/IJEBR-08-2016-0246

Muhammad, S., Ximei, K., Sharif, I., & Haq, Z. (2020). An overview of women entrepreneurship from islamic perspective. *Review of Economics and Development Studies, 6*(4), 857–866. doi:10.47067/reads.v6i4.285

Muhibbu-Din, M. O. (2019). Feminism and modern Islamic politics: The fact and the fallacy. *International Journal of Islamic Thought, 15*(1), 44–59. doi:10.24035/ijit.15.2019.005

Mukherjee, A., Rajendran, S. D., & Wahab, S. N. (2022). Technology Strategy in Boosting Halal Tourism Activities. In Technology Application in Aviation, Tourism and Hospitality: Recent Developments and Emerging Issues (pp. 41-56). Singapore: Springer Nature Singapore. doi:10.1007/978-981-19-6619-4_4

Mukherjee, R. R., & Patel, S. (2020). Critical Analysis of the Factors Affecting Gender Pay Gap. Gender Sensitive Education: A necessity to eradicate Gender Discrimination in India.". *Journal on 8th February*.

Murugesan, S., & Cherukuri, A. K. (2023). The Rise of Generative Artificial Intelligence and Its Impact on Education: The Promises and Perils. *Computer, 56*(5), 116–121. doi:10.1109/MC.2023.3253292

Musa, A. H., Baharuddin, F. N., Noh, S. N. S., & Asma'Rashidah Idris, S. M. S. (2022). Islamic Marketing, Electronic Word of Mouth (eWoM) and Religious Awareness Roles in Consuming Halal Food: A Conceptual Paper. *IJARBSS, 12*(12). doi:10.6007/IJARBSS/v12-i12/16038

Musari, K. (2016). *Redefining the Islamic nanofinance and its institutional strengthening: lesson learned from Asian countries.* 11th International Conference on Islamic Economics and Finance (ICIEF) Rethinking Islamic Economics and Finance: Paving The Way Forward for Inclusive and Sustainable Development. Institution Kulliyyah of Economics and Management Sciences International Islamic University Malaysia (IIUM).

Musari, K. (2016b). Redefining the Islamic nanofinance and its institutional strengthening: lesson learned from Asian countries. A paper was presented at *11th International Conference on Islamic Economics and Finance (ICIEF).* Institution Kulliyyah of Economics and Management Sciences International Islamic University Malaysia (IIUM).

Musari, K. (2017a). Nanofinance. *Jawa Pos Radar Jember Daily Newspaper*, Perspektif.

Musari, K. (2017b). Nanofinance, addressing the Islamic microfinance gap through global Islamic humanitarian institution. In Proceeding of Conference on *Philanthropy for Humanitarian Aid 2017 "Philantrophy for Humanitarian Aid as Mechanism to Alleviate Poverty and Maintain Human Dignity."* International Research Centre of Islamic Economics and Finance (IRCIEF).

Musari, K. (2017c). *Promoting qardhul hassan in nanofinance to against the moneylender (case study Indonesia, Cambodia, Brunei, Vietnam, and Thailand).* A paper was presented at the 2nd Studia Islamika International Conference 2017 "Southeast Asian Islam: Religious Radicalism, Democracy, and Global Trends," Post-Graduate School of State Islamic University Syarif Hidayatullah, Jakarta.

Musari, K. (2020a). Nanoeconomics, people's economy in post-pandemic. *Portal Jember, Pikiran Rakyat Media Network*, Opini. https://portaljember.pikiran-rakyat.com/opini/pr-16392575/refleksi-hari-lahir-pancasila-1-juni-ekonomi-nano-ekonomi-kerakyatan-pasca-pandemi?page=5

Musari, K. (2020a, January 17). Between Odisha, Jember, and Islamic Economy. *Jawa Pos Radar Jember Daily Newspaper*, 21 - 27.

Musari, K. (2022). P2P lending & philanthropy platform: a new face of Asian digital financial inclusion (evidence from Indonesia). In M. N. Almunawar, Z. Islam, and P. Ordóñez de Pablos (Eds.), Digital Transformation Management: Challenges and Futures in the Asian Digital Economy. New York, NY: Informa UK Limited, Taylor & Francis/Routledge.

Musari, K., & Sayah, F. (2022). *Finding the Islamic social finance partnership models for micro entrepreneurship through Islamic helix approach: case study in Indonesia and Algeria.* A paper was presented at Entrepreneurship, Sustainable Development, and Halal Economy Conference: Concepts, Framework and Practice held by College of Islamic Studies (CIS), Hamad Bin Khalifa University (HBKU), Doha - Qatar.

Musari, K. (2016a). Economic sustainability for Islamic nanofinance through sukuk-waqf linkage program (case study in Indonesia). [IJISEF]. *International Journal of Islamic Economics and Finance Studies*, *2*(3), 73–94.

Musari, K. (2019). Promoting qard al-hasan in nanofinance to counter the moneylender in Southeast Asia. *Studia Islamica*, *26*(1), 1–16. doi:10.15408di.v26i1.5990

Musari, K. (2020b). Islamic nanofinance for the very poor by women, hopes for addressing the Islamic microfinance gap. In T. Azid & J. L. Ward-Batts (Eds.), *Economic empowerment of women in the Islamic world: theory and practice* (pp. 265–286). World Scientific Publishing. doi:10.1142/9789811212154_0013

Musari, K. (2020c). The loan shark in ASEAN: can nanofinance with qardhul hassan deal with it? lesson learned from bank wakaf mikro in Indonesia. In P. Ordoñez de Pablos, M. Almunawar, & M. Abduh (Eds.), *Economics, business, and Islamic finance in ASEAN economics community* (pp. 252–277). IGI Global. doi:10.4018/978-1-7998-2257-8.ch012

Musari, K., & Fathorrazi, M. (2021). Islamic helix approach, the Islamic social finance partnership models for MSMEs: lesson learned from Indonesia. In T. Azid, M. Mukhlisin, N. Akbar, & M. Tahir (Eds.), *Monetary policy, Islamic finance, and Islamic corporate governance: an international overview* (pp. 303–322). Emerald Publishing Limited., doi:10.1108/978-1-80043-786-920211017

Musari, K., & Simanjuntak, R. (2016). Nanofinance, redefinition of microfinance for the very micro society through philanthropy linkage program (case study in Indonesia, Cambodia, Thailand, India). [AARJSH]. *Asian Academic Research Journal of Social Sciences and Humanities*, *3*(4), 455–463.

Musharraf, H. M., & Saiful Islam Arman, M. (2018). Prophetic medicine is the cheapest, safest and the best remedy in the prevention and treatment of hypertension (high blood pressure) – a mini review. *International Journal of Molecular Biology (Edmond, Okla.)*, *3*(6). doi:10.15406/ijmboa.2018.03.00084

Mustafa, D., Baita, A. J., & Adhama, H. D. (2020). Quantitative Economic Evaluation of Zakah-Poverty Nexus in Kano State, Nigeria. [IJIEF]. *International Journal of Islamic Economics and Finance*, *3*(1), 21–50. doi:10.18196/ijief.2120

Mustaqim, R., Kusyanti, A., & Aryadita, H. (2018). Analisis Faktor-Faktor yang Memengaruhi Niat Penggunaan E-Commerce XYZ Menggunakan Model UTAUT (Unified Theory Acceptance and Use Of Technology). *Jurnal Pengembangan Teknologi Informasi Dan Ilmu Komputer*, *2*(7), 2584–2593.

Mutmainah, L. (2018). The role of religiosity, halal awareness, halal certification, and food ingredients on purchase intention of halal food. *Journal of Islamic Economics, Finance, and Banking*, *1*(1), 33–50. doi:10.12928/ijiefb.v1i1.284

Mydyti, H., & Kadriu, A. (2021). The impact of chatbots in driving digital transformation. [IJESMA]. *International Journal of E-Services and Mobile Applications*, *13*(4), 88–104. doi:10.4018/IJESMA.2021100106

Myers, S. C. (2001). Capital structure. *The Journal of Economic Perspectives*, *15*(2), 81–102. doi:10.1257/jep.15.2.81

Nabi, G., Islam, A., Bakar, R., & Nabi, R. (2017). Islamic microfinance as a tool of financial inclusion in Bangladesh. *Journal of Islamic Economics, Banking, and Finance*, *113*(6218), 1–28. doi:10.12816/0051154

Nabi, N. (2019). Women in Islamic Economics: A Study of Some Prominent Muslim Women Scholars. *Insight Islamicus*, *19*, 33–46.

Naeem, G., & Mahvish, S. (2021). The honor and respect of Women: A comparative study based on Quran o Sunnah and current practices in Pakistan. *Rahatulquloob*, *5*(1), 40–46. doi:10.51411/rahat.5.1.2021/192

Nahapiet, J. (2011). *Social Capital, Intellectual Capital, and the Organizational Advantage*, *23*(2), 242–266.

Nakara, W. A., Gabriel, D., Street, M., & Cedex, T. (2012). Entrepreneurship and social media marketing: Evidence from French small business Fatim-Zohra Benmoussa Annabelle Jaouen. *International Journal of Entrepreneurship and Small Business*, *16*(4), 386–405. doi:10.1504/IJESB.2012.047608

Nanda, P., Patnaik, D., & Patnaik, S. (2021). Computational Management—An Overview. *Computational Management: Applications of Computational Intelligence in Business Management*, 3-21. doi:10.1007/978-3-030-72929-5_1

Nasution, A. C. (2013). A framework to analyse the efficiency of Baitul Maal wa Tamwil (BMT) As Islamic Microfinance Institutions in Indonesia. *Proceeding of Sharia Economic Conference, February*, 81–86.

Nathan, A. J., & Zhang, B. (2022). 'A shared future for mankind': Rhetoric and reality in Chinese foreign policy under Xi Jinping. *Journal of Contemporary China*, *31*(133), 57–71. doi:10.1080/10670564.2021.1926091

Nazaruddin, L. O., Gyenge, B., Fekete-Farkas, M., & Lakner, Z. (2023). The Future Direction of Halal Food Additive and Ingredient Research in Economics and Business: A Bibliometric Analysis. *Sustainability (Basel)*, *15*(7), 5680. doi:10.3390u15075680

Nguyen, Q. K. (2021). Oversight of bank risk-taking by audit committees and Sharia committees: Conventional vs Islamic banks. *Heliyon*, *7*(8), e07798. doi:10.1016/j.heliyon.2021.e07798 PMID:34458627

Nguyen, T. D., Nguyen, T., & Barrett, N. J. (2010). Consumer ethnocentrism, cultural sensitivity, and intention to purchase local products evidence from Vietnam. *Journal of Consumer Behaviour*, *7*(1), 88–100. doi:10.1002/cb.238

Nicolescu, L., & Tudorache, M. T. (2022). Human-Computer Interaction in Customer Service: The Experience with AI Chatbots—A Systematic Literature Review. *Electronics (Basel)*, *11*(10), 1579. doi:10.3390/electronics11101579

Nielsen, S., & Huse, M. (2010). Women directors' contribution to board decision-making and strategic involvement: The role of equality perception. *European Management Review*, *7*(1), 16–29. doi:10.1057/emr.2009.27

Nieto, M. J., & Santamaría, L. (2007). The importance of diverse collaborative networks for the novelty of product innovation. *Technovation, 27*(6), 367–377. doi:10.1016/j.technovation.2006.10.001

Nirala, K. K., Singh, N. K., & Purani, V. S. (2022). A survey on providing customer and public administration based services using AI: Chatbot. *Multimedia Tools and Applications, 81*(16), 22215–22246. doi:10.100711042-021-11458-y

Noor, N. (2022). Halal Service Marketing: A Strategic Perspective. In *Strategic Islamic Marketing: A Roadmap for Engaging Muslim Consumers* (pp. 11–29). Springer International Publishing. doi:10.1007/978-3-030-98160-0_3

Nsereko, I., Balunywa, J., Kyazze, L., Nsereko, H., & Nakato, J. (2021). Entrepreneurial alertness and social entrepreneurial venture creation: The mediating role of personal initiative. *Journal of Enterprising Communities People and Places in the Global Economy, 16*(3), 361–383. doi:10.1108/JEC-05-2020-0099

Nugrahaningsih, W., & Erlinawati, M. (2017). Implementasi Undang-Undang Nomor 8 Tahun 1999 Tentang Perlindungan Konsumen Terhadap Bisnis Online. *Jurnal Serambi Hukum, 11*(1), 27–40.

Nurjanah, S., Santoso, D., Fatarib, H., Jalil, M., & Murdiana, E. (2022). Lessons Learned From Child Protection Rights in Religion Paradigm and National Law. *Journal of Social Studies Education Research, 13*(1), 237–258.

O'Neill, A. (2021, Apr 22). *Maghreb region - Statistics & Facts.* Statista. https://www.statista.com/topics/4660/maghreb-region/#topicHeader__wrapper

Obeng, B. A., Robson, P., & Haugh, H. (2014). Strategic entrepreneurship and small firm growth in Ghana. *International Small Business Journal, 32*(5), 501–524. doi:10.1177/0266242612463946

Ojo, S. (2019). Navigating ethnic entrepreneurship in religion and culture meld. *Journal of Enterprising Communities, 13*(5), 625–646. doi:10.1108/JEC-11-2018-0089

Okafor, C., & Amalu, R. (2010). Entrepreneurial Motivations as Determinants of Women Entrepreneurship Challenges. *Petroleum-Gas University of Ploiesti Bulletin,* (2), 67–77.

Okem, A. (2015). Exploring the Opportunities and Challenges of Network Formation for Cooperatives in South Africa. *KJBM, 5*(1), 16–33.

Okeshola, F. B., & Sadiq, I. T. (2015). Determinants of Home Delivery among Hausa in Kaduna South Local Government Area of Kaduna State, Nigeria. *American International Journal of Contemporary Research, 3*(5), 78–85.

Okon, E. E. (2013). The Status of Woman in Islam. *IOSR Journal of Humanities and Social Science, 10*(2), 21–27. doi:10.9790/0837-01022127

Okunlola, O. A., & Oyeyemi, O. T. (2019). Spatio-temporal analysis of association between incidence of malaria and environmental predictors of malaria transmission in Nigeria. *Scientific Reports, 9*(1), 17500. Advance online publication. doi:10.103841598-019-53814-x PMID:31767899

Ordemann, S., Skjuve, M., Følstad, A., & Bjørkli, C. (2021). "Have a Nice Day:)": Social Interactions with Customer Service Chatbots. *Proceedings of the 19th International Conference on e-Society 2021.* Springer.

Ovuakporaye, K. (2022). The Impact, Comparison and Usefulness of Digital Marketing Communications Tools on Organizational Profit Maximization Using Facebook. *Asian Journal of Research in Computer Science, 13*(4), 46–64. doi:10.9734/ajrcos/2022/v13i430321

Owusu, J., Akanbasiam, A. C., & Anyesepari, A. A. (2013). Microfinance schemes and poverty reduction among women in the northern region of Ghana. *International Journal of Humanities and Social Science, 3*(19), 99–108.

Paliwal, S., Bharti, V., & Mishra, A. K. (2020). Ai chatbots: Transforming the digital world. *Recent Trends and Advances in Artificial Intelligence and Internet of Things*, 455-482. doi:10.1007/978-3-030-32644-9_34

Panda, S. (2018). Constraints faced by women entrepreneurs in developing countries: Review and ranking. *Gender in Management, 33*(4), 315–331. doi:10.1108/GM-01-2017-0003

Parpart, E. (2014, October 25). BOT considers 'nano-financing' for grass-roots people. *The Nation.* https://www.nationmultimedia.com/business/BOT-considers-nano-financing-for-grass-roots-peopl-30246202.html

Parvin. (2012). Women entrepreneurship development in Bangladesh: What are the challenges ahead? *African Journal of Business Management, 6*(11), 3862–3871.

Patoari, M. H. (2019). The Rights of Women in Islam and Some Misconceptions: An Analysis from Bangladesh Perspective. *Beijing Law Review, 10*(05), 1211–1224. doi:10.4236/blr.2019.105065

Patwary, A. K., & Rashid, B. (2016). The impacts of hospitality services on visit experience and future visit intention of student travellers. *International Journal of Business and Technopreneurship, 6*(8), 107–125.

Patwary, A. M., & Abdul, A., Hazbar, Abdulmalek S., N. Kamal, Mohammed, A., Azbar, H., & Kamal, N. (2018). Factors Influencing Consumers' Intentions towards Purchasing Islamic Hotel Service: Moderating Role of Religiosity. *International Journal of Management. Accounting and Economics, 5*(7), 482–497.

Peprah, J. A., Andoh, F. K., Avorkpo, E. A., Dafor, K. N., Afful, B. Jr, & Obeng, C. K. (2022). Compliance Burden and Tax gap among micro and small businesses: Evidence from Ghana. *SAGE Open, 12*(4), 21582440221126984. doi:10.1177/21582440221126985

Petty, R., & Guthrie, J. (2000). Intellectual capital literature review: Measurement, reporting and management. *Journal of Intellectual Capital, 1*(2), 155–176. doi:10.1108/14691930010348731

Piketty, T. (2014). Capital in the twenty-first century. In Mohiuddin, M.F. (ed.) Islamic social enterprises in Bangladesh: Conceptual and institutional challenges. The Belknap Press of Harvard University Press. doi:10.4159/9780674369542

Pillai, R., & Sivathanu, B. (2020). Adoption of AI-based chatbots for hospitality and tourism. *International Journal of Contemporary Hospitality Management, 32*(10), 3199–3226. doi:10.1108/IJCHM-04-2020-0259

Pita, M. (2021). Entrepreneurial initiative in islamic economics – the role of gender. a multi-country analysis. *Journal of Islamic Accounting and Business Research, 12*(6), 793–813. doi:10.1108/JIABR-01-2020-0010

Postelnicu, L., Hermes, N., & Szafarz, A. (2014). Defining social collateral in microfinance group lending. *Microfinance Institutions*, 187–207.

Pradana, M., Garciac, R. H., & Marimon, F. (2020). Spanish Muslims' halal food purchase intention. *The International Food and Agribusiness Management Review, 9*(11), 434–461. doi:10.22434/IFAMR2019.0200

Prativi, Y. P., Sukmadilaga, C., & Cupian, C. (2021). The Impact of Islamic Corporate Governance Disclosure, Islamic Intellectual Capital, Zakat, Financial Performance (SCnP Model) & Islamic Ethical Identity to Sustainable Business. *Jurnal Ekonomi Syariah Teori Dan Terapan, 8*(2), 171. doi:10.20473/vol8iss20212pp171-182

Pratiwi, A., Aidid, H., Uin, M., & Makassar, A. (n.d.). The Holy Quran perspective of business competition. *JISHIM, 2*(4).

Prayag, G., Hosany, S., Muskat, B., & Del, C. G. (2017). Understanding the relationships between tourists' emotional experiences, perceived overall image, satisfaction, and intention to recommend. *Journal of Travel Research, 56*(1), 41–54. doi:10.1177/0047287515620567

Preko, A., Mohammed, I., & Allaberganov, A. (2021). Antecedents of brand equity on halal tourism destination. *Journal of Islamic Marketing*, *8*(13), 1685–1702. doi:10.1108/JIMA-09-2020-0283

Priyadi, R., Daryanto, A., & Hermandi, I. (2017). View of Perilaku Penggunaan Portal E-office di Bank XYZ Dengan Pendekatan Model UTAUT. *Aplikasi Bisnis Dan Manajemen*, *3*(2), 186–193.

Putnam, R. (1993). The prosperous community; Social capital and public life. *The American Prospect*, *13*, 35–42.

Putra, G., & Ariyanti, M. (2013). Pengaruh Faktor-Faktor Dalam Modified Unified Theory of Acceptance and Use of Technology 2 (Utaut 2) Terhadap Niat Prospective Users Untuk Mengadopsi Home Digital Services Pt. Telkom Di Surabaya. *Jurnal Manajemen Indonesia*, *12*(4), 59–76.

Qurniawati, R. S., Sakinah, A. N., & Nurohman, Y. A. (2023). The Impact of Religious Beliefs on Halal Skincare Brand Loyalty in Central Java Indonesia: The Mediating Role of Brand Love. *Jurnal Ekonomi Syariah Teori dan Terapan*, *10*(2).

Qu, S. Q., & Dumay, J. (2011). The qualitative research interview. *Qualitative Research in Accounting & Management*, *8*(3), 238–264. doi:10.1108/11766091111162070

Rabeya, S., & Hossain, I. (2019). China's One Belt One Road (OBOR) Initiative and the Muslim World. *The Journal of Social, Political, and Economic Studies*, *44*(1/2), 3–38.

Rabiee, F. (2004). Focus-group interview and data analysis. *The Proceedings of the Nutrition Society*, *63*(4), 655–660. doi:10.1079/PNS2004399 PMID:15831139

Rafiq, F., Dogra, N., Adil, M., & Wu, J. Z. (2022). Examining consumer's intention to adopt AI-chatbots in tourism using partial least squares structural equation modeling method. *Mathematics*, *10*(13), 2190. doi:10.3390/math10132190

Rahbari, L. (2020). Women's Ijtihad and Lady Amin's islamic ethics on womanhood and motherhood. *Religions*, *11*(2), 1–13. doi:10.3390/rel11020088

Rahim, R. (2010). *Managing Conflict in Organizations*. Transaction Publishers.

Rahman, A. (1999). Micro-credit initiatives for equitable and sustainable development: Who pays? *World Development*, *27*(1), 67–82. doi:10.1016/S0305-750X(98)00105-3

Rahmayati, R. (2021). Competition Strategy In The Islamic Banking Industry: An Empirical Review. *International Journal Of Business, Economics, and Social Development*, *2*(2), 65–71.

Rajagopal, S., Ramanan, S., Visvanathan, R., & Satapathy, S. (2011). Halal certification: Implication for marketers in UAE. *Journal of Islamic Marketing*, *2*(2), 138–153. doi:10.1108/17590831111139857

Ramadani, V. (2021). Islamic entrepreneurship. In *World Encyclopedia of Entrepreneurship* (pp. 457–470). Edward Elgar Publishing. doi:10.4337/9781839104145.00059

Ramadani, V., Dana, L. P., Gërguri-Rashiti, S., & Ratten, V. (2017). An introduction to entrepreneurship and management in an Islamic context. In *Entrepreneurship and management in an Islamic context* (pp. 1–5). Springer. doi:10.1007/978-3-319-39679-8_1

Ramadani, V., Dana, L. P., Ratten, V., & Tahiri, S. (2015). The context of Islamic entrepreneurship and business: Concept, principles and perspectives. *International Journal of Business and Globalisation*, *15*(3), 244–261. doi:10.1504/IJBG.2015.071906

Ramadani, V., Hisrich, R. D., & Gërguri-Rashiti, S. (2015). Female entrepreneurs in transition economies: Insights from Albania, Macedonia and Kosovo. *World Review of Entrepreneurship, Management and Sustainable Development*, *11*(4), 391–413. doi:10.1504/WREMSD.2015.072066

Ramantoko, G., Putra, G., Ariyanti, M., & Sianturi, N. (2015). Early Adoption Characteristic of Consumers' Behavioral Intention to Use Home Digital Services in Indonesia. In *Advances in Social Science Education and Humanities Reasearch* (pp. 1–8). Atlanta Press.

Ramzy, O., & Eldahan, O. H. (2015). Marketing communications in the Islamic perspective: Communicating the halal branding. In Islamic Perspectives on Marketing and Consumer Behavior: Planning, Implementation, and Control (pp. 149-168). IGI Global. doi:10.4018/978-1-4666-8139-2.ch007

Rana, P. B., & Ji, X. (2020). *China's Belt and Road Initiative*. Springer Singapore. doi:10.1007/978-981-15-5171-0

Rapp, A., Curti, L., & Boldi, A. (2021). The human side of human-chatbot interaction: A systematic literature review of ten years of research on text-based chatbots. *International Journal of Human-Computer Studies, 151*, 102630. doi:10.1016/j.ijhcs.2021.102630

Rathiranee, Y., & Semasinghe, S. D. (2016). The impact of micro finance factors on women entrepreneurs' performance in northern Sri Lanka. *International Journal of Social Science Studies, 4*(3), 94–99.

Ratten, V., Ramadani, V., Dana, L. P., & Gerguri-Rashiti, S. (2017). Islamic entrepreneurship and management: Culture, religion and society. In *Entrepreneurship and management in an Islamic context* (pp. 7–17). Springer. doi:10.1007/978-3-319-39679-8_2

Rauf, A., Abubakar, Y., Abrar, A., Gohar, M., Slesman, L., & Mitra, J. (2022). Islam, entrepreneurship and economic development. *Journal of Entrepreneurship and Innovation in Emerging Economies, 8*(2), 270–273. doi:10.1177/23939575211047022

Ray, A. K. (2008). Self-help groups, micro finance and political economy. In B. J. Deb, K. Sengupta, & B. D. Ray (Eds.), *Globalization and north east India* (pp. 21–35). Ashok Kumar Mittal.

Reed, K. K., Lubatkin, M., & Srinivasun, N. (2006). Proposing and testing an intellectual capital-based view of the firm. *Journal of Management Studies, 43*(4), 867–893. doi:10.1111/j.1467-6486.2006.00614.x

Rejeb, A., Rejeb, K., Zailani, S., Treiblmaier, H., & Hand, K. J. (2021). Integrating the Internet of Things in the halal food supply chain: A systematic literature review and research agenda. *Internet of Things, 13*, 100361. doi:10.1016/j.iot.2021.100361

Report. (2019). *Celebrating Women in Islamic Business and Finance in Islamic Business and Finance who are leading*.

Rese, A., Ganster, L., & Baier, D. (2020). Chatbots in retailers' customer communication: How to measure their acceptance? *Journal of Retailing and Consumer Services, 56*, 102176. doi:10.1016/j.jretconser.2020.102176

Rezende, Y. (2001). Informação para negócios: Os novos agentes do conhecimento e a gestão do capital intelectua. *El Profesional de la Información, 8*(1), 75–83. doi:10.1076/epri.10.5.21.6523

Richards, G., & Hall, D. (2000). *The Community: A Sustainable Concept in Tourism Development*. Routledge. doi:10.4324/9780203464915_chapter_1

Rizkitysha, T. L., & Hananto, A. (2020). Do knowledge, perceived usefulness of halal label and religiosity affect attitude and intention to buy halal-labelled detergent? *Journal of Islamic Marketing*. . doi:10.1108/JIMA-03-2020-0070

Rizqi, S. S., & Riorini, S. V. (2022). The Stimulus of Loyalty to Beauty Product Influencer on Social Media. *The Management Journal of Binaniaga, 7*(2), 197–212. doi:10.33062/mjb.v7i2.10

Robinson, M. (2001). *The microfinance revolution: sustainable finance for the poor*. World Bank. doi:10.1596/0-8213-4524-9

Rocha, P. R. Z. (2012). *Métodos de avaliação de ativos intangíveis e capital intelectual: análise das competências individuais*. Dissertação (Mestrado) – Universidade Federal de Santa Catarina].

Rodrigo, P., & Turnbull, S. (2019). Halal holidays: How is value perceived by Muslim tourists? *International Journal of Tourism Research, 21*(5), 675–692. doi:10.1002/jtr.2290

Rodrigues, H. M. S. S., Dorrego, P. F. F., Fernández, C. M., & Fernández, J. (2009). La influencia del capital intelectual en la capacidad de innovación de las empresas del sector de automoción de la Eurorregión Galicia Norte de Portugal. Tese (Doutorado) – Universidade de Vigo, Vigo, 1–221.

Rokhman, W. (2013). Baitul mal wat tamwil (bmt) and poverty empowerment. *Qudus International Journal of Islamic Studies, 1*(2), 181–196.

Roos, G. (2017). Knowledge management, intellectual capital, structural holes, economic complexity and national prosperity. *Journal of Intellectual Capital, 18*(4), 745–770. doi:10.1108/JIC-07-2016-0072

Roos, G., & Roos, J. (1997). Measuring your company's intellectual performance. *Long Range Planning, 30*(3), 413–426. doi:10.1016/S0024-6301(97)90260-0

Roos, J., Roos, G., Dragonetti, N. C., & Edvinsson, L. (1997). *Intellectual Capital: Navigating in the New Business Landscape*. Macmillan. doi:10.1007/978-1-349-14494-5

Rosenberg, R. (2002). *Microcredit interest rates*. CGAP.

Rosenberg, R., Gaul, S., Ford, W., & Tomilova, O. (2013). *Microcredit interest rates and their determinants 2004–2011*. CGAP.

RosenbergR.GonzalezA.NarainS. (2009). The new moneylenders: are the poor being exploited by high microcredit interest rates? CGAP.

Roshayani, A., Ruhaini, M., Ramesh, N., & Idora, B. (2018). Value-based intermediation for islamic banking institutions directed towards sustainable development goals. *He International Revue of Entrepreneurial Finance, 1*(1).

Ruiz-Bejarano, B. (2017). Islamophobia as a Deterrent to Halal Global Trade. *Islamophobia Studies Journal, 1*(4). Advance online publication. doi:10.13169/islastudj.4.1.0129

Saba, I., Kouser, R., & Chaudhry, I. S. (2019). FinTech and Islamic finance-challenges and opportunities. *Review of Economics and Development Studies, 5*(4), 581–890. doi:10.26710/reads.v5i4.887

Sabbar, S. D., Kara, M. H., Said, S., Ahmed, S., & Asad, M. (2023). Awareness of Halal Branding and Marketing: Consumer Perception in Makassar, Indonesia. *Journal of Advances in Humanities Research, 2*(2), 98–124. doi:10.56868/jadhur.v2i2.128

Said, M., Hassan, F., Musa, R., & Rahman, N. A. (2014). Assessing Consumers' Perception, Knowledge and Religiosity on Malaysia's Halal Food Products. *Procedia: Social and Behavioral Sciences, 130*, 120–128. doi:10.1016/j.sbspro.2014.04.015

Saifee, A. U. R., Baloach, A. G., Sultan, S., & Khalid, I. (2012). Status, identity, and privileges of women in Islam. *European Journal of Soil Science, 30*(1), 146–154.

Sair, S. A., & Danish, R. Q. (2018). Effect of Performance Expectancy and Effort Expectancy on the Mobile Commerce Adoption Intention through Personal Innovativeness among Pakistani Consumers. *Pakistan Journal of Commerce and Social Sciences, 12*(2), 501–520.

Salleh, A. S. A., Suki, N. M., Hashim, N., & Abang, A. S. (2020). Sobel Statistical Test on the Mediation Effect of Halal Image Toward Intention to Patronage Retail Stores. *ECON-Journal of Economics, Management & Business*, *8*(3).

Sample, B. (2011). *Moving 100 million families out of severe poverty: how can we do it?*. 2011 Global Microcredit Summit, Auxiliary Session Paper, Valladolid, Spain.

Sandelowski, M. (1995). Sample size in qualitative research. *Research in Nursing & Health*, *18*(2), 179–183. doi:10.1002/nur.4770180211 PMID:7899572

Santosa, P. W. (2020). The moderating role of firm size on financial characteristics and Islamic firm value at Indonesian equity market. *Business: Theory and Practice*, *21*(1), 391–401. doi:10.3846/btp.2020.12197

Santoso, S. (2010), Statistik Multivariat. *PT Elex Media Compotindo*, Jakarta. https://books.google.co.id/books?hl=en&lr=&id=E5Dli6puzYUC&oi=fnd&pg=PR5&ots=cRyAe8KFm3&sig=2CI2sF4IQySFjvkgzcOIs1fSa-g&redir_esc=y#v=onepage&q&f=false

Saputra, A. D., Rahmatia, A., Wahyuningsih, S. H., & Azhar, A. (2022). Online Business Practices: A Study of Islamic Business Ethics Perspective in Indonesia. *Jurnal Penelitian*, 97–108.

Sarea, A. M., & Hanefah, M. M. (2013). The Need of Accounting Standards for Islamic Financial Institutions: Evidence from AAOIFI. *Journal of Islamic Accounting and Business Research*, *4*(1), 64–76. doi:10.1108/17590811311314294

Sarif, S., Noordin, K., & Abdullah, A. (2004). Managing organizational Conflict from Islamic perspective. *Jurnal Syariah*, *12*(2), 107–222.

Secundo, G., Ndou, V., Del Vecchio, P., & De Pascale, G. (2020). Sustainable development, intellectual capital and technology policies: A structured literature review and future research agenda. *Technological Forecasting and Social Change*, *153*(January), 119917. doi:10.1016/j.techfore.2020.119917

Sedana, I. G. N., & Wijaya, S. W. (2012). Penerapan Model Utaut Untuk Memahami Penerimaan Dan Penggunaan Learning Management System Studi Kasus: Experential E-Learning of Sanata Dharma University. *Jurnal Sistem Informasi*, *5*(2), 114–120. doi:10.21609/jsi.v5i2.271

Segovia-Villarreal, M., & Rosa-Díaz, I. M. (2022). Promoting Sustainable Lifestyle Habits:"Real Food" and Social Media in Spain. *Foods*, *11*(2), 224. doi:10.3390/foods11020224 PMID:35053956

Segrado, C. (2005). *Islamic microfinance and socially responsible investments.* Meda Project, University of Torino, August.

Self, S., & Grabowski, R. (2012). Opportunities for women and Islam: Variations upon variations. *Applied Economics*, *44*(1), 65–79. doi:10.1080/00036846.2010.498370

Septiarini, D. F., Ratnasari, R. T., Salleh, M. C. M., Herianingrum, S., & Sedianingsih, S. (2023). Drivers of behavioral intention among non-Muslims toward halal cosmetics: Evidence from Indonesia, Malaysia, and Singapore. *Journal of Islamic Accounting and Business Research*, *14*(2), 230–248. doi:10.1108/JIABR-02-2021-0064

Setyawati, L. M., Chairy, S. J., & Syahrivar, J. (2019). Factors affecting intention to buy halal food by the millennial generation: The mediating role of attitude. *Jurnal Manajemen*, *14*(2), 175–188. doi:10.1108/BFJ-10-2016-0455

Sfenrianto, S., Wijaya, T., & Wang, G. (2018). Assessing the buyer trust and satisfaction factors in the E-marketplace. *Journal of Theoretical and Applied Electronic Commerce Research*, *13*(2), 43–57. doi:10.4067/S0718-18762018000200105

Shafi, P. M., Jawalkar, G. S., Kadam, M. A., Ambawale, R. R., & Bankar, S. V. (2020). AI—Assisted Chatbot for E-Commerce to Address Selection of Products from Multiple Products. *Internet of Things, Smart Computing and Technology: A Roadmap Ahead*, 57-80. doi:10.1007/978-3-030-39047-1_3

Shahid, S., Ahmed, F., & Hasan, U. (2018). A qualitative investigation into consumption of halal cosmetic products: The evidence from India. *Journal of Islamic Marketing*, *9*(3), 484–503. doi:10.1108/JIMA-01-2017-0009

Shahid, S., Parray, M. A., Thomas, G., Farooqi, R., & Islam, J. U. (2023). Determinants of Muslim consumers' halal cosmetics repurchase intention: An emerging market's perspective. *Journal of Islamic Marketing*, *14*(3), 826–850. doi:10.1108/JIMA-08-2021-0265

Shah, K., & D'Souza, A. (2008). *Advertising and Promotions – An IMC Perspective*. Tata McGraw-Hill.

Shah, S. A. A., Sukmana, R., Fianto, B. A., Ahmad, M. A., Usman, I. U., & Mallah, W. A. (2020). Effects of Halal social media and customer engagement on brand satisfaction of Muslim customer: Exploring the moderation of religiosity. *Journal of Islamic Marketing*, *11*(6), 1671–1689. doi:10.1108/JIMA-06-2019-0119

Shah, S. A., Bhutto, M. H., & Azhar, S. M. (2022). Integrative review of Islamic marketing. *Journal of Islamic Marketing*, *13*(6), 1264–1287. doi:10.1108/JIMA-07-2020-0216

Shaikh, S. N., & Ali, A. (2020). Islamic Finance and Empowerment of Women: A Case Study of Pakistan. *Asian Journal of Economics, Business and Accounting*. doi:10.9734/ajeba/2020/v16i430243

Sharma, V., Goyal, M., & Malik, D. (2017). An intelligent behaviour shown by chatbot system. *International Journal of New Technology and Research*, *3*(4), 263312.

Sheehan, B., Jin, H. S., & Gottlieb, U. (2020). Customer service chatbots: Anthropomorphism and adoption. *Journal of Business Research*, *115*, 14–24. doi:10.1016/j.jbusres.2020.04.030

Shehu, F. M., & Al-Aidaros, A. H. (2015). Islamic Entrepreneurship in the Light of Maqasid Al-Shariâ€™ ah: A Critical Review. *Journal of Social and Development Sciences*, *6*(4), 6–14. doi:10.22610/jsds.v6i4.854

Sheth, J. N., Newman, B. I., & Gross, B. I. (1991). Why we buy what we buy: A theory of consumption values. *Journal of Business Research*, *22*(2), 159–170. doi:10.1016/0148-2963(91)90050-8

Shiner, L. (2020). *Something ordinary to something navy- exploring influencer arielle charnas' use of parasocial interaction techniques on instagram.*

Shipilov, A., & Danis, W. (2006). TMG social capital, strategic choice and firm performance. *European Management Journal*, *24*(1), 16–27. doi:10.1016/j.emj.2005.12.004

Shkodra, J., Ymeri, P., & Ibishi, L. (2021). Role of microfinance institutions for developing women entrepreneurship – The case study of Kosovo. *Economics & Sociology (Ternopil)*, *14*(1), 120–129. doi:10.14254/2071-789X.2021/14-1/8

Shook, C., Priem, R., & McGee, J. (2003). Venture creation and the enterprising individual: A review and synthesis. *Journal of Management*, *29*(3), 379–399. doi:10.1016/S0149-2063(03)00016-3

Shumanov, M., & Johnson, L. (2021). Making conversations with chatbots more personalized. *Computers in Human Behavior*, *117*, 106627. doi:10.1016/j.chb.2020.106627

Sidani, Y. (2005). Women, work, and Islam in Arab societies. *Women in Management Review*, *20*(7), 498–512. doi:10.1108/09649420510624738

Sidek, F., Pavlovich, K., & Gibb, J. (2018). Entrepreneurship as worship: A malay muslim perspective. *Journal of Management & Organization*, *24*(5), 698–710. doi:10.1017/jmo.2018.13

Sinclair, H. (2012). *Confessions of a microfinance heretic, how microlending lost its way and betrayed the poor*. Berrett-Koehler Publishers, Inc.

Sinha, N., Raju, D., & Morrison, A. (2007). Gender equality and economic growth. In *Women and Girls Rising*. Issue September., doi:10.4324/9781315708379-17

Siraj, A., Shaikh, F. A., Shukla, V. K., Nanda, I., & Punhani, R. (2022). Impact of Mobile Applications and Internet of Things (IoT. In H. Tourism (Ed.), *Tourist Behavior* (pp. 239–261). Apple Academic Press. doi:10.1201/9781003282082-11

Siswadi, Y., & Soemitra, A. (2022). Literature Study on Fiqh Muamalah Digital Business Transactions (e-commerce). *International Journal of Economics, Social Science* [IJESET]. *Entrepreneurship and Technology*, *1*(3), 220–236.

Smutny, P., & Schreiberova, P. (2020). Chatbots for learning: A review of educational chatbots for the Facebook Messenger. *Computers & Education*, *151*, 103862. doi:10.1016/j.compedu.2020.103862

Smylie, M. A., & Evans, A. E. (2006). Social Capital and Problem of Implementation. In M. Honig (Ed.), *Social capital and the problem of implementation. New directions in education policy implementation: Confronting complexity* (pp. 187–208). State University of New York Press.

Sofaer, S. (2010, December). *Articles Qualitative Methods: What Are They and Why Use Them?* Tocco, J. U. (2011). Every disease has its cure: Faith and HIV therapies in Islamic northern Nigeria. *African Journal of AIDS Research*, *9*(4), 385–395. doi:10.2989/16085906.2010.545646

Sohail, H., & Arshed, N. (2022). Contribution of Islamic debt financing in entrepreneurship promoting financial sector transformation. *International Journal of Management Research and Emerging Sciences*, *12*(2). Advance online publication. doi:10.56536/ijmres.v12i2.186

Soon, J. M., Chandia, M., & Mac Regenstein, J. (2017). Halal integrity in the food supply chain. *British Food Journal*, *119*(1), 39–51. doi:10.1108/BFJ-04-2016-0150

So, S. (2023). An Analysis on the Adoption of Chatbots in the Banking Sector of Hong Kong: A Contemporary System for Improving Customer Experiences in E-Banking. In *Digital Entrepreneurship and Co-Creating Value Through Digital Encounters* (pp. 245–262). IGI Global. doi:10.4018/978-1-6684-7416-7.ch012

Spence, L. J., & Schmidpeter, R. (2003). SMEs, social capital and the common good. *Journal of Business Ethics*, *45*(1), 93–108. doi:10.1023/A:1024176613469

Spence, L. J., Schmidpeter, R., & Habisch, A. (2003). Assessing social capital: Small and medium sized enterprises in Germany and the UK. *Journal of Business Ethics*, *47*(1), 17–29. doi:10.1023/A:1026284727037

Sridhar, K. (2012). Is the Triple Bottom Line a restrictive framework for non-financial reporting? In Asian Journal of Business Ethics, 1(2). doi:10.100713520-011-0010-4

Starovic, D., & Marr, B. (2004). *Understanding Corporate Value: Managing and Reporting Intellectual Capital.* The Chartered Institute of Management Accountants (CIMA) and Cranfield University, London. www.cimaglobal.com/Documents/ImportedDocuments/ intellectualcapital.pdf

Statista. (2022a). *Total population of the Maghreb countries from 2016 to 2026.* Statista. https://www.statista.com/statistics/796046/total-population-of-the-maghreb-countries/

Statista. (2022b). *Maghreb countries: Gross domestic product (GDP) per capita in current prices from 2016 to 2026.* Statista. https://www.statista.com/statistics/796087/gross-domestic-product-gdp-per-capita-in-the-maghreb-countries/

Steeger, J. H., & Hoffmann, M. (2016). Innovation and family firms: Ability and willingness and German SMEs. *Journal of Family Business Management*, *6*(3), 251–269. doi:10.1108/JFBM-09-2015-0036

Steinfield, C., DiMicco, J. M., Ellison, N. B., & Lampe, C. (2009). Bowling online: social networking and social capital within the organization. *In Proceedings of the Fourth International Conference on Communities and Technologies*, (pp. 245–254). ACM. 10.1145/1556460.1556496

Stella. (2018). The Most Powerful Women in Islamic Finance Women. *Islamic Finance Review*, 12–43.

Suandi, H., Herri, H., Yulihasri, Y., & Syafrizal, S. (2023, May 11). H., Yulihasri, Y., & Syafrizal, S. (2022). An empirical investigation of Islamic marketing ethics and convergence marketing as key factors in the improvement of Islamic banks performance. *Journal of Islamic Marketing*, *14*(6), 1438–1462. doi:10.1108/JIMA-07-2021-0225

Subramaniam, M., & Youndt, M. A. (2005). The influence of intellectual capital on the types of innovative capabilities. *Academy of Management Journal*, *48*(3), 450–463. doi:10.5465/amj.2005.17407911

Suhartanto, D. (2019). Predicting behavioural intention toward Islamic bank : A multi-group analysis approach. *Journal of Islamic Marketing*, *10*(4), 1091–1103. doi:10.1108/JIMA-02-2018-0041

Sujata, J., Nikita, M., & Shubham, S. (2019). Applications of chatbots in marketing: use cases, impacts, challenges and drivers. *International Journal of Advanced Trends in Computer Science and Engineering*, *8*(1.6), 195-200.

Sulasih, Pramono Hari Adi, Weni Novandari, & Suliyanto. (2023). Islamic Perspective on Marketing Strategy Through Quantitative Strategic Planning Matrix (QSPM). *Ijtimā Iyya Journal of Muslim Society Research*, *8*(1 SE-Articles), 11–32. doi:10.24090/ijtimaiyya.v8i1.6242

Sullivan, P. H. (1999). Profiting from intellectual capital. Journal of Knowledge Management. *Journal of Knowledge Management*, *3*(2), 132–142. doi:10.1108/13673279910275585

Sun, J., & Hou, J. W. (2019). Monetary and financial cooperation between China and the One Belt One Road countries. *Emerging Markets Finance & Trade*, *55*(11), 2609–2627. doi:10.1080/1540496X.2018.1540976

Swan, J. (1981). Disconfirmation of expectations and satisfaction with a retail service. *Journal of Retailing*, *57*(3), 49–66.

Syafitri, I. N. A. (2022). The Meaning of Profit for Krempyeng Market Gresik's Merchants through the Cultural Perspective. *Interdisciplinary Social Studies*, *1*(6), 793–808. doi:10.55324/iss.v1i6.145

Syahrivar, J., Hermawan, S. A., Gyulavári, T., & Chairy, C. (2022). Religious compensatory consumption in the Islamic context: The mediating roles of religious social control and religious guilt. *Asia Pacific Journal of Marketing and Logistics*, *34*(4), 739–758. doi:10.1108/APJML-02-2021-0104

Syukur, M., & Nimsai, S. (2018). Factors influencing the purchase intention of halal packaged food in Thailand. *Int. J Sup. Chain. Mgt*, *7*(4), 1–6.

Taillon, B. J., Mueller, S. M., Kowalczyk, C. M., & Jones, D. N. (2020). Understanding the relationships between social media influencers and their followers: The moderating role of closeness. *Journal of Product and Brand Management*, *29*(6), 767–782. doi:10.1108/JPBM-03-2019-2292

Tan, H. S. (2019). Overview of Indonesia's Online Consumers in Q4. *Janio*. https://janio.asia/sea/indonesia/indonesia-q4-consumer-overview/

Tariq, F., & Umar, S. (2012). Arming the other half: Attaining sustainability through women with microfinance. *WIT Transactions on Ecology and the Environment*, *155*, 811–819. doi:10.2495/SC120682

Temporal, P. (2011). *Islamic branding and marketing: Creating a global Islamic business*. John Wiley & Sons.

The Asia Foundation. (2003). *Microfinance services in Indonesia: a survey of institutions in 6 provinces*. The Asia Foundation.

The Star Online. (2018). Making Malaysia a top choice, no MATTA what. *The Star Online.* https://www.thestar.com.my/news/nation/2018/09/09/making-msia-a-top-choice-no-matta-what-minister-lauds-efforts-to-drive-tourism-industry-further

Timmons, S., & Park, J. (2008). A qualitative study of the factors influencing the submission for publication of research undertaken by students. *Nurse Education Today*, *28*(6), 744–750. doi:10.1016/j.nedt.2007.12.002 PMID:18226843

Tongco, M. D. C. (2007). Purposive Sampling as a Tool for Informant Selection. *Ethnobotany Research and Applications*, *5*, 147–158. doi:10.17348/era.5.0.147-158

Torres, A. I., & Delgado, C. J. (2023). Assessing Customer Interactions With Chatbots in Online Shopping Experiences: An Empirical Study. In Promoting Organizational Performance Through 5G and Agile Marketing (pp. 203-223). IGI Global. doi:10.4018/978-1-6684-5523-4.ch011

Torri, M. C. (2010). Increasing knowledge and traditional use of medicinal plants by local communities in tamil nadu: Promoting self-reliance at the grassroots level through a community-based entrepreneurship initiative. *Complementary Health Practice Review*, *15*(1), 40–51. doi:10.1177/1533210110379938

Tournois, L., & Aoun, I. (2012). From traditional to Islamic marketing strategies: Conceptual issues and implications for an exploratory study in Lebanon. *Education, Business and Society*, *5*(2), 134–140. doi:10.1108/17537981211251179

Trivedi, J. (2019). Examining the customer experience of using banking chatbots and its impact on brand love: The moderating role of perceived risk. *Journal of Internet Commerce*, *18*(1), 91–111. doi:10.1080/15332861.2019.1567188

Trofymenko, O., Prokop, Y., Zadereyko, O., & Loginova, N. (2022). Classification of chatbots. *System technologies*, *2*(139), 147-159. https://doi.org/ doi:10.34185/1562-9945-2-139-2022-14

Trudel, J., & Reio, T. Jr. (2011). Managing workplace incivility: The role of conflict management styles— antecedent or antidote? *Human Resource Development Quarterly*, *22*(4), 395–423. doi:10.1002/hrdq.20081

Tsai, W. H. S., Liu, Y., & Chuan, C. H. (2021). How chatbots' social presence communication enhances consumer engagement: The mediating role of parasocial interaction and dialogue. *Journal of Research in Interactive Marketing*, *15*(3), 460–482. doi:10.1108/JRIM-12-2019-0200

Tsai, W., & Ghoshal, S. (1998). Social capital and value creation: The role of intrafirm networks. *Academy of Management Journal*, *41*(4), 464–476. doi:10.2307/257085

Ud Din, M., Khan, F., Khan, U., Kadarningsih, A., & Astuti, S. D. VI. (2019). Effect of Islamic Work Ethics on Job Performance: Mediating Role of Intrinsic Motivation. *International Journal of Islamic Business Ethics*, *4*(2), 676–686. doi:10.30659/ijibe.4.2.676-688

Ullah, M. M., Mahmud, T. B., & Yousuf, F. (2013). Women entrepreneurship: Islamic perspective. *European Journal of Business and Management*, *5*(11), 44–52.

Umar, U. H., & Danlami, M. R. (2022). The need for revitalization of Islamic social finance instruments in the Covid-19 period in Nigeria: The role of digitalization. In *Artificial Intelligence for Sustainable Finance and Sustainable Technology: Proceedings of ICGER 2021 1* (pp. 177-187). Springer International Publishing.

United Nations Secretary-General. (2018). *Igniting SDG progress through digital financial* inclusion. NY: UNSGSA.

Usman, S. (2017). Kesamaan dan perbedaan pasar e-Commerce Indonesia dengan Tiongkok. *Merdeka.Com*, https://www.merdeka.com/teknologi/kesamaan-dan-perbedaan-pasar-e-commerce-indonesia-dengan-tiongkok.html

Ustaahmetoglu, E. (2020). The influence of different advertisement messages and levels of religiosity on attitude and purchase intention. *International Journal of Islamic and Middle Eastern Finance and Management*. . doi:10.1108/IMEFM-02-2019-0064

Vaismoradi, M., & Snelgrove, S. (2019). Theme in qualitative content analysis and thematic analysis. *Forum Qualitative Social Research, 20*(3). Advance online publication. doi:10.17169/fqs-20.3.3376

Vakulchuk, R., & Overland, I. (2018). China's Belt and Road Initiative through the lens of Central Asia. In *Regional Connection under the Belt and Road Initiative* (pp. 115–133). Routledge. doi:10.4324/9780429467172-5

Van den Broeck, E., Zarouali, B., & Poels, K. (2019). Chatbot advertising effectiveness: When does the message get through? *Computers in Human Behavior, 98*, 150–157. doi:10.1016/j.chb.2019.04.009

Van EeuwijkP.AngehrnZ. (2017). *How to Conduct a Focus Group Discussion (FGD). Methodological Manual*. doi:10.5167/uzh-150640

Van Es, M. A. (2019). Muslim women as 'ambassadors' of Islam: Breaking stereotypes in everyday life. *Identities (Yverdon), 26*(4), 375–392. doi:10.1080/1070289X.2017.1346985

Veirman, M., Cauberghe, V., & Hudders, L. (2017). Marketing through Instagram influencers: The impact of number of followers and product divergence on brand attitude. *International Journal of Advertising, 36*(5), 798–828. doi:10.1080/02650487.2017.1348035

Venkatesh, V., Morris, G., Davis, & Davis. (2003). User Acceptance of Information Technology: Toward A Unified View. *Management Information Systems Quarterly, 27*(3), 425–478. doi:10.2307/30036540

Venkatesh, V., Thong, J. Y., & Xin, X. U. (2012). Consumer Acceptance and Use of Information Technology: Extending the Unified Theory of Acceptance and Use of Technology. *Management Information Systems Quarterly, 36*(1), 157–178. doi:10.2307/41410412

Verbano, C., & Crema, M. (2016). Linking technology innovation strategy, intellectual capital and technology innovation performance in manufacturing SMEs. *Technology Analysis and Strategic Management, 28*(5), 524–540. doi:10.1080/09537325.2015.1117066

Vinerean, S. (2017). Importance of Strategic Social Media Marketing. *Expert Journal of Marketing, 5*(1), 28–35.

Vinerean, S., Cetina, I., Dumitrescu, L., & Tichindelean, M. (2013). The Effects of Social Media Marketing on Online Consumer Behavior. *International Journal of Business and Management, 8*(14). doi:10.5539/ijbm.v8n14p66

Wahyuni, E. T. (2008). The Accountability of Islamic Microfinance Institution: Evidence From Indonesia. *The Winners, 9*(1), 22–34. doi:10.21512/tw.v9i1.728

Walker, E., & Brown, A. (2004). What success factors are important to small business owners? *International Small Business Journal, 22*(6), 577–594. doi:10.1177/0266242604047411

Wang, S. W., Huang, C. Y., & Sun, C. T. (2022). Multiagent Diffusion and Opinion Dynamics Model Interaction Effects on Controversial Products. *IEEE Access : Practical Innovations, Open Solutions, 10*, 115252–115270. doi:10.1109/ACCESS.2022.3218719

Wathne, K. H., & Heide, J. B. (2004). Relationship governance in a supply chain network. *Journal of Marketing, 68*(1), 73–89. doi:10.1509/jmkg.68.1.73.24037

Wediawati, B., Effendi, N., Herwany, D., & Mashita, D. (2018). Sustainability of Islamic Microfinance in Indonesia: A Holistic Approach. *Academy of Strategic Management Journal, 17*(3), 1–15.

Whittaker, D. H., Sturgeon, T., Okita, T., & Zhu, T. (2020). *Compressed development: time and timing in economic and social development.* Oxford University Press. doi:10.1093/oso/9780198744948.001.0001

Wibowo, A., Widjaja, S., Utomo, S., Kusumojanto, D., Wardoyo, C., Wardana, L., & Narmaditya, B. (2021). Does islamic values matter for indonesian students' entrepreneurial intention? the mediating role of entrepreneurial inspiration and attitude. *Journal of Islamic Accounting and Business Research, 13*(2), 242–263. doi:10.1108/JIABR-03-2021-0090

Williams-Mcbean, C. T. (2019). The value of a qualitative pilot study in a multi-phase mixed methods research. *Qualitative Report, 24*(5), 1055–1064. doi:10.46743/2160-3715/2019.3833

Wilson, J. A. J. (2012). The new wave of transformational Islamic marketing. *Journal of Islamic Marketing, 3*(1), 5–11. doi:10.1108/17590831211225436

Wilson, J. A., & Grant, J. (2013). Islamic marketing – a challenger to the classical marketing canon? *Journal of Islamic Marketing, 4*(1), 7–21. doi:10.1108/17590831311306327

Wilson, J. A., & Liu, J. (2011). The challenges of Islamic branding: Navigating emotions and halal. *Journal of Islamic Marketing, 2*(1), 28–42. doi:10.1108/17590831111115222

Woolcock, M., & Narayan, D. (2000). Social Capital: Implications for Development Theory, Research, and Policy What Is Social Capital? *The World Bank Research Observer, 15*(2), 225–249. doi:10.1093/wbro/15.2.225

World Bank. (2018). *Implementation completion and results report on a loan in the amount of euro 37.9 million (us$ 50 million equivalent) to the kingdom of Morocco for the MA MSMEs development project.* World Bank.

World Bank. (2021). *The global findex database 2021 financial inclusion, digital payments, and resilience in the age of covid-19.* World Bank.

World Bank. 1978. Employment and development of small enterprises. Washington DC: World Bank.

Wu, P. C., Yeh, G. Y. Y., & Hsiao, C. R. (2011). The effect of store image and service quality on brand image and purchase intention for private label brands. [AMJ]. *Australasian Marketing Journal, 19*(1), 30–39. doi:10.1016/j.ausmj.2010.11.001

Wu, W., Zhou, L., & Chien, H. (2019). Impact of Consumer Awareness, Knowledge, and Attitudes on Organic Rice Purchasing Behaviour in China. *Journal of Food Products Marketing, 25*(5), 549–565. doi:10.1080/10454446.2019.1611515

Xu, Q., Yu, N., & Song, Y. (2018). User engagement in public discourse on genetically modified organisms: The role of opinion leaders on social media. *Science Communication, 40*(6), 691–717. doi:10.1177/1075547018806526

Yaacob, Y., & Azmi, I. A. G. (2012). Entrepreneur's Social Responsibilities From Islamic Perspective: A Study of Muslim Entrepreneurs In Malaysia. *Procedia: Social and Behavioral Sciences, 58*, 1131–1138. doi:10.1016/j.sbspro.2012.09.1094

Yadav, R. (2022). Zero Customer Defection. In *Adoption and Implementation of AI in Customer Relationship Management* (pp. 139–153). IGI Global., doi:10.4018/978-1-7998-7959-6.ch009

Yahya, S., & Kamalul Ariffin, S. (2020). Determinants of Consumer Purchase Intention of Halal Meat in Kano-Nigeria: a Conceptual Paper. *International Journal of Industrial Management, 6*(2015), 40–48. doi:10.15282/ijim.6.0.2020.5628

Yakovlev, I. A., & Nikulina, S. I. (2019). Indonesia's Strategy for Sustainable Finance. *Finansovyj žhurnal—Financial Journal*, (6), 83-95.

Yaseen, A., Mahmood, G., & Naheed, K. (2022). Who can practice islamic entrepreneurship: A review of recent literature on personality traits. *Journal of Law & Social Studies, 4*(3), 429–440. doi:10.52279/jlss.04.03.429440

Yaumidin, U. K., Suhodo, D. S., Yuniarti, P. I., & Hidayatina, A. (2017). Financial Inclusion for Women: Impact Evaluation on Islamic Microfinance to Women's Empowerment in Indonesia. In Financial Inclusion and Poverty Alleviation. doi:10.1007/978-3-319-69799-4_3

Yazdi, N. S., Shokoh, Z., Amiri, A., Nikpour, A., & Kamali, M. J. (2021). Identifying and examining the status of mental health and entrepreneurial organizational motivation components based on Islamic medicine culture. *International Journal of Hospital Research, 10*(4), 1–10. https://ijhr.iums.ac.ir/article_133543.html

Yildiz, S. Y. (2022). Instagram Influencerlarının Cinsiyetine Göre Tüketici Profillerinin Belirlenmesi. *Cumhuriyet Üniversitesi İktisadi ve İdari Bilimler Dergisi, 23*(4), 943–953. doi:10.37880/cumuiibf.1130303

Yilmaz, S., & Li, B. (2020). The BRI-led globalization and its implications for east Asian regionalization. *Chinese Political Science Review, 5*(3), 395–416. doi:10.100741111-020-00145-2

Youndt, M. A., Subramaniam, M., & Snell, S. A. (2004). Intellectual capital profiles: An examination of investments and returns. *Journal of Management Studies, 41*(2), 335–361. doi:10.1111/j.1467-6486.2004.00435.x

Younis Khan, M., Jamil, A., Ali Khan, U., Kareem, U., & Imran, G. (2012). Female Students Opinion about Women's Participation in Sports. *International Journal of Academic Research in Business & Social Sciences, 2*(9), 275–283.

Yousaf, S. (2016). Promotion mix management: A consumer focused Islamic perspective. *Journal of Marketing Communications, 22*(2), 215–231. doi:10.1080/13527266.2014.888575

Yu, H.-C., Wang, W.-Y., & Chang, C. (2015). The stock market valuation of intellectual capital in the IT industry. *Review of Quantitative Finance and Accounting, 45*(2), 279–304. doi:10.100711156-014-0437-5

Yunos, R. M., Mahmood, C. F. C., & Abd Mansor, N. H. (2014). Understanding mechanisms to promote halal industry-the stakeholders' views. *Procedia: Social and Behavioral Sciences, 130*, 160–166. doi:10.1016/j.sbspro.2014.04.020

Yunus, N. S. N. M., Rashid, W. E. W., Ariffin, N. M., & Rashid, N. M. (2014). Muslim's Purchase Intention towards Non-Muslim's Halal Packaged Food Manufacturer. *Procedia: Social and Behavioral Sciences, 130*, 145–154. doi:10.1016/j.sbspro.2014.04.018

Yu, S., & Lee, J. (2019). The effects of consumers' perceived values on intention to purchase upcycled products. *Sustainability (Basel), 11*(4), 1034. doi:10.3390u11041034

Yusfiarto, R., & Pambekti, G. T. (2019). Do internet marketing factors with islamic values improve sme performance? *Journal of Islamic Monetary Economics and Finance, 5*(4), 807–828. doi:10.21098/jimf.v5i4.1101

Yusof, N. S., Ramli, K. I., & Mohd Shariff, N. (2016). Image of Malaysia as a Halal destination (Paper presentation). *Prosiding Pengurusan Halal, Ekonomi dan Perniagaan 2016*, UUM.

Yusof, N., Mohd Shariff, N., & Omar., H. (2019). Examining the importance of Muslim friendly facilities perceived by international Muslim tourists to Malaysia. *International Academic Journal of Social Sciences and Education, 2*(1), 262–274.

Yusup, M., Mas'ud, R., & Johari, M. (2022). Brand Value and Tourists' Satisfaction in Lombok Indonesia as a Halal Tourism Destination. *Shirkah: Journal of Economics and Business, 7*(1), 1–16. doi:10.22515hirkah.v7i1.403

Zahra, S. A., & George, G. (2002). Absorptive capacity: A review, reconceptualization, and extension. *Academy of Management Review, 27*(2), 185. doi:10.2307/4134351

Zakaria, N. B., Yunos, R. M., Mahmood, C. F. C., Anita, R., & Said, J. (2017). The effect of consumers' interest, information access and spending willingness on halal products trustworthiness. *Asia-Pacific Management Accounting Journal, 12*(2), 183–200.

Zakaria, N., & Abdul-Talib, A. (2010). Applying Islamic market-oriented cultural model to sensitize strategies towards global customers, competitors, and environment. *Journal of Islamic Marketing*, *1*(1), 51–62. doi:10.1108/17590831011026222

Zak, S., & Hasprova, M. (2020). The role of influencers in the consumer decision-making process. In *SHS web of conferences* (Vol. 74, p. 03014). EDP Sciences. doi:10.1051hsconf/20207403014

Zapalska, A., & Wingrove-Haugland, E. (2013). Micro-Entrepreneurship And Islamic Economic System. *Business Journal for Entrepreneurs*, (1).

Zeller, M., Greeley, M., & Lapenu, C. (2003). *Measuring social performance of microfinance institutions.* CGAP Printer, Washington DC, USA. www.cerise-microfinance.org

Zerenler, M., Hasiloglu, S. B., & Sezgin, M. (2008). Intellectual capital and innovation performance: Empirical evidence in the Turkish automotive supplier. *Journal of Technology Management & Innovation*, *3*(4), 31–40. doi:10.4067/S0718-27242008000200003

Zhang, D., & Earp, B. E. (2020). Correlation between social media posts and academic citations of orthopaedic research. *JAAOS Global Research & Reviews, 4*(9).

Zhang, W. (2022). The Engagement Between Social Media Influencers and Their Followers on Instagram: A Case Study of# StopAsianHate. *Rangahau Aranga Aut Graduate Review, 1*(3).

Zhang, H., Wu, Y., & Buhalis, D. (2018). A model of perceived image, memorable tourism experiences and revisit intention. *Journal of Destination Marketing & Management*, *8*, 326–336. doi:10.1016/j.jdmm.2017.06.004

Zhang, Z. (2018). The belt and road initiative: China's new geopolitical strategy? *China Quarterly of International Strategic Studies*, *4*(03), 327–343. doi:10.1142/S2377740018500240

Zizumbo-Colunga, D., Zechmeister, E., & Mitchell, S. (2010). Social capital and economic crisis in the United States. *Americas Barometer Insights*, *43*, 1–9.

Zreik, M. (2021a). China and Europe in Africa: Competition or Cooperation?. *MJIR| Malaysian Journal of International Relations, 9*(1), 51-67.

Zreik, M. (2021b). Academic Exchange Programs between China and the Arab Region: A Means of Cultural Harmony or Indirect Chinese Influence? *Arab Studies Quarterly*, *43*(2). doi:10.13169/arabstudquar.43.2.0172

Zreik, M. (2022a). Contemporary geopolitics of Eurasia and the Belt and Road Initiative. *Eurasian Research Journal*, *4*(1), 7–26. doi:10.53277/2519-2442-2022.1-01

Zreik, M. (2022b). The Chinese presence in the Arab region: Lebanon at the heart of the Belt and Road Initiative. *International Journal of Business and Systems Research*, *16*(5-6), 644–662. doi:10.1504/IJBSR.2022.125477

About the Contributors

Ima Dwitawati is a faculty member of information technology department, State Islamic University Ar-Raniry, Banda Aceh, Indonesia. She has a bachelor's in Mathematics Computation from Syiah Kuala University, and Master Business Administration from Information and Society Department, College of Hakka Studies, National United University, Taiwan, R.O.C. She currently teaching the bachelor degree students at State Islamic University Ar-Raniry related to Business and Information Technology, Digital Culture, Digital Business, and Business Intelligent, Information Management, and Management of Information System.

Nur Alifah Fajariyah is a lecturer at the Department of Accounting, Faculty of Islamic Economics and Business (FEBI), Kiai Haji Achmad Siddiq State Islamic University (UIN KHAS), Jember – Indonesia. She is currently a member of the Indonesian Association of Islamic Economists (IAEI) for the Provincial Board of East Java and also a Companion to Halal Certification for Micro, Small, and Medium Enterprises (MSMEs). She has published several book chapters and journal articles related to her research interests in Islamic accounting for MSMEs, Islamic banks, and business ethics.

Azrin Jalasi is a Lecturer in Marketing at Politeknik Kota Kinabalu, Sabah and PhD.

Khusnul Khotimah is a lecturer at the Faculty of Tarbiyah and Education (FTIK) at once Faculty of Islamic Economics and Business (FEBI), Kiai Haji Achmad Siddiq State Islamic University (UIN KHAS), Jember – Indonesia. She is also the Staff for Cooperation Services and the International Office of UIN KHAS. Her research interests are in English for Economics and Management of English Education.

Nor Irvoni Mohd Ishar is a Certified Professional Marketer (CPM ASIA) and an Associate Professor of Marketing at Arshad Ayub Graduate Business School (AAGBS), UiTM Shah Alam, Malaysia. Before entering academia, Irvoni had over ten years of industry experience at Ericsson Academy Malaysia and the Central Bank of Malaysia. She lectures and supervises postgraduate students at present. Her teaching experience includes Marketing and Research Methodology related courses at the Ph.D., DBA, MBA, and Bachelor's Degree levels. She is also involved in academic research and corporate consultation work. Customer Experience, Customer Voice, Branding, Consumer Behaviour, Service Co-creation, Retailing, the Rasch Measurement Model, and Services Marketing are among her areas of interest.

Khairunnisa Musari is an Assistant Professor at Faculty of Islamic Economics and Business & Postgraduate Program, Kiai Haji Achmad Siddiq State Islamic University (UIN KHAS), Jember - Indonesia. She is a Secretary of the Indonesian Association of Islamic Economists (IAEI) for the Provincial Board of East Java since 2017. She has experience as a Senior Specialist for Islamic Finance of the United Nations Development Programme (UNDP) Indonesia and was listed as one of the Top 300 Most Influential Women in Islamic Business & Finance 2019, 2020, 2021, and WOMANi Significancica 2022 by Cambridge-IFA. She has an interest in issues related to sukuk, waqf, esham, fiscal & monetary policies, circular economy, halal logistics, sustainable financing, climate change, and Islamic microfinance & nanofinance.

Nazia Nasir was born in a small city of Punjab, Okara. She got her early education until Bachelor of Arts (BA) from Okara, Pakistan. After that she got admission and completed MBA program at University of South Asia, Lahore. Recently, she completed her MPhil program in Islamic Banking and Finance from School of Islamic Economics, Banking & Finance, Minhaj University Lahore. Moreover, she did MPhil research project under the supervision of Dr. Muhammad Bilal in the area of women role in Islamic banking & finance. She learn many new aspects of women involvement in Islamic banking & finance.

Muhammad Nawaz has a Ph.D. in Finance and Banking from University Utara Malaysia. (Accredited by AACSB)

Rahmawati Rahmawati is a lecturer at the Department of Accounting, Faculty of Economics and Business, Islamic State University Syarif Hidayatullah Jakarta, Indonesia. Her areas of research interest are Islamic accounting, financial accounting, and reporting, Islamic cooperative governance, internal audit, and finance in Islamic cooperative.

Fatima Sayah is an Assistant Professor at Ahmed Zabana University in Relizane (Algeria) since 2013. She obtained her Ph.D. in the Department of Management Sciences, specializing in Marketing, at the University of Tlemcen (Algeria) in 2009, and her second Ph.D. in the Department of Economic Sciences, specializing in Development Economics, at Djilali Liabes University, Sidi Bel Abbes (Algeria), in 2023. She has many writings, including journal articles, books, and book chapters, related to her concern on zakat, women, entrepreneurship, marketing, and economic development.

Nasir Yahaya is currently a master's student at the Indonesian International Islamic University. He obtained his dual bachelor's degree in theology and Arabic language at Uludag University, Bursa, Turkey, and the University of Tabuk, Saudi Arabia. Nasir Yahaya attended two international conferences in Indonesia and published an article titled" The rational sign and its inference in the interpretations of Al-Saadi and Al-Sabouni". His research focuses on Quranic studies, Muslim societies, and Arabic language literature.

Muhammad Bilal Zafar is an Assistant Professor of Islamic Economics, Banking and Finance at Minhaj University, Lahore-PK. He holds PhD in Islamic Economics from the University of Malaya, Kuala Lumpur-MY. He is a member of the Certified Shariah Adviser and Auditor (CSAA) fellowship under the auspices of AAOIFI, Bahrain.

Mohamad Zreik, is a recognized scholar in International Relations. His extensive knowledge spans Middle Eastern Studies, China-Arab relations, East Asian and Asian Affairs, Eurasian geopolitics, and Political Economy, providing him a unique viewpoint in his field. Dr. Zreik is a proud recipient of a PhD from Central China Normal University (Wuhan). He's written numerous acclaimed papers, many focusing on China's Belt and Road Initiative and its Arab-region impact. His groundbreaking research has established him as a leading expert in his field. His significant contributions make him a crucial figure in understanding contemporary international relations.

Index

K

M

N

O

P

Q

R

S

T

U

W

www.ingramcontent.com/pod-product-compliance
Lightning Source LLC
LaVergne TN
LVHW062143300926
849161LV00010B/2615